3rd Workshop for Natural Language Processing Open Source Software (NLP-OSS 2023)

Singapore
6 December 2023

ISBN: 978-1-7138-8605-1

Printed from e-media with permission by:

Curran Associates, Inc.
57 Morehouse Lane
Red Hook, NY 12571

Some format issues inherent in the e-media version may also appear in this print version.

Printed with permission by Curran Associates, Inc. (2024)

For permission requests, please contact the Association for Computational Linguistics at the address below.

Association for Computational Linguistics
209 N. Eighth Street
Stroudsburg, Pennsylvania 18360

Phone: 1-570-476-8006
Fax: 1-570-476-0860

acl@aclweb.org

Additional copies of this publication are available from:

Curran Associates, Inc.
57 Morehouse Lane
Red Hook, NY 12571 USA
Phone: 845-758-0400
Fax: 845-758-2633
Email: curran@proceedings.com
Web: www.proceedings.com

NLP-OSS 2023

The 3rd Workshop for Natural Language Processing Open Source Software (NLP-OSS)

Proceedings of the Workshop

December 6, 2023

Order copies of this and other ACL proceedings from:

Association for Computational Linguistics (ACL)
209 N. Eighth Street
Stroudsburg, PA 18360
USA
Tel: +1-570-476-8006
Fax: +1-570-476-0860
acl@aclweb.org

Program Committee

Program Chairs

Geeticka Chauhan
Jeremy Gwinnup
Dmitrijs Milajevs
Elijah Rippeth
Liling Tan

Reviewers

Sina Ahmadi, Zaid Alyafeai, Abhinav Arora

Guillaume Becquin, Steven Bethard, Tenzin Singhay Bhotia, Francis Bond, Daniel Braun

Geeticka Chauhan, Won Ik Cho, Marco Cognetta

Steve DeNeefe, Gérard Dupont

Ignatius Ezeani

Michael Wayne Goodman, Jeremy Gwinnup, Jana Götze

David M Howcroft, Phu Mon Htut

Cassandra L Jacobs

Thomas H Kober, Philipp Koehn

Arun Balajiee Lekshmi Narayanan, Pasquale Lisena

Nitin Madnani, Shubhanshu Mishra, Wafaa Mohammed, Anish Mohan, John Xavier Morris

Aakanksha Naik

Odunayo Ogundepo, Atul Kr Ojha, Akintunde Oladipo

Aline Paes, Flammie A Pirinen, Matt Post

Elijah Rippeth, Alexander M Rush

Lane Schwartz, Micah Shlain, Mallika Singh, Sudhakar Singh, Aitor Soroa, Shilpa Suresh

Liling Tan, Raphael Tang, Christoph Teichmann, Tommaso Teofili, Jörg Tiedemann, Vijay Murari Tiyyala, Atnafu Lambebo Tonja

Taha Zerrouki

Table of Contents

calamanCy: A Tagalog Natural Language Processing Toolkit
Lester James Validad Miranda 1

Jina Embeddings: A Novel Set of High-Performance Sentence Embedding Models
Michael Günther, Georgios Mastrapas, Bo Wang, Han Xiao and Jonathan Geuter 8

Deepparse : An Extendable, and Fine-Tunable State-Of-The-Art Library for Parsing Multinational Street Addresses
David Beauchemin 19

PyThaiNLP: Thai Natural Language Processing in Python
Wannaphong Phatthiyaphaibun, Korakot Chaovavanich, Charin Polpanumas, Arthit Suriyawongkul, Lalita Lowphansirikul, Pattarawat Chormai, Peerat Limkonchotiwat, Thanathip Suntorntip and Can Udomcharoenchaikit 25

Empowering Knowledge Discovery from Scientific Literature: A novel approach to Research Artifact Analysis
Petros Stavropoulos, Ioannis Lyris, Natalia Manola, Ioanna Grypari and Haris Papageorgiou . . 37

Zelda Rose: a tool for hassle-free training of transformer models
Loïc Grobol 54

GPT4All: An Ecosystem of Open Source Compressed Language Models
Yuvanesh Anand, Zach Nussbaum, Adam Treat, Aaron Miller, Richard Guo, Benjamin M Schmidt, Brandon Duderstadt and Andriy Mulyar 59

Kani: A Lightweight and Highly Hackable Framework for Building Language Model Applications
Andrew Zhu, Liam Dugan, Alyssa Hwang and Chris Callison-Burch 65

Beyond the Repo: A Case Study on Open Source Integration with GECToR
Sanjna Kashyap, Zhaoyang Xie, Kenneth Steimel and Nitin Madnani 78

Two Decades of the ACL Anthology: Development, Impact, and Open Challenges
Marcel Bollmann, Nathan Schneider, Arne Köhn and Matt Post 83

nanoT5: Fast & Simple Pre-training and Fine-tuning of T5 Models with Limited Resources
Piotr Nawrot 95

AWARE-TEXT: An Android Package for Mobile Phone Based Text Collection and On-Device Processing
Salvatore Giorgi, Garrick Sherman, Douglas Bellew, Sharath Chandra Guntuku, Lyle Ungar and Brenda Curtis 102

SOTASTREAM: A Streaming Approach to Machine Translation Training
Matt Post, Thamme Gowda, Roman Grundkiewicz, Huda Khayrallah, Rohit Jain and Marcin Junczys-Dowmunt 110

An Open-source Web-based Application for Development of Resources and Technologies in Underresourced Languages
Siddharth Singh, Shyam Ratan, Neerav Mathur and Ritesh Kumar 120

Rumour Detection in the Wild: A Browser Extension for Twitter
Andrej Jovanovic and Björn Ross 130

DeepZensols: A Deep Learning Natural Language Processing Framework for Experimentation and Reproducibility
Paul Landes, Barbara Di Eugenio and Cornelia Caragea 141

Improving NER Research Workflows with SeqScore
Constantine Lignos, Maya Kruse and Andrew Rueda 147

torchdistill Meets Hugging Face Libraries for Reproducible, Coding-Free Deep Learning Studies: A Case Study on NLP
Yoshitomo Matsubara 153

Using Captum to Explain Generative Language Models
Vivek Miglani, Aobo Yang, Aram H. Markosyan, Diego Garcia-Olano and Narine Kokhlikyan 165

nerblackbox: A High-level Library for Named Entity Recognition in Python
Felix Stollenwerk 174

News Signals: An NLP Library for Text and Time Series
Chris Hokamp, Demian Gholipour Ghalandari and Parsa Ghaffari 179

PyTAIL: An Open Source Tool for Interactive and Incremental Learning of NLP Models with Human in the Loop for Online Data
Shubhanshu Mishra and Jana Diesner 190

Antarlekhaka: A Comprehensive Tool for Multi-task Natural Language Annotation
Hrishikesh Terdalkar and Arnab Bhattacharya 199

GPTCache: An Open-Source Semantic Cache for LLM Applications Enabling Faster Answers and Cost Savings
Fu Bang 212

The Vault: A Comprehensive Multilingual Dataset for Advancing Code Understanding and Generation
Dung Nguyen Manh, Nam Le Hai, Anh T. V. Dau, Anh Minh Nguyen, Khanh Nghiem, Jin Guo and Nghi D. Q. Bui 219

SEA-LION (Southeast Asian Languages In One Network): A Family of Southeast Asian Language Models
William Tjhi, David Ong and Peerat Limkonchotiwat 245

trlX: A Framework for Large Scale Open Source RLHF
Louis Castricato 246

Towards Explainable and Accessible AI
Brandon Duderstadt and Yuvanesh Anand 247

Program

Thursday, May 26, 2022

09:15 - 10:15 *Invited Talk 1*

SEA-LION (Southeast Asian Languages In One Network): A Family of Southeast Asian Language Models
William Tjhi, David Ong and Peerat Limkonchotiwat

10:30 - 11:00 *Coffee Break*

11:00 - 11:30 *Lightning Session 1*

11:30 - 12:15 *Poster Session 1*

Jina Embeddings: A Novel Set of High-Performance Sentence Embedding Models
Michael Günther, Georgios Mastrapas, Bo Wang, Han Xiao and Jonathan Geuter

Deepparse : An Extendable, and Fine-Tunable State-Of-The-Art Library for Parsing Multinational Street Addresses
David Beauchemin

PyThaiNLP: Thai Natural Language Processing in Python
Wannaphong Phatthiyaphaibun, Korakot Chaovavanich, Charin Polpanumas, Arthit Suriyawongkul, Lalita Lowphansirikul, Pattarawat Chormai, Peerat Limkonchotiwat, Thanathip Suntorntip and Can Udomcharoenchaikit

Zelda Rose: a tool for hassle-free training of transformer models
Loïc Grobol

Kani: A Lightweight and Highly Hackable Framework for Building Language Model Applications
Andrew Zhu, Liam Dugan, Alyssa Hwang and Chris Callison-Burch

Beyond the Repo: A Case Study on Open Source Integration with GECToR
Sanjna Kashyap, Zhaoyang Xie, Kenneth Steimel and Nitin Madnani

Two Decades of the ACL Anthology: Development, Impact, and Open Challenges
Marcel Bollmann, Nathan Schneider, Arne Köhn and Matt Post

nanoT5: Fast & Simple Pre-training and Fine-tuning of T5 Models with Limited Resources
Piotr Nawrot

AWARE-TEXT: An Android Package for Mobile Phone Based Text Collection and On-Device Processing
Salvatore Giorgi, Garrick Sherman, Douglas Bellew, Sharath Chandra Guntuku, Lyle Ungar and Brenda Curtis

SOTASTREAM: A Streaming Approach to Machine Translation Training
Matt Post, Thamme Gowda, Roman Grundkiewicz, Huda Khayrallah, Rohit Jain and Marcin Junczys-Dowmunt

An Open-source Web-based Application for Development of Resources and Technologies in Underresourced Languages
Siddharth Singh, Shyam Ratan, Neerav Mathur and Ritesh Kumar

Rumour Detection in the Wild: A Browser Extension for Twitter
Andrej Jovanovic and Björn Ross

12:15 - 13:45 *Lunch Break*

13:45 - 14:45 *Invited Talk 2*

trlX: A Framework for Large Scale Open Source RLHF
Louis Castricato

14:45 - 15:15 *Lightning Session 2*

15:15 - 15:30 *Coffee Break*

15:30 - 16:15 *Poster Session 2*

GPT4All: An Ecosystem of Open Source Compressed Language Models
Yuvanesh Anand, Zach Nussbaum, Adam Treat, Aaron Miller, Richard Guo, Benjamin M Schmidt, Brandon Duderstadt and Andriy Mulyar

DeepZensols: A Deep Learning Natural Language Processing Framework for Experimentation and Reproducibility
Paul Landes, Barbara Di Eugenio and Cornelia Caragea

Improving NER Research Workflows with SeqScore
Constantine Lignos, Maya Kruse and Andrew Rueda

torchdistill Meets Hugging Face Libraries for Reproducible, Coding-Free Deep Learning Studies: A Case Study on NLP
Yoshitomo Matsubara

Using Captum to Explain Generative Language Models
Vivek Miglani, Aobo Yang, Aram H. Markosyan, Diego Garcia-Olano and Narine Kokhlikyan

nerblackbox: A High-level Library for Named Entity Recognition in Python
Felix Stollenwerk

News Signals: An NLP Library for Text and Time Series
Chris Hokamp, Demian Gholipour Ghalandari and Parsa Ghaffari

PyTAIL: An Open Source Tool for Interactive and Incremental Learning of NLP Models with Human in the Loop for Online Data
Shubhanshu Mishra and Jana Diesner

GPTCache: An Open-Source Semantic Cache for LLM Applications Enabling Faster Answers and Cost Savings
Fu Bang

The Vault: A Comprehensive Multilingual Dataset for Advancing Code Understanding and Generation
Dung Nguyen Manh, Nam Le Hai, Anh T. V. Dau, Anh Minh Nguyen, Khanh Nghiem, Jin Guo and Nghi D. Q. Bui

16:15 - 17:15 *Invited Talk 3*

Towards Explainable and Accessible AI
Brandon Duderstadt and Yuvanesh Anand

Wednesday, December 6, 2023

09:00 - 09:15 *Opening Remarks*

17:15 - 17:30 *Closing Remarks*

calamanCy: A Tagalog Natural Language Processing Toolkit

Lester James V. Miranda
ExplosionAI GmbH
lj@explosion.ai

Abstract

We introduce calamanCy, an open-source toolkit for constructing natural language processing (NLP) pipelines for Tagalog. It is built on top of spaCy, enabling easy experimentation and integration with other frameworks. calamanCy addresses the development gap by providing a consistent API for building NLP applications and offering general-purpose multitask models with out-of-the-box support for dependency parsing, parts-of-speech (POS) tagging, and named entity recognition (NER). calamanCy aims to accelerate the progress of Tagalog NLP by consolidating disjointed resources in a unified framework. The calamanCy toolkit is available on GitHub: `https://github.com/ljvmiranda921/calamanCy`.

1 Introduction

Tagalog is a low-resource language from the Austronesian family, with over 28 million speakers in the Philippines (Lewis, 2009). Despite its speaker population, few resources exist for the language (Cruz and Cheng, 2022). For example, Universal Dependencies (UD) treebanks for Tagalog are tiny ($\ll$ 20k words) (Samson, 2018; Aquino and de Leon, 2020), while domain-specific corpora are sparse (Cabasag et al., 2019; Livelo and Cheng, 2018). In addition, Tagalog language models (LMs) (Cruz and Cheng, 2022; Jiang et al., 2021) are few, while most multilingual LMs (Conneau et al., 2020; Devlin et al., 2019) underrepresent the language (Lauscher et al., 2020). Thus, consolidating these disjointed resources in a coherent framework is still an open problem. The lack of such framework hampers model development, experimental workflows, and the overall advancement of Tagalog NLP.

To address this problem, we introduce calamanCy,[1] an open-source toolkit for Tagalog NLP. It is built on top of spaCy (Honnibal et al., 2020) and offers end-to-end pipelines for NLP tasks such as dependency parsing, parts-of-speech (POS) tagging, and named entity recognition (NER). calamanCy also provides general-purpose pipelines in three different sizes to fit any performance or accuracy requirements. This work has two main contributions: (1) an open-source toolkit with out-of-the box support for common NLP tasks, and (2) comprehensive evaluations on several Tagalog benchmarks.

[1] "calamanCy" derives its name from *kalamansi*, a citrus fruit native to the Philippines.

2 Related Work

Open-source toolkits for NLP There has been a growing body of work in the development of NLP toolkits in recent years. For example, DaCy (Enevoldsen et al., 2021) and HuSpaCy (Orosz et al., 2022) serve the language-specific needs of Danish and Hungarian respectively. In addition, scispaCy (Neumann et al., 2019) and medspaCy (Eyre et al., 2021) were built to focus on scientific text. These tools employ spaCy (Honnibal et al., 2020), an industrial-strength open-source software for natural language processing. Using spaCy as a foundation is optimal, given its popularity and integration with other frameworks such as HuggingFace transformers (Wolf et al., 2020). However, no tool has existed for Tagalog until now. We aim to fill this development gap and serve the needs of the Tagalog language community through calamanCy.

Evaluations on Tagalog NLP Tasks Structured evaluations for core NLP tasks, such as dependency parsing, POS tagging, and NER, are meager. However, we have access to a reasonable amount of data to conduct comprehensive benchmarks. For example, TLUnified (Cruz and Cheng, 2022) is a pretraining corpus that combines news reports (Cruz et al., 2020), a preprocessed version of CommonCrawl (Suarez et al., 2019), and several other datasets. However, it was evaluated on domain-specific corpora that may not easily transfer to more

Proceedings of the 3rd Workshop for Natural Language Processing Open Source Software (NLP-OSS 2023), pages 1–7
December 6, 2023 ©2023 Association for Computational Linguistics

Entity	Description	Examples
Person (PER)	Person entities limited to humans. It may be a single individual or group.	Juan de la Cruz, Jose Rizal, Quijano de Manila
Organization (ORG)	Organization entities limited to corporations, agencies, and other groups of people defined by an organizational structure.	Meralco, DPWH, United Nations
Location (LOC)	Location entities are geographical regions, areas, and landmasses. Geo-political entities are also included within this group.	Pilipinas, Manila, CALABARZON, Ilog Pasig

Table 1: Entity types used for annotating TLUnified-NER (derived from the TLUnified pretraining corpus of Cruz and Cheng, 2022).

general tasks. In addition, Tagalog has two Universal Dependencies (UD) treebanks, Tagalog Reference Grammar (TRG) (Samson, 2018) and Ugnayan (Aquino and de Leon, 2020), both with POS tags and relational structures for parsing grammar. This paper will fill the evaluation gap by providing structured benchmarks on these core tasks.

3 Implementation

The best way to use calamanCy is through its trained pipelines. After installing the library, users can access the models in a few lines of code:

```
import calamancy as cl
nlp = cl.load("tl_calamancy_md-0.1.0")
doc = nlp("Ako si Juan de la Cruz.")
```

Here, the variable `nlp` is a spaCy processing pipeline[2] that contains trained components for POS tagging, dependency parsing, and NER. Applying this pipeline to a text will produce a `Doc` object with various linguistic features. calamanCy offers three pipelines of varying capacity: two static word vector-based models (md, lg), and one transformer-based model (trf). We will discuss how we developed these pipelines in the following section.

3.1 Pipeline development

Data annotation for NER There is no gold-standard corpus for NER, so we built one. To construct the NER corpus, we curated a portion of TLUnified (Cruz and Cheng, 2022) to contain Tagalog news articles. Including the author, we recruited two more annotators with at least a bachelor's degree and whose native language is Tagalog. The three annotators labeled for four months, given three entity types as seen in Table 1. We chose the

Dataset	Examples	PER	ORG	LOC
Training	6252	6418	3121	3296
Development	782	793	392	409
Test	782	818	423	438

Table 2: Dataset statistics for TLUnified-NER.

entity types to resemble ConLL (Tjong Kim Sang, 2002; Tjong Kim Sang and De Meulder, 2003), a standard NER benchmark. We excluded the `MISC` label to reduce uncertainty and confusion when labeling. Then, we measured inter-annotator agreement (IAA) by taking the pairwise Cohen's κ on all tokens and then averaged them for all three pairs. This process resulted in a Cohen's κ score of 0.81. To avoid confusion with the original TLUnified pretraining corpora, we will refer to this annotated NER dataset as TLUnified-NER. The final dataset statistics can be found in Table 2. For the dependency parser and POS tagger, we merged the TRG (Samson, 2018) and Ugnayan (Aquino and de Leon, 2020) treebanks to leverage their small yet relevant examples.

Model training We considered three design dimensions when training the calamanCy pipelines: (1) the presence of pretraining, (2) the word representation, and its (3) size or dimension. Model *pretraining* involves learning vectors from raw text to inform model initialization. Here, the pretraining objective asks the model to predict some number of leading and trailing UTF-8 bytes for the words—a variant of the cloze task (Devlin et al., 2019). A model's *word representation* may involve training static word embeddings using floret,[3] an efficient version of fastText (Bojanowski et al., 2017), or

[2]`https://spacy.io/usage/processing-pipelines`

[3]`https://github.com/explosion/floret`

Pipeline	Pretraining objective	Word embeddings	Dimensions
Medium-sized pipeline (tl_calamancy_md)	Predict some number of leading and trailing UTF-8 bytes for the words.	Uses floret vectors trained on the TLUnified corpora.	50k unique vectors (200 dimensions), Size: 77 MB
Large-sized pipeline (tl_calamancy_lg)	Same pretraining objective as the medium-sized pipeline.	Uses fastText vectors trained on CommonCrawl corpora.	714k unique vectors (300 dimensions), Size: 455 MB
Transformer-based pipeline (tl_calamancy_trf)	No separate pretraining because there's no token-to-vector component.	Context-sensitive vectors from a transformer network.	Uses roberta-tagalog-base. Size: 813 MB

Table 3: Language pipelines available in calamanCy (v0.1.0). The pretraining method for the word-vector models is a variant of the *cloze task*. All pipelines have a `tagger`, `parser`, `morphologizer`, and `ner` spaCy component.

Dataset	Task / Labels	Description
Hatespeech (Cabasag et al., 2019)	Binary text classification *(hate speech, not hate speech)*	Contains 10k tweets collected during the 2016 Philippine Presidential Elections labeled as hate speech or non-hate speech.
Dengue (Livelo and Cheng, 2018)	Multilabel text classification *(absent, dengue, health, sick, mosquito)*	Contains 4k dengue-related tweets collected for a health infoveillance application that classifies text into dengue subtopics.
TLUnified-NER (Cruz and Cheng, 2022)	Named entity recognition *(Person, Organization, Location)*	A held-out test split from the annotated TLUnified corpora containing news reports and other articles. See Table 2.
Merged UD (Samson, 2018; Aquino and de Leon, 2020)	Dependency parsing and POS tagging	Merged version of the Ugnayan and TRG treebanks from the Universal Dependencies framework.

Table 4: Datasets for benchmarking calamanCy.

using context-sensitive vectors from a transformer (Vaswani et al., 2017). Finally, a model's *dimension* is our way to tune the tradeoff between performance and accuracy.

The general process involves pretraining a filtered version of TLUnified, constructing static word embeddings if necessary, and training the downstream components. We used TLUnified-NER to train the NER component, and then trained the dependency parser and POS tagger using the combined treebanks. Ultimately, we devised three language pipelines as seen in Table 3.

4 Evaluation

Architectures We used spaCy's built-in architectures for each component in the calamanCy pipeline. The token-to-vector layer uses the multi-hash embedding trick (Miranda et al., 2022) to reduce the representation size. For the parser and named entity recognizer, we used a transition-based parser that maps text representations into a series of state transitions. As for the text categorizer, we utilized an ensemble of a bag-of-words model and a feed-forward network.

Experimental set-up We assessed the calamanCy pipelines on various Tagalog benchmarks as detailed in Table 4. We also tested on text categorization, an unseen task, for robustness. For NER evaluation, we used a held-out test split from TLUnified-NER. We measured their performance across five trials and then reported the average and standard deviation. For treebank-related benchmarks (POS tagging and dependency parsing), we followed UD's data split guidelines (Nivre et al., 2022) and performed 10-fold cross-validation to compensate for the size of the corpora ($\ll$ 20k tokens).

We also tested a cross-lingual transfer learning approach, i.e., finetuning a model from a source language closely related to Tagalog. According to

Model	Text categorization		NER	Dep. pars. & POS tag.	
	Hatespeech (binary)	Dengue (multilabel)	TLUnified-NER	Merged UD, UAS / LAS	Merged UD, POS Acc.
Monolingual (Ours)					
tl_calamancy_md	74.40±0.05	65.32±0.04	87.67±0.03	76.47 / 54.40	96.70
tl_calamancy_lg	75.62±0.02	68.42±0.01	88.90±0.01	82.13 / 70.32	97.20
tl_calamancy_trf	**78.25±0.06**	**72.45±0.02**	**90.34±0.02**	**92.48 / 80.90**	**97.80**
Cross-lingual transfer					
uk_core_news_trf	75.24±0.03	65.57±0.01	51.11±0.02	54.77 / 37.68	82.86
ro_core_news_lg	69.01±0.01	59.10±0.01	02.01±0.00	84.65 / 65.30	82.80
ca_core_news_trf	70.01±0.02	59.42±0.03	14.58±0.02	91.17 / 79.30	83.09
Multilingual finetuning					
xlm-roberta-base	77.57±0.01	67.20±0.01	88.03±0.03	88.34 / 76.07	94.29
bert-base-multilingual	76.40±0.02	71.07±0.04	87.40±0.02	90.79 / 78.52	95.30

Table 5: Benchmark evaluation scores for monolingual, cross-lingual, and multilingual pipelines across a variety of tasks and datasets. We evaluated the text categorization and NER tasks across five trials, and then conducted 10-fold cross-validation for dependency parsing. F1-scores are reported on the text categorization and NER tasks.

Aquino and de Leon (2020), the closest languages to Tagalog are Indonesian (id), Ukrainian (uk), Vietnamese (vi), Romanian (ro), and Catalan (ca). They obtained these results via a distance metric (Agić, 2017) based on the World Atlas for Language Structures (Haspelmath et al., 2005). However, only uk, ro, and ca have equivalent spaCy pipelines, so we only compared against those three. Finally, we also compared against multilingual language models by finetuning on XLM RoBERTa (Conneau et al., 2020) and an uncased version of multilingual BERT (Devlin et al., 2019). These LMs contain Tagalog in their training pool and are common alternatives for building Tagalog NLP applications.

5 Discussion

Table 5 shows the F1-scores for the text categorization and NER tasks, the unlabeled (UAS) and labeled attachment scores (LAS) for the dependency parsing task, and the tag accuracy for POS tagging.

The calamanCy pipelines are competitive across all core NLP tasks while maintaining a smaller compute footprint. As shown in the text categorization and NER results, users with low compute budgets can attain similar performance to multilingual LMs by using medium- or large-sized calamanCy models. The transformer-based calamanCy pipeline is the best option for users who prioritize accuracy. However, we were surprised that most alternative approaches perform better in dependency parsing. We attribute this performance to the added strength of multilingual and cross-lingual information, which we don't have when training solely on a smaller treebank. We plan to improve dependency parsing performance by building a larger treebank within the Universal Dependencies framework. For practical applications, we recommend users to start with a medium- or large-sized calamanCy model before trying out GPU-intensive pipelines. Only then can they switch to a transformer-based pipeline to get accuracy gains.

6 Conclusion

In this paper, we introduced calamanCy, a natural language processing toolkit for Tagalog. Our work has two main contributions: (1) an open-source toolkit containing general-purpose multitask pipelines with out-of-the-box support for common NLP tasks, and (2) comprehensive benchmarks that compare against alternative approaches, such as cross-lingual or multilingual finetuning. We hope that calamanCy is a step forward to improving the state of Tagalog NLP. As a low-resource language, consolidating resources into a unified framework is crucial to advance research and improve collaboration. In the future, we plan to create a more fine-grained NER benchmark corpus and extend calamanCy to natural language understanding (NLU) tasks. Finally, the project is hosted on GitHub (`https://github.com/ljvmiranda921/calamanCy`) and we are happy to receive community feedback and contributions.

Limitations

The TLUnified-NER corpus utilized for training the NER component of calamanCy comprises of new articles from early 2000s to the present. In addition the Universal Dependencies (UD) corpora for the POS tagger and dependency parser components are relatively modest in size, containing fewer than 10k tokens. Hence, the performance for these tasks during test-time could potentially be constrained by these factors.

Finally, reproducing the transformer pipelines may require a T4 or V100 GPU. The biggest bottleneck for reproduction is pretraining on the whole TLUnified corpus. In a 64vCPU machine with 256GB of RAM, the pretraining process can take three full days for 20 epochs.

References

Željko Agić. 2017. Cross-lingual parser selection for low-resource languages. In *Proceedings of the NoDaLiDa 2017 Workshop on Universal Dependencies (UDW 2017)*, pages 1–10, Gothenburg, Sweden. Association for Computational Linguistics.

Angelina Aquino and Franz de Leon. 2020. Parsing in the absence of related languages: Evaluating low-resource dependency parsers on Tagalog. In *Proceedings of the Fourth Workshop on Universal Dependencies (UDW 2020)*, pages 8–15, Barcelona, Spain (Online). Association for Computational Linguistics.

Piotr Bojanowski, Edouard Grave, Armand Joulin, and Tomas Mikolov. 2017. Enriching word vectors with subword information. *Transactions of the Association for Computational Linguistics*, 5:135–146.

Alex Brandsen, Suzan Verberne, Milco Wansleeben, and Karsten Lambers. 2020. Creating a dataset for named entity recognition in the archaeology domain. In *Proceedings of the Twelfth Language Resources and Evaluation Conference*, pages 4573–4577, Marseille, France. European Language Resources Association.

Neil Vicente P. Cabasag, Vicente Raphael C. Chan, Sean Christian Y. Lim, Mark Edward M. Gonzales, and Charibeth K. Cheng. 2019. Hate Speech in Philippine Election-Related Tweets: Automatic Detection and Classification Using Natural Language Processing. *Philippine Computing Journal Dedicated Issue on Natural Language Processing*, pages 1–14.

Alexis Conneau, Kartikay Khandelwal, Naman Goyal, Vishrav Chaudhary, Guillaume Wenzek, Francisco Guzmán, Edouard Grave, Myle Ott, Luke Zettlemoyer, and Veselin Stoyanov. 2020. Unsupervised cross-lingual representation learning at scale. In *Proceedings of the 58th Annual Meeting of the Association for Computational Linguistics*, pages 8440–8451, Online. Association for Computational Linguistics.

Jan Christian Blaise Cruz and Charibeth Cheng. 2022. Improving large-scale language models and resources for Filipino. In *Proceedings of the Thirteenth Language Resources and Evaluation Conference*, pages 6548–6555, Marseille, France. European Language Resources Association.

Jan Christian Blaise Cruz, Jose Kristian Resabal, James Lin, Dan John Velasco, and Charibeth Ko Cheng. 2020. Exploiting News Article Structure for Automatic Corpus Generation of Entailment Datasets. In *Pacific Rim International Conference on Artificial Intelligence*.

Louise Deleger, Qi Li, Todd Lingren, Megan Kaiser, Katalin Molnar, Laura Stoutenborough, Michal Kouril, Keith Marsolo, and Imre Solti. 2012. Building gold standard corpora for medical natural language processing tasks. In *AMIA Annual Symposium Proceedings*, pages 144–53.

Jacob Devlin, Ming-Wei Chang, Kenton Lee, and Kristina Toutanova. 2019. BERT: Pre-training of deep bidirectional transformers for language understanding. In *Proceedings of the 2019 Conference of the North American Chapter of the Association for Computational Linguistics: Human Language Technologies, Volume 1 (Long and Short Papers)*, pages 4171–4186, Minneapolis, Minnesota. Association for Computational Linguistics.

Kenneth C. Enevoldsen, L M Hansen, and Kristoffer Laigaard Nielbo. 2021. DaCy: A Unified Framework for Danish NLP. In *Workshop on Computational Humanities Research*.

Hannah Eyre, Alec B. Chapman, Kelly S. Peterson, Jianlin Shi, Patrick R. Alba, Makoto M. Jones, Tamára L Box, Scott L Duvall, and Olga V Patterson. 2021. Launching into clinical space with medspaCy: a new clinical text processing toolkit in Python. *Proceedings of the AMIA Annual Symposium*, 2021:438–447.

Martin Haspelmath, Matthew Dryer, David Gil, and Comrie Bernard. 2005. The World Atlas of Language Structures. In *Oxford University Press*.

Matthew Honnibal, Ines Montani, Sofie Van Landeghem, and Adriane Boyd. 2020. spaCy: Industrial-strength Natural Language Processing in Python.

Shengyi Jiang, Yingwen Fu, Xiaotian Lin, and Nankai Lin. 2021. Pre-trained Language Models for Tagalog with Multi-source Data. In *Natural Language Processing and Chinese Computing*.

Anne Lauscher, Vinit Ravishankar, Ivan Vulić, and Goran Glavaš. 2020. From zero to hero: On the limitations of zero-shot language transfer with multilingual Transformers. In *Proceedings of the 2020 Conference on Empirical Methods in Natural Language Processing (EMNLP)*, pages 4483–4499, Online. Association for Computational Linguistics.

Paul M. A. Lewis. 2009. Ethnologue: languages of the world. `https://ethnologue.com/language/tgl`. Accessed: June 2023.

Evan Dennison S. Livelo and Charibeth Ko Cheng. 2018. Intelligent Dengue Infoveillance Using Gated Recurrent Neural Learning and Cross-Label Frequencies. *2018 IEEE International Conference on Agents (ICA)*, pages 2–7.

Lester James V. Miranda, Ákos Kádár, Adriane Boyd, Sofie Van Landeghem, Anders Søgaard, and Matthew Honnibal. 2022. Multi hash embeddings in spaCy. *ArXiv*, abs/2212.09255.

Mark Neumann, Daniel King, Iz Beltagy, and Waleed Ammar. 2019. ScispaCy: Fast and robust models for biomedical natural language processing. In *Proceedings of the 18th BioNLP Workshop and Shared Task*, pages 319–327, Florence, Italy. Association for Computational Linguistics.

Joakim Nivre, Marie-Catherine de Marneffe, Filip Ginter, Jan Hajivc, Christopher D. Manning, Sampo Pyysalo, Sebastian Schuster, Francis M. Tyers, and Daniel Zeman. 2022. Data Release Checklist - Universal Dependencies. `https://universaldependencies.org/release_checklist.html#data-split`. Accessed: June 2023.

György Orosz, Zsolt Szántó, Péter Berkecz, Gergo Szabó, and Richárd Farkas. 2022. HuSpaCy: an industrial-strength Hungarian natural language processing toolkit. *ArXiv*, abs/2201.01956.

Nils Reiter. 2017. How to develop annotation guidelines. `https://sharedtasksinthedh.github.io/2017/10/01/howto-annotation/`. Accessed: June 2023.

Stephanie Dawn Samson. 2018. A treebank prototype of Tagalog. Bachelor's thesis, University of Tübingen, Germany.

Pedro Ortiz Suarez, Benoît Sagot, and Laurent Romary. 2019. Asynchronous Pipeline for Processing Huge Corpora on Medium to Low Resource Infrastructures. In *7th Workshop on the Challenges in the Management of Large Corpora*.

Erik F. Tjong Kim Sang. 2002. Introduction to the CoNLL-2002 shared task: Language-independent named entity recognition. In *COLING-02: The 6th Conference on Natural Language Learning 2002 (CoNLL-2002)*.

Erik F. Tjong Kim Sang and Fien De Meulder. 2003. Introduction to the CoNLL-2003 shared task: Language-independent named entity recognition. In *Proceedings of the Seventh Conference on Natural Language Learning at HLT-NAACL 2003*, pages 142–147.

Ashish Vaswani, Noam Shazeer, Niki Parmar, Jakob Uszkoreit, Llion Jones, Aidan N Gomez, Ł ukasz Kaiser, and Illia Polosukhin. 2017. Attention is all you need. In *Advances in Neural Information Processing Systems*, volume 30. Curran Associates, Inc.

Thomas Wolf, Lysandre Debut, Victor Sanh, Julien Chaumond, Clement Delangue, Anthony Moi, Pierric Cistac, Tim Rault, Remi Louf, Morgan Funtowicz, Joe Davison, Sam Shleifer, Patrick von Platen, Clara Ma, Yacine Jernite, Julien Plu, Canwen Xu, Teven Le Scao, Sylvain Gugger, Mariama Drame, Quentin Lhoest, and Alexander Rush. 2020. Transformers: State-of-the-art natural language processing. In *Proceedings of the 2020 Conference on Empirical Methods in Natural Language Processing: System Demonstrations*, pages 38–45, Online. Association for Computational Linguistics.

A Appendix

A.1 Reproducibility

All the experiments and models in this paper are available publicly. Readers can head over to `https://github.com/ljvmiranda921/calamanCy` for all related software. Note that the XLM-RoBERTa and multilingual BERT experiments may at least require a T4 or V100 GPU.

To reproduce the calamanCy models, head over to `models/v0.1.0`. To reproduce the benchmarking experiments, head over to the `report/benchmark` directory. Readers who are interested in the training set-up (e.g., hyperparameters, architectures used, etc.) can check the configuration (`.cfg`) files in the respective project's `configs/` directory.

A.2 Building the TLUnified-NER corpus

The TLUnified-NER dataset is a named entity recognition corpus containing the *Person (PER)*, *Organization (ORG)*, and *Location (LOC)* entities. It includes news articles and other texts in Tagalog from 2009 to 2020. It was based on the TLUnified pretraining corpora by (Cruz and Cheng, 2022). The author, together with two more annotators, annotated TLUnified in the course of four months. We employed an iterative approach as recommended by Reiter (2017), which included resolving disagreements and updating the annotation guidelines.

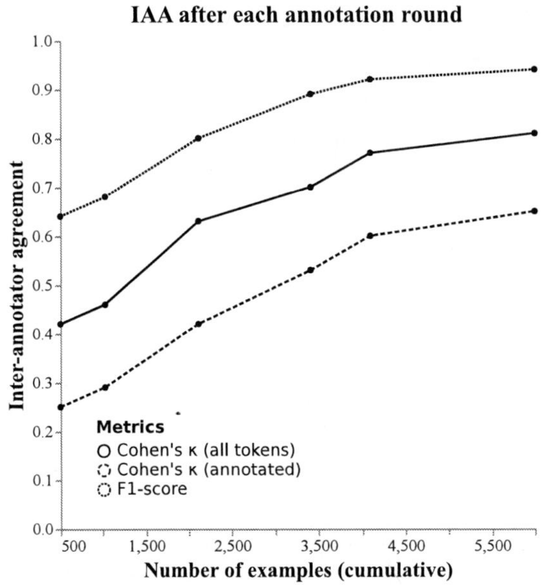

Figure 1: Inter-annotator agreement measurement after each annotation round. Each mark represents the end of a round. For each round, the annotators discuss disagreements, update the annotation guidelines, and evaluate the current set of annotations.

Metric	IAA
Cohen's κ on all tokens	0.81
Cohen's κ on annotated tokens only	0.65
F1 score	0.91

Table 6: Inter-annotator agreement (IAA) measurements. We obtained these values by computing for the pairwise comparisons between all annotator-pairs and averaging the results.

To get the inter-annotator agreement (IAA) score, we took Brandsen et al. (2020)'s work on the Archaeology dataset as inspiration. We computed Cohen's κ for all tokens, and only annotated tokens. In addition, we also measured the (3) pairwise F1 score without the 'O' label (Deleger et al., 2012). Table 6 shows the IAA measurements while Figure 1 shows their growth after each annotation round.

JINA EMBEDDINGS: A Novel Set of High-Performance Sentence Embedding Models

Michael Günther and **Louis Milliken** and **Jonathan Geuter**
Georgios Mastrapas and **Bo Wang** and **Han Xiao**

Jina AI
Ohlauer Str. 43, 10999 Berlin, Germany
{michael.guenther,louis.milliken,jonathan.geuter,
georgios.mastrapas,bo.wang,han.xiao}@jina.ai

Abstract

JINA EMBEDDINGS constitutes a set of high-performance sentence embedding models adept at translating textual inputs into numerical representations, capturing the semantics of the text. These models excel in applications like dense retrieval and semantic textual similarity. This paper details the development of JINA EMBEDDINGS, starting with the creation of high-quality pairwise and triplet datasets. It underlines the crucial role of data cleaning in dataset preparation, offers in-depth insights into the model training process, and concludes with a comprehensive performance evaluation using the Massive Text Embedding Benchmark (MTEB). Furthermore, to increase the model's awareness of grammatical negation, we construct a novel training and evaluation dataset of negated and non-negated statements, which we make publicly available to the community.

1 Introduction

Sentence embedding models are an effective instrument for encoding the semantic nuances of words, phrases, and larger textual units into a continuous vector space. They encapsulate the complexities of contexts and lexical and grammatical interrelationships within a text, facilitating downstream tasks like information retrieval, semantic similarity evaluation, and text classification.

Despite the potential of these models, questions remain about the effectiveness of different data preprocessing strategies, the optimal loss function for training sentence embedding models, and the impact on performance of increasing the number of model parameters. This paper addresses these challenges.

We have develop a novel dataset specifically to train our sentence embedding models. Furthermore, we design a dataset specifically to sensitize our models to distinguish negations of statements from confirming statements. This paper also presents JINA EMBEDDINGS, a set of high-performance sentence embedding models trained on these datasets. The JINA EMBEDDINGS set is expected to comprise five distinct models, ranging in size from 35 million to 6 billion parameters. Three of those models are already trained and published. [1]

The JINA EMBEDDINGS models employ contrastive training on the T5 architecture [Raffel et al., 2020]. It's important to note that we opt to use the T5 model as our base due to its pre-training on a mixed set of downstream tasks. We argue that incorporating this approach can potentially enhance our ability to accurately gauge the effectiveness of our training strategy.

Our large-scale contrastive fine-tuning approach surpasses zero-shot T5 and delivers a performance level on par with other leading T5-based sentence embedding models such as Sentence-T5 [Ni et al., 2022a] and GTR [Ni et al., 2022b]. Consequently, this work demonstrates that high-quality sentence embeddings can be achieved with the judicious use of resources and innovative training methodologies.

2 Dataset Preparation

In order to develop models that excel across a wide range of tasks, we collate a comprehensive set of both public and custom datasets. These datasets target various retrieval objectives, such as e-commerce search, duplicate detection, web retrieval, article retrieval for question-answering, and text classification. Consolidating these datasets into a unified format facilitates concurrent model training for all tasks.

Definition of Format: Given the lack of non-relevance information in many of the datasets, we reformat each training item into pairs, designated as $(q, p) \in D_{pairs}$. Each pair includes a query

[1] `jina-small-v1`, `jina-base-v1`, `jina-large-v1` are available at `https://huggingface.co/jinaai`, and are also ranked in the MTEB leaderboard on Hugging Face: `https://huggingface.co/spaces/mteb/leaderboard`.

Proceedings of the 3rd Workshop for Natural Language Processing Open Source Software (NLP-OSS 2023), pages 8–18
December 6, 2023

string q and an associated target string p. To leverage explicit non-relevance judgments, we create an auxiliary set of triplets $(q, p, n) \in D_{triplets}$, which pair a query string q with a match p (positive) and a non-matching string n (negative).

Data Extraction: The methods used to extract pairs and triplets are specific to each source dataset. For example, given a question-answer dataset, we use questions as query strings and answers as target strings. Retrieval datasets often contain queries that can serve as query strings and relevant and non-relevant annotated documents which can operate as matching and non-matching strings.

Training Steps: Our training process is a two-step approach. Initially, we train on pairs and then fine-tune the model using the triplets, as detailed in Section 3.3.

2.1 Pairwise Data Preparation

The substantial size and inconsistent quality of many large datasets necessitates a rigorous filtering pipeline. We apply the following steps to filter training data:

De-Duplication: Duplicated entries within training data can negatively impact model performance [Hernandez et al., 2022], and potentially lead to overfitting. Consequently, we remove duplicate entries from our dataset. Considering the dataset's volume, we employ hash functions to identify and eliminate text pairs that map to duplicate hash values. We normalize whitespace and capitalization before checking for duplicates. Empty pairs and pairs with identical elements are also removed.

Language Filtering: Since we design our embedding models for English, we use the `fasttext-language-identification` model[2] based on the fasttext text classification method [Joulin et al., 2017] to remove non-English training items from the dataset.

Consistency Filtering: Consistency filtering means excluding training pairs with low semantic similarity. Previous studies suggest that eliminating low-similarity pairs using an auxiliary, albeit less precise, model boosts performance [Dai et al., 2023, Wang et al., 2022]. We employ the `all-MiniLM-L6-v2` model[3] for consistency filtering in this manner: We generate embeddings for 1M pairs $(q_i, p_i)_i$ randomly sampled from D_{pairs}. For every pair $(q, p) \in D_{pairs}$ in the dataset, we verify whether p is among the top two passages most similar to q based on the cosine similarity of their embeddings compared to all passages p_i, $i = 1, ..., 1\text{M}$.

The application of these preprocessing steps reduces the size of the dataset from over 1.5 billion mixed-quality pairs to 385 million high-quality pairs. This reduction permits us to train our model with significantly less data than typical embedding models without sacrificing embedding quality.[4]

2.2 Triplet Data Preparation

For the triplet dataset, we forego de-duplication and language filtering and we assume the quality of these datasets already meets our quality requirements. However, we validate the relevance of the "positive" item with respect to the "query" for each triplet in a manner similar to consistency filtering. Instead of contrasting the embedding cosine similarity $s(q, p)$ against a sample set, we compare it solely with the similarity $s(q, n)$ of the embeddings derived from the same triplet $(q, p, n) \in D_{triplets}$. This is accomplished using a cross-encoder model, which evaluates the pair directly without generating embedding representations. More specifically, we leverage the `ms-marco-MiniLM-L-6-v2` model[5] to verify whether the difference in retrieval scores determined by the model exceeds a threshold $r(q, p) - r(q, n) > \kappa$, with threshold $\kappa = 0.2$, and eliminate all other pairs. This methodology draws inspiration from the de-noising strategy proposed in [Qu et al., 2021].

2.3 Negation Data Preparation

We observe that many embedding models struggle to accurately embed negations. For instance, when embedding the three sentences: "A couple walks hand in hand down a street.", "A couple is walking together.", and "A couple is not walking together.", the first two should be embedded close together, while the second and third, contradictory in

[2] `fasttext-language-identification` (https://huggingface.co/facebook/fasttext-language-identification)

[3] `all-MiniLM-L6-v2` model (https://huggingface.co/sentence-transformers/all-MiniLM-L6-v2)

[4] For instance, models like `all-MiniLM-L6-v2` and `all-mpnet-base-v2` are trained on nearly 1.2 billion pairs, whereas other T5-based models such as `sentence-t5-base` or `sentence-t5-large` are trained on 2.2 billion pairs.

[5] `ms-marco-MiniLM-L-6-v2` (https://huggingface.co/cross-encoder/ms-marco-MiniLM-L-6-v2)

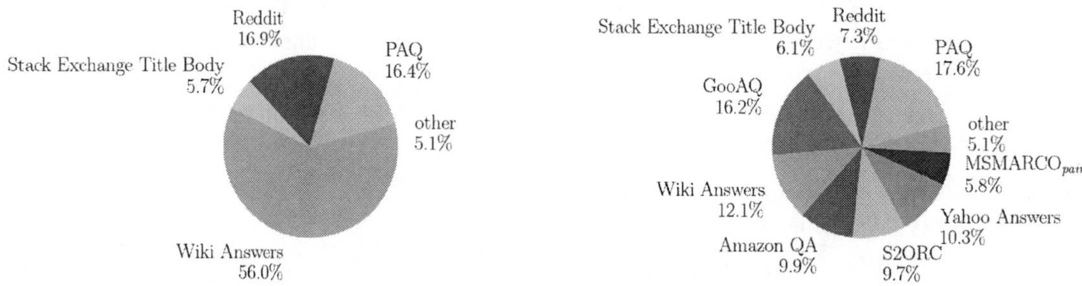

(a) Original Distribution after Filtering

(b) Adjusted by Sampling Rates

Figure 1: The composition of 385 million pairwise data

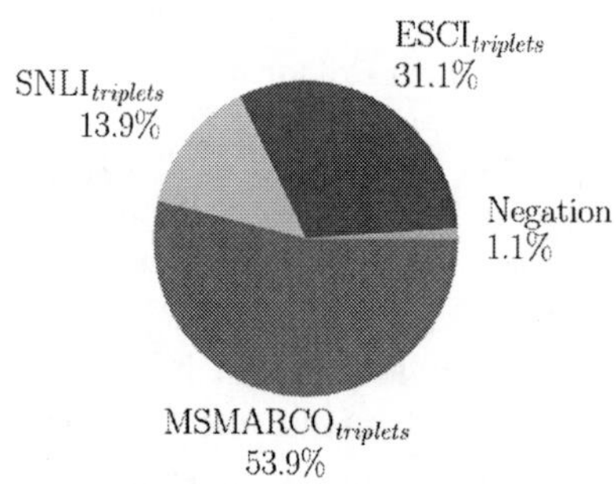

Figure 2: The composition of 927,000 triplets data

meaning, should be positioned further apart.[6] However, for instance, the `all-MiniLM-L6-v2` model assigns a cosine similarity of 0.7 to the first two sentences, while attributing a similarity of 0.86 to the second and third.[7]

We decide to address this problem by creating our own negation dataset[8]. This dataset, based on positive pairs from the SNLI dataset[9] and negatives created with GPT-3.5, comprises triplets (anchor, entailment, negative) akin to the example given above, where (anchor, entailment) form a positive pair and the "negative" contradicts both the "anchor" and "entailment", while remaining syntactically very similar to "entailment". This dataset forms a subset of our aforementioned triplet dataset, with training details provided in Section 3.3.

Our model evaluation on the negation dataset, which includes a comparative analysis with other popular open-source models, is presented in Section 4.3.

2.4 Data Composition

Our dataset of text pairs, represented as $D_{pairs} = D_1 \sqcup \cdots \sqcup D_n$, is aggregated from 32 individual datasets. This amounts to a total of 1.6 billion pairs before filtering, which is subsequently reduced to a robust 385 million high-quality pairs after rigorous filtering.

In comparison, our dataset of triplets initially comprises a total of 1.13 million entries before filtering, streamlined to 927,000 triplets after filtering.

The composition of our datasets after filtering is illustrated in Figure 1a for the text pairs, and in Figure 2 for the triplets. Together, these form the final dataset for the training of the JINA EMBEDDINGS models.

3 Training

Training takes place in two distinct phases. The first phase centers on training the model using the voluminous quantity of text pairs, consolidating the semantics of an entire text phrase into a single representative embedding. The second phase uses the relatively small triplet dataset, comprising an anchor, an entailment, and a hard-negative, teaching it to differentiate between similar and dissimilar text phrases.

3.1 Training on Pairwise Data

Each model within the JINA EMBEDDINGS set is based on, and trained using, the zero-shot T5 models of corresponding size, as detailed in [Raffel et al., 2020]. The zero-shot T5 models are composed of encoder-decoder pairs. However, Ni et al.

[6]Although it could be argued that for certain tasks, like document retrieval, it might still be desirable for contradicting texts to be embedded closely. Regardless, in this example, the first two sentences should be assigned a higher similarity.

[7]Interestingly, our large model does *correctly* assign a cosine similarity of 0.77 to the positive pair, and only a similarity of 0.62 to the negative pair, after fine-tuning with our negation dataset.

[8]The negation dataset is available at `https://huggingface.co/datasets/jinaai/negation-dataset`

[9]`https://huggingface.co/datasets/snli`

[2022a] has demonstrated that it is more effective to calculate text embeddings using only the encoder component of the T5 models, as opposed to deploying both encoder and decoder. Consequently, the JINA EMBEDDINGS models use only the encoders of their respective T5 models.

During tokenization, JINA EMBEDDINGS models use SentencePiece [Kudo and Richardson, 2018] to segment input text and encode them into WordPiece tokens [Kudo, 2018]. Following the encoder model, a mean pooling layer is implemented to generate fixed-length representations from the token embeddings.

For the training process involving pairs, we employ InfoNCE [van den Oord et al., 2018], a contrastive loss function. This function calculates the loss for a pair $(q, p) \sim B$ within a batch $B \in D^k$ of text pairs, where the batch size is k, as follows:

$$\mathcal{L}_{\text{NCE}}^{pairs}(B) := \mathbb{E}_{(q,p)\sim B}\left[-\ln \frac{e^{s(q,p)/\tau}}{\sum_{i=1}^{k} e^{s(q,p_i)/\tau}}\right]$$

The loss is calculated by comparing the cosine similarity between a given question q and its target p, with the similarity to all other targets in the batch. We found that calculating the loss in both directions results in greater improvements during training. Accordingly, the loss is defined as follows:

$$\mathcal{L}^{pairs}(B) := \mathcal{L}_{\text{NCE}}^{pairs}(B) + \mathcal{L}_{\overline{\text{NCE}}}^{pairs}(B), \text{ where}$$

$$\mathcal{L}_{\overline{\text{NCE}}}^{pairs}(B) := \mathbb{E}_{(q,p)\sim B}\left[-\ln \frac{e^{s(p,q)/\tau}}{\sum_{i=1}^{k} e^{s(p,q_i)/\tau}}\right].$$

Intuitively, $\mathcal{L}_{\overline{\text{NCE}}}^{pairs}$ matches the target string to all query strings instead. The constant τ denotes a temperature parameter which we set to $\tau = 0.05$. This method of calculating the loss is based on a similar method in [Neelakantan et al., 2022].

3.2 Data Sampling in Pairwise Training

Rather than sequentially training on individual datasets, we opt for a parallel approach, training on all datasets concurrently. We postulate that this parallel training promotes enhanced model generalization across diverse tasks. Despite this, each training batch is exclusively composed of data from a single dataset. This ensures that loss calculations, performed across the entire batch, do not conflate data from different tasks.

Our dataloader operates by initially selecting a dataset, followed by sampling the requisite number of data points from it to constitute a batch for the worker (refer to Section 4). Prior to training, the pairs within the datasets are thoroughly shuffled.

Sampling a dataset D_i follows a probability distribution ρ across all datasets D_i. The probability of sampling D_i is $\rho(D_i) = \frac{|D_i| s_i}{\sum_{j=1}^{n} |D_j| s_j}$ and is contingent upon the dataset's size $|D_i|$ and a scaling factor s_i.

Given the disparity in dataset sizes, it is critical to frequently sample from larger datasets to prevent overfitting on the smaller ones. Furthermore, we manipulate the sampling rates of datasets using scaling factors to prioritize training on high-quality datasets and achieve balance among text domains. In scenarios where datasets with higher sampling rates deplete their items before the completion of a training epoch, the dataset is reset, enabling the model to cycle through its items anew. This ensures that high-sampling-rate datasets contribute multiple times within a single training epoch.

Figure 1b displays the proportion of each dataset used based on their sampling rates. Following the creation of this adjusted distribution, the frequency of sampling from larger datasets significantly diminishes, resulting in only 180 million pairs actually being used during training.

3.3 Training on Triplet Data

Following the completion of pairwise training, the model progresses to the next phase which involves training on the triplet datasets. This phase uses a different loss function, leveraging negatives for improved model performance.

We experimented with various triplet loss functions and found that the best results are achieved through a combination of multiple commonly used triplet loss functions. Specifically, we use the extended version of the InfoNCE loss $\mathcal{L}_{NCE+}^{triplets}$, given by (2), which employs additional negatives [Reimers, 2023], the reverse InfoNCE loss $\mathcal{L}_{\overline{\text{NCE}}}^{triplets}$ from the initial training phase as given by (3), and the triplet margin loss function $\mathcal{L}_3^{triplets}$ as presented in (4) [Chechik et al., 2010].

The triplet function $\mathcal{L}_3^{triplets}$ determines the cosine similarity difference between the query and target $s(q, n)$, and the query and negative match $s(q, n)$. Furthermore, it establishes a minimal margin $\varepsilon = 0.05$ between these two values. If the negative is more similar to the query or the margin is violated, $\mathcal{L}_3^{triplets}$ returns a positive value. Otherwise, it yields 0, which is achieved through the application of the ReLU activation function. For the temperature parameter, we opted for a value of $\tau = 0.05$.

4 Evaluation

We conduct a comprehensive evaluation to compare our models against other state-of-the-art models (Section 4.1), investigate the impact of our filtering pipeline (Section 4.2), and evaluate the models' sensitivity to negation of statements (Section 4.3). Section 6 mentions details about the training.

To provide comprehensive results on the performance of models on various downstream tasks applicable to embeddings, we rely on the MTEB benchmark frameworks introduced by Muennighoff et al. [2023]. This also compromises all the retrieval tasks included in the BEIR [Thakur et al., 2021] benchmark. We also publish the code for executing it on our models on the Hugging Face pages of our model[10]. For evaluating models on the negation dataset, we use our own separate evaluation tool[11].

4.1 Performance Against State-of-the-Art Models

To gauge the performance of the JINA EMBEDDINGS set in relation to other similarly sized open-source and close-sourced models, we select representative models from five distinct size categories, as depicted in Table 1. Additionally, we include sentence-t5 and gtr-t5 xl and xxl models, which are based on T5 models with 3 billion and 11 billion parameters, respectively. This inclusion allows investigating the performance variation with models of such massive scales.

Table 6 presents the scores for MTEB's sentence similarity tasks, wherein the models within the JINA EMBEDDINGS set outshine their similarly sized counterparts across numerous tasks. Notably, the `jina-large-v1` model consistently delivers comparable, if not superior, results to models in the billion-parameter scale. `jina-base-v1` and `jina-small-v1` also exhibit competitive performances with models of analogous sizes, exceeding their peers on the BIOSSES[12] task. This highlights the benefits of training with highly diverse data sources.

Model	Parameters	Embedding Dimensions
sentence-t5-xxl	4.9b	768
gtr-t5-xxl	4.9b	768
gtr-t5-xl	1.2b	768
sentence-t5-xl	1.2b	768
`jina-large-v1`	330m	1024
gtr-t5-large	330m	768
sentence-t5-large	330m	768
all-mpnet-base-v2	110m	768
`jina-base-v1`	110m	768
gtr-t5-base	110m	768
sentence-t5-base	110m	768
`jina-small-v1`	35m	512
all-MiniLM-L6-v2	23m	384

Table 1: Model sizes and output dimensions

`jina-base-v1` consistently demonstrates performances similar to or better than gtr-t5-base, which was trained specifically for retrieval tasks [Ni et al., 2022b]. However, it seldom matches the scores of sentence-t5-base, which was trained on sentence similarity tasks [Ni et al., 2022a].

The evaluation of model performances on retrieval tasks, presented in Table 8, reflects a similar relationship among gtr-t5, sentence-t5, and JINA EMBEDDINGS. Here, gtr-t5 models, which have been specially trained on retrieval tasks, consistently score the highest for their respective sizes. JINA EMBEDDINGS models follow closely behind, whereas sentence-t5 models trail significantly. The JINA EMBEDDINGS set's capability to maintain competitive scores across these tasks underscores the advantage of multi-task training.

As illustrated in Table 7, `jina-large-v1` also achieves exceedingly high scores on reranking tasks, often outperforming larger models. Similarly, `jina-base-v1` surpasses gtr-t5-large and sentence-t5-large on several reranking tasks, which could once again be attributed to the specific training tasks of sentence-t5 and gtr-t5.

[10]`https://huggingface.co/jinaai/jina-embedding-b-en-v1/blob/main/mteb_evaluation.py`

[11]`https://huggingface.co/jinaai/jina-embedding-b-en-v1/blob/main/negation_evaluation.py`

[12]`https://tabilab.cmpe.boun.edu.tr/BIOSSES/DataSet.html`

$$\mathcal{L}^{triplets}(B) := \mathcal{L}^{triplets}_{NCE+}(B) + \mathcal{L}^{triplets}_{\overline{\text{NCE}}}(B) + \mathcal{L}^{triplets}_{3}(B), \quad \text{where} \tag{1}$$

$$\mathcal{L}^{triplets}_{NCE+}(B) := \mathbb{E}_{(q,p,n)\sim B}\left[-\ln \frac{\exp(s(q,p)/\tau)}{\sum_{i=1}^{k} \exp(s(q,p_i)/\tau) + \exp(s(q,n_i)/\tau)}\right], \tag{2}$$

$$\mathcal{L}^{triplets}_{\overline{\text{NCE}}}(B) := \mathbb{E}_{(q,p,n)\sim B}\left[-\ln \frac{\exp(s(p,q)/\tau)}{\sum_{i=1}^{k} \exp(s(p,q_i)/\tau)}\right], \tag{3}$$

$$\mathcal{L}^{triplets}_{3}(B) := \mathbb{E}_{(q,p,n)\sim B}\left[\text{ReLU}\Big(s(q,n) - s(q,p) + \varepsilon\Big)\right]. \tag{4}$$

Model	RR	RT	STS
sentence-t5-xxl	56.42	42.24	**82.63**
gtr-t5-xxl	**56.66**	**48.48**	78.38
gtr-t5-xl	55.96	47.96	77.80
sentence-t5-xl	54.71	38.47	81.66
jina-large-v1	**56.42**	44.81	80.96
gtr-t5-large	55.36	**47.42**	78.19
sentence-t5-large	54.00	36.71	**81.83**
all-mpnet-base-v2	**59.36**	43.81	80.28
jina-base-v1	55.84	44.03	79.93
gtr-t5-base	54.23	**44.67**	77.07
sentence-t5-base	53.09	33.63	**81.14**
jina-small-v1	53.07	38.91	78.06
all-MiniLM-L6-v2	**58.04**	**41.95**	**78.90**

Table 2: Average Scores for Reranking (RR), Retrieval (RT) and sentence similarity tasks (STS)

4.2 Impact of Filtering Steps

We evaluate the effectiveness of our dataset preprocessing pipeline by performing an ablation study. In this study, we fine-tune our smallest model on the Reddit dataset, where various preprocessing steps are individually applied. The corresponding results are presented in Table 3.

The ablation study's results underscore the value of both language and consistency filtering as crucial preprocessing steps. Their combined application results in the highest performance across the majority of benchmarks.

Specifically for the Reddit dataset, we observe a significant performance boost with the application of consistency filtering, while language filtering only marginally enhances the performance. We can account for this disparity by noting that the language filter removes only 17.4% of the Reddit data, while consistency filtering screens out 84.3[13]. Reddit samples are primarily in English, but many are positive pairs with very low similarity, making consistency filtering more effective than language filtering.

The effectiveness of these preprocessing steps, however, does exhibit variability across different datasets.

4.3 Effectiveness of Negation Data

To determine the effectiveness of our models on negation data, we evaluate them against the test split of our negation dataset, comparing the results with other open source models. We measure performance with respect to two metrics: one measures the percentage of samples where the model positions the *anchor* and *entailment* closer than the *anchor* and *negative* (which is an easy task, as the *anchor* and *negative* are syntactically dissimilar), the other measures the percentage of samples where the model positions the *anchor* and *entailment* closer than the *entailment* and *negative* (which is a hard task, as the *entailment* and *negative* are syntactically more similar than the *anchor* and *entailment*). The former is denoted by *EasyNegation*, the latter by *HardNegation*. The outcomes of these evaluations are displayed in Table 4. We assess our models both before and after fine-tuning on the triplet data, denoted as **<model>**$_{\text{pairwise}}$ and **<model>**$_{\text{all}}$, respectively.

From the results, we observe that across all model sizes, fine-tuning on triplet data (which includes our negation training dataset) dramatically enhances performance, particularly on the HardNegation task. Our models are on par with other state-of-the-art open-source models in terms of per-

[13]It is pertinent to note that the subsets filtered out overlap, thus the combined application of language and consistency filtering filters out *only* 86.8% of the data.

Data Preparation	Retrieval Quora	 SciFact	 Trec-Cov
No Extra Filter	0.734	0.218	0.242
Language	0.741	0.218	0.250
Consistency	0.805	**0.381**	0.297
Language + Consistency	**0.806**	0.379	**0.306**

Data Preparation	STS12	STS13	STS14	Sentence Similarity STS15	STS16	STS17	STS22
No Extra Filter	0.558	0.668	0.573	0.694	0.706	0.764	0.606
Language	0.561	0.668	0.579	0.697	0.704	0.765	0.609
Consistency	0.652	**0.728**	0.652	0.760	0.755	0.808	**0.610**
Language + Consistency	**0.653**	0.727	**0.656**	**0.764**	**0.757**	**0.810**	0.609

Table 3: Evaluation of Data-Preparation Effectiveness on the Reddit Dataset. Retrieval evaluated on nDCG@10, Sentence Similarity on Spearman.

formance, while achieving this with only a fraction of the training data required by their counterparts.

5 Related Work

The field of embedding models has seen significant advanced over the years, with the development of various models featuring diverse architectures and training pipelines. For instance, Sentence-BERT [Reimers and Gurevych, 2019] uses BERT to generate sentence embeddings. Similarly, Sentence-T5 [Ni et al., 2022a], based on the encoder architecture of T5, demonstrates superior performance over Sentence-BERT on numerous benchmarks. The study underscores the effectiveness of encoders for sentence embeddings, contrasting with another approach that explores the use of decoders [Muennighoff, 2022].

Knowledge distillation [Hinton et al., 2015] offers an alternative approach to model training. In this setup, a larger, pre-trained model acts as a mentor, instructing a smaller model during training. This methodology can be seamlessly integrated with a contrastive loss function, presenting an avenue for future investigation.

Embedding models can also be characterized based on their functionality. For instance, while some models are designed to solely embed queries, others are trained to embed queries along with specific instructions, generating task-dependent embeddings [Su et al., 2023]. An example of this using a T5-based model is the large dual encoder [Ni et al., 2022b], which is fine-tuned for retrieval tasks and computes a retrieval score directly.

Recent studies [Neelakantan et al., 2022, Wang et al., 2022] emphasize the benefits of contrastive pre-training coupled with fine-tuning on hard negatives. Both approaches have achieve state-of-the-art results on multiple benchmarks, with [Wang et al., 2022] also employing consistency filtering as part of their preprocessing pipeline.

6 Training Details

For training, we employ A100 GPUs and leverage the DeepSpeed stage 2 distributed training strategy [Rajbhandari et al., 2020] for effective multi-device management. For training our models we use the AdamW optimizer, coupled with a learning rate scheduler that adjusts the learning rate during the initial stages of training. The hyperparameters used across all three models throughout the training process are listed in Table 5.

7 Conclusion

This paper introduces the JINA EMBEDDINGS set of embedding models, demonstrating that competitive performance on various tasks can be achieved while substantially reducing the amount of training data, when compared to other models with comparable backbones. Through an extensive evaluation on the MTEB benchmark, we show that employing judicious data filtering techniques can lead to enhanced performance in comparison to training with a larger, yet lower-quality dataset. These findings significantly shift the paradigm, indicating that training large language models for embedding tasks can be conducted with less data than previously as-

	EasyNegation	HardNegation	Parameters	Training samples
jina-small-v1 pairwise	88.4%	8.4%	35m	385m
jina-base-v1 pairwise	93.0%	13.8%	110m	385m
jina-large-v1 pairwise	94.6%	16.6%	330m	385m
jina-small-v1 all	96.6%	35.2%	35m	386m
jina-base-v1 all	97.8%	54.6%	110m	386m
jina-large-v1 all	**98.2%**	65.4%	330m	386m
all-MiniLM-L6-v2	94.8%	29.4%	23m	1170m
all-mpnet-base-v2	97.4%	**67.6%**	110m	1170m
sentence-t5-base	96.0%	55%	110m	2275m
sentence-t5-large	**98.2%**	64.0%	330m	2275m

Table 4: Evaluating a Range of Models on the Negation Dataset: A Benchmark Analysis of JINA EMBEDDINGS Trained on Both Pairwise-Only and Combined Pairwise and Triplet Data. The negation dataset is available at https://huggingface.co/datasets/jinaai/negation-dataset

Hyperparameters	Value
# of devices	8
Sequence length	512
Model precision	32 bit
Learning rate	0.00005
# of steps for learning rate warm-up	500
Batch size for jina-small-v1	4096
Batch size for jina-base-v1	2048
Batch size for jina-large-v1	1024

Table 5: Hyperparameters

sumed, leading to potential savings in training time and resources.

However, we acknowledge the limitations of the current methodologies and the performance of the JINA EMBEDDINGS set. During the training on pairs, the sampling rate selection was based on a heuristic approach. Given the vast size of the search space for these sampling rates, we leaned on our intuition and dataset familiarity to prioritize higher-value datasets over their lower-value counterparts. This subjective approach, however, points to the need for more objective methods for future advancements.

Additionally, the JINA EMBEDDINGS set fell short on some tasks. For instance, calculating sentence similarity on our negation dataset (as described in Section 4.3) didn't meet our expectations (see Table 4) nor achieves competitive scores for classification and clustering tasks on the MTEB benchmark. These performance shortcomings suggest a possible deficit in the representation of these types of tasks in our training data, necessitating further investigation.

Looking ahead, we aim to refine our training processes to deliver models with improved performance and greater sequence length. Our future endeavors also include generating bilingual training data and training an embedding model capable of understanding and translating between two languages, thereby expanding the utility and versatility of the JINA EMBEDDINGS set.

References

Colin Raffel, Noam Shazeer, Adam Roberts, Katherine Lee, Sharan Narang, Michael Matena, Yanqi Zhou, Wei Li, and Peter J Liu. Exploring the limits of transfer learning with a unified text-to-text transformer. *The Journal of Machine Learning Research*, 21(1): 5485–5551, 2020.

Jianmo Ni, Gustavo Hernandez Abrego, Noah Constant, Ji Ma, Keith Hall, Daniel Cer, and Yinfei Yang. Sentence-t5: Scalable sentence encoders from pre-trained text-to-text models. In *Findings of the Association for Computational Linguistics: ACL 2022*, pages 1864–1874, 2022a.

Jianmo Ni, Chen Qu, Jing Lu, Zhuyun Dai, Gustavo Hernandez Abrego, Ji Ma, Vincent Zhao, Yi Luan, Keith Hall, Ming-Wei Chang, et al. Large dual encoders are generalizable retrievers. In *Proceedings of the 2022 Conference on Empirical Methods in Natural Language Processing*, pages 9844–9855, 2022b.

Danny Hernandez, Tom Brown, Tom Conerly, Nova DasSarma, Dawn Drain, Sheer El-Showk, Nelson Elhage, Zac Hatfield-Dodds, Tom Henighan, Tristan Hume, et al. Scaling laws and interpretability of learning from repeated data. *arXiv preprint arXiv:2205.10487*, 2022.

Armand Joulin, Édouard Grave, Piotr Bojanowski, and Tomáš Mikolov. Bag of tricks for efficient text classification. In *Proceedings of the 15th Conference of the European Chapter of the Association for Computational Linguistics: Volume 2, Short Papers*, pages 427–431, 2017.

Zhuyun Dai, Vincent Y Zhao, Ji Ma, Yi Luan, Jianmo Ni, Jing Lu, Anton Bakalov, Kelvin Guu, Keith Hall, and Ming-Wei Chang. Promptagator: Few-shot dense retrieval from 8 examples. In *The Eleventh International Conference on Learning Representations*, 2023. URL https://openreview.net/forum?id=gmL46YMpu2J.

Liang Wang, Nan Yang, Xiaolong Huang, Binxing Jiao, Linjun Yang, Daxin Jiang, Rangan Majumder, and Furu Wei. Text embeddings by weakly-supervised contrastive pre-training. *arXiv preprint arXiv:2212.03533*, 2022.

Yingqi Qu, Yuchen Ding, Jing Liu, Kai Liu, Ruiyang Ren, Wayne Xin Zhao, Daxiang Dong, Hua Wu, and Haifeng Wang. Rocketqa: An optimized training approach to dense passage retrieval for open-domain question answering. In *Proceedings of the 2021 Conference of the North American Chapter of the Association for Computational Linguistics: Human Language Technologies*, pages 5835–5847, 2021.

Taku Kudo and John Richardson. Sentencepiece: A simple and language independent subword tokenizer and detokenizer for neural text processing. In *Proceedings of the 2018 Conference on Empirical Methods in Natural Language Processing: System Demonstrations*, pages 66–71, 2018.

Taku Kudo. Subword regularization: Improving neural network translation models with multiple subword candidates. In *Proceedings of the 56th Annual Meeting of the Association for Computational Linguistics (Volume 1: Long Papers)*, pages 66–75, 2018.

Aäron van den Oord, Yazhe Li, and Oriol Vinyals. Representation learning with contrastive predictive coding. *CoRR*, abs/1807.03748, 2018. URL http://arxiv.org/abs/1807.03748.

Arvind Neelakantan, Tao Xu, Raul Puri, Alec Radford, Jesse Michael Han, Jerry Tworek, Qiming Yuan, Nikolas Tezak, Jong Wook Kim, Chris Hallacy, Johannes Heidecke, Pranav Shyam, Boris Power, Tyna Eloundou Nekoul, Girish Sastry, Gretchen Krueger, David Schnurr, Felipe Petroski Such, Kenny Hsu, Madeleine Thompson, Tabarak Khan, Toki Sherbakov andcalculating Joanne Jang, Peter Welinder, and Lilian Weng. Text and code embeddings by contrastive pre-training. *CoRR*, abs/2201.10005, 2022. URL https://arxiv.org/abs/2201.10005.

Nils Reimers. http://plastimatch.org/doxygen/classHausdorff__distance.html##details Last Access: 14th July 2023, 2023.

Gal Chechik, Varun Sharma, Uri Shalit, and Samy Bengio. Large scale online learning of image similarity through ranking. *Journal of Machine Learning Research*, 11(3), 2010.

Niklas Muennighoff, Nouamane Tazi, Loïc Magne, and Nils Reimers. Mteb: Massive text embedding benchmark, 2023.

Nandan Thakur, Nils Reimers, Andreas Rücklé, Abhishek Srivastava, and Iryna Gurevych. Beir: A heterogenous benchmark for zero-shot evaluation of information retrieval models, 2021.

Nils Reimers and Iryna Gurevych. Sentence-bert: Sentence embeddings using siamese bert-networks. In *Proceedings of the 2019 Conference on Empirical Methods in Natural Language Processing and the 9th International Joint Conference on Natural Language Processing (EMNLP-IJCNLP)*, pages 3982–3992, 2019.

Niklas Muennighoff. Sgpt: Gpt sentence embeddings for semantic search, 2022.

Geoffrey Hinton, Oriol Vinyals, and Jeff Dean. Distilling the knowledge in a neural network, 2015.

Hongjin Su, Weijia Shi, Jungo Kasai, Yizhong Wang, Yushi Hu, Mari Ostendorf, Wen tau Yih, Noah A. Smith, Luke Zettlemoyer, and Tao Yu. One embedder, any task: Instruction-finetuned text embeddings, 2023.

Samyam Rajbhandari, Jeff Rasley, Olatunji Ruwase, and Yuxiong He. Zero: Memory optimizations toward training trillion parameter models. In *SC20: International Conference for High Performance Computing, Networking, Storage and Analysis*, pages 1–16. IEEE, 2020.

Appendix

Model	BIOSSES	SICK-R	STS12	STS13	STS14	STS15	STS16	STS17	STS22	STS Benchm.
sentence-t5-xxl	80.43	**80.47**	78.85	**88.94**	**84.86**	**89.32**	84.67	**89.46**	65.33	**84.01**
sentence-t5-xl	73.12	79.98	**79.02**	88.80	84.33	88.89	**85.31**	88.91	64.32	83.93
gtr-t5-xxl	**81.91**	74.29	70.12	82.72	78.24	86.26	81.61	85.18	65.76	77.73
gtr-t5-xl	78.94	73.63	69.11	81.82	77.07	86.01	82.23	84.90	**66.61**	77.65
sentence-t5-large	78.93	**80.34**	**79.11**	**87.33**	**83.17**	**88.28**	**84.36**	88.99	62.39	**85.36**
gtr-t5-large	**84.86**	73.39	70.33	82.19	77.16	86.31	81.85	83.93	64.30	77.60
`jina-large-v1`	84.43	79.20	74.53	83.16	78.09	86.91	83.65	**90.16**	**64.89**	84.60
sentence-t5-base	75.89	80.18	**78.05**	**85.85**	**82.19**	**87.46**	**84.03**	**89.57**	62.66	**85.52**
gtr-t5-base	79.00	71.45	68.59	79.09	74.64	84.85	81.57	85.80	66.17	79.58
all-mpnet-base-v2	80.43	**80.59**	72.63	83.48	78.00	85.66	80.03	90.60	**67.95**	83.42
`jina-base-v1`	**83.58**	79.14	75.06	80.86	76.13	85.55	81.21	88.98	66.22	82.57
all-MiniLM-L6-v2	81.64	**77.58**	72.37	**80.60**	**75.59**	**85.39**	78.99	**87.59**	**67.21**	**82.03**
`jina-small-v1`	**82.96**	76.33	**74.28**	78.55	73.84	83.71	**80.03**	87.49	64.25	79.20
text-emb-ada-002*	86.35	80.60	69.80	83.27	76.09	86.12	85.96	90.25	68.12	83.17

Table 6: Spearman Correlation for Sentence Similarity Tasks

Model	AskUbuntu-DupQuestions	MindSmall-Reranking	SciDocsRR	StackOverflow-DupQuestions
sentence-t5-xxl	**66.16**	30.60	76.09	52.85
sentence-t5-xl	62.86	29.77	75.16	51.05
gtr-t5-xxl	63.23	**31.93**	**77.96**	**53.50**
gtr-t5-xl	63.08	31.50	76.49	52.79
sentence-t5-large	61.51	30.27	74.88	49.34
gtr-t5-large	61.64	**31.84**	76.39	**51.58**
`jina-large-v1`	**62.83**	31.48	**80.97**	50.38
sentence-t5-base	59.73	30.20	73.96	48.46
gtr-t5-base	60.86	31.33	73.71	51.01
all-mpnet-base-v2	**65.85**	30.97	**88.65**	**51.98**
`jina-base-v1`	62.40	**31.56**	79.31	50.11
all-MiniLM-L6-v2	**63.48**	**30.80**	**87.12**	**50.76**
`jina-small-v1`	60.25	30.68	74.16	47.18
text-emb-ada-002*	62.05	31.45	81.22	50.54

Table 7: Mean Average Precision (mAP@10) for Reranking Tasks

* text-emb-ada-002 appears in a separate category since no model size is known and the embedding size is much higher compared to other models.

Model	FEVER	HotpotQA	MSMARCO	NQ	Quora Retrieval	SciFact	TREC COVID	Argu Ana	Climate FEVER	DBPedia	FiQA 2018	NFCorpus	SCIDOCS	Touche 2020
sentence-t5-xxl	51.20	42.14	27.67	52.87	85.96	55.38	59.48	39.85	14.63	39.19	46.68	**35.08**	**17.17**	21.65
sentence-t5-xl	36.12	37.17	25.17	46.29	85.85	50.91	54.77	39.40	10.61	33.65	44.71	33.18	15.97	22.51
gtr-t5-xxl	**74.08**	**59.67**	**44.05**	**57.24**	**89.09**	**66.77**	51.90	**53.77**	**27.21**	**41.28**	**46.78**	34.18	15.88	**26.76**
gtr-t5-xl	72.18	58.91	43.52	56.16	88.91	64.2	**60.09**	52.81	27.01	39.74	44.19	33.34	15.71	25.26
sentence-t5-large	36.21	33.95	23.96	42.02	85.73	49.91	46.11	39.27	11.36	31.55	**43.55**	31.10	15.38	21.63
gtr-t5-large	**72.66**	**57.85**	**42.73**	**55.09**	**88.47**	**63.42**	56.68	**52.09**	**26.90**	**39.55**	42.79	**32.63**	15.51	**28.29**
jina-large-v1	71.90	54.95	40.34	51.40	88.09	59.76	**57.25**	46.48	21.26	34.13	37.27	32.24	**18.45**	20.73
sentence-t5-base	26.17	33.20	20.70	36.32	85.49	45.76	40.70	44.85	10.37	27.77	34.83	28.65	14.15	20.30
gtr-t5-base	68.93	**54.93**	**41.16**	**50.47**	**87.98**	59.74	56.05	**50.83**	**24.88**	**35.24**	35.15	30.22	14.00	**25.89**
all-mpnet-base-v2	50.86	39.29	39.75	50.45	87.46	**65.57**	51.33	46.52	21.97	32.09	**49.96**	**33.29**	**23.76**	19.93
jina-base-v1	**73.29**	52.78	37.77	47.87	87.63	59.40	**60.57**	49.01	21.48	32.44	34.06	30.38	17.63	18.59
all-MiniLM-L6-v2	51.93	46.51	**36.34**	**43.87**	**87.56**	**64.51**	47.25	**50.17**	**20.27**	**32.33**	**36.87**	**31.59**	**21.64**	**16.90**
jina-small-v1	**69.12**	**47.48**	31.80	38.89	85.69	52.40	**52.30**	43.57	17.25	28.28	25.19	25.96	15.29	16.67
text-emb-ada-002*	74.99	60.90	40.91	51.58	87.60	72.75	68.47	57.44	21.64	39.39	44.41	36.97	18.36	21.61

Table 8: Normalized Discounted Cumulative Gain (nDCG@10) for retrieval tasks

Deepparse : An Extendable, and Fine-Tunable State-Of-The-Art Library for Parsing Multinational Street Addresses

David Beauchemin, Marouane Yassine
Department of Computer Science and Software Engineering, Laval University
Group for Research in Artificial Intelligence of Laval University (GRAIL)
Québec, Canada
david.beauchemin@ift.ulaval.ca, marouane.yassine.1@ulaval.ca

Abstract

Segmenting an address into meaningful components, also known as address parsing, is an essential step in many applications from record linkage to geocoding and package delivery. Consequently, a lot of work has been dedicated to develop accurate address parsing techniques, with machine learning and neural network methods leading the state-of-the-art scoreboard. However, most of the work on address parsing has been confined to academic endeavours with little availability of free and easy-to-use open-source solutions.

This paper presents Deepparse, a Python open-source, extendable, fine-tunable address parsing solution under LGPL-3.0 licence to parse multinational addresses using state-of-the-art deep learning algorithms and evaluated on over 60 countries. It can parse addresses written in any language and use any address standard. The pre-trained model achieves average 99 % parsing accuracies on the countries used for training with no pre-processing nor post-processing needed. Moreover, the library supports fine-tuning with new data to generate a custom address parser.

1 Introduction

Address Parsing is the task of decomposing an address into its different components (Abid et al., 2018). This task is essential to many applications, such as geocoding and record linkage. Indeed, it is quite useful to detect the different parts of an address to find a particular location based on textual data to make an informed decision. Similarly, comparing two addresses to decide whether two or more database entries refer to the same entity can prove to be quite difficult and prone to errors if based on methods such as edit distance algorithms given the various address writing standards.

There have been many efforts to solve the address parsing problem. From rule-based techniques (Xu et al., 2012) to probabilistic approaches and neural network models (Abid et al., 2018), much progress has been made in reaching accurate addresses segmentation. These previous works did a remarkable job of finding solutions for the challenges related to the address parsing task. However, most of these approaches either do not take into account parsing addresses from different countries or do so but at the cost of a considerable amount of meta-data and substantial data pre-processing pipelines (Mokhtari et al.; Li et al., 2014; Wang et al., 2016; Sharma et al., 2018).

However, most of the work on address parsing has been confined to academic endeavours with little availability of free and easy-to-use open-source solutions. In an effort to solve some of the limitations of previous methods, as well as offer an open-source address parsing solution, we have created **Deepparse**[1] (Yassine and Beauchemin, 2020) an LGPL-3.0 licenced Python library. Our work allows anyone with a basic knowledge of Python or command line terminal to conveniently parse addresses from multiple countries using state-of-the-art deep learning models proposed by Yassine et al. (2020, 2022). Deepparse's goal is to parse multinational addresses written in any language or using any address writing format with an extendable and fine-tunable address parser. In addition, **Deepparse** proposes a functionality to easily customize the aforementioned models to new data along with an easy-to-use Docker FastAPI to parse addresses.

This paper's contributions are: First, we describe an open-source Python library for multinational address parsing. Second, we describe its implementation details and natural extensibility due to its fine-tuning possibilities. Third, we benchmark it against other open-source libraries.

[1] https://deepparse.org/

Proceedings of the 3rd Workshop for Natural Language Processing Open Source Software (NLP-OSS 2023), pages 19–24
December 6, 2023 ©2023 Association for Computational Linguistics

2 Related work

Address parsing has been approached on the academic front using probabilistic machine learning models such as Hidden Markov Models and Conditional Random Fields (CRF) (Li et al., 2014; Wang et al., 2016; Abid et al., 2018), as well as deep learning models mainly based on the recurrent neural network (RNN) architecture (Sharma et al., 2018; Mokhtari et al.; Abid et al., 2018). Regarding openly available software, most of the existing packages cater to US postal addresses. For instance, *pyaddress*[2] allows for the decomposition of US addresses into eight different attributes with a possibility to specify acceptable "street names", "cities" and "street suffixes" in order to improve parsing accuracy. Similarly, *address-parser*[3] identifies as "Yet another python address parser for US postal addresses" and enables users to extract multiple address components such as "house numbers", "street names", "cardinal directions" and "zip codes". These two packages are based on a combination of predefined component lists and regular expressions. In contrast, *usaddress*[4] uses a probabilistic model that users can fine-tune using their data. Another openly available avenue for address parsing is Geocoding APIs, which can result in highly precise parsed addresses based on reverse geocoding. However, while being openly available, Geocoding APIs are often not free and not always convenient to use for a programming layperson.

The aforementioned approaches are limited to parsing addresses from a single country and either cannot handle a multinational scope of address parsing or would need to be adjusted to do so. To tackle this problem, Libpostal[5], a C library for international address parsing, has been proposed. This library uses a CRF-based model trained with an averaged Perceptron for scalability. The model was trained on Libpostal dataset[6] and achieved a 99.45 % full parse accuracy[7] using an extensive pre and post-processing pipeline. However, this requires putting addresses through a heavy preprocessing pipeline before feeding them to the prediction model, and it does not seem possible to develop a new address parser based on the documentation. A thorough search of the relevant literature yielded no open-source neural network-based software for multinational address parsing.

3 Implementation

Deepparse is divided into three high-level components: pre-processors, embeddings model, and tagging model. The first component, the pre-processor, is a series of simple handcrafted pre-processing functions to be applied as a data cleaning procedure before the embedding component, such as lowercasing the address text and removing commas. By default, Deepparse simply lowercase and removes all commas in the address. The library does not require a complex pre-processing pipeline, but one can be defined and used more complex one if needed since Deepparse is built so users can handcraft and use a custom pre-processor during this phase.

The last two components are illustrated in Figure 1. We can see that the embeddings model component (black) encodes each token (i.e. word) of the address into a recurrent dense representation. At the end of the sentence, the component generates a single dense representation for the overall address generated from the individual address components. Then, this address-dense representation is used as input to the tagging model component (red), where each address component is decoded and classified into its appropriate tag. These two components do not rely on named entity recognition to parse addresses as opposed to the one proposed by Abid et al. (2018).

Deepparse proposes two embeddings model approaches and four pre-trained tagging model architectures; all approaches can be used with CPU or GPU setup. All pre-trained approaches have been trained on our publicly available dataset[8], based on to the Libpostal dataset, and achieved parse accuracies higher than 99% on the 20 trained countries without using pre or post-processing[9].

The following sub-section will briefly discuss how these two components work. For more details on the algorithms behind both components, readers can refer to Yassine et al. (2020, 2022). We will finish this section with a presentation on Deepparse's unique flexibility in developing a new

[2]https://github.com/SwoopSearch/pyaddress

[3]https://github.com/CivicKnowledge/address_parser

[4]https://github.com/datamade/usaddress

[5]https://github.com/openvenues/libpostal

[6]https://github.com/openvenues/libpostal#training-data

[7]The accuracy was computed considering the entire sequence and was not focused on individual tokens.

[8]https://github.com/GRAAL-Research/deepparse-address-data

[9]The accuracy for each sequence is computed as the proportion of the tags predicted correctly by the model. Predicting all the tags correctly for a sequence yields perfect accuracy.

address parser.

3.1 Embedding Model

Our objective was to build a single neural network to parse addresses from multiple countries. Thus, access to embeddings for different languages at runtime was necessary. Since the use of alignment vectors (Joulin et al., 2018; Conneau et al., 2017) would have introduced the unnecessary overhead of detecting of the source language to project word embeddings from different languages in the same space, Deepparse proposes the following two methods.

First, we use a fixed pre-trained monolingual French fastText model. We chose French embeddings since this language shares Latin roots with many languages in our test set. It is also due to the large corpus on which these embeddings were trained. We refer to this embeddings model technique as **fastText**.

Second, we use an encoding of words using MultiBPEmb and merge the obtained embeddings for each word into one word embedding using an RNN. This method has been shown to give good results in a multilingual setting (Heinzerling and Strube, 2019). Our RNN network of choice is a Bidirectional LSTM (Bi-LSTM) with a hidden state dimension of 300. We build the word embeddings by running the concatenated forward and backward hidden states corresponding to the last time step for each word decomposition through a fully connected layer of which the number of neurons equals the dimension of the hidden states. This approach produces 300-dimensional word embeddings. We refer to this embeddings model technique as **BPEmb**.

3.2 Tagging Model

Our downstream tagging model is a Seq2Seq model. Using Seq2Seq architecture as tagging model is effective for data with sequential pattern (Huang et al., 2019; Omelianchuk et al., 2021; Jin and Yu, 2021; Raman et al., 2022) such as address. The architecture consists of a one-layer unidirectional LSTM encoder and a one-layer unidirectional LSTM decoder followed by a fully-connected linear layer with a softmax activation. Both the encoder's and decoder's hidden states are of dimension 1024. The embedded address sequence is fed to the encoder that produces hidden states, the last of which is used as a context vector to initialize the decoder's hidden states. The decoder is then given a "Beginning Of Sequence" (BOS) token as input, and at each time step, the prediction from the last step is used as input. To better adapt the model to the task at hand and to facilitate the convergence process, we only require the decoder to produce a sequence with the same length as the input address. This approach differs from the traditional Seq2Seq architecture in which the decoder makes predictions until it predicts the ends-of-sequence token. The decoder's outputs are forwarded to the linear layer, of which the number of neurons equals the tag space dimensionality. The softmax activation function computes probabilities over the linear layer's outputs to predict the most likely token at each time step.

Deepparse proposes four pre-trained tagging model architectures: one using each embedding model approach, namely **fastText** and **BPEmb**, and one using each embedding model approach with an added attention mechanisms. Attention mechanisms are neural network components that can produce a distribution describing the interdependence between a model's inputs and outputs (general attention) or amongst model inputs themselves (self-attention). These mechanisms are common in natural language processing encoder-decoder architectures such as neural machine translation models (Bahdanau et al., 2015) since they have been shown to improve models' performance and help address some of the issues RNNs suffer from when dealing with long sequences. Also, Yassine et al. (2022) has shown that the attention mechanism has significantly increased performance for incomplete addresses. Incomplete addresses do not include all the components defined by a country-written standard—for example, an address missing its postal code. They are cumbersome and cause problems for many industries, such as delivery services and insurance companies (Nagabhushan, 2009).

Choosing a Model The difference between all four models is their capabilities to generate better results on unseen address patterns and unseen language. For example, as shown in Yassine et al. (2020), BPEmb embeddings models generate better parsing on address from India, even if the language and address pattern was unseen during training compared to FastText embeddings model. However, this increase in generalization performance comes at the cost of longer inference time (will be discussed in section 4). As shown in Yassine et al.

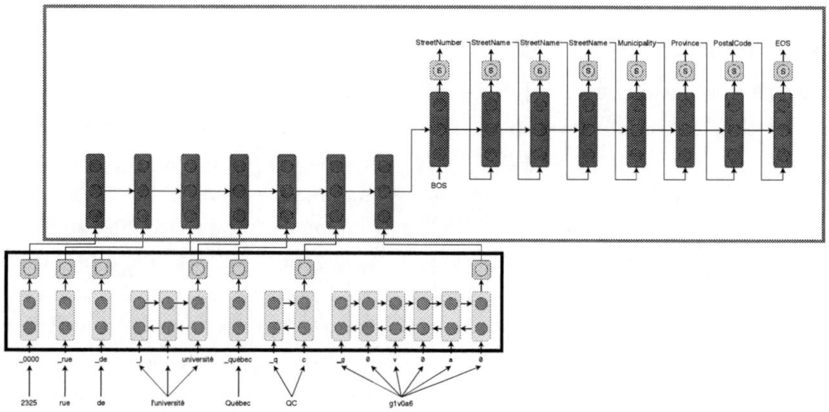

Figure 1: Illustration of our architecture using one of the two embedding model component (black) approach. Each word in the address is encoded using an embedding model, in this case, MultiBPEmb (the BPE segmentation algorithm replaces the numbers in the address with zeros). The embeddings are fed to a BiLSTM (rounded rectangle with two circles). The last hidden state for each word is run through a fully connected layer (rounded rectangle with one circle). The resulting embeddings are given as input to the tagging model components (red). The "S" in the fully connected layer following the Seq2Seq decoder stands for the Softmax function.

(2022), models using the attention mechanism also demonstrate the same improved generalization performance compared to their respective embeddings approaches but with the same cost of inference performance. Thus, one must trade off generalization performance over inference performance.

3.3 Developing a New Parser

One of the unique particularities of Deepparse is the ability to develop a new parser for one's specific needs. Namely, one can fine-tune one of our pretrained models for their specific needs using our public dataset or theirs. Doing so can improve Deepparse's performance on new data or unseen countries, giving Deepparse great flexibility. As shown in Figure 2, developing (i.e. fine-tuning) a new parser using our pre-trained public models is relatively easy and can be done with a few Python lines of code.

Moreover, as shown in Figure 3, one can also use Deepparse to retrain our pre-trained models on new prediction tags easily, and it is not restricted to the ones we have used during training, making it flexible for new addresses pattern.

Finally, as shown in Figure 4 it is also possible to easily reconfigure the tagging model architecture to either create a smaller architecture, thus potentially reducing memory usage and inference time, or increase it to improve performance on more complex address data. Also, one can do all of the above at the same time.

4 Practical results

In this section, since Libpostal and Deeparse are comparable in terms of accuracy, both are almost perfect; we benchmark Deepparse memory usage and inference time with 183,000 addresses of the Deepparse dataset. Our parsing experiment processes 183,000 addresses using different batch sizes ($2^0, \ldots, 2^9$) and assesses memory usage and inference time performance for Libpostal and Deepparse. Since Deepparse can batch address, we assess the inference time as the average processing time per address (i.e. $\frac{\text{Total time to process all addresses}}{183{,}000} =$ time per address). Libpostal does not offer batching functionality. The experiment used a GPU and a CPU to assess the accelerator's gain. Thus, we also assess GPU memory usage in our experiment that uses such devices.

Our experiment was conducted on Linux OS 22.04, with the latest Python version (i.e. 3.11), Python memory_profiler 0.61.0, Torch 2.0 and CUDA 11.7 (done March 21, 2023). Our GPU device is an RTX 2080.

Table 1 and Table 2 present our experiment results using respectively a GPU device or not (i.e. CPU) with or without using batch processing. In both tables, we can see that Libpostal achieved better inference time performance. However, Deepparse still achieved interesting performance, particularly with batching that reduced by one order of magnitude the average processing time of execution.

```
address_parser = AddressParser(model_type="fasttext")
address_parser.retrain(dataset, train_ratio=0.8, epochs=5)
```

Figure 2: Code example to fine-tune our "FastText" pre-trained model on a new dataset for 5 epochs using a 80-20 % train-evaluation dataset ratio.

```
address_parser = AddressParser(model_type="fasttext")
new_tag_dictionary = {"ATag": 0, "AnotherTag": 1, "EOS": 2}
address_parser.retrain(dataset, prediction_tags=tag_dictionary)
```

Figure 3: Code example to retrained our "FastText" pre-trained model on a new dataset with new tags.

	GPU Memory usage (GB)	RAM usage (GB)	Mean time of execution (not batched) (s)	Mean time of execution (batched) (s)
fastText	~1	~8	~0.0023	~0.0004
fastTextAttention	~1.1	~8	~0.0043	~0.0007
BPEmb	~1	~1	~0.0055	~0.0015
BPEmbAttention	~1.1	~1	~0.0081	~0.0019
Libpostal	0	~2.3	~0.00004	~N/A

Table 1: GPU and RAM usage and average processing time to parse 183,000 addresses using a GPU device with or without batching.

	RAM usage (GB)	Mean time of execution (not batched) (s)	Mean time of execution (batched) (s)
fastText	~8	~0.0128	~0.0026
fastTextAttention	~8	~0.0230	~0.0057
BPEmb	~1	~0.0179	~0.0044
BPEmbAttention	~1	~0.0286	~0.0075
Libpostal	~1	~0.00004	~N/A

Table 2: RAM usage and average processing time to parse 183,000 addresses using only CPU with or without batching.

5 Future Development and Maintaining the Library

As our development roadmap, we plan to improve the documentation by adding a training guide on how one can develop its address parser. Also, we plan to offer new deep learning architecture that leverages more recent progress, such as a Transformer based architecture and to support more words embedding models, such as contextualized embeddings like ELMO embeddings (Peters et al., 2018). Moreover, we plan to offer a minimalist application to address parsing for coding laypersons. Finally, we aim at improving inference time performance by using recent integration of quantization technique (Cheng et al., 2018; Wu et al., 2020) in PyTorch, namely, "performing computations and storing tensors at lower bitwidths than floating point precision" (PyTorch, 2023). The library is maintained mainly by the library authors, and three to four releases are published yearly to improve and maintain the solution.

6 Conclusion

In conclusion, we have described Deepparse, an extendable and fine-tunable state-of-the-art library for parsing multinational street addresses. It is an open-source library, has over 99.9% test coverage and integrates easily with existing natural language processing pipelines. Deepparse offers great flexibility to users who can develop their address parser using our easy-to-use fine-tuning interface. Although slower than the Libpostal alternative implemented in low-level language C, Deepparse successfully parses more than 99% of address components.

Acknowledgment

This research was supported by the Natural Sciences and Engineering Research Council of Canada (IRCPJ 529529-17) and a Canadian insurance company. We wish to thank the reviewers for their comments regarding our work and methodology.

References

N. Abid, A. ul Hasan, and F. Shafait. 2018. DeepParse: A Trainable Postal Address Parser. In *Digital Image Computing: Techniques and Applications*, pages 1–8.

Dzmitry Bahdanau, Kyunghyun Cho, and Yoshua Bengio. 2015. Neural machine translation by jointly learning to align and translate. In *International Conference on Learning Representations.*

Jian Cheng, Pei-song Wang, Gang Li, Qing-hao Hu, and Han-qing Lu. 2018. Recent Advances in Efficient Computation of Deep Convolutional Neural Networks. *Frontiers of Information Technology & Electronic Engineering*, 19:64–77.

```
address_parser = AddressParser(model_type="fasttext")
seq2seq_params = {"encoder_hidden_size": 512, "decoder_hidden_size": 512}
address_parser.retrain(dataset, seq2seq_params=seq2seq_params)
```

Figure 4: Code example to train a new model using our Seq2Seq architecture with a different configuration (i.e. encoder and decoder hidden size).

Alexis Conneau, Guillaume Lample, Marc'Aurelio Ranzato, Ludovic Denoyer, and Hervé Jégou. 2017. Word Translation Without Parallel Data.

Benjamin Heinzerling and Michael Strube. 2019. Sequence tagging with contextual and non-contextual subword representations: A multilingual evaluation. In *Proceedings of the Annual Meeting of the Association for Computational Linguistics*, pages 273–291.

Yi-Ting Huang, Yu-Yuan Chen, Chih-Chun Yang, Yeali Sun, Shun-Wen Hsiao, and Meng Chang Chen. 2019. Tagging Malware Intentions by Using Attention-Based Sequence-To-Sequence Neural Network. In *Information Security and Privacy*, pages 660–668. Springer.

Guozhe Jin and Zhezhou Yu. 2021. A Hierarchical Sequence-To-Sequence Model for Korean POS Tagging. *Transactions on Asian and Low-Resource Language Information Processing*, 20(2):1–13.

Armand Joulin, Piotr Bojanowski, Tomas Mikolov, Hervé Jégou, and Edouard Grave. 2018. Loss in Translation: Learning Bilingual Word Mapping with a Retrieval Criterion. In *Proceedings of the Conference on Empirical Methods in Natural Language Processing*.

Xiang Li, Hakan Kardes, Xin Wang, and Ang Sun. 2014. HMM-Based Address Parsing: Efficiently Parsing Billions of Addresses on MapReduce. In *Proceedings of the ACM SIGSPATIAL International Conference on Advances in Geographic Information Systems*, page 433–436. Association for Computing Machinery.

Shekoofeh Mokhtari, Ahmad Mahmoody, Dragomir Yankov, and Ning Xie. Tagging Address Queries in Maps Search. *Proceedings of the AAAI Conference on Artificial Intelligence*, 33:9547–9551.

P Nagabhushan. 2009. A Soft Computing Model for Mapping Incomplete/Approximate Postal Addresses to Mail Delivery Points. *Applied Soft Computing*, 9(2):806–816.

Kostiantyn Omelianchuk, Vipul Raheja, and Oleksandr Skurzhanskyi. 2021. Text Simplification by Tagging. *arXiv:2103.05070*.

Matthew E. Peters, Mark Neumann, Mohit Iyyer, Matt Gardner, Christopher Clark, Kenton Lee, and Luke Zettlemoyer. 2018. Deep Contextualized Word Representations. *arXiv:1802.05365*.

PyTorch. 2023. Quantization — PyTorch 2.0 documentation. Accessed online (30-07-2023) `https://pytorch.org/docs/stable/quantization.html`.

Karthik Raman, Iftekhar Naim, Jiecao Chen, Kazuma Hashimoto, Kiran Yalasangi, and Krishna Srinivasan. 2022. Transforming Sequence Tagging Into a Seq2Seq Task. *arXiv:2203.08378*.

S. Sharma, R. Ratti, I. Arora, A. Solanki, and G. Bhatt. 2018. Automated Parsing of Geographical Addresses: A Multilayer Feedforward Neural Network Based Approach. In *IEEE International Conference on Semantic Computing*, pages 123–130.

M. Wang, V. Haberland, A. Yeo, A. Martin, J. Howroyd, and J. M. Bishop. 2016. A Probabilistic Address Parser Using Conditional Random Fields and Stochastic Regular Grammar. In *International Conference on Data Mining Workshops*, pages 225–232.

Hao Wu, Patrick Judd, Xiaojie Zhang, Mikhail Isaev, and Paulius Micikevicius. 2020. Integer Quantization for Deep Learning Inference: Principles and Empirical Evaluation. *arXiv:2004.09602*.

Sen Xu, Soren Flexner, and Vitor R. Carvalho. 2012. Geocoding billions of addresses: Toward a spatial record linkage system with big data.

Marouane Yassine and David Beauchemin. 2020. Deepparse: A State-Of-The-Art Deep Learning Multinational Addresses Parser.

Marouane Yassine, David Beauchemin, François Laviolette, and Luc Lamontagne. 2022. Multinational Address Parsing: A Zero-Shot Evaluation. *International Journal of Information Science and Technology*, 6(3):40–50.

Marouane Yassine, David Beauchemin, François Laviolette, and Luc Lamontagne. 2020. Leveraging Subword Embeddings for Multinational Address Parsing. In *2020 IEEE Congress on Information Science and Technology*, pages 353–360.

PyThaiNLP: Thai Natural Language Processing in Python

Wannaphong Phatthiyaphaibun[♦], **Korakot Chaovavanich**[†], **Charin Polpanumas**[†],
Arthit Suriyawongkul[‡], **Lalita Lowphansirikul**[♦], **Pattarawat Chormai**[§¶],
Peerat Limkonchotiwat[♦], **Thanathip Suntorntip**[♣], **Can Udomcharoenchaikit**[♦]
[♦]VISTEC, [†]PyThaiNLP, [‡]Trinity College Dublin,
[§]Technische Universität Berlin, [¶]Max Planck School of Cognition, [♣]Wisesight
wannaphong.p_s21@vistec.ac.th

Abstract

We present PyThaiNLP, a free and open-source natural language processing (NLP) library for Thai language implemented in Python. It provides a wide range of software, models, and datasets for Thai language. We first provide a brief historical context of tools for Thai language prior to the development of PyThaiNLP. We then outline the functionalities it provided as well as datasets and pre-trained language models. We later summarize its development milestones and discuss our experience during its development. We conclude by demonstrating how industrial and research communities utilize PyThaiNLP in their work. The library is freely available at https://github.com/pythainlp/pythainlp.

1 Introduction

In recent years, the field of natural language processing has witnessed remarkable advancements, catalyzing breakthroughs for various applications. However, Thai has remained comparatively underserved due to the challenges posed by limited language resources (Arreerard et al., 2022).

Thai is the de facto national language of Thailand. It belongs to Tai linguistic group within the KraDai language family. According to Ethnologue (Eberhard et al., 2023), there are 60.2 million users of Central Thai, of which 20.8 million are native (2000). If including the Northern (6 million, 2004), Northeastern (15 million, 1983), and Southern (4.5 million, 2006) variants, there are estimated 85.7 million users of Thais speakers around the world.

Thai is a scriptio continua or has neither spaces nor other marks between the words or sentences in its most common writing style. (Sornlertlamvanich et al., 2000). The lack of clear word and sentence boundaries leads to ambiguity that cannot be disambiguated using merely just grammatical knowledge (Supnithi et al., 2004).

Although many closed-source open APIs for NLP have an ability to process Thai language[1], we believe that an open-source toolbox is essential for both researchers and practitioners to not only access the NLP capabilities but also gain full transparency and trust on both training data and algorithms.[2] This allows the community to adapt and further develop the functionalities as needed, making a crucial step towards democratizing NLP.

This paper introduces PyThaiNLP, an open-source Thai natural language processing library written in Python programming language. Its features span from a simple dictionary-based word tokenizer, to a statistical named-entity recognition, and an instruction-following large language model. The library was released in 2016 under an Open Source Initiative-approved Apache License 2.0 that allows free use and modification of software, including commercial use.

2 Open-source Thai NLP before PyThaiNLP

Before PyThaiNLP started in 2016, some free and open-source software do exist for different Thai NLP tasks, but there were no unified open-source toolkits that unified multiple tools or tasks in a single library, and the number of available Thai NLP datasets was low compared to high-resource languages like Chinese, English, or German.

Natural Language Toolkit (NLTK) (Bird and Loper, 2004), one of the most comprehensive and most popular NLP libraries in Python at the time, did not support Thai. OpenNLP, another popular free and open-source NLP toolkit written in Java,

[1]Such as those provided by commercial cloud service providers and "AI for Thai", the government-funded Thai AI service platform at https://aiforthai.in.th/.

[2]For a discussion about concentrated power and the political economy of 'open' AI, see Widder et al. (2023).

Proceedings of the 3rd Workshop for Natural Language Processing Open Source Software (NLP-OSS 2023), pages 25–36
December 6, 2023 ©2023 Association for Computational Linguistics

started having Thai models in version 1.4 (2008)[3] but in version 1.5 (2010) Thai was no longer listed in its supported languages[4].

Open Thai language resources, like annotated corpora, were also limited in size and number. "Publicly available" datasets tend to have restricted access, either through restrictive licenses[5] or the registration requirement, or both.

Because there is a few toolkits available, limited in documentation and performance, short of rigorous benchmarking, and/or lack of maintenance, Thai NLP reseachers had to spend their limited time and resources building basic components and/or collecting a dataset before they could proceed further for more advanced problems. The limited availability of source codes and datasets also affects reproducibility.

Examples of Thai NLP tools and datasets before PyThaiNLP:

- **Word tokenization:** ICU BreakIterator (IBM Corporation et al., 1999) [Unicode License] based on Gillam (1999), LibThai (Thai Linux Working Group, 2001) [LGPL], KU Wordcut (Sudprasert and Kawtrakul, 2003) [GPL], SWATH (Charoenpornsawat, 2003) [GPL] based on Meknavin et al. (1997), LexTo (National Electronics and Computer Technology Center, 2006) [LGPL], OpenNLP (Bierner et al., 2008) [LGPL], TLex (Haruechaiyasak and Kongyoung, 2009) [Freeware], and wordcutpy (Satayamas, 2015) [LGPL]. Haruechaiyasak et al. (2008) provided a comparative study of some of these tools.
- **Part-of-speech (POS) tagging:** OpenNLP and RDRPOSTagger (Nguyen et al., 2014) [GPL] support Thai POS tagging. There are corpora such as ORCHID (Sornlertlamvanich et al., 1999) and NAiST (Kawtrakul et al., 2002) which provide not only POS but also word boundaries.
- **Named-entity recognition (NER):** Polyglot (Al-Rfou, 2015) [GPL], a multilingual NLP software, supports Thai NER based on Al-Rfou et al. (2015). For datasets, BEST-2009 corpus (Kosawat et al., 2009) is available but cannot be used commercially, as its license is Creative Commons Attribution-NonCommercial-ShareAlike Public License.
- **Automatic speech recognition (ASR):** Thai Language Audio Resource Center (Thai ARC) corpus (Hoonchamlong et al., 1997) provides audio recordings of dialects and speech styles, with transcripts; it is not designed specifically for ASR. NECTEC-ATR (Kasuriya et al., 2003a), LOTUS (Kasuriya et al., 2003b), LOTUS-BN (Chotimongkol et al., 2009), LOTUS-Cell (Chotimongkol et al., 2010), CU-MFEC (Kertkeidkachorn et al., 2012) and TSync-2 are ASR corpora for different domains and tasks; their licenses are not fully open. See Charoenporn et al. (2004), Wutiwiwatchai and Furui (2007), and Kertkeidkachorn et al. (2012) for reviews.

Apart from the ones listed above, more open-source Thai word tokenizers were released after 2009 as a result of BEST (Benchmark for Enhancing the Standard of Thai language processing) evaluation for Thai word segmentation organized by the National Electronics and Computer Technology Center (NECTEC) in 2009 (Kosawat, 2009), and 2010[6]. Unfortunately, these tokenizers are no longer maintained and are not accessible at the time of writing. The most impactful contribution from BEST, however, is the BEST-2010 word segmentation dataset that was publicly released. This dataset provides a basis for a lot of modern Thai open-source word segmentation software.

We should also mention the Thai Language Toolkit (TLTK) (Aroonmanakun and Thamrongrattanarit, 2018). While releasing its source code a few years after, it is richer in features than PyThaiNLP at the time. Its first release on Python Package Index (version 0.3.4, February 2018) includes statistical syllable and word segmentation (Aroonmanakun, 2002), POS tagging, and spelling suggestion. Its latest version, as

[3] https://opennlp.sourceforge.net/models-1.4. Its README from December 2008 also mentioned Thai components: https://web.archive.org/web/20081219153426/http://opennlp.sourceforge.net/README.html

[4] https://opennlp.sourceforge.net/models-1.5. Arreerard et al. (2022), however, reports that Apache OpenNLP supports these basic Thai NLP tasks: word tokenization, part-of-speech tagging, and sentence detection.

[5] Even today, this practice continues: take, for instance, the LST20 corpus from NECTEC, which has multiple layers of linguistic annotation. However, the free version can only be used for non-commercial purposes. See https://opend-portal.nectec.or.th/en/dataset/lst20-corpus.

[6] https://thailang.nectec.or.th/archive/indexa290.html

of writing, features discourse unit segmentation, NER, grapheme-to-phoneme conversion, IPA transcription, romanization, and more. To date, TLTK and PyThaiNLP are the only two comprehensive Thai NLP libraries for Python. However, TLTK's documentation is still quite limited.

3 PyThaiNLP and Its Ecosystem

Our primary objective is to ensure the user-friendliness and simplicity of the library. Drawing inspiration from NLTK, we follow numerous established interfaces. For example, `word_tokenize` and `pos_tag`. In addition, we also create datasets and pre-trained models for the Thai language. Figure 1 illustrates the overview of PyThaiNLP's functionalities and its ecosystem. Table 1 displays the development milestones of PyThaiNLP.

We will discuss here only popular features and major datasets/models.

3.1 Features

3.1.1 Word and Sentence Tokenization

PyThaiNLP supports many word tokenization algorithms.[7] The default algorithm is NewMM which is dictionary-based maximum matching (Sornlertlamvanich, 1993) and utilizes Thai character cluster (Theeramunkong et al., 2000). The pure-Python tokenizer performs reasonably well on public benchmarks. Chormai et al. (2020) demonstrated that it is the fastest word tokenizer on the BEST 2010 benchmark, with 71.18 % accuracy (compared to state-of-the-art at 95.60 %). Thanathip Suntorntip ported NewMM to Rust programming language[8], resulting in an even faster word tokenizer in our toolbox.

For sentence tokenization, we trained a conditional random field (CRF) model, using python-crfsuite (Peng and Korobov, 2014), on translated TED transcripts and Thai sentence boundaries are assumed to be denoted by English sentence boundaries (Lowphansirikul et al., 2021b).

3.1.2 Spell Checking

For spell checking, we have many engines; the Norvig (2007) one uses a spelling dictionary from Thai National Corpus (Aroonmanakun et al., 2009), symspellpy (mmb L, 2018) that is a Python port of SymSpell v6.7.1, and phunspell (Wright, 2021) that is a port of Hunspell.

3.1.3 Phonetic Algorithm and Transliteration

PyThaiNLP supports a couple of grapheme-to-phoneme (g2p) conversion engines. We trained Thai-g2p model with data from Wiktionary[9], a free online dictionary.

PyThaiNLP implemented many Thai Soundex algorithms. For example, Lorchirachoonkul (1982), Udompanich (1983), Thai-English cross-language Soundex (Suwanvisat and Prasitjutrakul, 1998), and MetaSound (Metaphone-Soundex combination) (Snae and Brückner, 2009).

PyThaiNLP supports the following transliteration implementations: Thai romanization using the Royal Thai General System of Transcription (RTGS), transliteration of romanized Japanese/Korean/Mandarin/Vietnamese texts to Thai using Wunsen library (cakimpei, 2022)[10], and Thai word pronunciation.

3.1.4 Sequence Tagging (NER and POS)

We create a named-entity recognition model called Thai NER (Phatthiyaphaibun, 2022) by finetuning the WangchanBERTa model (Lowphansirikul et al., 2021a) and CRF model.

For part-of-speech tagging, we trained a CRF tagger, a perceptron tagger (Honnibal, 2013), a unigram tagger, and finetuned the WangchanBERTa model. The POS training sets are derived from ORCHID corpus (Sornlertlamvanich et al., 1999), Blackboard Treebank annotated based on the LST20 Annotation Guideline (Boonkwan et al., 2020), and Parallel Universal Dependencies (PUD) treebanks (Smith et al., 2018).

3.1.5 Coreference Resolution and Entity Linking

For coreference resolution, we create Han-Coref, a Thai coreference resolution corpus and model (Phatthiyaphaibun and Limkonchotiwat, 2023).

For entity linking, PyThaiNLP supports it using BELA model (Plekhanov et al., 2023).

3.1.6 Word Embeddings

We extract token embeddings from our thai2fit (Polpanumas and Phatthiyaphaibun, 2021), a

[7]For the ease of experimenting with different word tokenization algorithms, Pattarawat Chormai has created a Thai word tokenizers collection as a Docker container image: `https://github.com/PyThaiNLP/docker-thai-tokenizers`.

[8]`https://github.com/pythainlp/nlpo3`

[9]`https://www.wiktionary.org/`

[10]The library implements various transliteration systems that recommended by the Royal Society of Thailand.

Features in PyThaiNLP

Tokenizers	Phonetic Algorithm and Transliteration	Embedding	Sequence Tagging
Character Cluster and Syllable Level Word Level Sentence Level	Grapheme-to-Phoneme Soundex Thai-English Transliteration	Word Level Sentence Level	Named-Entity Recognition Part-of-Speech Tagging
Automatic Speech Recognition*	**Co-reference and Entity Linking**	**Spell Checking**	**Machine Translation***

Datasets

VISTEC-TPTH-2020 (Limkonchotiwat et al., 2021) Task: *Word Tokenization*; Domain: *social media*	**Thai NER** (Phatthiyaphaibun, 2022) Task: *Named-Entity Recognition*; Domain: *news and Wikipedia articles*
SCB-MT-EN-TH* (Lowphansirikul et al., 2020) Task: *Coreference Resolution*; Domain: *news and Wikipedia articles*	**Han-Coref** (Phatthiyaphaibun and Limkonchotiwat, 2023) Task: *Coreference Resolution*; Domain: *news and Wikipedia articles*

Pre-trained Langauge Models

WangchanBERTa* (Lowphansirikul et al., 2021a) *Thai Pre-trained Language Model*	**WangchanGLM** (Polpanumas et al., 2023) *Multilingual Instruction-Following Model*

*: in collaboration with the VISTEC-depa Thailand Artificial Intelligence Research Institute

Figure 1: Functionalities, datasets, and pre-trained language models available in PyThaiNLP's ecosystem.

word-level ULMFiT language model (Howard and Ruder, 2018) (Howard and Gugger, 2020) trained on Thai Wikipedia, and use them as word embeddings for PyThaiNLP. It was the state-of-the-art pre-trained model in many Thai classification benchmarks (Polpanumas and Suwansri, 2020) before the multilingual BERT model was released (PyCon Thailand, 2019).

3.1.7 Machine Translation

We collaborated with VISTEC-depa Thailand Artificial Intelligence Research Institute (AIResearch.in.th)[11] to create the English-Thai translation dataset and model. The model outperformed Google Translate on an out-of-sample test set at the time of release (Lowphansirikul et al., 2021b).

3.1.8 Automatic Speech Recognition

In order to develop a dataset for ASR, PyThaiNLP members contribute to the development of Common Voice corpus (Ardila et al., 2020), including Thai sentence cleanup and validation rules for its Sentence Collector[12], an online campaign inviting people to contribute Thai sentences, and offline events for volunteers to contribute their voices and voice validation.

Utilizing Common Voice Corpus 7.0, we created a Thai ASR model in collaboration with AIResearch.in.th and achieved the lowest character error rate in a benchmark (VISTEC-depa AI Research Institute of Thailand, 2023).

3.2 Datasets

3.2.1 VISTEC-TPTH-2020: Word Tokenization, Spell Checking and Correction

VISTEC-TPTH-2020 is a Thai word tokenization and spell checking dataset in the social media domain, the largest one to date (Limkonchotiwat et al., 2021). We collected 50,000 sentences from top trending posts on Twitter in 2020 and selected only posts with substantial character counts. This dataset is a multi-task dataset, including mention detection, spell checking, and spell correction.

3.2.2 Thai NER: Named Entity Recognition

Thai NER is a Thai named-entity recognition dataset. We curated text from various domains including news, Wikipedia articles, government documents, as well as text from other Thai NER datasets. The data is manually re-labeled for consistency (Phatthiyaphaibun, 2022).

3.2.3 Han-Coref: Coreference Resolution

Han-Coref is a coreference resolution dataset containing 1,339 documents in news and Wikipedia domains (Phatthiyaphaibun and Limkonchotiwat, 2023).

3.2.4 scb-mt-en-th-2020: English-Thai Machine Translation

scb-mt-en-th-2020 is an English-Thai sentence pair dataset consisting of 1,001,752 text pairs

[11]AIResearch.in.th is an initiative co-funded by a research university and a government agency, namely Vidyasirimedhi Institute of Science and Technology (VISTEC) in Wang Chan, Rayong, and the Digital Economy Promotion Agency (depa) under the Ministry of Digital Economy and Society, to create AI infrastructure for Thailand.

[12]`https://github.com/common-voice/sentence-collector`

(Lowphansirikul et al., 2021b). It is a collaborative work with AIResearch.in.th.

3.3 Pre-trained Language Models

WangchanBERTa is an encoder-only pre-trained Thai language model. Based on public benchmarks, it is the current state-of-the-art (Lowphansirikul et al., 2021a). It is also a collaborative work with AIResearch.in.th.

WangChanGLM (Polpanumas et al., 2023) is a multilingual instruction-following model finetuned from XGLM (Lin et al., 2022).

4 Community and Project Milestones

4.1 Foundation Years (2016-2019)

Wannaphong Phatthiyaphaibun, a high school student at the time, created PyThaiNLP in 2016 as a hobby project. He wanted to create a simple Thai chatbot in Python. He used PyICU as a word tokenizer and soon found out that Thai language did not have a comprehensive NLP toolkit in Python like NLTK (Bird and Loper, 2004). He decided to create PyThaiNLP and hosted the project on GitHub[13].

After the first few official releases, following Korakot Chaovavanich's suggestion, a "Thai Natural Language Processing" group has been created as a public Facebook group[14]. This serves as a main venue to showcase PyThaiNLP's capabilities and a hub for Thai NLP researchers and practitioners to discuss the field. Today, the group has over 16,000 members and is Thailand's largest NLP interest group. This communication channel also performs a recruiting function for us. The first offline meetup of the group occurred in 24 May 2018 as a bird-of-a-feather session after a Data Science BKK meetup[15].

Many of our main contributors, such as Charin Polpanumas and Arthit Suriyawongkul organically joined the project from the community. At this stage, we created foundational capabilities such as word tokenization, part-of-speech tagging, subword tokenization, named-entity recognition, and word vectors. A lot of code cleaning, reorganization, and documentation also happened around 2018-2019. This included the adoption of PEP 484 type hints[16] and other Python best practices to make the code even more readable and facilitate off-line type checkers. The adoption of PyThaiNLP can be reflected by the number of stars on GitHub the project received over the years (Figure 2).

4.2 Gaining Resources for Large Language Models (2019-present)

The growing activity of PyThaiNLP development can be seen from the number of code commits to the Git repository, which reached its peak in Q4 2019[17]. In 2020, the project began a collaboration with AIResearch.in.th. Their main focus was to create and distribute open-source models and datasets. This collaboration has provided PyThaiNLP with computational resources we need to scale up our operations as well as additional developers for maintaining the project, such as Lalita Lowphansirikul.

Under the collaboration, we have built an English-Thai sentence pair dataset and the state-of-the-art English-Thai translation model (Lowphansirikul et al., 2021b), the RoBERTa-based monolingual language model WangchanBERTa (Lowphansirikul et al., 2021a), and most recently the multilingual instruction-following model WangChanGLM (Polpanumas et al., 2023).

Due to limited computational and human resources, we prioritize features with the highest impact-to-effort ratio. For example, during 2019-2020, there were two types of dominant transformer-based language models: encoder-only BERT family and decoder-only GPT family. We opted to pursue the encoder-only models and trained WangchanBERTa because, at the time, it required relatively fewer resources to train and had better performance across impactful tasks such as text classification, sequence tagging, and extractive question answering. It was not until decoder-only models proved to create more value-added in 2022 that we started to train such models as WangChanGLM.

4.3 Community and Infrastructure for Software Quality

It is important to be noted that the community not only made contributions in the form of feature improvements but also in the areas of documenta-

[13] https://github.com/pythainlp/pythainlp

[14] https://www.facebook.com/groups/thainlp

[15] https://www.facebook.com/groups/thainlp/permalink/564348637279964/

[16] https://peps.python.org/pep-0484/

[17] https://github.com/PyThaiNLP/pythainlp/graphs/contributors

Years	Notable Features
2016	Word tokenization, part-of-speech tagging
2017	Soundex, spell checking, WordNet support
2018	Text classification language model, NER corpus/model, date and time parsing/formatting
2019	Syllable tokenization, date and time spell out
2020	ASR model, machine translation dataset/model, grapheme-to-phoneme conversion
2021	Autoencoding language model, word-to-phoneme conversion
2022	Dependency parsing, nested NER, text augmentation
2023	Coreference resolution dataset/model, generative language model

Table 1: Notable features introduced to PyThaiNLP over the years.

tion, including computational documentation (e.g., Jupyter notebooks), improving code quality and test suite, and streamlining software testing and delivery. Some of which may not be visible to the users but are crucial for the development of the project.

On the infrastructure side, test automation and continuous integration (CI) helps us systematically reinforce code style, detect code security vulnerabilities, maintain code coverage, and test the library in different computer configurations.

We were since 2017 rely on free Travis CI[18] and AppVeyor[19] for continuous integration workflow and later in June 2020 completely migrated to GitHub Actions[20]. Every GitHub pull requests will go through Black[21] for code formatting and Flake8[22] for PEP 8 code style[23] and cyclomatic complexity checks (McCabe, 1976). pip installation package will be built and tested against the test suite in Linux, macOS, and Windows[24]. The package then can be automatically publish to the Python Package Index directly from the CI, once it passed all the tests in every platform.

PyThaiNLP code coverage reached 80 % towards the end of 2018, compare to under 60 % in 2017. Code coverage is a metric that can help assess the quality of the test suite, and it therefore reflects how well the functionalities are thoroughly tested. The coverage went over 90 % in August 2019 and kept stable at this level until 2022[25].

From early 2022, we experienced a gradual drop of the code coverage to 80 %. The main reason is a growing number of features that require a large language model that cannot fit inside our standard GitHub-hosted runners. We have to remove some of the tests for those features. Before 2022, we also tested our library against versions of CPython and PyPy, but now it has been reduced to only CPython 3.8 due to the lack of support for other Python versions in some of our machine learning dependencies.

Some of the common code improvements we made after analyzing code coverage and other tests were the removal of unused code, fixing inconsistent behavior in different operating systems, better handling of a very long string, empty string, empty list, null, and/or negative values, and better handling of exceptions in control flow, resulting a code that is smaller and more robust.

5 PyThaiNLP in the Wild

5.1 PyThaiNLP and Its Research Impact

Researchers worldwide use PyThaiNLP to work with Thai language. For instance, for word tokenization in cross-lingual language model pretraining (Lample and Conneau, 2019), universal dependency parsing (Smith et al., 2018), and cross-lingual representation learning (Conneau et al., 2020). In addition, research and industry-grade tools namely SEACoreNLP[26], an open-source initiative by NLPHub of AI Singapore, and spaCy (Honnibal et al., 2020) include PyThaiNLP as part of their toolkit.

[18]https://www.travis-ci.com/

[19]https://www.appveyor.com/

[20]https://github.com/features/actions

[21]https://github.com/psf/black

[22]https://flake8.pycqa.org

[23]https://peps.python.org/pep-0008/

[24]Easy installation and consistent behavior across platforms are what we aim for. This is one of the reasons why we developed a pure-Python NewMM. The previous implementation of our default word tokenizer requires marisa-trie, a trie data structure library in C++. Unfortunately, marisa-trie does not officially support mingw32 compiler on Windows.

[25]Our code coverage is measured by coverage.py which is included in our continuous integration workflow. The coverage stats are made available online by Coveralls at: https://coveralls.io/github/PyThaiNLP/pythainlp

[26]https://seacorenlp.aisingapore.net/docs/

5.2 PyThaiNLP and Its Industry Impact

PyThaiNLP is used in many real-world business use cases in firms of all sizes both domestic and international. User feedback generally highlights how the library has sped up their product development cycles involving Thai NLP as well as its effectiveness in terms of business outcomes. The most frequently used functionalities are tokenization and text normalization. We introduce here selected use cases from national and multinational firms in banking, telecommunication, insurance, retail, and software development.

Siam Commercial Bank (BKK:SCB; USD 10B market cap) is one of Thailand's largest banks. The bank operates a chatbot to automatically answer customer queries. Their data analytics team finetuned WangchanBERTa for intent classification to enhance its question-answering capabilities as well as to detect personal information in customers' inputs in order to exclude them from their internal training sets. Moreover, the team relies on basic text processing functions such as tokenization and normalization to speed up their development process. They have also found the published performance benchmarks to be useful when selecting models for their tasks.

True Corporation (BKK:TRUE; 6B) is one of the two providers in Thailand's duopoly telecommunication market. Its subsidiary, True Digital Group, uses PyThaiNLP both for digital media analysis and for recommendation engine on production. They featurized their Thai-text contents using thai2fit word vectors and saw a noticeable uplift in user engagement and subsequent business outcomes. They also combined our word vectors with Top2Vec (Angelov, 2020) to perform topic modeling and improve customer experience.

Central Retail Digital (BKK:CRC; 6B) is a digital transformation unit serving Central Retail, Thailand's largest department store. Their data science team used PyThaiNLP mainly to enhance search and recommendation offerings across five business units and other six million customers. Word tokenization and text normalization were used to preprocess product information and search queries as input for the product search system. Since most search systems are built for languages with white spaces as word delimiters, this preprocessing step has allowed their product search to outperform out-of-the-box solutions which are not compatible with Thai. For content-based recommendations, the team featurized production information to create a model that recommends similar products to customers.

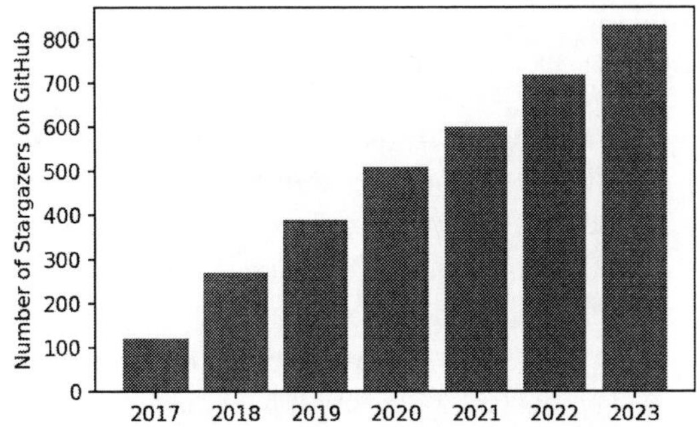

Figure 2: Number of stars PyThaiNLP has received from GitHub users over the years.

AIA Thailand (HKG:1299; 109B global) is the Thai headquarter of the global insurance firm American Insurance Association. Their data science team employs PyThaiNLP in analyzing their inbound and outbound call logs using word tokenization, text normalization, stop word handling, and local-time-format string handling functionalities. For the inbound calls, they normalize and tokenize the logs to perform topic modeling and identify critical topics of conversation to emphasize both automated voice bot and human staff training and allocation. This resulted in improved percentage of calls that the voice bot fulfilled successfully and reduced call waiting time. For the outbound calls, they perform keyword identification from the logs processed by PyThaiNLP to gain insights to improve customer retention.

VISAI is a VISTEC university spin-off that provides machine learning tools and consulting services. It has finetuned WangchanBERTa to perform text classification, named entity recognition, and relation extraction on unstructured data of their clients to create a queryable knowledge graph. They also use tokenization and text normalization functionalities to facilitate text processing for all their NLP-based products.

6 Conclusion and Future Works

This paper introduces the PyThaiNLP library, explains its features and datasets (as illustrated in Figure 1), and discusses the community and the engineering project supporting the library.

By 2023, we will have implemented the open-source version of most general NLP capabilities available in English for Thai[27]. We see the following items as the next major milestones:

- **Domain-specific datasets/models** Some capabilities are not performing well on specific use cases; for instances, named-entity recognition in financial reports, medical terms translation, and legal documents question answering. We believe more domain-specific datasets and models will help close this gap.
- **Robust benchmark for Thai NLP tasks** As NLP has garnered more attention, more models and datasets, both open- and closed-source, will be available. It will, therefore, be imperative to have a robust benchmark in comparing the models' performance and the datasets' quality.
- **Correctness and consistency** Search key generation (such as Soundex), sorting, and tokenization[28] have to be deterministic and strictly follow a specification, or an application may behave in an unexpected fashion. More test cases and verification might be needed for these features.
- **Efficient mechanism to load and manage datasets/models** To reduce the size of the library and to carter the use in a system with a restricted network connection[29].
- **Seamless integration with language-agnostic tools** The ultimate goal is for developers to no longer need PyThaiNLP as Thai language is supported by standard NLP libraries such as spaCy and Hugging Face (Wolf et al., 2020). We have begun this work with integrating our text processing functions and models to spaCy.

Acknowledgements

First and foremost, we appreciate the contributions from all PyThaiNLP contributors[30]. We would like to thank: 1) VISTEC-depa Thailand AI Research Institute and its director Sarana Nutanong for research collaboration and support in terms of academic guidance, computational resources, and personnel; 2) the companies featured in the industry impact section and respective interviewees Chrisada Sookdhis, Jayakorn Vongkulbhisal, Kowin Kulruchakorn, Phasathorn Suwansri, and Pongtachchai Panachaiboonpipop; 3) Ekapol Chuangsuwanich for academic guidance and contribution to models and datasets; and 4) MacStadium for infrastructure support. We are much obliged to free and open-source software community for software building blocks and best practices, including but not limited to NumFOCUS, fast.ai, Hugging Face, and Thai Linux Working Group. Moreover, we thank organizations who care enough to develop multilingual resources to accommodate low-resource languages, most notably Meta AI. Lastly, we cannot thank enough volunteers of various open-content communities, including Wikipedia, Common Voice, TED Translators, and similar local initiatives; modern NLP will not be possible without their accumulated effort.

Limitations

In our current CI workflow, every code commit to the repository triggers an automated test suit for all supported platforms. The process can be challenging if our package depends on large language models (LLMs) because a single LLM can exhaust the memory of our free-tier CI infrastructure. Some of the components can be cached to reduce build time, but they have to be loaded to the memory in any case. This forced us to drop some LLM-related tests and scarified the code coverage of the library as discussed in Section 4.3.

Even we have a resource to do such tests with the current design, it is neither economical nor sustainable. An improved test utilizing a stub, mock, or spy (proxy) test pattern that provides an off-line "fake inference" can help this. These techniques have been proven useful in other software testing involving expensive database/API queries or network connections. Lyra (2019) and Microsoft (2020) provide such examples, using the Python Standard Library's `unittest.mock`. This can reduce a number of times an LLM is actually being loaded/called. The required inference could be handled either by a non-free tier CI plan from the same or different provider (which should be more affordable now due to reduced number of calls) or by a computer outside the cloud.

[27] `https://nlpforthai.com/`

[28] Some phonetic algorithm and transliteration rely on syllable tokenization

[29] `https://github.com/PyThaiNLP/pythainlp/issues/298`

[30] `https://github.com/PyThaiNLP/pythainlp/graphs/contributors`

References

Rami Al-Rfou. 2015. Polyglot. Available at https://pypi.org/project/polyglot/.

Rami Al-Rfou, Vivek Kulkarni, Bryan Perozzi, and Steven Skiena. 2015. POLYGLOT-NER: Massive multilingual named entity recognition. In *Proceedings of the 2015 SIAM International Conference on Data Mining*, pages 586–594. SIAM.

Dimo Angelov. 2020. Top2Vec: Distributed representations of topics.

Rosana Ardila, Megan Branson, Kelly Davis, Michael Kohler, Josh Meyer, Michael Henretty, Reuben Morais, Lindsay Saunders, Francis Tyers, and Gregor Weber. 2020. Common Voice: A massively-multilingual speech corpus. In *Proceedings of the Twelfth Language Resources and Evaluation Conference*, pages 4218–4222, Marseille, France. European Language Resources Association.

Wirote Aroonmanakun. 2002. Collocation and Thai word segmentation. In *Proceedings of the Fifth Symposium on Natural Language Processing & The Fifth Oriental COCOSDA Workshop*, pages 68–75, Pathumthani, Thailand. Sirindhorn International Institute of Technology.

Wirote Aroonmanakun, Kachen Tansiri, and Pairit Nittayanuparp. 2009. Thai National Corpus: A progress report. In *Proceedings of the 7th Workshop on Asian Language Resources*, ALR7, page 153158, USA. Association for Computational Linguistics.

Wirote Aroonmanakun and Attapol Thamrongrattanarit. 2018. Thai Language Toolkit. Available at https://pypi.org/project/tltk/.

Ratchakrit Arreerard, Stephen Mander, and Scott Piao. 2022. Survey on Thai NLP language resources and tools. In *Proceedings of the Thirteenth Language Resources and Evaluation Conference*, pages 6495–6505, Marseille, France. European Language Resources Association.

Gann Bierner, Jason Baldridge, Thomas Morton, and Joern Kottmann. 2008. OpenNLP. Available at https://sourceforge.net/projects/opennlp/.

Steven Bird and Edward Loper. 2004. NLTK: The natural language toolkit. In *Proceedings of the ACL Interactive Poster and Demonstration Sessions*, pages 214–217, Barcelona, Spain. Association for Computational Linguistics.

Prachya Boonkwan, Vorapon Luantangsrisuk, Sitthaa Phaholphinyo, Kanyanat Kriengket, Dhanon Leenoi, Charun Phrombut, Monthika Boriboon, Krit Kosawat, and Thepchai Supnithi. 2020. The annotation guideline of LST20 corpus.

cakimpei. 2022. Wunsen. Available at https://github.com/cakimpei/wunsen.

Thatsanee Charoenporn, Virach Sornlertlamvanich, Sawit Kasuriya, Chatchawarn Hansakunbuntheung, and Hitoshi Isahara. 2004. Open collaborative development of the Thai language resources for natural language processing. In *Proceedings of the Fourth International Conference on Language Resources and Evaluation (LREC'04)*, Lisbon, Portugal. European Language Resources Association (ELRA).

Paisarn Charoenpornsawat. 2003. SWATH: Smart Word Analysis for THai. Available at http://www.cs.cmu.edu/~paisarn/software.html.

Pattarawat Chormai, Ponrawee Prasertsom, Jin Cheevaprawatdomrong, and Attapol Rutherford. 2020. Syllable-based neural Thai word segmentation. In *Proceedings of the 28th International Conference on Computational Linguistics*, pages 4619–4637, Barcelona, Spain (Online). International Committee on Computational Linguistics.

Ananlada Chotimongkol, Kwanchiva Saykhum, Patcharika Chootrakool, Nattanun Thatphithakkul, and Chai Wutiwiwatchai. 2009. LOTUS-BN: A Thai broadcast news corpus and its research applications. In *2009 Oriental-COCOSDA International Conference on Speech Database and Assessments*, pages 44–50, Urumqi, China.

Ananlada Chotimongkol, Nattanun Thatphithakkul, Sumonmas Purodakananda, Chai Wutiwiwatchai, Patcharika Chootrakool, Chatchawarn Hansakunbuntheung, Atiwong Suchato, and Panuthat Boonpramuk. 2010. The development of a large Thai telephone speech corpus: LOTUS-Cell 2.0. In *2010 Oriental-COCOSDA International Conference on Speech Database and Assessments*, Kathmandu, Nepal.

Alexis Conneau, Kartikay Khandelwal, Naman Goyal, Vishrav Chaudhary, Guillaume Wenzek, Francisco Guzmán, Edouard Grave, Myle Ott, Luke Zettlemoyer, and Veselin Stoyanov. 2020. Unsupervised cross-lingual representation learning at scale. In *Proceedings of the 58th Annual Meeting of the Association for Computational Linguistics*, pages 8440–8451, Online. Association for Computational Linguistics.

David Eberhard, Gary Simons, and Chuck Fennig. 2023. *Ethnologue: Languages of the World. Twenty-sixth edition.* SIL International.

Richard Gillam. 1999. Text boundary analysis in Java. In *Proceedings of Fifteenth International Unicode Conference*, San Jose, California, USA.

Choochart Haruechaiyasak and Sarawoot Kongyoung. 2009. TLex: Thai lexeme analyser based on the conditional random fields. In *Proceedings of 8th International Symposium on Natural Language Processing*, Bangkok, Thailand.

Choochart Haruechaiyasak, Sarawoot Kongyoung, and Matthew Dailey. 2008. A comparative study on

Thai word segmentation approaches. In *2008 5th International Conference on Electrical Engineering/Electronics, Computer, Telecommunications and Information Technology*, volume 1, pages 125–128.

Matthew Honnibal. 2013. A good part-of-speech tagger in about 200 lines of Python.

Matthew Honnibal, Ines Montani, Sofie Van Landeghem, and Adriane Boyd. 2020. spaCy: Industrial-strength Natural Language Processing in Python.

Yuphaphann Hoonchamlong, Sathaporn Koraksawet, Sarawuth Keawbumrung, and Krissadang Klaijinda. 1997. Thai Language Audio Resource Center.

Jeremy Howard and Sylvain Gugger. 2020. fastai: A Layered API for Deep Learning. *Information*, 11(2):108.

Jeremy Howard and Sebastian Ruder. 2018. Universal language model fine-tuning for text classification. In *Proceedings of the 56th Annual Meeting of the Association for Computational Linguistics (Volume 1: Long Papers)*, pages 328–339, Melbourne, Australia. Association for Computational Linguistics.

IBM Corporation et al. 1999. International Components for Unicode. Available at `https://icu.unicode.org`.

Sawit Kasuriya, Virach Sornlertlamvanich, Patcharika Cotsomrong, Takatoshi Jitsuhiro, Genichiro Kikui, and Yoshinori Sagisaka. 2003a. NECTEC-ATR Thai speech corpus. In *2003 Oriental-COCOSDA International Conference on Speech Database and Assessments*, pages 105–111, Singapore.

Sawit Kasuriya, Virach Sornlertlamvanich, Patcharika Cotsomrong, Supphanat Kanokphara, and Nattanun Thatphithakkul. 2003b. Thai speech corpus for speech recognition. In *2003 Oriental-COCOSDA International Conference on Speech Database and Assessments*, pages 54–61, Singapore.

Asanee Kawtrakul, Mukda Suktarachan, Patcharee Varasai, and Hutchatai Chanlekha. 2002. A state of the art of Thai language resources and Thai language behavior analysis and modeling. In *COLING-02: The 3rd Workshop on Asian Language Resources and International Standardization*.

Natthawut Kertkeidkachorn, Supadaech Chanjaradwichai, Teera Suri, Krerksak Likitsupin, Surapol Vorapatratorn, Pawanrat Hirankan, Worasa Limpanadusadee, Supakit Chuetanapinyo, Kitanan Pitakpawatkul, Natnarong Puangsri, Nathacha Tangsirirat, Konlawachara Trakulsuk, Proadpran Punyabukkana, and Atiwong Suchato. 2012. The CU-MFEC corpus for Thai and English spelling speech recognition. In *Proceedings of International Conference on Speech Database and Assessments*, pages 18–23.

Krit Kosawat. 2009. InterBEST 2009: Thai word segmentation workshop. In *Proceedings of 8th International Symposium on Natural Language Processing*, Bangkok, Thailand.

Krit Kosawat, Monthika Boriboon, Patcharika Chootrakool, Ananlada Chotimongkol, Supon Klaithin, Sarawoot Kongyoung, Kanyanut Kriengket, Sitthaa Phaholphinyo, Sumonmas Purodakananda, Tipraporn Thanakulwarapas, and Chai Wutiwiwatchai. 2009. BEST 2009: Thai word segmentation software contest. In *2009 Eighth International Symposium on Natural Language Processing*, pages 83–88.

Guillaume Lample and Alexis Conneau. 2019. Cross-lingual language model pretraining. *Advances in Neural Information Processing Systems (NeurIPS)*.

Peerat Limkonchotiwat, Wannaphong Phatthiyaphaibun, Raheem Sarwar, Ekapol Chuangsuwanich, and Sarana Nutanong. 2021. Handling cross- and out-of-domain samples in Thai word segmentation. In *Findings of the Association for Computational Linguistics: ACL-IJCNLP 2021*, pages 1003–1016, Online. Association for Computational Linguistics.

Xi Victoria Lin, Todor Mihaylov, Mikel Artetxe, Tianlu Wang, Shuohui Chen, Daniel Simig, Myle Ott, Naman Goyal, Shruti Bhosale, Jingfei Du, Ramakanth Pasunuru, Sam Shleifer, Punit Singh Koura, Vishrav Chaudhary, Brian O'Horo, Jeff Wang, Luke Zettlemoyer, Zornitsa Kozareva, Mona Diab, Veselin Stoyanov, and Xian Li. 2022. Few-shot learning with multilingual generative language models. In *Proceedings of the 2022 Conference on Empirical Methods in Natural Language Processing*, pages 9019–9052, Abu Dhabi, United Arab Emirates. Association for Computational Linguistics.

Vichit Lorchirachoonkul. 1982. A Thai soundex system. *Information Processing & Management*, 18(5):243–255.

Lalita Lowphansirikul, Charin Polpanumas, Nawat Jantrakulchai, and Sarana Nutanong. 2021a. WangchanBERTa: pretraining transformer-based Thai language models.

Lalita Lowphansirikul, Charin Polpanumas, Attapol T. Rutherford, and Sarana Nutanong. 2021b. A large English–Thai parallel corpus from the web and machine-generated text. *Language Resources and Evaluation*, 56(2):477–499.

Matti Lyra. 2019. Effective mocking of unit tests for machine learning.

Thomas J. McCabe. 1976. A complexity measure. *IEEE Transactions on Software Engineering*, SE-2(4):308–320.

Surapant Meknavin, Paisarn Charoenpornsawat, and Boonserm Kijsirikul. 1997. Feature-based Thai Word Segmentation. In *Proceedings of the Natural Language Processing Pacific Rim Symposium*, Phuket, Thailand.

Microsoft. 2020. Testing data science and MLOps code.

mmb L. 2018. symspellpy. Available at https://github.com/mammothb/symspellpy.

National Electronics and Computer Technology Center. 2006. Thai Lexeme Tokenizer: LexTo. [online]. Retrieved August 8, 2023, from http://www.sansarn.com/lexto/.

Dat Quoc Nguyen, Dai Quoc Nguyen, Dang Duc Pham, and Son Bao Pham. 2014. RDRPOSTagger: A ripple down rules-based part-of-speech tagger. In *Proceedings of the Demonstrations at the 14th Conference of the European Chapter of the Association for Computational Linguistics*, pages 17–20, Gothenburg, Sweden. Association for Computational Linguistics.

Peter Norvig. 2007. How to write a spelling corrector.

Terry Peng and Mikhail Korobov. 2014. python-crfsuite. Available at https://github.com/scrapinghub/python-crfsuite.

Wannaphong Phatthiyaphaibun. 2022. Thai NER 2.0.

Wannaphong Phatthiyaphaibun and Peerat Limkonchotiwat. 2023. Han-Coref: Thai coreference resolution by PyThaiNLP.

Mikhail Plekhanov, Nora Kassner, Kashyap Popat, Louis Martin, Simone Merello, Borislav Kozlovskii, Frédéric A. Dreyer, and Nicola Cancedda. 2023. Multilingual end to end entity linking.

Charin Polpanumas and Wannaphong Phatthiyaphaibun. 2021. thai2fit: Thai language implementation of ULMFiT.

Charin Polpanumas, Wannaphong Phatthiyaphaibun, Patomporn Payoungkhamdee, Peerat Limkonchotiwat, Lalita Lowphansirikul, Can Udomcharoenchaikit, Titipat Achakulwisut, Ekapol Chuangsuwanich, and Sarana Nutanong. 2023. WangChanGLM – the multilingual instruction-following model.

Charin Polpanumas and Phasathorn Suwansri. 2020. Pythainlp/classification-benchmarks: v0.1-alpha.

PyCon Thailand. 2019. How PyThaiNLP's thai2fit outperforms Google's BERT: State-of-the-art Thai text classification and beyond - Charin.

Vee Satayamas. 2015. wordcutpy. Available at https://github.com/veer66/wordcutpy.

Aaron Smith, Bernd Bohnet, Miryam de Lhoneux, Joakim Nivre, Yan Shao, and Sara Stymne. 2018. 82 treebanks, 34 models: Universal Dependency parsing with multi-treebank models. In *Proceedings of the CoNLL 2018 Shared Task: Multilingual Parsing from Raw Text to Universal Dependencies*, pages 113–123, Brussels, Belgium. Association for Computational Linguistics.

Chakkrit Snae and Michael Brückner. 2009. Novel phonetic name matching algorithm with a statistical ontology for analysing names given in accordance with Thai astrology. *Issues in Informing Science and Information Technology*, 6:497–515.

Virach Sornlertlamvanich. 1993. *Machine Translation*, chapter Word segmentation for Thai in machine translation system. National Electronics and Computer Technology Center.

Virach Sornlertlamvanich, Tanapong Potipiti, Chai Wutiwiwatchai, and Pradit Mittrapiyanuruk. 2000. The state of the art in Thai language processing. In *Proceedings of the 38th Annual Meeting of the Association for Computational Linguistics*, pages 1–2, Hong Kong. Association for Computational Linguistics.

Virach Sornlertlamvanich, Naoto Takahashi, and Hitoshi Isahara. 1999. Building a Thai part-of-speech tagged corpus (ORCHID). *Journal of the Acoustical Society of Japan (E)*, 20(3):189–198.

Sutee Sudprasert and Asanee Kawtrakul. 2003. Thai word segmentation based on global and local unsupervised learning. In *Proceedings of the 7th National Computer Science and Engineering Conference*, pages 1–8, Chonburi, Thailand.

Thepchai Supnithi, Krit Kosawat, Monthika Boriboon, and Virach Sornlertlamvanich. 2004. Language sense and ambiguity in Thai. In *Proceedings of the 8th Pacific Rim International Conference on Artificial Intelligence*, Auckland, New Zealand.

Prayut Suwanvisat and Somboon Prasitjutrakul. 1998. Thai-English cross-language transliterated word retrieval using soundex technique. In *Proceesings of the National Computer Science and Engineering Conference*, Bangkok, Thailand.

Thai Linux Working Group. 2001. LibThai. Available at https://linux.thai.net/projects/libthai/.

Thanaruk Theeramunkong, Virach Sornlertlamvanich, Thanasan Tanhermhong, and Wirat Chinnan. 2000. Character cluster based Thai information retrieval. In *Proceedings of the Fifth International Workshop on on Information Retrieval with Asian Languages*, IRAL '00, page 7580, New York, NY, USA. Association for Computing Machinery.

Wannee Udompanich. 1983. String searching for Thai alphabet using Soundex compression technique.

VISTEC-depa AI Research Institute of Thailand. 2023. wav2vec2-large-xlsr-53-th (revision 3155938).

David Gray Widder, Sarah West, and Meredith Whittaker. 2023. Open (for business): Big tech, concentrated power, and the political economy of open AI.

Thomas Wolf, Lysandre Debut, Victor Sanh, Julien Chaumond, Clement Delangue, Anthony Moi, Pierric Cistac, Tim Rault, Remi Louf, Morgan Funtowicz, Joe Davison, Sam Shleifer, Patrick von Platen,

Clara Ma, Yacine Jernite, Julien Plu, Canwen Xu, Teven Le Scao, Sylvain Gugger, Mariama Drame, Quentin Lhoest, and Alexander Rush. 2020. Transformers: State-of-the-art natural language processing. In *Proceedings of the 2020 Conference on Empirical Methods in Natural Language Processing: System Demonstrations*, pages 38–45, Online. Association for Computational Linguistics.

David Wright. 2021. Phunspell. Available at `https://github.com/dvwright/phunspell`.

Chai Wutiwiwatchai and Sadaoki Furui. 2007. Thai speech processing technology: A review. *Speech Communication*, 49(1):8–27.

Empowering Knowledge Discovery from Scientific Literature: A novel approach to Research Artifact Analysis

Petros Stavropoulos[1,2], **Ioannis Lyris**[1], **Natalia Manola**[3], **Ioanna Grypari**[1,3], **Haris Papageorgiou**[1]
[1]Institute for Language and Speech Processing, Athena R.C.
[2]Department of Informatics and Telecommunications, National and Kapodistrian University of Athens
[3]OpenAIRE AMKE
pestavr@di.uoa.gr, {ioannis.lyris, igrypari, haris}@athenarc.gr, natalia.manola@openaire.eu

Abstract

Knowledge extraction from scientific literature is a major issue, crucial to promoting transparency, reproducibility, and innovation in the research community. In this work, we present a novel approach towards the identification, extraction and analysis of dataset and code/software mentions within scientific literature. We introduce a comprehensive dataset, synthetically generated by ChatGPT and meticulously curated, augmented, and expanded with real snippets of scientific text from full-text publications in Computer Science using a human-in-the-loop process. The dataset contains snippets highlighting mentions of the two research artifact (RA) types: dataset and code/software, along with insightful metadata including their Name, Version, License, URL as well as the intended Usage and Provenance. We also fine-tune a simple Large Language Model (LLM) using Low-Rank Adaptation (LoRA) to transform the Research Artifact Analysis (RAA) into an instruction-based Question Answering (QA) task. Ultimately, we report the improvements in performance on the test set of our dataset when compared to other base LLM models. Our method provides a significant step towards facilitating accurate, effective, and efficient extraction of datasets and software from scientific papers, contributing to the challenges of reproducibility and reusability in scientific research.

1 Introduction

Scientific research is dynamically and rapidly evolving, generating an overwhelming amount of knowledge in the form of research outputs. The vastness and the intricacies of scientific literature makes it impossible for researchers to keep up with all advancements in their respective fields, which is critical to their research. Consequently, knowledge discovery from scientific literature and research artifact analysis (RAA) have gained significant prominence as fields. In recent years, many new research artifact (RA) datasets have been constructed, with the goal of training models and creating benchmarks for the identification of a variety of RAs, both intangible (e.g. methods, tasks) and tangible (e.g. datasets, software) (Wang et al., 2022; Krüger and Schindler, 2020). Moreover, recent efforts have been directed towards identifying corresponding metadata and classifying those RAs based on their functions, such as their usage and provenance (Du et al., 2021; Schindler et al., 2021).

In this paper, our primary focus lies in introducing a novel RA dataset specifically designed for dataset and software extraction. Our RA dataset is constructed by leveraging ChatGPT [1] and the full-text of scientific publications in the field of Computer Science. It employs a human-in-the-loop manual curation process and comprises snippets of scientific text that encompass mentions of datasets and software (RA mentions). Each snippet includes a trigger keyword or keyphrase indicating the RA mention, as well as a curated list of essential metadata, such as the Name, Version, License, URL, Usage, and Provenance of the respective dataset or software.

This RA dataset stands out from conventional RA datasets commonly used in the academic literature, due to its unique formulation. Unlike conventional approaches to RAA that focus on Named RAs through Named Entity Recognition (NER) and entity linking, our methodology addresses a significant oversight. Those approaches often neglect unnamed and undocumented resources, leading to implications for open science and reproducibility, and rendering them out of scope. Our approach unifies those tasks, including both named and unnamed RA mentions. Each RA mention is systematically mapped to a corresponding RA, along with its associated metadata, as defined by the context of the sentence (Fig. 1). The primary reason for this approach is to create a dataset where all RA men-

[1]https://chat.openai.com/

Proceedings of the 3rd Workshop for Natural Language Processing Open Source Software (NLP-OSS 2023), pages 37–53
December 6, 2023 ©2023 Association for Computational Linguistics

tions, whether explicitly named or not, are treated with equal importance. This allows models trained on this RA dataset to effectively identify the presence of RAs even in more complex and ambiguous scenarios.

Additionally, we utilized the LoRA (Hu et al., 2021) method to power the human-in-the-loop process and fine-tune base LLM models on the constructed RA dataset. Employing a model trained on this RA dataset can streamline the detection of RAs within the body of scientific publications, consequently improving the reproducibility of experiments and fostering a comprehensive understanding of the research process. Furthermore, this approach contributes to resource reusability by establishing a collection of crucial resources, accelerating scientific progress, mitigating repetition, and encouraging cross-disciplinary collaborations.

In the subsequent sections we provide detailed insights into the methodology employed for dataset construction (Secs. 3.1, 3.2, 3.3, 4.1). We also discuss the training and evaluation of our LoRA models (Secs. 3.5, 4.2), showcasing their effectiveness in extracting RAs through comprehensive benchmarking on our dataset's test set (Sec. 6). By comparing them to other base LLMs, we demonstrate the feasibility of employing simpler LLM models for successful and reliable RAA.

Our key contributions[2] are as follows:

1. We created two novel datasets for RAA, containing both synthetic and real RA mentions. The construction of those RA datasets was aimed to address issues present in other RA datasets found in the literature, such as the lack of unnamed RA mentions or even of all named RA mentions in a given snippet.

2. We demonstrated the effective performance of fine-tuned LLMs in RAA. Specifically, we discovered that even small LLMs, like the Flan-T5 Base model, when fine-tuned on our RA datasets, excel at RAA, surpassing the performance of larger, base models.

3. We conducted a comprehensive qualitative evaluation of our novel RA datasets and the models trained on them.

[2]All data and software resources can be accessed at the following link: `https://github.com/PetrosStav/Research-Artifact-Analysis-NLP-OSS-2023-Paper`.

2 Related Work

RAA has gained significant attention in recent years. This extensive research has led to the introduction of many important RA datasets related to the disciplines of Computer Science, Biology, Sociology and more. At the same time, important breakthroughs have been made in the construction of new novel machine learning models aimed to achieve this task, taking advantage of a variety of different technologies like Recurrent Neural Networks (RNNs) (Zeng and Acuna, 2020; Hou et al., 2022; Schindler et al., 2020) and BERT-like architectures (Schindler et al., 2021; Färber et al., 2021).

The aforementioned RA datasets can be differentiated into two types with respect to their formulation and goal. The first type is characterized by abstract RAs in the form of tasks, processes, or materials like SemEval 2017 Task 10 (Augenstein et al., 2017), SciERC (Luan et al., 2018), SciREX (Jain et al., 2020), the methods dataset from (Färber et al., 2021) and SciRes (Zhao et al., 2019). In contrast, the second type is aimed to the identification of more strictly defined RAs, with the Rich Context Competition dataset created by the Coleridge Initiative[3] at New York University, NER Dataset Recognition (Heddes et al., 2021) and DMDD (Pan et al., 2023) being characteristic examples for dataset extraction and SoMeSci (Schindler et al., 2021), Softcite (Du et al., 2021) being characteristic examples for software extraction. Nevertheless, a mapping between those two cases is not always possible. This divides RAA into two tasks that are similar in concept but very different in practice. Furthermore, some RA datasets further encompass the collection of RA metadata. Two notable works that address the lack of such RA datasets are Softcite and SoMeSci.

Our dataset differs significantly from common standards in RA datasets through a holistic approach that prioritizes both named and unnamed RA mentions. We annotate all RA mentions within a snippet, effectively creating a connection between those sharing the same name. That approach, similar to those employed in the construction of the Softcite and SoMeSci datasets, allows us to utilize the information from all RA mentions for a specific RA, providing a more comprehensive view. Considering the array of definitions for RA mention "validity" across various RA datasets, it is essential

[3]`https://coleridgeinitiative.org/`

for us to demonstrate the robustness and applicability of our annotation schema.

Therefore, we compared our RA dataset with five highly regarded datasets of RA mentions, in order to highlight its novelty and differences, and to explore how our broader scope could benefit future applications. For example, we observed that many of the existing RA datasets lack annotations of unnamed RA mentions in a given snippet or even aim only for the identification of named datasets or software. The RA datasets we used for comparison were Softcite and SoMeSci for software mentions, and the Rich Context Competition dataset, NER Dataset Recognition and DMDD for dataset mentions.

The exploitation of those RA datasets has been largely demonstrated through the utilization of RNN- and BERT-based models handling NER tasks embodied by those datasets. In contrast, the non-NER configuration of our RA dataset fosters the training and deployment of alternative model types. In our work, we use LLMs, fine-tuned with the LoRA method, and tackle the RAA task as an instruction-based QA task. This approach serves a dual purpose: it enables us to evaluate those models' performance when deployed on such tasks, while simultaneously assessing the quality of our newly introduced RA dataset.

3 Synthetic Dataset

In this section we describe the construction process of the Synthetic dataset (Subsecs. 3.1, 3.2) and the conversion of the RA mentions to question-answer (QA) pairs (Subsec. 3.3). Next, we detail the splitting of the dataset into training, development, and testing sets (Subsec. 3.4), and conclude with the training of the LoRA model (Subsec. 3.5).

3.1 Dataset Creation

For the creation of our RA dataset, we strategically harnessed the capabilities of ChatGPT to generate a corpus of synthetic data imbued with mentions of datasets and software. We formulated a prompt (Tab. 6, App. A) that explained to ChatGPT the notion of RAs, highlighting aspects such as their validity, metadata, usage and provenance, along with the task of RAA. Subsequently, we supplied ChatGPT with positive examples that illustrated valid RAs, as well as negative examples of invalid RAs. Positive examples consist of snippets containing valid dataset or software mentions, while negative examples typically comprise snippets with triggers that refer to general or encyclopedic references (e.g. "most existing datasets"), which are out of scope for most of the current approaches. We then instructed ChatGPT to act as a data creator, maintaining the structure and style of the examples.

Our dataset is meticulously structured to include a comprehensive set of fields: Snippet, Type, Valid, Name, Version, License, URL, Provenance, and Usage. Within each RA mention, the snippet contained one or multiple sentences, accompanied by a trigger encapsulated within <m> and </m> tags that also specifies the RA type (dataset or software). The Name, Version, License and URL fields of the RA require a text span within the snippet; in cases where those are not present, a default value of "N/A" is assigned. The Provenance and Usage fields can take values "Yes" or "No" to indicate if the RA was created or used by the authors of the publication. It is essential to note that those values must be supported by textual evidence in the snippet. Thus, even if a RA is generally created or used in the publication, the value is marked "Yes" only if this fact is evident from the snippet itself. Two characteristic examples of a valid and an invalid RA mention instance are presented in Figs. 1 and 2 respectively.

Snippet	In their study, the authors utilized the PyTorch <m>library</m> (version 1.9.0) for deep learning experiments. PyTorch is released under the BSD-3-Clause license. For more information, visit https://pytorch.org/.
Type	Software
Valid	Yes
Name	PyTorch
Version	1.9.0
License	BSD-3-Clause
URL	https://pytorch.org/
Provenance	No
Usage	Yes

Figure 1: An example of a RA mention containing all metadata.

Snippet	We leveraged the power of the Apache Spark framework for distributed <m>data</m> processing. The code implementation is available on our project's GitHub repository.
Type	Dataset
Valid	No

Figure 2: An example of an invalid RA mention.

Subsequently, our team of human curators[4] generated additional examples using ChatGPT, by specifying a range of attributes for ChatGPT to focus on. Those included creating specific types

[4]The team of human curators comprises two MSc students in Natural Language Processing (NLP) that worked on the task.

of RAs such as software or datasets, using a manually curated set of keywords and keyphrases for triggers, including metadata, and indicating usage and provenance. Additionally, the curators were able to determine the domain of the examples, such as Computer Vision, NLP, BioInformatics, and so on, or even specific linguistic features like using complex language or mentioning RAs in several sentences. Furthermore, effort was given to generating robust negative examples, taking into account their complexity, diversity, and linguistic function within the snippet.

The curated dataset of synthetic RA mentions served as the seed for generating an augmented set of positive and negative examples through a human-in-the-loop process, resulting in the creation of an expanded corpus of high-quality synthetic RA mentions.

Moreover, we made an effort to address the complex challenge of capturing snippets with multiple RA mentions that pertain to more than one RA of the same or different type. That mirrors more accurately the true complexity and nature of the task. The trigger words were derived from a manually curated set of keywords and keyphrases, which included the names of the RAs present within the snippets. Consequently, models trained on our RA dataset are equipped to adeptly extract RAs employing various trigger detection mechanisms and are also enabled to acquire entity linking capabilities, especially in scenarios where multiple triggers (e.g., names and keyphrases) pertain to the same RA.

3.2 Synthetic Data Augmentation

In the following stage, we employed a T5 model, which had been trained on the ChatGPT paraphrase dataset (Vladimir Vorobev, 2023), to augment our synthetic data via a paraphrasing technique. This involved substituting the trigger word in each snippet with the [MASK] token, followed by running the model to generate five paraphrased renditions of the snippet. Each paraphrased snippet was then checked, to ensure the presence of a single [MASK] token within each snippet, thereby filtering out any spurious hallucinations and noise.

3.3 QA Pairs Construction

Following the creation of the gold synthetic dataset, we converted all RA mentions into QA pairs for each metadata field, transforming the RAA to an instruction-based QA task. The questions used are depicted in Tab. 9 (App. C), with the value of each metadata field serving as the answer (Fig. 3). Those QA pairs were then structured into an input-output format suitable for the LoRA training of the LLM, further details of which will be presented in Sec. 3.5.

In an effort to enrich our dataset, we introduced a "special" type of QA pairs (Fig. 4) that are generated from the unique snippets of the RA dataset, devoid of any <m> and </m> tags, by enumerating all the RAs contained within each snippet. The construction of the QA pairs for those instances adhere to the aforementioned methodology. The question is consistent across all instances, as illustrated in Tab. 9 (App. C). The answer encompasses a list of all RAs found within the snippet, classified by their Type and Name, or marked as "unnamed" in the absence of a Name. Multiple RAs are separated by the "|" symbol. Those are then subjected to a similar augmentation process, discarding paraphrased snippets that exhibited a discrepancy in the count of RAs compared to the original instances.

<table>
<tr><th>Snippet</th><td>Our experiments were conducted using the data processing software datapro. The <m>software</m> version used was 1.5. It is distributed under the GNU Lesser General Public License.</td></tr>
<tr><th>Question</th><td>What is the name of the software defined in the <m> and </m> tags?</td></tr>
<tr><th>Answer</th><td>datapro</td></tr>
</table>

Figure 3: An example of QA pair.

<table>
<tr><th>Snippet</th><td>The CIFAR-10 dataset was used by the authors to assess the effectiveness of their image classification algorithm. This data set is freely available at https://www.cs.toronto.edu/kriz/cifar_fra.html.</td></tr>
<tr><th>Question</th><td>List all artifacts in the above snippet.</td></tr>
<tr><th>Answer</th><td>dataset : CIFAR-10 | software : unnamed</td></tr>
</table>

Figure 4: An example of a "special" QA pair.

As detailed in Tab. 1, prior to augmentation, the Synthetic dataset consisted of 305 unique snippets, 1616 RA mentions, and 10212 QA pairs. After the augmentation process, these figures were expanded to 4235 unique snippets, 5446 RA mentions, and 35475 QA pairs. More detailed statistics about the Synthetic dataset are depicted in Tab. 7 (App. B).

3.4 Train-Dev-Test Split

Given the meticulous process employed in the creation of the Synthetic dataset, special attention was required to split our data into training, development and testing sets. As mentioned previously and showcased in Tab. 1, although the dataset creation process yielded a total of 5446 RA mentions the original count of unique snippets was 305. For the process of data splitting, it is imperative to select instances from those unique snippets, rather than the final instances. This was purposely done to avoid the issue of knowledge leaking from the training set to the test set.

Furthermore, it is crucial to ensure balance among the three sets in terms of the RA types, their validity (i.e. positive vs. negative instances), the inclusion of each metadata field, as well as the RA provenance and usage. To achieve this, we conducted a systematic approach that considered the distribution and characteristics of the RA mentions within each set and across the three sets as a whole, ensuring a comprehensive and fair representation of the RA mentions.

3.5 LoRA Finetuning on the Synthetic Dataset

After transforming the Synthetic gold dataset to QA pairs, we used it to fine-tune a Flan-T5 Base model (Chung et al., 2022) using the LoRA method (Hu et al., 2021). This model was chosen as it has a relative good performance-to-parameter ratio and can be used even from smaller research teams, with limited computational resources.

We trained a LoRA model on top of the Flan-T5 Base model on the QA pairs using the Huggingface PEFT library (Sourab Mangrulkar, 2022) for training and the Weights and Biases (W&B)[5] platform for logging, visualizations and the sweep hyperparameter tuning.

We trained our LoRA model on a single Quadro RXT 5000 GPU for approximately 315 hours using a W&B sweep hyperparameter tuning setting. We optimized for the best evaluation loss on the development set in each run, and implemented an early stopping mechanism with a patience of three epochs to ensure efficiency. We achieved our best model with the hyperparameters $r = 16$, $alpha\_lora = 16$, $lora\_dropout = 0.4$, $max\_epochs = 5$.

4 Hybrid Dataset

This section explores the creation of a Hybrid dataset, focusing on the integration of RA mentions from synthetic and real snippets from scientific publications (Subsec. 4.1), and fine-tuning a LoRA model on the Hybrid dataset to enhance generalizability and performance for the RAA task (Subsec. 4.2).

[5]https://wandb.ai/site/research

4.1 Real Dataset Creation

As our Syntetic dataset was composed exclusively of synthetic RA mentions, we sought to expand it by incorporating gold-annotated RA mentions in real snippets from scientific publications (GARS dataset). This integration aimed to mitigate some of the biases in the Synthetic dataset construction, which originated from the repetitive and template-driven generated language used in the RA mentions. Such formatting is a concern as it could potentially impede the generalization capabilities and performance of models trained on the data.

Utilizing our best LoRA fine-tuned model on top of Flan-T5 Base (LoRA-Sy), we developed a tool that allows for automatic annotation of snippets. The same team of human curators employed this tool to annotate the full-text PDF files of a small collection of scientific publications within the Computer Science domain. Subsequently, this data underwent meticulous curation, expansion, and augmentation, as detailed in the previous sections. Similarly to the Synthetic dataset, the RA mentions were then converted to QA pairs to transform the RAA task into an instruction-based QA task. By combining the Synthetic dataset with the scientific publications dataset, we construct our Hybrid dataset (Tab. 1) comprising 15247 QA pairs from 2539 RA mentions spotted in 382 unique snippets, prior to augmentation and 45136 QA pairs from 7112 RA mentions spotted in 5230 unique snippets after the augmentation. More detailed statistics about the Hybrid dataset are depicted in Tab. 8 (App. B).

4.2 LoRA Finetuning on the Hybrid Dataset

We also performed fine-tuning on a LoRA model using our Hybrid dataset. The LoRA model was trained over a period of approximately 17 hours. The selection of hyperparameters was consistent with those that yielded the highest performance on the Synthetic dataset 3.5. The decision to use those particular settings was informed by the composition of the Hybrid dataset, which expanded upon the Synthetic dataset by integrating the GARS data into the training, dev, and test sets. This approach facilitated an ablation study on the test subset of the dataset, the findings of which will be explored in a subsequent section.

	Synthetic						Hybrid					
	Original			Augmented			Original			Augmented		
	dataset	software	all	dataset	software	all	dataset	software	all	dataset	software	all
Unique snippets	198	225	305	2051	2301	4235	258	298	382	2350	3047	5230
RA mentions	741	875	1616	2555	2891	5446	1010	1529	2539	3017	4095	7112
QA pairs	4548	5664	10212	15559	18592	35475	5921	9326	15247	18055	25504	45136

Table 1: Statistics for the Synthetic and Hybrid datasets.

5 Dataset Analysis & Comparisons

The previously introduced Synthetic and Hybrid datasets consist of 35475 and 45136 QA pairs respectively. Each QA pair revolves around a question pertaining to a RA mention, as delineated in Tab. 9 (App. C). Although large in quantity, they encompass only 5446 and 7112 RA mentions respectively, distinguishing them from large-scale collections like DMDD with 449798 dataset mentions. However, our aim deviates from such vast RA datasets, prioritizing quality over sheer quantity due to the different annotation methodology.

A key characteristic of our dataset is that it is comprised of QA pairs that have been generated from a smaller pool of snippets. Those snippets, containing references to RAs, have undergone various rounds of annotation and paraphrasing. This process produces a multitude of differently phrased snippets, each providing unique RA mentions of the same RA while preserving the original contextual information. This depth of RA mentions is unique to our RA dataset and sets it apart from others. To further illustrate where our dataset sits within the existing research landscape, we offer a comparison of our dataset's key statistics with those from other established RA datasets in Tab. 2.

Our manual annotation process has been executed rigorously to ensure quality enhancements across several aspects:

- All dataset and software mentions have been annotated for a given snippet, regardless of whether they are named, unnamed, or invalid. That approach ensures comprehensive coverage of all potential cases of RA mentions within our RA dataset.
- We have strictly defined what constitutes a negative example in our RA dataset, following the convention presented in subsection 3.1. This approach ensures clarity by precisely defining how the snippets without any RA mentions should be identified.
- We have meticulously curated our snippets to highlight the diversity and complexity of RA mentions, as outlined in previous sections. That includes snippets with multiple RA mentions: (a) of the same or different type, (b) of new, named, or unnamed RAs, and (c) of new RAs (named or unnamed) interspersed with already seen RAs. Those intricate patterns are often stumbling blocks for models not properly trained to handle them. Through our purposeful inclusion of such diverse and complex RA mention patterns, we aim to train models on our RA dataset to effectively manage a wide range of situations, thereby enhancing their generalizability.

The emphasis on manual annotation in our RA dataset is a result of our efforts to address the issues we have encountered in other RA datasets. Those issues include the following:

- In the case of named RAs an issue can be observed in the DMDD dataset (Pan et al., 2023), which was constructed by matching terms found in the Paper with Code repository[6]. Despite resulting in the inclusion of valid terms, this approach fails to capture all named datasets. An illustrative example can be found in the sentence "We evaluate trained translation models on wmt13 (Bojar et al., 2013) and wmt14 (Bojar et al., 2014) for en-es and en-fr, respectively." from the evaluation subset of the DMDD dataset. Here, only the "wmt14" dataset has been annotated due to the absence of a matching term for "wmt13" in the dataset construction.
- In terms of unnamed RAs, a significant number of RA datasets fail to acknowledge those RA mentions or even consider them as negative examples. The latter case is a notable characteristic of the NER Dataset Recognition dataset (Heddes et al., 2021), where unnamed dataset mentions are labeled as negative examples (Geen datasets), leading to differential metric definitions in comparison to other RA datasets. The broader issue of unnamed RAs omission can also be observed in the Rich Context Competition dataset, where phrases like "our data" would not be annotated as a RA mention. To a lesser extent, this issue is

[6] https://paperswithcode.com/

	Dataset	Instance Unit	Number of RA Mentions	Metadata Available
Dataset mentions	**Ner Dataset Recognition** (Heddes et al., 2021)	sentence	3416	-
	Rich Context Competition	paper	36597	-
	bioNerDS (Duck et al., 2013)	paper	920	-
	NLP-TDMS (Hou et al., 2019)	paper	1164	-
	TDM-Sci (Hou et al., 2021)	sentence	612	-
	SciERC (Luan et al., 2018)	abstract	770	-
	SciREX (Jain et al., 2020)	paper	10548	-
	DMDD (Pan et al., 2023)	paper	449798	-
	Synthetic Dataset (ours)	snippet	2555	URL, License, Version, Provenance, Usage
	Hybrid Dataset (ours)	snippet	3017	URL, License, Version, Provenance, Usage
Software mentions	**bioNerDS** (Duck et al., 2013)	paper	2625	-
	SoSciSoCi (Schindler et al., 2020)	method section/sentence	2385	-
	Softcite v.1 (Du et al., 2021)	paragraph	4093	URL, Version, Developer
	Softcite v.2 (Howison et al., 2023)	paragraph	5134	URL, Version, Type, Developer
	CZ Software Mentions (Istrate et al., 2022)	sentence	20.11M	Type
	SoMeSci (Schindler et al., 2021)	method section/full text/sentence	3756	URL, License, Version, Citation, Extension, Type, Provenance, Usage, Developer
	Synthetic Dataset (ours)	snippet	2891	URL, License, Version, Provenance, Usage
	Hybrid Dataset (ours)	snippet	4095	URL, License, Version, Provenance, Usage

Table 2: Comparison of dataset and software mention statistics between ours and other RA datasets.

also observed in the Softcite (Du et al., 2021) and SoMeSci (Schindler et al., 2021) datasets, which miss out on references to machine learning models in certain cases.

Finally, it is important to acknowledge that our definition of a RA mention within the context of a snippet aligns significantly with the construct employed by the SoMeSci dataset. The SoMeSci dataset, which is dedicated exclusively to software mentions, classifies those mentions into four categories: Application, Plugin, Operating System, and Programming Environment, while also annotating an extensive array of metadata. In our case, we have adopted this formalism to encompass RA mentions, without delving further into the corresponding subtypes. The metadata we have annotated includes the URL, Version, License, Provenance, and Usage of each RA mention.

6 Experimental Results on Test Set

We conducted a series of tests using the top-performing versions of the aforementioned LoRA fine-tuned models as well as the original Flan-T5 Base and XL models. Those were employed to evaluate the quality of information included within our Synthetic and Hybrid datasets.[7] Specifically, we computed the respective scores of those four models on the test sets of both RA datasets, aiming to discern the advantages of the fine-tuning process and to perform an ablation study to investigate the effect of fine-tuning a model using synthetic data versus synthetic data expanded by real data.

To ensure a balanced comparison between the original and fine-tuned models, we modified the prompts utilized by the original models (Tab. 10, App. C). Those adjusted prompts refrain from presupposing any specific training of the models to answer in a particular manner, and consequently, provide more comprehensive instructions. The F1 score measures successful identification of a valid RA mention or presence of specific metadata (Name, License, Version, URL). For Usage and Provenance metadata, it denotes successful identification of the RA's use or creation by authors. The exact match (EM) score, applicable for Name, License, Version, and URL metadata, determines exact lowercase match of the metadata text from a provided snippet, provided the model correctly identifies the presence of that metadata. The lenient match (LM) score checks if the model's answer in lowercase is within the gold truth, or vice versa. The results achieved by the four models on both RA datasets are outlined in Tabs. 3 and 4. Moreover, detailed evaluation results of named versus unnamed RA mentions can be found in App. D.

The original Flan-T5 Base and XL models achieved a high level of success in discerning the validity of RA mentions, as well as the associated metadata such as the License, Version, and URL. As anticipated, superior performance was observed on the less complicated Synthetic dataset. Furthermore, the XL model surpassed the Base model, particularly in identifying the Name, Usage, and Provenance. Those outcomes endorse the high semantic quality of both our RA datasets and showcase the efficacy of LLMs in the RAA task.

The significance of the LoRA fine-tuning procedure is evident in the scores presented in Tabs. 3 and 4. The fine-tuned models remarkably outperformed their base counterparts. In addition, the LoRA Hybrid model (LoRA-Hy) generally outperforms the LoRA-Sy model when evaluated on both the Synthetic and Hybrid datasets, indicating that the inclusion of additional real-world RA mention instances improves those models. Similar findings were observed in the model tests on the GARS dataset, as shown in Tab. 5. Notably, in the GARS

[7]Due to its substantial size, the Flan-T5 XXL model was not incorporated in this comparison.

	Flan T5 base			Flan T5 XL			LoRA-Sy			LoRA-Hy		
	Identification	Extraction		Identification	Extraction		Identification	Extraction		Identification	Extraction	
	F1	EM	LM	F1	EM	LM	F1	EM	LM	F1	EM	LM
Valid	0.841	-	-	0.870	-	-	0.967	-	-	**0.974**	-	-
Name	0.358	0.709	0.835	0.681	0.787	0.900	**0.887**	**0.917**	**0.962**	0.876	0.905	0.952
License	0.926	0.502	0.813	0.928	0.635	0.778	**0.946**	**0.700**	**0.818**	0.944	0.685	**0.818**
Version	0.677	0.620	0.816	0.942	0.687	**0.865**	0.975	0.620	0.626	**0.979**	**0.755**	0.767
URL	0.677	0.342	0.355	0.980	0.539	0.566	0.981	0.618	0.645	**0.982**	**0.632**	**0.658**
Usage	0.377	-	-	0.772	-	-	0.911	-	-	**0.914**	-	-
Provenance	0.537	-	-	0.647	-	-	0.939	-	-	**0.961**	-	-

Table 3: Experimental results on the test set of the Synthetic dataset.

	Flan T5 base			Flan T5 XL			LoRA-Sy			LoRA-Hy		
	Identification	Extraction		Identification	Extraction		Identification	Extraction		Identification	Extraction	
	F1	EM	LM	F1	EM	LM	F1	EM	LM	F1	EM	LM
Valid	0.766	-	-	0.822	-	-	0.938	-	-	**0.960**	-	-
Name	0.375	0.613	0.771	0.602	0.698	0.830	0.832	0.820	0.907	**0.852**	**0.840**	**0.911**
License	0.948	0.502	0.813	0.953	0.635	0.778	**0.963**	**0.700**	**0.818**	0.962	0.685	**0.818**
Version	0.738	0.620	0.816	0.935	0.687	**0.865**	0.973	0.538	0.571	**0.983**	**0.755**	0.767
URL	0.723	0.330	0.352	0.968	0.495	0.527	0.973	0.538	0.571	**0.982**	**0.571**	**0.604**
Usage	0.286	-	-	0.765	-	-	0.898	-	-	**0.921**	-	-
Provenance	0.523	-	-	0.650	-	-	0.895	-	-	**0.926**	-	-

Table 4: Experimental results on the test set of the Hybrid dataset.

results, the License and Version do not have extraction scores, as such metadata were not present in those particular instances.

Interestingly, despite the fine-tuned models being built on the simpler Flan-T5 Base architecture, they significantly outperformed Flan-T5 XL model in this particular task. This suggests that a model with a relatively small number of parameters, such as the base Flan-T5 model ($220M$ parameters), can surpass a larger LLM, like the Flan-T5 XL model ($3B$ parameters), given appropriate fine-tuning. The fine-tuning procedure effectively harnesses the parameters of the base model to learn task-specific information, resulting in a model that is both precise and efficient.

7 Qualitative Analysis

In this section, we delve into an analysis of some representative examples of our models' predictions, aiming to demonstrate the impact of the LoRA fine-tuning process on the model's understanding of this specific task. We initially explore two typical instances of RA mentions, the first for a dataset and the second for a software (refer to Figs. 5 and 6, App. E), to highlight the improvements brought about by the fine-tuning of the Flat-T5 model.

Considering the dataset mention illustrated in Fig. 5 (App. E), it is evident that the correct answer is an unnamed dataset represented by "N/A". Both of our LoRA fine-tuned models yielded the correct result, in contrast to the base models. More specifically, the Flan-T5 Base model erroneously returned "100,000 reviews", while the Flan-T5 XL model inaccurately produced the general term "costumer reviews" as a dataset name. The same error is observed in the software mention depicted in Fig. 6 (App. E), where both base models failed to give correct answers. The distinction in performance can be traced back to our fine-tuning process, as it allowed our models to understand that not every name-like term in the snippet necessarily represents a specific dataset.

An examination of different scenarios reveals that the LoRA-Hy model exhibits superior performance to the LoRA-Sy model in more complex cases, like the provenance and usage question instances in Figs. 7 and 8 (App. E).

The main shortcoming of our fine-tuned models is their occasional inability to extract text-spans from the given snippet to answer questions, despite explicitly being fine-tuned for the task. This issue is demonstrated in Fig. 9 (App. E). In this instance, all models provided correct responses. However, the answers generated by the LoRA-Hy model were not exact excerpts from the original snippet text. Consequently, this deviation from the snippet text was considered an error in the evaluation process.

8 Discussion & Conclusions

In this work, we have made significant steps towards knowledge discovery from scholarly literature and RAA by advancing the identification and extraction of dataset and software mentions within scientific literature, thereby addressing pressing challenges in reproducibility and reusability of RAs.

More specifically, by leveraging the capabilities of ChatGPT in conjunction with meticulous human curation, we streamlined the extraction of dataset and software mentions. This innovative approach made it possible to transform RAA from a NER task to an instruction-based QA task. Furthermore, we investigated how LLMs could be effectively employed for this task and how the LoRA fine-tuning method can enhance such models when trained on

	Flan T5 base			Flan T5 XL			LoRA-Sy			LoRA-Hy		
	Identification	Extraction		Identification	Extraction		Identification	Extraction		Identification	Extraction	
	F1	EM	LM	F1	EM	LM	F1	EM	LM	F1	EM	LM
Valid	0.375	-	-	0.621	-	-	0.847	-	-	**0.932**	-	-
Name	0.452	0.233	0.512	0.526	0.326	0.628	0.723	0.465	0.721	**0.884**	**0.628**	**0.814**
License	0.967	-	-	**1.000**	-	-	**1.000**	-	-	**1.000**	-	-
Version	0.811	-	-	0.950	-	-	0.967	-	-	**0.976**	-	-
URL	0.832	**1.000**	**1.000**	0.956	**1.000**	**1.000**	0.983	0.500	0.500	**0.991**	**1.000**	**1.000**
Usage	0.000	-	-	0.697	-	-	0.865	-	-	**0.945**	-	-
Provenance	0.341	-	-	0.735	-	-	**0.851**	-	-	0.836	-	-

Table 5: Experimental results on the test set of the GARS dataset.

RA datasets.

Through comprehensive examples and analysis, we demonstrated the efficacy of both the RA datasets and their associated models. Our results not only confirm the feasibility of this specific approach to the RAA task but also indicate its potential as a powerful tool in future applications.

In future work, our RA datasets can be further refined and expanded by including more representative snippets drawn from a broader and more diverse assortment of scientific publications. This will facilitate the creation of new and more generalized RA datasets, helping to mitigate potential biases and incorporate knowledge from various scientific disciplines.

Limitations

In this section, we turn our attention to the limitations inherent to our work. We provide a nuanced understanding of the boundaries of our RA datasets and methods, and we identify potential areas for improvement in future work.

The RA datasets we developed for this work are confined to snippets derived from scientific publications in Computer Science. As a result, models trained on those RA datasets may struggle to effectively generalize to complex, domain-specific scenarios in other scientific fields, such as those found in Biomedical and Health Sciences, or Sociology. Additionally, the RA datasets do not make distinctions between closely associated RA types, such as materials, repositories, and datasets or software, models, and methods.

While the fine-tuned LLM models that we specifically created and tested on our RA datasets yielded commendable results in our experiments in comparison to base Flan-T5 models, an evaluation against the Flan-T5 XXL model was not possible. Such an evaluation would have provided a significant opportunity to assess their performance against an even larger model.

Despite the considerable advancements in enriching the RA dataset with real examples drawn from scientific publications, resulting in the Hybrid dataset, the representation of RA mentions from scientific publications is still relatively narrow. Consequently, some uncommon cases of RA mentions may be underrepresented or entirely absent within our RA dataset. This observation emphasizes the need for further enhancements to our RA dataset. Future work could address this by incorporating a more diverse selection of scientific publications.

Acknowledgements

This work was supported by research grants from the European Union's H2020 IntelComp Project (`https://cordis.europa.eu/project/id/101004870`), European Union's HE PathOS Project (`https://cordis.europa.eu/project/id/101058728`) and European Union's HE TIER2 Project (`https://cordis.europa.eu/project/id/101094817`).

References

Isabelle Augenstein, Mrinal Das, Sebastian Riedel, Lakshmi Vikraman, and Andrew McCallum. 2017. SemEval 2017 task 10: ScienceIE - extracting keyphrases and relations from scientific publications. In *Proceedings of the 11th International Workshop on Semantic Evaluation (SemEval-2017)*, pages 546–555, Vancouver, Canada. Association for Computational Linguistics.

Hyung Won Chung, Le Hou, Shayne Longpre, Barret Zoph, Yi Tay, William Fedus, Eric Li, Xuezhi Wang, Mostafa Dehghani, Siddhartha Brahma, Albert Webson, Shixiang Shane Gu, Zhuyun Dai, Mirac Suzgun, Xinyun Chen, Aakanksha Chowdhery, Sharan Narang, Gaurav Mishra, Adams Yu, Vincent Zhao, Yanping Huang, Andrew Dai, Hongkun Yu, Slav Petrov, Ed H. Chi, Jeff Dean, Jacob Devlin, Adam Roberts, Denny Zhou, Quoc V. Le, and Jason Wei. 2022. Scaling instruction-finetuned language models.

Caifan Du, Johanna Cohoon, Patrice Lopez, and James Howison. 2021. Softcite dataset: A dataset of software mentions in biomedical and economic research publications. *Journal of the Association for Information Science and Technology*, 72(7):870–884.

Geraint Duck, Goran Nenadic, Andy Brass, David L Robertson, and Robert Stevens. 2013. Bionerds: Exploring bioinformatics' database and software use through literature mining. *BMC Bioinformatics*, 14(1).

Michael Färber, Alexander Albers, and Felix Schüber. 2021. Identifying used methods and datasets in scientific publications. In *Proceedings of the Workshop on Scientific Document Understanding: co-located with 35th AAAI Conference on Artificial Inteligence (AAAI 2021) ; Remote, February 9, 2021. Ed.: A. P. B. Veyseh*, volume 2831 of *CEUR Workshop Proceedings*. RWTH Aachen.

Jenny Heddes, Pim Meerdink, Miguel Pieters, and maarten marx. 2021. The automatic detection of dataset names in scientific articles. *Data*, 6:84.

Linlin Hou, Ji Zhang, Ou Wu, Ting Yu, Zhen Wang, Zhao Li, Jianliang Gao, Yingchun Ye, and Rujing Yao. 2022. Method and dataset entity mining in scientific literature: A cnn + bilstm model with self-attention. *Knowledge-Based Systems*, 235:107621.

Yufang Hou, Charles Jochim, Martin Gleize, Francesca Bonin, and Debasis Ganguly. 2019. Identification of tasks, datasets, evaluation metrics, and numeric scores for scientific leaderboards construction. In *Proceedings of the 57th Annual Meeting of the Association for Computational Linguistics*, pages 5203–5213, Florence, Italy. Association for Computational Linguistics.

Yufang Hou, Charles Jochim, Martin Gleize, Francesca Bonin, and Debasis Ganguly. 2021. TDMSci: A specialized corpus for scientific literature entity tagging of tasks datasets and metrics. In *Proceedings of the 16th Conference of the European Chapter of the Association for Computational Linguistics: Main Volume*, pages 707–714, Online. Association for Computational Linguistics.

James Howison, Patrice Lopez, Caifan Du, and Hannah Cohoon. 2023. Softcite dataset version 2.

Edward J. Hu, Yelong Shen, Phillip Wallis, Zeyuan Allen-Zhu, Yuanzhi Li, Shean Wang, and Weizhu Chen. 2021. Lora: Low-rank adaptation of large language models. *ArXiv*, abs/2106.09685.

Ana-Maria Istrate, Donghui Li, Dario Taraborelli, Michaela Torkar, Boris Veytsman, and Ivana Williams. 2022. A large dataset of software mentions in the biomedical literature.

Sarthak Jain, Madeleine van Zuylen, Hannaneh Hajishirzi, and Iz Beltagy. 2020. SciREX: A challenge dataset for document-level information extraction. In *Proceedings of the 58th Annual Meeting of the Association for Computational Linguistics*, pages 7506–7516, Online. Association for Computational Linguistics.

Frank Krüger and David Schindler. 2020. A literature review on methods for the extraction of usage statements of software and data. *Computing in Science & Engineering*, 22:26–38.

Yi Luan, Luheng He, Mari Ostendorf, and Hannaneh Hajishirzi. 2018. Multi-task identification of entities, relations, and coreference for scientific knowledge graph construction. In *Proceedings of the 2018 Conference on Empirical Methods in Natural Language Processing*, pages 3219–3232, Brussels, Belgium. Association for Computational Linguistics.

Huitong Pan, Qi Zhang, Eduard Constantin Dragut, Cornelia Caragea, and Longin Jan Latecki. 2023. Dmdd: A large-scale dataset for dataset mentions detection. *ArXiv*, abs/2305.11779.

David Schindler, Felix Bensmann, Stefan Dietze, and Frank Krüger. 2021. Somesci- a 5 star open data gold standard knowledge graph of software mentions in scientific articles. In *Proceedings of the 30th ACM International Conference on Information & Knowledge Management*, CIKM '21, page 4574–4583, New York, NY, USA. Association for Computing Machinery.

David Schindler, Benjamin Zapilko, and Frank Krüger. 2020. Investigating software usage in the social sciences: A knowledge graph approach. *The Semantic Web*, 12123:271 – 286.

Lysandre Debut Younes Belkada Sayak Paul Sourab Mangrulkar, Sylvain Gugger. 2022. Peft: State-of-the-art parameter-efficient fine-tuning methods. `https://github.com/huggingface/peft`.

Maxim Kuznetsov Vladimir Vorobev. 2023. A paraphrasing model based on chatgpt paraphrases.

Yuzhuo Wang, Chengzhi Zhang, and Kai Li. 2022. A review on method entities in the academic literature: extraction, evaluation, and application. *Scientometrics*, 127:2479 – 2520.

Tong Zeng and Daniel Ernesto Acuna. 2020. Finding datasets in publications: the syracuse university approach.

He Zhao, Zhunchen Luo, Chong Feng, Anqing Zheng, and Xiaopeng Liu. 2019. A context-based framework for modeling the role and function of on-line resource citations in scientific literature. In *Proceedings of the 2019 Conference on Empirical Methods in Natural Language Processing and the 9th International Joint Conference on Natural Language Processing (EMNLP-IJCNLP)*, pages 5206–5215, Hong Kong, China. Association for Computational Linguistics.

A ChatGPT Prompt

During the Synthetic dataset creation phase, the following ChatGPT prompt was employed (Tab. 6), initiating an iterative and detailed annotation process. Starting with a small set of carefully curated examples, we provided the prompt to ChatGPT, which generated new synthetic RA mentions with characteristics similar to the examples. We meticulously selected certain generated instances that exhibited specific properties, contributing to the richness and diversity of the dataset.

Furthermore, a key part of the process involved closely observing and collecting keywords and keyphrases that ChatGPT associated with RA mentions. Gradually, we created a set of keywords that acted as triggers for RA mentions, along with synthetic names for RA mentions.

When we gathered a sufficient collection of snippets, we leveraged the manually curated set of keywords and keyphrases to perform exhaustive annotation of the snippets. The keywords and keyphrases were used as triggers for RA mentions, including both named and unnamed RAs. That approach ensured a balanced representation of RAs and prevented bias towards specific RA mentions.

You are DataCreatorGPT. Your task is to generate snippets that contain structured information about research artifacts extracted from scientific publications. Each snippet includes a candidate research artifact highlighted by <m>and </m>tags.

For each publication snippet, you need to create the following metadata:

Artifact Type: Identify the type of research artifact specified within the <m>and </m>tags. The artifact could be a dataset, software, method, etc.

Valid Artifact: Determine if the artifact within the <m>and </m>tags is a valid research artifact. A valid artifact is a tangible input or output of the research publication. If the artifact is a general reference or functions as an adjective (for instance, "data" in "data analysis tool"), it is considered invalid.

Name Extraction: Extract the name of the research artifact from the snippet. If no name is provided, mark it as "N/A".

Version Extraction: Extract the version of the research artifact from the snippet. If no version is mentioned, mark it as "N/A".

License Extraction: Extract the license of the research artifact from the snippet. If no license is indicated, mark it as "N/A".

URL Extraction: Extract the URL of the research artifact from the snippet. If no URL is provided, mark it as "N/A".

Provenance Classification: Determine whether the authors of the publication have created, generated, or introduced the research artifact. This determination should be clearly evident from the snippet. The response should be "Yes" or "No".

Usage Classification: Determine whether the authors of the publication have used, implemented, utilized or compared/benchmarked the research artifact. This determination should be clearly evident from the snippet. The response should be "Yes" or "No".

Table 6: Prompt for ChatGPT used for the initial data creation and the human-in-the-loop process for the Synthetic dataset.

B RA Dataset Statistics

The details of the Synthetic and Hybrid datasets are summarized in Tabs. 7 and 8 respectively. Both datasets began with a specific number of unique snippets, each containing multiple mentions of datasets and software (RA mentions). These mentions may be accompanied by particular metadata (such as Valid, Name, Version, License, URL, Provenance, and Usage) relevant to the RA in question. Corresponding question-answer (QA) pairs are formulated for each RA mention and metadata field, utilizing Tab. 9 (App. C). The resulting collection of QA pairs provides a basis for fine-tuning a Large Language Model (LLM) using the LoRA method.

	Original									Augmented								
	Train			Dev			Test			Train			Dev			Test		
	dataset	software	all	dataset	software	all	dataset	software	all	dataset	software	all	dataset	software	all	dataset	software	all
RA mentions	554	647	1201	98	123	221	89	105	194	1981	2247	4228	292	335	627	282	309	591
valid	476	584	1060	87	107	194	69	98	167	1694	2022	3716	258	287	545	211	295	506
w. name	401	468	869	78	90	168	58	82	140	1422	1614	3036	226	237	463	171	243	414
w. version	42	235	277	11	61	72	0	57	57	122	762	884	33	151	184	0	178	178
w. license	142	192	334	38	46	84	20	47	67	519	616	1135	119	128	247	79	139	218
w. URL	224	171	395	38	38	76	16	20	36	764	593	1357	95	60	155	28	48	76
w. provenance	158	142	300	35	10	45	29	28	57	586	499	1085	118	30	148	115	81	196
w. usage	296	469	765	57	88	145	38	74	112	1016	1631	2647	160	222	382	88	241	329
Unique snippets	148	176	240	25	25	32	25	24	33	1589	1796	3298	232	258	474	230	247	463
Special QA pairs	-	-	-	-	-	-	-	-	-	489	616	1059	64	71	124	64	84	140
All QA pairs	3419	4193	7612	620	765	1385	509	706	1215	12147	14432	27639	1840	2057	4021	1572	2103	3815

Table 7: Statistics for the Synthetic dataset.

	Original									Augmented								
	Train			Dev			Test			Train			Dev			Test		
	dataset	software	all	dataset	software	all	dataset	software	all	dataset	software	all	dataset	software	all	dataset	software	all
RA mentions	757	1126	1883	128	222	350	125	181	306	2332	3125	5457	331	507	838	354	463	817
valid	615	951	1566	108	189	297	93	149	242	1958	2712	4670	286	439	725	258	403	661
w. name	488	769	1257	88	152	240	75	120	195	1592	2199	3791	238	352	590	194	329	523
w. version	42	235	277	11	61	72	0	57	57	122	762	884	33	151	184	0	178	178
w. license	142	201	343	38	55	93	20	47	67	519	633	1152	119	131	250	79	139	218
w. URL	225	173	398	38	38	76	16	24	40	767	601	1368	95	60	155	28	63	91
w. provenance	175	235	410	36	39	75	33	53	86	620	673	1293	119	75	194	131	138	269
w. usage	427	770	1197	77	158	235	60	115	175	1262	2208	3470	186	344	530	130	332	462
Unique snippets	194	230	298	32	34	41	32	34	43	1815	2337	4027	257	369	605	278	341	598
Special QA pairs	-	-	-	-	-	-	-	-	-	575	773	1267	73	90	147	72	106	162
All QA pairs	4456	6882	11338	776	1356	2132	689	1088	1777	14082	19458	34808	2047	3141	5335	1926	2905	4993

Table 8: Statistics for the Hybrid dataset.

C Prompts for instruction-based QA

The transformation of the RAA task from RA mentions to an instruction-based QA task, characterized by QA pairs, was achieved through the utilization of specific questions. These questions, as presented in Tab. 9, were used in the training and testing of our LoRA fine-tuned models. To ensure a fair comparison with the base Flan-T5 models during evaluation on our RA datasets' test sets, necessary modifications were made to these questions, as detailed in Tab. 10. The subsequent tables provide insight into this transformation process, illustrating how each metadata field is restructured into a question, such that the answer to that question, based on the RA mention's snippet, corresponds to the metadata field value in the RA mention.

In addition to the standard metadata-related questions, a "special" type of QA pair question, which is not associated with a specific metadata field, is also included. That "special" type plays a crucial role in the conversion of unique snippets into "special" QA pairs, which enumerate all the RAs in the snippet, denoting their Type and Name.

Metadata Field	Question
Valid	Is there a valid [software/dataset] defined in the <m> and </m> tags?
Name	What is the name of the [software/dataset] defined in the <m> and </m> tags?
Version	What is the version of the [software/dataset] defined in the <m> and </m> tags?
License	What is the license of the [software/dataset] defined in the <m> and </m> tags?
URL	What is the URL of the [software/dataset] defined in the <m> and </m> tags?
Provenance	Is the [software/dataset] defined in the <m> and </m> tags introduced or created by the authors of the publication in the snippet above?
Usage	Is the [software/dataset] defined in the <m> and </m> tags used or adopted by the authors of the publication in the snippet above?
Special QA pairs	List all the artifacts in the above snippet.

Table 9: Questions to convert the RA mentions to QA pairs.

Metadata Field	Question
Valid	Is there a valid datasetlsoftware defined in the <m> and </m> tags? Answer only using "Yes" or "No".
Name	What is the name of the [dataset/software] defined in the <m> and </m> tags? The answer must be a text span from the Snippet. If you can't answer the question then respond with "N/A".
Version	What is the version of the [dataset/software] defined in the <m> and </m> tags? The answer must be a text span from the Snippet. If you can't answer the question then respond with "N/A".
License	What is the license of the [dataset/software] defined in the <m> and </m> tags? The answer must be a text span from the Snippet. If you can't answer the question then respond with "N/A".
URL	What is the URL of the [dataset/software] defined in the <m> and </m> tags? The answer must be a text span from the Snippet. If you can't answer the question then respond with "N/A".
Provenance	Is the [dataset/software] defined in the <m> and </m> tags introduced or created by the authors of the publication in the snippet above? Answer only using "Yes" or "No".
Usage	Is the [dataset/software] defined in the <m> and </m> tags used or adopted by the authors of the publication in the snippet above? Answer only using "Yes" or "No".
Special QA pairs	List all artifacts in the above snippet. Answer with a list of artifacts in the format "artifact_type: artifact_name" separated by "|" tokens.

Table 10: Modified questions to convert the RA mentions to QA pairs.

D Evaluation results of named vs unnamed RA Mentions

In this Appendix, we present a detailed overview of the evaluation results for all models across the Synthetic, Hybrid, and GARS test sets, categorizing them by named and unnamed RA mentions. The unnamed RA Mentions do not have "Extraction" scores for the "Name" since there is no name to predict. Similarly, in the GARS test set tables, specific metrics pertaining to Licence, Version, and URL extraction do not have a score. This indicates that there is no such metadata in those particular instances.

	Flan T5 base			Flan T5 XL			LoRA-Sy			LoRA-Hy		
	Identification	Extraction		Identification	Extraction		Identification	Extraction		Identification	Extraction	
	F1	EM	LM	F1	EM	LM	F1	EM	LM	F1	EM	LM
Valid	0.918	-	-	0.932	-	-	0.994	-	-	0.995	-	-
Name	0.987	0.709	0.835	0.972	0.787	0.900	0.990	0.917	0.962	0.989	0.905	0.952
License	0.947	0.502	0.813	0.944	0.635	0.778	0.958	0.700	0.818	0.961	0.685	0.818
Version	0.688	0.544	0.779	0.944	0.625	0.838	0.985	0.581	0.588	0.989	0.735	0.750
URL	0.617	0.385	0.400	0.980	0.477	0.492	0.984	0.569	0.600	0.983	0.585	0.615
Usage	0.429	-	-	0.811	-	-	0.910	-	-	0.919	-	-
Provenance	0.484	-	-	0.649	-	-	0.941	-	-	0.958	-	-

Table 11: Experimental results on the named RA mentions of the Synthetic test set.

	Flan T5 base			Flan T5 XL			LoRA-Sy			LoRA-Hy		
	Identification	Extraction		Identification	Extraction		Identification	Extraction		Identification	Extraction	
	F1	EM	LM	F1	EM	LM	F1	EM	LM	F1	EM	LM
Valid	0.534	-	-	0.728	-	-	0.915	-	-	0.933	-	-
Name	0.387	-	-	0.773	-	-	0.925	-	-	0.919	-	-
License	0.883	-	-	0.895	-	-	0.919	-	-	0.907	-	-
Version	0.636	1.000	1.000	0.934	1.000	1.000	0.939	0.815	0.815	0.945	0.852	0.852
URL	0.849	0.091	0.091	0.977	0.909	1.000	0.971	0.909	0.909	0.977	0.909	0.909
Usage	0.154	-	-	0.597	-	-	0.915	-	-	0.899	-	-
Provenance	0.713	-	-	0.644	-	-	0.937	-	-	0.966	-	-

Table 12: Experimental results on the unnamed RA mentions of the Synthetic test set.

	Flan T5 base			Flan T5 XL			LoRA-Sy			LoRA-Hy		
	Identification	Extraction		Identification	Extraction		Identification	Extraction		Identification	Extraction	
	F1	EM	LM	F1	EM	LM	F1	EM	LM	F1	EM	LM
Valid	0.827	-	-	0.879	-	-	0.993	-	-	0.989	-	-
Name	0.977	0.613	0.771	0.949	0.698	0.830	0.968	0.820	0.907	0.975	0.840	0.911
License	0.959	0.502	0.813	0.964	0.635	0.778	0.972	0.700	0.818	0.973	0.685	0.818
Version	0.760	0.544	0.779	0.937	0.625	0.838	0.977	0.581	0.588	0.988	0.735	0.750
URL	0.693	0.362	0.388	0.983	0.438	0.463	0.979	0.487	0.525	0.985	0.525	0.562
Usage	0.340	-	-	0.799	-	-	0.883	-	-	0.917	-	-
Provenance	0.454	-	-	0.700	-	-	0.914	-	-	0.947	-	-

Table 13: Experimental results on the named RA mentions of the Hybrid dataset test set.

	Flan T5 base			Flan T5 XL			LoRA-Sy			LoRA-Hy		
	Identification	Extraction		Identification	Extraction		Identification	Extraction		Identification	Extraction	
	F1	EM	LM	F1	EM	LM	F1	EM	LM	F1	EM	LM
Valid	0.580	-	-	0.721	-	-	0.932	-	-	0.948	-	-
Name	0.422	-	-	0.730	-	-	0.926	-	-	0.930	-	-
License	0.923	-	-	0.930	-	-	0.946	-	-	0.938	-	-
Version	0.663	1.000	1.000	0.928	1.000	1.000	0.962	0.815	0.815	0.966	0.852	0.852
URL	0.807	0.091	0.091	0.916	0.909	1.000	0.977	0.909	0.909	0.974	0.909	0.909
Usage	0.099	-	-	0.637	-	-	0.943	-	-	0.933	-	-
Provenance	0.720	-	-	0.554	-	-	0.860	-	-	0.889	-	-

Table 14: Experimental results on the unnamed RA mentions of the Hybrid dataset test set.

	Flan T5 base			Flan T5 XL			LoRA-Sy			LoRA-Hy		
	Identification	Extraction		Identification	Extraction		Identification	Extraction		Identification	Extraction	
	F1	EM	LM	F1	EM	LM	F1	EM	LM	F1	EM	LM
Valid	0.333	-	-	0.696	-	-	0.989	-	-	0.989	-	-
Name	0.951	0.233	0.512	0.897	0.326	0.628	0.868	0.465	0.721	0.951	0.628	0.814
License	0.951	-	-	1.000	-	-	1.000	-	-	1.000	-	-
Version	0.822	-	-	0.938	-	-	0.951	-	-	0.964	-	-
URL	0.836	1.000	1.000	1.000	1.000	1.000	0.975	0.500	0.500	1.000	1.000	1.000
Usage	0.000	-	-	0.738	-	-	0.812	-	-	0.933	-	-
Provenance	0.222	-	-	0.947	-	-	0.941	-	-	0.947	-	-

Table 15: Experimental results on the named RA mentions of the GARS test set.

	Flan T5 base			Flan T5 XL			LoRA-Sy			LoRA-Hy		
	Identification	Extraction		Identification	Extraction		Identification	Extraction		Identification	Extraction	
	F1	EM	LM	F1	EM	LM	F1	EM	LM	F1	EM	LM
Valid	0.462	-	-	0.571	-	-	0.919	-	-	0.947	-	-
Name	0.519	-	-	0.667	-	-	0.919	-	-	0.974	-	-
License	1.000	-	-	1.000	-	-	1.000	-	-	1.000	-	-
Version	0.788	-	-	0.974	-	-	1.000	-	-	1.000	-	-
URL	0.824	-	-	0.857	-	-	1.000	-	-	0.974	-	-
Usage	0.000	-	-	0.583	-	-	0.971	-	-	0.971	-	-
Provenance	0.571	-	-	0.000	-	-	0.615	-	-	0.588	-	-

Table 16: Experimental results on the unnamed RA mentions of the GARS test set.

E Qualitative Analysis Examples

In this Appendix, we present a collection of QA pairs, along with the results produced by both the LoRA fine-tuned and Flan-T5 base models. The QA pairs have been thoughtfully selected to support the qualitative analysis elaborated in Sec. 7.

Snippet	We manually collected a remarkable dataset consisting of <m>customer reviews</m> from various e-commerce websites. This extensive dataset comprises 100,000 reviews encompassing diverse product categories. Researchers can request access to this dataset by sending an email to alex@abc.com.
Question	What is the name of the dataset defined in the <m> and </m> tags?
Answer	"N/A"
Flan-T5 Base	"100,000 reviews"
Flan-T5 XL	"customer reviews"
LoRA-Sy	"N/A"
LoRA-Hy	"N/A"

Figure 5: Example of a dataset type RA mention, where the LoRA fine-tuned models outperform the original Flan-T5 models.

Snippet	In their study, the authors incorporated various research artifacts. They employed the Apache Spark (v3.1.2) distributed computing framework and the hadoop (v3.3.1) big data processing <m>platform</m>. Apache Spark, licensed under the Apache 2.0 license, allowed efficient processing and analysis of large-scale datasets. hadoop, also released under the Apache 2.0 license, provided a robust infrastructure for distributed storage and processing. Those artifacts were instrumental in handling and analyzing massive amounts of data in their research.
Question	What is the name of the software defined in the <m> and </m> tags?
Answer	"hadoop"
Flan-T5 Base	"Apache Spark"
Flan-T5 XL	"Apache Spark (v3.1.2) distributed computing framework and the hadoop (v3.3.1) big data processing m>platform/m>"
LoRA-Sy	"hadoop"
LoRA-Hy	"hadoop"

Figure 6: Example of a software type RA mention, where the LoRA fine-tuned models outperform the original Flan-T5 models.

Snippet	The first comprehensive pre-trained multilingual model for phoneme representations, also known as <m>XPhoneBERT</m>, is presented. On the downstream TTS task, XPhoneBERT significantly enhances the strong baseline vits and confirms its effectiveness.
Question	Is the software defined in the <m> and </m> tags introduced or created by the authors of the publication in the snippet above?
Answer	"Yes"
Flan-T5 Base	"No"
Flan-T5 XL	"Yes"
LoRA-Sy	"No"
LoRA-Hy	"Yes"

Figure 7: Example of LoRA-Hy model's success in a provenance QA pair.

Snippet	To overcome the issue of accuracy, we present the <m>Sparse-Quantized Representation (SpQR)</m> approach, a new quantization and compressed format technique that delivers near-lossless compression of LLM models across model scales, while maintaining similar levels of compression as previous techniques.
Question	Is the software defined in the <m> and </m> tags used or adopted by the authors of the publication in the snippet above?
Answer	"Yes"
Flan-T5 Base	"No"
Flan-T5 XL	"No"
LoRA-Sy	"No"
LoRA-Hy	"Yes"

Figure 8: Example of LoRA-Hy model's success in a usage QA pair.

Snippet	To train <m>HeadlineSense</m>, our news headline classification model, we used the News Headlines Dataset, which consists of headlines from news articles. The dataset is widely used for text classification tasks. It is released under the Open Data Commons Attribution License (ODC-BY).
Question	What is the name of the software defined in the <m> and </m> tags?
Answer	"HeadlineSense"
Flan-T5 Base	"HeadlineSense"
Flan-T5 XL	"HeadlineSense"
LoRA-Sy	"HeadlineSense"
LoRA-Hy	"headline sense"

Figure 9: Example of a correct prediction of the LoRA-Hy model that was not a text-span from the snippet.

Zelda Rose: a tool for hassle-free training of transformer models

Loïc Grobol
MoDyCo, CNRS, Université Paris Nanterre
Lattice, ENS, CNRS and Université Sorbonne Nouvelle
lgrobol@parisnanterre.fr

Abstract

Zelda Rose is a command line interface for pretraining transformer-based models. Its purpose is to enable an easy start for users interested in training these ubiquitous models, but unable or unwilling to engage with more comprehensive — but more complex — frameworks and the complex interactions between libraries for managing models, datasets and computations. Training a model requires no code on the user's part and produce models directly compatible with the HuggingFace ecosystem, allowing quick and easy distribution and reuse. A particular care is given to lowering the cost of maintainability and future-proofing, by making the code as modular as possible and taking advantage of third-party libraries to limit ad-hoc code to the strict minimum.

1 Introduction

Since their advent in machine translation (Vaswani et al., 2017) and as a mean to obtain contextual word representations (Devlin et al., 2019), transformer models have become ubiquitous in Natural Language Processing. The latter use in particular is almost impossible to avoid to develop state-of-the-art NLP systems, the usual workflow being a self-supervised *pretraining* step using unannotated data, followed by a *fine-tuning* step for a downstream task, either as a module in a larger neural architecture or as an end-to-end predictor.

Using these models and *fine-tuning* them on downstream tasks has been made easier by libraries such as *AllenNLP* (Gardner et al., 2018), *FairSeq* (Ott et al., 2019), *MaChAmp* (van der Goot et al., 2021), *Trankit* (Nguyen et al., 2021)... and most of all *Transformers* (Wolf et al., 2020). However, among these, only *FairSeq* and *Transformers* provide interfaces to *pretrain* them.

While these libraries have considerably lowered the barrier of entry for using these models, producing new ones remains an involved process. In particular training existing models on new data is not trivial, making it hard to develop models for new languages or specialty domains. This difficulty is largely due to the number of moving pieces and options required for training these models with limited resources in a reasonable time.

Zelda Rose is meant to make pretraining transformers models as simple as possible, in particular for users who would benefit from being able to train or refine them on their own specialized domains, but who are not necessarily interested in controlling or customizing every possible aspect of the training process. This include among researchers in domains other than NLP, software engineers in the process of porting existing NLP tools to new languages, and, generally speaking, *consumers* of transformer models as opposed to *researchers* interested in improving the models themselves. It must therefore be a small tool, with a limited and clearly defined purpose, as easy to use and cheap to maintain as possible.

To this end, pretraining a transformer model using Zelda Rose does not require writing any code (although it is easy to write code to extend its capability or customize it), but running a simple command. The configuration is done with entirely with configuration files and command line options. It can use any local datasets, models and configurations as well as refer to HuggingFace Hub repository. It is also transparently compatible with the SLURM scheduler to make it easier to run on computing clusters.

2 Related works

To our knowledge, only two mainstream libraries providing interfaces for pretraining transformer models are *FairSeq* (Ott et al., 2019) and *Transformers* (Wolf et al., 2020) (via its Trainer module). Both of these are complete frameworks, providing model implementations, data process-

Proceedings of the 3rd Workshop for Natural Language Processing Open Source Software (NLP-OSS 2023), pages 54–58
December 6, 2023 ©2023 Association for Computational Linguistics

ing tools and training interfaces. While this allows for a complete customization of the architecture of the models and of the training process, it can makes it less straightforward to train a known model on new data or to get a precise sense of what is happening during training, since it requires an extensive knowledge of their often convoluted code bases. In other words, while they are essential tools to build on, they are not necessarily the most ergonomic for the need of all users. The tight coupling of their model training utilities with their library code also makes it hard to extend them, for instance to make them compatible with new hardware platforms or training techniques.

To avoid these complications, some works (such as He et al. (2020) for DeBERTa), chose to build projects entirely around the purpose of training a single model, writing ad-hoc code more or less from scratch. This obviates the need for learning all the details of a specific framework, but is much more involved in terms of engineering to design the model and training code, run them and ensure the reusability of the resulting artifacts. Overall, this model would not be suitable for the use cases that we target with Zelda Rose.

Between these two extremes of being completely integrated in an end-to-end framework or to build from ad-hoc code, the choice we made for Zelda Rose is a loose coupling with frameworks. In practice, this means that users can train new models by providing a configuration and a dataset to a command line tool, which trains a model using only high-level interfaces of third-party libraries, each specialized in a specific aspect. For instance we use *Pytorch-Lightning* (Falcon and The PyTorch Lightning team, 2019) to manage the training process, while the models implementations come from *Transformers*, which allows to benefits from all their respective innovations while avoiding being restricted by their limitations.

3 Design

3.1 User interface

From the point of view of a user, Zelda Rose mainly consists of a command line interface, which takes parameters related to the *model architecture*, *task and training configurations* and *training platform*. In its most basic form, it trains a model on a masked language task using the same hyperparameters as Liu et al. (2019):

```
zeldarose transformer \
    --tokenizer roberta_base \
    --model-config roberta_base \
    --val-text dev_corpus.txt \
    train_corpus.txt
```

The training parameters can be customized by passing a configuration file in the TOML format. For instance the default configuration would be

```
type = "mlm"

[task]
change_ratio = 0.15
mask_ratio = 0.8
switch_ratio = 0.1

[tuning]
batch_size = 64
betas = [0.9, 0.98]
epsilon = 1e-8
learning_rate = 1e-4
lr_decay_steps = 1048567
warmup_steps = 1024
weight_decay = 1e-5
```

The use of configuration files rather than command line flags or environment variables help keeping track of the settings used (they can be directly redistributed with the models) for documentation and reproduction. They are also easier to version and to validate (in our case via *Pydantic* (Colvin et al., 2023)).

On the other hands, parameters related to the training platform are given as command line optiuons, since they are specific to each invocation. For instance `--num-devices` specifies the number of devices (GPU, CPU cores…) used for a training run. Other options include the type of devices to use, the number of nodes to use when running in SLURM…

So far, the tasks implemented are masked language modeling (inspired by BERT Devlin et al. (2019)), replaced token detection (from ELECTRA (Clark et al., 2019) and DeBERTa v3 (He et al., 2021)) and span-masking denoising (from mBART (Liu et al., 2020)). Not all hyperparameters are configurable and some opinionated choices are made (for instance at this point the gradient descent algorithm used is AdamW (Loshchilov and Hutter, 2019)) in order to keep the configuration space manageable, which simplify the choice of a setting for user and reduces the maintainability burden.

The model configurations given in input refer to *Transformers* models, which can be loaded either from a local file or from a repository on HuggingFace Hub[1]. This allow an easy reference to most popular models. Users can also ask for the initialization of their model with already pretrained weights for post-training (Zhuang et al., 2021), which has been shown to significantly improve model performances on domain-specific tasks. Finally, the outputs of Zelda Rose are *Transformers*-compatible models, ready to be loaded in this library or uploaded to HuggingFace Hub for immediate distribution.

3.2 Internal organization

The library is organized around two main building blocks: *tasks* and *datasets*.

Datasets are managers for collections of samples, e.g. raw sentences or parallel sentences. They contain the logic to load (from local files or remote repositories), preprocess (including at least tokenization, digitization and batching) and serve batch of samples to the training modules. In order to process large datasets with a limited memory footprint and enable caching, the data management and processing parts currently use of HuggingFace's *Datasets* library (Lhoest et al., 2021), wrapped in regular Pytorch and Pytorch-Lightning objects to make this transparent to the rest of the code and reduce the cost of changing this in future extensions of Zelda Rose.

Tasks are abstractions for the process of — given a model architecture and a configuration —, providing an object (in practice a Pytorch-Lightning training module) that implement the actual training process: generating targets from the inputs (for self-supervised tasks), obtain parameters for the optimization algorithm, run training steps, compute losses and metrics... In practice, since the models used are those implemented in HuggingFace's *Transformers* library (Wolf et al., 2020), which handles the forward pass and the loss computations, most tasks only have to specify target generation, optimization and monitoring-related parts.

Finally, given a configuration, the main module loads the appropriate task and dataset, to which it delegates all task- and data-related aspects, while taking care of the platform considerations, such as how many training processes to spawn, which devices to use and how many sample should they each process at once, etc. according to the configuration. This architecture allows for a clear separation of concerns, making adding new tasks and datasets quite easy. In practice, this is implemented by having the main module build a Pytorch-Lightning Trainer, which natively deals with a large number of hardware and training strategies and is actively maintained to follow the state of the art, in turn allowing us to benefits from the latest innovations at a relatively low maintenance cost.

4 Challenges

The main challenge with such a library is its maintainability given a limited time budget. Indeed, while the systematic reliance on third-party libraries rather than ad-hoc code as often as possible lets us benefit from their latest improvement with very little engineering code *a priori*, it also makes Zelda Rose dependent upon them for correctness and backward compatibility. This means that every new release of a dependency has to be checked with great care, as it could be introducing new bugs and it is often the case that slight but significant behavior changes go unnoticed or undocumented.

Undocumented behavior and implementation details in the dependencies were also a burden for the initial engineering effort and for subsequent extension of Zelda Rose (for instance when adding new tasks). Indeed, for libraries of these sizes and providing so many functionality, the documentation does not always follow the speed of bleeding edge evolutions, and checking their source code directly is often necessary to ensure that we use their interfaces correctly.

In other cases it was the lack of support for certain features required for the reproduction of existing work (such as embedding tying in the ELECTRA and DeBERTa models) that made reaching into private interfaces and monkey-patching necessary. While the dynamic nature of these libraries allow this, it makes part of our code much more brittle than we would hope for and these parts have to be checked for correctness with each new release.

This regular checking of non-regressions is made harder by the nature of the tool. Since train-

[1] `https://huggingface.co/models`

ing neural networks is not in general deterministic and since bugs tend to manifest not as outright errors but as degradation in performances, ensuring that a modification did not introduce a bug can be challenging. Indeed, it is often the case that such a degradation would not be observed on toy examples but only on the larger scale of real world examples. However, continuously running automated tests (in a continuous integration pipeline for instance) at these scales is not realistic, reducing the safety provided by tests.

Moreover, the complexity of the dependencies makes unit testing challenging, since it would often require mocking internals of these libraries. Automated tests ran as part of the continuous integration pipeline of Zelda Rose are therefore limited to so-called smoke tests, which verify if the tool runs, is able to train model in a variety of configuration and produces viable output. Non-regression tests, in contrast, are run manually, by training a few select models in realistic conditions. Since these are much more costly, they are only ran before a new version of Zelda Rose is released.

5 Conclusion

Zelda Rose makes possible it to pretrain transformer models with very little effort, even in complex environments. No custom code is needed to train a model on new data, which should allow more people to participate in resource development efforts. However, the modular design of this tool also makes it easy to extend and to integrate future developments in transformer models.

Building upon high level state-of-the-art frameworks rather than custom engineering allows to benefit from the latest innovations without too much maintenance work. It is not without downsides as it still requires some work to ensure that new releases of these dependencies do not introduce bugs and it makes the parts of Zelda Rose more complex to test individually. Overall, however, this design choice is still a net gain.

Planned future development in Zelda Rose will focus on adding more tasks, which will be the occasion to make the design even more modular by allowing tasks to be external plugins. More efforts will also be made on the instrumentation and testing, to make the testing process more cumbersome and add as many checks as possible of the reproducibility of training results. Finally, since the aim of this tool is to be useful beyond its developers, future improvements will also in a large part be guided by the requests of users, which we hope will be numerous and relevant!

References

Kevin Clark, Minh-Thang Luong, Quoc V. Le, and Christopher D. Manning. 2019. ELECTRA: Pre-training Text Encoders as Discriminators Rather Than Generators. In *Proceedings of the 8th International Conference on Learning Representations.*

Samuel Colvin, Eric Jolibois, Hasan Ramezani, Adrian Garcia, Terrence Dorsey, and David Montague. 2023. Pydantic.

Jacob Devlin, Ming-Wei Chang, Kenton Lee, and Kristina Toutanova. 2019. BERT: Pre-training of deep bidirectional transformers for language understanding. In *Proceedings of the 2019 Conference of the North American Chapter of the Association for Computational Linguistics: Human Language Technologies, Volume 1 (Long and Short Papers)*, pages 4171–4186, Minneapolis, Minnesota. Association for Computational Linguistics.

William Falcon and The PyTorch Lightning team. 2019. PyTorch Lightning.

Matt Gardner, Joel Grus, Mark Neumann, Oyvind Tafjord, Pradeep Dasigi, Nelson F. Liu, Matthew Peters, Michael Schmitz, and Luke Zettlemoyer. 2018. AllenNLP: A deep semantic natural language processing platform. In *Proceedings of Workshop for NLP Open Source Software (NLP-OSS)*, pages 1–6, Melbourne, Australia. Association for Computational Linguistics.

Pengcheng He, Jianfeng Gao, and Weizhu Chen. 2021. Debertav3: Improving deberta using electra-style pre-training with gradient-disentangled embedding sharing.

Pengcheng He, Xiaodong Liu, Jianfeng Gao, and Weizhu Chen. 2020. DeBERTa: Decoding-enhanced BERT with disentangled attention. In *Proceedings of the 2021 International Conference on Learning Representations.*

Quentin Lhoest, Albert Villanova del Moral, Yacine Jernite, Abhishek Thakur, Patrick von Platen, Suraj Patil, Julien Chaumond, Mariama Drame, Julien Plu, Lewis Tunstall, Joe Davison, Mario Šaško, Gunjan Chhablani, Bhavitvya Malik, Simon Brandeis, Teven Le Scao, Victor Sanh, Canwen Xu, Nicolas Patry, Angelina McMillan-Major, Philipp Schmid, Sylvain Gugger, Clément Delangue, Théo Matussière, Lysandre Debut, Stas Bekman, Pierric Cistac, Thibault Goehringer, Victor Mustar, François Lagunas, Alexander Rush, and Thomas Wolf. 2021. Datasets: A community library for natural language processing. In *Proceedings of the 2021 Conference on Empirical Methods in Natural Language Processing: System Demonstrations*, pages 175–184, Online and Punta Cana, Dominican Republic. Association for Computational Linguistics.

Yinhan Liu, Jiatao Gu, Naman Goyal, Xian Li, Sergey Edunov, Marjan Ghazvininejad, Mike Lewis, and Luke Zettlemoyer. 2020. Multilingual denoising pre-training for neural machine translation. *Transactions of the Association for Computational Linguistics*, 8:726–742.

Yinhan Liu, Myle Ott, Naman Goyal, Jingfei Du, Mandar Joshi, Danqi Chen, Omer Levy, Mike Lewis, Luke Zettlemoyer, and Veselin Stoyanov. 2019. Roberta: A robustly optimized bert pretraining approach. *ArXiv*, abs/1907.11692.

Ilya Loshchilov and Frank Hutter. 2019. Decoupled weight decay regularization. In *International Conference on Learning Representations*.

Minh Van Nguyen, Viet Dac Lai, Amir Pouran Ben Veyseh, and Thien Huu Nguyen. 2021. Trankit: A light-weight transformer-based toolkit for multilingual natural language processing. In *Proceedings of the 16th Conference of the European Chapter of the Association for Computational Linguistics: System Demonstrations*, pages 80–90, Online. Association for Computational Linguistics.

Myle Ott, Sergey Edunov, Alexei Baevski, Angela Fan, Sam Gross, Nathan Ng, David Grangier, and Michael Auli. 2019. fairseq: A fast, extensible toolkit for sequence modeling. In *Proceedings of the 2019 Conference of the North American Chapter of the Association for Computational Linguistics (Demonstrations)*, pages 48–53, Minneapolis, Minnesota. Association for Computational Linguistics.

Rob van der Goot, Ahmet Üstün, Alan Ramponi, Ibrahim Sharaf, and Barbara Plank. 2021. Massive choice, ample tasks (MaChAmp): A toolkit for multi-task learning in NLP. In *Proceedings of the 16th Conference of the European Chapter of the Association for Computational Linguistics: System Demonstrations*, pages 176–197, Online. Association for Computational Linguistics.

Ashish Vaswani, Noam Shazeer, Niki Parmar, Jakob Uszkoreit, Llion Jones, Aidan N Gomez, Łukasz Kaiser, and Illia Polosukhin. 2017. Attention is All you Need. In *Advances in Neural Information Processing Systems 30*, pages 5998–6008, Long Beach, California. Curran Associates, Inc.

Thomas Wolf, Lysandre Debut, Victor Sanh, Julien Chaumond, Clement Delangue, Anthony Moi, Pierric Cistac, Tim Rault, Remi Louf, Morgan Funtowicz, Joe Davison, Sam Shleifer, Patrick von Platen, Clara Ma, Yacine Jernite, Julien Plu, Canwen Xu, Teven Le Scao, Sylvain Gugger, Mariama Drame, Quentin Lhoest, and Alexander Rush. 2020. Transformers: State-of-the-art natural language processing. In *Proceedings of the 2020 Conference on Empirical Methods in Natural Language Processing: System Demonstrations*, pages 38–45, Online. Association for Computational Linguistics.

Liu Zhuang, Lin Wayne, Shi Ya, and Zhao Jun. 2021. A robustly optimized BERT pre-training approach with post-training. In *Proceedings of the 20th Chinese National Conference on Computational Linguistics*, pages 1218–1227, Huhhot, China. Chinese Information Processing Society of China.

GPT4All: An Ecosystem of Open Source Compressed Language Models

Yuvanesh Anand
Nomic AI
yuvanesh@nomic.ai

Zach Nussbaum
Nomic AI
zach@nomic.ai

Adam Treat
Nomic AI
adam@nomic.ai

Aaron Miller
Nomic AI
aaron@nomic.ai

Richard Guo
Nomic AI
richard@nomic.ai

Ben Schmidt
Nomic AI
ben@nomic.ai

GPT4All Community
Planet Earth

Brandon Duderstadt*
Nomic AI
brandon@nomic.ai

Andriy Mulyar*
Nomic AI
andriy@nomic.ai

Abstract

Large language models (LLMs) have recently achieved human-level performance on a range of professional and academic benchmarks. The accessibility of these models has lagged behind their performance. State-of-the-art LLMs require costly infrastructure, are only accessible via rate-limited, geo-locked, and censored web interfaces, and lack publicly available code and technical reports.

In this paper, we tell the story of GPT4All, a popular open source repository that aims to democratize access to LLMs. We outline the technical details of the original GPT4All model family, as well as the evolution of the GPT4All project from a single model into a fully fledged open source ecosystem. It is our hope that this paper acts as both a technical overview of the original GPT4All models as well as a case study on the subsequent growth of the GPT4All open source ecosystem.

1 Introduction

On March 14 2023, OpenAI released GPT-4, a large language model capable of achieving human level performance on a variety of professional and academic benchmarks. Despite the popularity of the release, the GPT-4 technical report (OpenAI, 2023) contained virtually no details regarding the architecture, hardware, training compute, dataset construction, or training method used to create the model. Moreover, users could only access the model through the internet interface at chat.openai.com, which was severely rate limited and unavailable in several locales (e.g. Italy) (BBC News, 2023). Additionally, GPT-4 refused to answer a wide variety of queries, responding only with the now infamous "As an AI Language Model, I cannot..." prefix (Vincent, 2023). These transparency and accessibility concerns spurred several developers to begin creating open source large language model (LLM) alternatives. Several grassroots efforts focused on fine tuning Meta's open code LLaMA model (Touvron et al., 2023; McMillan, 2023), whose weights were leaked on BitTorrent less than a week prior to the release of GPT-4 (Verge, 2023). GPT4All started as one of these variants.

In this paper, we tell the story of GPT4All. We comment on the technical details of the original GPT4All model (Anand et al., 2023), as well as the evolution of GPT4All from a single model to an ecosystem of several models. We remark on the impact that the project has had on the open source community, and discuss future directions. It is our hope that this paper acts as both a technical overview of the original GPT4All models as well as a case study on the subsequent growth of the GPT4All open source ecosystem.

2 The Original GPT4All Model

2.1 Data Collection and Curation

To train the original GPT4All model, we collected roughly one million prompt-response pairs using the GPT-3.5-Turbo OpenAI API between March 20, 2023 and March 26th, 2023. In particular, we gathered GPT-3.5-Turbo responses to prompts of three publicly available datasets: the unified chip2 subset of LAION OIG, a random sub-sample of Stackoverflow Questions, and a sub-sample of Bigscience/P3 (Sanh et al., 2021). Following the approach in Stanford Alpaca (Taori et al., 2023), an open source LLaMA variant that came just before GPT4All, we focused substantial effort on dataset curation.

The collected dataset was loaded into Atlas (Nomic, 2023)—a visual interface for exploring and tagging massive unstructured datasets —for data curation. Using At-

* Shared Senior Authorship

Proceedings of the 3rd Workshop for Natural Language Processing Open Source Software (NLP-OSS 2023), pages 59–64
December 6, 2023

las, we identified and removed subsets of the data where GPT-3.5-Turbo refused to respond, had malformed output, or produced a very short response. This resulted in the removal of the entire Bigscience/P3 subset of our data, as many P3 prompts induced responses that were simply one word. After curation, we were left with a set of 437,605 prompt-response pairs, which we visualize in Figure 1a.

2.2 Model Training

The original GPT4All model was a fine tuned variant of LLaMA 7B. In order to train it more efficiently, we froze the base weights of LLaMA, and only trained a small set of LoRA (Hu et al., 2021) weights during the fine tuning process. Detailed model hyper-parameters and training code can be found in our associated code repository[1].

2.3 Model Access

We publicly released all data, training code, and model weights for the community to build upon. Further, we provided a 4-bit quantized version of the model, which enabled users to run it on their own commodity hardware without transferring data to a 3rd party service.

Our research and development costs were dominated by ~\$800 in GPU spend (rented from Lambda Labs and Paperspace) and ~\$500 in OpenAI API spend. Our final GPT4All model could be trained in about eight hours on a Lambda Labs DGX A100 8x 80GB for a total cost of ~\$100.

2.4 Model Evaluation

We performed a preliminary evaluation of our model using the human evaluation data from the Self Instruct paper (Wang et al., 2023). We reported the ground truth perplexity of our model against what was, to our knowledge, the best openly available alpaca-lora model at the time, provided by user *chainyo* on HuggingFace. Both models had very large perplexities on a small number of tasks, so we reported perplexities clipped to a maximum of 100. We found that GPT4All produces stochastically lower ground truth perplexities than alpaca-lora (Anand et al., 2023).

3 From a Model to an Ecosystem

3.1 GPT4All-J: Repository Growth and the implications of the LLaMA License

The GPT4All repository grew rapidly after its release, gaining over 20000 GitHub stars in just one week, as shown in Figure 2. This growth was supported by an in-person hackathon hosted in New York City three days after the model release, which attracted several hundred participants. As the Nomic discord, the home of online discussion about GPT4All, ballooned to over 10000 people, one thing became very clear - there was massive demand for a model that could be used commercially.

The LLaMA model that GPT4All was based on was licensed for research only, which severely limited the set of domains that GPT4All could be applied in. As a response to this, the Nomic team repeated the model training procedure of the original GPT4All model, but based on the already open source and commercially licensed GPT-J model (Wang and Komatsuzaki, 2021). GPT4All-J also had an augmented training set, which contained multi-turn QA examples and creative writing such as poetry, rap, and short stories. The creative writing prompts were generated by filling in schemas such as "Write a [CREATIVE STORY TYPE] about [NOUN] in the style of [PERSON]." We again employed Atlas to curate the prompt-response pairs in this data set.

Our evaluation methodology also evolved as the project grew. In particular, we began evaluating GPT4All models using a suite of seven reasoning tasks that were used for evaluation of the Databricks Dolly (Conover et al., 2023b) model, which was released on April 12, 2023. Unfortunately, GPT4All-J did not outperform other prominent open source models on this evaluation. As a result, we endeavoured to create a model that did.

3.2 GPT4All-Snoozy: the Emergence of the GPT4All Ecosystem

GPT4All-Snoozy was developed using roughly the same procedure as the previous GPT4All models, but with a few key modifications. First, GPT4All-Snoozy used the LLaMA-13B base model due to its superior base metrics when compared to GPT-J. Next, GPT4All-Snoozy incorporated the Dolly's training data into its train mix. After data curation and deduplication with Atlas, this yielded a training set of 739,259 total prompt-response pairs. We dubbed the model that resulted from training on this improved dataset GPT4All-Snoozy. As shown in Figure 1, GPT4All-Snoozy had the best average score on our evaluation benchmark of any model in the ecosystem at the time of its release.

Concurrently with the development of GPT4All, several organizations such as LMSys, Stability AI, BAIR, and Databricks built and deployed open source language models. We heard increasingly from the community that they wanted quantized versions of these models for local use. As we realized that organizations with ever more resources were developing source language models, we decided to pivot our effort away from training increasingly capable models and towards providing easy access to the plethora of models being produced by the open source community. Practically, this meant spending our time compressing open source models for use on commodity hardware, providing stable and simple high level model APIs, and supporting a GUI for no code model experimentation.

3.3 The Current State of GPT4All

Today, GPT4All is focused on improving the accessibility of open source language models. The repository

[1]https://github.com/nomic-ai/gpt4all

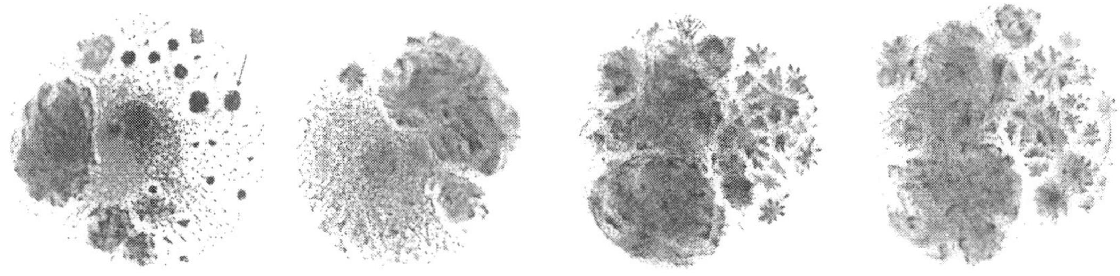

(a) (b) (c) (d)

Figure 1: TSNE visualizations showing the progression of the GPT4All train set. Panel (a) shows the original uncurated data. The red arrow denotes a region of highly homogeneous prompt-response pairs. The coloring denotes which open dataset contributed the prompt. Panel (b) shows the original GPT4All data after curation. This panel, as well as panels (c) and (d) are 10 colored by topic, which Atlas automatically extracts. Notice that the large homogeneous prompt-response blobs no longer appearl. Panel (c) shows the GPT4All-J dataset. The "starburst" clusters introduced on the right side of the panel correspond to the newly added creative data. Panel (d) shows the final GPT4All-snoozy dataset. All datasets have been released to the public, and can be interactively explored online. In the web version of this article, you can click on a panel to be taken to its interactive visualization.

Model	BoolQ	PIQA	HellaSwag	WinoG.	ARC-e	ARC-c	OBQA	Avg.
GPT4All-J 6B v1.0*	73.4	74.8	63.4	64.7	54.9	36	40.2	58.2
GPT4All-J v1.1-breezy*	74	75.1	63.2	63.6	55.4	34.9	38.4	57.8
GPT4All-J v1.2-jazzy*	74.8	74.9	63.6	63.8	56.6	35.3	41	58.6
GPT4All-J v1.3-groovy*	73.6	74.3	63.8	63.5	57.7	35	38.8	58.1
GPT4All-J Lora 6B*	68.6	75.8	66.2	63.5	56.4	35.7	40.2	58.1
GPT4All LLaMa Lora 7B*	73.1	77.6	72.1	67.8	51.1	40.4	40.2	60.3
GPT4All 13B snoozy*	83.3	79.2	75	71.3	60.9	44.2	43.4	65.3
GPT4All Falcon	77.6	79.8	74.9	70.1	67.9	43.4	42.6	65.2
Nous-Hermes (Nous-Research, 2023b)	79.5	78.9	80	71.9	74.2	50.9	**46.4**	68.8
Nous-Hermes2 (Nous-Research, 2023c)	**83.9**	**80.7**	80.1	71.3	75.7	**52.1**	46.2	**70.0**
Nous-Puffin (Nous-Research, 2023d)	81.5	**80.7**	**80.4**	**72.5**	**77.6**	50.7	45.6	69.9
Dolly 6B* (Conover et al., 2023a)	68.8	77.3	67.6	63.9	62.9	38.7	41.2	60.1
Dolly 12B* (Conover et al., 2023b)	56.7	75.4	71	62.2	64.6	38.5	40.4	58.4
Alpaca 7B* (Taori et al., 2023)	73.9	77.2	73.9	66.1	59.8	43.3	43.4	62.5
Alpaca Lora 7B* (Wang, 2023)	74.3	79.3	74	68.8	56.6	43.9	42.6	62.8
GPT-J* 6.7B (Wang and Komatsuzaki, 2021)	65.4	76.2	66.2	64.1	62.2	36.6	38.2	58.4
LLama 7B* (Touvron et al., 2023)	73.1	77.4	73	66.9	52.5	41.4	42.4	61.0
LLama 13B* (Touvron et al., 2023)	68.5	79.1	76.2	70.1	60	44.6	42.2	63.0
Pythia 6.7B* (Biderman et al., 2023)	63.5	76.3	64	61.1	61.3	35.2	37.2	56.9
Pythia 12B* (Biderman et al., 2023)	67.7	76.6	67.3	63.8	63.9	34.8	38	58.9
Fastchat T5* (Zheng et al., 2023)	81.5	64.6	46.3	61.8	49.3	33.3	39.4	53.7
Fastchat Vicuña* 7B (Zheng et al., 2023)	76.6	77.2	70.7	67.3	53.5	41.2	40.8	61.0
Fastchat Vicuña 13B* (Zheng et al., 2023)	81.5	76.8	73.3	66.7	57.4	42.7	43.6	63.1
StableVicuña RLHF* (Stability-AI, 2023)	82.3	78.6	74.1	70.9	61	43.5	44.4	65.0
StableLM Tuned* (Stability-AI, 2023)	62.5	71.2	53.6	54.8	52.4	31.1	33.4	51.3
StableLM Base* (Stability-AI, 2023)	60.1	67.4	41.2	50.1	44.9	27	32	46.1
Koala 13B* (Geng et al., 2023)	76.5	77.9	72.6	68.8	54.3	41	42.8	62.0
Open Assistant Pythia 12B*	67.9	78	68.1	65	64.2	40.4	43.2	61.0
Mosaic MPT7B (MosaicML-Team, 2023)	74.8	79.3	76.3	68.6	70	42.2	42.6	64.8
Mosaic mpt-instruct (MosaicML-Team, 2023)	74.3	80.4	77.2	67.8	72.2	44.6	43	65.6
Mosaic mpt-chat (MosaicML-Team, 2023)	77.1	78.2	74.5	67.5	69.4	43.3	44.2	64.9
Wizard 7B (Xu et al., 2023)	78.4	77.2	69.9	66.5	56.8	40.5	42.6	61.7
Wizard 7B Uncensored (Xu et al., 2023)	77.7	74.2	68	65.2	53.5	38.7	41.6	59.8
Wizard 13B Uncensored (Xu et al., 2023)	78.4	75.5	72.1	69.5	57.5	40.4	44	62.5
GPT4-x-Vicuna-13b (Nous-Research, 2023a)	81.3	75	75.2	65	58.7	43.9	43.6	63.2
Falcon 7b (Almazrouei et al., 2023)	73.6	**80.7**	76.3	67.3	71	43.3	44.4	65.2
Falcon 7b instruct (Almazrouei et al., 2023)	70.9	78.6	69.8	66.7	67.9	42.7	41.2	62.5
text-davinci-003	88.1	83.8	83.4	75.8	83.9	63.9	51.0	75.7

Table 1: Evaluations of all language models in the GPT4All ecosystem as of August 1, 2023. Code models are not included. OpenAI's text-davinci-003 is included as a point of comparison. The best overall performing model in the GPT4All ecosystem, Nous-Hermes2, achieves over 92% of the average performance of text-davinci-003. Models marked with an asterisk were available in the ecosystem as of the release of GPT4All-Snoozy. Note that at release, GPT4All-Snoozy had the best average performance of any model in the ecosystem. Bolded numbers indicate the best performing model as of August 1, 2023.

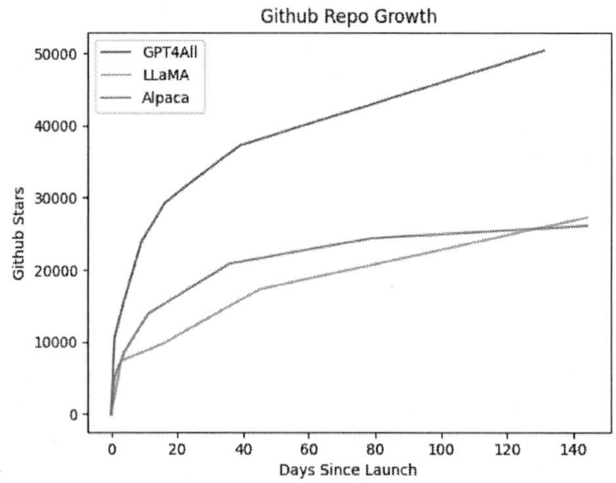

Figure 2: Comparison of the github start growth of GPT4All, Meta's LLaMA, and Stanford's Alpaca. We conjecture that GPT4All achieved and maintains faster ecosystem growth due to the focus on access, which allows more users to meaningfully participate.

provides compressed versions of open source models for use on commodity hardware, stable and simple high level model APIs, and a GUI for no code model experimentation. The project continues to increase in popularity, and as of August 1 2023, has garnered over 50000 GitHub stars and over 5000 forks.

GPT4All currently provides native support and benchmark data for over 35 models (see Figure 1), and includes several models co-developed with industry partners such as Replit and Hugging Face. GPT4All also provides high level model APIs in languages including Python, Typescript, Go, C#, and Java, among others. Furthermore, the GPT4All no code GUI currently supports the workflows of over 50000 monthly active users, with over 25% of users coming back to the tool every day of the week. (Note that all GPT4All user data is collected on an *opt in* basis.) GPT4All has become the top language model integration in the popular open source AI orchestration library LangChain (Chase, 2022), and powers many popular open source projects such as PrivateGPT (imartinez, 2023), Quiver (StanGirard, 2023), and MindsDB (MindsDB, 2023), among others. GPT4All is the 3rd fastest growing GitHub repository of all time (Leo, 2023), and is the 185th most popular repository on the platform, by star count.

4 The Future of GPT4All

In the future, we will continue to grow GPT4All, supporting it as the de facto solution for LLM accessibility. Concretely, this means continuing to compress and distribute important open-source language models developed by the community, as well as compressing and distributing increasingly multimodal AI models. Furthermore, we will expand the set of hardware devices that GPT4All models run on, so that GPT4All models "just work" on any machine, whether it comes equipped with Apple Metal silicon, NVIDIA, AMD, or other edge-accelerated hardware. Overall, we envision a world where anyone, anywhere, with any machine, can access and contribute to the cutting edge of AI.

Limitations

By enabling access to large language models, the GPT4All project also inherits many of the ethical concerns associated with generative models. Principal among these is the concern that unfiltered language models like GPT4All enable malicious users to generate content that could be harmful and dangerous (e.g., instructions on building bioweapons). While we recognize this risk, we also acknowledge the risk of concentrating this technology in the hands of a limited number of increasingly secretive research groups. We believe that the risk of concentrating the benefits of language model technology in the hands of a small number of people significantly outweighs the risk of misuse, and hence we prefer to make the technology as widely available as possible.

Finally, we realize the challenge in assigning credit for large-scale open source initiatives. We make a first attempt at fair credit assignment by explicitly including the GPT4All open source developers as authors on this work, but recognize that this is insufficient fully characterize everyone involved in the GPT4All effort. Furthermore, we acknowledge the difficulty in citing open source works that do not necessarily have standardized citations, and do our best in this paper to provide URLs to projects whenever possible. We encourage further research in the area of open source credit assignment, and hope to be able to support some of this research ourselves in the future.

References

Ebtesam Almazrouei, Hamza Alobeidli, Abdulaziz Alshamsi, Alessandro Cappelli, Ruxandra Cojocaru, Merouane Debbah, Etienne Goffinet, Daniel Heslow, Julien Launay, Quentin Malartic, Badreddine Noune, Baptiste Pannier, and Guilherme Penedo. 2023. Falcon-40B: an open large language model with state-of-the-art performance.

Yuvanesh Anand, Zach Nussbaum, Brandon Duderstadt, Benjamin Schmidt, and Andriy Mulyar. 2023. Gpt4all: Training an assistant-style chatbot with large scale data distillation from gpt-3.5-turbo. https://github.com/nomic-ai/gpt4all.

BBC News. 2023. Chatgpt banned in italy over privacy concerns. *BBC News*.

Stella Biderman, Hailey Schoelkopf, Quentin Anthony, Herbie Bradley, Kyle O'Brien, Eric Hallahan, Mohammad Aflah Khan, Shivanshu Purohit, USVSN Sai Prashanth, Edward Raff, Aviya Skowron, Lintang Sutawika, and Oskar van der Wal. 2023. Pythia: A suite for analyzing large language models across training and scaling.

Harrison Chase. 2022. langchain. https://github.com/langchain-ai/langchain.

Mike Conover, Matt Hayes, Ankit Mathur, Xiangrui Meng, Jianwei Xie, Jun Wan, Ali Ghodsi, Patrick Wendell, and Matei Zaharia. 2023a. Hello dolly: Democratizing the magic of chatgpt with open models.

Mike Conover, Matt Hayes, Ankit Mathur, Jianwei Xie, Jun Wan, Sam Shah, Ali Ghodsi, Patrick Wendell, Matei Zaharia, and Reynold Xin. 2023b. Free dolly: Introducing the world's first truly open instruction-tuned llm.

Xinyang Geng, Arnav Gudibande, Hao Liu, Eric Wallace, Pieter Abbeel, Sergey Levine, and Dawn Song. 2023. Koala: A dialogue model for academic research. Blog post.

Edward J. Hu, Yelong Shen, Phillip Wallis, Zeyuan Allen-Zhu, Yuanzhi Li, Shean Wang, Lu Wang, and Weizhu Chen. 2021. Lora: Low-rank adaptation of large language models.

imartinez. 2023. privategpt. https://github.com/imartinez/privateGPT.

Oscar Leo. 2023. GitHub: The Fastest Growing Repositories of All Time.

Robert McMillan. 2023. A meta platforms leak put powerful ai in the hands of everyone. *The Wall Street Journal*.

MindsDB. 2023. Mindsdb. https://github.com/mindsdb/mindsdb. GitHub repository.

MosaicML-Team. 2023. Introducing mpt-7b: A new standard for open-source, commercially usable llms. Accessed: 2023-08-07.

Nomic. 2023. Atlas. https://atlas.nomic.ai/.

Nous-Research. 2023a. gpt4-x-vicuna-13b. https://huggingface.co/NousResearch/gpt4-x-vicuna-13b. Model on Hugging Face.

Nous-Research. 2023b. Nous-hermes-13b. https://huggingface.co/NousResearch/Nous-Hermes-13b. Model on Hugging Face.

Nous-Research. 2023c. Nous-hermes-llama-2-7b. https://huggingface.co/NousResearch/Nous-Hermes-llama-2-7b. Model on Hugging Face.

Nous-Research. 2023d. Redmond-puffin-13b. https://huggingface.co/NousResearch/Redmond-Puffin-13B. Model on Hugging Face.

OpenAI. 2023. Gpt-4 technical report.

Victor Sanh, Albert Webson, Colin Raffel, Stephen H. Bach, Lintang Sutawika, Zaid Alyafeai, Antoine Chaffin, Arnaud Stiegler, Teven Le Scao, Arun Raja, Manan Dey, M Saiful Bari, Canwen Xu, Urmish Thakker, Shanya Sharma Sharma, Eliza Szczechla, Taewoon Kim, Gunjan Chhablani, Nihal Nayak, Debajyoti Datta, Jonathan Chang, Mike Tian-Jian Jiang, Han Wang, Matteo Manica, Sheng Shen, Zheng Xin Yong, Harshit Pandey, Rachel Bawden, Thomas Wang, Trishala Neeraj, Jos Rozen, Abheesht Sharma, Andrea Santilli, Thibault Fevry, Jason Alan Fries, Ryan Teehan, Stella Biderman, Leo Gao, Tali Bers, Thomas Wolf, and Alexander M. Rush. 2021. Multitask prompted training enables zero-shot task generalization.

Stability-AI. 2023. Stablelm. https://github.com/Stability-AI/StableLM. GitHub repository.

StanGirard. 2023. quivr. https://github.com/StanGirard/quivr. GitHub repository.

Rohan Taori, Ishaan Gulrajani, Tianyi Zhang, Yann Dubois, Xuechen Li, Carlos Guestrin, Percy Liang, and Tatsunori B. Hashimoto. 2023. Stanford alpaca: An instruction-following llama model. https://github.com/tatsu-lab/stanford_alpaca.

Hugo Touvron, Thibaut Lavril, Gautier Izacard, Xavier Martinet, Marie-Anne Lachaux, Timothée Lacroix, Baptiste Rozière, Naman Goyal, Eric Hambro, Faisal Azhar, Aurelien Rodriguez, Armand Joulin, Edouard Grave, and Guillaume Lample. 2023. Llama: Open and efficient foundation language models.

The Verge. 2023. Meta's powerful ai language model has leaked online — what happens now? *The Verge*.

James Vincent. 2023. As an ai generated language model: The phrase that shows how ai is polluting the web. *The Verge*.

Ben Wang and Aran Komatsuzaki. 2021. GPT-J-6B: A 6 Billion Parameter Autoregressive Language Model. https://github.com/kingoflolz/mesh-transformer-jax.

Eric J. Wang. 2023. alpaca-lora. https://github.com/tloen/alpaca-lora. GitHub repository.

Yizhong Wang, Yeganeh Kordi, Swaroop Mishra, Alisa Liu, Noah A. Smith, Daniel Khashabi, and Hannaneh Hajishirzi. 2023. Self-instruct: Aligning language models with self-generated instructions.

Can Xu, Qingfeng Sun, Kai Zheng, Xiubo Geng, Pu Zhao, Jiazhan Feng, Chongyang Tao, and Daxin Jiang. 2023. Wizardlm: Empowering large language models to follow complex instructions.

Lianmin Zheng, Wei-Lin Chiang, Ying Sheng, Siyuan Zhuang, Zhanghao Wu, Yonghao Zhuang, Zi Lin, Zhuohan Li, Dacheng Li, Eric. P Xing, Hao Zhang, Joseph E. Gonzalez, and Ion Stoica. 2023. Judging llm-as-a-judge with mt-bench and chatbot arena.

Kani: A Lightweight and Highly Hackable Framework for Building Language Model Applications

Andrew Zhu*, Liam Dugan*, Alyssa Hwang, Chris Callison-Burch
University of Pennsylvania
{andrz,ldugan,ahwang16,ccb}@seas.upenn.edu

Abstract

Language model applications are becoming increasingly popular and complex, often including features like tool usage and retrieval augmentation. However, existing frameworks for such applications are often opinionated, deciding for developers how their prompts ought to be formatted and imposing limitations on customizability and reproducibility. To solve this we present Kani: a lightweight, flexible, and model-agnostic open-source framework for building language model applications. Kani helps developers implement a variety of complex features by supporting the core building blocks of chat interaction: model interfacing, chat management, and robust function calling. All Kani core functions are easily overridable and well documented to empower developers to customize functionality for their own needs. Kani thus serves as a useful tool for researchers, hobbyists, and industry professionals alike to accelerate their development while retaining interoperability and fine-grained control.

Figure 1: Kani is a *lightweight* and *flexible* framework that tracks chat history, calls inference engines, and manages callable functions in an un-opinionated manner—allowing researchers and developers to implement custom functionality easily and quickly.

1 Introduction

We introduce Kani, an open-source[1] framework for building language model (LM) applications. Kani takes care of the basics of chat interaction—querying models, managing chat history, and calling external functions—allowing developers to write robust application code that is interoperable across any underlying language model. From this minimal base, developers can easily override the core features to implement more complex functionality like retrieval, web hosting, dynamic model routing, and tool usage tracking.

Unlike existing frameworks, Kani is lightweight and highly hackable, allowing developers to control their prompts, customize their models, and handle errors with ease. Our design philosophy is minimalist implementation with maximalist documentation: we implement a small number of universally useful core features while providing more complex application-specific examples in documentation.

Kani is appealing to a wide range of developers. Hobbyists can get started with models like GPT-4, LLaMA v2, and Vicuna with as few as five lines of code. Industry professionals will enjoy the added robustness of automatic chat management and function retrying. Finally, researchers can appreciate the improved reproducibility afforded by fine-grained control over prompting.

In this paper we provide a quick-start guide for developing with Kani (Section 2), an overview of our philosophy with comparisons to other frameworks (Sections 3-4), and a detailed tutorial on how to build more complex applications (Sections 5-8).

2 Getting Started with Kani

Let's start by discussing the basics of installing and querying language models with Kani. To start, Kani requires Python 3.10+ and is installed via pip.

*Equal contribution.

[1]Kani is available at `https://github.com/zhudotexe/kani`, free for use under the MIT license.

Proceedings of the 3rd Workshop for Natural Language Processing Open Source Software (NLP-OSS 2023), pages 65–77
December 6, 2023 ©2023 Association for Computational Linguistics

Platform	Engine	Extra
ChatGPT	`OpenAIEngine`	`openai`
GPT-4	`OpenAIEngine`	`openai`
HuggingFace	`HuggingEngine`	`huggingface`
LLaMA v2	`LlamaEngine`	`llama`
Vicuna v1.3	`VicunaEngine`	`llama`
ctransformers	`CTransformersEngine`	`ctransformers`
LLaMA v2	`LlamaCTransformersEngine`	`ctransformers`

Table 1: The list of models and engines included in Kani with associated pip extras to add when installing. For example, to install Kani with support for HuggingFace Transformers, use `pip install 'kani[huggingface]'`.

```
$ pip install kani
```

This command will install the core Kani dependencies. In order to use our pre-built engine classes for HuggingFace or OpenAI (Table 1), you must also include one or more "extras" with your pip installation command.

```
$ pip install kani[openai]
```

In Figure 2 we provide a minimal example to quickly get started with Kani in only five lines of code. We initialize the `OpenAIEngine` with our OpenAI API key, pass it into a new Kani object, and chat with the Kani using the built-in `chat_in_terminal()` function. With this, novice and advanced developers alike are able to easily query a variety of language models through Kani.

3 Conceptual Overview

3.1 What is the Kani object?

The main atomic unit of processing in our framework is the titular Kani.[2] When developing applications with Kani you will mostly be spawning and manipulating different Kani objects. A Kani object consists of the following three parts:

1. **Inference Engine**: The underlying language model and associated framework.
2. **Chat History**: The state of the conversation including system prompts.
3. **Function Context**: The list of available callable functions, if any.

To initialize a Kani all you need to pass in is an inference engine—the chat history will default to an empty list and callable functions are optional.

[2]Kani (カニ) is Japanese for "crab". **snip snip**

```
from kani import Kani, chat_in_terminal
from kani.engines.openai import OpenAIEngine

engine = OpenAIEngine(api_key, model="gpt-4")
ai = Kani(engine)
chat_in_terminal(ai)
```

Figure 2: A basic example showing how to initialize a Kani object and chat with GPT-4 (OpenAI, 2023) in only three lines of code.

3.2 What does a Kani object do?

When designing Kani, we wanted to implement the minimal set of features that allowed for the largest amount of flexibility and customization. Following this design principle, a Kani object does the following three things:

1. **Interfaces with Models**: Kani queries LMs via inference engines, allowing developers to swap models without editing the application.
2. **Manages Chat History**: Kani tracks the token counts and turns of the conversation ensuring that models never exceed their context.
3. **Exposes and Calls Functions**: Kani exposes functions to models, validates function calls, runs code, and returns output back to the inference engine. Kani also propagates all errors back to the model to allow for auto-retrying of failed function calls ensuring that such calls are robustly implemented.

This core is flexible and minimalist, allowing for a wide array of emergent capabilities while simultaneously optimizing for robustness and scalability. For example, you can create a Kani that calls a retrieval function to augment its chat responses, following Lewis et al. (2020), or a Kani that dynamically routes queries to different engines. All core functions of the Kani base class are asynchronous by default, allowing for easy web hosting and responsive applications.

3.3 Where does Kani fit in the LM Stack?

In Figure 3 we lay out our categorization of LM application libraries into four distinct layers: Model, Engine, Control, and Application. In this subsection, we will give a brief overview of what each component of the stack accomplishes to help better contextualize how Kani fits in to the broader ecosystem of tools.

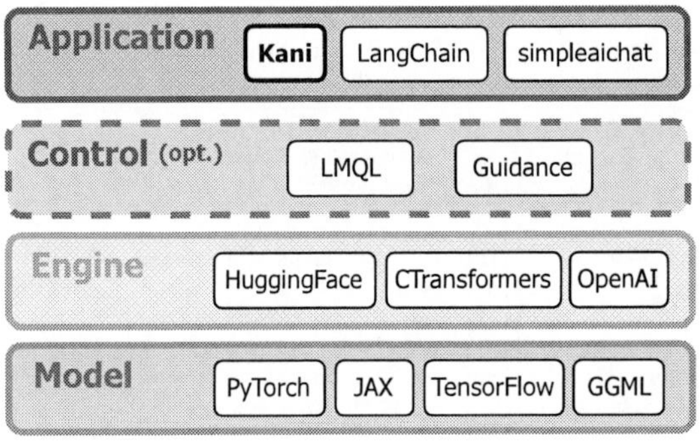

Figure 3: The different layers of the modern LM application stack. Kani sits at the Application layer and is simpler and more flexible than the competing frameworks. Additionally, Kani supports the usage of any lower level control or engine library, allowing developers to use their favorite frameworks alongside Kani.

Model Layer. In this layer, LM libraries assist with low-level procedures like matrix operations and hardware acceleration. Examples include PyTorch (Paszke et al., 2019), TensorFlow (Abadi et al., 2016), and JAX (Bradbury et al., 2018). Kani is agnostic to the underlying model implementation so all Model libraries are compatible.

Engine Layer. Libraries like HuggingFace (Wolf et al., 2020) and OpenAI (OpenAI, 2022) in this layer manage elements of model inference such as sampling strategies and tokenization. Kani is interoperable across any Engine library by extending the `BaseEngine` class (see Section 7). In an era characterized by an ever-changing state of the art, the ability to easily swap Engines without changing the application code is invaluable.

Control Layer. Libraries in this optional layer handle complex control logic like dynamic prompt branching and tabular data prediction. Control libraries include LMQL (Beurer-Kellner et al., 2023) and Guidance (Lundberg et al., 2023). Kani supports these libraries and can be configured to dynamically route queries on its own (see Section 8.1), allowing for more robust inference.

Application Layer. In the final layer, LM libraries provide the highest level of functionality by managing chat history, compiling prompts, creating function contexts, and handling errors. Examples of Application libraries include LangChain (Chase et al., 2022), simpleaichat (Woolf et al., 2023), and, of course, Kani. Kani provides a more flexible, interoperable, and streamlined experience to help any developer build LM applications.

	Kani	simpleaichat	LangChain
Size (in MB)	13	26	156
Dependencies	2	8	12
Lightweight	✓	✓	✗
Chat Management	✓	✗	✗
Function Retry	✓	✗	✗
Model-Agnostic	✓	✗	✓
Un-opinionated	✓	✗	✗
Extensive Docs	✓	✗	✓

Table 2: A feature comparison between Kani and competing frameworks. Kani is the only package that includes function retrying and chat management while still being lightweight and un-opinionated.

4 Framework Comparison

In this section, we compare Kani with simpleaichat (Woolf et al., 2023) and LangChain (Chase et al., 2022) to highlight Kani's strengths (see Table 2).

Lightweight. Kani is minimalist in both functionality and footprint: we implement essential features with fewer dependencies and less library-specific tooling while accomplishing more (see Table 2). Paired with our detailed documentation, Kani's lean and efficient core of features allows developers to start easily and grow rapidly.

Chat History Management. Unlike our contemporaries, Kani automatically tracks token counts and ensures that the maximum context length is never exceeded—letting developers focus on more exciting parts of their applications. Kani also lets developers easily customize this behavior by overriding `Kani.get_prompt()` (see Section 7.1).

Robust Function Calling. In contrast to other frameworks, Kani *guarantees* that function calls are valid by the time they reach developers' Python code. If a model calls a function incorrectly, Kani automatically provides feedback to the model and allows it to try again or follows developers' custom error handling (see Sections 6.4 and 7.3).

Model-Agnostic. Kani provides a straightforward interface to use and interchange *any* model. Developers can easily swap models without altering their source code, simplifying the process of switching models as newer ones are released.

Un-opinionated Prompting. Unlike our contemporaries, Kani does not modify developers' prompts under the hood (see Figure 4). We instead give developers full control to override and con-

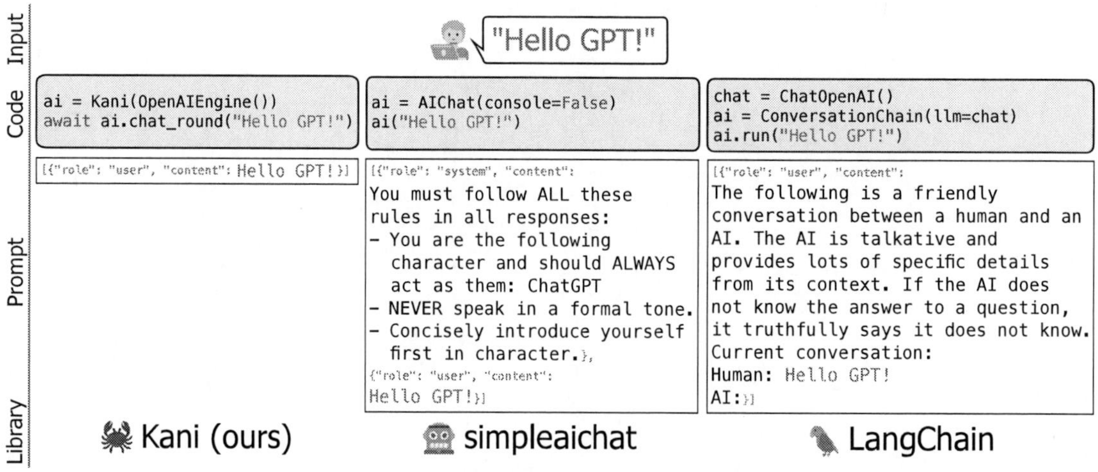

Figure 4: A comparison of prompting behavior between Kani and other competing frameworks. Kani does not edit developers' prompts under the hood in unexpected ways and allows for full control over what is passed to the model.

struct prompts themselves, leading to more robust, transparent, and reproducible source code.

Extensive Documentation. Kani provides thorough and up-to-date documentation[3] on core library features with a particular focus on customizability. Our docs go beyond basic descriptions of features by including numerous examples of complex applications and guides on how to override and customize default behaviors.

5 Developing Applications with Kani

Now that we understand Kani's place in the broader ecosystem of tools, we will dive deeper into exactly how to develop LM applications with Kani.

5.1 The Chat History

Kani interacts with the user through `ChatMessage` objects, which are tracked in the chat history:

```
>>> chat_in_terminal(ai, rounds=1)
USER: Hello Kani!
AI: Hello! How can I help?
>>> ai.chat_history
[ChatMessage(role=ChatRole.USER,
             content="Hello Kani!"),
 ChatMessage(role=ChatRole.ASSISTANT,
             content="Hello! How can I help?")]
```

Following the OpenAI convention, each message contains the `role` (system, assistant, user, or function) and `content` of the message.[4] Kani will pass in as much of this chat history as the engine's context window can hold as a default, which can be easily overridden (see Section 7). The chat history can also be saved or loaded in JSON format with `Kani.save()` and `Kani.load()` for ultimate control over the conversation context.

5.2 Prompting

Kani queries the underlying language model by providing a prompt, which is made of four parts:

1. **System Prompt** (optional): Content specifically for the `system` role that typically defines high-level instructions for model responses.
2. **Persistent Messages** (optional): Content that always appears at the top of the context window and will never be truncated.
3. **Chat History**: The most recent messages that have not exceeded the context length.
4. **User Message**: The current user input.

The bulk of chat application interactions are a combination of these four components. For example, the system prompt can define a chatbot persona and the persistent messages can include a set of few-shot examples in the context (see Figure 5).

A system prompt and list of persistent messages can be passed into the Kani constructor at initialization: `Kani(engine, system='...', always_included_messages=[...])`. You can

[3]`https://kani.readthedocs.io/`

[4]Optionally, a user message can also contain a name (for multi-user conversations), and an assistant message can contain a `function_call` (discussed in Section 6).

```python
shots = [ChatMessage.user("thank you"),
         ChatMessage.assistant("arigato"),
         ChatMessage.user("good morning"),
         ChatMessage.assistant("ohayo")]
ai = Kani(engine, always_included_messages=shots)
chat_in_terminal(ai)
# USER: crab
# AI: kani
```

Figure 5: A basic example showing how to initialize a Kani with a few-shot prompt (Brown et al., 2020). We can see that the Kani obeys the pattern and continues to translate English to Japanese in the chat session despite never being explicitly prompted to do so.

also define custom prompt behavior by overriding `Kani.get_prompt()` (see Section 7.1).

5.3 Writing a Kani Application

So far we have interacted with Kani exclusively through `chat_in_terminal()`. While this function is useful for testing, when building applications you may want to intercept the model output for logging, content filtering, or any other operation before serving it to the user. This can be done with `Kani.chat_round()`[5], which executes one turn of the conversation and returns a `ChatMessage` from the system or assistant. We can then complete additional tasks and return the finalized response to the user, as demonstrated in Figure 6.

```python
def is_toxic(message):
    # ... Run toxicity detection

async def chat_with_toxicity_filter(ai):
  while True:
    user_message = input("USER: ")
    message = await ai.chat_round(user_message)
    if is_toxic(message.content):
        message.content = "<Removed>"
    print("AI:", message.content)

ai = Kani(OpenAIEngine(api_key, model="gpt-4"))
asyncio.run(chat_with_toxicity_filter(ai))
```

Figure 6: An example showing how to use Kani with additional output parsing. We query the engine using the `Kani.chat_round()` function and filter out toxic content.

6 Function Calling

Until this point, Kani objects had no abilities beyond text generation. Function calling (or "tool usage") makes Kani objects even more powerful as intelligent assistants.

6.1 What is Function Calling?

Function calling is the process of a model autonomously deciding to call a set of developer-defined functions. Models that have been fine-tuned to support function calling typically allow developers to provide function headers and docstrings in the prompt. When appropriate, the model will indicate that a certain function should be run with the given parameters in a JSON request. The developer then needs to receive this request, run the specified function with their own resources, and return the output back to the model. Without Kani, developers usually need to define and maintain their own logic to handle these requests.

Giving language models access to callable functions allows them to hook into various tools, like sending text messages, browsing the web, or creating a calendar event. Kani provides easy ways to document functions and handle errors, which let developers focus on writing full-featured applications without the fuss of tedious boilerplate.

6.2 Function Calling with Kani

There are two ways to create a Kani with function calling capabilities. One way is to load them statically by making a subclass of the `Kani` base class and writing your functions as class methods with the `@ai_function()` decorator (see Figure 7). The other way to incorporate function calling is to load the functions dynamically by passing them in a list to the Kani constructor when instantiating a `Kani` base class or subclass (see Appendix D). Querying a function-calling-enabled Kani is similar to what we have previously seen, except that `Kani.full_round()` should be used instead of `Kani.chat_round()`.[6]

6.3 Documenting a Function

Kani functions must be documented with native Python type annotations[7] and docstrings (triple-quoted strings immediately following a function

[5]`Kani.chat_round()` is an asynchronous method. This means that applications do not have to wait on it to finish and can instead perform other tasks while responses are being generated. To call these functions you must `await` them from an asynchronous context such as `asyncio.run()`.

[6]`https://kani.readthedocs.io/en/latest/api_reference.html#kani.Kani.full_round`

[7]We support primitive, compound, and enum Python types.

```
class Unit(enum.Enum):
  FAHRENHEIT = "fahrenheit"
  CELSIUS = "celsius"

class WeatherKani(Kani):
  @ai_function()
  def get_weather(self, loc: Annotated[str,
  AIParam(desc="The desired city")], unit: Unit):
    """Get the weather in a given location."""
    # ... Query some weather API
    return weather

chat_in_terminal(WeatherKani(engine))
# USER: What's the weather in San Francisco?
# AI: Thinking (get_weather)...
# AI: It's currently 72F in San Francisco.
```

Figure 7: An example showing how to create a subclass of the base Kani and expose a function with `@ai_function`. Functions are given type annotations, triple-quoted docstrings, and `AIParam` descriptions to indicate to the model how they should be used.

definition). You can optionally describe parameters even further by providing an `AIParam` annotation.

Proper function documentation not only helps language models use functions but also allows Kani to validate that a function is being called properly. For functions with proper type annotations, Kani *guarantees* that all parameters are of the correct type before they reach your code. This feature is unique to Kani and allows for considerably more robust function calling.

6.4 Retry & Model Feedback

When a function call returns an error, Kani will raise one of the following exception types:

- **NoSuchFunction**: The requested function was hallucinated and does not exist.
- **WrappedCallException**: The requested function raised an exception during execution.
- **TypeError**: The function exists, but the model hallucinated parameters that do not.
- **ValidationError**: The parameter names exist, but the model got the data types wrong.

If the model calls a function incorrectly, Kani will give it feedback by adding the error message to the chat history. This gives the model a chance to correct itself by retrying the call with new arguments or another function. Developers can customize the retry behavior or error messages with the `handle_function_call_exception()` method (see Section 7.3). By anticipating common errors and automatically retrying function calls, Kani helps developers build more robust applications without the extra effort.

```
class AmnesiaKani(Kani):
  async def get_prompt(self):
    return self.always_included_messages
      + self.chat_history[-2:]

chat_in_terminal(AmnesiaKani(engine))
# USER: Hi kani! My name is Andrew.
# AI: Hello Andrew! How can I assist you today?
# USER: What does "kani" mean in Japanese?
# AI: "Kani" in Japanese means "Crab".
# USER: What is my name?
# AI: As an AI, I don't have access to that data.
```

Figure 8: A example showing how to customize the default `get_prompt()` function to only include the most recent two messages in the model prompt.

7 Customization

Kani is built on the philosophy that the developer should be in control of every aspect of an application. To accomplish this, Kani allows you to override and customize virtually all default behaviors of the library code. In this section we will briefly go over some common customizations developers may want to make.

7.1 Customizing the Prompt

Kani allows developers to control exactly what is being exposed to the language model by customizing the prompt builder. This can best be done by overriding the `Kani.get_prompt()` function.

In Figure 8 we show how you can customize the `Kani.get_prompt()` function to include only the most recent two messages, but this is just the tip of the iceberg. With custom prompt builders, developers can implement anything from dynamic prompt templating to fine-grained LMQL-style control prompts (see Appendix B).

7.2 Implementing a Custom Engine

Kani interacts with language models through Engines. While Kani comes pre-packaged with a few starter engines, developers are encouraged to implement their own custom engines to adapt new language models or inference libraries for use with

```
class CustomExceptionKani(Kani):
  async def handle_function_call_exception(
    self, call, err, attempt):
    self.chat_history.append(ChatMessage.system(
      "The call encountered an error. Relay"
      f"it to the user sarcastically: {err}"))
    return attempt < self.retry_attempts

  @ai_function()
  def get_time(self):
    """Get the current time."""
    raise RuntimeError("The API is offline")

chat_in_terminal(CustomExceptionKani(engine))
# USER: What time is it?
# AI: Thinking (get_time)...
# AI: Well, it seems like our handy-dandy time
# API decided to take a coffee break...
```

Figure 9: A example showing how to customize the `Kani.handle_function_call_exception()` function to return errors to the user in a sarcastic manner.

Kani. To create an engine, you must subclass the `BaseEngine` class. A new engine must implement:

1. `BaseEngine.message_len()`: Takes as input a `ChatMessage` and returns the token length of the message.
2. `BaseEngine.predict()`: Takes in a list of `ChatMessage` and returns a new `Completion`.
3. `BaseEngine.max_context_size`: Specifies the model's maximum token context length.

Optionally, you can also choose to implement `BaseEngine.close()` to clean up resources or `BaseEngine.function_token_reserve()` if your engine needs to reserve some tokens for functions. Kani also comes with a few extra base classes and utilities to help you quickly build engines for models on HuggingFace (Wolf et al., 2020) (See Appendix E) or with an available HTTP API.[8]

7.3 Custom Error Handling

Kani calls `handle_function_call_exception()` whenever it encounters an error from a function. In Figure 9, we provide an example of overriding this function to tell our model to return function errors to the user in a sarcastic tone. While this is just a fun example, custom error messages can and often do serve a more utilitarian purpose by helping models retry functions more effectively.

```
class KaniWithSummary(Kani):
  @ai_function()
  async def summarize_conversation(self):
    """Get the summary of the conversation."""
    long_context_engine = OpenAIEngine(api_key,
                              model="gpt-4-32k")
    sub_kani = Kani(long_context_engine,
        chat_history=self.chat_history[:-2])
    summary = await sub_kani.chat_round(
    "Please summarize the conversation so far.")
    return summary.content

chat_in_terminal(KaniWithSummary(engine))
# USER: Tell me about trains.
# AI: Trains are modes of long-distance transport
# [Multiple turns of conversation...]
# USER: Summarize the conversation.
# AI: Thinking (summarize_conversation)...
# AI: Our chat began with a general overview
# about trains and how railway systems work...
```

Figure 10: A example showing how to use sub-kani spawning to dynamically resize the context window of the model depending on a user query. Note that the base `"gpt-4"` kani spawns a `"gpt-4-32k"` sub-kani in order to capture the full conversation for summarization.

8 Advanced Usage

In this section, we'll look at some more advanced examples. For each of these use cases, we provide the full implementation in the GitHub repository.[9]

8.1 Sub-Kanis

When used in conjunction with function calling, Kani can choose to spawn "sub-Kani"—self-contained "agents" capable of performing their own tasks then reporting to the parent with their results.

For example, you might have the parent Kani use a cheaper, faster model with a smaller context length. If you need it to perform a task that requires more context, you can spawn a sub-Kani using a more expensive, slower model with a larger context. In Figure 10, we show how you can spawn a sub-Kani inside a callable function and copy the chat history to accomplish this.

Of course, the sub-Kani you spawn doesn't have to be a vanilla Kani—you could imagine having multiple different Kani types with different sets of

[8]Built an engine for a popular model Kani doesn't support yet? Kani is open-source and greatly appreciates PRs with engine implementations for the latest models—see the contribution page in our documentation.

[9]https://github.com/zhudotexe/kani/tree/main/examples

```python
class WikipediaKani(Kani):
  @ai_function()
  async def wikipedia(self, title: Annotated[
      str, AIParam(desc='The article title')]):
    """Get information from Wikipedia."""
    if page := await wikipedia_client.get(title):
      return page
    return f"Page {title!r} does not exist"

  @ai_function()
  async def search(self, query: str):
    """Find article titles given a query."""
    titles = await wikipedia_client.search(query)
    return json.dumps(titles)

chat_in_terminal(WikipediaKani(engine))
# USER: Tell me about the Tokyo Yamanote line.
# AI: Thinking (search)...
# AI: Thinking (wikipedia)...
# AI: The Yamanote is a loop service in Tokyo...
```

Figure 11: A example showing how to make a retrieval agent in Kani using custom AI function declarations. The WikipediaKani exposes the two functions (`search()` and `wikipedia()`) to the model which then calls both in order to retrieve the page for generation.

functions or engines, each capable of performing their own specialized tasks.

8.2 Retrieval

Language models can be augmented with an external factual database that they can retrieve information from, allowing them to access more relevant and up-to-date information without having to retrain on more recent events.

In Figure 11, we demonstrate how Kani's function calling can be used to retrieve information from a data source like Wikipedia. Since retrieved articles might be longer than the model's maximum context window, you may want to combine this with the previous summarization example for maximum efficacy.

8.3 Hosting a Kani Online

What if you want to host a web service to allow users to chat with a Kani online? In Figure 12, we show how you can host and connect to a Kani on a webserver using a WebSocket connection.

We use FastAPI[10] to run this webserver. To connect to our server, we can use any client that

```python
engine = OpenAIEngine(api_key, model="gpt-4")
app = FastAPI()

@app.websocket("/chat")
async def kani_chat(websocket: WebSocket):
  await websocket.accept()
  ai = Kani(engine)
  while True:
    data = await websocket.receive_text()
    resp = await ai.chat_round(data)
    await websocket.send_text(resp.content)
```

Figure 12: A example showing how to host and query Kani on the web using FastAPI and WebSockets.

supports WebSockets, like Insomnia.[11] Web frameworks like FastAPI and Flask 2 allow route methods to be asynchronous, meaning you can await a Kani method from within your route method without needing to call `asyncio.run()`.

9 Conclusion

In this paper we presented Kani, a lightweight and highly customizable framework for building chat applications. At its core, Kani lets developers use the same application code across all language model backends and robustly implements convenient quality-of-life features like chat history management, function validation, and error handling.

We believe that the design of our tools is as important as the tools themselves. Well-designed tools impose far less friction when using them, freeing up developers' hands from fighting bugs and racking up tech debt. This is especially important now that the LLM landscape is so turbulent with new and improved models being released more often than ever. Kani offloads the burden of tedious language model management without locking developers into onerous default paradigms, giving developers back control over their applications—hopefully making the landscape a bit less turbulent.

Limitations

One limitation of the Kani framework is that not all models are natively chat models. Given our design decision to maintain the internal state as a chat, with such attributes as roles and system prompts present, implementing interfaces for traditional completion-based language models is more

[10] https://fastapi.tiangolo.com/

[11] https://insomnia.rest/

difficult than it otherwise could have been with a different internal memory organization scheme.

Another limitation of our work is the lack of native function calling support in all models, making our defining features around robust function calling irrelevant for such models (e.g. LLaMA). However, the customizable nature of Kani allows developers who want such a feature to simply create a new Engine class and implement custom output parsing logic to recognize and route function calls themselves. Kani thus gives developers maximum flexibility in the creation of their applications.

Acknowledgments

We would like to thank the members of the lab of Chris Callison-Burch for their testing and detailed feedback on the contents of both this paper and the Kani repository. In addition, we'd like to thank Henry Zhu (no relation to the first author) for his early and enthusiastic support of the project.

This research is based upon work supported in part by the Air Force Research Laboratory (contract FA8750-23-C-0507), the IARPA HIATUS Program (contract 2022-22072200005), and the NSF (Award 1928631). Approved for Public Release, Distribution Unlimited. The views and conclusions contained herein are those of the authors and should not be interpreted as necessarily representing the official policies, either expressed or implied, of IARPA, NSF, or the U.S. Government.

References

Martín Abadi, Paul Barham, Jianmin Chen, Zhifeng Chen, Andy Davis, Jeffrey Dean, Matthieu Devin, Sanjay Ghemawat, Geoffrey Irving, Michael Isard, Manjunath Kudlur, Josh Levenberg, Rajat Monga, Sherry Moore, Derek G. Murray, Benoit Steiner, Paul Tucker, Vijay Vasudevan, Pete Warden, Martin Wicke, Yuan Yu, and Xiaoqiang Zheng. 2016. TensorFlow: A System for Large-Scale Machine Learning. In *Proceedings of the 12th USENIX Conference on Operating Systems Design and Implementation (OSDI '16)*, pages 265–283, USA. USENIX Association.

Luca Beurer-Kellner, Marc Fischer, and Martin Vechev. 2023. Prompting Is Programming: A Query Language for Large Language Models. *Proceedings of the ACM on Programming Languages*, 7(PLDI):1946–1969.

James Bradbury, Roy Frostig, Peter Hawkins, Matthew James Johnson, Chris Leary, Dougal Maclaurin, George Necula, Adam Paszke, Jake VanderPlas, Skye Wanderman-Milne, and Qiao Zhang. 2018. JAX: Composable Transformations of Python+NumPy Programs.

Tom Brown, Benjamin Mann, Nick Ryder, Melanie Subbiah, Jared D Kaplan, Prafulla Dhariwal, Arvind Neelakantan, Pranav Shyam, Girish Sastry, Amanda Askell, Sandhini Agarwal, Ariel Herbert-Voss, Gretchen Krueger, Tom Henighan, Rewon Child, Aditya Ramesh, Daniel Ziegler, Jeffrey Wu, Clemens Winter, Chris Hesse, Mark Chen, Eric Sigler, Mateusz Litwin, Scott Gray, Benjamin Chess, Jack Clark, Christopher Berner, Sam McCandlish, Alec Radford, Ilya Sutskever, and Dario Amodei. 2020. Language Models are Few-Shot Learners. In *Advances in Neural Information Processing Systems*, volume 33, pages 1877–1901. Curran Associates, Inc.

Harrison Chase, Bagatur, Davis Chase, Zander Chase, Leonid Gandeline, Eugene Yurtsev, and Nuno Campos. 2022. LangChain.

Patrick Lewis, Ethan Perez, Aleksandra Piktus, Fabio Petroni, Vladimir Karpukhin, Naman Goyal, Heinrich Küttler, Mike Lewis, Wen-tau Yih, Tim Rocktäschel, Sebastian Riedel, and Douwe Kiela. 2020. Retrieval-Augmented Generation for Knowledge-Intensive NLP Tasks. In *Proceedings of the 34th International Conference on Neural Information Processing Systems (NeurIPS '20)*, Red Hook, NY, USA. Curran Associates Inc.

Scott Lundberg, Marco Tulio Ribeiro, and Contributors. 2023. Guidance.

OpenAI. 2022. ChatGPT: Optimizing Language Models for Dialogue.

OpenAI. 2023. GPT-4 Technical Report.

Adam Paszke, Sam Gross, Francisco Massa, Adam Lerer, James Bradbury, Gregory Chanan, Trevor Killeen, Zeming Lin, Natalia Gimelshein, Luca Antiga, Alban Desmaison, Andreas Kopf, Edward Yang, Zachary DeVito, Martin Raison, Alykhan Tejani, Sasank Chilamkurthy, Benoit Steiner, Lu Fang, Junjie Bai, and Soumith Chintala. 2019. PyTorch: An Imperative-Style, High-Performance Deep Learning Library. In *Proceedings of the 33rd International Conference on Neural Information Processing Systems (NeurIPS '19)*, volume 32. Curran Associates, Inc.

Hugo Touvron, Louis Martin, Kevin Stone, Peter Albert, Amjad Almahairi, Yasmine Babaei, Nikolay Bashlykov, Soumya Batra, Prajjwal Bhargava, Shruti Bhosale, Dan Bikel, Lukas Blecher, Cristian Canton Ferrer, Moya Chen, Guillem Cucurull, David Esiobu, Jude Fernandes, Jeremy Fu, Wenyin Fu, Brian Fuller, Cynthia Gao, Vedanuj Goswami, Naman Goyal, Anthony Hartshorn, Saghar Hosseini, Rui Hou, Hakan Inan, Marcin Kardas, Viktor Kerkez, Madian Khabsa, Isabel Kloumann, Artem Korenev, Punit Singh Koura,

Marie-Anne Lachaux, Thibaut Lavril, Jenya Lee, Diana Liskovich, Yinghai Lu, Yuning Mao, Xavier Martinet, Todor Mihaylov, Pushkar Mishra, Igor Molybog, Yixin Nie, Andrew Poulton, Jeremy Reizenstein, Rashi Rungta, Kalyan Saladi, Alan Schelten, Ruan Silva, Eric Michael Smith, Ranjan Subramanian, Xiaoqing Ellen Tan, Binh Tang, Ross Taylor, Adina Williams, Jian Xiang Kuan, Puxin Xu, Zheng Yan, Iliyan Zarov, Yuchen Zhang, Angela Fan, Melanie Kambadur, Sharan Narang, Aurelien Rodriguez, Robert Stojnic, Sergey Edunov, and Thomas Scialom. 2023. LLaMa 2: Open Foundation and Fine-Tuned Chat Models.

Thomas Wolf, Lysandre Debut, Victor Sanh, Julien Chaumond, Clement Delangue, Anthony Moi, Pierric Cistac, Tim Rault, Remi Louf, Morgan Funtowicz, Joe Davison, Sam Shleifer, Patrick von Platen, Clara Ma, Yacine Jernite, Julien Plu, Canwen Xu, Teven Le Scao, Sylvain Gugger, Mariama Drame, Quentin Lhoest, and Alexander Rush. 2020. Transformers: State-of-the-Art Natural Language Processing. In *Proceedings of the 2020 Conference on Empirical Methods in Natural Language Processing: System Demonstrations*, pages 38–45, Online. Association for Computational Linguistics.

Max Woolf, Nadav Timor, Agustin Bacigalup, Zeit der Forschung, Víctor Navarro Aránguiz, Ikko Eltociear Ashimine, and Arne Neumann. 2023. simpleaichat.

A Size Measurement

This section describes how we measured the number of dependencies of a library and its size in the framework comparison table (Table 2). We define a library's dependency count as the number of top-level dependencies that are installed when installing the library from pip without any extras. We measure the size of a library by installing it in a fresh Python virtual environment, running a command to measure the size of installed packages, and removing the size of the `pip` and `setuptools` packages (packaging utilities included in every Python environment). Specifically, we used the following shell commands:

```
python3.10 -m venv venv
source venv/bin/activate
pip install {kani|simpleaichat|langchain}
du -h venv/lib/python3.10/site-packages
```

B Dynamic Prompt Templating

Below is an example of dynamically customizing a system prompt to include the phrase "Always act like <persona>" if a user types a chat message containing the phrase "act like." This is a flexible alternative to hard-coding persona logic as is common in other repositories.

```
class PersonaKani(Kani):
  def get_persona_prompt(self):
    if self.persona:
        return ChatMessage.system(
             f"Always act like {self.persona}.")

  async def get_prompt(self):
    prev = self.chat_history[-1].content
    if match := re.search(r"act like (.+)", prev):
      self.persona = match[1]
    return [self.get_persona_prompt()] +
          await super().get_prompt()
```

C Tracking Function Calls

Below we show an example of overriding the default `do_function_call()` method to additionally keep track of how many times a model called a function and how often it was successful.

```
class TrackCallsKani(Kani):
  def __init__(self, *args, **kwargs):
    super().__init__(*args, **kwargs)
    self.successful_calls = collections.Counter()
    self.failed_calls = collections.Counter()

  async def do_function_call(self, call):
    try:
      res = await super().do_function_call(call)
      self.successful_calls[call.name] += 1
      return res
    except FunctionCallException:
      self.failed_calls[call.name] += 1
      raise

  @ai_function()
  def get_time(self):
    """Get the current time."""
    raise RuntimeError("The time API is offline")

  @ai_function()
  def get_date_and_time(self):
    """Get the current day and time."""
    return str(datetime.datetime.now())
```

After chatting with our Kani, we can print out the new `successful_calls` and `failed_calls` variables to recover statistics on how well our models are calling our custom AI functions.

```
>>> chat_in_terminal(TrackCallsKani(engine))
USER: What time is it?
```

```
AI: Thinking (get_time)...
AI: Thinking (get_date_and_time)...
AI: The current time is 22:42.
>>> ai.successful_calls
Counter({'get_date_and_time': 1})
>>> ai.failed_calls
Counter({'get_time': 1})
```

This behavior is particularly useful for researchers studying language model tool usage and similar customizations can be easily made to other core functions to add more tracking.

D Dynamic Function Loading

Rather than statically defining the list of functions a Kani can use in a class, you can also pass a list of functions to the Kani constructor when you initialize a Kani. To do this we need to use the special `Kani.AIFunction` class (which is similar to the traditional `@ai_function` decorator).

```
def my_cool_function(foo: str,
  bar: Annotated[int, AIParam(desc="Cool int")]):
  """Do some cool things."""

engine = OpenAIEngine(api_key, model="gpt-4")
functions = [AIFunction(my_cool_function)]
ai = Kani(engine, functions=functions)
```

This is particularly useful when spawning sub-Kani, as such agents can be dynamically given only a particular subset of the functions defined in the parent to help increase function call accuracy.

E Example Engine Implementations

In this section, we include the HuggingFace (Wolf et al., 2020) and LLaMA v2 (Touvron et al., 2023) engine implementations to demonstrate how a developer might implement new engines. The HuggingFace engine acts as a base engine class that implements common logic for all HuggingFace models, while the LLaMA v2 engine extends the base HuggingFace class with the model-specific prompt and delimiting tokens.

```python
class HuggingEngine(BaseEngine, abc.ABC):
  def __init__(
    self,
    model_id: str,
    max_context_size: int,
    device: str | None = None,
    tokenizer_kwargs: dict = {},
    model_load_kwargs: dict = {},
    **hyperparams,
  ):
    self.model_id = model_id
    self.max_context_size = max_context_size
    self.tokenizer = AutoTokenizer.from_pretrained(model_id, **tokenizer_kwargs)
    self.model = AutoModelForCausalLM.from_pretrained(model_id, **model_load_kwargs)
    self.hyperparams = hyperparams

    if device is None:
      device = "cuda" if torch.has_cuda else "cpu"
    self.device = device
    if self.model.device.type != self.device:
      self.model.to(device)

  @abc.abstractmethod
  def build_prompt(
    self, messages: list[ChatMessage], functions: list[AIFunction] | None = None
  ) -> str | torch.Tensor:
    """Given the list of messages from kani, build either a single string
    representing the prompt for the model, or build the token tensor."""
    raise NotImplementedError

  async def predict(
    self, messages: list[ChatMessage], functions: list[AIFunction] | None = None, **hyperparams
  ) -> Completion:
    """Given the current context of messages and available functions, get the next
    predicted chat message from the LM."""
    prompt = self.build_prompt(messages, functions)
    if isinstance(prompt, str):
      tokenized = self.tokenizer(prompt, return_tensors="pt", return_length=True)
      input_len = int(tokenized.length)
      input_toks = tokenized.input_ids
    elif isinstance(prompt, torch.Tensor):
      input_toks = prompt
      input_len = len(input_toks[0])
    else:
      raise TypeError("build_prompt should either return a str or a Tensor.")
    # move the input tensor to the right device
    if input_toks.device.type != self.device:
      input_toks = input_toks.to(self.device)
    # set up hyperparams for HF decode
    hyperparams = {**self.hyperparams, **hyperparams}
    # run it through the model
    output = self.model.generate(input_toks, **hyperparams)
    # decode to tokens
    # the completion shouldn't include the prompt or stop token
    content = self.tokenizer.decode(output[0][input_len:-1]).strip()
    return Completion(ChatMessage.assistant(content), prompt_tokens=input_len,
            completion_tokens=len(output[0]) - (input_len + 1))
```

```
class LlamaEngine(HuggingEngine):
  def __init__(self, model_id: str = "meta-llama/Llama-2-7b-chat-hf", *args, **kwargs):
    kwargs.setdefault("max_context_size", 4096)  # LLaMA has 4096 token window
    super().__init__(model_id, *args, **kwargs)

  def build_prompt(self, messages: list[ChatMessage], functions: list[AIFunction] | None = None):
    tokens = []
    prompt_buf = []  # parts of the user-assistant pair
    for message in messages:
      if message.role == ChatRole.USER:
        prompt_buf.append(f"{B_INST} {message.content} {E_INST}")
      elif message.role == ChatRole.ASSISTANT:
        prompt_buf.append(f" {message.content} ")
        # turn the current round into tokens
        prompt_round = "".join(prompt_buf)
        # if we see a " {E_INST}{B_INST} " we should replace it with empty string
        # (it happens immediately after a system + user message)
        prompt_round.replace(f" {E_INST}{B_INST} ", "")
        tokens.extend(self.tokenizer(prompt_round))
        # tokenizer adds the BOS token but not the EOS token
        tokens.append(eos_token_id)
        prompt_buf.clear()
      else:
        prompt_buf.append(f"{B_INST} {B_SYS}{message.content}{E_SYS} {E_INST}")
    # flush rest of prompt buffer (probably a user message) into tokens
    if prompt_buf:
      tokens.extend(self.tokenizer("".join(prompt_buf)))
    return torch.tensor([tokens], device=self.device)

  def message_len(self, message: ChatMessage) -> int:
    if message.role == ChatRole.USER:
      # <s> [INST] {} [/INST] -> 7
      return self.tokenizer(message.content, return_length=True).length[0] + 7
    elif message.role == ChatRole.ASSISTANT:
      # {} </s> -> 2
      return self.tokenizer(f" {message.content} ", return_length=True).length[0] + 2
    # <s> [INST] <<SYS>>\n{}\n<</SYS>>\n\n [/INST] -> 20
    return self.tokenizer(message.content, return_length=True).length[0] + 20
```

Beyond the Repo: A Case Study on Open Source Integration with GECToR

Sanjna Kashyap **Zhaoyang Xie** **Kenneth Steimel** **Nitin Madnani**
Educational Testing Service
Princeton, NJ, USA
skashyap@ets.org zxie@etscanada.ca ksteimel@ets.org nmadnani@ets.org

Abstract

We present a case study describing our efforts to integrate the open source GECToR code and models into our production NLP pipeline that powers many of Educational Testing Service's products and prototypes. The paper's contributions includes a discussion of the issues we encountered during integration and our solutions, the overarching lessons we learned about integrating open source projects, and, last but not least, the open source contributions we made as part of the journey.

1 Introduction

GECToR (Grammatical Error Correction Tag, not Rewrite)[1] is a set of deep learning models developed by Grammarly for the task of Grammatical Error Correction or GEC (Omelianchuk et al., 2020). GECToR achieves state-of-the-art results for the GEC task and its inference speed is up to 10 times as fast as that of equivalent Transformer-based sequence-to-sequence (seq2seq) GEC systems.

The most commonly proposed systems for the GEC task leverage seq2seq Neural Machine Translation (NMT) models to "translate" from errorful text to corrected text. However, such systems generally suffer from slow inference and require a large amount of data. To deal with these issues, GECToR simplified the task from sequence generation to sequence tagging. To train this tagging system, GECToR utilizes three training stages: pre-training on synthetic data, fine-tuning on parallel datasets that contain both errorful and corrected texts, and further fine-tuning on a combination of high-quality, parallel datasets containing both errorful/corrected as well as error-free texts. However, one of the largest benefits of GECToR to the NLP community is that it was open sourced under a commercially-unrestricted Apache 2.0 license.

[1] `https://github.com/grammarly/gector`

2 Requirements

Educational Testing Service (ETS) has developed a pipeline that uses a service-based architecture to combine multiple NLP services into scalable and robust backend applications (Madnani et al., 2018). These applications are used to evaluate the speaking and writing proficiency of students' written essays or spoken responses and provide both automatic scores as well as actionable feedback. Specifically, our pipeline provides descriptive feedback on multiple dimensions such as the student's grammar, mechanics, vocabulary, text complexity, style, organization, among others. Our pipeline is used for various high-stakes assessments, e.g., the Analytical Writing section from GRE (Graduate Record Examinations)[2] and the Independent and Integrated Writing prompts from TOEFL iBT (Test of English as a Foreign Language Internet-Based Test).[3]

Our pipeline has two main requirements: (1) every NLP service should return its results in less than a few seconds to enable near real-time feedback and (2) all models used in services should be optimized for precision over recall to minimize unfair penalization of students. After a careful evaluation of GECToR's GEC performance and inference speed, we felt comfortable in replacing our existing GEC system with GECToR.

GECToR provides three already trained English GEC models based on BERT, RoBERTa, and XLNET. It also has scripts for training and inference. Since our pipeline is English-only for now, the existing GEC models perfectly fit our needs. Therefore, our integration efforts focus entirely on the inference side.

[2] `https://www.ets.org/gre.html`
[3] `https://www.ets.org/toefl.html`

Proceedings of the 3rd Workshop for Natural Language Processing Open Source Software (NLP-OSS 2023), pages 78–82
December 6, 2023 ©2023 Association for Computational Linguistics

3 Related Work

Adopting open source software in commercial environments has been a topic of much interest. There are several barriers to open source use: lack of knowledge, inability to incorporate it into existing legacy systems, too many forks created by different groups, technological immaturity, et cetera (Nagy et al., 2010). One formal approach that can be used to assess an open source project before putting it into production is the Open Source Maturity Model (OSMM) which assesses factors like the product, support, training, documentation, product integration and professional services, and gives them a weighted score. However, this model is only a first step in identifying which projects are worth a more in-depth evaluation (Golden, 2005). In this paper, we hope to provide a detailed case study with illustrative, concrete steps for using open source projects.

There are major forks and re-implementations of the original GECToR project available on GitHub. **fast-gector**[4] claims to be a faster and simpler implementation of the original project leveraging AMP[5] and DeepSpeed (Rasley et al., 2020). However, we were unable to reproduce the same results as the original model in our experiments with fast-gector. **gector-large** (Tarnavskyi et al., 2022) focuses on improving GECToR by upgrading the Transformer encoders, and using an ensemble model for span-level edits. According to the paper, while the larger encoders do yield better performance, they do so at the cost of speed with inference being 2.3-2.5x slower.

4 Integration

In this section, we discuss the challenges we faced when integrating GECToR into our pipeline and our solutions.

4.1 Issues

Before we delve into the integration issues, we want to impress upon the reader that the existence of such issues should not detract from or minimize the usefulness of GECToR (or other open source software) to the NLP community. However, we feel that an honest discussion of such real-world issues can provide both the authors and users of such software with useful, actionable information.

GECToR was open sourced as part of a research publication and aligns well with the needs of the academic community. However, as we attempted to adapt it for use in a commercial NLP pipeline, we felt that some critical requirements were not fully addressed in its original design. This mismatch between the original authors' intended use and users seeking to *productionize* it led to challenges in utilizing GECToR effectively in its original form.

The system was not under active development, which posed challenges for commercial adoption. The dynamic nature of commercial environments needs ongoing development and maintenance to keep pace with rapidly evolving requirements and security issues. A specific challenge in adopting GECToR for our purposes was that it used *significantly* older versions of Python, PyTorch, and AllenNLP (Gardner et al., 2018). Its reliance on these outdated dependencies prevented seamless integration into our existing environments and limited access to the latest features and optimizations.

GECToR was also not packaged for easy installation, further complicating its integration into existing environments. The library could only be used by cloning the repository, downloading the model, and running some scripts created by the authors. Packaging GECToR and streamlining its installation process would be vital to ensure smooth continuous integration and deployment.

GECToR was designed to leverage AllenNLP, a powerful NLP library. However, its usage did not fully exploit the capabilities that AllenNLP offered, namely its high-level abstractions and API, leading to potentially sub-optimal performance. Properly utilizing AllenNLP would significantly enhance the library's overall effectiveness and result in more standardized and maintainable code.

4.2 Solutions

To address the issues we identified with GECToR in the previous section, we undertook several mitigation strategies. These efforts focused on enhancing its functionality, compatibility, and maintainability while still preserving the overall integrity of the original codebase. To implement these strategies, we forked GECToR on GitHub[6] and added the following improvements to our fork.

[4] https://github.com/cofe-ai/fast-gector

[5] https://developer.nvidia.com/automatic-mixed-precision

[6] https://github.com/EducationalTestingService/gector

4.2.1 Regression & unit tests

To ensure that any modifications or updates made by us do not lead to differences in predictions made by the existing models, the *very first* thing we did in our fork was to implement a comprehensive test suite comprising of a total of 95 tests (37 unit tests as well as 58 regression tests). We decided that a good way to get started was to test each AllenNLP component separately, e.g., the tokenizer, the token indexer, the embedder etc. This gave us not only a clear structure to follow but also a reasonable granularity for the test cases.

The test suite not only helps in verifying the correctness of the system but also acts as a safety net to prevent potential differences in the future. We also added a continuous integration plan using Github Actions to automatically run the complete test suite for any changes made to the codebase.

4.2.2 Updated dependencies

One of the critical steps in making GECToR suitable for production was to update its dependencies to modern, supported versions. We carefully updated the library to work seamlessly with the latest versions of Python (3.7 only → 3.8 through 3.10), PyTorch (1.10.0 → 1.12.1), AllenNLP (0.8.4 → 2.10.0), and many other dependencies. By doing so, we ensured compatibility with more modern infrastructure and took advantage of the latest advancements in frameworks and tools. This allows the installation of GECToR in existing CI and deployment environments via package managers such as conda,[7] and minimizes dependency conflicts. Our regression tests ensured that there were no changes to the output as a result of our updating the package versions.

4.2.3 True AllenNLP-ification

We followed AllenNLP's recommended abstractions and guidelines to re-architect our fork of GECToR, enabling a more streamlined integration with AllenNLP. The architecture adopted was largely influenced by the design and modules of AllenNLP. Utilities for training and inference were already provided by AllenNLP so our changes largely reshaped the existing GECToR codebase to function as an extension of AllenNLP. Specifically:

1. To facilitate better configurability and ease of use, we registered GECToR modules with the AllenNLP framework: each file in our fork contains one type of AllenNLP component like tokenizers, token indexers, models, predictors, and dataset readers. The registration allowed model architecture, tokenizer settings and preprocessing options to be referenced and contained in a single `jsonnnet` file used for both training and inference.

2. Users can now access GECToR *directly* through AllenNLP-supported configuration files, enhancing its usability.

3. GECToR models can now be bundled into an AllenNLP model archive for easy distribution and inference.

Since we completed this work on GECToR, AllenNLP has been archived and is no longer being maintained. We discuss the implications of this in §5.4.

4.2.4 Packaging & easy installation

We architected our GECToR fork to better support packaging, created a conda recipe, and deployed a publicly-available package on our public conda channel.[8] This makes the installation of GECToR significantly easier and reproducible (Arvan et al., 2022), unlike installing from the Github source repository every time since it is challenging to keep track of any changes made to the code since the last installation from source. We also packaged the GECToR RoBERTa model for easy installation via conda.[9]

By implementing rigorous testing, updating dependencies, aligning with AllenNLP guidelines, and creating easily installable packages, we were able to successfully mitigate the challenges associated with productionizing the original version of GECToR. We argue that these efforts have transformed GECToR into a more robust and adaptable library for grammatical error correction, suitable for use in any production Python environment.

5 Lessons learned

While bolstering GECToR, we learned a few general lessons about open source development and integration that we would like to share.

5.1 Projects should explicitly state a purpose.

In our opinion, open source authors should explicitly state the purpose of their projects. Document-

[7] `https://docs.conda.io/en/latest/`

[8] `https://anaconda.org/ets/gector`

[9] `https://anaconda.org/ets/gector-roberta`

ing whether the codebase is intended solely for research purposes or whether it is ready for production can help potential users easily estimate the level of effort required for integration. We hope our message is clear. Open source research projects like GECToR are invaluable for the community. However, the level of involvement required to productionize research codebases can vary significantly.

5.2 Estimation of effort is hard but necessary.

It is crucial to perform a careful analysis of the effort involved in integrating an open source project into a production codebase. Most popular open source projects are under active development and are used by a large number of users and organizations. Such projects are usually created or maintained by commercial organizations with dedicated teams working on them. Any issues or feature requests have a higher chance of being addressed and implemented respectively.

However, sometimes a smaller project or one open sourced as part of a research publication might be more suitable for your needs. In such cases, you must do your best to examine the codebase and develop a reasonable estimate for the integration effort. It is essential to carefully test the project and develop a plan to gauge whether the level of work as indicated by the resulting estimate can be offset by the value provided to your own product or project.

5.3 Test, test, test!

Many open source projects do not implement any form of testing since it's not perceived to be necessary for research projects. However, in our opinion, a good testing setup is critical *irrespective* of the eventual use case since it assures users that the code actually behaves as expected. This may seem like a large cost to take on upfront, but can significantly reduce technical debt in the future. We strongly recommend that everyone who contributes to open source consider adding unit/regression testing along with a CI plan which can help identify bugs and failures as and when they happen, regardless of whether their project is meant only for experimental purposes.

5.4 Always have a contingency plan.

One of the primary concerns with open source projects is the risk of abandonment by their original authors. While many projects have active maintainers and thriving communities, there have been instances where developers discontinue support and maintenance. The case of AllenNLP[10] serves as an example of how a once prominent open source library can become stagnant or archived due to shifting priorities or organizational changes.

This can have serious consequences for those who have integrated such projects into their production environment since bugs and security vulnerabilities will likely go unaddressed in the future. Therefore, it is important to be prepared for such scenarios and have a well-defined strategy in place for either taking on the entire maintenance of the library or transitioning to an alternate solution.

6 Future Work

In the future, we plan to take our own advice from §5.4 and transition our fork of GECToR away from AllenNLP. We plan to replicate the functionality we need by using actively maintained open source projects from Huggingface such as Transformers (Wolf et al., 2020), Datasets (Lhoest et al., 2021), and Accelerate[11] directly.

7 Conclusion

We presented a case study on integrating an open source project into a commercial, production NLP pipeline. While we consider the primary contributions of this paper to be a clear and concise description of the issues we faced (and solved) as well as the larger lessons we learned, we also hope that the NLP community will benefit from our fork of GECToR that is actively maintained, more modern, more robustly tested, and easier to use for inference.

References

Mohammad Arvan, Luís Pina, and Natalie Parde. 2022. Reproducibility in computational linguistics: Is source code enough? In *Proceedings of the 2022 Conference on Empirical Methods in Natural Language Processing*, pages 2350–2361, Abu Dhabi, United Arab Emirates. Association for Computational Linguistics.

Matt Gardner, Joel Grus, Mark Neumann, Oyvind Tafjord, Pradeep Dasigi, Nelson F. Liu, Matthew Peters, Michael Schmitz, and Luke Zettlemoyer. 2018.

[10] https://github.com/allenai/allennlp

[11] https://huggingface.co/docs/accelerate/index

AllenNLP: A Deep Semantic Natural Language Processing Platform. In *Proceedings of Workshop for NLP Open Source Software (NLP-OSS)*, pages 1–6, Melbourne, Australia. Association for Computational Linguistics.

B. Golden. 2005. *Succeeding with Open Source*. Addison-Wesley information technology series. Addison-Wesley.

Quentin Lhoest, Albert Villanova del Moral, Yacine Jernite, Abhishek Thakur, Patrick von Platen, Suraj Patil, Julien Chaumond, Mariama Drame, Julien Plu, Lewis Tunstall, Joe Davison, Mario Sasko, Gunjan Chhablani, Bhavitvya Malik, Simon Brandeis, Teven Le Scao, Victor Sanh, Canwen Xu, Nicolas Patry, Angelina McMillan-Major, Philipp Schmid, Sylvain Gugger, Clement Delangue, Théo Matussière, Lysandre Debut, Stas Bekman, Pierric Cistac, Thibault Goehringer, Victor Mustar, François Lagunas, Alexander M. Rush, and Thomas Wolf. 2021. Datasets: A Community Library for Natural Language Processing. *CoRR*, abs/2109.02846.

Nitin Madnani, Aoife Cahill, Daniel Blanchard, Slava Andreyev, Diane Napolitano, Binod Gyawali, Michael Heilman, Chong Min Lee, Chee Wee Leong, Matthew Mulholland, and Brian Riordan. 2018. A Robust Microservice Architecture for Scaling Automated Scoring Applications. *ETS Research Report Series*, 2018(1).

Del Nagy, Areej M. Yassin, and Anol Bhattacherjee. 2010. Organizational adoption of open source software: Barriers and remedies. *Commun. ACM*, 53(3):148–151.

Kostiantyn Omelianchuk, Vitaliy Atrasevych, Artem Chernodub, and Oleksandr" Skurzhanskyi. 2020. GECToR – Grammatical Error Correction: Tag, Not Rewrite. In *Proceedings of the Fifteenth Workshop on Innovative Use of NLP for Building Educational Applications*, pages 163–170. Association for Computational Linguistics.

Jeff Rasley, Samyam Rajbhandari, Olatunji Ruwase, and Yuxiong He. 2020. Deepspeed: System optimizations enable training deep learning models with over 100 billion parameters. In *Proceedings of the 26th ACM SIGKDD International Conference on Knowledge Discovery & Data Mining*, pages 3505–3506.

Maksym Tarnavskyi, Artem Chernodub, and Kostiantyn Omelianchuk. 2022. Ensembling and knowledge distilling of large sequence taggers for grammatical error correction. In *Accepted for publication at 60th Annual Meeting of the Association for Computational Linguistics (ACL 2022)*, Dublin, Ireland.

Thomas Wolf, Lysandre Debut, Victor Sanh, Julien Chaumond, Clement Delangue, Anthony Moi, Pierric Cistac, Tim Rault, Rémi Louf, Morgan Funtowicz, Joe Davison, Sam Shleifer, Patrick von Platen, Clara Ma, Yacine Jernite, Julien Plu, Canwen Xu, Teven Le Scao, Sylvain Gugger, Mariama Drame, Quentin Lhoest, and Alexander M. Rush. 2020. HuggingFace's Transformers: State-of-the-art Natural Language Processing.

Two Decades of the ACL Anthology: Development, Impact, and Open Challenges

Marcel Bollmann
Linköping University
marcel.bollmann@liu.se

Nathan Schneider
Georgetown University
nathan.schneider@georgetown.edu

Arne Köhn
New Work SE
arne.koehn@new-work.se

Matt Post
Microsoft
mattpost@microsoft.com

Abstract

The ACL Anthology is a prime resource for research papers within computational linguistics and natural language processing, while continuing to be an open-source and community-driven project. Since Gildea et al. (2018) reported on its state and planned directions, the Anthology has seen major technical changes. We discuss what led to these changes and how they impact long-term maintainability and community engagement, describe which open-source data and software tools the Anthology currently provides, and provide a survey of literature that has used the Anthology as a main data source.

1 Introduction

The ACL Anthology[1] is a repository for scientific contributions within computational linguistics and natural language processing maintained by the Association for Computational Linguistics (ACL). It currently hosts over 88k papers from from relevant conferences and journals within the field, including both ACL-sponsored and non-ACL venues, nearly 400 in total, a growth of almost 70% since 2019 (see Figure 1). It also includes many related materials such as software, posters, slides, and recordings of talks. All papers and materials are open-access, provided to the world without barrier under various open licenses.[2]

Development of the ACL Anthology takes place in a public repository,[3] which contains (i) metadata for all items in the Anthology, in XML and YAML formats; (ii) code for accessing and transforming this metadata, in form of a Python library and scripts; and (iii) code and templates for generating the ACL Anthology website. All code is made available under the permissive Apache-2.0 license.[4] Development has been almost entirely volunteer-driven, though since 2021 the ACL has funded assistants who have contributed to ingestions at the rate of about 20 hours a month.

In this paper, we first describe the metadata currently provided by the ACL Anthology and efforts to improve it (§2); the technical framework and development of the website (§3); as well as a Python library for accessing data from the Anthology (§4). We then look at the impact the ACL Anthology has had on other open-source software projects and provide a survey of known datasets and studies that rely on the Anthology as a main data source (§5). Finally, we discuss lessons and challenges (§6) as well as future directions that we would like to see realized for the Anthology (§7), for which we rely on help from the community.

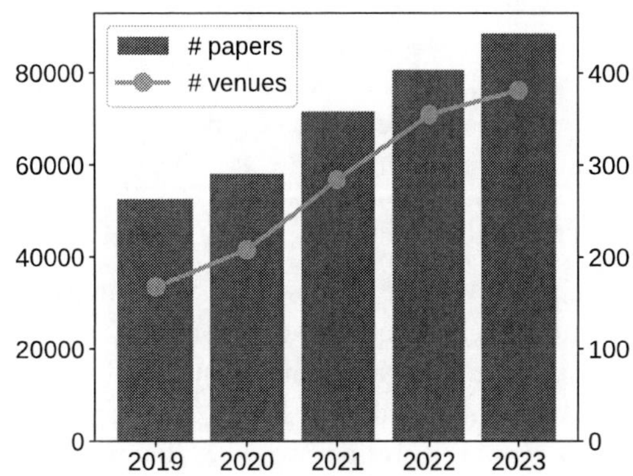

Figure 1: Growth of the ACL Anthology since 2019 as measured by the number of papers (left y-axis) and venues (right y-axis).

[1] https://aclanthology.org/

[2] ACL materials ingested since 2016 are CC BY 4.0; https://creativecommons.org/licenses/by/4.0/

[3] https://github.com/acl-org/acl-anthology/

[4] https://opensource.org/license/apache-2-0/

Proceedings of the 3rd Workshop for Natural Language Processing Open Source Software (NLP-OSS 2023), pages 83–94
December 6, 2023 ©2023 Association for Computational Linguistics

```
<paper id="2">
  <title>Towards a Computational History of the <fixed-case>ACL</fixed-case>: 1980-2008</title>
  <author><first>Ashton</first><last>Anderson</last></author>
  <author><first>Dan</first><last>Jurafsky</last></author>
  <author><first>Daniel A.</first><last>McFarland</last></author>
  <pages>13-21</pages>
  <url hash="0fe03143">W12-3202</url>
  <bibkey>anderson-etal-2012-towards</bibkey>
</paper>
```

Figure 2: XML metadata for the paper by Anderson et al. (2012) as stored in the ACL Anthology repository.

2 Publication Metadata

At the core of the Anthology repository is the metadata on the publications it hosts. Here, we describe the different kinds of data provided by the Anthology, which efforts we have taken to enrich this data and ensure correctness, and how new materials are added to the Anthology.

2.1 Organization

At a high level, the papers in the Anthology are organized into *collections* of *volumes*. A *volume* is a set of related papers that would traditionally have been bound and published as a physical book. A *collection* is a group of volumes that were published at the same time under the same *venue*. Each collection is saved to a file in the data directory, e.g., `data/xml/2022.acl.xml` for ACL main proceedings volumes from 2022.

Each volume in a collection has a list of metadata, including its book title and its list of editors, which are typically the program chairs of a conference. It also notes the month, year, and address of the event of the event where the associated event was presented.[5] Volumes also identify their associated venues, and can be linked to multiple venues to denote joint events (cf. §2.5).

2.2 Paper Metadata

For all papers hosted on the Anthology, corresponding metadata can be found in the `data/xml/` folder of the repository. Figure 2 gives an example for the metadata of a single paper; it will contain, at a minimum, the *title* and *bibkey* (i.e., the bibliographic key as found in the official BibTeX export[6]) of the paper. *Authors* of a paper are stored with first and last name components clearly marked up so as to aid in formatting them correctly in bibliographic information. All files hosted on the Anthology server, such as a paper's PDF, will also have a *hash* attribute in the metadata, which is a simple CRC-32 checksum that can be used to verify any files downloaded from the Anthology. The full set of tags and attributes in the XML metadata is documented in the form of a RELAX NG schema (Clark, 2002).[7]

Language	Est. Count
French	2195
Chinese	716
Portuguese	68
Swedish	34
Norwegian	33
Danish	32
German	7

Table 1: Estimated counts of non-English papers.

Paper metadata stored this way can be processed with any XML processing software or library. As the Anthology website is built from these XML files, the data is guaranteed to be identical to what users see online. GitHub CI checks automatically validate the XML files against the schema, ensuring that they always conform to the tags and attributes defined there.

Languages At the time of this writing, the Anthology contains 85,324 papers with a `<title>` tag. The majority of these are written in English, but a few other languages are also represented. Such papers can be annotated with a `<language>` tag. As this tag is not yet systematically applied, we rely on heuristics to obtain estimated counts of non-English papers, shown in Table 1. The major venues for these papers are the JEP, RECITAL, TAL, and TALN venues (French), and the ROCLING, IJCLCLP, and CCL venues (Chinese).

Data Types Whereas older versions of the Anthology hosted only PDFs of papers/volumes and

[5] These fields were originally intended to note the date of publication and the publisher address, but have morphed in purpose over the years.

[6] `https://aclanthology.org/anthology.bib.gz`

[7] `https://github.com/acl-org/acl-anthology/blob/master/data/xml/schema.rnc`

their metadata, papers now support richer supplementary content, including slides, video, software, and data downloads. In case the paper itself needs to be corrected subsequent to publication, there is support for adding revisions of or errata for the original paper, as well as for retractions and removals.

Fixed-casing in Titles One of the most important parts of the site is its BibTeX export functionality. In the paper metadata input by authors upon submission and provided by publication venues to the Anthology for ingestion, many paper titles typically feature *title casing*—that is, capitalization of all content words. However, ACL bibliography style files call for *sentence casing*, in which only proper names (words that would be customarily capitalized even outside of a title) are capitalized, along with the beginning of the title. In order to avoid sloppy lowercasing of languages and other proper names, it is necessary to detect which letters in the original title should have their original casing protected in BibTeX entries, and which should be subject to alteration by the stylesheet. The Anthology codebase implements a set of heuristics based on wordlists to determine which characters should be flagged as *fixed-case* per English spelling conventions.[8] Approximately 45% of titles in the data contain at least one fixed-case designation.

The current heuristics were implemented in 2020, informed by reviewing the data in the Anthology at the time, and the wordlists are updated from time to time as new proper names are encountered. The main components of the heuristics are:

- The `truelist`, a set of 13k words and phrases that should have fixed capitals. The list was seeded with words commonly capitalized in abstracts, and augmented from gazetteers of names of languages and geopolitical entities, as well as manual additions. Salient entries that are not languages or places include "ACL Anthology", "Abstract Meaning Representation", "Carnegie", "Chinese Discourse Treebank", "Viterbi", and "Wizard of Oz".

- Lists of several adjectives and nouns commonly occurring as part of names whose capitalization should match the rest of the name. These are mostly geographic terms like "North", place descriptors like "University" and "Island", and "Ancient" and "Modern" (common modifiers in language names).

- General spelling rules, the most important of which are: (i) Any word with a capital letter in a non-initial position (e.g., "TextTiling", "QA") is marked as fixed-case. (ii) Any tokenized word consisting of a single uppercase letter other than "A", "K" or "N", or a single uppercase letter plus ".", is also fixed-case.

These rules are applied at ingestion time and marked with `<fixed-case>` tags in the XML. Skimming through the XML titles in recent proceedings, we find that errors are rare.[9] There are thus no plans to incorporate more sophisticated named entity recognition software.

2.3 Author Metadata

The Anthology website also provides author pages, which compile all items authored (or edited) by a given person. In contrast to paper metadata, information about authors is only *indirectly* stored in the XML, in the form of names attached to paper entries. This poses two challenges: (i) *names* need to be mapped to *identities*—this involves both merging, as the same person can have published under different names, and disambiguation, as different people can have the same name; and (ii) person identities need to be *indexed* in order to provide a mapping from people to their papers.

Name Merging and Disambiguation There are two forms of name ambiguity: (i) individual authors may publish papers under different variants of their name, and (ii) a particular name variant may be used by more than one person. To resolve (i), we compile a YAML metadata file (`data/yaml/name_variants.yaml`) to collapse known variants under a canonical representation, which is used for the author's page on the website. Additionally, we merge names automatically if they only differ in diacritics (e.g., *José* vs. *Jose*), as we find that in practice they almost always refer to the same person. To address (ii), or false positives from the merge heuristic, an *ID* can be assigned to create an author identity. This ID can then be used in a paper's `<author>` tag to link it to that identity. Figure 3 contains examples.

[8] https://github.com/acl-org/acl-anthology/tree/master/bin/fixedcase

[9] In the ACL 2023 proceedings, an example of a false positive is the English word "Even", which is also the name of a language. A false negative is "New Yorker".

```
- canonical: {first: James H., last: Martin}
  variants:
  - {first: James, last: Martin}
- canonical: {first: Yang, last: Liu}
  comment: Edinburgh
  id: yang-liu-edinburgh
- canonical: {first: Yang, last: Liu}
  comment: 刘扬; Ph.D Purdue; ICSI, \
    Dallas, Facebook, Liulishuo, Amazon
  id: yang-liu-icsi
```

Figure 3: Example of YAML metadata for merging multiple surface forms of a name under a single canonical representation (*James H. Martin*), and for identifying a person with an ambiguous name (*Yang Liu*).

We typically use the Ph.D. institution as the disambiguator in the ID, but plan to move to an ORCID representation.

Author Indexing Finding metadata for a specific paper in the XML files is easy: for example, given a paper with the Anthology ID "2020.acl-main.699," its metadata will be located in the `2020.acl.xml` file under a `<volume>` with ID "main" and a `<paper>` with ID "699." This XML block could be retrieved with a single XPath expression. However, to find all papers authored by a given person, it is necessary to parse *all* XML files and look for instances of their name plus respective variants. This motivates the need for building an *index* that maps people to their (co-)authored papers. To avoid data redundancy, we do not store such an index in the repository directly, but rather compute it dynamically through a Python library specifically made for the Anthology, which we describe in §4.

2.4 Event Metadata

An *event* is a set of otherwise unrelated Anthology volumes that were presented together at a conference. Events are inferred from collections: each non-journal collection is assumed to have been presented in the real world. Additionally, an `<event>` block in a collection's XML file allows to note other volumes that were associated with that event (e.g., colocated workshop volumes).

Until 2023, events had no explicit representation. The Anthology now has the ability to represent event metadata and link to materials related to it, such as the conference handbook and videos from plenary talks and meetings. Importantly, we will also be able to generate citations for these materials. Completion of this work is planned for this year.

2.5 Venue and SIG Metadata

Every volume is linked to a venue using a <venue> tag in the volume's metadata. Every venue has its own file under `data/yaml/venues` listing key information about that venue, including its name (e.g., "Conference on Machine Translation"), its acronym ("WMT"), and tags determining whether it belongs to ACL and whether it is displayed on the main page. A URL-friendly "slug" containing only lowercased, alphanumeric characters is constructed from the venue acronym. Similarly, workshop volumes can be associated with an ACL Special Interest Group (SIG). Information on these can be found under `data/yaml/sigs`. Each SIG file lists all the volumes associated with that SIG.

2.6 Ingestion of New Materials

Ingestion refers to the process of importing new materials in the Anthology. A single ingestion typically includes the main volumes of a conference (e.g., ACL long and short papers, tutorials, system demonstrations, and its student research workshop) together with its colocated workshops. Publication chairs compile the proceedings in a single, formatted directory and submit them to the Anthology, where they will be assembled in a branch of the GitHub repository and submitted as a pull request for review by the Anthology team.

As of 2022, the preferred ingestion format is ACLPUB2,[10] a modernization of ACLPUB.[11] The Anthology has also developed scripts for a number of other ingestion formats, including for the TACL and CL journals, for the MT Archive, and for a generic TSV format. These scripts can be found under `bin/ingest_*.py`.

3 Website

Most users interact with the ACL Anthology through its website. Here, we describe how the website is built, the technical developments it has seen in recent years, and new features we have introduced for the community.

3.1 Static Rewrite

The Anthology website underwent a major rewrite in early 2019, switching from a dynamic to a fully static site. Gildea et al. (2018) describe the technical framework of the Anthology prior to this

[10] https://github.com/rycolab/aclpub2
[11] https://github.com/acl-org/ACLPUB

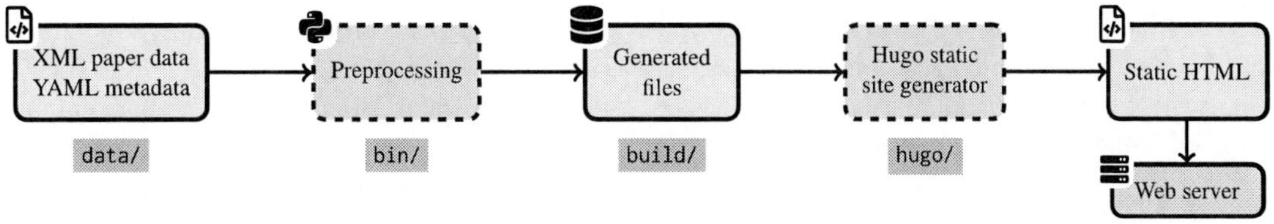

Figure 4: Simplified illustration of the ACL Anthology build pipeline, with the folders where relevant files can be found in the official repository (at https://github.com/acl-org/acl-anthology/).

rewrite, which consisted of a Ruby on Rails application powered by a PostgreSQL database and the Apache Solr search platform. New data could be added to the Anthology via an intermediate XML format containing all bibliographic metadata for proceedings volumes and the contained papers. These XML files had to be ingested into the PostgreSQL database and indexed by the Solr engine.

This new static site generation approach is illustrated in Figure 4. The XML files with the bibliographic metadata (cf. §2.2) now constitute the primary data source for the Anthology; there is no derived database. Some additional metadata, e.g. for publication venues (cf. §2.5) and for disambiguating author names (cf. §2.3), is also stored in YAML files. For building the website, the data files are first processed by a number of Python scripts using an internal Python library (described in §4), which generate page stubs for the site generator and convert the bibliographic data to a number of export formats (e.g. BIBTEX). Afterwards, the website is built using the site generator Hugo,[12] resulting in entirely static HTML files. A CI/CD pipeline on GitHub automatically builds and uploads these to the production web server. To provide search functionality, the website embeds a custom search using Google's Programmable Search Engine (PSE).[13] Notably, the PDF files of the papers, as well as any supplementary material, are *not* part of the repository or the build pipeline as they constitute an enormous volume of data;[14] they are currently copied over manually to the web server.

Advantages Using a static website offers many performance benefits. Since there is no database backend that needs to be queried, the user experience when browsing the website is considerably faster. Building the website locally is also faster: with the former approach, seeding the database would take "at least 30 minutes,"[15] while a full build of the static website takes around nine minutes on a modern laptop.[16] Most of this speed comes from using Hugo as the site generator, which takes 133 seconds to generate 165k HTML pages (i.e., $\approx$0.8 ms per page).

The complexity of running the Anthology is also greatly reduced, which both makes maintenance easier (the production system only needs a web server and no other software) and lowers the barrier of entry, as potential contributors do not need to set up any services to test their contributions. The complete Anthology can be built and served with a single `make` call, provided that Python and Hugo are installed on the system. Generating a static website means that it is trivial to serve copies of the Anthology, which is extensively used in the continuous integration (CI) pipeline; every pull request is rendered to a preview website and the effect on the production system can be easily checked.

Search Functionality Providing search functionality on the website is difficult in our simplified static setting.[17] Google's PSE provides search within both HTML pages and PDF files, but also comes with a number of drawbacks: (i) customization options are limited; e.g., there is no way to display a paper's landing page and its PDF as a single item in the search results, even though they logically belong together; (ii) no immediate control over the indexing of new or changed items, leading to delays of updates being reflected in the search; (iii) region-blocking of Google Search making the search unusable for affected users, e.g. in China. Addressing these issues is challenging and most likely requires either (i) re-introducing a dynamic

[12]https://gohugo.io/

[13]https://programmablesearchengine.google.com/

[14]86,819 files consuming 87 GB.

[15]cf. https://github.com/acl-org/acl-anthology/blob/4a751ac/README.md?plain=1#L58; also note that at this point in time, the Anthology had less than half the number of papers it has now.

[16]Tested on AMD Ryzen 7 Pro 5850U, 12 GB RAM, with Python 3.11.4 and Hugo v0.115.3.

[17]For further discussion, also see https://github.com/acl-org/acl-anthology/issues/165.

server component to host our own search platform, which comes with an increased maintenance burden; or (ii) using a commercial search-as-a-service platform, which comes with a financial cost.

3.2 Features

Citation Export Formats Each paper's page provides a number of user-friendly citation formats beyond BIBTEX, including Markdown and EndNote. These are available for download or for one-click copying. We also provide preformatted long and informal textual citation formats.

GitHub Issue Tracker Corrections to the metadata can be requested by anyone by opening a Github issue. We make extensive use of issue templates to facilitate opening and handling a range of common corrections and suggestions from users.

Zotero Integration Zotero[18] is a popular open source reference manager that allows users to import scholarly content and metadata as they browse the web. Content from the Anthology is easily imported into Zotero, with metadata parsed from BIBTEX files.[19]

Papers With Code Integration Papers With Code (PWC)[20] is a website that links papers to related datasets and code repositories. For papers in the ACL Anthology, data is fetched from PWC through an API and automatically merged into the Anthology metadata; dataset and code links provided by PWC are subsequently displayed on the Anthology website.

Paper Awards The Anthology marks papers that have received awards from their respective conferences. A page compiling all awarded papers does currently not exist, but could be a future addition.

4 Python Library

Building the Anthology website requires transforming all the metadata described above into a format suitable for generating the HTML pages using Hugo. To do this, we rely on a custom-built Python library that is currently found in the `bin/anthology/` folder of the repository. Besides wrapping access to the XML and YAML data files, the Python library (i) implements author indexing and name disambiguation functionality (cf. §2.3); (ii) converts markup found in paper titles and abstracts into appropriate representations for HTML or LATEX; (iii) converts a limited subset of LATEX expressions in paper titles and abstracts into appropriate Unicode and/or HTML representations; (iv) generates bibliographic information (e.g. BIBTEX entries).

4.1 Adoption of the Library

Like the other parts of the repository, the library is open-source and free to use for anyone wanting to access the Anthology data. As with the metadata files, the library is used to build the ACL Anthology website, so re-using it is guaranteed to provide data identical to that on the website. In practice, however, we see some obstacles for a wider adoption of this library (e.g. for projects such as those surveyed in §5.3). One is a lack of proper documentation; while Python scripts found in the repository's `bin/` folder can serve as concrete examples for how the library is used, individual functions are often undocumented. This has consequences not just for third-party adoption, but also for maintainability (cf. §6). Another is the partly unintuitive interface of the library; when it was first built in 2019, the top priority was to recreate the exact functionality of the Ruby application that existed at the time (cf. §3.1), and as such, it is mainly geared towards the needs of building the Anthology website. For these reasons, we are in the process of reimplementing this library.

4.2 PyPI Package

Based on the challenges touched upon above (and further discussed in §6), we have begun reimplementing the Python library in a way that (i) is user-friendlier and better documented, and (ii) easily installable (e.g. via `pip`). A fully usable version of this package is already available on PyPI, the main Python package repository, as `acl-anthology-py`.[21] Figure 5 shows some examples of how this library might be used. We are currently working on making this library feature-complete with respect to the functionality needed to replace the old library in the website's build chain (cf. §3.1), but the current version of the library already comes with full API documentation as well as a user guide.[22] Furthermore, it is implemented

[18] https://www.zotero.org/

[19] Implemented by Guy Aglionby: https://github.com/zotero/translators/blob/master/ACLWeb.js

[20] https://paperswithcode.com/

[21] https://pypi.org/project/acl-anthology-py/

[22] Please refer to the PyPI page for the latest link.

```
# Instantiate the Anthology, automatically fetching data from the official repository
from acl_anthology import Anthology
anthology = Anthology.from_repo()

# Find all papers with "ACL Anthology" in the title, and print their bibkey
for paper in anthology.papers():
    if "ACL Anthology" in str(paper.title):
        print(paper.bibkey)

# Find all people named "Dan Klein", and pick the first one (-- as of now, there's only one)
person = anthology.find_people("Klein, Dan")[0]

# Get a list of URLs to all paper PDFs by a given person
urls = [paper.pdf.url for paper in person.papers()]

# Generate the BibTeX entry of a paper based on its Anthology ID
bibtex = anthology.get("2020.acl-main.699").to_bibtex()
```

Figure 5: Examples illustrating the usage of the `acl-anthology-py` Python library. Please refer to the latest API documentation for the most up-to-date information.

using many "best practices" of software development, including a high test coverage (>90%) and automated CI checks that enforce coding style conventions and type hints.

We hope that this redesigned library will make the ACL Anthology easier to maintain and thus more future-proof. Releasing the library on PyPI should also greatly increase discoverability and, consequently, adoption in related work that wants to access Anthology data.

5 Impact of the ACL Anthology

A lot of research has built on data from the ACL Anthology over the years, but even the technical infrastructure has had impact on other open-source projects. Here, we try to provide an extensive survey of software, datasets, and scientific studies that directly rely on data or code from the Anthology.

5.1 On Open-Source Software

Being open-source and easy to use made it possible for other publication repositories to re-use the ACL Anthology infrastructure. At least three such projects currently exist: (i) the SemDial workshop series,[23] which publishes its proceedings dating back to 2004; (ii) the IR Anthology,[24] which currently collects ≈63k papers from information retrieval venues (Potthast et al., 2021); and (iii) the Global Water Futures archive,[25] which hosts 1.2k publications from their project on addressing water threats. The last project in particular highlights that the codebase of the ACL Anthology has even found adoption outside of computer science domains.

5.2 On Corpora and Datasets

The ACL Anthology Reference Corpus (ACL ARC; Bird et al., 2008) was one of the first efforts to build on the ACL Anthology for academic research, providing the extracted full-text and metadata for 11k papers up to February 2007. The ACL Anthology Network Corpus (AAN; Radev et al., 2009) expands on this by providing citation and collaboration networks. Schäfer et al. (2011) introduce the ACL Anthology Searchbench, which Weitz and Schäfer (2012) build on to provide a "citation browser." Singh et al. (2018) present CL Scholar, an ACL Anthology "knowledge graph miner." Unfortunately, as of now, most of these initiatives appear to be abandoned and/or unavailable; the ANN is still accessible through the broader "All About NLP" project (also AAN; Fabbri et al., 2018).

More recently, the NLP4NLP corpus (Mariani et al., 2019a) incorporates data from the ACL Anthology as part of a dataset of articles in "speech and natural language processing over a period of 50 years (1965–2015)," which Mariani et al. (2022) extend to cover publications until 2020. The NLP Scholar project combines data from the ACL Anthology and Google Scholar in a new dataset (Mohammad, 2020b) and an associated visual exploration tool (Mohammad, 2020c). NLPExplorer (Parmar et al., 2020) offers a curated dataset and web portal[26] with annotations including manually curated topic classification. Finally, the ACL

[23] http://semdial.org/anthology/venues/semdial/

[24] https://ir.webis.de/anthology/

[25] https://gwf-uwaterloo.github.io/gwf-publications/

[26] http://nlpexplorer.org/

OCL corpus (Rohatgi et al., 2023) provides automatically extracted text for ACL Anthology papers currently up to September 2022.

Several other annotated datasets based on subsets of the Anthology exist: Schäfer et al. (2012) present a small corpus of 266 papers annotated with coreference; QasemiZadeh and Schumann (2016) introduce a dataset for terminology extraction and classification; Gábor et al. (2016) add semantic annotation such as entity tagging and relations, which was subsequently used in a SemEval shared task (Gábor et al., 2018); Iwatsuki et al. (2020) build a dataset with formulaic expressions and their communicative functions; van Dongen et al. (2020) add citation information; Hao et al. (2020) introduce a corpus annotated with "future work sentences"; and Hou et al. (2021) present a corpus for entity tagging of tasks, datasets, and evaluation metrics in 30k ACL Anthology papers.

5.3 On Academic Research

The ACL Anthology has frequently been used for scholarly literature analysis within the NLP domain, such as citation analysis. As the Anthology does not provide any data on citations, such studies require either data mining of the PDFs, a combination with data from external sources such as Google Scholar or Semantic Scholar,[27] or the use of a dataset that already provides this, like NLP Scholar (Mohammad, 2020b). Despite this necessary extra step, studies have focused on the ACL Anthology to analyze incoming citations (Mohammad, 2020a), outgoing citations (Bollmann and Elliott, 2020; Singh et al., 2023), or geographic citation gaps (Rungta et al., 2022).Van Dongen et al. (2020) present a model for citation count prediction. Guo et al. (2020) provide a Java API for extracting citation context from academic literature, trained on an annotated dataset based on the Anthology.

Beyond citation analysis, studies have used the Anthology to analyze the gender distribution among authors (Vogel and Jurafsky, 2012), to analyze the influence of industry on academic research (Abdalla et al., 2023), and to track the evolution of research topics and domains over time (Anderson et al., 2012; Omodei et al., 2014; Schumann, 2016; Mariani et al., 2019b; Schopf et al., 2023). Joshi et al. (2020) combine data from the Anthology and the Semantic Scholar API to analyze linguistic diversity in NLP research. Fortuna et al. (2021) analyze 50k Anthology papers to find instances of "NLP for Social Good."

Data from the ACL Anthology has also been used to build and evaluate models for a variety of tasks, such as relation extraction (Schäfer et al., 2008), scientific term mining (Jin et al., 2013), name disambiguation and topic modeling (King et al., 2014), semantic labeling (Schumann and Martínez Alonso, 2018), building search systems (Yoneda et al., 2017; Ding et al., 2020), and analyzing document similarity (Ostendorff et al., 2020).

6 Lessons & Challenges

Impact of Open Development All development – including changes to the data – happening in public is highly beneficial. By far the most common contributions by non-project members are metadata corrections such as name changes and typos. Some of these come directly as pull requests ($\approx$1k so far), which can often be merged within a day and reduce the workload of the Anthology volunteers; others come as (pre-formatted) GitHub issues (also $\approx$1k so far), which are then automatically linked to pull requests that are merged monthly.

As everyone can build the Anthology themselves, we occasionally get feedback or suggestions regarding the robustness of the infrastructure on different systems, but overall contributions to the code parts of the project are rare. One notable exception is the integration with Papers With Code (PWC): this functionality was suggested and in large parts contributed by the team behind PWC.

Discoverability and Usability of Open-Source Data and Software There is a discrepancy between the data and tools that the ACL Anthology directly and openly provides and what researchers use in practice. While not all the studies mentioned in §5.3 are explicit about how they obtain data from the Anthology, we do find instances of using web-scraping tools on the Anthology website or using the BibTeX export as the primary data source. In both situations, we would expect that using the XML metadata (cf. §2.2) and/or the Python library (cf. §4) would be a faster and potentially easier[28] way to obtain the same results. The fact that several studies build their own solutions for this points to a problem of *discoverability* or *usability* of the data

[27] `https://www.semanticscholar.org/`

[28] For example, the BibTeX export contains TeX-encoded characters such as `\"{a}` for the letter ä, while the XML contains Unicode strings.

and tools we provide; i.e., people are either not aware that these data and tools exist, or they find them too hard to use (e.g. due to lack of documentation).

Encouraging Contributions All of the features the ACL Anthology has today are the result of volunteer effort, yet we rarely see new volunteers contributing features to the code. Potentially, one factor in this is (again) the lack of documentation: while there is some information distributed across a GitHub Wiki, code-internal comments, and even the ACL Anthology website,[29] it is neither very accessible nor complete. Such "documentation debt" is known to cause problems for maintainability (e.g., Rios et al., 2020), and is likely to pose a hurdle for potential new contributors as well.

7 Ongoing and Future Work

Automatic Name Disambiguation An increasing problem with the growth of the field is author name disambiguation. As described in §2.3, our XML format supports maintaining separate identities for authors with the same name, but currently these names have to be manually disambiguated at ingestion time. Ingestion input materials often include disambiguating information such as ORCIDs, author affiliation, and so on, but we cannot depend on their presence. A great project (likely publishable) would be to build an automated disambiguation process based on metadata, context (such as co-author lists), and paper content itself.

Incomplete Venue/SIG Information Prior to the new Anthology ID format introduced in 2020, all workshop venues were grouped together under a common `W` prefix, without more specific venue information. Many of these have been manually linked to venues (e.g., all early WMT volumes), but the information is incomplete. These could similarly be linked to SIGs.

Abstracts for Older Papers Since around 2016, papers start systematically including abstracts in the metadata, but most older papers do not have them. Some datasets (e.g., Rohatgi et al., 2023) provide text extracted automatically from the PDFs, potentially enabling us to add abstracts for older papers too. However, some form of quality check of the extracted text appears necessary to maintain a high level of quality of our metadata.

[29]https://aclanthology.org/info/

Copyright The copyright situation with Anthology data has operated under the best efforts of non-expert volunteers, largely from academia. However, the licensing information is imperfect. The ACL owns the copyright to most papers submitted to ACL venues, but there are exceptions where the ACL was only granted a license, such as for papers published by Canadian and British academics, for whom copyright belongs to the English Crown. The ideal situation would be to incorporate this information in paper-level metadata.

Incomplete Older Volumes Many early volumes are missing, and it is not always even known which ones they are.

Front Page Redesign The front page of the Anthology is showing its age, and could use reworking from a graphic designer and/or front-end developer.

8 Conclusion

The ACL Anthology has grown into an invaluable resource for the CL/NLP community. Volunteer contributions are responsible for virtually all of the improvements of the metadata (§2), the Anthology website (§3), and the provided Python library (§4). The survey in §5 highlights the utility and importance of this resource for academic research. To address the ongoing challenges (§6) and future directions (§7), we continue to rely on help from the community. We encourage anyone who is interested in contributing to the ACL Anthology to explore our GitHub repository.[30]

Acknowledgements

We would like to thank everyone who has contributed to the ACL Anthology over the years,[31] and thereby helped to make it into what it is today.

Limitations

The literature survey in §5 was performed by searching for papers with "ACL Anthology" in the title or abstract, as well as inspecting references in and citations of these papers. It is conceivable that there is more relevant work that we missed. Likewise, there may be more open-source projects based off the Anthology that we are not aware of.

[30]https://github.com/acl-org/acl-anthology/

[31]An imperfect overview of contributors can be derived from: https://github.com/acl-org/acl-anthology/graphs/contributors

References

Mohamed Abdalla, Jan Philip Wahle, Terry Lima Ruas, Aurélie Névéol, Fanny Ducel, Saif Mohammad, and Karen Fort. 2023. The elephant in the room: Analyzing the presence of big tech in natural language processing research. In *Proceedings of the 61st Annual Meeting of the Association for Computational Linguistics (Volume 1: Long Papers)*, pages 13141–13160, Toronto, Canada. Association for Computational Linguistics.

Ashton Anderson, Dan Jurafsky, and Daniel A. McFarland. 2012. Towards a computational history of the ACL: 1980–2008. In *Proceedings of the ACL-2012 Special Workshop on Rediscovering 50 Years of Discoveries*, pages 13–21, Jeju Island, Korea. Association for Computational Linguistics.

Steven Bird, Robert Dale, Bonnie Dorr, Bryan Gibson, Mark Joseph, Min-Yen Kan, Dongwon Lee, Brett Powley, Dragomir Radev, and Yee Fan Tan. 2008. The ACL Anthology reference corpus: A reference dataset for bibliographic research in computational linguistics. In *Proceedings of the Sixth International Conference on Language Resources and Evaluation (LREC'08)*, Marrakech, Morocco. European Language Resources Association (ELRA).

Marcel Bollmann and Desmond Elliott. 2020. On forgetting to cite older papers: An analysis of the ACL Anthology. In *Proceedings of the 58th Annual Meeting of the Association for Computational Linguistics*, pages 7819–7827, Online. Association for Computational Linguistics.

James Clark. 2002. RELAX NG compact syntax. Committee specification, The Organization for the Advancement of Structured Information Standards [OASIS].

Shane Ding, Edwin Zhang, and Jimmy Lin. 2020. Cydex: Neural search infrastructure for the scholarly literature. In *Proceedings of the First Workshop on Scholarly Document Processing*, pages 168–173, Online. Association for Computational Linguistics.

Alexander Fabbri, Irene Li, Prawat Trairatvorakul, Yijiao He, Weitai Ting, Robert Tung, Caitlin Westerfield, and Dragomir Radev. 2018. TutorialBank: A manually-collected corpus for prerequisite chains, survey extraction and resource recommendation. In *Proceedings of the 56th Annual Meeting of the Association for Computational Linguistics (Volume 1: Long Papers)*, pages 611–620, Melbourne, Australia. Association for Computational Linguistics.

Paula Fortuna, Laura Pérez-Mayos, Ahmed AbuRa'ed, Juan Soler-Company, and Leo Wanner. 2021. Cartography of natural language processing for social good (NLP4SG): Searching for definitions, statistics and white spots. In *Proceedings of the 1st Workshop on NLP for Positive Impact*, pages 19–26, Online. Association for Computational Linguistics.

Kata Gábor, Davide Buscaldi, Anne-Kathrin Schumann, Behrang QasemiZadeh, Haïfa Zargayouna, and Thierry Charnois. 2018. SemEval-2018 task 7: Semantic relation extraction and classification in scientific papers. In *Proceedings of the 12th International Workshop on Semantic Evaluation*, pages 679–688, New Orleans, Louisiana. Association for Computational Linguistics.

Kata Gábor, Haïfa Zargayouna, Davide Buscaldi, Isabelle Tellier, and Thierry Charnois. 2016. Semantic annotation of the ACL Anthology corpus for the automatic analysis of scientific literature. In *Proceedings of the Tenth International Conference on Language Resources and Evaluation (LREC'16)*, pages 3694–3701, Portorož, Slovenia. European Language Resources Association (ELRA).

Daniel Gildea, Min-Yen Kan, Nitin Madnani, Christoph Teichmann, and Martín Villalba. 2018. The ACL Anthology: Current state and future directions. In *Proceedings of Workshop for NLP Open Source Software (NLP-OSS)*, pages 23–28, Melbourne, Australia. Association for Computational Linguistics.

Chenrui Guo, Haoran Cui, Li Zhang, Jiamin Wang, Wei Lu, and Jian Wu. 2020. SmartCiteCon: Implicit citation context extraction from academic literature using supervised learning. In *Proceedings of the 8th International Workshop on Mining Scientific Publications*, pages 21–26, Wuhan, China. Association for Computational Linguistics.

Wenke Hao, Zhicheng Li, Yuchen Qian, Yuzhuo Wang, and Chengzhi Zhang. 2020. The acl fws-rc: A dataset for recognition and classification of sentence about future works. In *Proceedings of the ACM/IEEE Joint Conference on Digital Libraries in 2020*, JCDL '20, page 261–269, New York, NY, USA. Association for Computing Machinery.

Yufang Hou, Charles Jochim, Martin Gleize, Francesca Bonin, and Debasis Ganguly. 2021. TDMSci: A specialized corpus for scientific literature entity tagging of tasks datasets and metrics. In *Proceedings of the 16th Conference of the European Chapter of the Association for Computational Linguistics: Main Volume*, pages 707–714, Online. Association for Computational Linguistics.

Kenichi Iwatsuki, Florian Boudin, and Akiko Aizawa. 2020. An evaluation dataset for identifying communicative functions of sentences in English scholarly papers. In *Proceedings of the Twelfth Language Resources and Evaluation Conference*, pages 1712–1720, Marseille, France. European Language Resources Association.

Yiping Jin, Min-Yen Kan, Jun-Ping Ng, and Xiangnan He. 2013. Mining scientific terms and their definitions: A study of the ACL Anthology. In *Proceedings of the 2013 Conference on Empirical Methods in Natural Language Processing*, pages 780–790, Seattle, Washington, USA. Association for Computational Linguistics.

Pratik Joshi, Sebastin Santy, Amar Budhiraja, Kalika Bali, and Monojit Choudhury. 2020. The state and fate of linguistic diversity and inclusion in the NLP world. In *Proceedings of the 58th Annual Meeting of the Association for Computational Linguistics*, pages 6282–6293, Online. Association for Computational Linguistics.

Ben King, Rahul Jha, and Dragomir R. Radev. 2014. Heterogeneous networks and their applications: Scientometrics, name disambiguation, and topic modeling. *Transactions of the Association for Computational Linguistics*, 2:1–14.

Joseph Mariani, Gil Francopoulo, and Patrick Paroubek. 2019a. The NLP4NLP corpus (I): 50 years of publication, collaboration and citation in speech and language processing. *Frontiers in Research Metrics and Analytics*, 3.

Joseph Mariani, Gil Francopoulo, Patrick Paroubek, and Frédéric Vernier. 2019b. The NLP4NLP corpus (II): 50 years of research in speech and language processing. *Frontiers in Research Metrics and Analytics*, 3.

Joseph Mariani, Gil Francopoulo, Patrick Paroubek, and Frédéric Vernier. 2022. NLP4NLP+5: The deep (r)evolution in speech and language processing. *Frontiers in Research Metrics and Analytics*, 7.

Saif M. Mohammad. 2020a. Examining citations of natural language processing literature. In *Proceedings of the 58th Annual Meeting of the Association for Computational Linguistics*, pages 5199–5209, Online. Association for Computational Linguistics.

Saif M. Mohammad. 2020b. NLP scholar: A dataset for examining the state of NLP research. In *Proceedings of the Twelfth Language Resources and Evaluation Conference*, pages 868–877, Marseille, France. European Language Resources Association.

Saif M. Mohammad. 2020c. NLP scholar: An interactive visual explorer for natural language processing literature. In *Proceedings of the 58th Annual Meeting of the Association for Computational Linguistics: System Demonstrations*, pages 232–255, Online. Association for Computational Linguistics.

Elisa Omodei, Jean-Philippe Cointet, and Thierry Poibeau. 2014. Mapping the natural language processing domain: Experiments using the ACL Anthology. In *Proceedings of the Ninth International Conference on Language Resources and Evaluation (LREC'14)*, pages 2972–2978, Reykjavik, Iceland. European Language Resources Association (ELRA).

Malte Ostendorff, Terry Ruas, Till Blume, Bela Gipp, and Georg Rehm. 2020. Aspect-based document similarity for research papers. In *Proceedings of the 28th International Conference on Computational Linguistics*, pages 6194–6206, Barcelona, Spain (Online). International Committee on Computational Linguistics.

Monarch Parmar, Naman Jain, Pranjali Jain, P Jayakrishna Sahit, Soham Pachpande, Shruti Singh, and Mayank Singh. 2020. NLPExplorer: Exploring the universe of NLP papers. In *Advances in Information Retrieval*, pages 476–480, Cham. Springer International Publishing.

Martin Potthast, Sebastian Günther, Janek Bevendorff, Jan Philipp Bittner, Alexander Bondarenko, Maik Fröbe, Christian Kahmann, Andreas Niekler, Michael Völske, Benno Stein, and Matthias Hagen. 2021. The Information Retrieval Anthology. In *Proceedings of the 44th International ACM SIGIR Conference on Research and Development in Information Retrieval*, SIGIR '21, page 2550–2555, New York, NY, USA. Association for Computing Machinery.

Behrang QasemiZadeh and Anne-Kathrin Schumann. 2016. The ACL RD-TEC 2.0: A language resource for evaluating term extraction and entity recognition methods. In *Proceedings of the Tenth International Conference on Language Resources and Evaluation (LREC'16)*, pages 1862–1868, Portorož, Slovenia. European Language Resources Association (ELRA).

Dragomir R. Radev, Pradeep Muthukrishnan, and Vahed Qazvinian. 2009. The ACL Anthology network corpus. In *Proceedings of the 2009 Workshop on Text and Citation Analysis for Scholarly Digital Libraries (NLPIR4DL)*, pages 54–61, Suntec City, Singapore. Association for Computational Linguistics.

Nicolli Rios, Leonardo Mendes, Cristina Cerdeiral, Ana Patrícia F. Magalhães, Boris Perez, Darío Correal, Hernán Astudillo, Carolyn Seaman, Clemente Izurieta, Gleison Santos, and Rodrigo Oliveira Spínola. 2020. Hearing the voice of software practitioners on causes, effects, and practices to deal with documentation debt. In *Requirements Engineering: Foundation for Software Quality*, pages 55–70, Cham. Springer International Publishing.

Shaurya Rohatgi, Yanxia Qin, Benjamin Aw, Niranjana Unnithan, and Min-Yen Kan. 2023. The ACL OCL corpus: advancing open science in computational linguistics. arXiv:2305.14996.

Mukund Rungta, Janvijay Singh, Saif M. Mohammad, and Diyi Yang. 2022. Geographic citation gaps in NLP research. In *Proceedings of the 2022 Conference on Empirical Methods in Natural Language Processing*, pages 1371–1383, Abu Dhabi, United Arab Emirates. Association for Computational Linguistics.

Ulrich Schäfer, Bernd Kiefer, Christian Spurk, Jörg Steffen, and Rui Wang. 2011. The ACL Anthology searchbench. In *Proceedings of the ACL-HLT 2011 System Demonstrations*, pages 7–13, Portland, Oregon. Association for Computational Linguistics.

Ulrich Schäfer, Christian Spurk, and Jörg Steffen. 2012. A fully coreference-annotated corpus of scholarly papers from the ACL Anthology. In *Proceedings of COLING 2012: Posters*, pages 1059–1070, Mumbai, India. The COLING 2012 Organizing Committee.

Ulrich Schäfer, Hans Uszkoreit, Christian Federmann, Torsten Marek, and Yajing Zhang. 2008. Extracting and querying relations in scientific papers on language technology. In *Proceedings of the Sixth International Conference on Language Resources and Evaluation (LREC'08)*, Marrakech, Morocco. European Language Resources Association (ELRA).

Tim Schopf, Karim Arabi, and Florian Matthes. 2023. Exploring the landscape of natural language processing research. arXiv:2307.10652.

Anne-Kathrin Schumann. 2016. Brave new world: Uncovering topical dynamics in the ACL Anthology reference corpus using term life cycle information. In *Proceedings of the 10th SIGHUM Workshop on Language Technology for Cultural Heritage, Social Sciences, and Humanities*, pages 1–11, Berlin, Germany. Association for Computational Linguistics.

Anne-Kathrin Schumann and Héctor Martínez Alonso. 2018. Automatic annotation of semantic term types in the complete ACL Anthology reference corpus. In *Proceedings of the Eleventh International Conference on Language Resources and Evaluation (LREC 2018)*, Miyazaki, Japan. European Language Resources Association (ELRA).

Janvijay Singh, Mukund Rungta, Diyi Yang, and Saif Mohammad. 2023. Forgotten knowledge: Examining the citational amnesia in NLP. In *Proceedings of the 61st Annual Meeting of the Association for Computational Linguistics (Volume 1: Long Papers)*, pages 6192–6208, Toronto, Canada. Association for Computational Linguistics.

Mayank Singh, Pradeep Dogga, Sohan Patro, Dhiraj Barnwal, Ritam Dutt, Rajarshi Haldar, Pawan Goyal, and Animesh Mukherjee. 2018. CL scholar: The ACL Anthology knowledge graph miner. In *Proceedings of the 2018 Conference of the North American Chapter of the Association for Computational Linguistics: Demonstrations*, pages 16–20, New Orleans, Louisiana. Association for Computational Linguistics.

Thomas van Dongen, Gideon Maillette de Buy Wenniger, and Lambert Schomaker. 2020. SChuBERT: Scholarly document chunks with BERT-encoding boost citation count prediction. In *Proceedings of the First Workshop on Scholarly Document Processing*, pages 148–157, Online. Association for Computational Linguistics.

Adam Vogel and Dan Jurafsky. 2012. He said, she said: Gender in the ACL Anthology. In *Proceedings of the ACL-2012 Special Workshop on Rediscovering 50 Years of Discoveries*, pages 33–41, Jeju Island, Korea. Association for Computational Linguistics.

Benjamin Weitz and Ulrich Schäfer. 2012. A graphical citation browser for the ACL Anthology. In *Proceedings of the Eighth International Conference on Language Resources and Evaluation (LREC'12)*, pages 1718–1722, Istanbul, Turkey. European Language Resources Association (ELRA).

Takuma Yoneda, Koki Mori, Makoto Miwa, and Yutaka Sasaki. 2017. Bib2vec: Embedding-based search system for bibliographic information. In *Proceedings of the Software Demonstrations of the 15th Conference of the European Chapter of the Association for Computational Linguistics*, pages 112–115, Valencia, Spain. Association for Computational Linguistics.

nanoT5: A PyTorch Framework for Pre-training and Fine-tuning T5-style Models with Limited Resources

Piotr Nawrot
University of Edinburgh
https://github.com/PiotrNawrot/nanoT5

Abstract

State-of-the-art language models like T5 have revolutionized the NLP landscape, but their computational demands hinder a large portion of the research community. To address this challenge, we present nanoT5, a specially-optimized PyTorch framework for efficient pre-training and fine-tuning of T5 models. Drawing on insights from optimizer differences and prioritizing efficiency, nanoT5 allows a T5-Base model to be pre-trained on a single GPU in just 16 hours, without any loss in performance. With the introduction of this open-source framework, we hope to widen the accessibility to language modelling research and cater to the community's demand for more user-friendly T5 (Encoder-Decoder) implementations. We make our contributions, including configurations, codebase, pre-training insights, and pre-trained models, available to the public.

1 Introduction

The transformative power of large pre-trained language models such as GPT-3 (Brown et al., 2020), T5 (Raffel et al., 2019), and PaLM (Chowdhery et al., 2022) is undeniable. However, their massive computational requirements remain a barrier for many researchers. Notably, models like T5 require extensive datasets and significant computational resources for their pre-training (Raffel et al., 2019). Furthermore, many open-source implementations lean heavily on TPU accelerators (Shazeer, 2020), which are not as available to the academic community as GPUs.

Recognizing this gap, we introduce nanoT5, a resource-efficient, open-source PyTorch framework designed for the pre-training and fine-tuning of T5 models. Inspired by pioneering efforts such as nanoGPT (Karpathy, 2021) and Cramming (Geiping and Goldstein, 2022), nanoT5 uniquely concentrates on enhancing the training pipeline specifically for T5 encoder-decoder models. Our framework includes optimized configurations and scripts, enabling researchers to pre-train a T5-Base model with 248M parameters on a single GPU in just 16 hours. Every facet, from data preprocessing and model architecture to the learning rate schedule, has been tuned for both efficiency and adaptability. With nanoT5, users can seamlessly initiate model pre-training within minutes of accessing our GitHub repository.

This paper underscores two main innovations: First, we delve into the nuances between the Adam and Adafactor optimizer performances as detailed in (Havinga), suggesting a version of AdamW (Loshchilov and Hutter, 2017), augmented with matrix-wise learning rate scaling based on root mean square. This variant showcases better speed and robustness compared to the default Adafactor (Shazeer and Stern, 2018). Second, we demonstrate that T5 models trained with nanoT5, housing around 250M parameters, can achieve performance akin to the publicly-available checkpoints while requiring 150x less pre-training data.

Our primary motivation stems from the growing demand for reproducible and tuned baselines (Kaddour et al., 2023), enabling fast and small-scale hypothesis validation in the evolving realm of large pre-trained Transformers. With nanoT5, we address a gap highlighted by community requests [1][2][3], providing an approachable platform for working with T5 (Encoder-Decoder) architecture. To our understanding, nanoT5 pioneers the effort to reproduce T5 v1.1 pre-training using PyTorch, deviating from prior Jax/Flax implementations. We invite the community to explore our training configurations, codebase, and pre-trained models, all of which are available at https://github.com/PiotrNawrot/nanoT5.

[1] https://github.com/google-research/text-to-text-transfer-transformer/issues/172

[2] https://github.com/huggingface/transformers/issues/18030

[3] https://github.com/huggingface/transformers/issues/5079

Proceedings of the 3rd Workshop for Natural Language Processing Open Source Software (NLP-OSS 2023), pages 95–101
December 6, 2023 ©2023 Association for Computational Linguistics

2 Related Work

The landscape of open-source repositories tailored for efficient pre-training of Transformer language models is vast. Notably, nanoGPT (Karpathy, 2021) sheds light on decoder-only models, while Cramming (Geiping and Goldstein, 2022) homes in on the optimal pre-training of the encoder-only BERT architecture (Devlin et al., 2019). Contrastingly, with nanoT5, we sought to bridge the existing gap by providing a standalone research template tailored for the T5-style (Encoder-Decoder) models.

To expedite the training process of nanoT5 we incorporated various optimizations. These encompass mixed precision training (Micikevicius et al., 2017), compiled runtimes (Narang et al., 2021), and more. Additionally, we delved into the potential of efficient training methodologies such as recent optimizers (Chen et al., 2023; Liu et al., 2023), and fast attention mechanism (Dao et al., 2022), which are elaborated further in Section 4.3. It's crucial to note that while we evaluated various efficient algorithms, we consciously opted against those, such as (Nawrot et al., 2022; Shazeer et al., 2017), that would modify the core model structure. Instead, our intent with nanoT5 was to cultivate a straightforward baseline for further research endeavors. The standout contribution of our work in terms of efficient training algorithms is the AdamW variant, with the RMS matrix scaling, which improves T5 pre-training convergence.

3 Methodology

Our validation strategy seeks to replicate the T5-base pre-training outcomes detailed in (Shazeer, 2020) and the fine-tuning results of Tk-Instruct on the Super Natural-Instructions (SNI) meta-dataset (Wang et al., 2022).

3.1 Training pipeline

We've devised a comprehensive training pipeline prioritizing efficient data management, low-level optimizations, and coding simplicity, all while preserving the core model and training logic:

- **Dataset Handling:** Given the extensive volume of the C4 dataset, which exceeds 300GB, our repository implements concurrent data downloading with model training. This optimization speeds up the commencement of T5 model pre-training to a few minutes.
- **Exposure and Simplicity:** Our methodology aims to strike a balance between adaptability and abstraction. With tools such as the HuggingFace Accelerator (Sylvain Gugger, 2022), we abstract tasks like checkpoint management and tensor operations. Experiment tracking is realized via neptune.ai (Neptune team, 2019), and we've employed hydra (Yadan, 2019) for coordinated hyperparameter handling.
- **Efficiency:** We've leveraged the optimizations of PyTorch 2.0 (Paszke et al., 2019), and employed mixed-precision training in line with established optimization guidelines [4][5].
- **Flexibility:** Our repository is designed with adaptability in mind, offering support for multi-GPU training, gradient accumulation, and gradient checkpointing. This ensures users can reproduce our results on a variety of GPUs beyond the A100 and can experiment with configurations larger than the T5-base size emphasized in this study. Additionally, we provide support for both CPUs and Apple's ARM M1 chips.

3.2 Pre-training

Our experiments strictly follow the T5-v1.1-base training configuration (Shazeer, 2020), where the model itself comprises of roughly 248M parameters. The C4 dataset (Raffel et al., 2019), sourced directly from Huggingface, undergoes tokenization via the Wordpiece tokenizer (Schuster and Nakajima, 2012), with the original model's vocabulary. During pre-processing, 15% of input data is masked using sentinel tokens, setting the neural network's target as the prediction of these tokens, leveraging its decoder. Consistent with the original study, we've set the batch size at 128 examples, with inputs of 512 tokens and outputs of 114 tokens. Optimization is facilitated through the Adafactor optimizer (Shazeer and Stern, 2018), combined with the Inverse-Square-Root (ISR) learning rate schedule. The model is trained for 2^{16} steps. For more details please refer to the original work.

3.3 Fine-tuning

Our fine-tuning employs the Super Natural-Instructions (SNI) meta-dataset (Wang et al., 2022), which has been previously used for fine-tuning

[4] https://huggingface.co/docs/transformers/perf_train_gpu_one

[5] https://pytorch.org/tutorials/recipes/recipes/tuning_guide.html

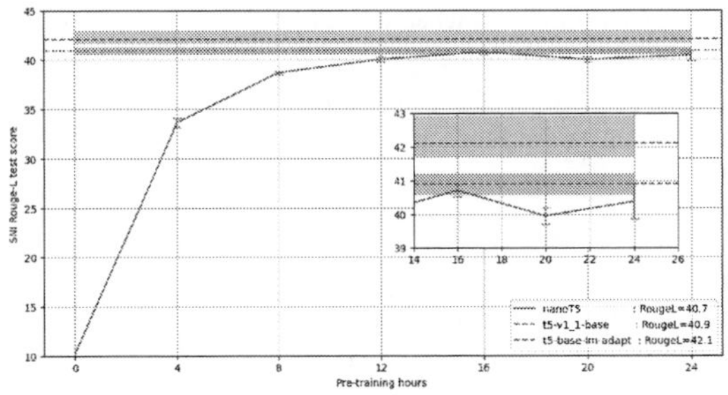

Figure 1: Downstream performance of models across various pre-training durations, including existing T5-base variants accessible through Huggingface Hub.

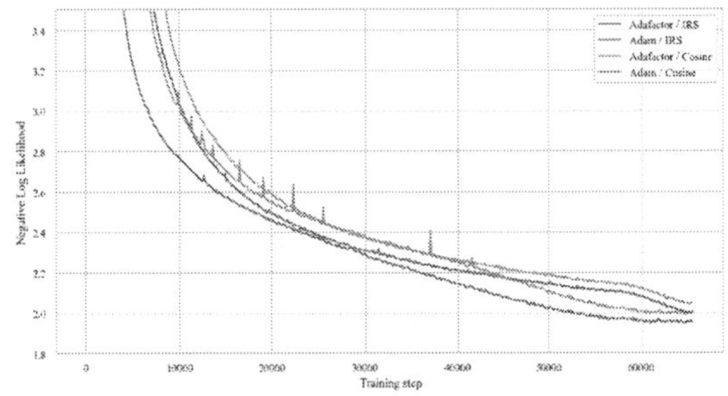

Figure 2: Training loss curves contrasting different optimizers and learning rate schedules.

models like FlanT5 (Chung et al., 2022), BLOOM (Scao et al., 2022), and Tk-Instruct (Wang et al., 2022). To assess the correctness of our fine-tuning setup, and the efficiency of our pre-training, we decided to reproduce the Tk-Instruct methodology.

3.4 Reproducibility

Ensuring that our work can be reliably replicated is a core focus of our methodology. To facilitate this, we have taken the following measures:

- **Model Weights:** We make the model's weights available on the HuggingFace Hub. These can be downloaded and used for fine-tuning on the SNI dataset with nanoT5.
- **Loss Curves:** We openly share both the pre-training and fine-tuning loss curves to provide insight into the model's learning dynamics.
- **Hyperparameters:** All hyperparameters used in our experiments have been released.
- **Environment and Hardware:** In our repository we offer comprehensive instructions on how to recreate our environment, including detailed information about our hardware. This encompasses specifications of our CPU and GPU, as well as the relevant driver versions.
- **Statistical Robustness:** To ensure the validity of our results, each experiment was conducted three times with different random seeds.

4 Results

4.1 Reproducing Pre-Training

By following the original experimental setup described above, we achieved a negative log-likelihood of 1.995 on the held-out set, which is slightly inferior to the reference.

In exploring alternative optimization methods, we tested the AdamW optimizer as a potential replacement for the original Adafactor. While AdamW theoretically promises greater training stability by directly estimating the second moment of the gradients (as opposed to Adafactor's low-rank approximation), our training with AdamW diverged. This behavior mirrors findings from a study on T5 pre-training (Havinga). Upon further investigation, we identified that matrix-wise learning rate (LR) scaling using its root mean square (RMS) [6] was the crucial element ensuring Adafactor's convergence. After augmenting AdamW with this extra LR scaling, which we will refer to as RMS scaling, it not only converged but also exhibited improved stability during pre-training and operated slightly faster, thanks to the direct retrieval of the second moment from memory instead of approximating it.

Nonetheless, when combined with the Inverse-Square-Root LR schedule, AdamW's performance was still outpaced by Adafactor. By replacing the ISR schedule with a Cosine LR Schedule, we achieved a superior negative log-likelihood of 1.953 on the held-out set, significantly surpassing Adafactor with the ISR schedule. The specific results of these experiments can be found in Table 2. A comparison of the training loss curves using different optimizers (Adafactor vs. AdamW) and schedules (ISR vs. Cosine) is provided in Figure 2.

4.2 Fine-Tuning Performance Across Different Pre-Training Durations

Our fine-tuning configuration strictly aligns with that of Tk-Instruct. However, there remains some ambiguity regarding whether Tk-Instruct was initialized from a regular checkpoint (google/t5-v1_1-base) or from a version specifically tailored for Lan-

[6]For more details please refer to (Shazeer and Stern, 2018), Section 8, titled "Relative Step Size"

Mixed Precision	Torch 2.0 compile	Grad Acc	Time per 1 Pre-training step	Total Pre-training time
FP32	No	2	~4.10s	~74.6h
TF32	No	2	~1.39s	~25.3h
BF16	No	2	~1.30s	~23.7h
TF32	Yes	2	~0.95s	~17.3h
BF16	Yes	1	~0.56s	~10.2h

Table 1: Efficiency metrics across various configuration settings during pre-training, with the "Total Pre-training Time" column referencing 2^{16} steps following the default config.

	Inverse-Square-Root	Cosine
Adafactor	1.995	1.993
AdamW	2.040	**1.953**

Table 2: Comparison of negative log-likelihood scores on the held-out set of C4 using different optimization methods and learning rate schedules.

guage Modelling (google/t5-base-lm-adapt). To cover all bases, we evaluated both, and successfully reproduced the original results.

Figure 1 presents a performance comparison of the model we trained in various time increments (ranging from 4 to 24 hours) against the original T5-base-v1.1 model weights from Huggingface Hub and its language modeling-adapted version. Notably, our model, trained for 16 hours on a single GPU, lagged by only 0.2 RougeL on average compared to the original T5-base-v1.1. This is an impressive result given the vast disparity in training data (the T5 paper indicates training on approximately 150x more data than we did). The language modeling-adapted checkpoint outperformed both the original T5-base-v1.1 model and ours, but this language modeling model adaptation extends beyond the scope of this study. A single fine-tuning step in our setup took approximately 0.18s, culminating in roughly an hour for the entire fine-tuning process.

4.3 Efficiency Statistics

Table 1 showcases the efficiency metrics from our pre-training experiments. It details the time taken for a single pre-training step and the overall pre-training time based on our default configuration desribed in Section 3.2. A noteworthy observation is that, because of the large batch size (128) used for pre-training, for numerical precisions other than BF16 we need to increase the number of gradient accumulation steps from 1 to 2.

Attempts at Boosting Efficiency In our pursuit of efficiency, we experimented with various strategies, albeit with limited success:

- **Optimization Algorithms**: We assessed the performance of recent optimizers like Lion (Chen et al., 2023) and Sophia (Liu et al., 2023). However, neither outperformed the AdamW with RMS scaling.

- **Positional Embeddings**: We tried replacing T5's learned relative positional embeddings with ALiBi (Press et al., 2021). Although such a switch had the potential to reduce the number of parameters, leading to faster training and inference rates, and paving the way for integrating Flash Attention (Dao et al., 2022) (currently limited to non-parametric bias), our trials revealed that training with ALiBi was more volatile and yielded suboptimal pre-training loss.

- **FP16 Precision**: Unfortunately, all our attempts using FP16 precision consistently diverged.

5 Conclusions

In this study, we demonstrated the feasibility of pre-training a substantial model like T5 under resource constraints, specifically using a single A100 GPU within a 24-hour timeframe. Through selection of optimization methods and configurations, we achieved results comparable to large-scale training settings. Our intention in sharing the codebase, configurations, and training logs is to bridge the gap between research accessibility and computational resource limitations in the NLP domain. We invite and welcome community suggestions to further refine and enhance our approach.

Moving forward, we aim to enrich our codebase by incorporating additional training objectives, such as those suggested by (Tworkowski et al., 2023; Tay et al., 2022), in hopes of further optimizing the training pipeline.

Acknowledgements

This work was supported by the UKRI Centre for Doctoral Training in Natural Language Processing, funded by the UKRI (grant EP/S022481/1) and the University of Edinburgh, School of Informatics and School of Philosophy, Psychology & Language Sciences.

References

Tom B. Brown, Benjamin Mann, Nick Ryder, Melanie Subbiah, Jared Kaplan, Prafulla Dhariwal, Arvind Neelakantan, Pranav Shyam, Girish Sastry, Amanda Askell, Sandhini Agarwal, Ariel Herbert-Voss, Gretchen Krueger, T. J. Henighan, Rewon Child, Aditya Ramesh, Daniel M. Ziegler, Jeff Wu, Clemens Winter, Christopher Hesse, Mark Chen, Eric Sigler, Mateusz Litwin, Scott Gray, Benjamin Chess, Jack Clark, Christopher Berner, Sam McCandlish, Alec Radford, Ilya Sutskever, and Dario Amodei. 2020. Language models are few-shot learners. *ArXiv*, abs/2005.14165.

Xiangning Chen, Chen Liang, Da Huang, Esteban Real, Kaiyuan Wang, Yao Liu, Hieu Pham, Xuanyi Dong, Thang Luong, Cho-Jui Hsieh, Yifeng Lu, and Quoc V. Le. 2023. Symbolic discovery of optimization algorithms. *ArXiv*, abs/2302.06675.

Aakanksha Chowdhery, Sharan Narang, Jacob Devlin, Maarten Bosma, Gaurav Mishra, Adam Roberts, Paul Barham, Hyung Won Chung, Charles Sutton, Sebastian Gehrmann, Parker Schuh, Kensen Shi, Sasha Tsvyashchenko, Joshua Maynez, Abhishek Rao, Parker Barnes, Yi Tay, Noam M. Shazeer, Vinodkumar Prabhakaran, Emily Reif, Nan Du, Benton C. Hutchinson, Reiner Pope, James Bradbury, Jacob Austin, Michael Isard, Guy Gur-Ari, Pengcheng Yin, Toju Duke, Anselm Levskaya, Sanjay Ghemawat, Sunipa Dev, Henryk Michalewski, Xavier García, Vedant Misra, Kevin Robinson, Liam Fedus, Denny Zhou, Daphne Ippolito, David Luan, Hyeontaek Lim, Barret Zoph, Alexander Spiridonov, Ryan Sepassi, David Dohan, Shivani Agrawal, Mark Omernick, Andrew M. Dai, Thanumalayan Sankaranarayana Pillai, Marie Pellat, Aitor Lewkowycz, Erica Moreira, Rewon Child, Oleksandr Polozov, Katherine Lee, Zongwei Zhou, Xuezhi Wang, Brennan Saeta, Mark Díaz, Orhan Firat, Michele Catasta, Jason Wei, Kathleen S. Meier-Hellstern, Douglas Eck, Jeff Dean, Slav Petrov, and Noah Fiedel. 2022. Palm: Scaling language modeling with pathways. *ArXiv*, abs/2204.02311.

Hyung Won Chung, Le Hou, S. Longpre, Barret Zoph, Yi Tay, William Fedus, Eric Li, Xuezhi Wang, Mostafa Dehghani, Siddhartha Brahma, Albert Webson, Shixiang Shane Gu, Zhuyun Dai, Mirac Suzgun, Xinyun Chen, Aakanksha Chowdhery, Dasha Valter, Sharan Narang, Gaurav Mishra, Adams Wei Yu, Vincent Zhao, Yanping Huang, Andrew M. Dai, Hongkun Yu, Slav Petrov, Ed Huai hsin Chi, Jeff Dean, Jacob Devlin, Adam Roberts, Denny Zhou, Quoc V. Le, and Jason Wei. 2022. Scaling instruction-finetuned language models. *ArXiv*, abs/2210.11416.

Tri Dao, Daniel Y. Fu, Stefano Ermon, Atri Rudra, and Christopher R'e. 2022. Flashattention: Fast and memory-efficient exact attention with io-awareness. *ArXiv*, abs/2205.14135.

Jacob Devlin, Ming-Wei Chang, Kenton Lee, and Kristina Toutanova. 2019. Bert: Pre-training of deep bidirectional transformers for language understanding. *ArXiv*, abs/1810.04805.

Jonas Geiping and Tom Goldstein. 2022. Cramming: Training a language model on a single gpu in one day. *ArXiv*, abs/2212.14034.

Yeb Havinga. Pre-training dutch t5 models.

Jean Kaddour, Oscar Key, Piotr Nawrot, Pasquale Minervini, and Matt J. Kusner. 2023. No train no gain: Revisiting efficient training algorithms for transformer-based language models. *ArXiv*, abs/2307.06440.

Andrej Karpathy. 2021. nanogpt. `https://github.com/karpathy/nanoGPT`. GitHub repository.

Hong Liu, Zhiyuan Li, David Leo Wright Hall, Percy Liang, and Tengyu Ma. 2023. Sophia: A scalable stochastic second-order optimizer for language model pre-training. *ArXiv*, abs/2305.14342.

Ilya Loshchilov and Frank Hutter. 2017. Decoupled weight decay regularization. In *International Conference on Learning Representations*.

Paulius Micikevicius, Sharan Narang, Jonah Alben, Gregory Frederick Diamos, Erich Elsen, David García, Boris Ginsburg, Michael Houston, Oleksii Kuchaiev, Ganesh Venkatesh, and Hao Wu. 2017. Mixed precision training. *ArXiv*, abs/1710.03740.

Sharan Narang, Hyung Won Chung, Yi Tay, William Fedus, Thibault Févry, Michael Matena, Karishma Malkan, Noah Fiedel, Noam M. Shazeer, Zhenzhong Lan, Yanqi Zhou, Wei Li, Nan Ding, Jake Marcus, Adam Roberts, and Colin Raffel. 2021. Do transformer modifications transfer across implementations and applications? *ArXiv*, abs/2102.11972.

Piotr Nawrot, Jan Chorowski, Adrian La'ncucki, and E. Ponti. 2022. Efficient transformers with dynamic token pooling. In *Annual Meeting of the Association for Computational Linguistics*.

Neptune team. 2019. neptune.ai.

Adam Paszke, Sam Gross, Francisco Massa, Adam Lerer, James Bradbury, Gregory Chanan, Trevor Killeen, Zeming Lin, Natalia Gimelshein, Luca Antiga, Alban Desmaison, Andreas Kopf, Edward Yang, Zachary DeVito, Martin Raison, Alykhan Tejani, Sasank Chilamkurthy, Benoit Steiner, Lu Fang,

Junjie Bai, and Soumith Chintala. 2019. PyTorch: An Imperative Style, High-Performance Deep Learning Library. In *Advances in Neural Information Processing Systems 32*, pages 8024–8035. Curran Associates, Inc.

Ofir Press, Noah A. Smith, and Mike Lewis. 2021. Train short, test long: Attention with linear biases enables input length extrapolation. *ArXiv*, abs/2108.12409.

Colin Raffel, Noam M. Shazeer, Adam Roberts, Katherine Lee, Sharan Narang, Michael Matena, Yanqi Zhou, Wei Li, and Peter J. Liu. 2019. Exploring the limits of transfer learning with a unified text-to-text transformer. *ArXiv*, abs/1910.10683.

Teven Le Scao, Angela Fan, Christopher Akiki, Elizabeth-Jane Pavlick, Suzana Ili'c, Daniel Hesslow, Roman Castagn'e, Alexandra Sasha Luccioni, Franccois Yvon, Matthias Gallé, Jonathan Tow, Alexander M. Rush, Stella Rose Biderman, Albert Webson, Pawan Sasanka Ammanamanchi, Thomas Wang, Benoît Sagot, Niklas Muennighoff, Albert Villanova del Moral, Olatunji Ruwase, Rachel Bawden, Stas Bekman, Angelina McMillan-Major, Iz Beltagy, Huu Nguyen, Lucile Saulnier, Samson Tan, Pedro Ortiz Suarez, Victor Sanh, Hugo Laurenccon, Yacine Jernite, Julien Launay, Margaret Mitchell, Colin Raffel, Aaron Gokaslan, Adi Simhi, Aitor Soroa Etxabe, Alham Fikri Aji, Amit Alfassy, Anna Rogers, Ariel Kreisberg Nitzav, Canwen Xu, Chenghao Mou, Chris C. Emezue, Christopher Klamm, Colin Leong, Daniel Alexander van Strien, David Ifeoluwa Adelani, Dragomir R. Radev, Eduardo Gonz'alez Ponferrada, Efrat Levkovizh, Ethan Kim, Eyal Bar Natan, Francesco De Toni, Gérard Dupont, Germán Kruszewski, Giada Pistilli, Hady ElSahar, Hamza Benyamina, Hieu Trung Tran, Ian Yu, Idris Abdulmumin, Isaac Johnson, Itziar Gonzalez-Dios, Javier de la Rosa, Jenny Chim, Jesse Dodge, Jian Zhu, Jonathan Chang, Jorg Frohberg, Josephine L. Tobing, Joydeep Bhattacharjee, Khalid Almubarak, Kimbo Chen, Kyle Lo, Leandro von Werra, Leon Weber, Long Phan, Loubna Ben Allal, Ludovic Tanguy, Manan Dey, Manuel Romero Muñoz, Maraim Masoud, Mar'ia Grandury, Mario vSavsko, Max Huang, Maximin Coavoux, Mayank Singh, Mike Tian-Jian Jiang, Minh Chien Vu, Mohammad Ali Jauhar, Mustafa Ghaleb, Nishant Subramani, Nora Kassner, Nurulaqilla Khamis, Olivier Nguyen, Omar Espejel, Ona de Gibert, Paulo Villegas, Peter Henderson, Pierre Colombo, Priscilla Amuok, Quentin Lhoest, Rheza Harliman, Rishi Bommasani, Roberto L'opez, Rui Ribeiro, Salomey Osei, Sampo Pyysalo, Sebastian Nagel, Shamik Bose, Shamsuddeen Hassan Muhammad, Shanya Sharma, S. Longpre, Somaieh Nikpoor, Stanislav Silberberg, Suhas Pai, Sydney Zink, Tiago Timponi Torrent, Timo Schick, Tristan Thrush, Valentin Danchev, Vassilina Nikoulina, Veronika Laippala, Violette Lepercq, Vrinda Prabhu, Zaid Alyafeai, Zeerak Talat, Arun Raja, Benjamin Heinzerling, Chenglei Si, Elizabeth Salesky, Sabrina J. Mielke, Wilson Y. Lee, Abheesht Sharma, Andrea Santilli, Antoine Chaffin, Arnaud Stiegler, Debajyoti Datta, Eliza Szczechla, Gunjan Chhablani, Han Wang, Harshit Pandey, Hendrik Strobelt, Jason Alan Fries, Jos Rozen, Leo Gao, Lintang Sutawika, M Saiful Bari, Maged S. Al-shaibani, Matteo Manica, Nihal V. Nayak, Ryan Teehan, Samuel Albanie, Sheng Shen, Srulik Ben-David, Stephen H. Bach, Taewoon Kim, Tali Bers, Thibault Févry, Trishala Neeraj, Urmish Thakker, Vikas Raunak, Xiang Tang, Zheng Xin Yong, Zhiqing Sun, Shaked Brody, Y Uri, Hadar Tojarieh, Adam Roberts, Hyung Won Chung, Jaesung Tae, Jason Phang, Ofir Press, Conglong Li, Deepak Narayanan, Hatim Bourfoune, Jared Casper, Jeff Rasley, Max Ryabinin, Mayank Mishra, Minjia Zhang, Mohammad Shoeybi, Myriam Peyrounette, Nicolas Patry, Nouamane Tazi, Omar Sanseviero, Patrick von Platen, Pierre Cornette, Pierre Franccois Lavall'ee, Rémi Lacroix, Samyam Rajbhandari, Sanchit Gandhi, Shaden Smith, Stéphane Requena, Suraj Patil, Tim Dettmers, Ahmed Baruwa, Amanpreet Singh, Anastasia Cheveleva, Anne-Laure Ligozat, Arjun Subramonian, Aur'elie N'ev'eol, Charles Lovering, Daniel H Garrette, Deepak R. Tunuguntla, Ehud Reiter, Ekaterina Taktasheva, Ekaterina Voloshina, Eli Bogdanov, Genta Indra Winata, Hailey Schoelkopf, Jan-Christoph Kalo, Jekaterina Novikova, Jessica Zosa Forde, Xiangru Tang, Jungo Kasai, Ken Kawamura, Liam Hazan, Marine Carpuat, Miruna Clinciu, Najoung Kim, Newton Cheng, Oleg Serikov, Omer Antverg, Oskar van der Wal, Rui Zhang, Ruochen Zhang, Sebastian Gehrmann, S. Osher Pais, Tatiana Shavrina, Thomas Scialom, Tian Yun, Tomasz Limisiewicz, Verena Rieser, Vitaly Protasov, Vladislav Mikhailov, Yada Pruksachatkun, Yonatan Belinkov, Zachary Bamberger, Zdenvek Kasner, Alice Rueda, Amanda Pestana, Amir Feizpour, Ammar Khan, Amy Faranak, Ananda Santa Rosa Santos, Anthony Hevia, Antigona Unldreaj, Arash Aghagol, Arezoo Abdollahi, Aycha Tammour, Azadeh HajiHosseini, Bahareh Behroozi, Benjamin Olusola Ajibade, Bharat Kumar Saxena, Carlos Muñoz Ferrandis, Danish Contractor, David M. Lansky, Davis David, Douwe Kiela, Duong Anh Nguyen, Edward Tan, Emily Baylor, Ezinwanne Ozoani, Fatim T Mirza, Frankline Ononiwu, Habib Rezanejad, H.A. Jones, Indrani Bhattacharya, Irene Solaiman, Irina Sedenko, Isar Nejadgholi, Jan Passmore, Joshua Seltzer, Julio Bonis Sanz, Karen Fort, Lívia Macedo Dutra, Mairon Samagaio, Maraim Elbadri, Margot Mieskes, Marissa Gerchick, Martha Akinlolu, Michael McKenna, Mike Qiu, M. K. K. Ghauri, Mykola Burynok, Nafis Abrar, Nazneen Rajani, Nour Elkott, Nourhan Fahmy, Olanrewaju Samuel, Ran An, R. P. Kromann, Ryan Hao, Samira Alizadeh, Sarmad Shubber, Silas L. Wang, Sourav Roy, Sylvain Viguier, Thanh-Cong Le, Tobi Oyebade, Trieu Nguyen Hai Le, Yoyo Yang, Zachary Kyle Nguyen, Abhinav Ramesh Kashyap, Alfredo Palasciano, Alison Callahan, Anima Shukla, Antonio Miranda-Escalada, Ayush Kumar Singh, Benjamin Beilharz, Bo Wang, Caio Matheus Fonseca de Brito, Chenxi Zhou, Chirag Jain, Chuxin Xu, Clémentine Fourrier, Daniel Le'on Perin'an, Daniel Molano, Dian Yu, Enrique Manjavacas, Fabio

Barth, Florian Fuhrimann, Gabriel Altay, Giyaseddin Bayrak, Gully A. Burns, Helena U. Vrabec, Iman I.B. Bello, Isha Dash, Ji Soo Kang, John Giorgi, Jonas Golde, Jose David Posada, Karthi Sivaraman, Lokesh Bulchandani, Lu Liu, Luisa Shinzato, Madeleine Hahn de Bykhovetz, Maiko Takeuchi, Marc Pàmies, María Andrea Castillo, Marianna Nezhurina, Mario Sanger, Matthias Samwald, Michael Cullan, Michael Weinberg, M Wolf, Mina Mihaljcic, Minna Liu, Moritz Freidank, Myungsun Kang, Natasha Seelam, Nathan Dahlberg, Nicholas Michio Broad, Nikolaus Muellner, Pascale Fung, Patricia Haller, R. Chandrasekhar, R. Eisenberg, Robert Martin, Rodrigo L. Canalli, Rosaline Su, Ruisi Su, Samuel Cahyawijaya, Samuele Garda, Shlok S Deshmukh, Shubhanshu Mishra, Sid Kiblawi, Simon Ott, Sinee Sang-aroonsiri, Srishti Kumar, Stefan Schweter, Sushil Pratap Bharati, T. A. Laud, Th'eo Gigant, Tomoya Kainuma, Wojciech Kusa, Yanis Labrak, Yashasvi Bajaj, Y. Venkatraman, Yifan Xu, Ying Xu, Yun chao Xu, Zhee Xao Tan, Zhongli Xie, Zifan Ye, Mathilde Bras, Younes Belkada, and Thomas Wolf. 2022. Bloom: A 176b-parameter open-access multilingual language model. *ArXiv*, abs/2211.05100.

Mike Schuster and Kaisuke Nakajima. 2012. Japanese and Korean voice search. In *2012 IEEE International Conference on Acoustics, Speech and Signal Processing (ICASSP)*, pages 5149–5152.

Noam M. Shazeer. 2020. Glu variants improve transformer. *ArXiv*, abs/2002.05202.

Noam M. Shazeer, Azalia Mirhoseini, Krzysztof Maziarz, Andy Davis, Quoc V. Le, Geoffrey E. Hinton, and Jeff Dean. 2017. Outrageously large neural networks: The sparsely-gated mixture-of-experts layer. *ArXiv*, abs/1701.06538.

Noam M. Shazeer and Mitchell Stern. 2018. Adafactor: Adaptive learning rates with sublinear memory cost. *ArXiv*, abs/1804.04235.

Thomas Wolf Philipp Schmid Zachary Mueller Sourab Mangrulkar Marc Sun Benjamin Bossan Sylvain Gugger, Lysandre Debut. 2022. Accelerate: Training and inference at scale made simple, efficient and adaptable. `https://github.com/huggingface/accelerate`.

Yi Tay, Mostafa Dehghani, Vinh Q. Tran, Xavier García, Jason Wei, Xuezhi Wang, Hyung Won Chung, Dara Bahri, Tal Schuster, Huaixiu Steven Zheng, Denny Zhou, Neil Houlsby, and Donald Metzler. 2022. Ul2: Unifying language learning paradigms. In *International Conference on Learning Representations*.

Szymon Tworkowski, Konrad Staniszewski, Mikolaj Pacek, Yuhuai Wu, Henryk Michalewski, and Piotr Milo's. 2023. Focused transformer: Contrastive training for context scaling. *ArXiv*, abs/2307.03170.

Yizhong Wang, Swaroop Mishra, Pegah Alipoormolabashi, Yeganeh Kordi, Amirreza Mirzaei, Anjana Arunkumar, Arjun Ashok, Arut Selvan Dhanasekaran, Atharva Naik, David Stap, Eshaan Pathak, Giannis Karamanolakis, Haizhi Gary Lai, Ishan Purohit, Ishani Mondal, Jacob Anderson, Kirby Kuznia, Krima Doshi, Maitreya Patel, Kuntal Kumar Pal, M. Moradshahi, Mihir Parmar, Mirali Purohit, Neeraj Varshney, Phani Rohitha Kaza, Pulkit Verma, Ravsehaj Singh Puri, Rushang Karia, Shailaja Keyur Sampat, Savan Doshi, Siddharth Deepak Mishra, Sujan Reddy, Sumanta Patro, Tanay Dixit, Xudong Shen, Chitta Baral, Yejin Choi, Noah A. Smith, Hanna Hajishirzi, and Daniel Khashabi. 2022. Supernaturalinstructions: Generalization via declarative instructions on 1600+ nlp tasks. In *Conference on Empirical Methods in Natural Language Processing*.

Omry Yadan. 2019. Hydra - a framework for elegantly configuring complex applications. Github.

AWARE-TEXT: An Android Package for Mobile Phone Based Text Collection and On-Device Processing

Salvatore Giorgi[1,2,*], **Garrick Sherman**[1,*], **Douglas Bellew**[1],
Sharath Chandra Guntuku[2], **Lyle Ungar**[2] and **Brenda Curtis**[1]
[1]National Institute on Drug Abuse, [2]University of Pennsylvania
{sal.giorgi, garrick.sherman, doug.bellew, brenda.curtis}@nih.gov
{sharathg, ungar}@cis.upenn.edu

Abstract

We present the AWARE-TEXT package, an open-source software package for collecting textual data on Android mobile devices. This package allows for collecting short message service (SMS or text messages) and character-level keystrokes. In addition to collecting this raw data, AWARE-TEXT is designed for *on device* lexicon processing, which allows one to collect standard textual-based measures (e.g., sentiment, emotions, and topics) without collecting the underlying raw textual data. This is especially important in the case of mobile phones, which can contain sensitive and identifying information. Thus, the AWARE-TEXT package allows for privacy protection while simultaneously collecting textual information at multiple levels of granularity: person (lifetime history of SMS), conversation (both sides of SMS conversations and group chats), message (single SMS), and character (individual keystrokes entered across applications). Finally, the unique processing environment of mobile devices opens up several methodological and privacy issues, which we discuss.

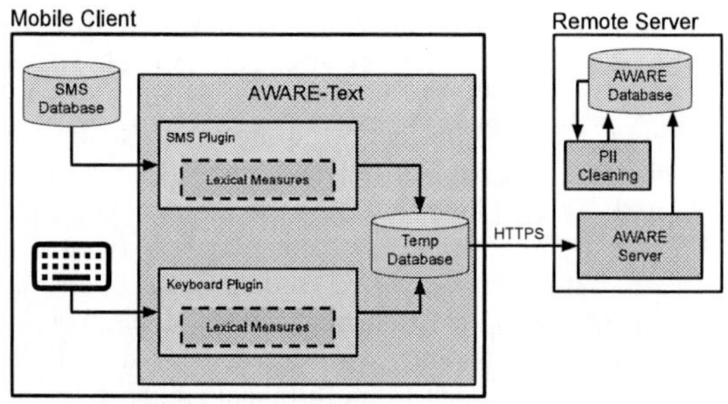

Figure 1: Data flow diagram. Data stored and collected on a mobile client is sent through AWARE-TEXT which then processes the textual data and transmits raw (i.e., raw SMS or keystrokes) and lexical data to a remote sever via a secure, encrypted connection. Privacy preserving methods are shown in red.

1 Introduction

Unlike traditional NLP tasks (e.g., machine translation or question answering), NLP in the context of psychological, social, and health sciences is aimed at understanding how textual data can characterize people. This includes stance or sarcasm at document-level (Lynn et al., 2019), state-level tasks, such as emotion prediction (Mohammad, 2016), trait-level tasks, such as personality prediction (Park et al., 2015) or mental health applications (De Choudhury and De, 2014), or even population-level tasks, for example, monitoring the opioid epidemic via social media data (Giorgi et al., 2023). Similarly, keystroke data (or typing dynamics, i.e., a succession of individual depressions on a keyboard) has been used to predict emotions (Epp et al., 2011) and cognition (Brizan et al., 2015). Historically, human-generated textual data for such social science-oriented tasks is collected from social media (e.g., Facebook, Reddit, or Twitter), open-ended survey questions (Kjell et al., 2022), or interviews (Son et al., 2023). However, more recently, short message service (SMS or text messaging) has received attention as a viable data source (Liu et al., 2023; Meyerhoff et al., 2023; Benoit et al., 2020; Nook et al., 2021; Stamatis et al., 2022a,b; Tlachac and Rundensteiner, 2020; Tlachac et al., 2022; Ameer et al., 2022). SMS, and, more generally, mobile phone-based data, is important for Just-in-Time Adaptive Interventions (JITAIs), which can be used to deliver personalized support and interventions in response to a person's changing physical and mental health (Nahum-Shani et al., 2018).

AWARE-TEXT[1] is an Android mobile phone application (or "app") built to collect passive mobile data (e.g., GPS locations and accelerometer data) with particular emphasis on textual[2] data

[*] Authors contributed equally.

[1]https://github.com/TTRUCurtis/aware-text

[2]To disambiguate *text messages* (or SMS) from *text data* (data in the form of written text), we use the term *textual data*

Proceedings of the 3rd Workshop for Natural Language Processing Open Source Software (NLP-OSS 2023), pages 102–109
December 6, 2023 ©2023 Association for Computational Linguistics

such as SMS and keystrokes. This app allows researchers to collect raw textual data, both historical data and prospective data *in real time*, as well as lexical-based measures calculated on the device. On-device processing of lexical-based measures, such as sentiment or topics, inherently preserves privacy: summary scores (e.g., sentiment) are transmitted to a remote server and the underlying raw data, which can be highly sensitive and contain personally identifiable information (PII), does not need to leave the mobile device.

In summary, AWARE-TEXT focuses on two types of textual data (SMS data and keyboard input) across four levels of granularity (person, conversation, message, and character). Across all data types and levels AWARE-TEXT offers the ability to collect raw data as well as lexical measures, which inherently preserve privacy, as shown in Figure 2. This package offers researchers the ability to collect fine-grained textual data which can be used to gain insight into tasks across natural language processing, psychology, computational social sciences, and psycho-linguistics.

2 Overall System Design

The AWARE-TEXT package is an extension of the AWARE mobile sensing framework, an open-source package developed to passively collect mobile phone sensor data, such as accelerometer, gyroscope, and GPS data (Ferreira et al., 2015). This extension consists of two on-device plugins (to collect SMS data and process lexical measures) and a series of post-processing scripts for data aggregation and cleaning. Thus, AWARE-TEXT is able to collect everything AWARE is able to collect, plus additional textual data. While the AWARE framework is available for both iOS and Android devices, the AWARE-TEXT package is only available on Android devices due to iOS restrictions on access to raw SMS and keyboard data.

The high-level features of AWARE-TEXT are shown in Figure 1. Here we see that AWARE-TEXT pulls data from both the mobile device's keyboard and local SMS database (described below). Both data types are then optionally processed into lexical measures, after which the raw and processed lexical data are stored in a temporary local database. This data is transferred (via a secure HTTPS connection) to a remote server and stored in a final database. AWARE-TEXT is designed to

when referring to data in text form.

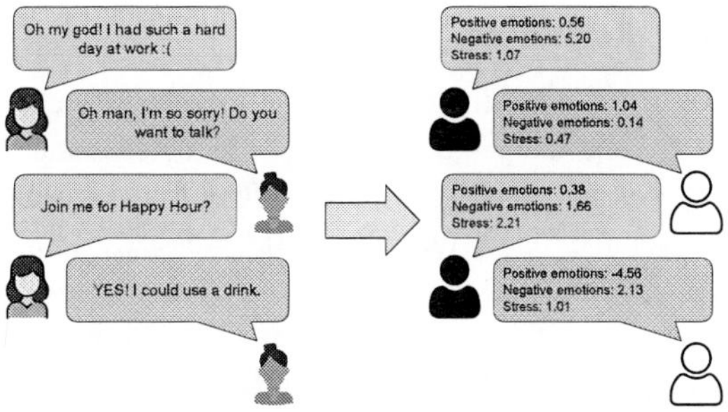

Figure 2: AWARE-TEXT has anonymized both people in the conversation and the exact text written within each utterance, while preserving the conversation structure.

optimally transfer data whenever wifi connections are available to minimize the amount of cellular data the application uses. The temporary database is then cleared so as not to duplicate data.

3 Data Types

AWARE-TEXT collects two types of raw text data: SMS and keystrokes. While the keystroke data is available in the original AWARE implementation, the keystrokes lexical processing is novel to AWARE-TEXT, as is the SMS collection.

3.1 SMS

SMS data includes traditional SMS and more recent types of messaging, including MMS (Multimedia Messaging Service) and RCS (Rich Communication Services). This includes group messages (text messages between three or more people) and reactions to messages, such as emojis. Each message is timestamped to indicate the time sent or received. We note that only textual data is collected, and no images or audio files are stored. Finally, information on who is on the opposite end of the received or sent SMS is stored via a hashed identifier. This is done in such as way that hashes are consistent across communications, which enables one to reconstruct conversations or identify SMS messages sent to a particular (non-identifiable) person.

SMS collection can occur retrospectively (the complete history of SMS stored on the mobile device) and prospectively (all SMS messages exchanged while AWARE-TEXT is running). Additionally, SMS is collected from both the person running AWARE-TEXT on their device (i.e., sent messages) as well as from others (i.e., all received messages). Data collection is fully configurable, and all combinations of retrospective/prospective and sent/received are available.

3.2 Keystrokes

Keystrokes are single depressions of a key on a keyboard and include non-standard characters such as deletions and auto-completes, along with information on the time between each key press. Keystroke data is collected per application. This allows one to measure typing dynamics in applications such as Facebook Messenger or the local web browser. For example (as seen in Table 1), if a user searched "Taylor Swift'", while misspelling the name, then AWARE-TEXT would collect rows for each of "T", "Ta", "Tai", "Ta" (i.e., a deletion occurred), "Tay", etc. No passwords are collected via AWARE-TEXT. Finally, we note that when applying lexical measures to the keystroke data, we only consider the complete keyboard input for a single typing session (for example, input to a search engine) instead of running lexica across each character.

Device ID	Timestamp	Application Name	Before Text	After Text
1	08/06/2023 12:46:56	Chrome		T
1	08/06/2023 12:46:57	Chrome	T	Ta
1	08/06/2023 12:46:58	Chrome	Ta	Tai
1	08/06/2023 12:46:58	Chrome	Tai	Ta
1	08/06/2023 12:46:59	Chrome	Ta	Tay
2	08/12/2023 07:02:23	Instagram		p
2	08/12/2023 07:02:23	Instagram	p	pi
2	08/12/2023 07:02:23	Instagram	pi	piz
2	08/12/2023 07:02:24	Instagram	piz	pizza

Table 1: Example keystroke data. Each row contains a single depression of a key on the keyboard and includes both the current text and the previous text, allowing one to easily identify deletions and autocompletes.

4 Levels of Data Collection

AWARE-TEXT has been designed to enable analysis of textual data at various levels of granularity: person, conversation, messages, and characters. This is true of both raw data and lexical measures. This flexibility is enabled by collecting data at a low level and preserving summary statistics that may be aggregated to higher levels of analysis.

Person-level data is available by aggregating raw text (SMS or keystrokes) or lexical measures across a person's individual inputs (for example, their lifetime SMS history). Conversations can be constructed by combining SMS data between pairs and groups of people. This can include SMS from non-consenting individuals (see Ethical considerations below). Message data (raw or lexical) is obtained by single SMS or complete keyboard input and is the most basic unit available for lexical measures. Finally, raw character-level data is obtained through keystroke inputs.

5 Privacy Preserving Lexical Measures

Running lexical measures *on the device* allows researchers the ability to collect data across each SMS or keystroke without necessitating the collection of the underlying raw data. This raw data could include sensitive information (e.g., revealing search histories or SMS with PII) and data from non-consenting individuals (e.g., SMS from people communicating with the study participant). As shown in Figure 2, the lexical measures can be applied to both ends of the conversation, thus obfuscating both the *exact people* in the conversation and their *exact utterances* while still preserving both the overall conversation and individual turns within the conversation. While mobile phones can collect data in multiple languages, this tokenizer is designed for English text, and thus would need to be replaced for on-device processing of non-English languages.

Preprocessing Applications on the Android OS are Java and, more recently, Kotlin based. Therefore, we use a Java-based tokenizer from the Natural Language Processing for JVM languages (NLP4J) project[3] developed by EmoryNLP. While this tokenizer is not designed for noisy user-generated textual data such as SMS, several key features make it useful for this setting, such as emoji recognition.

Lexical Data Table 2 shows a sample of the SMS lexical data. Here we see both the Device ID (the mobile device running AWARE-TEXT) and the Contact ID as numeric or hashed identifiers, thus removing any identifying information. Total Words and Lexicon Words are, respectively, defined as the total number of words in the message and the number of words in the intersection between the message and the lexicon. This allows one to normalize the lexicon score in various ways. Additionally, this allows one to aggregate scores across levels. For example, one could aggregate the *stress* scores across messages in a given day, normalized using the Total Words, to produce a daily *stress* score. Similarly, this can be done across people, conversations, or applications (via keystroke data).

[3]https://emorynlp.github.io/nlp4j/

Device ID	Lexicon Category	Total Words	Lexicon Words	Score	Contact ID	Type	Timestamp
1	stress	11	5	17.0798	9f27e	sent	08/06/2023 12:46:56
1	happiness	11	7	1.17805	9f27e	sent	08/06/2023 12:46:56
1	stress	4	1	0.382509	c3d17	received	08/07/2023 17:52:01
1	happiness	4	3	0.585531	c3d17	received	08/07/2023 17:52:01
2	loneliness	25	20	-45.5145	73e48;ca96d	sent	08/07/2023 01:43:12
2	life satisfaction	25	6	0.0454235	73e48;ca96d	sent	08/07/2023 01:43:12

Table 2: Example of lexical measures across the SMS data. Lexical measures include stress, happiness, loneliness, and life satisfaction. The person on the other end of the conversation is consistently hashed (e.g., 9f27e) in order to preserve conversations. Group messages include a list of all recipients. Total and Lexicon Words allow for different types of normalization, as well as the aggregation of category scores across time and people.

Post-processing Given the sensitive nature of the raw keystroke features, we include a post-processing script that can be automatically run on the remote AWARE server (Figure 1) to remove potentially identifying information. This script uses spaCy's Named Entity Recognizer and regular expressions[4] to remove mentions of names, numbers, places, etc. The explicit mentions are replaced with their respective category names (e.g., "Taylor Swift" is replaced with {NAME}), and the category names are backpropagated through the data to the first keypress in the explicit mention.

Data Aggregation The lexical data can be further post-processed using the open-source RAPIDS package (Vega et al., 2021). This package is used to process raw mobile sensing data in order to extract behavioral features. In particular, RAPIDS is designed to work with the AWARE and AWARE-TEXT apps. This package can be used to aggregate lexical measures across time, people, and applications and combinations of each. For example, RAPIDS can aggregate lexical measures across hours, days, or even applications and days together.

Prepackaged Lexical Measures AWARE-TEXT comes prepackaged with state-of-the-art lexica for measuring psychological well-being from textual data (see original publications for details): happiness (Giorgi et al., 2021), life satisfaction (Jaidka et al., 2020), loneliness (Guntuku et al., 2019b), politeness (Li et al., 2020), and stress (Guntuku et al., 2019a).

Extending the Lexical Measures The prepackaged lexical measures in AWARE-TEXT can be easily extended to include any measure that can be decomposed into a category with weighted words (note that weights can be trivially set to one for all words). For example, this can include Latent Dirichlet Allocation (LDA) topics, where weights are conditional probabilities estimated through the LDA process. This can also include other popular lexical measures such as LIWC (Pennebaker et al., 2001), the NRC Emotion/Valence-Arousal-Dominance/Sentiment lexica (Mohammad and Kiritchenko, 2015; Mohammad, 2018), and ANEW (Warriner et al., 2013).

6 Methodological Considerations

Running on-device computation opens up methodological and computational issues. First, while many NLP tools exist in Java, such as the Stanford CoreNLP toolkit (Manning et al., 2014), most modern libraries are written in Python, making them inaccessible in an Android environment. Thus, many new technologies, such as contextual embeddings, are unavailable for on-device processing. Second, one must consider the person using the device. For example, high computation can quickly drain the phone's battery or slow down other applications. Similarly, transferring large amounts of data to a re-

	Facebook	SMS
Age	.68	.45*
Gender†	.91	.80*
Depression	.36	.29
Life Satis.	.21	.14
Stress	.21	.18

Table 3: Product moment correlations (or † accuracy) between language estimates and self-reports across both platforms reported in Liu et al. (2023). * significant difference in bootstrapping test between the SMS and Facebook correlations.

[4]https://github.com/madisonmay/CommonRegex

	Open Source	SMS	Keystrokes	On-device Lexical Processing
AWARE-TEXT	✓	✓	✓	✓
AWARE (Ferreira et al., 2015)	✓		✓	
Beiwe (Onnela et al., 2021)	✓	✓		
EARS (Lind et al., 2018)		✓	✓	
Passive Data Kit (Audacious Software, 2018)	✓			✓
m-Path (Mestdagh et al., 2023)		✓		
mindLAMP (Torous et al., 2019)	✓	✓		

Table 4: Comparison of recent mobile sensing platforms in their textual data collecting capabilities. AWARE-TEXT is the only open-source app which collects multiple types of data while offering on-device processing.

mote server can quickly increase data usage and the user's mobile phone bill. These issues can cause participants to uninstall AWARE-TEXT which can lead to low study completion rates. Thus, algorithms should reduce run-time and throughput.

7 Case Study

To date, one study has used the AWARE-TEXT app with a sample of 120 participants who installed AWARE-TEXT, answered a series of self-reports, and shared Facebook language data. This study compared preexisting social media-based lexical models in their ability to predict self-reports when applied to out-of-domain textual data (Liu et al., 2023). It applied five models trained from Facebook language to predict self-reported age, gender, depression, life satisfaction, and stress. Each model was separately applied to SMS and Facebook posts, and the resulting model predictions were compared to self-reports. We report their findings in Table 3. The results from this study show that for three out of five models, the SMS-based predictions did not statistically differ from the Facebook-based predictions, indicating that SMS is a potential data source for investigating social-psychological traits of people. This paper represents a preliminary analysis, and further investigation is needed into the strengths and weaknesses of SMS data.

8 Comparison of Mobile Text Apps

There are several apps which allow for either SMS retrieval or keystroke logging. SMS retrieval apps are typically designed for personal use, such as data backups and phone transfers, such as SMS Backup & Restore[5], or legal discovery, such as Logikcull[6]. Finally, there are also apps used for survey collection via SMS, such as ODK[7]. These apps send questions and receive answers via SMS, and data collection is typically limited to retrieving the survey question responses. Keylogging apps are typically designed for the purpose of monitoring, such as Kidlogger[8] which allows parents to monitor their children's phone activity. Thus, most apps which collect this data are not used for general data collection and research purposes.

Apps which collect SMS or keystroke data that are designed for research purposes are typically in the domain of mobile phone–based sensing software. There are several popular apps in this domain which have been used for social scientific research. In Table 4, we summarize the textual data collecting capabilities of several apps (those updated since 2018[9]). We note that AWARE-TEXT is the only open-source app which collects multiple types of text data while offering on-device processing.

9 Conclusions

AWARE-TEXT is a novel data collection application for Android mobile phones designed to capture textual data through SMS and keystrokes. This application allows researchers to collect data from consenting participants at multiple levels of granularity (person, conversation, message, and character) with the additional ability to collect both raw and aggregate lexical measures which preserve privacy. Over 85% of Americans own smartphones, and a growing number identify as smartphone dependent (i.e., smartphone serves as their primary means of online access). Thus, mobile phones offer a rich data source, which can be used as a lens into the daily lives of large sections of the population.

[5] https://www.synctech.com.au/sms-backup-restore/
[6] https://www.logikcull.com/
[7] https://odk.org/
[8] https://kidlogger.net/
[9] https://w.wiki/7qPn

Ethical Considerations

While AWARE-TEXT allows one to collect anonymized data (in the form of lexical based measures) and offers post-processing cleaning scripts, it does offer the ability to collect raw data. Raw SMS and keystroke data can contain highly sensitive and identifying information, such as names and social security numbers. Similarly, passwords (while not collected in the keystroke data) can be found in SMS data. It also offers the ability to collect data from non-consenting individuals in the form of received SMS. While no identifying information is explicitly collected from these individuals (e.g., all mobile phone numbers are hashed), the SMS data may contain sensitive information. Working with such data therefore requires a high level of care.

Collecting SMS data across conversations involves collecting data from non-consenting individuals. As discussed above, AWARE-TEXT offers the ability to collect de-identified lexical features as opposed to the underlying raw data. If the raw SMS data must be collected then AWARE-TEXT offers post-processing scripts that attempt to automatically remove sensitive and identifying information, which we *highly* recommend using. The resulting text (associated to an individual only with a hashed identifier) may be considered de-identified and, therefore, might not always be considered human subjects research. These distinctions should ultimately be decided by an Institutional Review Board. Note that further privacy preserving actions can be taken in order to help ensure equitable data collection. One study which collected both sides of SMS conversations (Song et al., 2014), offered participants the ability to remove or alter text and asked participants to consider the preferences of their conversation partners when removing sensitive text[10].

While outside of the scope of the AWARE-TEXT app, when storing this data on remote servers we recommended following standard security protocols such limited access, encryption, and two factor authentication. When collecting other measures from participants (such as surveys, demographics, or medical records), we recommend that raw data from AWARE-TEXT be stored separately and, if possible, on separate machines.

Mobile sensing, in general, opens up several ethical and privacy issues, especially in the context of health or when used to collect data from vulnerable populations; see Breslin et al. (2019) and Fuller et al. (2017) for in-depth discussions on such issues. At a minimum, we believe all uses of AWARE-TEXT should obtain approval from an ethical review board (e.g., Institutional Review Board or Ethics Committee). Similarly, researchers should follow informed consent principals when recruiting study participants.

[10]This study did not use AWARE-TEXT.

Acknowledgements

This research was supported by the Intramural Research Program of the NIH, NIDA (ZIA DA000628). We thank Olivia Dodge and Miguel Galván for their programming expertise. We also thank both Denzil Ferreira and the AWARE team, as well as Julio Vega and the RAPIDS team for their guidance.

References

Iqra Ameer, Grigori Sidorov, Helena Gomez-Adorno, and Rao Muhammad Adeel Nawab. 2022. Multi-label emotion classification on code-mixed text: Data and methods. *IEEE Access*, 10:8779–8789.

Audacious Software. 2018. Passive data kit. https://passivedatakit.org/.

James Benoit, Henry K. Onyeaka, Matcheri S. Keshavan, and John B Torous. 2020. Systematic review of digital phenotyping and machine learning in psychosis spectrum illnesses. *Harvard Review of Psychiatry*, 28:296 – 304.

Samantha Breslin, Martine Shareck, and Daniel Fuller. 2019. Research ethics for mobile sensing device use by vulnerable populations. *Social Science & Medicine*, 232:50–57.

David Guy Brizan, Adam Goodkind, Patrick Koch, Kiran Balagani, Vir V Phoha, and Andrew Rosenberg. 2015. Utilizing linguistically enhanced keystroke dynamics to predict typist cognition and demographics. *International Journal of Human-Computer Studies*, 82:57–68.

Munmun De Choudhury and Sushovan De. 2014. Mental health discourse on reddit: Self-disclosure, social support, and anonymity. In *Proceedings of the international AAAI conference on web and social media*, volume 8, pages 71–80.

Clayton Epp, Michael Lippold, and Regan L Mandryk. 2011. Identifying emotional states using keystroke dynamics. In *Proceedings of the sigchi conference on human factors in computing systems*, pages 715–724.

Denzil Ferreira, Vassilis Kostakos, and Anind K Dey. 2015. Aware: mobile context instrumentation framework. *Frontiers in ICT*, 2:6.

Daniel Fuller, Martine Shareck, and Kevin Stanley. 2017. Ethical implications of location and accelerometer measurement in health research studies with mobile sensing devices. *Social Science & Medicine*, 191:84–88.

Salvatore Giorgi, Sharath Chandra Guntuku, Johannes C Eichstaedt, Claire Pajot, H Andrew Schwartz, and Lyle H Ungar. 2021. Well-being depends on social comparison: Hierarchical models of twitter language suggest that richer neighbors make you less happy. In *Proceedings of the International AAAI Conference on Web and Social Media*, volume 15, pages 1069–1074.

Salvatore Giorgi, David B Yaden, Johannes C Eichstaedt, Lyle H Ungar, H Andrew Schwartz, Amy Kwarteng, and Brenda Curtis. 2023. Predicting us county opioid poisoning mortality from multi-modal social media and psychological self-report data. *Scientific reports*, 13(1):9027.

Sharath Chandra Guntuku, Anneke Buffone, Kokil Jaidka, Johannes C Eichstaedt, and Lyle H Ungar. 2019a. Understanding and measuring psychological stress using social media. In *Proceedings of the international AAAI conference on web and social media*, volume 13, pages 214–225.

Sharath Chandra Guntuku, Rachelle Schneider, Arthur Pelullo, Jami Young, Vivien Wong, Lyle Ungar, Daniel Polsky, Kevin G Volpp, and Raina Merchant. 2019b. Studying expressions of loneliness in individuals using twitter: an observational study. *BMJ open*, 9(11):e030355.

Kokil Jaidka, Salvatore Giorgi, H Andrew Schwartz, Margaret L Kern, Lyle H Ungar, and Johannes C Eichstaedt. 2020. Estimating geographic subjective well-being from twitter: A comparison of dictionary and data-driven language methods. *Proceedings of the National Academy of Sciences*, 117(19):10165–10171.

Oscar NE Kjell, Sverker Sikström, Katarina Kjell, and H Andrew Schwartz. 2022. Natural language analyzed with ai-based transformers predict traditional subjective well-being measures approaching the theoretical upper limits in accuracy. *Scientific reports*, 12(1):3918.

Mingyang Li, Louis Hickman, Louis Tay, Lyle Ungar, and Sharath Chandra Guntuku. 2020. Studying politeness across cultures using english twitter and mandarin weibo. *Proceedings of the ACM on Human-Computer Interaction*, 4(CSCW2):1–15.

Monika N Lind, Michelle L Byrne, Geordie Wicks, Alec M Smidt, and Nicholas B Allen. 2018. The effortless assessment of risk states (ears) tool: An interpersonal approach to mobile sensing. *JMIR Mental Health*, 5(3):e10334.

Tingting Liu, Salvatore Giorgi, Xiangyu Tao, Sharath Chandra Guntuku, Douglas Bellew, Brenda Curtis, and Lyle Ungar. 2023. Different affordances on facebook and sms text messaging do not impede generalization of language-based predictive models. *Proceedings of the International AAAI Conference on Web and Social Media*, 17(1):1153–1157.

Veronica Lynn, Salvatore Giorgi, Niranjan Balasubramanian, and H Andrew Schwartz. 2019. Tweet classification without the tweet: An empirical examination of user versus document attributes. In *Proceedings of the third workshop on natural language processing and computational social science*, pages 18–28.

Christopher D Manning, Mihai Surdeanu, John Bauer, Jenny Rose Finkel, Steven Bethard, and David McClosky. 2014. The stanford corenlp natural language processing toolkit. In *Proceedings of 52nd annual meeting of the association for computational linguistics: system demonstrations*, pages 55–60.

Merijn Mestdagh, Stijn Verdonck, Maarten Piot, Koen Niemeijer, Ghijs Kilani, Francis Tuerlinckx, Peter Kuppens, and Egon Dejonckheere. 2023. m-path: an easy-to-use and highly tailorable platform for ecological momentary assessment and intervention in behavioral research and clinical practice. *Frontiers in Digital Health*, 5.

Jonah Meyerhoff, Tingting Liu, Caitlin A. Stamatis, Tony Liu, Harry Wang, Yixuan Meng, Brenda L. Curtis, Chris J. Karr, Garrick T. Sherman, Pallavi V. Kulkarni, and David C. Mohr. 2023. Analyzing text message linguistic features: Do people with depression communicate differently with their close and non-close contacts? *Behaviour research and therapy*, 166:104342.

Saif Mohammad. 2018. Obtaining reliable human ratings of valence, arousal, and dominance for 20,000 english words. In *Proceedings of the 56th annual meeting of the association for computational linguistics (volume 1: Long papers)*, pages 174–184.

Saif M Mohammad. 2016. Sentiment analysis: Detecting valence, emotions, and other affectual states from text. In *Emotion measurement*, pages 201–237. Elsevier.

Saif M Mohammad and Svetlana Kiritchenko. 2015. Using hashtags to capture fine emotion categories from tweets. *Computational Intelligence*, 31(2):301–326.

Inbal Nahum-Shani, Shawna N Smith, Bonnie J Spring, Linda M Collins, Katie Witkiewitz, Ambuj Tewari, and Susan A Murphy. 2018. Just-in-time adaptive interventions (jitais) in mobile health: key components and design principles for ongoing health behavior support. *Annals of Behavioral Medicine*, 52(6):446–462.

Erik C. Nook, Thomas Derrick Hull, Matthew K. Nock, and Leah H. Somerville. 2021. Linguistic measures of psychological distance track symptom levels and treatment outcomes in a large set of psychotherapy transcripts. *Proceedings of the National Academy of Sciences of the United States of America*, 119.

Jukka-Pekka Onnela, Caleb Dixon, Keary Griffin, Tucker Jaenicke, Leila Minowada, Sean Esterkin, Alvin Siu, Josh Zagorsky, and Eli Jones. 2021. Beiwe: A data collection platform for high-throughput digital phenotyping. *Journal of Open Source Software*, 6(68):3417.

Gregory Park, H Andrew Schwartz, Johannes C Eichstaedt, Margaret L Kern, Michal Kosinski, David J Stillwell, Lyle H Ungar, and Martin EP Seligman. 2015. Automatic personality assessment through social media language. *Journal of personality and social psychology*, 108(6):934.

James W Pennebaker, Martha E Francis, and Roger J Booth. 2001. Linguistic inquiry and word count: Liwc 2001. *Mahway: Lawrence Erlbaum Associates*, 71(2001):2001.

Youngseo Son, Sean AP Clouston, Roman Kotov, Johannes C Eichstaedt, Evelyn J Bromet, Benjamin J Luft, and H Andrew Schwartz. 2023. World trade center responders in their own words: predicting ptsd symptom trajectories with ai-based language analyses of interviews. *Psychological medicine*, 53(3):918–926.

Zhiyi Song, Stephanie M Strassel, Haejoong Lee, Kevin Walker, Jonathan Wright, Jennifer Garland, Dana Fore, Brian Gainor, Preston Cabe, Thomas Thomas, et al. 2014. Collecting natural sms and chat conversations in multiple languages: The bolt phase 2 corpus. In *LREC*, pages 1699–1704. Citeseer.

Caitlin A. Stamatis, Jonah Meyerhoff, Tingting Liu, Zhaoyi Hou, Garrick T. Sherman, Brenda L. Curtis, Pallavi V. Kulkarni, and David C. Mohr. 2022a. The association of language style matching in text messages with mood and anxiety symptoms. *Procedia computer science*, 206:151–161.

Caitlin A. Stamatis, Jonah Meyerhoff, Tingting Liu, Garrick T. Sherman, Harry Wang, Tony Liu, Brenda L. Curtis, Pallavi V. Kulkarni, and David C. Mohr. 2022b. Prospective associations of text-message-based sentiment with symptoms of depression, generalized anxiety, and social anxiety. *Depression and Anxiety*, 39:794 – 804.

M. L. Tlachac and Elke A. Rundensteiner. 2020. Screening for depression with retrospectively harvested private versus public text. *IEEE Journal of Biomedical and Health Informatics*, 24:3326–3332.

M. L. Tlachac, Avantika Shrestha, Mahum Shah, Benjamin R. Litterer, and Elke A. Rundensteiner. 2022. Automated construction of lexicons to improve depression screening with text messages. *IEEE Journal of Biomedical and Health Informatics*, 27:2751–2759.

John Torous, Hannah Wisniewski, Bruce Bird, Elizabeth Carpenter, Gary David, Eduardo Elejalde, Dan Fulford, Synthia Guimond, Ryan Hays, Philip Henson, et al. 2019. Creating a digital health smartphone app and digital phenotyping platform for mental health and diverse healthcare needs: an interdisciplinary and collaborative approach. *Journal of Technology in Behavioral Science*, 4:73–85.

Julio Vega, Meng Li, Kwesi Aguillera, Nikunj Goel, Echhit Joshi, Kirtiraj Khandekar, Krina C Durica, Abhineeth R Kunta, and Carissa A Low. 2021. Reproducible analysis pipeline for data streams: open-source software to process data collected with mobile devices. *Frontiers in Digital Health*, 3:769823.

Amy Beth Warriner, Victor Kuperman, and Marc Brysbaert. 2013. Norms of valence, arousal, and dominance for 13,915 english lemmas. *Behavior research methods*, 45:1191–1207.

SOTASTREAM: A Streaming Approach to Machine Translation Training

Matt Post **Thamme Gowda** **Roman Grundkiewicz**
Huda Khayrallah **Rohit Jain** **Marcin Junczys-Dowmunt**

Microsoft

Abstract

Many machine translation toolkits make use of a data preparation step wherein raw data is transformed into a tensor format that can be used directly by the trainer. This preparation step is increasingly at odds with modern research and development practices because it produces a static, unchangeable version of the training data, making common training-time needs difficult (e.g., subword sampling), time-consuming (preprocessing with large data can take days), expensive (e.g., disk space), and cumbersome (managing experiment combinatorics). We propose an alternative approach that separates the *generation* of data from the *consumption* of that data. In this approach, there is no separate pre-processing step; data generation produces an infinite stream of permutations of the raw training data, which the trainer tensorizes and batches as it is consumed. Additionally, this data stream can be manipulated by a set of user-definable operators that provide on-the-fly modifications, such as data normalization, augmentation or filtering. We release an open-source toolkit, SOTASTREAM, that implements this approach: `https://github.com/marian-nmt/sotastream`. We show that it cuts training time, adds flexibility, reduces experiment management complexity, and reduces disk space, all without affecting the accuracy of the trained models.

1 Introduction

A cumbersome component of training machine translation systems is working with large amounts of data. Modern high-resource parallel datasets are often on the order of hundreds of millions of parallel sentences, and backtranslation easily doubles that (Kocmi et al., 2022, Appendix A). Because this data is too large to fit into main memory, toolkits such as FAIRSEQ (Ott et al., 2019) and SOCKEYE (Hieber et al., 2022) make use of a pre-processing step, which transforms the training data from its raw state into a static sequence of tensors.

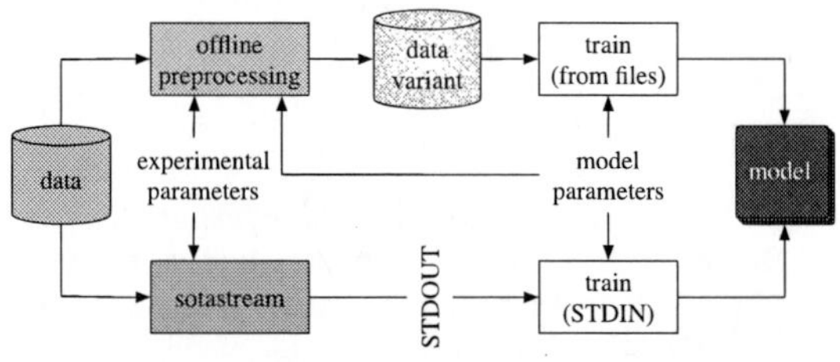

Figure 1: The SOTASTREAM approach separates data generation from consumption. Whereas offline tensorization requires model-specific parameters such as the vocabulary, which ties processed data to a particular training, SOTASTREAM produces data on the fly, avoiding time-consuming production and space-wasting storage of preprocessed data.

These tensors can then be read in via an index and memory-mapped shards, allowing for quick assembly into batches at training time.

While this offline preprocessing prevents data loading from becoming a bottleneck in training, it creates a number of other problems:

- *it breaks an abstraction*: the tensorized data is tied to specific modeling decisions, such as the vocabulary;
- *it is cumbersome*: the tensorized data cannot be easily changed, and even minor variations of the data must be processed separately and then managed;
- *it is time-consuming*: pre-processing can take considerable time and must be completed before training can start; and
- *it is wasteful*: each data variant replicates the original's disk space.

These problems exist for construction of any model, but are exacerbated in research settings, which often explore variations of the training data.

We describe an alternative that factors *generation* of data from the *consumption* of that data by

Proceedings of the 3rd Workshop for Natural Language Processing Open Source Software (NLP-OSS 2023), pages 110–119
December 6, 2023 ©2023 Association for Computational Linguistics

the training toolkit. This view presents the training data as an infinite stream of permutations of the raw training samples. This stream is then consumed by the training toolkit, which tensorizes it on the fly, consuming data into a buffer from which it can assemble batches. This framework eliminates all the problems above: variants of the data are independent of any model; arbitrary manipulations can be applied on the fly; preprocessing time is amortized over training, which can start as soon as the first batch can be constructed;and no extra disk space or management is required.

We release an open-source implementation of the proposed data generation framework called SOTASTREAM[1]. SOTASTREAM is written in Python and uses Infinibatch[2] to provide a stream of data over permutations of data sources. It additionally provides an easily-extendable set of *mixers*, *augmentors*, and *filters* that allow data to be probabilistically manipulated on the fly. A particular configuration of manipulators is provided by the user in the form of a dynamically-loadable *pipeline*, which defines a parameterizable recipe that can be used for training. SOTASTREAM uses multiprocessing to reach high throughput levels that prevent starvation of the training toolkit. And finally, it employs a standard UNIX API, writing data to STDOUT.

After presenting this framework (§ 2), we conduct a quality comparison to demonstrate that it does not reduce model quality (§ 4). We then investigate stream bandwidth under various pipelines as well as necessary toolkit consumption needs (§ 5). We conclude by demonstrating a number of use cases (§ 6).

2 Training from data streams

The core idea underlying SOTASTREAM is to cleanly separate data generation from consumption of that data during training. The *data generator* is responsible for producing training samples, and the *trainer* consumes them. This factorization allows us to separate properties of the data (such as their sources, mixing ratios, and augmentations) from properties of training and the model (such as tensor format, batch size, and so on).

The current approach relies on standard UNIX I/O pipes as an interface between these two pieces. However, SOTASTREAM could also be used to generate data for offline uses, or modified to allow consumption through some other API, such as a library call that returns a generator.

[1]`https://github.com/marian-nmt/sotastream`
[2]`https://github.com/microsoft/infinibatch`

2.1 Data generation

SOTASTREAM is a data generator. At a high level, it works by defining a *pipeline*. This pipeline reads from a set of zero or more input data sources, applies any augmentations, and produces a single output stream.

Pipelines Pipelines are implemented by inheriting from the base `Pipeline` class. The class implementation is responsible for defining the input data sources, reading from them, applying augmentations, and returning a single output stream. These are depicted in Figure 2, a simplified presentation that elides other support features, such as providing the mixing weights for the input data sources.

The pipeline has three basic components:

1. Build a stream for each input data source;
2. apply a sequence of augmentors; and
3. merge the streams to a single output stream.

Data sources SOTASTREAM uses Infinibatch to return a generator over a permutation of the samples in a data source. Each `DataSource` object receives two key arguments: a file path to the data source on disk, d, and a processor function, f, to read it. This can be seen in Figure 2 in the call to `create_data_stream`(d, f).

The data is received as a path to a directory of compressed TSV file shards. Infinibatch requires that data be presented in this way.[3] For each data epoch, Infinibatch produces a permutation of these shards. The shards are then passed, in turn, to the function f, which is responsible for opening, reading, and processing the shard. It is important to note that Infinibatch provides an *infinite stream* of data; that is, it will iterate indefinitely over its input data, subject to the constraint that no shard (within a data source) will be seen $n + 1$ times until all shards have been seen n times. See the Multiprocessing section (§ 2.3) below for important caveats related to multiprocessing and MPI training).

Augmentations The second argument to `create_data_stream` is a generator function, f,

[3]SOTASTREAM can also receive a path to a single compressed TSV file, in which case it splits the file into shards under a temporary directory. The default shard size is `1e6` lines. The results of this automatic sharding are cached using an MD5 checksum.

```
@pipeline("robust-case")
class RobustCasePipeline(Pipeline):
  def __init__(self, pa_dir: str, bt_dir: str, **kwargs):
    super().__init__(**kwargs)
    pa_stream = self.create_data_stream(pa_dir, processor=Augment)
    bt_stream = self.create_data_stream(bt_dir,
      processor=partial(Augment, tag="[BT]"))  # tag the BT data
    self.stream = Mixer([pa_stream, bt_stream], self.mix_weights)
  # definitions of other class methods go here ...

def LowerCase(stream: Generator[Line]) -> Generator[Line]:
  for line in stream:
    line[0] = line[0].lower()  # lowercase the source side
    yield line

def TitleCase(stream: Generator[Line]) -> Generator[Line]:
  for line in stream:
    line[0], line[1] = line[0].title(), line[1].title()  # titlecase both sides
    yield line

def TagData(stream: Generator[Line], tag: str) -> Generator[Line]}:
  for line in stream:
    line[0] = f"{tag} {line}"  # add a target language tag to the source
    yield line

def Augment(path: str, tag: str = None) -> Generator[Line]:
  stream = UTF8File(path)   # open the path to the shard

  stream = Mixer(  # randomly mix casing variants
    [ stream, LowerCase(stream), TitleCase(stream) ],
    [ 0.95,   0.04,              0.01 ],
  )

  if tag is not None:
    stream = TagData(stream, tag)
  return stream
```

Figure 2: A simplified pipeline. Streams are built by composing generator functions over input data sources (here, parallel and backtranslated data). This example tags the backtranslated stream, then mixes it with the parallel stream using weights provided on the command line (defaulting to 1:1). It then applies random source-lowercasing (4%) and title-casing (1%).

```
class Line:
  def __init__(self, line: str):
    if line is not None:
      self.fields = line.split("\t")
    else:
      self.fields = []
```

Figure 3: The (simplified) `Line` object, a lightweight wrapper around a single row of tab-separated input data.

an Infinibatch primitive whose task is to open each shard and produce an output data stream. The output is in the form of `Line` objects (Figure 3), each of which is a class representation of the TSV input. By convention in machine translation, fields 0 and 1 are treated as *source* and *target* segments, respectively, but the code itself makes no such assumptions.

The function is not limited in just reading and returning the data. A key feature of SOTASTREAM is augmentations, which are arbitrary manipulations of a data stream that are easy to stack and accumulate. This is accomplished by composing generators. Figure 2 contains a number of examples in the `Augment` function. It first opens a stream on a path (passed from Infinibatch, containing a path to a sharded file name). It then applies lowercasing and title-casing to the input stream probabilistically, using a `Mixer` class to select among them with specified weights. Finally, it prepends a tag to the data, if requested by the caller.

Outputting the stream Finally, at the top level, the (augmented) streams from different data sources are merged into a single stream. This works in the same way as the above `Mixer` class example. One additional feature is that the `Pipeline` class provides the ability to set these top-level data weights from the command line (`--mix-weights`).

2.2 Data consumption

The main requirements for the trainer are to consume data into a pool, apply subword processing, organize into batches, and run backpropagation against the training objective. Because these are done on the fly, rather than in preprocessing, special considerations must be implemented to ensure that this extra processing does not become a bottleneck for training.

In Section 5, we experiment with an implementation in the Marian toolkit (Junczys-Dowmunt et al., 2018). Marian makes use of multiple worker threads, which pre-fetch data from STDIN into an internal memory pool, where the data is tokenized and integerized. When the pool is filled, it is sorted and batched (according to run-time settings). In the meantime, prefetching continues into a second pool. As training proceeds, these two pools are used alternately for filling via prefetching and batch generation.

2.3 Multiprocessing

In order to sustain a sufficient throughput, SOTASTREAM makes use of multiprocessing. This can be increasingly important if the augmentations applied are expensive to compute. We quantify the effects of multiprocessing for generation under a handful of pipelines of varying complexity in Section 5.

Internally, this is accomplished with the `multiprocessing` library. We create separate subprocesses, each of which is provided with independent access to the data sources. The parent process maintains a pipe to each subprocess, and queries them in sequence, reading a fixed number of lines from each in turn, and passing them to the standard output.

An important issue is raised when working with subprocesses. If each subprocess were to return an independent permutation over the input data, merging subprocesses would not itself result in a permutation. To address this, each of n subprocesses is initalized with $\frac{1}{n}$ of the data shards, themselves assigned in round-robin order across the subprocesses. In this way, we guarantee a permutation in settings where the number of processes evenly divides the number of shards.

When working over MPI, no such coordination takes place. Each MPI instantiation will receive a different randomly-seeded shard permutation.

3 Experimental setup

Our experimental goal is to demonstrate that the many advantages of SOTASTREAM do not come at a cost in accuracy (§ 4) or speed (§ 5). We do this by comparing to a number of other data loading methods. In order to isolate the effects of changing the data loader, we conduct all of our experiments within the Marian toolkit. Marian does not support offline data preprocessing; instead, we compare a number of different streaming settings that cover best-case scenarios for data loading.

3.1 Streaming variations

We compare the following data-loading variations.

- *Full loading*. In this scenario, the trainer has direct memory access to the entire data source. For our experiments, Marian loads the complete datasets into main memory. There is some startup cost, after which all access to the data is immediate.

- *Sequential streaming*. In this approach, the training data is read sequentially, in a loop over the entire training set. Data is prefetched into a pool of a specified size, from which mini-batches are assembled. Since data is read sequentially, there is no randomization across data epochs. The pool size determines an upper bound on memory usage.

- *Randomized sequential streaming*. In this variant of sequential streaming, the lines in each data source are randomly permuted prior to being read, providing a corpus-level permutation on top of sequential streaming's pool-based reordering.

- SOTASTREAM. Our Infinibatch-based streaming approach.

For toolkits that support preprocessing, it is typical to construct an index, which organizes the presorted and tensorized data into memory-mappable shards. Marian does not have a preprocessing option, which means that we have no comparison to a setting where tensorization is done offline. We thus consider full-loading to be the closest equivalent, since preprocessing is in fact a stand-in for full loading. This can only possible affect speed comparisons (§ 5).

3.2 Model parameters

We conduct experiments in a large-data and small-data setting. Our large-data setting is English–German. We train on 297m lines of Paracrawl v9 (Bañón et al., 2020) from WMT22 (Kocmi et al., 2022). We use a 32k shared unigram subword model (Kudo, 2018) using SentencePiece (Kudo and Richardson, 2018), trained jointly over both sides. We train a standard base Transformer model (Vaswani et al., 2017) with 6/6 encoder/decoder layers, an embedding size of 1024, a feed-forward size of 4096, and 8 attention heads. The large model is trained for 20 virtual epochs. Since there are roughly 7.4 billion target-side tokens after tokenizing the data, this equates to roughly three passes over the data.

For the small-data setting, we train on Czech–Ukrainian, also from WMT22. This dataset has roughly 12m parallel lines. We use the same model and parameter settings, but train for only five virtual epochs, or roughly 30 data epochs, since the model converges by then.

3.3 Evaluation

We evaluate on the WMT21/en-de and WMT22/cs-uk test sets. We use a number of metrics to capture variation:

- **BLEU** (Papineni et al., 2002) and **chrF** (Popović, 2015), both computed with sacrebleu[4] (Post, 2018).
- **COMET20/22** (Rei et al., 2020), using model `wmt20-comet-da` (EN-DE) or `wmt22-comet-da` (CS-UK).

4 Quality Comparison

Table 1 contains metric results for both our high- and low-resource settings. For English–German, we observe rough equivalence across all training methods and metrics, which establishes SOTASTREAM as a viable data preparation tool. A similar pattern holds for Czech–Ukrainian, except for the odd outlier of the sequential streaming approach. This approach simply 'cat'ed the training data repeatedly until model convergence. This result is strongest for COMET and less pronounced for BLEU and chrF. We have no clear explanation for this; one guess is that in smaller data settings, with no filtering, curriculum effects may be more pronounced, and this is the only data generation approach with no randomization. Among approaches that permuted the data, SOTASTREAM is on par with the others. We therefore consider it to pass the quality benchmark.

5 Speed

Next we ask whether SOTASTREAM has a negative effect on speed. We examine speed in three settings: generation speed (§ 5.1), Marian's consumption speed (§ 5.2), and total runtime (§ 5.3).

5.1 Data generation

We first examine how fast SOTASTREAM can write data to STDOUT.

Our benchmark consists of a producer and a consumer connected by UNIX pipe. The producer varies among the tools we compare in our benchmark (described below), while the consumer is a lightweight script, whose sole purpose is to count records from STDIN and report the yield rate (the number of lines per second). All benchmarks are run one at a time, on the same machine,[5] with no other CPU- or I/O-intensive processes are competing for resources. We run each benchmark multiple times and report the average.

We compare the following generation tools:

- `zcat`: A wrapper to GNU gzip[6] that decompresses and outputs lines. This serves as the best case scenario, where the producer is implemented in an efficient way (e.g. C/C++) and has no time-consuming augmentations.
- `zcat.py`: Similar to `zcat`, but based on `gzip` API from Python's standard library.[7]
- `default` pipeline: SOTASTREAM' default, returning lines from a single data source (§ 2.1) with no augmentations.
- `case augmentor` pipeline: the pipeline from Figure 2. It mixes two data sources, applies case transformations, and prepends a "[BT]" tag to the backtranslated data.

We benchmark multiple worker subprocesses: $n \in \{1, 2, 4, 8, 16, 32\}$. The throughput measured is

[4] Version 2.3.1 with default settings.

[5] An Intel Xeon E5-2620 CPU with 32 cores, 660 GB of RAM, and running Ubuntu 20.04 LTS.

[6] `https://git.savannah.gnu.org/cgit/gzip.git/tree/zcat.in`

[7] `https://docs.python.org/3/library/gzip.html`

Model	English–German (newstest2021) COMET20	BLEU	chrF	Czech–Ukranian (wmttest2022) COMET22	BLEU	chrF
Best constrained	54.8	31.3	60.7	91.6	34.7	61.5
Full loading	55.9 ± 0.4	34.9 ± 0.1	62.0 ± 0.0	85.5 ± 0.2	27.9 ± 0.4	55.6 ± 0.2
Sequential streaming	56.1 ± 0.2	35.0 ± 0.2	62.1 ± 0.0	86.4 ± 0.1	28.7 ± 0.3	56.6 ± 0.2
Randomized streaming	55.8 ± 0.2	35.1 ± 0.0	62.2 ± 0.0	85.6 ± 0.1	27.8 ± 0.0	55.6 ± 0.2
SOTASTREAM	55.9 ± 0.1	34.9 ± 0.1	62.1 ± 0.1	85.7 ± 0.2	28.5 ± 0.4	56.2 ± 0.2

Table 1: Mean over three runs for our high- and low-resource scenarios. The best constrained system is WeChat-AI (Zeng et al., 2021) for EN-DE and AMU (Nowakowski et al., 2022) for CS-UK.

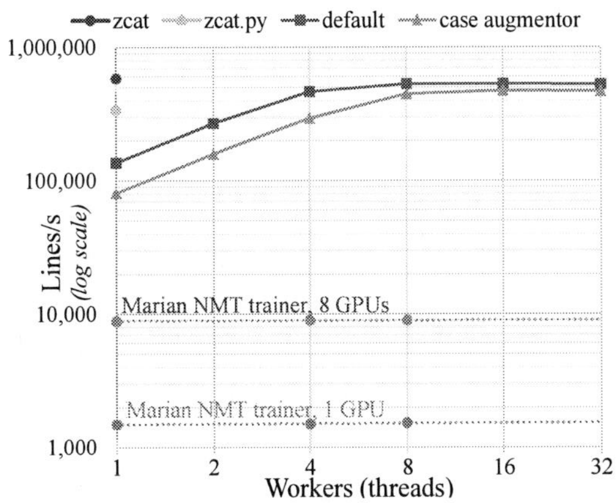

Figure 4: Generation and consumption rates with SOTASTREAM and Marian, respectively. SOTASTREAM is not a bottleneck, but is easily able to generate data and transmit it through the POSIX API to sustain training.

as lines/s and is given Figure 4. `zcat`, being the fastest, yields over 585k lines/s, and Python's alternative (`zcat.py`) yields 342k lines/s.[8] Our SOTASTREAM `default` with a single worker yields approximately 136k lines/s, which can be increased with more workers and plateaus after a certain rate (possibly due to a bottleneck in number of parallel reads supported by underlying storage device). As we add more augmentations and mixture processes, we observe a lower yield rate than no-augmentation baselines (expected). However, yield rate can be improved with more worker processes.

5.2 Consumption

We have shown the rate at which SOTASTREAM can generate data. In this section, we show the rate at which one particular NMT trainer (Marian) consumes training data. Training time and the consumption rate varies based the size of model being trained, and the number of GPUs used for training.

We train smaller Transformer models than used

Model	Time (Hours)
Full loading	36.84 ±0.16
Sequential streaming	35.51 ±0.15
Randomized streaming	35.73 ±0.05
SOTASTREAM	35.86 ±0.27

Table 2: End-to-end training time.

for Table 1, since smaller models train faster and therefore have higher data consumption needs. We use 6/6 encoder/decoder layers, 512-dimensional embeddings, and feedforward sublayers of size 2048. We report consumption rate for six settings: one vs. eight GPUs,[9] and using one, four, or eight prefetching worker threads. As shown in Figure 4, a trainer with single GPU consumes about 1523 lines/s, and with eight GPUs, the consumption rate increases to 8957 lines/s. Even in the best case scenario (smaller model, more GPUs, and more prefetcher threads), the consumption rates of training process are lower than SOTASTREAM production rate.

We recommend running multiple workers when augmentations are slow in order to maintain sufficient output rates. We do not experiment with them here, but in multi-node training settings coordinated with MPI, one (multiprocess) instance of SOTASTREAM should be run per node.

5.3 Total time to run

Table 2 verifies that SOTASTREAM's amortized approach is neither slower nor faster than other approaches when total runtime is considered.

6 Example Use Cases

In this section we show example use cases how SOTASTREAM can be used to simply and easily modify data on the fly. This provides all the advantages of training for robustness without the cumbersome task of generating (and managing) data that has

[8]Measured on CPython v3.11; prior versions of CPython are found to be slower.

[9]NVIDIA Tesla V100s with 32GB.

been preprocessed in many different forms, which are combinatorial and impose high costs on the complexity of managing training runs.

6.1 Mixing multiple streams of data

Training machine translation models often requires combining different data sets in desired proportions in order to balance their size or quality or other properties. The example in Figure 2 demonstrates that combining original parallel data and back-translated data can be efficiently achieved in SOTASTREAM by mixing multiple data streams with specific data weighting. The weights for each data stream can be then specified using the command-line options:

```
sotastream robust-case \
  parallel.tsv.gz backtrans.tsv.gz \
  --mix-weights 1 1
```

The weights are normalized and used as probabilities with the `Mixer` augmentor.

This approach, when compared to the traditional offline preparation of the data, is much simpler, more scalable, saves disk space and does not require complicated ratio-computation and data over- or downsampling.

6.2 Data augmentation for robustness

SOTASTREAM's augmentors provide a flexible framework for developing different methods for data augmentation, for example, case manipulation for robustness against different casing variants of the input text. It is demonstrated in the example in Figure 2, where `LowerCase` is an augmentor that lowercases the source text, and `TitleCase` converts both source and target sides to the English title-cased format. The frequency of each variant is easily controlled with the same `Mixer` used to join separate data sources. The on-the-fly approach simplifies experiments when testing multiple variations, which is often needed in order to find optimal augmentation methods and ratios, it minimizes the burden of experiment management.

Many other types of robustness augmentation (Li et al., 2019), such as source-side punctuation removal, spelling errors generation, etc., can be implemented in a similar way.

6.3 Filtering bad data examples

In SOTASTREAM it is straightforward to do data filtering on the fly. This type of filtering is especially useful in scenarios in which external data is used for model training or fine-tuning that cannot be manually filtered in a controlled way.

For example, a `URLFilter` filter that removes lines that have unmatched URLs between the source and target fields can be implemented using the provided `MatchFilter`:

```
def URLFilter(stream):
  pattern = r'\bhttps?:\S+[a-z]\b'
  return MatchFilter(stream, pattern)
```

6.4 Subword tokenization sampling

The boundary separating data generation from consumption can be blurred. For example, instead of producing raw text output, the tool could generate subwords, if provided with a subword model. This facilitates randomized sampling of different subword segmentations from a Unigram LM model with SentencePiece's Python wrapper:

```
import sentencepiece as sp
spm = sp.SentencePieceProcessor(
      model_file=SPM_VOCAB)

def spm_enc(stream, spm, fields=[0, 1]):
  for line in stream:
    for field in fields:
      line[field] = spm.encode(
          line[field], out_type=str,
          enable_sampling=True))
    yield line
```

6.5 Training document-context models

When training document models (e.g., Post and Junczys-Dowmunt (2023)), we can easily construct pseudo-documents on the fly if the training data is augmented with a document identifier field:

```
def read_docs(stream):
    doc, previd = [], None
    for line in stream:
        docid = line[2]
        if len(doc) and docid != previd:
            yield doc
            doc = []
        doc.append(line)
        previd = docid
    if len(doc):
        yield doc
```

A wrapper around this function could merge the source and target sides of the `Line` object, perhaps subject to parameters such as a maximum sequence length, a maximum number of sentences, and structural tokens to be used as affixes.

6.6 Alignments and other data types

SOTASTREAM has been primarily designed for machine translation, which requires providing source and target texts as separate fields. Other data types or metadata can be generated on the fly or provided as additional fields in the input stream. By design the existing augmentors pass forward the unused fields, which makes introducing new fields that are used only by a subset of augmentors simple.

The example below demonstrates on-the-fly generation of word alignment using SimAlign (Jalili Sabet et al., 2020):

```
import simalign as sa
aln = sa.SentenceAligner()

def align(stream, aln, fields=[0, 1]):
  i, j = fields
  for line in stream,
    res = aln.get_word_aligns(line[i],
                              line[j])
    res = " ".join(f"{p[0]}-{p[1]}"
                   for p in res['mwmf'])
    line.append(res)
    yield line
```

The word alignment can be used directly by the trainer, e.g., for guided alignment training (Chen et al., 2016), or used by subsequent augmentors that may require it, e.g., constrained terminology translation annotations (Bergmanis and Pinnis, 2021).

6.7 Integration with data collection tools

SOTASTREAM can integrate tools like MTData, which automates the collection and preparation of machine translation data sets (Gowda et al., 2021). The following example shows `mtdata` pipeline which downloads the specified data sets and mixes them as per `--mix-weights` argument:

```
sotastream -n 1 mtdata --langs rus-eng \
  Statmt-news_commentary-16-eng-rus \
  Statmt-backtrans_ruen-wmt20-rus-eng \
  OPUS-paracrawl-v9-eng-rus \
  --mix-weights 2 1 1
```

6.8 Generating data sets for offline use

If the training tool does not support consuming training data from the standard input, SOTASTREAM can be used for static data generation. While the real advantages of SOTASTREAM accrue when making use of its on-the-fly data manipulations, this approach retains some of its benefits.

6.9 Other uses

The SOTASTREAM approach to factoring data generation, as well as SOTASTREAM itself, could also be used for generating non-textual content. The benefits of not writing data to disk would be greater in settings where input disk space is larger than plain text, such as translation from visual representations (Salesky et al., 2021). Nor does it need to be limited to sequence-to-sequence settings; we imagine the approach could be useful for training of LLMs.

7 Related Work

To our knowledge, SOTASTREAM is novel in presenting a framework for the generation of training data as a distinct component in the model training pipeline. It emphasizes a clean separation between data generation and training, multithreading for throughput, and the use of the standard UNIX pipeline interface.

It is not the first to propose streaming data, however. Although Fairseq's documentation emphasizes a preprocessing step,[10], Fairseq can also read and process raw data on the fly if it can be loaded completely into memory. Pytorch (Paszke et al., 2019) also provides "iterable-style" DataPipes for iterating over data samples,[11] but as far as we know, they are not widely used for machine translation training. They could, however, provide an interface to SOTASTREAM for Python-based training toolkits.

There are many libraries focused on data augmentation. A number of these are focused just on text augmentations, including nlpaug (Ma, 2019), TextAttack (Morris et al., 2020), and TextFlint (Gui et al., 2021). Another tool is AugLy (Papakipos and Bitton, 2022), a multimodal tool for text, audio, images, and video that provides robust training against adversarial perturbations. Many of these libraries could be useful within SOTASTREAM's general framework.

8 Conclusion

The data-preprocessing approach that is common in machine translation model training makes it possible to work with increasingly large datasets, but this ability does not come without costs. It is time-consuming to copy and process data, and can be expensive to store on disk. If data is compiled with model-specific parameters that tie the data to a particular model training, it prevents or at least complicates reusability. This problem is further exacerbated by research settings where one of the experimental parameters is manipulations of the training data, since each variant (and potentially

[10]https://web.archive.org/web/20230609072600/https://fairseq.readthedocs.io/en/latest/getting_started.html

[11]https://pytorch.org/data/main/torchdata.datapipes.iter.html

their cross-products) must be written to disk and then managed.

We have described an approach that separates data generation from data consumption, and shared SOTASTREAM, an implementation that makes use of the standard UNIX pipeline. The requirement is that preprocessing must now be computed on the fly. Our experiments show that this does not slow down training, nor does it affect the accuracy of the models trained. The approach provides flexibility, saves processing time and disk space, and simplifies experiment management.

Limitations

We have only investigated data consumption rates in a single toolkit, Marian, written in C++. It's possible that the online preprocessing requirements may be too much for toolkits written in languages without a proper thread implementation.

References

Marta Bañón, Pinzhen Chen, Barry Haddow, Kenneth Heafield, Hieu Hoang, Miquel Esplà-Gomis, Mikel L. Forcada, Amir Kamran, Faheem Kirefu, Philipp Koehn, Sergio Ortiz Rojas, Leopoldo Pla Sempere, Gema Ramírez-Sánchez, Elsa Sarrías, Marek Strelec, Brian Thompson, William Waites, Dion Wiggins, and Jaume Zaragoza. 2020. ParaCrawl: Web-scale acquisition of parallel corpora. In *Proceedings of the 58th Annual Meeting of the Association for Computational Linguistics*, pages 4555–4567, Online. Association for Computational Linguistics.

Toms Bergmanis and Mārcis Pinnis. 2021. Facilitating terminology translation with target lemma annotations. In *Proceedings of the 16th Conference of the European Chapter of the Association for Computational Linguistics: Main Volume*, pages 3105–3111, Online. Association for Computational Linguistics.

Wenhu Chen, Evgeny Matusov, Shahram Khadivi, and Jan-Thorsten Peter. 2016. Guided alignment training for topic-aware neural machine translation. In *Conferences of the Association for Machine Translation in the Americas: MT Researchers' Track*, pages 121–134, Austin, TX, USA. The Association for Machine Translation in the Americas.

Thamme Gowda, Zhao Zhang, Chris Mattmann, and Jonathan May. 2021. Many-to-English machine translation tools, data, and pretrained models. In *Proceedings of the 59th Annual Meeting of the Association for Computational Linguistics and the 11th International Joint Conference on Natural Language Processing: System Demonstrations*, pages 306–316, Online. Association for Computational Linguistics.

Tao Gui, Xiao Wang, Qi Zhang, Qin Liu, Yicheng Zou, Xin Zhou, Rui Zheng, Chong Zhang, Qinzhuo Wu, Jiacheng Ye, Zexiong Pang, Yongxin Zhang, Zhengyan Li, Ruotian Ma, Zichu Fei, Ruijian Cai, Jun Zhao, Xinwu Hu, Zhiheng Yan, Yiding Tan, Yuan Hu, Qiyuan Bian, Zhihua Liu, Bolin Zhu, Shan Qin, Xiaoyu Xing, Jinlan Fu, Yue Zhang, Minlong Peng, Xiaoqing Zheng, Yaqian Zhou, Zhongyu Wei, Xipeng Qiu, and Xuanjing Huang. 2021. Textflint: Unified multilingual robustness evaluation toolkit for natural language processing. *CoRR*, abs/2103.11441.

Felix Hieber, Michael Denkowski, Tobias Domhan, Barbara Darques Barros, Celina Dong Ye, Xing Niu, Cuong Hoang, Ke Tran, Benjamin Hsu, Maria Nadejde, Surafel Lakew, Prashant Mathur, Anna Currey, and Marcello Federico. 2022. Sockeye 3: Fast neural machine translation with pytorch.

Masoud Jalili Sabet, Philipp Dufter, François Yvon, and Hinrich Schütze. 2020. SimAlign: High quality word alignments without parallel training data using static and contextualized embeddings. In *Findings of the Association for Computational Linguistics: EMNLP 2020*, pages 1627–1643, Online. Association for Computational Linguistics.

Marcin Junczys-Dowmunt, Kenneth Heafield, Hieu Hoang, Roman Grundkiewicz, and Anthony Aue. 2018. Marian: Cost-effective high-quality neural machine translation in C++. In *Proceedings of the 2nd Workshop on Neural Machine Translation and Generation*, pages 129–135, Melbourne, Australia. Association for Computational Linguistics.

Tom Kocmi, Rachel Bawden, Ondřej Bojar, Anton Dvorkovich, Christian Federmann, Mark Fishel, Thamme Gowda, Yvette Graham, Roman Grundkiewicz, Barry Haddow, Rebecca Knowles, Philipp Koehn, Christof Monz, Makoto Morishita, Masaaki Nagata, Toshiaki Nakazawa, Michal Novák, Martin Popel, and Maja Popović. 2022. Findings of the 2022 conference on machine translation (WMT22). In *Proceedings of the Seventh Conference on Machine Translation (WMT)*, pages 1–45, Abu Dhabi, United Arab Emirates (Hybrid). Association for Computational Linguistics.

Taku Kudo. 2018. Subword regularization: Improving neural network translation models with multiple subword candidates. In *Proceedings of the 56th Annual Meeting of the Association for Computational Linguistics (Volume 1: Long Papers)*, pages 66–75, Melbourne, Australia. Association for Computational Linguistics.

Taku Kudo and John Richardson. 2018. SentencePiece: A simple and language independent subword tokenizer and detokenizer for neural text processing. In *Proceedings of the 2018 Conference on Empirical Methods in Natural Language Processing: System Demonstrations*, pages 66–71, Brussels, Belgium. Association for Computational Linguistics.

Xian Li, Paul Michel, Antonios Anastasopoulos, Yonatan Belinkov, Nadir Durrani, Orhan Firat, Philipp Koehn, Graham Neubig, Juan Pino, and Hassan Sajjad. 2019. Findings of the first shared task on machine translation robustness. In *Proceedings of the Fourth Conference on Machine Translation (Volume 2: Shared Task Papers, Day 1)*, pages 91–102, Florence, Italy. Association for Computational Linguistics.

Edward Ma. 2019. Nlp augmentation. https://github.com/makcedward/nlpaug.

John Morris, Eli Lifland, Jin Yong Yoo, Jake Grigsby, Di Jin, and Yanjun Qi. 2020. TextAttack: A framework for adversarial attacks, data augmentation, and adversarial training in NLP. In *Proceedings of the 2020 Conference on Empirical Methods in Natural Language Processing: System Demonstrations*, pages 119–126, Online. Association for Computational Linguistics.

Artur Nowakowski, Gabriela Pałka, Kamil Guttmann, and Mikołaj Pokrywka. 2022. Adam Mickiewicz University at WMT 2022: NER-assisted and quality-aware neural machine translation. In *Proceedings of the Seventh Conference on Machine Translation (WMT)*, pages 326–334, Abu Dhabi, United Arab Emirates (Hybrid). Association for Computational Linguistics.

Myle Ott, Sergey Edunov, Alexei Baevski, Angela Fan, Sam Gross, Nathan Ng, David Grangier, and Michael Auli. 2019. fairseq: A fast, extensible toolkit for sequence modeling. In *Proceedings of the 2019 Conference of the North American Chapter of the Association for Computational Linguistics (Demonstrations)*, pages 48–53, Minneapolis, Minnesota. Association for Computational Linguistics.

Zoe Papakipos and Joanna Bitton. 2022. Augly: Data augmentations for robustness. *CoRR*, abs/2201.06494.

Kishore Papineni, Salim Roukos, Todd Ward, and Wei-Jing Zhu. 2002. Bleu: a method for automatic evaluation of machine translation. In *Proceedings of the 40th Annual Meeting of the Association for Computational Linguistics*, pages 311–318, Philadelphia, Pennsylvania, USA. Association for Computational Linguistics.

Adam Paszke, Sam Gross, Francisco Massa, Adam Lerer, James Bradbury, Gregory Chanan, Trevor Killeen, Zeming Lin, Natalia Gimelshein, Luca Antiga, Alban Desmaison, Andreas Köpf, Edward Z. Yang, Zach DeVito, Martin Raison, Alykhan Tejani, Sasank Chilamkurthy, Benoit Steiner, Lu Fang, Junjie Bai, and Soumith Chintala. 2019. Pytorch: An imperative style, high-performance deep learning library. *CoRR*, abs/1912.01703.

Maja Popović. 2015. chrF: character n-gram F-score for automatic MT evaluation. In *Proceedings of the Tenth Workshop on Statistical Machine Translation*, pages 392–395, Lisbon, Portugal. Association for Computational Linguistics.

Matt Post. 2018. A call for clarity in reporting BLEU scores. In *Proceedings of the Third Conference on Machine Translation: Research Papers*, pages 186–191, Brussels, Belgium. Association for Computational Linguistics.

Matt Post and Marcin Junczys-Dowmunt. 2023. Escaping the sentence-level paradigm in machine translation.

Ricardo Rei, Craig Stewart, Ana C Farinha, and Alon Lavie. 2020. COMET: A neural framework for MT evaluation. In *Proceedings of the 2020 Conference on Empirical Methods in Natural Language Processing (EMNLP)*, pages 2685–2702, Online. Association for Computational Linguistics.

Elizabeth Salesky, David Etter, and Matt Post. 2021. Robust open-vocabulary translation from visual text representations. In *Proceedings of the 2021 Conference on Empirical Methods in Natural Language Processing*, pages 7235–7252, Online and Punta Cana, Dominican Republic. Association for Computational Linguistics.

Ashish Vaswani, Noam Shazeer, Niki Parmar, Jakob Uszkoreit, Llion Jones, Aidan N. Gomez, Lukasz Kaiser, and Illia Polosukhin. 2017. Attention is all you need. *CoRR*, abs/1706.03762.

Xianfeng Zeng, Yijin Liu, Ernan Li, Qiu Ran, Fandong Meng, Peng Li, Jinan Xu, and Jie Zhou. 2021. WeChat neural machine translation systems for WMT21. In *Proceedings of the Sixth Conference on Machine Translation*, pages 243–254, Online. Association for Computational Linguistics.

An Open-source Web-based Application for Development of Resources and Technologies in Underresourced Languages

Siddharth Singh
CTRANS, Dr. Bhimrao Ambedkar University
Agra, India
siddharth.unreal@outlook.com

Shyam Ratan
CALTS, University of Hyderabad
Hyderabad, India
shyam.unral@outlook.com

Neerav Mathur
UnReaL-TecE LLP
Agra, India
neerav.unreal@outlook.com

Ritesh Kumar
UnReaL-TecE LLP
Agra, India
ritesh.unreal@outlook.com

Abstract

The paper discusses the Linguistic Field Data Management and Analysis System (LiFE), a new open-source, web-based software that systematises storage, management, annotation, analysis and sharing of linguistic data gathered from the field as well as that crawled from various sources on the web such as YouTube, Twitter, Facebook, Instagram, Blog, Newspaper, Wikipedia, etc. The app supports two broad workflows - (a) the field linguists' workflow in which data is collected directly from the speakers in the field and analysed further to produce grammatical descriptions, lexicons, educational materials and possibly language technologies; (b) the computational linguists' workflow in which data collected from the web using automated crawlers or digitised using manual or semi-automatic means, annotated for various tasks and then used for developing different kinds of language technologies.

In addition to supporting these workflows, the app provides some additional features as well - (a) it allows multiple users to collaboratively work on the same project via its granular access control and sharing option; (b) it allows the data to be exported to various formats including CSV, TSV, JSON, XLSX, LaTeX, PDF, Textgrid, RDF (different serialisation formats) etc as appropriate; (c) it allows data import from various formats viz. LIFT XML, XLSX, JSON, CSV, TSV, Textgrid, etc; (d) it allows users to start working in the app at any stage of their work by giving the option to either create a new project from scratch or derive a new project from an existing project in the app.

The app is currently available for use and testing on our server[1] and its source code has been released under AGPL license on our GitHub repository[2]. It is licensed under separate, specific conditions for commercial usage.

[1]http://life.unreal-tece.co.in/

[2]https://github.com/unrealtecellp/life

1 Introduction

Field linguists constantly need tools for collecting, storing, annotating, analysing, sharing and managing linguistic data. As field linguists gather a lot of data for lots of languages, including comparatively under-represented, lesser-known, minoritised, and endangered languages around the globe, this data has to be properly preserved, quickly and accurately analysed and processed and made available to the larger community for social good. On the other hand, there are very few publicly available and accessible datasets for developing language tools and technology for a vast array of languages around the world including most of those which have been worked upon by field linguists - the field linguists', if made available in a structured format, could help in alleviating this situation to a certain extent.

To address this dual issue of accelerating the process of collecting and processing datasets of under-resourced languages (possibly with assistance from available state-of-the-art language technologies) and developing language technologies for these under-resourced languages, a unified platform with an easily available/accessible and handy interface targeted for linguists is required. Our application, Linguistic Field Data Management and Analysis System "LiFE" aims to offer a practical intervention in the field. The app creates a structured framework for the management, analysis and sharing of primary linguistic field data. It also provides interfaces for producing the derivatives of this data such as digital and print lexicons, sketch grammars, and basic language processing tools like part-of-speech taggers and morphological analyzers and generators, automatic speech recognition systems, machine translation and others.

The software focuses on automating the different

Proceedings of the 3rd Workshop for Natural Language Processing Open Source Software (NLP-OSS 2023), pages 120–129
December 6, 2023 ©2023 Association for Computational Linguistics

tasks as much as possible through a handy, intuitive interface for carrying out all the tasks. For instance, by giving initial input, the system gradually trains automatic techniques for inter-linear glossing of the dataset and subsequent production of sketch grammar as well as NLP tools for the language.

The app integrates popular machine learning model hubs such as HuggingFace Hub[3] and Universal Language Contribution API (ULCA)[4] as well as other popular models for individual tasks to provide automation for various tasks. This has enabled us to, for example, give access to the most recent unsupervised and transfer learning-based ASR models based on transformers (such as wav2vec 2.0 (Baevski et al., 2020), wav2vec-U (Baevski et al., 2021) and Whisper (Radford et al., 2022)). It has given field linguists direct access to the most recent state-of-the-art models available for language processing tasks. On the other hand, the app has also provided access to a no-code environment for training or fine-tuning models for new languages and new tasks using some of the most popular libraries such as HuggingFace Transformers and scikit-learn - this environment provides simple point-and-click options to train baseline models that could be quickly integrated into the field linguists' workflow. These two together have helped us provide an automated pipeline for transcription, inter-linear glossing and free translation of the dataset collected from the field.

2 Related Work

The growth of field linguistics and NLP has mostly taken place independently of one another. Thus the tools for speech and multimodal data collection, management and analysis used by linguists and the tools used for data collection and annotation by NLP practitioners are not developed to be interoperable and are generally used exclusively by the two communities.

For the storage, management and gathering of multimodal data as well as the creation of a lexicon, there are certain programmes and technologies designed specifically for field linguists (or community members engaged in fieldwork for their own language). One of the earliest pieces of software created by SIL (The Summer Institute of Linguistics), `Toolbox` (Robinson et al., 2007), formerly known as `Shoebox`[5], served as a forerunner to `FLEx` and was primarily designed for use by anthropologists and field linguists to input their text data and create dictionaries. FieldWorks Language Explorer (`FLEx`)[6] (Butler and Volkinburg, 2007) and (Manson, 2020), which is used for the gathering, management, analysis, and sharing of linguistic and cultural data, is one of the most well-liked tools in the field. A software called `LexiquePro`[7] (Guérin and Lacrampe, 2007) makes it simple to create and format lexicon databases for sharing with others. `WeSay`[8] was developed by SIL to assist native speakers and non-linguists in creating dictionaries for their own languages (Perlin, 2012) & (Albright and Hatton, 2008). There have been various attempts to create tools that are primarily used for data collection. (Vries et al., 2014) talks about the creation of an app called `Woefzela`[9]. It is a smartphone-based (Android Operating System) data-gathering tool that (Vries et al., 2014). It supports several sessions for data collection and can operate without an Internet connection. For the purpose of data collection quality control, it works well. In the South African data collection experiment, where nearly 800 hours of voice data were gathered from remote and rural locations, this technique is displayed. Similarly, `SayMore`[10] is designed to collect data for building dictionaries.

While these different tools provide adequate support for different tasks, there are some serious limitations -

- All of these are standalone desktop/mobile applications and most of these tools are not compatible with Linux systems, thereby, forcing users to use them on Windows /Mac.
- There are different tools for different tasks and it is expected from the users to learn all these different tools and transfer and manage their datasets across these different tools on their own. For example, `FLEx` and WeSay are mainly lexicon-development software (but `FLEx` also supports interlinear glossing), `SayMore` is a data collection tool and `LexiquePro` is mainly for dictionary distri-

[3] https://huggingface.co/docs/hub

[4] https://bhashini.gov.in/ulca/model/explore-models

[5] https://software.sil.org/shoebox/, https://software.sil.org/toolbox/

[6] https://software.sil.org/fieldworks/

[7] https://software.sil.org/lexiquepro/

[8] https://software.sil.org/wesay/

[9] https://sites.google.com/site/woefzela/

[10] https://software.sil.org/saymore/

bution (which gives a basic dictionary editing functionality). Moreover, generally, other tools such as ELAN[11] for video transcription, something like Audacity[12] or Praat[13] for slicing the sound recordings, etc are required (Wittenburg et al., 2006), (Thompson, 2014) and (Boersma and Van Heuven, 2001). Navigating through these different tools and software is a difficult task and has a long learning curve.

- The data formats used by these tools are generally non-standard and trying to use the data processed or produced through these tools with NLP systems is not feasible without significant processing of the dataset (which would require good programming skills).

- Sharing the data, in general, and in a format that works without these tools, more specifically, is not completely straightforward.

On the other side of the spectrum, NLP practitioners, make use of a different set of tools and applications for data management and annotation. For example, Label Studio[14] is a specific open-source, web-based application for data labelling. With a clear and simple user interface, it enables users to label a variety of data kinds, including speech, text, image, video, and time series, and export to several model formats. To create more accurate machine learning models, it can be used to prepare raw data or enhance current training data (Tkachenko et al., 2020-2022).

Similarly, an open-source platform named Shoonya[15] is being created with the goal of enhancing the digital presence of India's underrepresented languages. It allows users to annotate and classify data at scale. This is a crucial necessity to produce larger datasets for neural machine translation training on a wide range of Indian languages.

Some other open-source tools for token, span and document-level text annotation include BRAT rapid annotation tool (brat)[16] (Stenetorp et al., 2011, 2012), doccano[17] is an open-source text annotation tool. For text categorization, sequence labelling, and sequence-to-sequence applications, it offers annotation features. Users can produce labelled data for sentiment analysis, named entity recognition, text summarising, and other purposes (Nakayama et al., 2018), INCEpTION[18] (Klie et al., 2018), among several others.

As is evident, none of these tools even attempt to support data collection from the field and its management and analysis. Given this, LiFE attempts to provide the following -

- An integrated interface that caters to the needs of both the field linguists and NLP practitioners for their data management and processing workflows.

- Give field and documentary linguists access to an integrated workspace for the complete workflow from questionnaire preparation to data analysis and production of community-centred outputs such as grammars, lexicons, etc, without them having to wade through the convoluted workflow of different tools for different aspects of the same work. This interface also provides a user-friendly interface for putting their data in a structured format.

- Give field and documentary linguists access to the most advanced NLP models without the need for them to set up different NLP tools for their work. It also gives them a scope to train baseline models for underrepresented and undocumented languages using a no-code environment and use it for their own work as well as make it available for others.

- Give computational linguists access to a unified data collection and annotation app with support for AI-in-the-loop annotation.

- Give computational linguists access to data from endangered, low-resource, un(der)-represented languages in a structured way (if the community and researchers agree to render it accessible). Additionally, an interface allows using the interface to train and test the model on this data.

[11]https://archive.mpi.nl/tla/elan

[12]https://www.audacityteam.org

[13]https://www.fon.hum.uva.nl/praat

[14]https://labelstud.io/,https://github.com/heartexlabs/label-studio

[15]https://ai4bharat.iitm.ac.in/shoonya,https://github.com/AI4Bharat/Shoonya

[16]http://brat.nlplab.org,https://github.com/nlplab/brat

[17]https://doccano.herokuapp.com,https://github.com/doccano/doccano

[18]https://inception-project.github.io,https://github.com/inception-project/inception

We discuss the architecture and features of the app in more detail in the following sections.

3 LiFE Interface

LiFE has a full-fledged interlinked pipeline of four customisable modules for questionnaire creation, multimodal data labelling (speech, text, image etc) and validation, production of output based on data annotation and analysis (viz lexicon generation) and model training (Figure 1). All these four modules of LiFE are discussed in detail in the following subsections and their interrelationship is demonstrated in Figure 2.

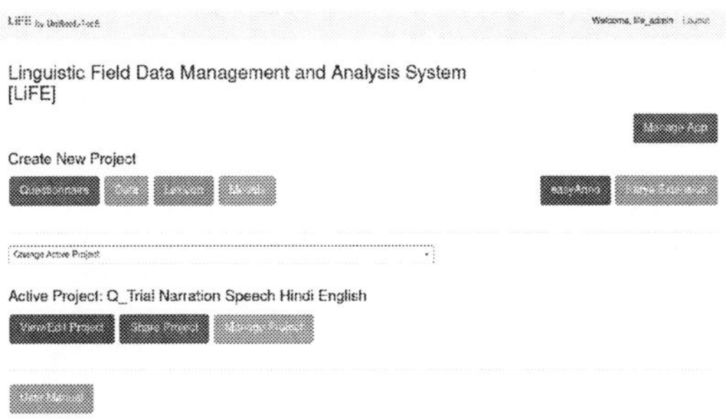

Figure 1: LiFE Interface with All Modules

3.1 Questionnaire

This module is for creating questionnaires that could be used for collecting data in the field (Figure 3). A field linguist could create a new customised questionnaire project or could derive a questionnaire project from the existing questionnaire project for a target language with the purpose of adaptation/manipulation/modification or addition of/in the existing questionnaire. This module facilitates uploading and downloading the questionnaire in multiple formats (viz JSON, CSV, XLSX, Karya JSON[19]). The questionnaire could also be downloaded in printable formats such as PDF and carried to the field for elicitation.

3.2 Data

The basic interface of this module is also the same as the questionnaire module, where a field linguist or a computational linguist could create a new customised data project or could derive a customised data project from an existing questionnaire or another data project (Figure 4). This module allows the creation of three broad kinds of projects including the following -

1. **Data Collection Projects:** The app supports data collection both from the field and through the web through two different kinds of projects.
   (a) collection of speech and text from the field.
   (b) crawling data from different sources on the web.
2. **Data Labelling projects:** The app supports the following kinds of labelling tasks -
   (a) labelling of text at both span and document level (Figure 5 (Kumar et al., 2021a)).
   (b) transcription and labelling of images.
   (c) transcription, labelling and inter-linear glossing of audio-video data.
   (d) text-to-text tasks such as translation, summarisation, etc.
3. **Data Validation Projects:** The app supports two kinds of validation projects.
   (a) giving scores to the data or annotations based on pre-defined metrics (similar to a labelling project).
   (b) arbitration and selection of the best labels among labels assigned by multiple annotators.

If the project is derived from the questionnaire or a new project is created then the module allows the upload of the data in various structured formats such as XLSX, CSV, TSV, JSON, etc. If the project is derived from another kind of data project then data and labels are copied to the new project. The module allows the data, transcriptions and annotations to be downloaded in multiple formats viz Praat Textgrid, CSV, TSV, JSON, XLSX, LaTeX, HTML and Markdown. The data could also be pushed to different platforms and repositories such as HuggingFace Hub, ULCA, GitHub, etc for public usage.

3.3 Lexicon

The data processed in different kinds of data projects is input data for this module and the field linguist could gloss transcribed/labeled data with lemma, pos category and morphological features

[19]This is the format that could be directly uploaded on the Karya Crowd-sourcing android app for data collection. `https://karya.in`

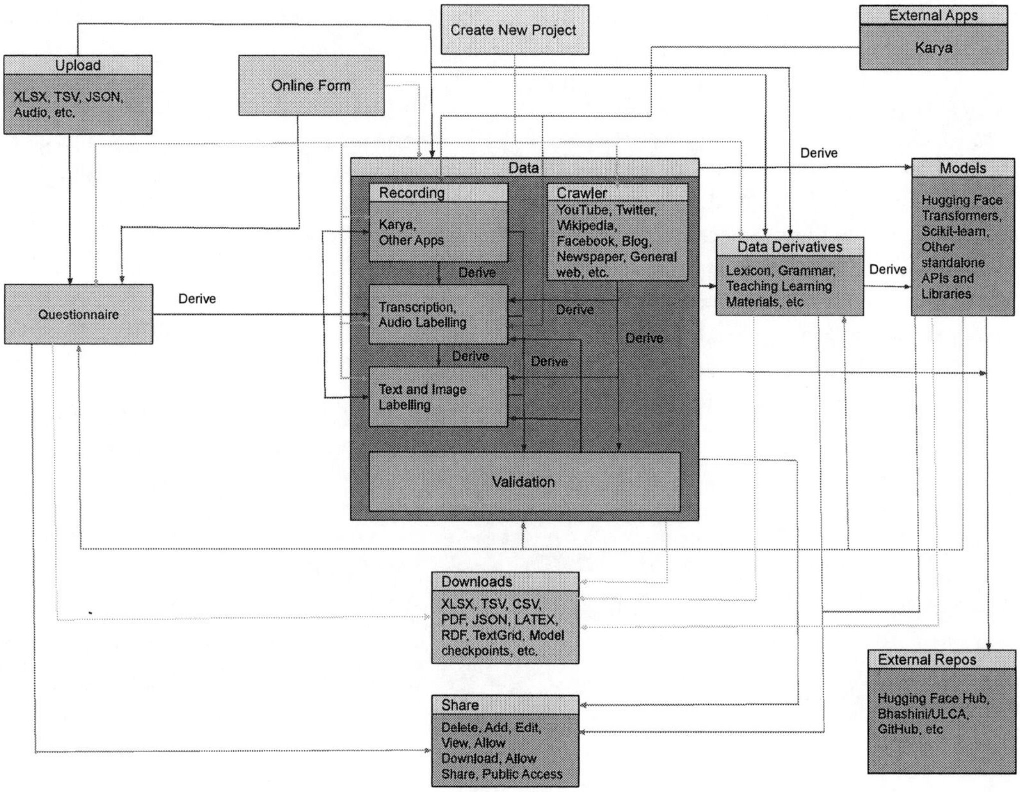

Figure 2: LiFE Workflows

to create a new lexicon (Figure 6). The information already provided during interlinear glossing or other kinds of labelling tasks (such as part-of-speech annotation) is automatically copied in the new project. A new lexicon project from scratch could also be created using the module. In that case, lexical entries could be imported from XLSX, CSV, TSV, JSON and also LIFT XML (this is the format generated by FLEx and it allows the apps' interoperability with the popular, legacy apps used by field linguists for data management and generating lexicons) formats. The data could be downloaded for further editing in multiple formats such as XLSX, CS, TSV, JSON, etc, in a publishable format for further dissemination such as Markdown or HTML or in a printable format such as PDF and LaTeX. This module also automatically generates an RDF representation of the lexicon and downloads it in different serialisation formats such as RDF/XML, Turtle, N3, etc.

3.4 Models

This module provides a no-code environment for training models for different tasks, using data from one or more projects of the same kind or different kinds of projects with similar kinds of data Figure 8. It could be derived from the projects both in the data and the lexicon modules. The models trained in this module are automatically made available across different projects in the app for immediate use. They could also be directly pushed to different platforms such as HuggingFace Hub, ULCA, GitHub, etc for public usage.

4 Supported Workflows in LiFE

LiFE does not enforce any specific workflows or pipelines. The app is currently being used by over 200 users and at least three organisations for various purposes and they all have different workflows. The app allows users to start working at any point in their data collection and analysis project. While users could define their own workflow and use different modules accordingly, the has been consciously designed to support two broad kinds of workflow -

- The Field Linguists' Workflow and
- The Computational Linguists' Workflow

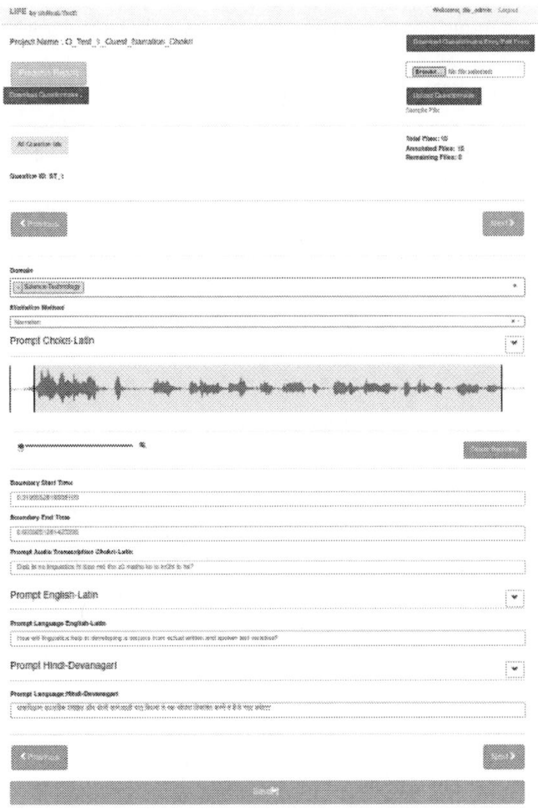

Figure 3: LiFE Questionnaire Interface

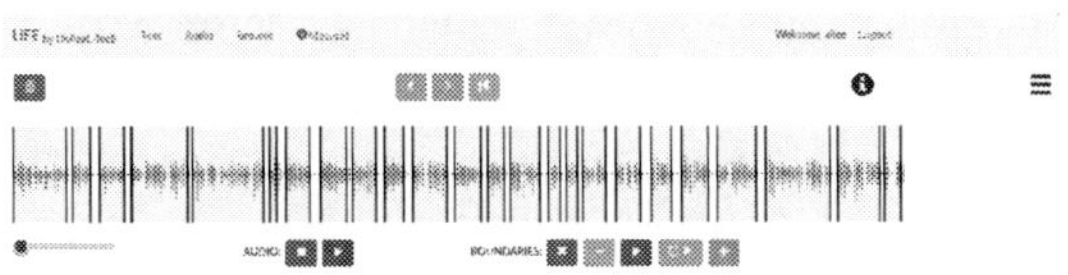

Figure 4: LiFE Data Interface

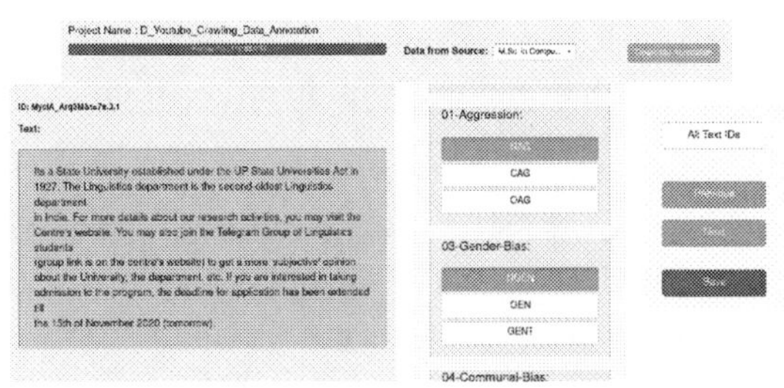

Figure 5: LiFE Text Annotation Interface

These two are discussed in the following subsections.

4.1 The Field Linguists' Workflow

A typical workflow of field linguists starts with the creation of questionnaires and other elicitation tools that could be used in the field for data collection. For this, the users have two options

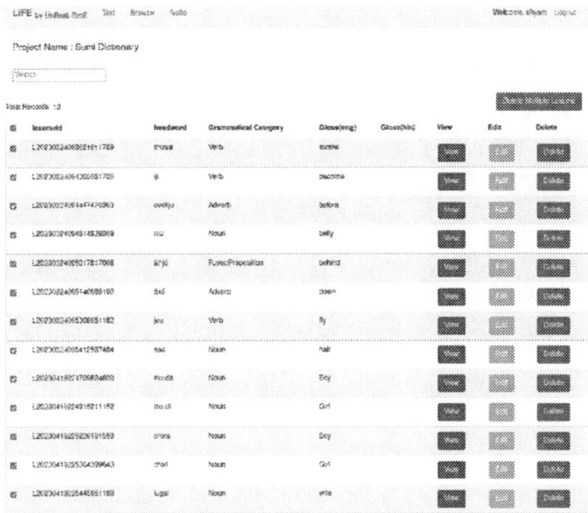

Figure 6: LiFE Lexicon Inteface

Figure 7: LiFE Models Module Form

to create questionnaires for field data collection. The first is to develop new questionnaires as per their target/goal for writing grammatical descriptions, generating lexicons, and preparing educational materials of any language. The other way is to modify and adapt some existing questionnaires to their needs. The questionnaire module in the app supports all these. After this data is collected directly from the speakers in the field using that questionnaire and imported into the data project for storage, transcription, inter-linear glossing and analysis. Once data is prepared the lexicon is generated by encoding grammatical, syntactic and semantic categories, morphological features, lexical relations, inter-linear glossing and free translation including examples. Users could also develop text and speech technologies like pos-tagger, morphological analyser and generator, automatic speech recognition (ASR), etc out of labelled data for multiple domains. Thus the app provides a simple, linear workflow for field linguists across its four modules.

The app is being used in large projects that make use of this workflow. One such project is "The Speech Datasets and Models for Indian Languages" (SpeeD-IL)[20], which is working on developing transcribed speech corpora of around 1000 hours each

[20] `https://sites.google.com/view/speed-il,https://github.com/unrealtecellp/SpeeD-IL`

for more than ten languages of the four major language families of India: Tibeto-Burman, Austro-Asiatic, Dravidian, and Indo-Aryan, as well as other tools and models (Kumar et al., 2022b). The project is being jointly executed by six institutions and more than twenty-five linguists are working on data collection and transcription across different languages. The other project is that of the Linguistic Data Consortium for Indian Languages (LDC-IL) [21] is an initiative by the Government of India to create all kinds of datasets across all Indian languages for technology development. The `LiFE` app has been recently adapted as the application for speech transcription, part-of-speech tagging and other kinds of activities in the consortium.

4.2 The Computational Linguists' Workflow

A typical workflow of computational linguists starts with data collection, generally from the web sources such as YouTube, Twitter, Facebook, Instagram, Blog, Newspaper, Wikipedia, etc. using automated crawlers A large number of such crawlers are integrated with the data module of the app and could be employed out-of-the-box for collecting multimodal data including speech, text and images. After collection, the data is annotated, transcribed, translated or processed in some way to make it suitable for training models of different kinds. A typical workflow also involves validating the data and its annotations. The data module provides support for these as well. Further, annotated data is used for developing different kinds of language technologies by training different models using the models module of the app.

Workflow like this has also been utilised in projects like "The Communal and Misogynistic Aggression in Hindi-English-Bangla-Meitei" (ComMA)[22], which was a multi-institutional project that focused on aggression identification in Hindi, English, Bangla, and Meitei ((Bhattacharya et al., 2020), (Kumar et al., 2021b) and (Kumar et al., 2022a)). Another similar project using the app is "Measuring Harm Potential of Social Media Content in India", being carried out by the Council for Strategic and Defense Research (CSDR). It aims to predict the possibility of a text (in Hindi or English) leading to some real-world harm. The annotation schema of the project is a complex mix of cross-document, single-document and span-level annotations and is handled efficiently in the app.

5 LiFE Technology Stack

The app's backend is built on the Python-based Flask[23] framework, with MongoDB (as the database) and the frontend using HTML, CSS, and Javascript. Bootsrap v3 and JQeury are used for developing the user interface in the app. Wavesurfer.js[24] is used for creating interactive, customizable waveforms which is an open-source audio visualization library. To train models for different types (audio recording and transcription, crawling and annotation) of data created in the LiFE app, Hugging Face[25] and scikit-learn[26] are used. We are also using the models hosted on the HuggingFace App to provide most of the automation facilities in the app - the app basically provides user interfaces to access these models for various tasks. The app is being developed using Agile methodology - this is ensured by keeping different modules as different Blueprints in the Flask app.

5.1 Database Architecture

Since the app contains various kinds of data and includes both structured and unstructured datasets, we are using a NoSQL database, MongoDB. It allows for storing the data entries as documents across different collections. The database of the tool contains fifteen core collections for storing different kinds of information. These are discussed below:

- **userlogin:** contains all the usernames with metadata and user profile information in the application,
- **userprojects:** contains projects that each user has developed and shared, as well as their active projects at any given point of time,
- **projectsform:** stores the forms created by users for their projects (questionnaire, data, lexicon and model) in JSON-like format. This stored information is used to render the HTML for all kinds of projects and is crucial to ensure that the interface and other properties of all projects remain completely customisable,

[21] `https://www.ldcil.org/`

[22] `https://sites.google.com/view/comma-ctrans`, `https://github.com/unrealtecellp/ComMA`

[23] `https://flask.palletsprojects.com/en/2.0.x/`

[24] `https://wavesurfer-js.org/`

[25] `https://huggingface.co/`

[26] `https://scikit-learn.org/stable/`

- **projects:** collection that has information about the project, its owner and project type (questionnaires, annotation, transcriptions, recordings, etc), project derivatives (other projects in the LiFE app that derive this project), project derive from (project from which this project is being derived),

- **questionnaires:** collection has a document for each prompt in the questionnaire which contains the prompt itself, a unique id, domain and elicitation information, prompt type (text, audio, image, multimedia) of the questionnaire,

- **recordings:** collection contains one document for each recorded audio and metadata of the audio (channels, sample rate, length etc),

- **crawling:** has information of data which is crawled with sources details from where the data is crawled,

- **tagsets:** has info regarding the tagset uploaded for text and image annotation, these tagsets can also be used by other projects if the user has to do a similar kind of annotation; since the app allows for using completely customised tagsets, with relatively complex structure, we have defined a structured format for uploading the tagset - this collection contains all the information provided through that structure,

- **annotation:** collection has one document for each data point to be annotated and as the same data can be annotated by multiple annotators so each annotators annotation is recorded in the same document by their username,

- **transcriptions:** collection contains the information about the transcription that has been done for each recording, speaker id, textgrid which has information about the transcription done for the audio at discourse, sentence, word, or phoneme level. The same audio could be transcribed by multiple users and the record is maintained accordingly,

- **lexemes:** collection contains information about each lexeme, with the aid of the appropriate vocabulary.

- **speakerdetails:** stores a list of metadata of all speakers,

- **sourcedetails:** is listing all the sources from where data is fetched or uploaded in the system,

- **models:** contains all the details about different models that have been trained in the app,

- **fs.files:** saves fs.chunks and the file's metadata. a file's binary portions, including pictures, videos, and audio files, are stored.

Besides these, some other collections are defined for interfacing with external apps such as Karya, interacting with external repositories like HF Hub and also for storing the app-level settings. The app stores all kinds of data and metadata in the database, without the need of storing anything in the file system.

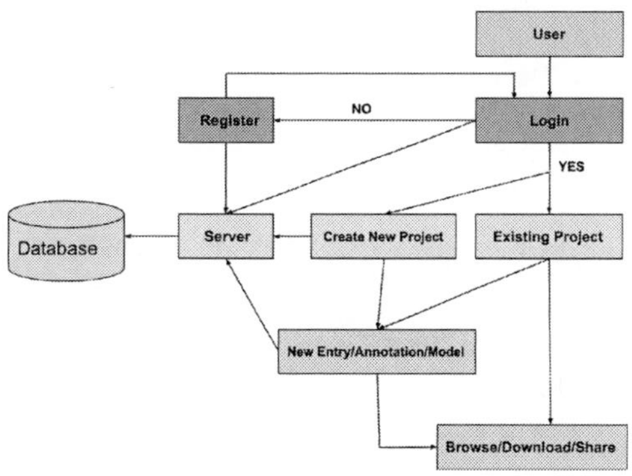

Figure 8: Model Diagram of LiFE

6 Summary

In this paper, we have presented an open-source app, `LiFE` for linguistic data management, analysis and sharing. The app intends to accelerate the development of language technologies for extremely underresourced languages by providing a link between field linguists and computational linguists. The app allows field linguists to use state-of-the-art NLP models for aiding and accelerating their work and also training baseline models for new languages and tasks in a no-code environment. At the same, it stores the data collected in the field in a structured format that could be used by computational linguists for their research. The app is currently being actively developed and is also used by multiple teams for their research.

7 Acknowledgements

We would like to thank the Linguistic Data Consortium for Indian Languages, Central Institute of Indian Languages and Ministry of Electronics and Information Technology, Government of India for providing grants and necessary support for the development of this app. We would also like to thank Karya Inc and the Council for Strategic and Defense Research for providing the support essential for developing the app.

References

Eric Albright and John Hatton. 2008. Wesay, a tool for collaborating on dictionaries with non-linguists. *Documenting and revitalizing Austronesian languages*, 6:189 – 201.

Alexei Baevski, Wei-Ning Hsu, Alexis Conneau, and Michael Auli. 2021. Unsupervised speech recognition. *CoRR*, abs/2105.11084.

Alexei Baevski, Henry Zhou, Abdelrahman Mohamed, and Michael Auli. 2020. wav2vec 2.0: A framework for self-supervised learning of speech representations. *CoRR*, abs/2006.11477.

Shiladitya Bhattacharya, Siddharth Singh, Ritesh Kumar, Akanksha Bansal, Akash Bhagat, Yogesh Dawer, Bornini Lahiri, and Atul Kr. Ojha. 2020. Developing a multilingual annotated corpus of misogyny and aggression. In *Proceedings of the Second Workshop on Trolling, Aggression and Cyberbullying*, pages 158–168, Marseille, France. European Language Resources Association (ELRA).

Paul Boersma and Vincent Van Heuven. 2001. Speak and unspeak with praat. *Glot Int*, 5:341–347.

Lynnika Butler and Heather Volkinburg. 2007. Review of fieldworks language explorer (flex). *Language Documentation and Conservation*, 1.

Valérie Guérin and Sébastien Lacrampe. 2007. Lexique pro. *Language Documentation and Conservation*, 1(2):293 – 300.

Jan-Christoph Klie, Michael Bugert, Beto Boullosa, Richard Eckart de Castilho, and Iryna Gurevych. 2018. The INCEpTION platform: Machine-assisted and knowledge-oriented interactive annotation. In *Proceedings of the 27th International Conference on Computational Linguistics: System Demonstrations*, pages 5–9, Santa Fe, New Mexico.

Ritesh Kumar, Enakshi Nandi, Laishram Niranjana Devi, Shyam Ratan, Siddharth Singh, Akash Bhagat, and Yogesh Dawer. 2021a. The comma dataset v0.2: Annotating aggression and bias in multilingual social media discourse.

Ritesh Kumar, Shyam Ratan, Siddharth Singh, Enakshi Nandi, Laishram Niranjana Devi, Akash Bhagat, Yogesh Dawer, Bornini Lahiri, and Akanksha Bansal. 2021b. ComMA@ICON: Multilingual gender biased and communal language identification task at ICON-2021. In *Proceedings of the 18th International Conference on Natural Language Processing: Shared Task on Multilingual Gender Biased and Communal Language Identification*, pages 1–12, NIT Silchar. NLP Association of India (NLPAI).

Ritesh Kumar, Shyam Ratan, Siddharth Singh, Enakshi Nandi, Laishram Niranjana Devi, Akash Bhagat, Yogesh Dawer, bornini lahiri, Akanksha Bansal, and Atul Kr. Ojha. 2022a. The comma dataset v0.2: Annotating aggression and bias in multilingual social media discourse. In *Proceedings of the Language Resources and Evaluation Conference*, pages 4149–4161, Marseille, France. European Language Resources Association.

Ritesh Kumar, Siddharth Singh, Shyam Ratan, Mohit Raj, Sonal Sinha, Sumitra Mishra, Bornini Lahiri, Vivek Seshadri, Kalika Bali, and Atul Kr. Ojha. 2022b. Annotated Speech Corpus for Low Resource Indian Langauges: Awadhi, Bhojpuri, Braj and Magahi. In *Proc. 1st Workshop on Speech for Social Good (S4SG)*, pages 1–5.

Ken Manson. 2020. Fieldworks linguistic explorer (flex) training 2020 (ver 1.1 august 2020).

Hiroki Nakayama, Takahiro Kubo, Junya Kamura, Yasufumi Taniguchi, and Xu Liang. 2018. doccano: Text annotation tool for human. Software available from https://github.com/doccano/doccano.

Ross Perlin. 2012. Wesay, a tool for collaborating on dictionaries with non-linguists. *Language Documentation & Conservation*, 6:181 – 186.

Alec Radford, Jong Wook Kim, Tao Xu, Greg Brockman, Christine McLeavey, and Ilya Sutskever. 2022. Robust speech recognition via large-scale weak supervision.

Stuart Robinson, Greg Aumann, and Steven Bird. 2007. Managing fieldwork data with toolbox and the natural language toolkit. *Language Documentation and Conservation*, 1.

Pontus Stenetorp, Sampo Pyysalo, Goran Topić, Tomoko Ohta, Sophia Ananiadou, and Jun'ichi Tsujii. 2012. brat: a web-based tool for NLP-assisted text annotation. In *Proceedings of the Demonstrations at the 13th Conference of the European Chapter of the Association for Computational Linguistics*, pages 102–107, Avignon, France. Association for Computational Linguistics.

Pontus Stenetorp, Goran Topić, Sampo Pyysalo, Tomoko Ohta, Jin-Dong Kim, and Jun'ichi Tsujii. 2011. Bionlp shared task 2011: Supporting resources.

In *Proceedings of BioNLP Shared Task 2011 Workshop*, pages 112–120, Portland, Oregon, USA. Association for Computational Linguistics.

Douglas Earl Thompson. 2014. An overview of audacity. *General Music Today*, 27(3):40–43.

Maxim Tkachenko, Mikhail Malyuk, Andrey Holmanyuk, and Nikolai Liubimov. 2020-2022. Label Studio: Data labeling software. Open source software available from https://github.com/heartexlabs/label-studio.

Nic Vries, Marelie Davel, Jaco Badenhorst, Willem Basson, Etienne Barnard, and Alta de Waal. 2014. A smartphone-based asr data collection tool for under-resourced languages. *Speech Communication*, 56:119–131.

Peter Wittenburg, Hennie Brugman, Albert Russel, Alex Klassmann, and Han Sloetjes. 2006. Elan: A professional framework for multimodality research. *Proceedings of the Fifth International Conference on Language Resources and Evaluation (LREC 2006).*

Rumour Detection in the Wild: A Browser Extension for Twitter

Andrej Jovanović and Björn Ross
University of Edinburgh
Edinburgh, United Kingdom
contact.me.maddox@gmail.com
b.ross@ed.ac.uk

Abstract

Rumour detection, particularly on social media, has gained popularity in recent years. The machine learning community has made significant contributions in investigating automatic methods to detect rumours on such platforms. However, these state-of-the-art (SoTA) models are often deployed by social media companies; ordinary end-users cannot leverage the solutions in the literature for their own rumour detection. To address this issue, we put forward a novel browser extension that allows these users to perform rumour detection on Twitter. Particularly, we leverage the performance from SoTA architectures, which has not been done previously. Initial results from a user study confirm that this browser extension provides benefit. Additionally, we examine the performance of our browser extension's rumour detection model in a simulated deployment environment. Our results show that additional infrastructure for the browser extension is required to ensure its usability when deployed as a live service for Twitter users at scale[1].

1 Introduction

The advent of social media has forever transformed the way in which we are able to communicate with one another. Content-sharing has effectively been democratised with the removal of existing traditional barriers (Bates, 2007). Indeed, this provides many benefits: for those individuals involved in a newsworthy event, for example, information can be shared in real-time. This allows for news to propagate faster, with the intention of informing the wider public and inciting action from relevant stakeholders. However, with the low barrier of entry to content production and dissemination on social media, the overall quality of information on these platforms has degraded (Shu et al., 2017).

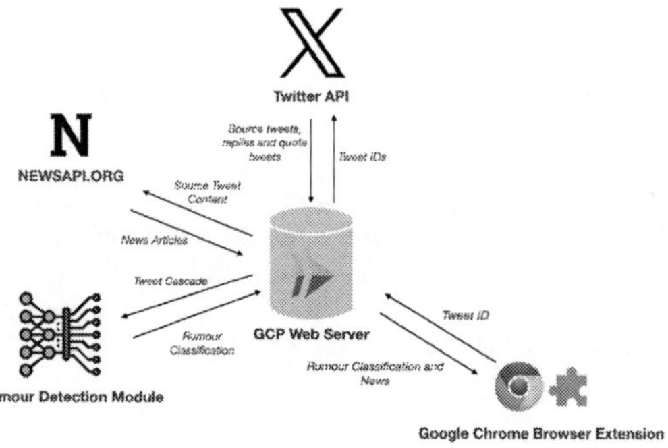

Figure 1: Server architecture of the Twitter rumour detection browser extension. Icons are taken from the following sources a, b, c, d and e

Users of social media platforms are now able to, inadvertently or deliberately, publish misinformation and falsehoods (Kydd and Shepherd, 2023). This has led to very damaging consequences for society in the past: Sharma et al. (2019) have provided examples of these effects in the financial, political and social domains. With this in mind, the machine learning community has created automatic detection systems which are designed to identify misinformation on social media platforms. However, it is the case that companies who own and manage these platforms are the ones that implement and deploy their own misinformation detection services (Kydd and Shepherd, 2023; Kumar et al., 2020). As such, regular content-consumers do not have access to these services directly. This takes away the autonomy of an individual who wishes to perform rumour detection for themselves, for example.

In this work, we present a Google Chrome browser extension, and the associated server architecture, (seen in Figure 1) that addresses this problem as highlighted by Fernandez and Alani (2018). It allows regular Twitter users to perform on-demand rumour detection for any tweet, whilst enhancing their experience through proving semantically-related news articles.

[1]We make all the materials related to this work available at the following GitHub repository under an open-source license.

Proceedings of the 3rd Workshop for Natural Language Processing Open Source Software (NLP-OSS 2023), pages 130–140
December 6, 2023 ©2023 Association for Computational Linguistics

2 Related Work

Considerable progress has been made in investigating methods to perform rumour detection on social media platforms. Seminal papers in this discipline initially focussed on generating informative, handcrafted features for this task (Castillo et al., 2011; Qazvinian et al., 2011; Yang et al., 2012). Stemming from these works, researchers refocussed their attention on temporal features. Kwon et al. (2013) showed that these features are highly predictive of rumours as they described the periodic bursts that are typical for these phenomena. These new features now allowed researchers to capture how rumours change over time, which is particularly important for early rumour detection. Ma et al. (2015) identified rumours through modelling their lifecycle as a time series, whilst Wu et al. (2015) approached this through modelling the propagation pattern as a tree. Furthermore, certain features were shown to have greater importance at different steps in a rumours' propagation (Kwon et al., 2017). However, the collective flaw in these works is that the feature engineering processes are detail-specific, could introduce biases and are extremely laborious (Bian et al., 2020; Ma et al., 2016). As such, SoTA solutions turn to deep learning for the automatic feature representations, increased model complexity and subsequent increase in performance for rumour detection.

Ma et al. (2016) implemented the same time series ideas from their earlier works (Ma et al., 2015) with recurrent neural networks (RNNs), later improved with attention (Chen et al., 2017), which leveraged the deep hidden representations that were learnt by the neural network. Ma et al. (2018) found that recursive neural networks (RvNNs) were more performant than RNNs as they are able to embed both content-based and propagation-based information due to their tree-like structure. This architecture was also improved with an attention mechanism (Ma et al., 2020). Bian et al. (2020) achieved SoTA performance on the *Twitter15* and *Twitter16* datasets for rumour detection on Twitter through not only modelling the propagation properties of a rumour, but also the dispersion properties with their Bi-Directional Graph Convolutional Network (Bi-GCN).

However, deploying said rumour detection models as a service has not been extensively researched in an academic setting. Gupta et al. (2014) introduced TweetCred, a Google Chrome browser extension that assigned a credibility score to each tweet on a user's feed using an SVM-rank model using 45 handcrafted features. Thilakarathna et al. (2020) created a browser extension for Twitter, called Veritas, that is able to detect fake news on the social media platform. Most notably, their architecture involves a model trainer pipeline to ensure that their neural models are constantly up-to-date. Kydd and Shepherd (2023) explored a very similar tool that used a deep learning solution as the backbone to a browser extension focusing on clickbait detection.

Additionally, we note that news articles are a typical resource that one would use to determine the status of a rumour. These resources enhance the experience for the user, informing them of the context in which the tweet occurs. To this end, our work attempts to address the following flaws found in previous work. i) Previous works that tackle rumour detection specifically do not leverage SoTA rumour detection models at the core of their service, which renders them outdated. ii) In certain cases, the rumour detection model is deployed on the user-side. We posit that with SoTA models, this will render the service inutile due to the computational complexity of the models (Kydd and Shepherd, 2023). iii) None of the aforementioned works enhance the user's experience through recommending articles that are semantically related to the tweet in question. Our browser extension will explore this addition.

3 Browser Extension Architecture

When creating a browser extension, and the associated architecture, we wish for the following properties to be met. These are chosen to maximise the extension's ease-of-use, performance and informativeness.

D1: Twitter users should be able to use the service in-real time in concert with their ordinary browsing experience.

D2: Users of the service should not have to bear the computational load of the underlying architecture.

D3: The detection model should be interchangeable, allowing for the browser extension to improve continually with the latest advancements in the field.

D4: News articles that are semantically related to the source tweet should enhance the user's rumour detection experience.

To meet the above desiderata, we put forward the

(a) The browser extension's landing page.

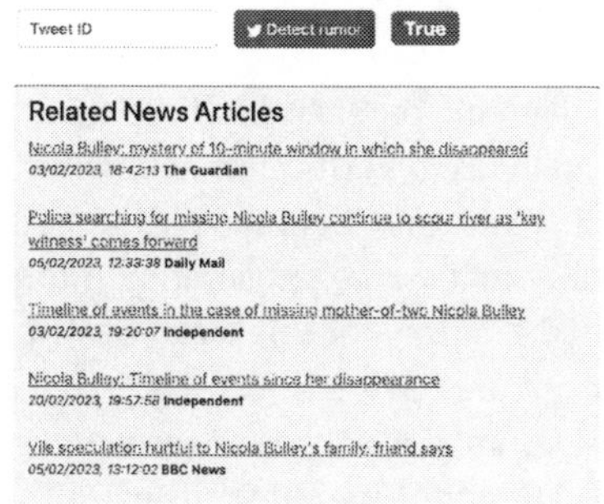

(b) The browser extension with results: a rumour classification label of "True" and a list of five semantically related news articles.

Figure 2: Screenshots showing the graphical user interface (GUI) of the browser extension.

browser extension architecture seen in Figure 1. Furthermore, we designed a user-friendly interface in the form of a Google Chrome browser extension seen in Figure 2.

A user will interact with the system as follows:

(i) A user browses Twitter via Google Chrome. Once they identify a particular tweet on which they wish to perform rumour detection, the user opens the browser extension and clicks the "Detect rumour" button seen in Figure 2a (**D1**). Once the button has been pressed, the tweet ID is extracted from the URL of the tweet and the client's web browser sends a POST request to the web server (**D2**), with the specific tweet ID as a parameter.

(ii) Once the web server receives this POST request, three functions occur sequentially:

   (a) Using the tweet ID, the web server interacts with the Twitter API to retrieve the source tweet, and its respective tweet cascade as outlined in section 3.2.

   (b) Once the tweet cascade has been retrieved and preprocessed, this is then fed into the rumour detection model (**D3**) seen in section 3.1, and inference is performed. This returns a particular rumour classification label.

   (c) Finally, using the source tweet, the web server finds semantically-related keywords and retrieves relevant news articles from NewsAPI.org (**D4**), as outlined in Section 3.3. This returns a list of relevant news articles to the web server.

(iii) Once the rumour classification label and the relevant news articles have been retrieved, these are returned to the user as a JSON object in response to the original POST request.

3.1 Rumour Detection Model Choice

For this iteration of the rumour detection browser extension, we choose the Bi-GCN architecture (Bian et al., 2020) as the machine learning model used in our service. The training code can be found in our GitHub repository, or at in the original repository. This model was chosen as it reported SoTA performance for the rumour detection task on the *Twitter15* and *Twitter16* datasets. The model is able to represent both the top-down and bottom-up views of a tweet cascade, each of which is passed to a dedicated two-layer GCN, along with a shared tweet feature matrix (linguistic tokens). Bian et al. (2020) also implement DropEdge to prevent overfitting, and root feature enhancement after each GCN layer to emphasise the information contained in the source tweet[2]. To deploy the model, we train it using the *Twitter16* data, with the same specifications as in (Bian et al., 2020) (see Section 4) with 5-fold cross validation, taking the average model as final. The Bi-GCN, with a hidden dimension size of 64, is trained using stochastic gradient descent with the Adam optimiser ($\eta = 5 \times 10^{-4}$) to minimise the cross entropy loss. The model is trained for 200 epochs, with early stopping on the validation loss and patience set to 10 epochs. DropEdge rate is set to 0.2, dropout rate is set to 0.5 and L2 regularisation is applied to all model parameters with $\lambda = 1 \times 10^{-4}$.

[2]We point the interested reader to their original paper for more details on the model's functionality.

3.2 Twitter API

We make use of the Twitter API to retrieve the raw data required to classify the rumour status of a particular tweet. Since the Bi-GCN represents each tweet as a cascade, we first collect the source tweet from the API to act as the root of the cascade. We then retrieve all the replies, quote tweets and retweets related to the root. We continue this process recursively, until the algorithm bottoms out at the leaf tweets. Once we have retrieved the cascade, each tweet is assigned its textual features according to the vocabulary used at training (Section 4).

3.3 Semantically-Related News Articles

To find the semantically-related news articles, we made use of the open-source KeyBERT tool[3]. This package leverages embeddings that are created using a Sentence-BERT architecture (Reimers and Gurevych, 2019; Devlin et al., 2018), particularly the *all-MiniLM-L6-v2* model found on HuggingFace[4], to generate the semantically related keywords. Before passing raw tweet text to KeyBERT, we first preprocess it with NLTK's tweet tokenizer[5]. Candidate keyword phrases are extracted from N-gram sequences (one to three grams in particular) in the document text, and word embeddings are computed for these. KeyBERT returns the candidate phrases that are most similar to the document text using the cosine similarity metric, and have been re-ranked using Maximal Marginal Relevance (MMR) (Carbonell and Goldstein, 1998) to increase the diversity. The keywords are then passed to News-API.org which returns relevant news articles according to a keyword-based query.

4 Datasets

We make use of the *Twitter15* and *Twitter16* datasets (Ma et al., 2017) to train our rumour detection model. The datasets comprise rumours linked to newsworthy events at specific time periods; the statistics of these can be found in Table 1. In particular, these datasets are graphical in nature. Each node refers to a tweet, where each node is described by textual features derived from a pretrained vocabulary of the top 5000 words in terms of TF-IDF (Sammut and Webb, 2010) score. Edges between tweets represent their retweet or response relationships. A collection of tweets in a cascade describes an event, and is assigned a veracity tag (rumour **(UR)**, non-rumour **(NR)**, false rumour **(FR)** or true rumour **(TR)**) which were derived from cross-referencing rumour debunking websites.

Statistic	Twitter15	Twitter16
# of posts	331,612	204,820
# of users	276,663	173,487
# of cascades	1,490	818
# of non-rumours	374	205
# of false rumours	370	205
# of true rumours	372	205
# of unverified rumours	374	203
Avg. time length / cascade (Hours)	1,337	848
Avg. # of posts / cascade	223	251
Max # of posts / cascade	1,768	2,765
Min # of posts / cascade	55	81

Table 1: Statistics of the *Twitter16* and *Twitter16* datasets.

5 Rumour Detection Model Evaluation

5.1 Out-of-Distribution Performance

An imperative part of the browser extension's functionality relies on the underlying performance of the machine learning model used for inference. It is well accepted that models are able to generalise well (if trained appropriately) to data that is unseen, but comes from a similar distribution to the training data (Hendrycks and Dietterich, 2019; Klaise et al., 2020; Engstrom et al., 2019). However, using our browser extension for rumour detection in the wild necessitates that the model will be used to evaluate tweets that are OOD relative to the data which it was trained. Concept drift is frequently occurring in social media, particularly when the nature of discourse underlying different rumours changes (Horne et al., 2019). Furthermore, end-users of the browser extension could use the tool outside the environment in which it was intended to be deployed. In these scenarios, we would expect that the browser extension would perform suboptimally on the rumour detection task.

To simulate this effect, we conduct a data mixing experiment. Specifically, we leverage two datasets that are frequently occurring in the rumour detection literature: *Twitter15* and *Twitter16*. In this experiment, we create a third *TwitterMix* dataset through a linear-interpolation-like combination of the *Twitter15* and *Twitter16* datasets $TM = p_{T15} * T_{15} + p_{T16} * T_{16}$, controlling for

[3]KeyBERT
[4]all-MiniLM-L6-v2
[5]NLTK Tokenize

the size of the dataset by enforcing the following constraint: $p_{T15} + p_{T16} = 1$. p_{T15} and p_{T16} act as the proportion of the dataset that is selected. We posit that a model trained on *TwitterMix*, as a simple baseline, would be able to mitigate partially the effects of concept drift. This baseline is akin to a single-shot retraining procedure. Following the training regime set out in Section 3.1, we train three separate models based on the following datasets: i) a *Twitter15* model on the unmixed $1 - p_{T15}$ *Twitter15* data, ii) a *Twitter16* model on the unmixed $1 - p_{T16}$ *Twitter16* data, and iii) a *TwitterMix* model on the mixed data. In the case of the *Twitter15* and *Twitter16*, all models were evaluated on the p_{T15} and p_{T16} data. All models were evaluated on the *TwitterMix* data, where we report the cross-validation performance in the case of the *TwitterMix* model. In Figure 3, we view the experimental results where we set $p_{T15} = p_{T16} = 0.5$. This particular proportion was chosen for the sake of simplicity. On both the *Twitter15* and *Twitter16* datasets, we find that their respective models perform well, as expected. Similarly, we find that the *Twitter15* model's performance decays dramatically on the *Twitter16* data, and *vice versa*. Both models perform equally well on the *TwitterMix* data. Furthermore, we find that the *TwitterMix* model is able to mitigate some adverse effects when evaluating a model on OOD data, seen particularly on the *Twitter15* data. While not as performant as the *Twitter16* model on *Twitter16* data, it is able to recover some performance relative to the *Twitter15* model. These results confirm findings of Horne et al. (2019); Paleyes et al. (2022); Lobo et al. (2020), and show the importance of retraining schedules and engines when deploying machine learning models in browser extension tools (Thilakarathna et al., 2020). We perform additional experiments (seen in Appendix B) altering the proportion of p_{T15} and p_{T16}. These experiments show that if adequate care is not placed on constantly maintaining a representative/diverse training sample through retraining, or if additional methods are not put into place to detect when samples are OOD, the performance of the model decays significantly.

5.2 Imperfect Data Performance

5.2.1 Textual Ablation Experiments

Another implication to consider is that the rumour detection model's performance is also constrained by the Twitter API limits. For example, the quote tweet endpoint has a 75 request per 15-minute window threshold[6]. This would not affect those users who wish to perform rumour detection on a handful of tweets, but rather "power users". In the cases, we could observe that the true tweet cascade cannot be sufficiently represented, which in turn could affect the performance of the rumour detection model. Similarly, due to the effects of concept drift mentioned in Section 5.1, the rumour detection model would be unable to represent the textual content of certain tweets in a rumour cascade. As seen in Section 3.1, the Bi-GCN architecture is trained on a fixed, static vocabulary (as are many other NLP solutions). If a tweet were composed of tokens that were out-of-vocabulary for the rumour detection model, this tweet would then be underrepresented.

To simulate these effects, we run two ablation studies. First, we run a text ablation study where generate new versions of the *Twitter15* and *Twitter16* datasets according to some textual ablation proportion. In these new datasets, we randomly replace, according to the specified proportion, the textual features of a given tweet with `[0:1]`, which is the corresponding `[index:count]` pair for an `<END>` tag. Once the new datasets have been created, we train a *Twitter15* and *Twitter16* model, and report the performance on five-fold cross validation as done in section 3.1. This was done for the textual ablation proportions: 0%, 50%, 70%, 90%, 100%. We view the results of this experiment in Figure 4.

We see that the performance of the two models dramatically decays as we increase the proportion of tweets that have their textual features removed. These results were expected due to the importance of textual features to rumour detection models. Textual features have always provided an important signal in predicting the rumour status of a particular tweet (Section 2). The same is true with the Bi-GCN model. These results stress that without the proper, and full, representation of tweet cascades, the performance of the rumour detection model drops dramatically.

5.2.2 Node Ablation Experiment

Similar to the textual feature ablation experiment, we conduct a node ablation experiment. We first generate new versions of the *Twitter15* and *Twitter16* datasets according to some node ablation proportion. However, instead of removing textual

[6] Quote Tweets API

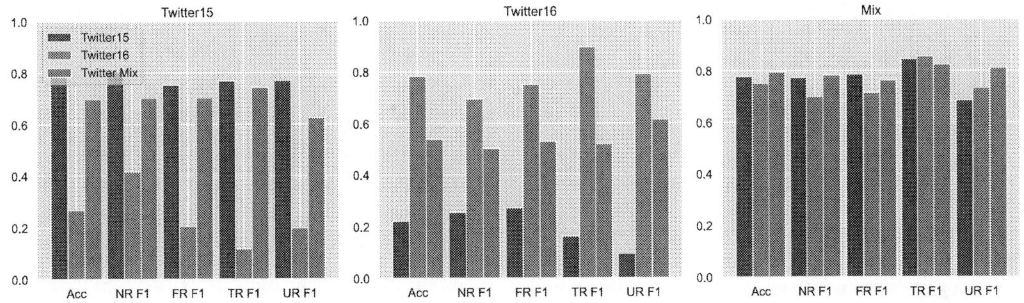

Figure 3: Result from the dataset mixing experiment for the *Twitter15*, *Twitter16* and TwitterMix models, with $p_{T15} = p_{T16} = 0.5$. Each subplot indicates the evaluation dataset, and the legend the model versions.

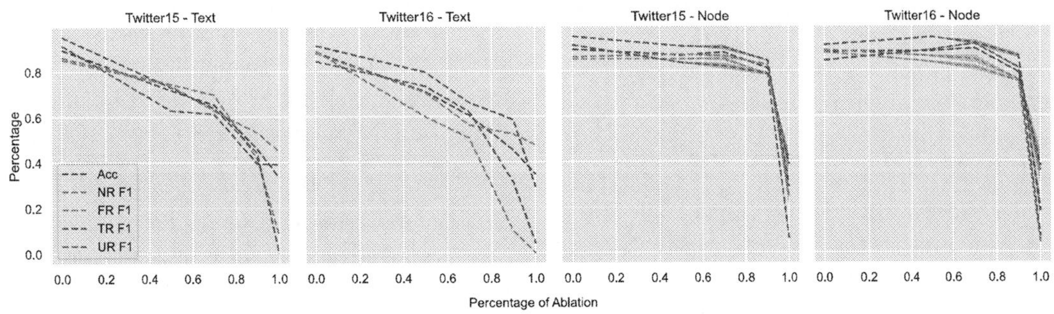

Figure 4: Results from the textual and node ablation experiments, across varying ablation proportions, for the *Twitter15* and *Twitter16* datasets.

features, we randomly remove nodes, and their descendents, from every tweet cascade[7]. This was done to simulate the scenario where certain tweets would not be retrieved by the Twitter API. We train a *Twitter15* and *Twitter16* model on these new datasets and report the performance on five-fold cross validation as done in section 3.1. We repeat this experiment for the following node ablation proportions: 0%, 50%, 70%, 90% and 99.9%. The results of these experiments are specified in Figure 4.

Surprisingly, we did not observe the same effect as was seen in the textual ablation experiments (Figure 4). Instead, we see that the Bi-GCN was able to was able to maintain, and sometimes improve, performance relative to the baseline, across both datasets. This was achieved until over 90% of the tweets in each cascade had been removed. After this point, the models' predictive capability sharply decreased – once enough tweets had been removed, both models lose enough signal from the input data to classify the rumour status accurately. However, we can contrast these results with the early rumour detection study in the original paper by Bian et al. (2020). Their work examined the Bi-GCN's performance on the task of early rumour detection. Although our experiment does not remove tweets from the cascade temporally (as we do not have access to the timestamp for each tweet), we are, essentially, creating an experiment that is very similar to this experiment in Bian et al. (2020).

However, an interesting result is that in both datasets, we observed that the models were able to score better than the baseline even with fewer tweets representing the cascade. When randomly removing a tweet, and its descendents, from a cascade, we have no rules enforcing what type of tweets are removed from the cascade. If we observe the rumour tweet in Figure 5, tweets that express doubt in response to a root tweet indicates that the tweet is potentially a rumour (Kwon et al., 2017). As such, removing the tweets that express support make the tweet seem more rumour-like. Similarly, removing the tweets that express doubt from the non-rumour would make this tweet more non-rumour like. These situations would make each of the tweet cascades seem more like a prototypical example of their respective class.

[7]We did not remove the root nodes from the tweet cascades as the label for each tweet cascade is tied to the root node.

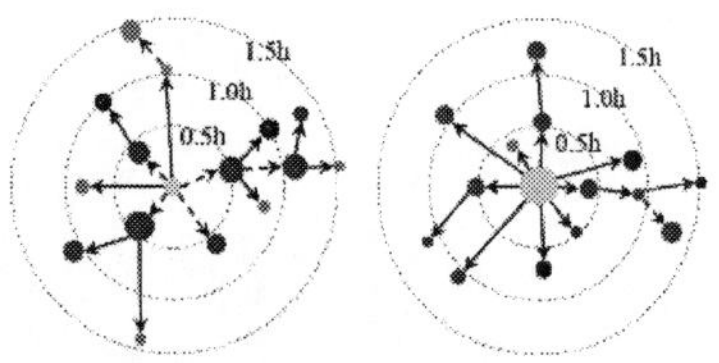

(a) A rumor (b) A non-rumor

Figure 5: Prorogation structure of two source tweets taken from Ma et al. (2017). Red nodes express doubt, blue nodes express neutrality and black nodes express support. The green node is the root of the cascade.

A similar effect could, by chance, be observed in our node ablation experiments. By randomly removing certain nodes, we inadvertently simplify the rumour detection task for that tweet as it would seem more prototypical of its class.

6 Latency Experiments

Similar to the work done by Gupta et al. (2014), we wish to evaluate the browser extension's performance with respect to response time. This is calculated as the amount of time taken for our browser extension to respond to a particular rumour detection request. In our experiment, we measure the response time across 50 randomly selected newsworthy tweets of varying size. We view the cumulative distribution function (CDF) of the response times in Figure 6.

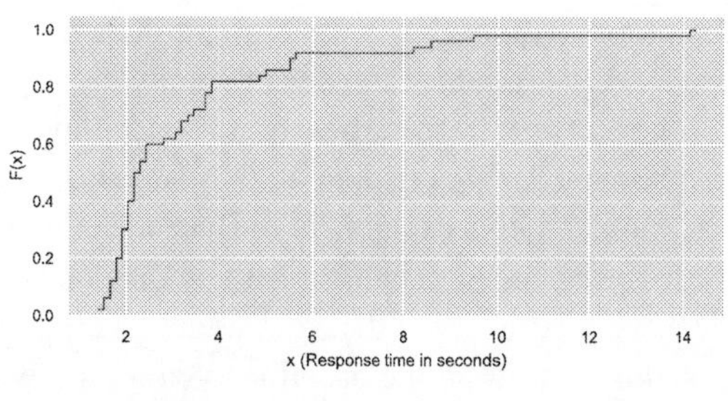

Figure 6: CDF for response time taken for rumour detection across 50 tweets.

Observing Figure 6, we see that our browser extension is able to provide a response for 90% of requests in six seconds or less. This is an improvement over the 82% of requests in Gupta et al. (2014); however, their experiment analysed the CDF across 5.4 million requests. Due to time constraints, our sample size is significantly smaller. Yet, we can make some initial comparisons between the two solutions. Our work retrieves the entire tweet cascade for a tweet, and predicts the rumour status using the Bi-GCN model. TweetCred, on the other hand calculates 45 handcrafted features based on the tweet itself, and uses SVM-rank to assign a credibility score. Given the fact that our approach uses far more information per tweet, and a more sophisticated and computationally intensive model[8], this is still an encouraging result for our browser extension. Unfortunately, the other browser extensions mentioned in Section 2 do not report results for a response time experiment. As such, we are unable to compare our extension to other solutions on this particular axis.

7 User Study

To determine whether the browser extension provides benefit to Twitter users, we ran an anonymised user study. We asked 19 participants to perform five rumour detection tasks (RDTs). In this context, a RDT is divided into two questions.

(i) Before performing rumour detection using the browser extension, determine the rumour status of the current tweet.

(ii) After performing rumour detection, assess whether the browser extension aid in determining the true status of the tweet.

Each set of questions was asked on a preselected tweet that was newsworthy at that instance in time. This was done to ensure that the tweets used in the study were as similar as possible to the training data distribution on which the model was trained (see Section 5.1 for out-of-distribution performance).

After performing these tasks, we asked the users to comment on their overall experience using the browser extension. The user study was facilitated through the use of anonymised survey. The users accessed the server architecture through a remote Google Cloud Platform server (GCP), and the browser extension itself from a shareable Google Chrome Store link. The user study was approved by a research ethics board (see Section 8). The results from the RDT and overall experience feedback are seen in Figures 7 and 8, respectively. See Appendix A for full details on the user study.

Prior to performing rumour detection, we see that there is considerable disagreement amongst the annotators. Particularly, we find that Randolph's Kappa is $\kappa = 0.345$ (Randolph, 2010). These results confirm an assumed truth in the field: rumour

[8]Most notably, our browser extension was able to classify a tweet cascade with over 579 retweets, 343 quote tweets and 454 replies in approximately 14 seconds.

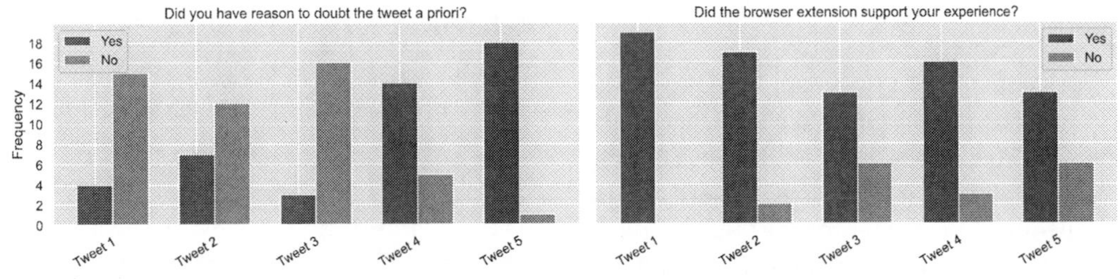

Figure 7: Results from the RDT in the user study.

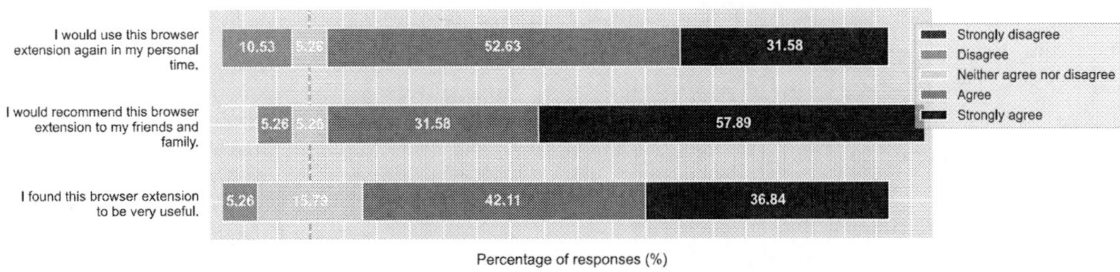

Figure 8: Results from global feedback in the user study.

detection, a highly subjective task, is difficult for humans as the labels are not necessarily objective (Touvron et al., 2023). This further motivates the need for assistive tools such as this browser extension. Contrastingly, we see that, generally, annotators found that the browser extension supported their rumour detection experience. $\kappa = 0.443$ which supports the fair agreement on the browser extension's positive impact on their rumour detection experience. An interesting result is that this kappa score is similar to the user agreement on the credibility score (43%) obtained for TweetCred (Gupta et al., 2014). Whilst the questions posed to the users are different, these results show that there is some benefit to be gained through using additional rumour detection tools. However, there needs to be additional measures put into place to make users more confident in the tool's performance, which would lead to higher user agreement (see Section 8).

Furthermore, we asked the users to rate their agreement to three questions on a five-point Likert scale. Observing Figure 8, we see that the feedback for the browser extension is generally positive. 78.95% of the participants in the user study agreed or strongly agreed with finding the browser extension to be useful. However, we see that there was a small portion of users who either disagreed or were ambivalent to the three statements. This study did not require the participant to be a Twitter user. As such, the study could have attracted participants who: do not use Twitter frequently, do not use Twitter as a news source, or those users that do not have a Twitter account at all. These users would not see the need to have access to a tool such as this browser extension as they would have no use for it personally.

8 Conclusion and Future Work

In this work, we put forward a novel browser extension that allows Twitter users to perform rumour detection, leveraging the performance from SoTA models. Our work shows that this tool provides benefit to those Twitter users wanting autonomy over their rumour detection. However, we note that our work is merely the first iteration in a series of deployments. Future work could explore additional mechanisms to allow the browser extension to cope with OOD data. Online retraining (Horne et al., 2019) has been shown to be effective in minimising the effects of concept drift; this is similar to the trainer pipeline in Veritas (Thilakarathna et al., 2020). Furthermore, Diethe et al. (2019) show a more sophisticated paradigm with their continual learning approach. Additionally, we could extend the browser extension's functionality through allowing its users to submit examples of tweets they believe to be (non-)rumours (with evidence) to some community-moderated data store. This process could be used to create more up-to-date datasets for rumour detection.

Limitations

The work suffers from two main limitations, the first of which is the current system's reliance on the Twitter API, and its changing access requirements. At the time of writing, Twitter API users will no longer be able to make use of the GET API endpoints, which include the endpoints used to fetch the information needed for a tweet's cascade representation (Section 3.2), under the free tier. Instead, users will have to pay $100 per month[9]. As such, this limits the use-case of the browser extension that we have created. However, the flexible architecture that we have created allows the browser extension to be ported to a different context. Instead of focussing on Twitter, a similar use-case would be found with Sina Weibo, for example. The browser extension could focus on fake news detection, rather than on rumour detection. Each of these disciplines have their own state-of-the-art solutions in the literature, and exploring practical tools that would leverage their performance would be a worthwhile research direction.

A second limitation lies in the small sample size of the user study. Furthermore, the participants themselves could be biased in their evaluation of the browser extension because of their relation to the author; the browser extension was shared via a university mailing list. However, due to the anonymity of the study, we hope that the participants of the user study would be objective in their assessment of the browser extension. Nevertheless, we find that these initial results support and encourage the viability of a Twitter rumour detection extension. However, a potential direction for future work would be extending the browser extension to a wider, more diverse audience.

Ethics Statement

This project obtained approval from the Informatics Research Ethics committee at the University of Edinburgh.
Ethics application number: 2023/260884
Date when approval was obtained: 2023-01-30

Acknowledgements

We are grateful to the following people (in no particular order) for their helpful insight and corrections to the manuscript: Alessandro Palmarini, Maxime Labonne, and Simon Chi Lok U.

[9]https://developer.twitter.com/en/portal/products/basic

References

Benjamin Bates. 2007. Yochai benkler. the wealth of networks: How social production transforms markets and freedom. *Journal of Media Economics*, 20:161–165.

Tian Bian, Xi Xiao, Tingyang Xu, Peilin Zhao, Wenbing Huang, Yu Rong, and Junzhou Huang. 2020. Rumor detection on social media with bi-directional graph convolutional networks. *Proceedings of the AAAI Conference on Artificial Intelligence*, 34(01):549–556.

Jaime Carbonell and Jade Goldstein. 1998. The use of mmr, diversity-based reranking for reordering documents and producing summaries. In *Proceedings of the 21st Annual International ACM SIGIR Conference on Research and Development in Information Retrieval*, SIGIR '98, page 335–336, New York, NY, USA. Association for Computing Machinery.

Carlos Castillo, Marcelo Mendoza, and Barbara Poblete. 2011. Information credibility on twitter. In *Proceedings of the 20th International Conference on World Wide Web*, WWW '11, page 675–684, New York, NY, USA. Association for Computing Machinery.

Tong Chen, Lin Wu, Xue Li, Jun Zhang, Hongzhi Yin, and Yang Wang. 2017. Call attention to rumors: Deep attention based recurrent neural networks for early rumor detection. *CoRR*, abs/1704.05973.

Jacob Devlin, Ming-Wei Chang, Kenton Lee, and Kristina Toutanova. 2018. Bert: Pre-training of deep bidirectional transformers for language understanding.

Tom Diethe, Tom Borchert, Eno Thereska, Borja Balle, and Neil Lawrence. 2019. Continual learning in practice.

Logan Engstrom, Brandon Tran, Dimitris Tsipras, Ludwig Schmidt, and Aleksander Madry. 2019. Exploring the landscape of spatial robustness. In *Proceedings of the 36th International Conference on Machine Learning*, volume 97 of *Proceedings of Machine Learning Research*, pages 1802–1811. PMLR.

Miriam Fernandez and Harith Alani. 2018. Online misinformation: Challenges and future directions. In *Companion Proceedings of the The Web Conference 2018*, WWW '18, page 595–602, Republic and Canton of Geneva, CHE. International World Wide Web Conferences Steering Committee.

Aditi Gupta, Ponnurangam Kumaraguru, Carlos Castillo, and Patrick Meier. 2014. Tweetcred: Real-time credibility assessment of content on twitter. pages 228–243.

Dan Hendrycks and Thomas Dietterich. 2019. Benchmarking neural network robustness to common corruptions and perturbations. In *International Conference on Learning Representations*.

Benjamin D. Horne, Jeppe Nørregaard, and Sibel Adali. 2019. Robust fake news detection over time and attack. *ACM Trans. Intell. Syst. Technol.*, 11(1).

Janis Klaise, Arnaud Van Looveren, Clive Cox, Giovanni Vacanti, and Alexandru Coca. 2020. Monitoring and explainability of models in production.

Sachin Kumar, Rohan Asthana, Shashwat Upadhyay, Nidhi Upreti, and Mohammad Akbar. 2020. Fake news detection using deep learning models: A novel approach. *Trans. Emerg. Telecommun. Technol.*, 31(2).

Sejeong Kwon, Meeyoung Cha, and Kyomin Jung. 2017. Rumor detection over varying time windows. *PLOS ONE*, 12(1):1–19.

Sejeong Kwon, Meeyoung Cha, Kyomin Jung, Wei Chen, and Yajun Wang. 2013. Prominent features of rumor propagation in online social media. In *2013 IEEE 13th International Conference on Data Mining*, pages 1103–1108.

Marc Kydd and Lynsay A. Shepherd. 2023. Deep breath: A machine learning browser extension to tackle online misinformation.

Jesus L. Lobo, Javier Del Ser, Albert Bifet, and Nikola Kasabov. 2020. Spiking neural networks and online learning: An overview and perspectives. *Neural Networks*, 121:88–100.

Jing Ma, Wei Gao, Shafiq Joty, and Kam-Fai Wong. 2020. An attention-based rumor detection model with tree-structured recursive neural networks. *ACM Trans. Intell. Syst. Technol.*, 11(4).

Jing Ma, Wei Gao, Prasenjit Mitra, Sejeong Kwon, Jim Jansen, Kam-Fai Wong, and Meeyoung Cha. 2016. Detecting rumors from microblogs with recurrent neural networks.

Jing Ma, Wei Gao, Zhongyu Wei, Yueming Lu, and Kam-Fai Wong. 2015. Detect rumors using time series of social context information on microblogging websites. In *Proceedings of the 24th ACM International on Conference on Information and Knowledge Management*, CIKM '15, page 1751–1754, New York, NY, USA. Association for Computing Machinery.

Jing Ma, Wei Gao, and Kam-Fai Wong. 2017. Detect rumors in microblog posts using propagation structure via kernel learning. In *Proceedings of the 55th Annual Meeting of the Association for Computational Linguistics (Volume 1: Long Papers)*, pages 708–717, Vancouver, Canada. Association for Computational Linguistics.

Jing Ma, Wei Gao, and Kam-Fai Wong. 2018. Rumor detection on Twitter with tree-structured recursive neural networks. In *Proceedings of the 56th Annual Meeting of the Association for Computational Linguistics (Volume 1: Long Papers)*, pages 1980–1989, Melbourne, Australia. Association for Computational Linguistics.

Andrei Paleyes, Raoul-Gabriel Urma, and Neil D. Lawrence. 2022. Challenges in deploying machine learning: A survey of case studies. *ACM Comput. Surv.*, 55(6).

Vahed Qazvinian, Emily Rosengren, Dragomir R. Radev, and Qiaozhu Mei. 2011. Rumor has it: Identifying misinformation in microblogs. In *Proceedings of the 2011 Conference on Empirical Methods in Natural Language Processing*, pages 1589–1599, Edinburgh, Scotland, UK. Association for Computational Linguistics.

Justus Randolph. 2010. Free-marginal multirater kappa (multirater κfree): An alternative to fleiss fixed-marginal multirater kappa. volume 4.

Nils Reimers and Iryna Gurevych. 2019. Sentence-bert: Sentence embeddings using siamese bert-networks.

Claude Sammut and Geoffrey I. Webb, editors. 2010. *TF–IDF*, pages 986–987. Springer US, Boston, MA.

Karishma Sharma, Feng Qian, He Jiang, Natali Ruchansky, Ming Zhang, and Yan Liu. 2019. Combating fake news: A survey on identification and mitigation techniques. *ACM Trans. Intell. Syst. Technol.*, 10(3).

Kai Shu, Amy Sliva, Suhang Wang, Jiliang Tang, and Huan Liu. 2017. Fake news detection on social media: A data mining perspective. *SIGKDD Explor. Newsl.*, 19(1):22–36.

Madusha Prasanjith Thilakarathna, Vihanga Ashinsana Wijayasekara, Yasiru Gamage, Kavindi Hanshani Peiris, Chanuka Abeysinghe, Intizar Rafaideen, and Prathieshna Vekneswaran. 2020. Hybrid approach and architecture to detect fake news on twitter in real-time using neural networks. In *2020 5th International Conference on Information Technology Research (ICITR)*, pages 1–6.

Hugo Touvron, Louis Martin, Kevin Stone, Peter Albert, Amjad Almahairi, Yasmine Babaei, Nikolay Bashlykov, Soumya Batra, Prajjwal Bhargava, Shruti Bhosale, Dan Bikel, Lukas Blecher, Cristian Canton Ferrer, Moya Chen, Guillem Cucurull, David Esiobu, Jude Fernandes, Jeremy Fu, Wenyin Fu, Brian Fuller, Cynthia Gao, Vedanuj Goswami, Naman Goyal, Anthony Hartshorn, Saghar Hosseini, Rui Hou, Hakan Inan, Marcin Kardas, Viktor Kerkez, Madian Khabsa, Isabel Kloumann, Artem Korenev, Punit Singh Koura, Marie-Anne Lachaux, Thibaut Lavril, Jenya Lee, Diana Liskovich, Yinghai Lu, Yuning Mao, Xavier Martinet, Todor Mihaylov, Pushkar Mishra, Igor Molybog, Yixin Nie, Andrew Poulton, Jeremy Reizenstein, Rashi Rungta, Kalyan Saladi, Alan Schelten, Ruan Silva, Eric Michael Smith, Ranjan Subramanian, Xiaoqing Ellen Tan, Binh Tang, Ross Taylor, Adina Williams, Jian Xiang Kuan, Puxin Xu, Zheng Yan, Iliyan Zarov, Yuchen Zhang, Angela Fan, Melanie Kambadur, Sharan Narang, Aurelien Rodriguez, Robert Stojnic, Sergey Edunov, and Thomas Scialom. 2023. Llama 2: Open foundation and fine-tuned chat models.

Ke Wu, Song Yang, and Kenny Q. Zhu. 2015. False rumors detection on sina weibo by propagation structures. In *2015 IEEE 31st International Conference on Data Engineering*, pages 651–662.

Fan Yang, Yang Liu, Xiaohui Yu, and Min Yang. 2012. Automatic detection of rumor on sina weibo. In *Proceedings of the ACM SIGKDD Workshop on Mining Data Semantics*, MDS '12, New York, NY, USA. Association for Computing Machinery.

A User Study Information

The participants, all of whom are fluent in English, accessed the survey via an anonymised Google Form sent via a university undergraduate mailing list. The web server architecture was deployed on Google Cloud Platform; all participants received the same underlying tweet cascade and recommended articles as a response for every tweet. The users could not comment on the speed of the service as these results were cached for the sake of reproducibility and efficiency.

B OOD: Additional Proportion Experiments

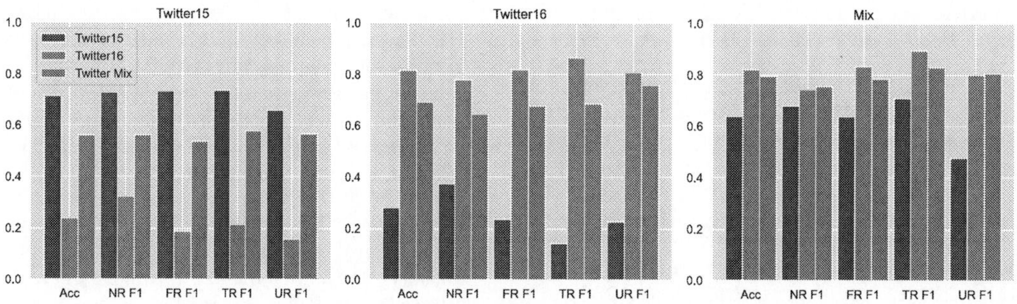

Figure 9: Result from the dataset mixing experiment for the *Twitter15* and *Twitter16* models, with $p_{T15} = 0.3$ and $p_{T16} = 0.7$.

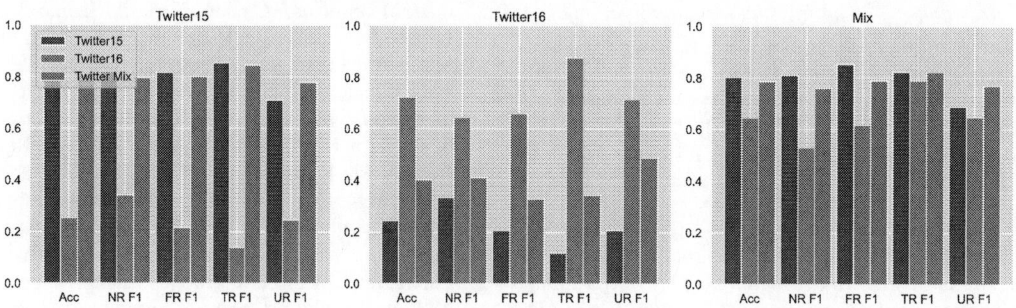

Figure 10: Result from the dataset mixing experiment for the *Twitter15* and *Twitter16* models, with $p_{T15} = 0.7$ and $p_{T16} = 0.3$.

DeepZensols: A Deep Learning Natural Language Processing Framework for Experimentation and Reproducibility

Paul Landes, Barbara Di Eugenio, Cornelia Caragea
Department of Computer Science
University of Illinois at Chicago
{plande2, bdieugen, cornelia}@uic.edu

Abstract

Given the criticality and difficulty of reproducing machine learning experiments, there have been significant efforts in reducing the variance of these results. The ability to consistently reproduce results effectively strengthens the underlying hypothesis of the work and should be regarded as important as the novel aspect of the research itself. The contribution of this work is an open source framework that has the following characteristics: a) facilitates reproducing consistent results, b) allows hot-swapping features and embeddings without further processing and re-vectorizing the dataset, c) provides a means of easily creating, training and evaluating natural language processing deep learning models with little to no code changes, and d) is freely available to the community.

1 Introduction

Consistently reproducing results is a fundamental criterion of the scientific method, without which, a hypothesis may be weakened or even invalidated (Arvan et al., 2022). Reproduction of results becomes even more necessary as a growing number of publications are inflated by false positives (Head et al., 2015). Efforts to abate this trend include introducing new statistical methods to detect false findings (Ulrich and Miller, 2015).

The inability to reproduce results has been referred to as the "replication crisis" (Hutson, 2018). The problem of reproducibility in results is becoming more acknowledged as a serious issue in the machine learning (ML) community with efforts to understand and overcome the challenge (Rogers et al., 2021; Drummond, 2018). Not only has the community addressed the issue in the literature, it has endeavored to assess if experiments are reproducible and provide recommendations to enhance reproducibility as with the Reproducibility Challenge[1]. To address these issues, we present DeepZensols, a freely available[2] deep learning (DL) framework for NLP research by and for the academic research community including citizen scientists, academic researchers, and students. It has been used for research projects(Landes et al., 2022, 2023) funded by the National Institute of Health (NIH)[3].

A key feature that sets DeepZensols apart from others is a novel method to rapidly and easily swap features sets and compare performance across models (see Section 2.4). Other systems must re-parse and re-vectorize each mini-batch over each epoch. While there exist similar frameworks to ours (Ning et al., 2020; Falcon, 2019; Paszke et al., 2019; Alberti et al., 2018), none of these provides this batch strategy, vectorization of natural language text features and reproducibility of results across advanced programming interfaces (APIs) and datasets in one framework. Popular neural network (NN) architectures are available out of the box and easily configurable with little to no coding necessary (see Section 2.2 for NLP specific framework details).

2 Library Design

DeepZensols is a combination of Python APIs built on top of PyTorch that provide a means of easily and quickly creating NLP task specific pipelines. The framework's source code and installable libraries are released under the MIT Open Source License, and includes extensive and in depth overview and API documentation, tutorials, Jupyter Notebook examples and class diagrams for NLP reference models and datasets. The framework is validated with 381 unit tests and six integration tests, which are automated using continuous integration.

2.1 Reproducibility

All random state, including utility libraries, scientific libraries, PyTorch, and GPU state, is consistent

[1]https://www.cs.mcgill.ca/.../ReproducibilityChallenge.html

[2]https://github.com/plandes/deepnlp

[3]NIH award R01CA225446, MyPHA: Automatically generating personalized accounts of in-patient hospitalizations.

Proceedings of the 3rd Workshop for Natural Language Processing Open Source Software (NLP-OSS 2023), pages 141–146
December 6, 2023

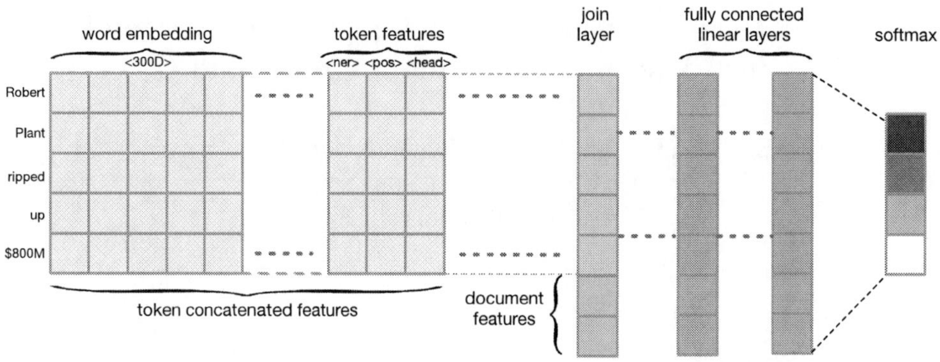

Figure 1: Word embeddings concatenated to vectorized linguistic features, and then joined with vectorized document features constructed using configuration with no coding.

across each run of the interpreter execution of the model's training, evaluation and testing when using the framework. Results are consistent by saving this random state when saving the model, then retrieving and resetting it before using the model.

The order of mini-batches, and their constituent data can affect the model performance as an aspect of training or the results of validation and testing (Pham et al., 2020). This performance inconsistency is addressed by recording the order of all data[4] and tracking the training, validation and test data splits. Not only are mini-batches given in the same order, the ordering in each mini-batch is also preserved. These dataset partitions and their order are saved to the file system so the community has the option of distributing it along with the source code for later experiment duplication.

The framework also saves the configuration used to recreate the same in-memory state along with the model. This duplicates all train-time memory model structures, parameters, and hyperparameters during testing. For the framework's reproducibility, unit tests are executed for individual components and integration tests by comparing the validation and training loss across six data sets[5]. In addition, this demonstrates to users of the framework how to add their own components and tests.

2.2 NLP-Focused Abstractions and Features

The framework provides many APIs for natural language tasks, including concatenation of vectorized language features to input embedding (see Figure 1). Vectorization of contextual embeddings such as BERT (Devlin et al., 2019) and non-contextual embeddings such as word2vec (Mikolov et al., 2013), GloVe (Pennington et al., 2014) and fastText (Bojanowski et al., 2017) are available.

The framework includes many layer implementations, which are compatible with the PyTorch API as module classes. Examples of layers provided include BiLSTM CRF, BERT transformer models, 1D convolution NN, word embedding layer for concatenating features (see Section 2.3), and TF/IDF frequency weighting (Sparck Jones, 1972).

HuggingFace transformer layers are available as embeddings, document, sentence and token features. The framework also provides direct access to these models' data and utilizes it in a variety of tasks such as text classification, token classification, language generation, latent semantic analysis, etc. A linguistic feature mapper that translates spaCy[6] to wordpieces, which are token sub-units with associated vectors (Wu et al., 2016), is also accessible as an easy to configure module.

2.3 Vectorization

The DeepZensols framework allows for easily configurable components that provide a higher level abstraction that tokenizes, sentence chunks, and vectorizes linguistic features. These *vectorizers* have a class taxonomy based on data they vectorize so their output data can be automatically constructed in various off-the-shelf architectures. See Section 2.2 for more information on NLP specific feature generation.

2.4 Batching

We provide a novel method to vectorize and batch data without wasteful pre-processing of feature and

[4]Regardless of any given data pre-processing or shuffling.

[5]Data sets include the MNIST, Adult, Iris datasets and those mentioned in Section 3.

[6]https://spacy.io

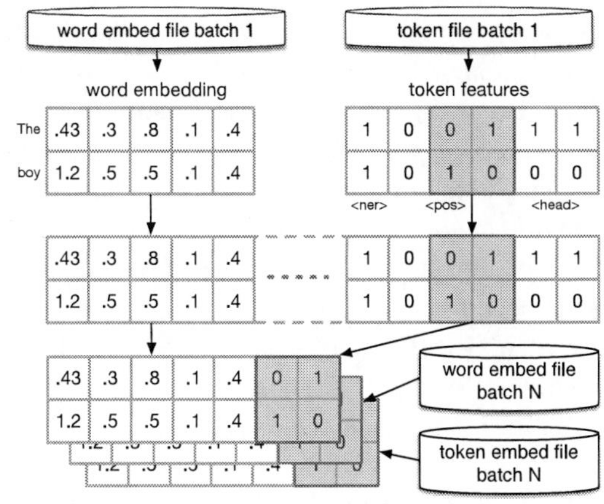

Figure 2: Batch decoding "stitches" mini-batches together from files containing features for the current run.

embedding combinations. Other similar frameworks pre-process data in an intermediate form only once before training. However, this leads to a brittle and difficult to reproduce dataset of ad-hoc text processing scripts that are challenging to re-execute, and thus, reproduce performance metrics.

Our framework addresses this with an organized intermediate file scheme and partitioned feature set so the input data is vectorized only once efficiently using a multi-processing pipeline. The output format of this process allows for quick feature swapping and hyperparameter tuning for re-training. It leverages the fact that mini-batches are independent and fit nicely as independent units of work by segmenting datasets into smaller chunks, vectorizing each chunk in parallel sub-processes, and creating batches independently across each sub processes.

This process by which data is written to the file system in a format that is fast to reassemble is called *batch encoding* and accomplished by: a) split sentences and/or tokens into equal size "chunks" units of work, b) parsing natural language features from chunks across multiple processes, and c) vectorizing each chunk as tensor data in separate files by feature.

After batch encoding is complete, the model is ready to be trained from data obtained from a *batch decoding* step, which is accomplished by: a) choosing a feature set for a training run, b) reassembling features by mini-batch, c) decode each mini-batch into a tensor (see Figure 2), and d) load, cache and copy tensors to the GPU.

Reassembling mini-batches by feature greatly reduces load time and memory space, which speeds up model training (see Section 3) and ameliorates issues of complex models. The train, validation and test cycle is faster for other vectorized linguistic data such as spaCy features as well.

2.5 Execution

The framework provides both a command line and a Jupyter notebook interface to train, test and predict. A "glue" API is used to make a Python dataclass[7] class a dynamically generated command line with help usage message documentation. A set of default application classes are available with the framework, but they can be extended to include project specific workflows. The default application set provides interactive early stopping or epoch resetting during training.

Results are organized by each run and carry a common file system structured named by either what is provided in the configuration or by model name. This directory structure contains the full model with all configuration, the PyTorch model, and results provided as human readable indented text, JSON and binary formats.

3 Runtime Analysis

Runtime analysis was performed for parsing, feature vectorization (see Section 2.3), batching (see Section 2.4), training and testing three different types of models using a Nvidia TITAN RTX graphics processor on an Intel 3.6GHz CPU using the following criteria:

- Model: the model trained and evaluated.
- Batch: whether or not the mini-batches were (re)created (see Section 2.4).
- GPU: whether or not the mini-batches were cached in GPU memory.[8]

Since obtaining fast results allows for more experimentation with a variety of feature sets, embeddings, and NN architectures, our experiments included several combinations of caching strategies. Table 1 shows the latency to batch, retrain and test the model for each dataset in the "Duration" column. Experiments were rerun obtain the time needed for training, validation and testing of each model, then a second time using the precomputed mini-batched data. The GPU caching option was toggled across these experiments to find the CPU to GPU latency for loading mini-batches.

[7]https://docs.python.org/3/library/dataclasses.html

[8]The framework offers GPU caching, CPU caching, and iterative buffering of mini-batches.

Data	Model	Duration	Batch	GPU	Both
NER	BERT	1:06:04	04:23	00:12	04:35
	GloVe	34:08	04:19	05:41	10:00
Mov	BERT	21:19	02:04	-00:26	01:38
	GloVe	05:03	03:07	01:20	04:27
CB	BERT	05:48	01:50	-00:01	01:49
	GloVe	05:45	01:51	03:03	04:54

Table 1: Efficiency benchmarks showing the **N**amed **E**ntity **R**ecognition, **Mov**ie review sentiment, and **C**lick**B**ate datasets. The "Duration" column lists processing latency with no batch or GPU caching in hours, minutes and seconds. The "Batch" and "GPU" columns have the caching speedup times in minutes and seconds. The "Both" column is the speedup with both batch and GPU caching are enabled.

The datasets used in the runtime analysis include the CoNNL 2003 (Tjong Kim Sang and De Meulder, 2003) for NER, the movie review corpus (Pang and Lee, 2005; Socher et al., 2013) for sentiment, and the clickbate corpus (Chakraborty et al., 2016) for text classification.

The results show significant processing improvements in all three datasets with the GloVe model leading. This is likely due to how the static embedding are not computed for each sentence (unlike BERT). The NER dataset with the BERT model was faster by 4.5 minutes and the GloVe model was 10 minutes faster (1.4X speedup). However, the movie review sentiment dataset shows the best improvement (7.8X speedup) on the GloVe model. This is primarily from the batch caching 2.6X speedup, but benefited from a GPU 1.3X caching speedup. We hypothesize that the GPU slowdowns for the movie review and clickbate datasets are potentially due to larger BERT (768D vs 300D embeddings) mini-batches copied from the CPU.

4 Related Frameworks

Popular DL frameworks such as TensorFlow[9] have a dashboard that provides metrics, such as training and validation loss. However, these general purpose frameworks offer basic performance metrics and do not provide a means of producing higher abstraction level NLP specific models. More specifically, frameworks such as Keras, supply a very coarse API allowing solely for cookie-cutter models. They lack the ability to easily create and evaluate models past this surface interface.

Frameworks such as PyTorch[10], which are more common in academia, provide a more straightforward simple API that is similar to the core TensorFlow libraries, and thus have the same shortcomings as a tool to bridge the gap between pure research and reproducibility. Specifically, they do not provide batching for accessible feature swapping and ablation studies, or retention of ML algorithm state necessary to reproduce results.

AllenNLP (Gardner et al., 2018) is a flexible configuration driven framework that provides construction of NLP NN architectures and is the closest framework to ours. However, it does not have fast feature swapping (see Section 2.4) and batch creation capability, and lacks most of the components necessary to consistently reproduce results[11].

Popular packages providing support for transformer architectures such as BERT (Devlin et al., 2019) include HuggingFace[12]. However, this framework only provides transformer models for contextual word embeddings.

5 Conclusion and Limitations

The DeepZensols framework is a viable solution to easily create NLP specific models with APIs and analysis tools to produce consistent results. Such frameworks create the types of models that give confidence and legitimacy by providing a way to produce reliable reproducible results for researchers not familiar with deep learning tools, practitioners, medical personnel, students, and those new to the field. Runtime analysis shows the framework offers significant processing time savings compared to systems that do not provide feature caching with stable results, but not all HuggingFace pretrained models[13] have been tested. The following have been tested: BERT, RoBERTa (Liu et al., 2019), DistilBERT (Sanh et al., 2019), Big Bird (Zaheer et al., 2020), BioBERT (Lee et al., 2020), XML-R (Conneau et al., 2020), ClinicalBioBERT (Alsentzer et al., 2019), and GatorTron (Yang et al., 2022) have been tested. A planned future work is to integrate the framework with TensorBoard[14].

6 Acknowledgments

This work is partially supported by award R01CA225446 from the NIH.

[9] https://www.tensorflow.org

[10] https://pytorch.org

[11] https://github.com/allenai/allennlp/issues/3100

[12] https://huggingface.co

[13] https://huggingface.co/models

[14] https://www.tensorflow.org/tensorboard

References

Michele Alberti, Vinaychandran Pondenkandath, Marcel Würsch, Rolf Ingold, and Marcus Liwicki. 2018. DeepDIVA: A Highly-Functional Python Framework for Reproducible Experiments. In *2018 16th International Conference on Frontiers in Handwriting Recognition (ICFHR)*, pages 423–428.

Emily Alsentzer, John Murphy, William Boag, Wei-Hung Weng, Di Jindi, Tristan Naumann, and Matthew McDermott. 2019. Publicly Available Clinical BERT Embeddings. In *Proceedings of the 2nd Clinical Natural Language Processing Workshop*, pages 72–78. Association for Computational Linguistics.

Mohammad Arvan, Luís Pina, and Natalie Parde. 2022. Reproducibility in Computational Linguistics: Is Source Code Enough? In *Proceedings of the 2022 Conference on Empirical Methods in Natural Language Processing*, pages 2350–2361. Association for Computational Linguistics.

Piotr Bojanowski, Edouard Grave, Armand Joulin, and Tomas Mikolov. 2017. Enriching Word Vectors with Subword Information. *Transactions of the Association for Computational Linguistics*, 5:135–146.

Abhijnan Chakraborty, Bhargavi Paranjape, Sourya Kakarla, and Niloy Ganguly. 2016. Stop clickbait: Detecting and preventing clickbaits in online news media. In *Proceedings of the 2016 IEEE/ACM International Conference on Advances in Social Networks Analysis and Mining*, ASONAM '16, pages 9–16. IEEE Press.

Alexis Conneau, Kartikay Khandelwal, Naman Goyal, Vishrav Chaudhary, Guillaume Wenzek, Francisco Guzmán, Edouard Grave, Myle Ott, Luke Zettlemoyer, and Veselin Stoyanov. 2020. Unsupervised Cross-lingual Representation Learning at Scale. In *Proceedings of the 58th Annual Meeting of the Association for Computational Linguistics*, pages 8440–8451. Association for Computational Linguistics.

Jacob Devlin, Ming-Wei Chang, Kenton Lee, and Kristina Toutanova. 2019. BERT: Pre-training of Deep Bidirectional Transformers for Language Understanding. In *Proceedings of the 2019 Conference of the North American Chapter of the Association for Computational Linguistics: Human Language Technologies, Volume 1 (Long and Short Papers)*, pages 4171–4186.

Chris Drummond. 2018. Reproducible research: A minority opinion. *Journal of Experimental & Theoretical Artificial Intelligence*, 30(1):1–11.

William A Falcon. 2019. Pytorch lightning. *GitHub*, 3.

Matt Gardner, Joel Grus, Mark Neumann, Oyvind Tafjord, Pradeep Dasigi, Nelson F. Liu, Matthew E. Peters, Michael Schmitz, and Luke Zettlemoyer. 2018. AllenNLP: A Deep Semantic Natural Language Processing Platform. In *Proceedings of Workshop for NLP Open Source Software (NLP-OSS)*, pages 1–6.

Megan L. Head, Luke Holman, Rob Lanfear, Andrew T. Kahn, and Michael D. Jennions. 2015. The Extent and Consequences of P-Hacking in Science. *PLoS Biology*, 13(3).

Matthew Hutson. 2018. Artificial intelligence faces reproducibility crisis. *Science*, 359(6377):725–726.

Paul Landes, Aaron Chaise, Kunal Patel, Sean Huang, and Barbara Di Eugenio. 2023. Hospital Discharge Summarization Data Provenance. In *The 22nd Workshop on Biomedical Natural Language Processing and BioNLP Shared Tasks*, pages 439–448. Association for Computational Linguistics.

Paul Landes, Kunal Patel, Sean S. Huang, Adam Webb, Barbara Di Eugenio, and Cornelia Caragea. 2022. A New Public Corpus for Clinical Section Identification: MedSecId. In *Proceedings of the 29th International Conference on Computational Linguistics*, pages 3709–3721. International Committee on Computational Linguistics.

Jinhyuk Lee, Wonjin Yoon, Sungdong Kim, Donghyeon Kim, Sunkyu Kim, Chan Ho So, and Jaewoo Kang. 2020. BioBERT: A pre-trained biomedical language representation model for biomedical text mining. *Bioinformatics*, 36(4):1234–1240.

Yinhan Liu, Myle Ott, Naman Goyal, Jingfei Du, Mandar Joshi, Danqi Chen, Omer Levy, Mike Lewis, Luke Zettlemoyer, and Veselin Stoyanov. 2019. RoBERTa: A Robustly Optimized BERT Pretraining Approach. arXiv: 1907.11692 (Only available as arXiv preprint).

Tomas Mikolov, Ilya Sutskever, Kai Chen, Greg S Corrado, and Jeff Dean. 2013. Distributed Representations of Words and Phrases and their Compositionality. In *Advances in Neural Information Processing Systems*, volume 26. Curran Associates, Inc.

Qiang Ning, Hao Wu, Pradeep Dasigi, Dheeru Dua, Matt Gardner, Robert L. Logan Iv, Ana Marasović, and Zhen Nie. 2020. Easy, Reproducible and Quality-Controlled Data Collection with CROWDAQ. In *Proceedings of the 2020 Conference on Empirical Methods in Natural Language Processing: System Demonstrations*, pages 127–134.

Bo Pang and Lillian Lee. 2005. Seeing Stars: Exploiting Class Relationships for Sentiment Categorization with Respect to Rating Scales. In *Proceedings of the 43rd Annual Meeting of the Association for Computational Linguistics (ACL'05)*, pages 115–124. Association for Computational Linguistics.

Adam Paszke, Sam Gross, Francisco Massa, Adam Lerer, James Bradbury, Gregory Chanan, Trevor Killeen, Zeming Lin, Natalia Gimelshein, Luca Antiga, Alban Desmaison, Andreas Kopf, Edward

Yang, Zachary DeVito, Martin Raison, Alykhan Tejani, Sasank Chilamkurthy, Benoit Steiner, Lu Fang, Junjie Bai, and Soumith Chintala. 2019. PyTorch: An Imperative Style, High-Performance Deep Learning Library. In *Advances in Neural Information Processing Systems*, volume 32. Curran Associates, Inc.

Jeffrey Pennington, Richard Socher, and Christopher Manning. 2014. Glove: Global Vectors for Word Representation. In *Proceedings of the 2014 Conference on Empirical Methods in Natural Language Processing (EMNLP)*, pages 1532–1543. Association for Computational Linguistics.

Hung Viet Pham, Shangshu Qian, Jiannan Wang, Thibaud Lutellier, Jonathan Rosenthal, Lin Tan, Yaoliang Yu, and Nachiappan Nagappan. 2020. Problems and opportunities in training deep learning software systems: An analysis of variance. In *Proceedings of the 35th IEEE/ACM International Conference on Automated Software Engineering*, pages 771–783. Association for Computing Machinery.

Anna Rogers, Timothy Baldwin, and Kobi Leins. 2021. 'Just What do You Think You're Doing, Dave?' A Checklist for Responsible Data Use in NLP. In *Findings of the Association for Computational Linguistics: EMNLP 2021*, pages 4821–4833. Association for Computational Linguistics.

Victor Sanh, Lysandre Debut, Julien Chaumond, and Thomas Wolf. 2019. DistilBERT, a distilled version of BERT: Smaller, faster, cheaper and lighter. In *The 5th EMC2 - Energy Efficient Training and Inference of Transformer Based Models*.

Richard Socher, Alex Perelygin, Jean Wu, Jason Chuang, Christopher D. Manning, Andrew Ng, and Christopher Potts. 2013. Recursive Deep Models for Semantic Compositionality Over a Sentiment Treebank. In *Proceedings of the 2013 Conference on Empirical Methods in Natural Language Processing*, pages 1631–1642. Association for Computational Linguistics.

Karen Sparck Jones. 1972. A statistical interpretation of term specificity and its application in retrieval. *Journal of documentation*, 28(1):11–21.

Erik F. Tjong Kim Sang and Fien De Meulder. 2003. Introduction to the CoNLL-2003 Shared Task: Language-Independent Named Entity Recognition. In *Proceedings of the Seventh Conference on Natural Language Learning at HLT-NAACL 2003*, pages 142–147.

Rolf Ulrich and Jeff Miller. 2015. P-hacking by post hoc selection with multiple opportunities: Detectability by skewness test?: Comment on Simonsohn, Nelson, and Simmons (2014). *Journal of Experimental Psychology: General*, 144(6):1137–1145.

Yonghui Wu, Mike Schuster, Zhifeng Chen, Quoc V. Le, Mohammad Norouzi, Wolfgang Macherey, Maxim Krikun, Yuan Cao, Qin Gao, Klaus Macherey, Jeff Klingner, Apurva Shah, Melvin Johnson, Xiaobing Liu, Łukasz Kaiser, Stephan Gouws, Yoshikiyo Kato, Taku Kudo, Hideto Kazawa, Keith Stevens, George Kurian, Nishant Patil, Wei Wang, Cliff Young, Jason Smith, Jason Riesa, Alex Rudnick, Oriol Vinyals, Greg Corrado, Macduff Hughes, and Jeffrey Dean. 2016. Google's Neural Machine Translation System: Bridging the Gap between Human and Machine Translation. arXiv: 1609.08144 (Only available as arXiv preprint).

Xi Yang, Aokun Chen, Nima PourNejatian, Hoo Chang Shin, Kaleb E. Smith, Christopher Parisien, Colin Compas, Cheryl Martin, Mona G. Flores, Ying Zhang, Tanja Magoc, Christopher A. Harle, Gloria Lipori, Duane A. Mitchell, William R. Hogan, Elizabeth A. Shenkman, Jiang Bian, and Yonghui Wu. 2022. GatorTron: A Large Clinical Language Model to Unlock Patient Information from Unstructured Electronic Health Records. arXiv: 2203.03540 (Only available as arXiv preprint).

Manzil Zaheer, Guru Guruganesh, Kumar Avinava Dubey, Joshua Ainslie, Chris Alberti, Santiago Ontañón, Philip Pham, Anirudh Ravula, Qifan Wang, Li Yang, and Amr Ahmed. 2020. Big Bird: Transformers for Longer Sequences. In *Advances in Neural Information Processing Systems 33: Annual Conference on Neural Information Processing Systems 2020, NeurIPS 2020*.

Improving NER Research Workflows with SeqScore

Constantine Lignos† and **Maya Kruse*** and **Andrew Rueda***
Michtom School of Computer Science
Brandeis University
{lignos,mayakruse,andrewrueda}@brandeis.edu

Abstract

We describe the features of SeqScore, an MIT-licensed Python toolkit for working with named entity recognition (NER) data. While SeqScore began as a tool for NER scoring, it has been expanded to help with the full lifecycle of working with NER data: validating annotation, providing at-a-glance and detailed summaries of the data, modifying annotation to support experiments, scoring system output, and aiding with error analysis. SeqScore is released via PyPI and development occurs on GitHub.

1 Introduction

While much attention in language technology development is focused on the creation of better models and datasets, it is essential to also have tools for understanding the output of those models and the contents of the datasets. For classification tasks, the combination of scikit-learn (Pedregosa et al., 2011) and Pandas (Wes McKinney, 2010) can provide preprocessing, data exploration, powerful modeling, and error analysis. However, chunking tasks like named entity recognition (NER) pose a challenge for data workflows and error analysis. While NER is often treated like a sequence-labeling problem like part of speech (POS) tagging, unlike POS tagging, the annotation and evaluation are performed at the chunk level, not individual tokens.

For example, if a sentence begins "Alan Turing was...", an NER task may require that *Alan Turing* is correctly identified as a mention of a person's name. Less or no credit would be received for identifying just the person name *Alan* or separately identifying the names *Alan* and *Turing* without noting that they form a single unit. Typically, each mention (also called an entity, phrase, or chunk) is encoded using BIO encoding, so for example *Alan Turing* might receive the tags `B-PER I-PER` to reflect the beginning and continuation of a mention of type person, while non-mention tokens are tagged `O`.[1]

The nature of chunking tasks means that every step of data processing is necessarily more complicated than traditional classification tasks. Unlike a per-token classification task, looking at the individual token labels is a poor summary of the dataset. Scoring is more difficult as the scorer must interpret a sequence of tagged tokens as mentions, which becomes non-trivial when the tags produced by a system do not follow the norms of the mention encoding method (e.g., BIO) used (Lignos and Kamyab, 2020).

This paper describes the SeqScore toolkit and its applications for validating, summarizing, and transforming NER data. A previous publication (Palen-Michel et al., 2021), introduced SeqScore and described its value as a reproducibility-focused NER scorer. While this paper is also about SeqScore, it has a different focus. We describe the development of new features for SeqScore and what was needed to extend it from being just a scorer to a more complete toolkit for working with NER data. We discuss new feature development on SeqScore and the process of expanding it to fill gaps common in NER workflows. In addition to discussing the details of SeqScore, we discuss the challenges of trying to build open-source software for research.

2 Why a Toolkit?

For decades, NER researchers have been able to be productive without any popular toolkits for working with NER data. There has been a commonly-used scorer, conlleval, which was provided for the 2002–3 CoNLL shared tasks (Tjong Kim Sang, 2002; Tjong Kim Sang and De Meulder, 2003), available for two decades now. While standard-

†Corresponding author.
*Equal contribution.

[1] Lester (2020) provides a more detailed explanation of common encodings and their intricacies in the context of software development.

Proceedings of the 3rd Workshop for Natural Language Processing Open Source Software (NLP-OSS 2023), pages 147–152
December 6, 2023 ©2023 Association for Computational Linguistics

izing around a single scorer provides significant benefits (Lignos and Kamyab, 2020; Post, 2018), conlleval is not actively maintained and has not been updated as approaches to NER have changed.

While common scorers and shared tasks are uniquely capable of uniting the research community, there is still a vital need for tools for tools for many stages of working with NER data. For example, given a dataset, how can we examine it? How can we determine what mention encoding it uses and whether it was used consistently? How can we modify it efficiently? How can we examine performance beyond just a few numbers? SeqScore aims to provide efficient, command-line solutions to these problems.

The most similar software package to SeqScore is iobes (Lester, 2020). While the two projects began development concurrently, iobes was released first and has previously been published at NLP-OSS. The iobes package is designed for API-level access and manipulation of spans. SeqScore is focused on a command-line interface for scoring NER data and performing common manipulations on that data. Both provide logic around converting chunk encodings (BIO, BIOES, etc.) to and from mentions.

3 SeqScore's Features

This section describes the features of SeqScore, focusing on the newest features that enable it to assist in many NER data workflows. Previous work (Palen-Michel et al., 2021) has described the scoring features of SeqScore, so they are not discussed in detail in this paper. SeqScore is released via PyPI (`https://pypi.org/project/seqscore/`) and development occurs on GitHub (`https://github.com/bltlab/seqscore`).

3.1 Overview

SeqScore is accessed via a command-line interface (CLI), and like git provides a command for each action. After running `pip install seqscore`, the `seqscore` script is now available. Table 1 lists SeqScore's commands and their purposes.

All SeqScore commands share a common set of capabilities. The most important is robust reading and writing of CoNLL-style NER formats. SeqScore supports several options to work with a wide variety of data files: setting the file encoding (older files often use ISO-8859-1), ignoring comment lines (which some files use for sentence provenance information), and automatic detection of field delimiters (older files use space, newer ones use tabs). Different strategies can be set regarding how to deal with invalid label transitions like `O I-PER` in BIO (for more details see Palen-Michel et al., 2021). SeqScore can maintain or discard the document boundaries specified using `-DOCSTART-` sentences inside CoNLL-format files, which enables scoring a reference with document boundaries against system output without them.

While each of these features is simple, those attempting to write "quick scripts" to manipulate NER data often find them to be stumbling blocks. For example, many older workflows used tools like `cut` and `paste` to extract and replace NER labels; these encounter problems when dealing with comment lines, inconsistent delimiters, document boundaries in one file but not the other, etc.

3.2 Validation

One of the most common questions that arises when dealing with NER data is determining which mention encoding (BIO, etc.) is used and whether it has been used consistently. While BIO is currently the most commonly-used encoding for dataset creation, many papers describing datasets do not explicitly state what the encoding is. Many older datasets use IOB, often erratically.[2]

An example of running the validate command on a file `train.bio` would be: `seqscore validate --labels BIO train.bio`. The mention encoding in use must be explicitly given; it is important that users be sure of the mention encoding they are using.

As part of an effort to test SeqScore to make sure it can reliably load a variety of datasets, we collected a mix of recent and older datasets and validated them. The following datasets passed validation without any modifications: NYTK-NerKor+Cars-OntoNotes++ (Novák and Novák, 2022; Simon and Vadász, 2021), TurkuNLP (Luoma et al., 2020), GermanLER (Leitner et al., 2019; Leitner, 2019), TweebankNER (Jiang et al., 2022), HiNER (Murthy et al., 2022), GermEval 2014

[2]Our experiments in validating older datasets led to interesting findings. There seems to be disagreement on how IOB encoding should be implemented. Some data files use `B-` only when strictly necessary, that is when two adjacent mentions of the same entity type appear, as would be for the fragment "[Australian]MISC [Davis Cup]MISC captain" from the CoNLL-02 English data. Others use `B-` for the second mention of two adjacent mentions, even if the entity types are different. SeqScore currently only allows the former variety to pass IOB validation, but this may change in future releases.

Command	Purpose
`convert`	Convert between different mention encodings (BIO, BIOES, etc.)
`count`	Show counts of the mentions in a file in descending order
`process`	Modify the mentions in a file by choosing which entity types to keep/remove or mapping entity types
`repair`	Correct invalid label transitions
`score`	Produce a score or a summary of the scoring events (false positives, etc.)
`summarize`	Give a high-level summary of a dataset that includes its length and the count of each entity type
`validate`	Check whether a file contains any invalid labels or invalid label transitions

Table 1: Description of SeqScore commands

(Benikova et al., 2014), CoNLL-03 English and German (Tjong Kim Sang and De Meulder, 2003, we used the 2006 German data re-release), CoNLL-02 Dutch (Tjong Kim Sang, 2002), and Europarl annotation (Agerri et al., 2018).

Three datasets contained invalid label transitions, but using SeqScore's `repair` command could be converted to valid versions that pass validation: CoNLL-02 Spanish (Tjong Kim Sang, 2002), KazNERD (Yeshpanov et al., 2022), and MultiCoNER II (Fetahu et al., 2023).

SeqScore's validation tool helped identify more significant issues with other datasets. When validating the BIO-encoded MasakhaNER 1.0 (Adelani et al., 2021) dataset, we found sentences beginning with `I-` labels that appeared to be a continuation of a mention at the end of the previous sentence. When we investigated, we discovered that after creation of the original dataset, long sentences were split without regard to mention boundaries in order to meet the maximum sentence length requirements of the models used in their study. We were able to locate an earlier version of the data in their GitHub repository that did not have these additional sentence breaks, and that data passed validation.

Other datasets passed validation after modifications were made to them. MahaNER (Litake et al., 2022) has tags of the form `BPER` instead of `B-PER`. After changing the tags to add `-`, SeqScore's `repair` command was used to correct invalid label transitions. The tags in KIND (Paccosi and Palmero Aprosio, 2022) are "bare" tags like `PER`. After changing all tags to IO tags like `I-PER`, the dataset was successfully validated as IO.

The only dataset we found to be unusable was SiNER (Ali et al., 2020), as it appears to have some text processing issue resulting in some of the lines having tokens but no label, and others the reverse.

3.3 Data Modification

While core entity types likes person, organization, and location appear in many NER datasets, different datasets use different ontologies. Often some entity types are annotated less reliably, like MISC in CoNLL 2002–3, and others may simply be of less interest, like DATE in MasakhaNER.

SeqScore supports specifying either a set of entity types to keep or remove. For example, to include only PER, LOC, and ORG, the user can run `seqscore process --keep-types PER,LOC,ORG input.bio output.bio`. Similarly, to remove the DATE type, the user can run `seqscore process --remove-types DATE input.bio output.bio`.

Another common task is collapsing a fine-grained set of types into a smaller set. For example, the MultiCoNER II dataset (Fetahu et al., 2023) is annotated with 33 fine-grained types which can be mapped to 6 coarse-grained types. The annotation is provided using fine-grained types, so to evaluate for the coarse types, the types must be mapped.

SeqScore supports this type mapping using a JSON file. For example, this JSON can be used to convert to the higher-level types PROD and LOC from fine-grained types: `{"PROD": ["Clothing", "Drink", "Food", "OtherPROD", "Vehicle"], "LOC": ["Facility", "HumanSettlement", "OtherLOC", "Station"]}`. This mapping can be used as follows: `seqscore process --type-map map.json input.bio output.bio`.

3.4 Error Analysis at a Glance

In text classification tasks, confusion matrices allow for quick understanding of error patterns in a system's output. For a chunking task like NER, it is difficult to define exactly what a confusion matrix should look like. For SeqScore, we attempted to come up with a way to summarize the errors in a system's output in a way similar to identifying the "hot spots" in a heat map of the confusion matrix. When scoring, SeqScore can produce a table of false positives and negatives sorted by descending frequency by using the `--error-counts` flag: `seqscore score --error-counts --labels BIO --reference ref.bio pred.bio`.

Count	Error	Type	Text
7	FP	MISC	ALPINE
5	FN	ORG	Real Madrid
5	FN	ORG	Barcelona
4	FP	LOC	Tasmania
4	FP	LOC	Victoria
4	FP	MISC	National Hockey
4	FP	MISC	League
4	FP	MISC	ATLANTIC DIVISION
4	FP	MISC	PACIFIC DIVISION
4	FP	LOC	Santa Fe
4	FN	ORG	Victoria
4	FN	ORG	Tasmania
4	FN	ORG	National Hockey
4	FN	ORG	League
4	FN	MISC	ATLANTIC
4	FN	LOC	PACIFIC
4	FN	ORG	Santa Fe
3	FP	MISC	World Cup
3	FP	ORG	William Hill
3	FP	MISC	Italian
3	FP	MISC	EST
3	FP	MISC	Conservative
3	FP	MISC	SKIING-WOMEN
3	FN	MISC	SKIING-WORLD CUP
3	FN	ORG	NFL

Table 2: Most-frequent false positive (FP) and false negative (FN) errors identified using `seqscore score --error-counts`

Table 2 shows output of this command from an NER model based on XLM-R (Conneau et al., 2020) and fine-tuned on CoNLL++ English data using FLERT (Schweter and Akbik, 2020). It immediately shows that some of the most-repeated errors happen in all-caps contexts. The output also suggests that sports is a problem domain, with leagues, sub-leagues, and clubs appearing in both false positives and negatives. Looking at this output allowed us to identify problems with the annotation of *National Hockey League* in the CoNLL++ test data; a deeper look revealed that improper sentence boundaries in the gold data repeatedly resulted in split mentions of *National Hockey* and *League*.

As most papers reporting NER scores do not report any error analysis, we hope the ease with which the most frequent errors can be looked at in SeqScore will help researchers at least identify the largest sources of error.

4 Design Challenges

Explicit or Implicit? Unlike conlleval, which will score many mention encodings without any direction from the user—even encodings it does not support (Akbik et al., 2019, footnote 2)—SeqScore requires users to be specify the mention encoding and how they want invalid transitions to be repaired. This can be confusing to new users, because if they do not specify a repair method, scoring may raise an error. SeqScore has always erred on the side of making users be explicit and avoiding any silent defaults that could affect the results, but this comes at a price of some user frustration.

Limiting Scope While SeqScore is so far the most richly-featured toolkit for working with NER files, we have intentionally limited the scope of its capabilities where there is risk of misuse. One example is scoring NER in cases where the reference and system output may disagree in the tokens of a sentence, such as when performing NER on the output of speech recognition. SeqScore currently insists that the reference and system output have the same text to avoid issues where sentences have become misaligned between the two, and this cannot be disabled. Providing a flag to disable this check could result in users specifying it "just in case" to make sure scoring never raises an error, potentially leading to incorrect scores. Benaicha et al. (2023) forked SeqScore for their study of NER on speech so they could score more flexibly.

Test Coverage While SeqScore stands apart from much research software in having a test suite and code coverage instrumentation, as the complexity of the toolkit has increased, so has the time required for tests to keep up with functionality. While very time-intensive to maintain, writing tests that exercise the command-line interface has been essential to avoiding regressions. SeqScore uses click[3] to implement the CLI, and testing is greatly aided by its `CliRunner` class which allows direct invocation of the CLI in unit tests.

SeqScore's test coverage stands at 95%, but it will take substantial effort to reach 100%. A handful of warnings and error cases are not exercised by the current tests due to the high time cost of developing inputs that would reach them and maintaining these inputs as the codebase changes.

Performance SeqScore is written highly defensively to protect against user errors that could result in incorrect evaluation results. This unfortunately comes at the cost of speed; SeqScore is slower at scoring and processing long files than other scorers. While we are interested in improving speed by using profiling, we are unwilling to optimize for speed at the expense of safety.

[3] `https://palletsprojects.com/p/click/`

5 Conclusion

SeqScore provides a feature-rich toolkit for working with NER data, and we believe it will enable easier and more reproducible NER research. As more users adopt SeqScore, we look forward to addressing their needs and the bugs they find.

Development of SeqScore is ongoing. A major area of interest is developing a stable API for scoring. Unlike iobes and seqeval (Nakayama, 2018), the primary use case of SeqScore has been through the command line. We plan to add a stable API before a version 1.0 release.

References

David Ifeoluwa Adelani, Jade Abbott, Graham Neubig, Daniel D'souza, Julia Kreutzer, Constantine Lignos, Chester Palen-Michel, Happy Buzaaba, Shruti Rijhwani, Sebastian Ruder, Stephen Mayhew, Israel Abebe Azime, Shamsuddeen H. Muhammad, Chris Chinenye Emezue, Joyce Nakatumba-Nabende, Perez Ogayo, Aremu Anuoluwapo, Catherine Gitau, Derguene Mbaye, Jesujoba Alabi, Seid Muhie Yimam, Tajuddeen Rabiu Gwadabe, Ignatius Ezeani, Rubungo Andre Niyongabo, Jonathan Mukiibi, Verrah Otiende, Iroro Orife, Davis David, Samba Ngom, Tosin Adewumi, Paul Rayson, Mofetoluwa Adeyemi, Gerald Muriuki, Emmanuel Anebi, Chiamaka Chukwuneke, Nkiruka Odu, Eric Peter Wairagala, Samuel Oyerinde, Clemencia Siro, Tobius Saul Bateesa, Temilola Oloyede, Yvonne Wambui, Victor Akinode, Deborah Nabagereka, Maurice Katusiime, Ayodele Awokoya, Mouhamadane MBOUP, Dibora Gebreyohannes, Henok Tilaye, Kelechi Nwaike, Degaga Wolde, Abdoulaye Faye, Blessing Sibanda, Orevaoghene Ahia, Bonaventure F. P. Dossou, Kelechi Ogueji, Thierno Ibrahima DIOP, Abdoulaye Diallo, Adewale Akinfaderin, Tendai Marengereke, and Salomey Osei. 2021. MasakhaNER: Named entity recognition for African languages. *Transactions of the Association for Computational Linguistics*, 9:1116–1131.

Rodrigo Agerri, Yiling Chung, Itziar Aldabe, Nora Aranberri, Gorka Labaka, and German Rigau. 2018. Building named entity recognition taggers via parallel corpora. In *Proceedings of the Eleventh International Conference on Language Resources and Evaluation (LREC 2018)*.

Alan Akbik, Tanja Bergmann, and Roland Vollgraf. 2019. Pooled contextualized embeddings for named entity recognition. In *Proceedings of the 2019 Conference of the North American Chapter of the Association for Computational Linguistics: Human Language Technologies, Volume 1 (Long and Short Papers)*, pages 724–728, Minneapolis, Minnesota. Association for Computational Linguistics.

Wazir Ali, Junyu Lu, and Zenglin Xu. 2020. SiNER: A large dataset for Sindhi named entity recognition. In *Proceedings of the Twelfth Language Resources and Evaluation Conference*, pages 2953–2961, Marseille, France. European Language Resources Association.

Moncef Benaicha, David Thulke, and M. A. Tuğtekin Turan. 2023. Exploring spoken named entity recognition: A cross-lingual perspective. ArXiv preprint 2307.01310.

Darina Benikova, Chris Biemann, Max Kisselew, and Sebastian Pado. 2014. GermEval 2014 named entity recognition shared task: companion paper. In *Workshop Proceedings of the 12th edition of the KONVENS conference*, pages 104–112.

Alexis Conneau, Kartikay Khandelwal, Naman Goyal, Vishrav Chaudhary, Guillaume Wenzek, Francisco Guzmán, Edouard Grave, Myle Ott, Luke Zettlemoyer, and Veselin Stoyanov. 2020. Unsupervised cross-lingual representation learning at scale. In *Proceedings of the 58th Annual Meeting of the Association for Computational Linguistics*, pages 8440–8451, Online. Association for Computational Linguistics.

Besnik Fetahu, Sudipta Kar, Zhiyu Chen, Oleg Rokhlenko, and Shervin Malmasi. 2023. SemEval-2023 task 2: Fine-grained multilingual named entity recognition (MultiCoNER 2). In *Proceedings of the The 17th International Workshop on Semantic Evaluation (SemEval-2023)*, pages 2247–2265, Toronto, Canada. Association for Computational Linguistics.

Hang Jiang, Yining Hua, Doug Beeferman, and Deb Roy. 2022. Annotating the Tweebank corpus on named entity recognition and building NLP models for social media analysis. In *Proceedings of the Thirteenth Language Resources and Evaluation Conference*, pages 7199–7208, Marseille, France. European Language Resources Association.

Elena Leitner. 2019. Eigennamen- und Zitaterkennung in Rechtstexten. Master's thesis, Universität Potsdam, Potsdam.

Elena Leitner, Georg Rehm, and Julian Moreno-Schneider. 2019. Fine-grained Named Entity Recognition in Legal Documents. In *Semantic Systems. The Power of AI and Knowledge Graphs. Proceedings of the 15th International Conference (SEMANTiCS 2019)*, number 11702 in Lecture Notes in Computer Science, pages 272–287, Karlsruhe, Germany. Springer. 10/11 September 2019.

Brian Lester. 2020. iobes: Library for span level processing. In *Proceedings of Second Workshop for NLP Open Source Software (NLP-OSS)*, pages 115–119, Online. Association for Computational Linguistics.

Constantine Lignos and Marjan Kamyab. 2020. If you build your own NER scorer, non-replicable results will come. In *Proceedings of the First Workshop on Insights from Negative Results in NLP*, pages 94–99, Online. Association for Computational Linguistics.

Onkar Litake, Maithili Ravindra Sabane, Parth Sachin Patil, Aparna Abhijeet Ranade, and Raviraj Joshi. 2022. L3Cube-MahaNER: A Marathi named entity recognition dataset and BERT models. In *Proceedings of the WILDRE-6 Workshop within the 13th Language Resources and Evaluation Conference*, pages 29–34, Marseille, France. European Language Resources Association.

Jouni Luoma, Miika Oinonen, Maria Pyykönen, Veronika Laippala, and Sampo Pyysalo. 2020. A broad-coverage corpus for Finnish named entity recognition. In *Proceedings of the Twelfth Language Resources and Evaluation Conference*, pages 4615–4624, Marseille, France. European Language Resources Association.

Rudra Murthy, Pallab Bhattacharjee, Rahul Sharnagat, Jyotsana Khatri, Diptesh Kanojia, and Pushpak Bhattacharyya. 2022. HiNER: A large Hindi named entity recognition dataset. In *Proceedings of the Thirteenth Language Resources and Evaluation Conference*, pages 4467–4476, Marseille, France. European Language Resources Association.

Hiroki Nakayama. 2018. seqeval: A Python framework for sequence labeling evaluation. Software available from `https://github.com/chakki-works/seqeval`.

Attila Novák and Borbála Novák. 2022. NerKor+Cars-OntoNotes++. In *Proceedings of the Thirteenth Language Resources and Evaluation Conference*, pages 1907–1916, Marseille, France. European Language Resources Association.

Teresa Paccosi and Alessio Palmero Aprosio. 2022. KIND: an Italian multi-domain dataset for named entity recognition. In *Proceedings of the Thirteenth Language Resources and Evaluation Conference*, pages 501–507, Marseille, France. European Language Resources Association.

Chester Palen-Michel, Nolan Holley, and Constantine Lignos. 2021. SeqScore: Addressing barriers to reproducible named entity recognition evaluation. In *Proceedings of the 2nd Workshop on Evaluation and Comparison of NLP Systems*, pages 40–50, Punta Cana, Dominican Republic. Association for Computational Linguistics.

F. Pedregosa, G. Varoquaux, A. Gramfort, V. Michel, B. Thirion, O. Grisel, M. Blondel, P. Prettenhofer, R. Weiss, V. Dubourg, J. Vanderplas, A. Passos, D. Cournapeau, M. Brucher, M. Perrot, and E. Duchesnay. 2011. Scikit-learn: Machine learning in Python. *Journal of Machine Learning Research*, 12:2825–2830.

Matt Post. 2018. A call for clarity in reporting BLEU scores. In *Proceedings of the Third Conference on Machine Translation: Research Papers*, pages 186–191, Brussels, Belgium. Association for Computational Linguistics.

Stefan Schweter and Alan Akbik. 2020. FLERT: Document-level features for named entity recognition.

Eszter Simon and Noémi Vadász. 2021. Introducing NYTK-NerKor, a gold standard Hungarian named entity annotated corpus. In *Text, Speech, and Dialogue: 24th International Conference, TSD 2021, Olomouc, Czech Republic, September 6–9, 2021, Proceedings 24*, pages 222–234. Springer.

Erik F. Tjong Kim Sang. 2002. Introduction to the CoNLL-2002 shared task: Language-independent named entity recognition. In *COLING-02: The 6th Conference on Natural Language Learning 2002 (CoNLL-2002)*.

Erik F. Tjong Kim Sang and Fien De Meulder. 2003. Introduction to the CoNLL-2003 shared task: Language-independent named entity recognition. In *Proceedings of the Seventh Conference on Natural Language Learning at HLT-NAACL 2003*, pages 142–147.

Wes McKinney. 2010. Data Structures for Statistical Computing in Python. In *Proceedings of the 9th Python in Science Conference*, pages 56 – 61.

Rustem Yeshpanov, Yerbolat Khassanov, and Huseyin Atakan Varol. 2022. KazNERD: Kazakh named entity recognition dataset. In *Proceedings of the Thirteenth Language Resources and Evaluation Conference*, pages 417–426, Marseille, France. European Language Resources Association.

torchdistill Meets Hugging Face Libraries for Reproducible, Coding-Free Deep Learning Studies: A Case Study on NLP

Yoshitomo Matsubara *
University of California, Irvine
yoshitom@uci.edu

Abstract

Reproducibility in scientific work has been becoming increasingly important in research communities such as machine learning, natural language processing, and computer vision communities due to the rapid development of the research domains supported by recent advances in deep learning. In this work, we present a significantly upgraded version of torchdistill[1], a modular-driven coding-free deep learning framework significantly upgraded from the initial release, which supports only image classification and object detection tasks for reproducible knowledge distillation experiments. To demonstrate that the upgraded framework can support more tasks with third-party libraries, we reproduce the GLUE benchmark results of BERT models using a script based on the upgraded torchdistill, harmonizing with various Hugging Face libraries. All the 27 fine-tuned BERT models and configurations to reproduce the results are published at Hugging Face[2], and the model weights have already been widely used in research communities. We also reimplement popular small-sized models and new knowledge distillation methods and perform additional experiments for computer vision tasks.

1 Introduction

The rapid developments of various research domains such as natural language procession (NLP), computer vision, and speech recognition (He et al., 2016; Ballé et al., 2017; Devlin et al., 2019; Dosovitskiy et al., 2020; Raffel et al., 2020; Rombach et al., 2022; Radford et al., 2023) have been supported by advances in deep learning (Krizhevsky et al., 2012; Mikolov et al., 2013; Kingma and Welling, 2014; Sutskever et al., 2014; Kingma and Ba, 2015; Sohl-Dickstein et al., 2015; Vaswani et al., 2017; Brown et al., 2020). While it has been developed rapidly, poor reproducibility of deep learning-based studies is a severe problem that research communities have been facing (Crane, 2018; Yang et al., 2019; Daoudi et al., 2021; Matsubara, 2021), and the reproducibility has been attracting significant attention from researchers (Gundersen et al., 2018; Gundersen, 2019; Dodge et al., 2019; Kamphuis et al., 2020; Lopresti and Nagy, 2021; Pineau et al., 2021).

To address the serious problem, research communities introduced reproducibility checklists. At the time of writing, some venues require authors to complete checklists when submitting their work *e.g.*, Responsible NLP Research Checklist[3] (Rogers et al., 2021) at NLP venues (ACL, NAACL, ARR) and Paper Checklist at NeurIPS.[4]

Matsubara (2021) developed torchdistill, a modular, configuration-driven knowledge distillation framework built on PyTorch (Paszke et al., 2019) for reproducible deep learning research. Knowledge distillation (Hinton et al., 2014) is a well known model compression method usually to train a small model (called *student*) leveraging outputs from a more complex model (called *teacher*) as part of loss functions to be minimized. Recent knowledge distillation approaches are more complex *e.g.*, using intermediate layers' outputs (embeddings or feature maps) besides the final output (logits) of teacher models with auxiliary module branches attached to teacher and/or student models during training (Kim et al., 2018; Zhang et al., 2020; Chen et al., 2021), using multiple teachers (Mirzadeh et al., 2020; Matsubara et al., 2022b), and training multilingual or non-English models solely with an English teacher model (Reimers and Gurevych, 2020; Li et al., 2022b; Gupta et al., 2023).

For implementing such approaches, researchers

*This work was done prior to joining Amazon.

[1] https://github.com/yoshitomo-matsubara/torchdistill/

[2] https://huggingface.co/yoshitomo-matsubara

[3] https://aclrollingreview.org/responsibleNLPresearch/

[4] https://neurips.cc/public/guides/PaperChecklist

Proceedings of the 3rd Workshop for Natural Language Processing Open Source Software (NLP-OSS 2023), pages 153–164
December 6, 2023

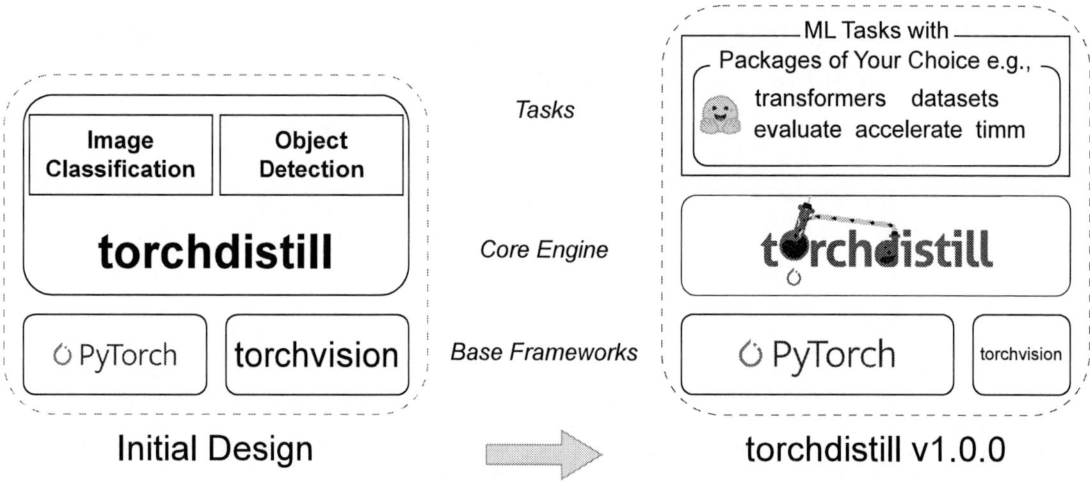

Figure 1: Initial design of torchdistill (Matsubara, 2021) vs. v1.0.0 in this work.

unpacked existing model implementations and modified their input-output interfaces to extract and/or hard-code new auxiliary modules (trainable modules to be used only during training) (Zagoruyko and Komodakis, 2016; Passalis and Tefas, 2018; Heo et al., 2019; Park et al., 2019; Tian et al., 2019; Xu et al., 2020; Chen et al., 2021). torchdistill (Matsubara, 2021) was initially designed as a unified knowledge distillation framework to enable users to design experiments by declarative PyYAML configuration files without such hardcoding effort and help researchers complete the ML Code Completeness Checklist[5] for high-quality reproducible knowledge distillation studies. One of its key concepts is that a declarative PyYAML configuration file designs an experiment and explains key hyperparameters and components used in the experiment. While the initial framework is well generalized and supports 18 different knowledge distillation methods implemented in a unified way, the implementation of the initial framework is highly dependent on torchvision[6], a package for popular datasets, model architectures, and common image transformations for computer vision tasks.

In this work, we significantly upgrade torchdistill from the initial framework (Matsubara, 2021) to enable further generalized implementations, supporting more flexible module abstractions and enhance the advantage of decralative PyYAML configuration files to design experiments with third-party packages of user's choice, as promised in (Matsubara, 2021). Using GLUE tasks (Wang et al., 2019) as an example, we demonstrate that the upgraded torchdistill and a new script harmonize with Hugging Face Transformers (Wolf et al., 2020), Datasets (Lhoest et al., 2021), Accelerate (Gugger et al., 2022), and Evaluate (Von Werra et al., 2022) to reproduce the GLUE test results reported in (Devlin et al., 2019) by fine-tuning pretrained BERT-Base and BERT-Large models with the upgraded torchdistill. We also conduct knowledge distillation experiments using the fine-tuned BERT-Large models as teachers to train BERT-Base models. All these experiments are performed on Google Colaboratory.[7] We also publish all the code and configuration files at GitHub[1] and trained model weights and training logs at Hugging Face[2] for reproducibility and helping researchers build on this work. Our BERT models fine-tuned for the GLUE tasks have already been downloaded 138,000 times in total and widely used in research communities not only in research papers but also in tutorials of deep learning frameworks and ACL 2022. Besides the NLP tasks, we reimplement popular small-sized computer vision models and a few more recent knowledge distillation methods as part of torchdistill, and perform additional experiments to demonstrate that the upgraded torchdistill still supports computer vision tasks.

2 Related Work

In this section, we briefly summarize related work on open source software that supports end-to-end

[5] https://github.com/paperswithcode/releasing-research-code

[6] https://github.com/pytorch/vision

[7] https://colab.google/

research frameworks. Yang et al. (2018) propose Anserini, an information retrieval toolkit built on Lucene[8] for reproducible information retrieval research. Pyserini (Lin et al., 2021) is a Python toolkit built on PyTorch (Paszke et al., 2019) and Faiss (Johnson et al., 2019) for reproducible information retrieval research with sparse and dense representations, and the sparse representation-based retrieval support comes from Lucene via Anserini.

AllenNLP (Gardner et al., 2018) is a toolkit built on PyTorch for research on deep learning methods in NLP and designed to lower barriers to high quality NLP research *e.g.*, useful NLP module abstractions and defining experiments using declarative configuration files. Highly inspired by AllenNLP, Matsubara (2021) design torchdistill, a module, configuration-driven framework built on PyTorch for reproducible knowledge distillation studies. Similar to AllenNLP, torchdistill enables users to design experiments by declarative PyYAML configuration files and supports high-level module abstractions. For image classification and object detection tasks, its generalized starter scripts and configurations help users implement knowledge distillation methods without much coding cost. Matsubara (2021) also reimplement 18 knowledge distillation methods with torchdistill and point out that the standard knowledge distillation (Hinton et al., 2014) can outperform many of the recent state of the art knowledge distillation methods for a popular teacher-student pair (ResNet-34 and ResNet-18) with ILSVRC 2012 dataset (Russakovsky et al., 2015). In Section 3, we describe major upgrades in torchdistill from the initial release (Matsubara, 2021).

3 Major Upgrades from the Initial Release

In this section, we summarize the major upgrades from the initial release of torchdistill (Matsubara, 2021). Figure 1 highlights high-level differences between the initial design (Matsubara, 2021) of torchdistill and a largely upgraded version in this work. The initial torchdistill is dependent on PyTorch and torchvision and contains key modules and functionalities specifically designed to support image classification and object detection tasks. For example, dataset modules that the initial version officially supports are only those in torchvision, and some of dataset-relevant functionalities such as building a sequence of data transforms and dataset loader are based on datasets in torchvision.

In this work, we make torchdistill less dependent on torchvision and support more tasks with third-party packages of users' choice, by generalizing some of the key components in the framework and exporting task-specific implementations to the corresponding executable scripts and local packages. We also reimplement popular small-sized models whose official PyTorch implementations are not either available or maintained.

3.1 PyYAML-based Instantiation

A declarative PyYAML configuration file plays an important role in torchdistill. Users can design experiments with the declarative PyYAML configuration file, which defines various types of abstracted modules with hyperparameters such as dataset, model, optimizer, scheduler, and loss modules. To allow more flexibility in PyYAML configurations, we add more useful constructors such as importing arbitrary local packages to register modules but without edits on an executable script, and instantiating an arbitrary class with a log message. Those can be done simply at the very beginning of an experiment when loading the PyYAML configuration file and make the configuration files more self-explanatory since the configuration format used for the initial version does not explicitly tell users whether the experiment needs specific local packages. Those features also help us generalize ways to define key module such as datasets and their components (*e.g.*, pre-processing transforms, samplers).

Figure 2 shows an example that build a sequence of image/tensor transforms with the initial version and torchdistill in this work. While the former requires both a Python function specifically designed for torchvision modules (`build_transform`) and a list of dict objects defined in a PyYAML configuration to be given to the function as (`transform_params_config`), the latter can build exactly the same transform when loading the PyYAML configuration and store the instantiated object as part of a dict object with **`transform`** key.

3.2 Generalized Modules for Supporting More Tasks

The PyYAML-based instantiation feature described in Section 3.1 enables us to remove torchvision-specific modules mentioned in Section 3 (*e.g.*, `build_transform` in Fig. 2) so that we can reduce

[8] `https://lucene.apache.org/`

```python
import torchvision
from torchdistill.datasets.transform import TRANSFORM_CLASS_DICT

TRANSFORM_CLASS_DICT.update(torchvision.transforms.__dict__)


def build_transform(transform_params_config, compose_cls=None):
    if not isinstance(transform_params_config, (dict, list)) or len(transform_params_config) == 0:
        return None

    component_list = list()
    if isinstance(transform_params_config, dict):
        for component_key in sorted(transform_params_config.keys()):
            component_config = transform_params_config[component_key]
            params_config = component_config.get('params', dict())
            if params_config is None:
                params_config = dict()

            component = TRANSFORM_CLASS_DICT[component_config['type']](**params_config)
            component_list.append(component)
    else:
        for component_config in transform_params_config:
            params_config = component_config.get('params', dict())
            if params_config is None:
                params_config = dict()

            component = TRANSFORM_CLASS_DICT[component_config['type']](**params_config)
            component_list.append(component)
    return transforms.Compose(component_list) if compose_cls is None else compose_cls(component_list)
```

```yaml
transform_params:
  - type: 'RandomCrop'
    params:
      size: 32
      padding: 4
  - type: 'RandomHorizontalFlip'
    params:
      p: 0.5
  - type: 'ToTensor'
    params:
  - type: 'Normalize'
    params:
      mean: [0.49139968, 0.48215841, 0.44653091]
      std: [0.24703223, 0.24348513, 0.26158784]
```

```yaml
transform: !import_call
  key: 'torchvision.transforms.Compose'
  init:
    kwargs:
      transforms:
        - !import_call
          key: 'torchvision.transforms.RandomCrop'
          init:
            kwargs:
              size: 32
              padding: 4
        - !import_call
          key: 'torchvision.transforms.RandomHorizontalFlip'
          init:
            kwargs:
              p: 0.5
        - !import_call
          key: 'torchvision.transforms.ToTensor'
          init:
        - !import_call
          key: 'torchvision.transforms.Normalize'
          init:
            kwargs:
              mean: [0.49139968, 0.48215841, 0.44653091]
              std: [0.24703223, 0.24348513, 0.26158784]
```

Figure 2: Example of two different ways to build a sequence of transforms in torchvision (**transform**) for CIFAR-10 dataset. The initial version (top, left) defines a function for torchvision `build_transform` in torchdistill and gives the function a list of dict objects in the left PyYAML as `transform_params_config`. torchdistill in this work (right) can build exactly the same **transform** by instantiating each of the transform classes step-by-step with `!import_call`, one of our pre-defined PyYAML constructors in the upgraded torchdistill.

torchdistill's dependency on torchvision and generalize its modules for supporting more tasks.

The initial version of torchdistill is designed to support image classification and object detection tasks based on torchvision, and torchvision models for the tasks such as ResNet (He et al., 2016) and Faster R-CNN (Ren et al., 2015) require an image (tensor) and an annotation as part of the model inputs during training. However, this interface does not generalize well to support other tasks. Taking a text classification task as an example, Transformer (Vaswani et al., 2017) models in Hugging Face Transformers (Wolf et al., 2020) have much more input data fields such as (not limited to) token IDs, attention mask, token type IDs, position IDs, and labels for BERT (Devlin et al., 2019), and different models have different input data fields *e.g.*, BART (Lewis et al., 2020) has additional input data fields such as token IDs for its decoder.

In order to support diverse models and tasks, we generalize interfaces of model input/output and the subsequent processes in torchdistill such as computing training losses. For demonstrating that the upgraded torchdistill can support more tasks, we provide starter scripts based on the upgraded framework for GLUE (Wang et al., 2019) and semantic segmentation tasks. For the GLUE tasks, we harmonize popular Python libraries with torchdistill in the script such as Hugging Face Transformers (Wolf et al., 2020), Datasets (Lhoest et al., 2021), and Evaluate (Von Werra et al., 2022) for model, dataset, and evaluation modules. We also leverage Accelerate (Gugger et al., 2022) for efficient training and inference. In Section 4.1, we demonstrate GLUE experiments with torchdistill and the third-party libraries.

3.3 Reimplemented Models and Methods

We find in recent knowledge distillation studies (Tian et al., 2019; Xu et al., 2020; Chen et al., 2021) that there is still a demand of small models for relatively simple datasets such as ResNet (He et al., 2016)[9], WRN (Zagoruyko and Komodakis, 2016)[10], and DenseNet (Huang et al., 2017)[11] for image classification tasks with CIFAR-10 and CIFAR-100 datasets (Krizhevsky, 2009) since the official repositories are no longer maintained and/or not implemented with PyTorch.

For helping the community conduct better benchmarking, we reimplement the models for CIFAR-10 and CIFAR-100 datasets as part of torchdistill and attempt to reproduce the reported results following the original training recipes (See Section 4). With the upgraded torchdistill, we also reimplement and test a few more knowledge distillation methods (He et al., 2019; Chen et al., 2021).

4 Google Colab Demos

In this section, we demonstrate that the upgraded torchdistill can collaborate with third-party libraries for supporting more tasks. We also attempt to reproduce the CIFAR-10 and CIFAR-100 results reported in the original papers. To lower the barrier to reusing and building on the scripts with torchdistill, we conduct all the experiments on Google Colaboratory[7], which gives users access to GPUs free of charge. We publish the Jupyter Notebook[12] files to run the experiments as part of torchdistill repository[1] so that researchers can easily use them.

4.1 GLUE Tasks

The GLUE benchmark (Wang et al., 2019) uses nine datasets in three different task categories. The benchmark consists of 1) two single-sentence tasks: CoLA (Warstadt et al., 2019) and SST-2 (Socher et al., 2013), 2) three similarity and paraphrase tasks: MRPC (Dolan and Brockett, 2005), QQP[13], and STS-B (Cer et al., 2017), and 3) four inference tasks: MNLI (Williams et al., 2018), QNLI (Rajpurkar et al., 2016; Wang et al., 2019), RTE (Dagan et al., 2005; Haim et al., 2006; Giampiccolo et al., 2007; Bentivogli et al.), and WNLI (Levesque et al., 2012).

We attempt to reproduce GLUE test results reported in a popular study, BERT (Devlin et al., 2019), using the upgraded torchdistill harmonizing with Hugging Face libraries (transformers, datasets, evaluate, and accelerate) (Wolf et al., 2020; Lhoest et al., 2021; Von Werra et al., 2022; Gugger et al., 2022). Following the experiments, we also conduct knowledge distillation experiments that fine-tune pretrained BERT-Base models for GLUE tasks, using the fine-tuned BERT-Large models as teachers for the knowledge distillation method of Hinton et al. (2014) minimizing

$$\mathcal{L} = \alpha \cdot \mathcal{L}_{\text{CE}}(\hat{\mathbf{y}}, \mathbf{y}) + (1-\alpha) \cdot \tau^2 \cdot \mathcal{L}_{\text{KL}}(\mathbf{p}, \mathbf{q}), \quad (1)$$

where $\mathcal{L}_{\text{CE}}$ is a standard cross entropy. $\hat{\mathbf{y}}$ indicates the student model's estimated class probabilities, and $\mathbf{y}$ is the annotated category. $\mathcal{L}_{\text{KL}}$ is the Kullback-Leibler divergence, and α and τ are a balancing factor and a temperature, respectively. $\mathbf{p}$ and $\mathbf{q}$ represent the *softened* output distributions from teacher and student models, respectively. $\mathbf{p}$ is used as a target distribution for $\mathcal{L}_{\text{KL}}$. Specifically, $\mathbf{p} = [p_1, p_2, \dots, p_{|\mathcal{C}|}]$ where $\mathcal{C}$ is a set of categories in the target task. p_i indicates the student model's softened output value (scalar) for the i-th category:

$$p_i = \frac{\exp\left(\frac{v_i}{\tau}\right)}{\sum_{k \in \mathcal{C}} \exp\left(\frac{v_k}{\tau}\right)}, \quad (2)$$

[9] https://github.com/facebookarchive/fb.resnet.torch

[10] https://github.com/szagoruyko/wide-residual-networks

[11] https://github.com/liuzhuang13/DenseNet

[12] https://jupyter.org/

[13] https://quoradata.quora.com/First-Quora-Dataset-Release-Question-Pairs

Model (Method, Reference)	MNLI-(m/mm) Acc./Acc.	QQP F1	QNLI Acc.	SST-2 Acc.	CoLA M Corr.	STS-B P-S Corr.	MRPC F1	RTE Acc.	WNLI Acc.
BERT-Large (FT, Devlin et al. (2019))	86.7/85.9	72.1	92.7	94.9	60.5	86.5	89.3	70.1	N/A
BERT-Large (FT, Ours)	86.4/85.7	72.2	92.4	94.6	61.5	85.0	89.2	68.9	65.1
BERT-Base (FT, Devlin et al. (2019))	84.6/83.4	71.2	90.5	93.5	52.1	85.8	88.9	66.4	N/A
BERT-Base (FT, Ours)	84.2/83.3	71.4	91.0	94.1	51.1	84.4	86.8	66.7	65.8
BERT-Base (KD, Ours)	85.9/84.7	72.8	90.7	93.7	57.0	85.6	87.5	66.7	65.1

Table 1: GLUE test results. Our results are hyperlinked to our Hugging Face Model repositories. FT: Fine-Tuning, KD: Knowledge Distillation using BERT-Large (FT, ours) as teacher.

where τ is one of the hyperparameters defined in Eq. (1). v_i denotes a logit value for the i-th category. The same rules are applied to $\mathbf{q}$ for the student model.

For reproducing the GLUE test results in (Devlin et al., 2019), we use pretrained BERT-Base[14] and BERT-Large[15] models in Hugging Face Transformers (Wolf et al., 2020). Following (Devlin et al., 2019) we minimize a standard cross-entropy and the Adam optimizer (Kingma and Ba, 2015) with slightly extended hyperparameter choices: batch size of either 16 or 32 and 2-5 epochs for fine-tuning and select a learning rate among $\{2.0\times10^{-5}, 3.0\times10^{-5}, 4.0\times10^{-5}, 5.0\times10^{-5}\}$ on the *dev* set for each of the tasks. For knowledge distillation, we also choose learning rate from $\{1.0 \times 10^{-5}, 2.0 \times 10^{-5}, 3.0 \times 10^{-5}, 4.0 \times 10^{-5}, 5.0 \times 10^{-5}\}$, temperature $\tau \in \{1, 3, 5, 7, 9, 11\}$, and a balancing weight $\alpha \in \{0.1, 0.3, 0.5, 0.7, 0.9\}$ based on the *dev* sets. Note that since STS-B is not a classification task, we use the sum of 1) a mean squared error between the annotation and the student model's output and 2) a mean squared error between outputs of the teacher and student models instead of Eq. (1) for the dataset.

Table 1 shows the GLUE test results reported by Devlin et al. (2019) and those obtained from GLUE Benchmark[16] for our three configurations: fine-tuning pretrained BERT-Base (FT, Ours) and pretrained BERT-Large (FT, Ours) models and knowledge distillation to fine-tune pretrained BERT-Base (KD, Ours) as a student, using the fine-tuned BERT-Large as the teacher. Note that Devlin et al. (2019) do not report the results for the WNLI test dataset.

Overall, our fine-tuned BERT-Base and BERT-Large models achieved GLUE test results comparable to the official test results reported by Devlin et al. (2019). The knowledge distillation method (Hinton et al., 2014) helped BERT-Base models improve the performance for most of the tasks, compared to those fine-tuned without the teacher models. All the trained model weights and training logs are published at Hugging Face[2], and the training configurations are published as part of the torchdistill GitHub repository.[1]

The fine-tuned BERT models we published are widely used in the research communities and have already been downloaded about 138,000 times in total at the time of writing. For instance, some of the models are used for benchmarks, ensembling, model quantization, token pruning (Matena and Raffel, 2022; Church et al., 2022; Guo et al., 2022; Lee et al., 2022), DeepSpeed Tutorials[17], Intel® Neural Compressor Examples[18], and ACL 2022 Tutorial.[19]

4.2 CIFAR-10 and CIFAR-100

We also attempt to reproduce the CIFAR-10 and CIFAR-100 results reported in (He et al., 2016; Zagoruyko and Komodakis, 2016; Huang et al., 2017) using the upgraded torchdistill with the reimplemented ResNet, WRN, and DenseNet models. We follow the original papers and reuse the hyperparameter choices and training recipes such as data augmentations. Note that we do not confider models that can not fit to the GPU memory which Google Colab can offer *e.g.*, ResNet-1202 (He et al., 2016) for CIFAR-10 and DenseNet-BC(k = 24 and k = 40) (Huang et al., 2017) for CIFAR-10 and CIFAR-100.

Tables 2 and 3 compare the results reported in the original papers (He et al., 2016; Zagoruyko and Komodakis, 2016; Huang et al., 2017) with

[14]https://huggingface.co/bert-base-uncased

[15]https://huggingface.co/bert-large-uncased

[16]https://gluebenchmark.com/

[17]https://www.deepspeed.ai/tutorials/model-compression/

[18]https://github.com/intel/neural-compressor/tree/master/examples

[19]https://github.com/kwchurch/ACL2022_deepnets_tutorial

CIFAR-10 Model	Test Accuracy Original	torchdistill
ResNet-20	91.25	91.92
ResNet-32	92.49	93.03
ResNet-44	92.83	93.20
ResNet-56	93.03	93.57
ResNet-110	93.57	93.50
WRN-40-4	95.47	95.24
WRN-28-10	96.00	95.53
WRN-16-8	95.73	94.76
DenseNet-BC (k=12, depth=100)	95.49	95.53

Table 2: CIFAR-10 results for ResNet (He et al., 2016), WRN (Zagoruyko and Komodakis, 2016), and DenseNet (Huang et al., 2017).

CIFAR-100 Model	Test Accuracy Original	torchdistill
WRN-40-4	79.82	79.44
WRN-28-10	80.75	81.27
WRN-16-8	79.57	79.26
DenseNet-BC (k=12, depth=100)	77.73	77.14

Table 3: CIFAR-100 results for WRN (Zagoruyko and Komodakis, 2016) and DenseNet (Huang et al., 2017).

those we reproduced for CIFAR-10 and CIFAR-100 test datasets, respectively. We can confirm that for most of the reimplemented models, our results are comparable to those reported in the original papers. Those model weights and training configuration files are publicly available, and users can automatically download the weights via the upgraded torchdistill PyPI package.

5 ILSVRC 2012

As highlighted in Section 3, torchdistill was initially focused on supporting implementations of diverse knowledge distillation in a unified way and dependent on torchvision to specifically support image classification and object detection tasks with its relevant modules (see Fig. 1). To demonstrate that the upgraded torchdistill still preserves the feature, we reimplement a few more knowledge distillation methods with the upgraded torchdistill: knowledge review (KR) framework (Chen et al., 2021) and knowledge translation and adaptation with affinity distillation (KTAAD) (He et al., 2019). Note that Matsubara (2021) present the results of various knowledge distillation methods reimplemented with the initial version of torchdistill for ILSVRC 2012 and COCO 2017 (Lin et al., 2014) datasets. Those results are not included in this work, and we refer interested readers to (Matsubara, 2021).

T: ResNet-34 CE	S: ResNet-18 CE	KR (Original)	KR (Ours)
73.31	69.75	71.61	71.64

Table 4: ILSVRC 2012 top-1 accuracy of ResNet-18 (student) trained by KR (Chen et al., 2021) with pretrained ResNet-34 (teacher). CE: torchvision models pretrained with cross-entropy.

Chen et al. (2021) demonstrate that the KR method can outperform other knowledge distillation using ResNet-34 and ResNet-18 (He et al., 2016), a popular pair of teacher and student models for the ImageNet (ILSVRC 2012) dataset (Russakovsky et al., 2015). Using the reimplemented KR method based on the upgraded torchdistill with hyperparameters in (Chen et al., 2021), we successfully reproduce their reported result of ResNet-18 for the ImageNet dataset as shown in Table 4. The trained model weights and configuration are published as part of the torchdistill repository.[1]

6 PASCAL VOC 2012 & COCO 2017

The initial torchdistill (Matsubara, 2021) supports image classification and object detection tasks. As mentioned in Section 3.2, we also provide a starter script for semantic segmentation tasks. Using two popular datasets, PASCAL VOC 2012 (Everingham et al., 2012) and COCO 2017 (Lin et al., 2014), we demonstrate that the upgraded torchdistill supports semantic segmentation tasks as well.

In the experiments with PASCAL VOC 2012 dataset, we use DeepLabv3 (Chen et al., 2017) with ResNet-50 and ResNet-101 backbones (He et al., 2016), using torchvision's pretrained model weights for COCO 2017 dataset. We choose hyperparameters such as learning rate policy and crop size based on the original study of DeepLabv3 (Chen et al., 2017). Our results are shown in Table 5, and DeepLabv3 with ResNet-101 achieved comparable mIoU (mean Intersection over Union) to the best DeepLabv3 model for PASCAL VOC 2012 dataset (*val* set) in the original study (mIoU: 82.70). Following torchvision documentation[20], we measure global pixelwise accuracy as well. In terms of both the metrics, DeepLabv3 with ResNet-101 outperforms DeepLabv3 with ResNet-50.

[20]https://pytorch.org/vision/stable/models.html#table-of-all-available-semantic-segmentation-weights

Model	mean IoU	Pixelwise Acc.
DeepLabv3 w/ ResNet-50	80.6	95.7
DeepLabv3 w/ ResNet-101	82.4	96.2

Table 5: PASCAL VOC 2012 (Segmentation, *val* set) validation results for DeepLabv3 with ResNet backbones (Chen et al., 2017) initialized with torchvision pretrained model weights for COCO 2017 dataset.

Method	mean IoU	Pixelwise Acc.
CE (torchvision)	57.9	91.2
KTAAD (Ours)	58.2	92.1

Table 6: COCO 2017 (Segmentation, *val* set) results for LRASPP with MobileNetV3-Large backbone (Howard et al., 2019).

We also examine our reimplemented KTAAD method (He et al., 2019) for the Lite R-ASPP model (LRASPP in torchvision) (Howard et al., 2019) as a student model, using the COCO 2017 dataset and the pretrained DeepLabv3 with ResNet-50 in torchvision as a teacher model, whose mIoU and global pixelwise accuracy are 66.4 and 92.4, respectively. Since the KTAAD method is not tested on COCO 2017 dataset for LRASPP with MobileNetV3-Large backbone in the original paper of KTAAD (He et al., 2019), our hyperparameter choice is based on torchvision's reference script.[21]

Table 6 presents the semantic segmentation results of LRASPP with MobileNetV3-Large backbone trained without the teacher model and by the KTAAD method we reimplemented. We confirm that the student model trained by KTAAD outperforms the same model trained on COCO 2017 available in torchvision in terms of mean IoU and global pixelwise accuracy.

As with other experiments, the trained model weights and configuration used in this section are published as part of the torchdistill repository.[1]

7 Conclusion

In this work, we significantly upgraded torchdistill (Matsubara, 2021), a modular, configuration-driven framework built on PyTorch (Paszke et al., 2019) for reproducible deep learning and knowledge distillation studies. We enhanced PyYAML-based instantiation, generalized internal modules for supporting more tasks, and reimplemented popular models and methods.

To demonstrate that the upgraded framework can support more tasks as we claim, we provided starter scripts for new tasks based on the upgraded framework. One of the new starter scripts supports GLUE tasks (Wang et al., 2019) and harmonizes with Hugging Face Transformers (Wolf et al., 2020), Datasets (Lhoest et al., 2021), Accelerate (Gugger et al., 2022), and Evaluate (Von Werra et al., 2022). Using the script on Google Colaboratory, we reproduced the GLUE test results of fine-tuned BERT models (Devlin et al., 2019) and performed knowledge distillation experiments with our fine-tuned BERT-Large models as teacher models. Similarly, we reproduced CIFAR-10 and -100 results of popular small-sized models we reimplemented, using Google Colaboratory. Furthermore, we reproduced the result of ResNet-18 trained with the reimplemented KR method (Chen et al., 2021) for the ImageNet dataset. We also demonstrated a new starter script for semantic segmentation tasks using PASCAL VOC 2012 and COCO 2017 datasets, and the reimplemented KTAAD method (He et al., 2019) improves a pretrained semantic segmentation model in torchvision.

In this study, we also published 27 trained models for NLP tasks[2] and 14 trained models for computer vision tasks.[1] According to Hugging Face Model repositories, the BERT models fine-tuned for the GLUE tasks have already been downloaded about 138,000 times in total at the time of writing. Research communities leverage torchdistill not only for knowledge distillation studies (Liu et al., 2021; Li et al., 2022a; Lin et al., 2022; Dong et al., 2022; Miles and Mikolajczyk, 2023), but also for machine learning reproducibility challenge (MLRC) (Lee and Lee, 2023) and reproducible deep learning studies (Matsubara et al., 2022a,c; Furutanpey et al., 2023b,a; Matsubara et al., 2023). torchdistill is publicly available as a pip-installable PyPI package and will be maintained and upgraded for encouraging coding-free reproducible deep learning and knowledge distillation studies.

Acknowledgements

We thank the anonymous reviewers for their comments. This project has been supported by Travis CI's OSS credits and JetBrain's Free License Programs (Open Source) since November 2021 and June 2022, respectively.

[21] https://github.com/pytorch/vision/tree/main/references/segmentation

References

Johannes Ballé, Valero Laparra, and Eero P Simoncelli. 2017. End-to-end Optimized Image Compression. In *International Conference on Learning Representations*.

Luisa Bentivogli, Peter Clark, Ido Dagan, and Danilo Giampiccolo. The Sixth PASCAL Recognizing Textual Entailment Challenge.

Tom Brown, Benjamin Mann, Nick Ryder, Melanie Subbiah, Jared D Kaplan, Prafulla Dhariwal, Arvind Neelakantan, Pranav Shyam, Girish Sastry, Amanda Askell, et al. 2020. Language Models are Few-Shot Learners. *Advances in neural information processing systems*, 33:1877–1901.

Daniel Cer, Mona Diab, Eneko Agirre, Iñigo Lopez-Gazpio, and Lucia Specia. 2017. SemEval-2017 Task 1: Semantic Textual Similarity Multilingual and Crosslingual Focused Evaluation. In *Proceedings of the 11th International Workshop on Semantic Evaluation (SemEval-2017)*, pages 1–14.

Liang-Chieh Chen, George Papandreou, Florian Schroff, and Hartwig Adam. 2017. Rethinking Atrous Convolution for Semantic Image Segmentation. *arXiv preprint arXiv:1706.05587*.

Pengguang Chen, Shu Liu, Hengshuang Zhao, and Jiaya Jia. 2021. Distilling Knowledge via Knowledge Review. In *Proceedings of the IEEE/CVF Conference on Computer Vision and Pattern Recognition*, pages 5008–5017.

Kenneth Church, Valia Kordoni, Gary Marcus, Ernest Davis, Yanjun Ma, and Zeyu Chen. 2022. A Gentle Introduction to Deep Nets and Opportunities for the Future. In *Proceedings of the 60th Annual Meeting of the Association for Computational Linguistics: Tutorial Abstracts*, pages 1–6.

Matt Crane. 2018. Questionable Answers in Question Answering Research: Reproducibility and Variability of Published Results. *Transactions of the Association for Computational Linguistics*, 6:241–252.

Ido Dagan, Oren Glickman, and Bernardo Magnini. 2005. The PASCAL Recognising Textual Entailment Challenge. In *Machine learning challenges workshop*, pages 177–190. Springer.

Nadia Daoudi, Kevin Allix, Tegawendé F Bissyandé, and Jacques Klein. 2021. Lessons Learnt on Reproducibility in Machine Learning Based Android Malware Detection. *Empirical Software Engineering*, 26(4):74.

Jacob Devlin, Ming-Wei Chang, Kenton Lee, and Kristina Toutanova. 2019. BERT: Pre-training of Deep Bidirectional Transformers for Language Understanding. In *Proceedings of the 2019 Conference of the North American Chapter of the Association for Computational Linguistics: Human Language Technologies, Volume 1 (Long and Short Papers)*, pages 4171–4186.

Jesse Dodge, Suchin Gururangan, Dallas Card, Roy Schwartz, and Noah A Smith. 2019. Show Your Work: Improved Reporting of Experimental Results, author=Dodge, Jesse and Gururangan, Suchin and Card, Dallas and Schwartz, Roy and Smith, Noah A. In *Proceedings of the 2019 Conference on Empirical Methods in Natural Language Processing and the 9th International Joint Conference on Natural Language Processing (EMNLP-IJCNLP)*, pages 2185–2194. Association for Computational Linguistics.

William B Dolan and Chris Brockett. 2005. Automatically Constructing a Corpus of Sentential Paraphrases. In *Proceedings of the Third International Workshop on Paraphrasing (IWP2005)*.

Chengyu Dong, Liyuan Liu, and Jingbo Shang. 2022. SoTeacher: Toward Student-oriented Teacher Network Training for Knowledge Distillation.

Alexey Dosovitskiy, Lucas Beyer, Alexander Kolesnikov, Dirk Weissenborn, Xiaohua Zhai, Thomas Unterthiner, Mostafa Dehghani, Matthias Minderer, Georg Heigold, Sylvain Gelly, et al. 2020. An Image is Worth 16x16 Words: Transformers for Image Recognition at Scale. In *International Conference on Learning Representations*.

Mark Everingham, Luc Van Gool, CKI Williams, John Winn, and Andrew Zisserman. 2012. The PASCAL Visual Object Classes Challenge 2012 (VOC2012).

Alireza Furutanpey, Johanna Barzen, Marvin Bechtold, Schahram Dustdar, Frank Leymann, Philipp Raith, and Felix Truger. 2023a. Architectural Vision for Quantum Computing in the Edge-Cloud Continuum. *arXiv preprint arXiv:2305.05238*.

Alireza Furutanpey, Philipp Raith, and Schahram Dustdar. 2023b. FrankenSplit: Saliency Guided Neural Feature Compression with Shallow Variational Bottleneck Injection. *arXiv preprint arXiv:2302.10681*.

Matt Gardner, Joel Grus, Mark Neumann, Oyvind Tafjord, Pradeep Dasigi, Nelson F Liu, Matthew E Peters, Michael Schmitz, and Luke Zettlemoyer. 2018. AllenNLP: A Deep Semantic Natural Language Processing Platform. In *Proceedings of Workshop for NLP Open Source Software (NLP-OSS)*, pages 1–6.

Danilo Giampiccolo, Bernardo Magnini, Ido Dagan, and William B Dolan. 2007. The Third PASCAL Recognising Textual Entailment Challenge. In *Proceedings of the ACL-PASCAL workshop on textual entailment and paraphrasing*, pages 1–9.

Sylvain Gugger, Lysandre Debut, Thomas Wolf, Philipp Schmid, Zachary Mueller, and Sourab Mangrulkar. 2022. Accelerate: Training and inference at scale made simple, efficient and adaptable. `https://github.com/huggingface/accelerate`.

Odd Erik Gundersen. 2019. Standing on the Feet of Giants - Reproducibility in AI. *AI Magazine*, 40(4):9–23.

Odd Erik Gundersen, Yolanda Gil, and David W. Aha. 2018. On Reproducible AI: Towards Reproducible Research, Open Science, and Digital Scholarship in AI Publications. *AI Magazine*, 39(3):56–68.

Cong Guo, Chen Zhang, Jingwen Leng, Zihan Liu, Fan Yang, Yunxin Liu, Minyi Guo, and Yuhao Zhu. 2022. ANT: Exploiting Adaptive Numerical Data Type for Low-bit Deep Neural Network Quantization. In *2022 55th IEEE/ACM International Symposium on Microarchitecture (MICRO)*, pages 1414–1433. IEEE.

Shivanshu Gupta, Yoshitomo Matsubara, Ankit Chadha, and Alessandro Moschitti. 2023. Cross-lingual knowledge distillation for answer sentence selection in low-resource languages. In *Findings of the Association for Computational Linguistics: ACL 2023*, pages 7259–7272.

R Bar Haim, Ido Dagan, Bill Dolan, Lisa Ferro, Danilo Giampiccolo, Bernardo Magnini, and Idan Szpektor. 2006. The Second PASCAL Recognising Textual Entailment Challenge. In *Proceedings of the Second PASCAL Challenges Workshop on Recognising Textual Entailment*, volume 7, pages 785–794.

Kaiming He, Xiangyu Zhang, Shaoqing Ren, and Jian Sun. 2016. Deep residual learning for image recognition. In *Proceedings of the IEEE Conference on Computer Vision and Pattern Recognition*, pages 770–778.

Tong He, Chunhua Shen, Zhi Tian, Dong Gong, Changming Sun, and Youliang Yan. 2019. Knowledge Adaptation for Efficient Semantic Segmentation. In *Proceedings of the IEEE/CVF Conference on Computer Vision and Pattern Recognition*, pages 578–587.

Byeongho Heo, Minsik Lee, Sangdoo Yun, and Jin Young Choi. 2019. Knowledge Transfer via Distillation of Activation Boundaries Formed by Hidden Neurons. In *Proceedings of the AAAI Conference on Artificial Intelligence*, volume 33, pages 3779–3787.

Geoffrey Hinton, Oriol Vinyals, and Jeff Dean. 2014. Distilling the Knowledge in a Neural Network. In *Deep Learning and Representation Learning Workshop: NIPS 2014*.

Andrew Howard, Mark Sandler, Grace Chu, Liang-Chieh Chen, Bo Chen, Mingxing Tan, Weijun Wang, Yukun Zhu, Ruoming Pang, Vijay Vasudevan, et al. 2019. Searching for MobileNetV3. In *Proceedings of the IEEE/CVF International Conference on Computer Vision*, pages 1314–1324.

Gao Huang, Zhuang Liu, Laurens Van Der Maaten, and Kilian Q Weinberger. 2017. Densely connected convolutional networks. In *Proceedings of the IEEE conference on computer vision and pattern recognition*, pages 4700–4708.

Jeff Johnson, Matthijs Douze, and Hervé Jégou. 2019. Billion-Scale Similarity Search with GPUs. *IEEE Transactions on Big Data*, 7(3):535–547.

Chris Kamphuis, Arjen P de Vries, Leonid Boytsov, and Jimmy Lin. 2020. Which BM25 Do You Mean? A Large-Scale Reproducibility Study of Scoring Variants. In *Advances in Information Retrieval: 42nd European Conference on IR Research, ECIR 2020, Lisbon, Portugal, April 14–17, 2020, Proceedings, Part II 42*, pages 28–34. Springer.

Jangho Kim, SeongUk Park, and Nojun Kwak. 2018. Paraphrasing Complex Network: Network Compression via Factor Transfer. In *Advances in Neural Information Processing Systems*, pages 2760–2769.

Diederik P. Kingma and Jimmy Ba. 2015. Adam: A Method for Stochastic Optimization. In *Third International Conference on Learning Representations*.

Diederik P Kingma and Max Welling. 2014. Auto-Encoding Variational Bayes. In *International Conference on Learning Representations*.

Alex Krizhevsky. 2009. Learning Multiple Layers of Features from Tiny Images.

Alex Krizhevsky, Ilya Sutskever, and Geoffrey E Hinton. 2012. ImageNet Classification with Deep Convolutional Neural Networks. In *Advances in Neural Information Processing Systems 25*, pages 1097–1105.

Heejun Lee, Minki Kang, Youngwan Lee, and Sung Ju Hwang. 2022. Sparse Token Transformer with Attention Back Tracking. In *The Eleventh International Conference on Learning Representations*.

Seungjae Ryan Lee and Seungmin Lee. 2023. [Re] Pure Noise to the Rescue of Insufficient Data. In *ML Reproducibility Challenge 2022*.

Hector Levesque, Ernest Davis, and Leora Morgenstern. 2012. The Winograd Schema Challenge. In *Proceedings of the Thirteenth International Conference on Principles of Knowledge Representation and Reasoning*, pages 552–561.

Mike Lewis, Yinhan Liu, Naman Goyal, Marjan Ghazvininejad, Abdelrahman Mohamed, Omer Levy, Veselin Stoyanov, and Luke Zettlemoyer. 2020. BART: Denoising Sequence-to-Sequence Pre-training for Natural Language Generation, Translation, and Comprehension. In *Proceedings of the 58th Annual Meeting of the Association for Computational Linguistics*, pages 7871–7880.

Quentin Lhoest, Albert Villanova del Moral, Yacine Jernite, Abhishek Thakur, Patrick von Platen, Suraj Patil, Julien Chaumond, Mariama Drame, Julien Plu, Lewis Tunstall, et al. 2021. Datasets: A Community Library for Natural Language Processing. In *Proceedings of the 2021 Conference on Empirical Methods in Natural Language Processing: System Demonstrations*, pages 175–184.

Wei Li, Shitong Shao, Weiyan Liu, Ziming Qiu, Zhihao Zhu, and Wei Huan. 2022a. What Role Does Data Augmentation Play in Knowledge Distillation? In *Proceedings of the Asian Conference on Computer Vision*, pages 2204–2220.

Yulong Li, Martin Franz, Md Arafat Sultan, Bhavani Iyer, Young-Suk Lee, and Avirup Sil. 2022b. Learning Cross-Lingual IR from an English Retriever. In *Proceedings of the 2022 Conference of the North American Chapter of the Association for Computational Linguistics: Human Language Technologies*, pages 4428–4436.

Jimmy Lin, Xueguang Ma, Sheng-Chieh Lin, Jheng-Hong Yang, Ronak Pradeep, and Rodrigo Nogueira. 2021. Pyserini: A Python Toolkit for Reproducible Information Retrieval Research with Sparse and Dense Representations. In *Proceedings of the 44th International ACM SIGIR Conference on Research and Development in Information Retrieval*, pages 2356–2362.

Sihao Lin, Hongwei Xie, Bing Wang, Kaicheng Yu, Xiaojun Chang, Xiaodan Liang, and Gang Wang. 2022. Knowledge Distillation via the Target-aware Transformer. In *Proceedings of the IEEE/CVF Conference on Computer Vision and Pattern Recognition*, pages 10915–10924.

Tsung-Yi Lin, Michael Maire, Serge Belongie, James Hays, Pietro Perona, Deva Ramanan, Piotr Dollár, and C Lawrence Zitnick. 2014. Microsoft coco: Common objects in context. In *European conference on computer vision*, pages 740–755. Springer.

Li Liu, Qingle Huang, Sihao Lin, Hongwei Xie, Bing Wang, Xiaojun Chang, and Xiaodan Liang. 2021. Exploring Inter-Channel Correlation for Diversity-preserved Knowledge Distillation. In *Proceedings of the IEEE/CVF International Conference on Computer Vision*, pages 8271–8280.

Daniel Lopresti and George Nagy. 2021. Reproducibility: Evaluating the Evaluations. In *International Workshop on Reproducible Research in Pattern Recognition*, pages 12–23. Springer.

Michael S Matena and Colin A Raffel. 2022. Merging Models with Fisher-Weighted Averaging. *Advances in Neural Information Processing Systems*, 35:17703–17716.

Yoshitomo Matsubara. 2021. torchdistill: A Modular, Configuration-Driven Framework for Knowledge Distillation. In *International Workshop on Reproducible Research in Pattern Recognition*, pages 24–44. Springer.

Yoshitomo Matsubara, Davide Callegaro, Sameer Singh, Marco Levorato, and Francesco Restuccia. 2022a. BottleFit: Learning Compressed Representations in Deep Neural Networks for Effective and Efficient Split Computing. *arXiv preprint arXiv:2201.02693*.

Yoshitomo Matsubara, Luca Soldaini, Eric Lind, and Alessandro Moschitti. 2022b. Ensemble Transformer for Efficient and Accurate Ranking Tasks: an Application to Question Answering Systems. In *Findings of the Association for Computational Linguistics: EMNLP 2022*, pages 7259–7272.

Yoshitomo Matsubara, Ruihan Yang, Marco Levorato, and Stephan Mandt. 2022c. Supervised Compression for Resource-Constrained Edge Computing Systems. In *Proceedings of the IEEE/CVF Winter Conference on Applications of Computer Vision*, pages 2685–2695.

Yoshitomo Matsubara, Ruihan Yang, Marco Levorato, and Stephan Mandt. 2023. SC2 Benchmark: Supervised Compression for Split Computing. *Transactions on Machine Learning Research.*

Tomas Mikolov, Ilya Sutskever, Kai Chen, Greg S Corrado, and Jeff Dean. 2013. Distributed Representations of Words and Phrases and Their Compositionality. *Advances in Neural Information Processing Systems*, 26.

Roy Miles and Krystian Mikolajczyk. 2023. A closer look at the training dynamics of knowledge distillation. *arXiv preprint arXiv:2303.11098*.

Seyed Iman Mirzadeh, Mehrdad Farajtabar, Ang Li, Nir Levine, Akihiro Matsukawa, and Hassan Ghasemzadeh. 2020. Improved Knowledge Distillation via Teacher Assistant. In *Proceedings of the AAAI Conference on Artificial Intelligence*, volume 34, pages 5191–5198.

Wonpyo Park, Dongju Kim, Yan Lu, and Minsu Cho. 2019. Relational Knowledge Distillation. In *Proceedings of the IEEE Conference on Computer Vision and Pattern Recognition*, pages 3967–3976.

Nikolaos Passalis and Anastasios Tefas. 2018. Learning Deep Representations with Probabilistic Knowledge Transfer. In *Proceedings of the European Conference on Computer Vision (ECCV)*, pages 268–284.

Adam Paszke, Sam Gross, Francisco Massa, Adam Lerer, James Bradbury, Gregory Chanan, Trevor Killeen, Zeming Lin, Natalia Gimelshein, Luca Antiga, et al. 2019. PyTorch: An imperative style, high-performance deep learning library. In *Advances in Neural Information Processing Systems*, pages 8024–8035.

Joelle Pineau, Philippe Vincent-Lamarre, Koustuv Sinha, Vincent Larivière, Alina Beygelzimer, Florence d'Alché Buc, Emily Fox, and Hugo Larochelle. 2021. Improving Reproducibility in Machine Learning Research(A Report from the NeurIPS 2019 Reproducibility Program). *The Journal of Machine Learning Research*, 22(1):7459–7478.

Alec Radford, Jong Wook Kim, Tao Xu, Greg Brockman, Christine McLeavey, and Ilya Sutskever. 2023. Robust speech recognition via large-scale weak supervision. In *International Conference on Machine Learning*, pages 28492–28518. PMLR.

Colin Raffel, Noam Shazeer, Adam Roberts, Katherine Lee, Sharan Narang, Michael Matena, Yanqi Zhou, Wei Li, and Peter J Liu. 2020. Exploring the Limits of Transfer Learning with a Unified Text-to-Text Transformer. *The Journal of Machine Learning Research*, 21(1):5485–5551.

Pranav Rajpurkar, Jian Zhang, Konstantin Lopyrev, and Percy Liang. 2016. SQuAD: 100,000+ Questions for Machine Comprehension of Text. In *Proceedings of the 2016 Conference on Empirical Methods in Natural Language Processing*, pages 2383–2392.

Nils Reimers and Iryna Gurevych. 2020. Making Monolingual Sentence Embeddings Multilingual using Knowledge Distillation. In *Proceedings of the 2020 Conference on Empirical Methods in Natural Language Processing (EMNLP)*, pages 4512–4525.

Shaoqing Ren, Kaiming He, Ross Girshick, and Jian Sun. 2015. Faster R-CNN: Towards Real-Time Object Detection with Region Proposal Networks. In *Advances in neural information processing systems*, pages 91–99.

Anna Rogers, Timothy Baldwin, and Kobi Leins. 2021. 'Just What do You Think You're Doing, Dave?'A Checklist for Responsible Data Use in NLP. In *Findings of the Association for Computational Linguistics: EMNLP 2021*, pages 4821–4833.

Robin Rombach, Andreas Blattmann, Dominik Lorenz, Patrick Esser, and Björn Ommer. 2022. High-Resolution Image Synthesis with Latent Diffusion Models. In *Proceedings of the IEEE/CVF Conference on Computer Vision and Pattern Recognition*, pages 10684–10695.

Olga Russakovsky, Jia Deng, Hao Su, Jonathan Krause, Sanjeev Satheesh, Sean Ma, Zhiheng Huang, Andrej Karpathy, Aditya Khosla, Michael Bernstein, Alexander C. Berg, and Li Fei-Fei. 2015. ImageNet Large Scale Visual Recognition Challenge. *International Journal of Computer Vision*, 115(3):211–252.

Richard Socher, Alex Perelygin, Jean Wu, Jason Chuang, Christopher D Manning, Andrew Y Ng, and Christopher Potts. 2013. Recursive Deep Models for Semantic Compositionality Over a Sentiment Treebank. In *Proceedings of the 2013 conference on empirical methods in natural language processing*, pages 1631–1642.

Jascha Sohl-Dickstein, Eric Weiss, Niru Maheswaranathan, and Surya Ganguli. 2015. Deep Unsupervised Learning using Nonequilibrium Thermodynamics. In *International Conference on Machine Learning*, pages 2256–2265. PMLR.

Ilya Sutskever, Oriol Vinyals, and Quoc V Le. 2014. Sequence to Sequence Learning with Neural Networks. *Advances in Neural Information Processing Systems*, 27.

Yonglong Tian, Dilip Krishnan, and Phillip Isola. 2019. Contrastive Representation Distillation. In *International Conference on Learning Representations*.

Ashish Vaswani, Noam Shazeer, Niki Parmar, Jakob Uszkoreit, Llion Jones, Aidan N Gomez, Łukasz Kaiser, and Illia Polosukhin. 2017. Attention Is All You Need. *Advances in neural information processing systems*, 30.

Leandro Von Werra, Lewis Tunstall, Abhishek Thakur, Sasha Luccioni, Tristan Thrush, Aleksandra Piktus, Felix Marty, Nazneen Rajani, Victor Mustar, and Helen Ngo. 2022. Evaluate & Evaluation on the Hub: Better Best Practices for Data and Model Measurements. In *Proceedings of the The 2022 Conference on Empirical Methods in Natural Language Processing: System Demonstrations*, pages 128–136.

Alex Wang, Amanpreet Singh, Julian Michael, Felix Hill, Omer Levy, and Samuel R Bowman. 2019. GLUE: A Multi-Task Benchmark and Analysis Platform for Natural Language Understanding. In *International Conference on Learning Representations*.

Alex Warstadt, Amanpreet Singh, and Samuel Bowman. 2019. Neural network acceptability judgments. *Transactions of the Association for Computational Linguistics*, 7:625–641.

Adina Williams, Nikita Nangia, and Samuel Bowman. 2018. A Broad-Coverage Challenge Corpus for Sentence Understanding through Inference. In *Proceedings of the 2018 Conference of the North American Chapter of the Association for Computational Linguistics: Human Language Technologies, Volume 1 (Long Papers)*, pages 1112–1122.

Thomas Wolf, Julien Chaumond, Lysandre Debut, Victor Sanh, Clement Delangue, Anthony Moi, Pierric Cistac, Morgan Funtowicz, Joe Davison, Sam Shleifer, et al. 2020. Transformers: State-of-the-art natural language processing. In *Proceedings of the 2020 Conference on Empirical Methods in Natural Language Processing: System Demonstrations*, pages 38–45.

Guodong Xu, Ziwei Liu, Xiaoxiao Li, and Chen Change Loy. 2020. Knowledge Distillation Meets Self-supervision. In *European Conference on Computer Vision*, pages 588–604. Springer.

Peilin Yang, Hui Fang, and Jimmy Lin. 2018. Anserini: Reproducible Ranking Baselines Using Lucene. *Journal of Data and Information Quality (JDIQ)*, 10(4):1–20.

Wei Yang, Kuang Lu, Peilin Yang, and Jimmy Lin. 2019. Critically Examining the "Neural Hype": Weak Baselines and the Additivity of Effectiveness Gains from Neural Ranking Models. In *Proceedings of the 42nd International ACM SIGIR Conference on Research and Development in Information Retrieval*, pages 1129–1132.

Sergey Zagoruyko and Nikos Komodakis. 2016. Wide residual networks. In *Proceedings of the British Machine Vision Conference (BMVC)*, pages 87.1–87.12. BMVA Press.

Youcai Zhang, Zhonghao Lan, Yuchen Dai, Fangao Zeng, Yan Bai, Jie Chang, and Yichen Wei. 2020. Prime-Aware Adaptive Distillation. In *The European Conference on Computer Vision (ECCV)*.

Using Captum to Explain Generative Language Models

Vivek Miglani*, Aobo Yang*, Aram H. Markosyan, Diego Garcia-Olano, Narine Kokhlikyan

Meta AI

{vivekm, aoboyang, amarkos, diegoolano, narine}@meta.com

Abstract

Captum is a comprehensive library for model explainability in PyTorch, offering a range of methods from the interpretability literature to enhance users' understanding of PyTorch models. In this paper, we introduce new features in Captum[1] that are specifically designed to analyze the behavior of generative language models. We provide an overview of the available functionalities and example applications of their potential for understanding learned associations within generative language models.

1 Introduction

Model interpretability and explainability have become significantly more important as machine learning models are used in critical domains such as healthcare and law. It is insufficient to simply make a prediction through a black-box model and important to better understand why the model made a particular decision.

Interest in Large Language Models (LLMs) has also grown exponentially in the past few years with the release of increasingly large and more powerful models such as GPT-4 (OpenAI, 2023). A lack of explainability continues to exist despite larger models, and with the use of these models expanding to more and more use-cases, it is increasingly important to have access to tooling providing model explanations.

Captum is an open-source model explainability library for PyTorch providing a variety of generic interpretability methods proposed in recent literature such as Integrated Gradients, LIME, DeepLift, TracIn, TCAV and more (Kokhlikyan et al., 2020).

In this work, we discuss newly open-sourced functionalities in Captum v0.7 to easily apply explainability methods to large generative language models, such as GPT-3.

*Denotes equal contribution

[1]`https://captum.ai`

2 Attribution Methods

One important class of explainability methods is attribution or feature importance methods, which output a score corresponding to each input feature's contribution or impact to a model's final output.

Formally, given a function $f : \mathbb{R}^d \rightarrow \mathbb{R}$, where $f \in \mathbb{F}$ and $X \in \mathbb{R}^d$ is a single input vector consisting of d dimensions or features, an attribution method is defined as a function $\phi : \mathbb{F} \times \mathbb{R}^d \rightarrow \mathbb{R}^d$. Each element in the attribution output corresponds to a score of the contribution of corresponding feature $i \in D$, where D denotes the set of all feature indices $D = \{1, 2, ..., d\}$.

Many attribution methods also require a baseline or reference input $B \in \mathbb{R}^d$ defining a comparison input point to measure feature importance with respect to.

We utilize the notation X_S to denote selecting the feature values with indices from the set $S \subseteq D$ and the remaining indices from B. Formally, the value of feature i in X_S is $(X_S)_i = I_{i \in S} X_i + I_{i \notin S} B_i$, where I is the indicator function.

In this section, we provide background context on attribution methods available in Captum. These methods can be categorized broadly into (i) perturbation-based methods, which utilize repeated evaluations of a black-box model on perturbed inputs to estimate attribution scores, and (ii) gradient-based methods, which utilize backpropagated gradient information to estimate attribution scores. Perturbation-based methods do not require access to model weights, while gradient-based models do.

2.1 Perturbation-Based Methods

2.1.1 Feature Ablation

The most straightforward attribution is feature ablation, where each feature is substituted with the corresponding element of the baseline feature vector to estimate the corresponding importance.

Proceedings of the 3rd Workshop for Natural Language Processing Open Source Software (NLP-OSS 2023), pages 165–173
December 6, 2023 ©2023 Association for Computational Linguistics

Formally, this method is defined as

$$\phi_i(f, X) = f(X) - f(X_{D\setminus\{i\}}) \tag{1}$$

Feature Ablation has clear advantages as a simple and straightforward method, but the resulting attributions may not fully capture the impacts of feature interactions since features are ablated individually.

2.1.2 Shapley Value Sampling

Shapley Values originated from cooperative game theory as an approach to distribute payouts fairly among players in a cooperative game. Analogously, in the attribution setting, Shapley Values assign scores to input features, with payouts corresponding to a feature's contribution to the model output. Shapley Values satisfy a variety of theoretical properties including efficiency, symmetry and linearity. Formally, this method is defined as

$$\phi_i(f, X) = \sum_{S \subseteq D\setminus\{i\}} \Big[\frac{|S|!(|D| - |S| - 1)!}{|D|!} \\ f(X_{S\cup\{i\}}) - f(X_S)\Big] \tag{2}$$

While computing this quantity exactly requires an exponential number of evaluations in the number of features, we can estimate this quantity using a sampling approach (Castro et al., 2009). The approach involves selecting a permutation of the d features and adding the features one-by-one to the original baseline. The output change as a result of adding each feature accounts for its contribution, and averaging this over sampled perturbations results in an unbiased estimate of Shapley Values.

2.1.3 LIME

LIME or Locally Interpretable Model Explanations proposes a generic approach to sample points in the neighborhood of the input point X and train an interpretable model (such as a linear model) based on the results of the local evaluations (Ribeiro et al., 2016).

This method proposes reparametrizing the input space to construct interpretable features such as super-pixels in images and then evaluating the original model on a variety of perturbations of the interpretable features. The method can be utilized with any perturbation sampling and weighting approaches and interpretable model / regularization parameters. The interpretable model can then be used as an explanation of the model's behavior in the local region surrounding the target input point. For a linear model, the coefficients of this model can be considered as attribution scores for the corresponding feature.

2.1.4 Kernel SHAP

Kernel SHAP is a special case of the LIME framework, which sets the sampling approach, intepretable model, and regularization in a specific way such that the results theoretically approximate Shapley Values (Lundberg and Lee, 2017).

2.2 Gradient Based Methods

2.2.1 Saliency

Saliency is a simple gradient-based approach, utilizing the model's gradient at the input point as the corresponding feature attribution (Simonyan et al., 2013). This method can be understood as taking a first order approximation of the function, in which the gradients would serve as the coefficients of each feature in the model.

$$\phi_i(f, X) = f'(X) \tag{3}$$

2.2.2 Integrated Gradients

Integrated Gradients estimates attribution by computing the path integral of model gradients between the baseline point and input point (Sundararajan et al., 2017). This approach has been shown to satisfy desirable theoretical properties including sensitivity and implementation invariance. Formally, the method can be defined as

$$\phi_i(f, X) = (X_i - B_i) \\ \times \int_{\alpha=0}^{1} \frac{f'(B + (X - B)\alpha)}{\partial x_i} d\alpha \tag{4}$$

2.2.3 Other Gradient-Based Methods

Other popular gradient-based attribution methods include DeepLift and Layerwise Relevance Propogation (LRP) (Shrikumar et al., 2017; Bach et al., 2015). These methods both require a backward pass of the model on the original inputs but customize the backward propagation of specific functions, instead of using their default gradient functions.

3 Language Model Attribution

In Captum v0.7, we propose new functionalities to apply the attribution methods within Captum to analyze the behaviors of LLMs. Users can choose any interested tokens or segments from the input

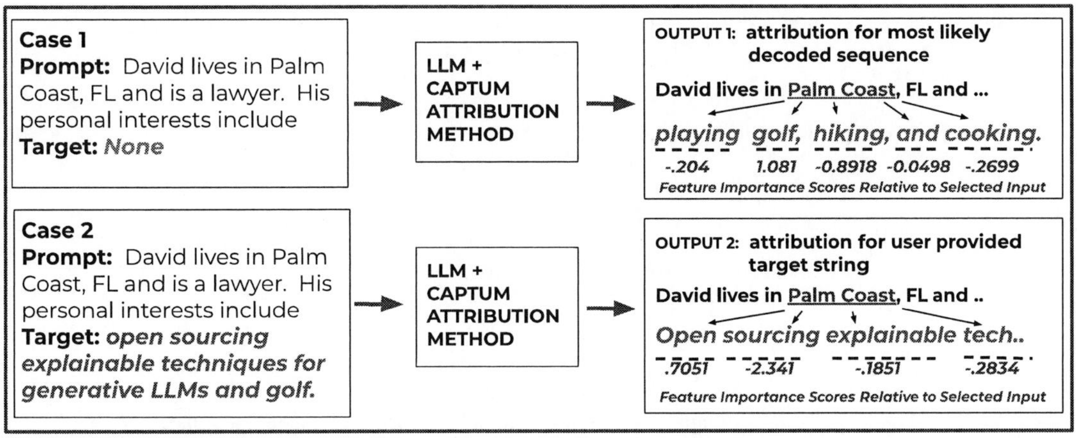

Figure 1: Example of applying Captum attribution methods to analyze the input prompt's effect on the output of LLMs, showing two types of target strings accepted by Captum attribution API and token level attribution outputs for both with respect to the input "Palm Coast". In Case 1, no Target string is provided, so attributions are provided for the most likely decoded sequence. In Case 2, attributions are provided for the chosen target output.

prompt as features, e.g., "Palm Coast" in the example shown in Figure 1, and use attribution methods to quantify their impacts to the generation targets, which can be either a specified output sequence or a likely generation from the model.

3.1 Perturbation-Based Methods

We introduce simple APIs to experiment with perturbation-based attribution methods including Feature Ablation, Lime, Kernel SHAP and Shapley Value Sampling.

We prioritize ease-of-use and flexibility, allowing users to customize the chosen features for attribution, mask features into groups as necessary, and define appropriate baselines to ensure perturbed inputs remain within the natural data distribution.

In Figure 2, we demonstrate an example usage of the LLMAttribution API for the simple prompt *"Dave lives in Palm Coast, FL and is a lawyer. His personal interests include"*. Providing this input prompt to a language model to generate the most likely subsequent tokens, we can apply Captum to understand the impact of different parts of the prompt string on the model generation. Figure 3 presents a more customized usage where we use the same function to understand a specific output we are interested in (*"playing golf, hiking, and cooking."*).

3.1.1 Defining Features

Users are able to define and customize 'features' for attribution in the prompt text. The simplest approach would be defining the features as individual tokens.

Unfortunately, in many cases, it doesn't make sense to perturb individual tokens, since this may no longer form a valid sentence in the natural distribution of potential input sequences. For example, perturbing the token "Palm" in the above sentence would result in a city name that is not in the natural distribution of potential cities in Florida, which may lead to unexpected impacts on the perturbed model output. Moreover, tokenizers used in modern LLMs may further break a single word in many cases. For example, the tokenizer can break the word *"spending"* into *"_sp"* and *"ending"*.

The API provides flexibility to define units of attribution as custom interpretable features which could be individual words, tokens, phrases, or even full sentences. For example, in Figure 2, we select the relevant features to be the name, city, state, occupation, and pronoun in the sentence prompt and desire to determine the relative contribution of these contextual features on the model's predicted sentence completion.

Users can define the units for attribution as a list or dictionary of features and provide a format string or function to define a mapping from the attribution units to the full input prompt as shown in Figure 3.

3.1.2 Baselines

The baseline choice is particularly important for computing attribution for text features, as it serves as the reference value used when perturbing the chosen feature. The perturbation-based feature API allows defining custom baselines corresponding to

```
from captum.attr import FeatureAblation, LLMAttribution, TextTemplateFeature

fa = FeatureAblation(model)
llm_attr = LLMAttribution(fa, tokenizer)

inp = TextTemplateFeature(
    # the text template
    "{} lives in {}, {} and is a {}. {} personal interests include",
    # the values of the features
    ["Dave", "Palm Coast", "FL", "lawyer", "His"],
    # the reference baseline values of the features
    baselines=["Sarah", "Seattle", "WA", "doctor", "Her"],
)
llm_attr.attribute(inp)
```

Figure 2: Example of applying Captum with a list of features in a text template

```
inp = TextTemplateFeature(
    "{name} lives in {city}, {state} and is a {occupation}. {pronoun} personal
                                              interests include",
   {"name":"Dave", "city": "Palm Coast", "state": "FL", "occupation":"lawyer", "
                                             pronoun":"His"},
   baselines={"name":"Sarah", "city": "Seattle", "state": "WA", "occupation":"doctor
                                             ", "pronoun":"Her"}
)
attr_result = llm_attr.attribute(inp, target="playing golf, hiking, and cooking.")
attr_result.plot_token_attr()
```

Figure 3: Example of applying Captum with a dictionary of features in a text template and a specific target, and visualize the token attribution

each input feature.

It is recommended to select a baseline which fits the context of the original text and remains within the natural data distribution. For example, replacing the name of a city with another city ensures the sentence remains naturally coherent, but allows measuring the contribution of the particular city selected.

In addition to a single baseline, the Captum API also supports providing a distribution of baselines, provided as either a list or function to sample a replacement option. For example, in the example above, the name "Dave" could be replaced with a sample from the distribution of common first names to measure any impact of the name "Dave" in comparison to the chosen random distribution as shown in Figure 6.

3.1.3 Masking Features

Similar to the underlying Captum attribution methods, we support feature masking, which enables grouping features together to perturb as a single unit and obtain a combined, single attribution score. This functionality may be utilized for highly correlated features in the text input, where it often makes sense to ablate these features together, rather than independently.

For example, in Figure 2, the feature pairs (city, state) and (name, pronoun) are often highly correlated, and thus it may make sense to group them and consider them as a single feature.

3.1.4 Target Selection

For any attribution method, it is also necessary to select the target function output for which attribution outputs are computed. Since language models typically output a probability distribution over the space of tokens for each subsequently generated token, there are numerous choices for the appropriate target.

By default, when no target is provided, the target function behavior is for the attribution method to return attributions with respect to the most likely decoded token sequence.

When a target string is provided, the target function is the log probability of the output sequence from the language model, given the input prompt. For a sequence with multiple tokens, this is numerically computed through the sum of the log probabilities of each token in the target string. Figure 1 shows these two input use cases and shows token level attribution relative to an input subsequence for both.

We also support providing a custom function on the output logit distribution, which allows attribution with respect to an alternate quantity such as the entropy of the output token distribution.

3.2 Gradient-Based Methods

Captum 0.7 also provides a simple API to apply gradient-based methods to LLMs. Applying these methods to language models is typically more challenging than for models with dense feature inputs, since embedding lookups in LLMs are typically non-differentiable functions, and gradient-based attributions need to be obtained with respect to embedding outputs. Captum allows these attributions to be aggregated across embedding dimensions to obtain per-token attribution scores. Figure 4 demonstrates an example of applying Integrated Gradients on a sample input prompt.

3.3 Visualization

We also open source utilities for easily visualizing the attribution outputs from language models. Figure 3 shows how to use the utilities to visualize the attribution result, and Figure 5 demonstrates the heatmap plotted with the prompt along the top, the target string along the left side and feature importance scores in each cell.

(Feature) Value	Golfing	Hiking	Cooking
(Name) Dave	0.4660	-0.2640	-0.4515
(City) Palm Coast	1.0810	-0.8762	-0.2699
(State) FL	0.6070	-0.3620	-0.3513
(Occupation) lawyer	0.7584	-0.1966	0.0331
(Pronoun) His	0.2217	-0.0650	-0.2577

Table 1: Associations between input and generated text features

4 Applications

In this section, we discuss two applications of the attribution methods described above in different contexts. These applications provide additional transparency as well as contribute to a better understanding of a model's learned associations and robustness.

4.1 Understanding Model Associations

This perturbation-based tooling can be particularly useful for improved understanding of learned associations in LLMs.

Consider the example prompt:

"David lives in Palm Coast, FL and is a lawyer. His personal interests include "

We can define features including gender, city, state and occupation. Obtaining attributions on these features against the subsequent target

"playing golf, hiking, and cooking. "

allows us to better understand why the model predicted these personal interests and how each feature correlates with each of these interests. The model might be associating this activity as a common hobby for residents in the specific city or as an activity common to lawyers. Through this choice of features, we can obtain a better understanding of why the model predicted these particular hobbies and how this associates with the context provided in the prompt.

We apply Shapley Value Sampling to better understand how each of the features contributed to the prediction. The corresponding code snippet is shown in the Appendix in Figure 6. Table 1 presents the effects of each feature on the LLM's probability of outputting the corresponding interest, with positive and negative values indicating increases and decreases of the probability respectively. We can therefore identify some interesting and even potentially biased associations. For example, the male name and pronoun, i.e., "Dave" and "His", have positive attribution to "golfing" but negative attribution to "cooking".

4.2 Evaluating Effectiveness of Few-Shot Prompts

Significant prior literature has demonstrated the ability of LLMs to serve as few-shot learners (Brown et al., 2020). We utilize Captum's attribution functionality to better understand the impact and contributions of few-shot examples to model predictions. Table 2 demonstrates four example few shot prompts and corresponding attribution scores when predicting positive sentiment for "I really liked the movie, it had a captivating plot!" movie review.

Here we aim to understand the impact of each example prompt on the *Positive* sentiment prediction. The LLM is asked to predict positive or negative sentiment using the following prompt:

"Decide if the following movie review enclosed in quotes is Positive or Negative. Output only either Positive or Negative:

```
from captum.attr import LayerIntegratedGradients, TextTokenFeature

ig = LayerIntegratedGradients(model, "model.embed_tokens")
llm_attr = LLMGradientAttribution(ig, tokenizer)

inp = TextTokenFeature("Dave lives in Palm Coast, FL and is a lawyer. His personal
                                                        interests include", tokenizer)
llm_attr.attribute(inp)
```

Figure 4: Example of applying Captum with a gradient-based approach

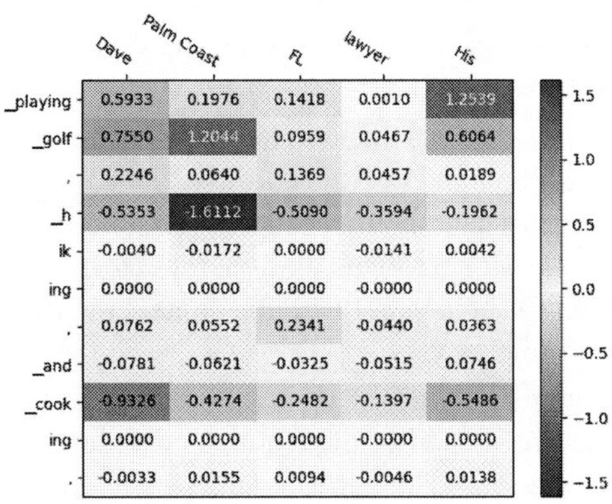

Figure 5: Text Attribution Visualization Example

'I really liked the movie, it had a captivating plot!'
"

We consider each of the provided example prompts as features and we utilize zero-shot prompt as a baseline in the attribution algorithm. The detailed implementation can be found in Appendix in Figure 7.

We obtain results as shown in Table 2 by applying Shapley Values. Surprisingly, the results suggest that all the provided examples actually reduced confidence in the prediction of "Positive".

Example	Shapley Value
'The movie was ok, the actors weren't great' -> Negative	-0.0413
'I loved it, it was an amazing story!' -> Positive	-0.2751
'Total waste of time!!' -> Negative	-0.2085
'Won't recommend' -> Negative	-0.0399

Table 2: Example prompts' contribution to model response "Positive."

5 Related Work

Numerous prior works have developed and investigated attribution methods with a variety of properties, but few efforts have been made to develop open-source interpretability tools providing a variety of available methods, particularly for the text domain. Captum was initially developed to fill this gap and provide a centralized resource for recent interpretability methods proposed in literature (Kokhlikyan et al., 2020).

Ecco and inseq are two libraries that have provided attribution functionalities for text / language models (Sarti et al., 2023; Alammar, 2021), and both libraries are built on top of the attribution methods available in Captum. These libraries primarily focus on gradient-based attribution methods, which provide token-level attribution based on gradient information.

In contrast, our main contribution in this work has been a focus on perturbation-based methods and providing flexibility on aspects such as feature definition, baseline choice and masking. We do not necessarily expect that these attribution methods provide a score for each token individually, which is typically the case for gradient-based methods. This shift in structure allows us to generalize to a variety of cases and allows the users to define features for attribution as it fits best.

Some prior work on attribution methods have also demonstrated limitations and counterexamples of these methods in explaining a model's reliance on input features, particularly with gradient-based attribution methods (Adebayo et al., 2018).

Perturbation-based methods generally have an advantage of being justifiable through the model's output on counterfactual perturbed inputs. But perturbing features by removing individual tokens or replacing them with pad or other baseline tokens may result in inputs outside of the natural data distribution, and thus, model outputs in this region may not be accurate. The tools developed have been designed to make it easier for developers to select features, baselines, and masks which can ensure perturbations remain within the natural data distribution in order to obtain more reliable feature attribution results.

Recent advances in data augmentation (Pluščec and Šnajder, 2023) for natural language processing have led to the development of a number of open-source libraries (Wang et al., 2021; Papakipos and Bitton, 2022; Zeng et al., 2021; Morris et al., 2020; Ma, 2019; Dhole et al., 2022; Wu et al., 2021). Among many functionalities, these libraries provide a rich set of text perturbations. Some libraries have specific focus, e.g. perturbing demographic references (Qian et al., 2022). An interesting direction of future work will be the extension of our present API to provide fully automated feature and baseline selections, allowing users to simply provide an input string and automatically identify appropriate text features and corresponding baselines for attribution.

6 Conclusion

In this work, we introduce new features in the open source library Captum that are specifically designed to analyze the behavior of generative LLMs. We provide an overview of the available functionalities and example applications of their potential in understanding learned associations and evaluating effectiveness of few-shot prompts within generative LLMs. We demonstrate examples for using perturbation and gradient-based attribution methods with Captum which highlight the API's flexibility on aspects such as feature definition, baseline choice and masking. This flexibility in structure allows users to generalize to a variety of cases, simplifying their ability to conduct explainability experiments on generative LLMs.

In the future, we plan to expand our API for additional automation in baseline and feature selection as well as incorporate other categories of interpretability techniques for language models. Runtime performance optimization of attribution algorithms is another area of research that could be beneficial for the OSS community.

References

Julius Adebayo, Justin Gilmer, Michael Muelly, Ian Goodfellow, Moritz Hardt, and Been Kim. 2018. Sanity checks for saliency maps.

J Alammar. 2021. Ecco: An open source library for the explainability of transformer language models. In *Proceedings of the 59th Annual Meeting of the Association for Computational Linguistics and the 11th International Joint Conference on Natural Language Processing: System Demonstrations*. Association for Computational Linguistics.

Sebastian Bach, Alexander Binder, Grégoire Montavon, Frederick Klauschen, Klaus-Robert Müller, and Wojciech Samek. 2015. On pixel-wise explanations for non-linear classifier decisions by layer-wise relevance propagation. *PloS one*, 10(7):e0130140.

Tom Brown, Benjamin Mann, Nick Ryder, Melanie Subbiah, Jared D Kaplan, Prafulla Dhariwal, Arvind Neelakantan, Pranav Shyam, Girish Sastry, Amanda Askell, et al. 2020. Language models are few-shot learners. *Advances in neural information processing systems*, 33:1877–1901.

Javier Castro, Daniel Gómez, and Juan Tejada. 2009. Polynomial calculation of the shapley value based on sampling. *Computers & Operations Research*, 36(5):1726–1730.

Kaustubh D. Dhole, Varun Gangal, Sebastian Gehrmann, Aadesh Gupta, Zhenhao Li, Saad Mahamood, Abinaya Mahendiran, Simon Mille, Ashish Shrivastava, Samson Tan, Tongshuang Wu, Jascha Sohl-Dickstein, Jinho D. Choi, Eduard Hovy, Ondrej Dusek, Sebastian Ruder, Sajant Anand, Nagender Aneja, Rabin Banjade, Lisa Barthe, Hanna Behnke, Ian Berlot-Attwell, Connor Boyle, Caroline Brun, Marco Antonio Sobrevilla Cabezudo, Samuel Cahyawijaya, Emile Chapuis, Wanxiang Che, Mukund Choudhary, Christian Clauss, Pierre Colombo, Filip Cornell, Gautier Dagan, Mayukh Das, Tanay Dixit, Thomas Dopierre, Paul-Alexis Dray, Suchitra Dubey, Tatiana Ekeinhor, Marco Di Giovanni, Tanya Goyal, Rishabh Gupta, Rishabh Gupta, Louanes Hamla, Sang Han, Fabrice Harel-Canada, Antoine Honore, Ishan Jindal, Przemyslaw K. Joniak, Denis Kleyko, Venelin Kovatchev, Kalpesh Krishna, Ashutosh Kumar, Stefan Langer, Seungjae Ryan Lee, Corey James Levinson, Hualou Liang, Kaizhao Liang, Zhexiong Liu, Andrey Lukyanenko, Vukosi Marivate, Gerard de Melo, Simon Meoni, Maxime Meyer, Afnan Mir, Nafise Sadat Moosavi, Niklas Muennighoff, Timothy Sum Hon Mun, Kenton Murray, Marcin Namysl, Maria Obedkova, Priti Oli, Nivranshu Pasricha, Jan Pfister, Richard Plant, Vinay Prabhu, Vasile Pais, Libo Qin, Shahab Raji, Pawan Kumar Rajpoot, Vikas Raunak, Roy Rinberg, Nicolas Roberts, Juan Diego Rodriguez, Claude Roux, Vasconcellos P. H. S., Ananya B. Sai, Robin M. Schmidt, Thomas Scialom, Tshephisho Sefara, Saqib N. Shamsi, Xudong Shen, Haoyue Shi, Yiwen Shi, Anna Shvets, Nick Siegel, Damien Sileo, Jamie Simon, Chandan Singh, Roman Sitelew, Priyank Soni, Taylor Sorensen, William Soto, Aman Srivastava, KV Aditya Srivatsa, Tony Sun, Mukund Varma T, A Tabassum, Fiona Anting Tan, Ryan Teehan, Mo Tiwari, Marie Tolkiehn,

Athena Wang, Zijian Wang, Gloria Wang, Zijie J. Wang, Fuxuan Wei, Bryan Wilie, Genta Indra Winata, Xinyi Wu, Witold Wydmański, Tianbao Xie, Usama Yaseen, Michael A. Yee, Jing Zhang, and Yue Zhang. 2022. Nl-augmenter: A framework for task-sensitive natural language augmentation.

Narine Kokhlikyan, Vivek Miglani, Miguel Martin, Edward Wang, Bilal Alsallakh, Jonathan Reynolds, Alexander Melnikov, Natalia Kliushkina, Carlos Araya, Siqi Yan, and Orion Reblitz-Richardson. 2020. Captum: A unified and generic model interpretability library for pytorch.

Scott Lundberg and Su-In Lee. 2017. A unified approach to interpreting model predictions.

Edward Ma. 2019. Nlp augmentation. https://github.com/makcedward/nlpaug.

John X. Morris, Eli Lifland, Jin Yong Yoo, Jake Grigsby, Di Jin, and Yanjun Qi. 2020. Textattack: A framework for adversarial attacks, data augmentation, and adversarial training in nlp.

OpenAI. 2023. Gpt-4 technical report.

Zoe Papakipos and Joanna Bitton. 2022. Augly: Data augmentations for robustness.

Domagoj Pluščec and Jan Šnajder. 2023. Data augmentation for neural nlp.

Rebecca Qian, Candace Ross, Jude Fernandes, Eric Michael Smith, Douwe Kiela, and Adina Williams. 2022. Perturbation augmentation for fairer NLP. In *Proceedings of the 2022 Conference on Empirical Methods in Natural Language Processing*, pages 9496–9521, Abu Dhabi, United Arab Emirates. Association for Computational Linguistics.

Marco Tulio Ribeiro, Sameer Singh, and Carlos Guestrin. 2016. "why should i trust you?": Explaining the predictions of any classifier.

Gabriele Sarti, Nils Feldhus, Ludwig Sickert, Oskar van der Wal, Malvina Nissim, and Arianna Bisazza. 2023. Inseq: An interpretability toolkit for sequence generation models. *ArXiv*, abs/2302.13942.

Avanti Shrikumar, Peyton Greenside, and Anshul Kundaje. 2017. Learning important features through propagating activation differences. In *International conference on machine learning*, pages 3145–3153. PMLR.

Karen Simonyan, Andrea Vedaldi, and Andrew Zisserman. 2013. Deep inside convolutional networks: Visualising image classification models and saliency maps. *arXiv preprint arXiv:1312.6034*.

Mukund Sundararajan, Ankur Taly, and Qiqi Yan. 2017. Axiomatic attribution for deep networks. In *International conference on machine learning*, pages 3319–3328. PMLR.

Xiao Wang, Qin Liu, Tao Gui, Qi Zhang, Yicheng Zou, Xin Zhou, Jiacheng Ye, Yongxin Zhang, Rui Zheng, Zexiong Pang, Qinzhuo Wu, Zhengyan Li, Chong Zhang, Ruotian Ma, Zichu Fei, Ruijian Cai, Jun Zhao, Xingwu Hu, Zhiheng Yan, Yiding Tan, Yuan Hu, Qiyuan Bian, Zhihua Liu, Shan Qin, Bolin Zhu, Xiaoyu Xing, Jinlan Fu, Yue Zhang, Minlong Peng, Xiaoqing Zheng, Yaqian Zhou, Zhongyu Wei, Xipeng Qiu, and Xuanjing Huang. 2021. TextFlint: Unified multilingual robustness evaluation toolkit for natural language processing. In *Proceedings of the 59th Annual Meeting of the Association for Computational Linguistics and the 11th International Joint Conference on Natural Language Processing: System Demonstrations*, pages 347–355, Online. Association for Computational Linguistics.

Tongshuang Wu, Marco Tulio Ribeiro, Jeffrey Heer, and Daniel S Weld. 2021. Polyjuice: Generating counterfactuals for explaining, evaluating, and improving models. In *Proceedings of the 59th Annual Meeting of the Association for Computational Linguistics and the 11th International Joint Conference on Natural Language Processing (Volume 1: Long Papers)*, pages 6707–6723.

Guoyang Zeng, Fanchao Qi, Qianrui Zhou, Tingji Zhang, Zixian Ma, Bairu Hou, Yuan Zang, Zhiyuan Liu, and Maosong Sun. 2021. OpenAttack: An open-source textual adversarial attack toolkit. In *Proceedings of the 59th Annual Meeting of the Association for Computational Linguistics and the 11th International Joint Conference on Natural Language Processing: System Demonstrations*. Association for Computational Linguistics.

A Appendix

```
from captum.attr import ShapleyValueSampling, LLMAttribution, TextTemplateFeature,
                                              ProductBaselines

svs = ShapleyValueSampling(model)
baselines = ProductBaselines(
    {
        ("name", "pronoun"): [("Sarah", "Her"), ("John", "His")],
        "city": ["Seattle", "Boston"],
        "state": ["WA", "MA"],
        "occupation": ["doctor", "engineer", "teacher", "technician", "plumber"],
    }
)

llm_attr = LLMAttribution(svs, tokenizer)

inp = TextTemplateFeature(
    "{name} lives in {city}, {state} and is a {occupation}. {pronoun} personal
                                                  interests include",
    {"name":"Dave", "city": "Palm Coast", "state": "FL", "occupation":"lawyer", "
                                                  pronoun":"His"},
    baselines=baselines,
)

attr_result = llm_attr.attribute(inp, target="playing golf, hiking, and cooking.")
```

Figure 6: Applying Captum for the model associations example

```
from captum.attr import ShapleyValues, LLMAttribution, TextTemplateFeature

sv = ShapleyValues(model)
llm_attr = LLMAttribution(sv, tokenizer)

def prompt_fn(*examples):
    main_prompt = "Decide if the following movie review enclosed in quotes is
                                                  Positive or Negative:\n'I really liked
                                                   the Avengers, it had a captivating
                                                  plot!'\nReply only Positive or
                                                  Negative."
    subset = [elem for elem in examples if elem]
    if not subset:
        prompt = main_prompt
    else:
        prefix = "Here are some examples of movie reviews and classification of
                                                      whether they were Positive or
                                                      Negative:\n"
        prompt = prefix + "\n".join(subset) + "\n" + main_prompt
    return "[INST] " + prompt + "[/INST]"

input_examples = [
    "'The movie was ok, the actors weren't great' -> Negative",
    "'I loved it, it was an amazing story!' -> Positive",
    "'Total waste of time!!' -> Negative",
    "'Won't recommend' -> Negative",
]
inp = TextTemplateFeature(prompt_fn, input_examples)

attr_result = llm_attr.attribute(inp)
```

Figure 7: Applying Captum for the few-shot prompt example

nerblackbox: A High-level Library for Named Entity Recognition in Python

Felix Stollenwerk
AI Sweden
felix.stollenwerk@ai.se

Abstract

We present *nerblackbox*, a python library to facilitate the use of state-of-the-art transformer-based models for named entity recognition. It provides simple-to-use yet powerful methods to access data and models from a wide range of sources, for fully automated model training and evaluation as well as versatile model inference. While many technical challenges are solved and hidden from the user by default, *nerblackbox* also offers fine-grained control and a rich set of customizable features. It is thus targeted both at application-oriented developers as well as machine learning experts and researchers.

1 Introduction

Named Entity Recognition (NER) is an important natural language processing task with a multitude of applications (Lorica and Nathan, 2021). While generative AI is currently ubiquitous in the scientific literature and public debate, it has not (yet) replaced discriminative AI for information extraction tasks like NER. Fine-tuned, transformer-based encoder models are both SOTA in research[1] and commonly used by developers to solve real-world problems, see e.g. (Raza et al., 2022; Stollenwerk et al., 2022). Popular open source frameworks, like the ones provided by HuggingFace (Wolf et al., 2020; Lhoest et al., 2021; Von Werra et al., 2022), greatly facilitate the use of such models. They cover the whole workflow consisting of dataset integration, model training, evaluation and inference, see Fig. 1.

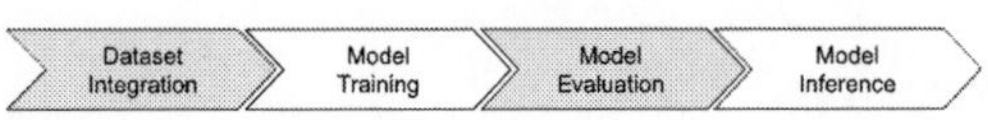

Figure 1: Essential stages in the life cycle of a machine learning model.

[1]http://nlpprogress.com/english/named_entity_recognition.html

However, they do require a certain degree of expertise and often some significant, use-case specific effort. Some of the (general and NER-specific) challenges are:

(i) There exist various sources for datasets. Regarding public datasets, HuggingFace and GitHub repositories are important sources. Private datasets may be stored on local filesystems or be created using annotation tools. Additional complexity is introduced by the circumstance that datasets often come in different formats. This may be true even for datasets from the same source. These issues typically require customized data preprocessing code for every new use case.

(ii) Data for NER is processed on three different levels: tokens, words and entities. Different parts of the workflow may operate on different levels, as shown in Tab. 1. Datasets may be pre-

stage	token	word	entity
dataset		×	×
training	×	×	
evaluation			×
inference		×	×

Table 1: Overview of the data levels that the different parts of a NER model workflow can operate on.

tokenized (word level) or not (entity level). At training time, labels for tokens that are not the first token of a word may be ignored (word level) or included (token level) in the computation of the loss. Model evaluation takes place primarily on the entity level (although it is labels on the token or word level that are employed for the computation). Finally, while model predictions are often made on the entity level, some use cases may require predictions on the word level, for instance if the associated probabilities are to be used for active learning. Handling these technical intricacies requires expert knowledge.

Proceedings of the 3rd Workshop for Natural Language Processing Open Source Software (NLP-OSS 2023), pages 174–178
December 6, 2023 ©2023 Association for Computational Linguistics

(iii) There exists a multitude of NER-specific annotation schemes and variants and it is important to be aware of the differences. For instance, during data preprocessing, existing word or entity labels need to be mapped to token labels, which is an annotation scheme dependent process. At evaluation time, there are different ways to cope with predictions that do not obey the rules of the given annotation scheme (we will get back to this in Sec. 4.6).

(iv) Training hyperparameters which lead to reasonable performance may depend on the employed model and dataset. For instance, while a small dataset often requires more training epochs, larger datasets can usually be trained for fewer epochs.

The aim of *nerblackbox* is to provide a high-level framework which makes the usage of SOTA NER models as simple as possible. As we will see in detail in Sec. 3, it offers easy access to datasets from various sources, automated training and evaluation as well as simple but versatile model inference. It does so by hiding all technical complications from the user[2] and is targeted at developers as well as people who are not necessarily experts in machine learning or NLP. However, *nerblackbox* also allows fine-grained control over all sorts of low-level parameters and provides many advanced features, some of which we will cover in Sec. 4. This might make the library appealing also for researchers and experts.

2 Related Work

The most commonly used framework for transformer-based NLP is arguably the HuggingFace ecosystem, in particular the open source libraries *transformers* (Wolf et al., 2020), *datasets* (Lhoest et al., 2021) and *evaluate* (Von Werra et al., 2022). Another popular alternative is *spacy* (Honnibal et al., 2020).

High-level libraries that are build on top of *transformers* exist in the form of *Simple Transformers* (Rajapakse, 2019) and *T-NER* (Ushio and Camacho-Collados, 2021). *Simple Transformers* is a high-level library that covers a broad range of NLP tasks with basic support for NER. *T-NER* is specific to NER with an emphasis on cross-domain and cross-lingual model evaluation. Of all the mentioned libraries, it is arguably the most similar to *nerblackbox*. However, as will be discussed in the following sections, *nerblackbox* offers many unique and powerful features that—to the best of our knowledge—make it distinct from any existing frameworks.

3 Basic Usage

nerblackbox provides a simple API to automate each step in the life cycle of a NER model (cf. Fig. 1) using very few lines of code. It does so in terms of the following classes:

```
>> from nerblackbox import Dataset,
    Training, Model
```

A high-level overview of the involved components is shown in Fig. 2.

3.1 Dataset Integration

nerblackbox allows seamless access to datasets from the following sources: HuggingFace (HF), the local filesystem (LF), built-in datasets (BI) and annotation tools (AT)[3].

Basically, a dataset can be set up for training and evaluation like in the following example:

```
>> dataset = Dataset(
       "conll2003",
       source="HF",
   )
>> dataset.set_up()
```

While this works out-of-the-box for the sources HF and BI, some additional information needs to be provided for the sources LF and AT in order for *nerblackbox* to be able to find the data. Integrating different datasets can be challenging as they may have different formatting (even on HuggingFace) and annotation schemes. Some datasets are pretokenized and split into training/validation/test subsets, while others are not. The `set_up()` method automatically deals with these challenges and makes sure that every dataset, irrespective of the source, is transformed into a standard format[4]. Apart from downloading, reformatting, and dataset splitting (if needed), it also includes an analysis of the data. For details, we refer to the library's documentation.

[2] This is where the name *nerblackbox* stems from: The framework does not require any knowledge about internal processes and can be used as a black box by only specifying inputs (pretrained model, dataset) and using the outputs (fine-tuned model). Note that there is no direct relation to explainability.

[3] Currently, the two commonly used (open source) annotation tools *LabelStudio* (Tkachenko et al., 2020) and *Doccano* (Nakayama et al., 2018) are supported.

[4] Datasets may still have different annotation schemes (IO, BIO, BILOU), and be pretokenized or not.

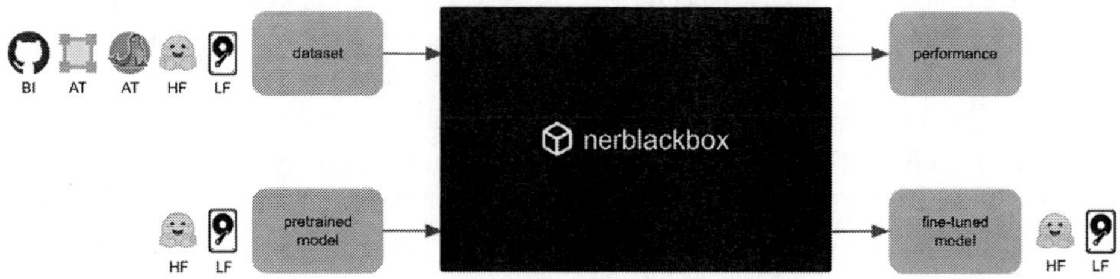

Figure 2: High-level overview of the *nerblackbox* library. It allows to easily fine-tune, evaluate and apply models for named entity recognition. The symbols to the left and right represent the sources that *nerblackbox* provides seamless access to. These are the Local Filesystem (LF), HuggingFace (HF), Annotation Tools (AT) as well as Built-in (BI) datasets that are fetched from GitHub.

3.2 Training

In order to train a model, one only needs to choose a name for the training run (for later reference) and specify the model and dataset names, like so:

```
>> training = Training(
       "my_training",
       model="bert-base-cased",
       dataset="conll2003",
   )
>> training.run()
```

In order to ensure stable results irrespective of the dataset, the training employs well-established hyperparameters by default (Mosbach et al., 2021). In particular, a specific learning rate schedule (Stollenwerk, 2022) based on early stopping and warm restarts (Loshchilov and Hutter, 2017) is used to accommodate different dataset sizes.

3.3 Evaluation

Any NER model, whether it was trained using *nerblackbox* or is taken directly from HuggingFace (HF), can be evaluated on any dataset that is accessible via *nerblackbox* (see Sec. 3.1)

```
>> model = Model.from_training(
       "my_training"
   )
>> results = model.evaluate_on_dataset(
       "conll2003",
       phase="test",
   )
>> results["micro"]["entity"]["f1"]
## 0.9045
```

The standard metrics for NER are used, i.e. precision, recall and the f1 score. Each metric is computed as a micro- and macro-average as well as for the individual classes. All metrics are determined both on the entity and word level.

3.4 Inference

Similar to evaluation, both NER models trained using *nerblackbox* and models taken directly from HuggingFace (HF) can be used for inference.

```
>> model = Model.from_training(
       "my_training"
   )
>> model.predict("The United Nations")
## [[{
##     'char_start': '4',
##     'char_end': '18',
##     'token': 'United Nations',
##     'tag': 'ORG'
## }]]
```

Apart from the predictions on the entity level for a single document shown above, *nerblackbox* also supports predictions on the word level (with or without probabilities) and batch inference. In addition, a model can be applied directly to a file containing raw data, which may be useful for inference at large scale (e.g. in production).

4 Advanced Usage

The *nerblackbox* workflow and the API are designed to be as simple as possible and to conceal technical complications from the user. However, they are also highly customizable in terms of optional function arguments, which may be particularly interesting for machine learning experts and researchers. In this section, we are going to cover a non-exhaustive selection of *nerblackbox*'s advanced features, with a slight emphasis on the training part. For further information, the reader is referred to the library's documentation.

4.1 Training Hyperparameters and Presets

While *nerblackbox* uses sensible default values for the training hyperparameters (see Sec. 3.2), one may also opt to specify them manually. In particular, all aspects of the learning rate schedule (e.g. maximum learning rate, epochs, early stopping parameters etc.) can be chosen at one's own discretion. In addition, the `Training` class offers several popular hyperparameter presets via the instantiation argument `from_preset`. Among them are the learning rate schedules from (Devlin et al., 2019) and (Mosbach et al., 2021), which may work well for larger and smaller datasets, respectively. Hyperparameters search is also supported.

4.2 Dataset Pruning

nerblackbox provides the option to only use a subset of the training, validation or test data by specifying parameters like `train_fraction`. This may be useful to accelerate the training (for instance in the development phase of a product) or if one wants to investigate the effect of the dataset size (for instance to see if the model has saturated, or for research).

4.3 Annotation Schemes

While every dataset is associated with a certain annotation scheme, *nerblackbox* provides the option to translate between schemes at training time. The desired annotation scheme can simply be specified via the training parameter `annotation_scheme`. This may be interesting for users who aim to optimize their model's performance as well as researchers who systematically want to investigate the impact of the annotation scheme.

4.4 Multiple Runs

Since the training of a neural network includes stochastic processes, the performance of the resulting model depends on the employed random seed. In order to gain control over the associated statistical uncertainties, one may train multiple models using different random seeds. With *nerblackbox*, this can trivially be done by setting the training parameter `multiple_runs` to an integer greater than 1. In that case, the evaluation metrics will be given in terms of the mean and its associated uncertainty. For inference, the best model is automatically used.

4.5 Detailed Results

nerblackbox saves detailed training and evaluation results (e.g. loss curves, confusion matrices) using *MLflow*[5] and TensorBoard. This is useful in order to keep an overview of trained models, inspect their detailed properties as well as optimize and cross-check the training process.

4.6 Careful Evaluation

A model may predict labels for a sequence of tokens that are inconsistent with the employed annotation scheme. For instance, if the BIO annotation scheme is used, the combination `O I-PER` is incorrect[6]. When translated to *entity* predictions, *nerblackbox* ignores incorrect labels by default, both at evaluation and inference time. However, the popular *evaluate* (Von Werra et al., 2022) and *seqeval* (Nakayama, 2018) libraries do take inconsistent predictions into account during evaluation. For this reason, the `evaluate_on_dataset()` method (see Sec. 3.3) returns results for both approaches.

4.7 Compatibility with *transformers*

nerblackbox is heavily based on *transformers* (Wolf et al., 2020) such that compatibility is guaranteed. In particular, the `Model` class has the attributes `tokenizer` and `model`, which are ordinary *transformers* classes and can be used as such. GPU support (i.e. automatic detection and use) is also provided through *transformers*.

5 Resources and Code Quality

nerblackbox is available as a package on PyPI[7]. The associated GitHub repository is public at `https://github.com/flxst/nerblackbox` and contains the source code as well as multiple example notebooks. A detailed documentation is provided[8]. It includes a pedagogical introduction to the library, an in-depth discussion of its features as well as docs for the python API. Consistent code syntax and typing are ensured by usage of *black*[9] and *mypy*[10], respectively. We employ unit and end-to-end testing. As an additional cross-check, numerical results from the literature are reproduced using *nerblackbox* (details can be found in the documentation).

Acknowledgements

This work was supported by Vinnova through the grants 2019-02996 and 2021-03630.

[5] `https://pypi.org/project/mlflow/`

[6] The variant of the BIO scheme which we assume here is also known as IOB2

[7] `https://pypi.org/project/nerblackbox/`

[8] `https://flxst.github.io/nerblackbox/`

[9] `https://pypi.org/project/black/`

[10] `https://pypi.org/project/mypy/`

References

Jacob Devlin, Ming-Wei Chang, Kenton Lee, and Kristina Toutanova. 2019. BERT: Pre-training of Deep Bidirectional Transformers for Language Understanding. In *Proceedings of the 2019 Conference of the North American Chapter of the Association for Computational Linguistics: Human Language Technologies, Volume 1 (Long and Short Papers)*, pages 4171–4186, Minneapolis, Minnesota. Association for Computational Linguistics.

Matthew Honnibal, Ines Montani, Sofie Van Landeghem, and Adriane Boyd. 2020. spaCy: Industrial-strength Natural Language Processing in Python.

Quentin Lhoest, Albert Villanova del Moral, Yacine Jernite, Abhishek Thakur, Patrick von Platen, Suraj Patil, Julien Chaumond, Mariama Drame, Julien Plu, Lewis Tunstall, Joe Davison, Mario Šaško, Gunjan Chhablani, Bhavitvya Malik, Simon Brandeis, Teven Le Scao, Victor Sanh, Canwen Xu, Nicolas Patry, Angelina McMillan-Major, Philipp Schmid, Sylvain Gugger, Clément Delangue, Théo Matussière, Lysandre Debut, Stas Bekman, Pierric Cistac, Thibault Goehringer, Victor Mustar, François Lagunas, Alexander Rush, and Thomas Wolf. 2021. Datasets: A Community Library for Natural Language Processing. In *Proceedings of the 2021 Conference on Empirical Methods in Natural Language Processing: System Demonstrations*, pages 175–184, Online and Punta Cana, Dominican Republic. Association for Computational Linguistics.

Ben Lorica and Paco Nathan. 2021. 2021 NLP Survey Report.

Ilya Loshchilov and Frank Hutter. 2017. SGDR: Stochastic Gradient Descent with Warm Restarts. ArXiv:1608.03983 [cs, math].

Marius Mosbach, Maksym Andriushchenko, and Dietrich Klakow. 2021. On the Stability of Fine-tuning BERT: Misconceptions, Explanations, and Strong Baselines. ArXiv:2006.04884 [cs, stat].

Hiroki Nakayama. 2018. seqeval: A Python framework for sequence labeling evaluation.

Hiroki Nakayama, Takahiro Kubo, Junya Kamura, Yasufumi Taniguchi, and Xu Liang. 2018. doccano: Text Annotation Tool for Human.

T. C. Rajapakse. 2019. Simple Transformers.

Shaina Raza, Deepak John Reji, Femi Shajan, and Syed Raza Bashir. 2022. Large-Scale Application of Named Entity Recognition to Biomedicine and Epidemiology. Pages: 2022.09.22.22280246.

Felix Stollenwerk. 2022. Adaptive Fine-Tuning of Transformer-Based Language Models for Named Entity Recognition. ArXiv:2202.02617 [cs].

Felix Stollenwerk, Niklas Fastlund, Anna Nyqvist, and Joey Öhman. 2022. Annotated Job Ads with Named Entity Recognition. *SLTC*.

Maxim Tkachenko, Mikhail Malyuk, Andrey Holmanyuk, and Nikolai Liubimov. 2020. Label Studio: Data labeling software.

Asahi Ushio and Jose Camacho-Collados. 2021. T-NER: An All-Round Python Library for Transformer-based Named Entity Recognition. In *Proceedings of the 16th Conference of the European Chapter of the Association for Computational Linguistics: System Demonstrations*, pages 53–62, Online. Association for Computational Linguistics.

Leandro Von Werra, Lewis Tunstall, Abhishek Thakur, Sasha Luccioni, Tristan Thrush, Aleksandra Piktus, Felix Marty, Nazneen Rajani, Victor Mustar, and Helen Ngo. 2022. Evaluate & Evaluation on the Hub: Better Best Practices for Data and Model Measurements. In *Proceedings of the 2022 Conference on Empirical Methods in Natural Language Processing: System Demonstrations*, pages 128–136, Abu Dhabi, UAE. Association for Computational Linguistics.

Thomas Wolf, Lysandre Debut, Victor Sanh, Julien Chaumond, Clement Delangue, Anthony Moi, Pierric Cistac, Tim Rault, Remi Louf, Morgan Funtowicz, Joe Davison, Sam Shleifer, Patrick von Platen, Clara Ma, Yacine Jernite, Julien Plu, Canwen Xu, Teven Le Scao, Sylvain Gugger, Mariama Drame, Quentin Lhoest, and Alexander Rush. 2020. Transformers: State-of-the-Art Natural Language Processing. In *Proceedings of the 2020 Conference on Empirical Methods in Natural Language Processing: System Demonstrations*, pages 38–45, Online. Association for Computational Linguistics.

News Signals: An NLP Library for Text and Time Series

Chris Hokamp* and **Demian Gholipour Ghalandari*** and **Parsa Ghaffari**
Quantexa
`<firstname><lastname>@quantexa.com`

Abstract

We present an open-source Python library for building and using datasets where inputs are clusters of textual data, and outputs are sequences of real values representing one or more time series signals. The `news-signals` library supports diverse data science and NLP problem settings related to the prediction of time series behaviour using textual data feeds. For example, in the news domain, inputs are document clusters corresponding to daily news articles about a particular entity, and targets are explicitly associated real-valued time series: the volume of news about a particular person or company, or the number of pageviews of specific Wikimedia pages. Despite many industry and research use cases for this class of problem settings, to the best of our knowledge, News Signals is the only open-source library designed specifically to facilitate data science and research settings with natural language inputs and time series targets. In addition to the core codebase for building and interacting with datasets, we also conduct a suite of experiments using several popular Machine Learning libraries, which are used to establish baselines for time series anomaly prediction using textual inputs.

1 Introduction

The natural ordering of many types of data along a time dimension is a consequence of the known physics of our universe. Real-world applications of machine learning often involve data with implicit or explicit temporal ordering. Examples include weather forecasting, market prediction, self-driving cars, and language modeling.

A large body of work on time series forecasting studies models which consume and predict real-valued target signals that are explicitly ordered in time; however, aside from some existing work mainly related to market signal prediction using social media (Chen et al., 2021, 2022; Arno et al., 2022; Li et al., 2014; Bing et al., 2014; Kim et al., 2016; Wang and Luo, 2021), inter alia, the NLP research community has generally not focused on tasks with textual inputs and time series outputs. This is confirmed by the lack of any popular NLP tasks related to time series in result-tracking projects such as nlp-progress[1] and papers-with-code[2].

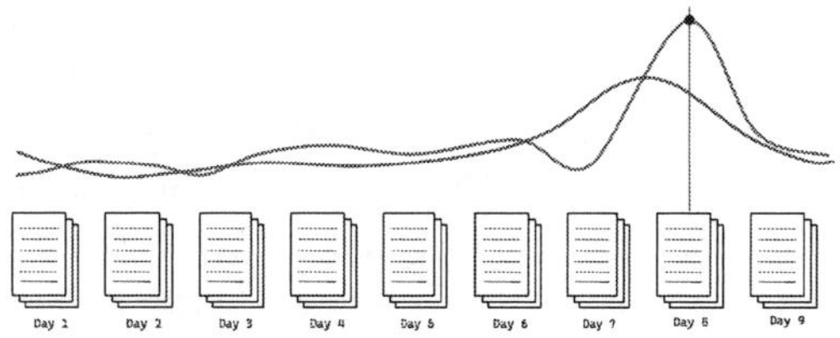

Figure 1: News Signals Datasets: clusters of documents, bucketed by time period, are associated with time series signals. ML models can be trained to predict time series signals using the textual data.

We believe there is potential for novel, impactful research into tasks beyond market signal forecasting, in which textual inputs and real-valued output signals are explicitly organized along a time dimension with fixed-length "ticks". Two reasons for the lack of attention to such tasks to date may be:

1. researchers do not have access to canonical NLP datasets for time series forecasting.

2. data scientists are missing a high level software library for NLP datasets with time series.

Examples of tasks where natural language input can be used to predict a time series signal include:

- weather or pandemic forecasting using social media posts from a recent time period,
- market signal prediction using newsfeeds or bespoke textual data feeds,

[*] equal contribution

[1] `https://nlpprogress.com/`
[2] `https://paperswithcode.com/`

Proceedings of the 3rd Workshop for Natural Language Processing Open Source Software (NLP-OSS 2023), pages 179–189
December 6, 2023 ©2023 Association for Computational Linguistics

- media monitoring for consumer behavior prediction and forecasting,
- forecasting the impact of a news event on the pageviews of a particular website,

and many others. We refer to this general task setting as `text2signal` (T2S).

1.1 `news-signals`

This work introduces `news-signals`[3], a high-level MIT-licensed software package for building and interacting with datasets where inputs are clusters of texts, and outputs are time series signals (Figure 1). Despite the package's news-focused origins, it is built to be a general purpose library for interacting with time-ordered clusters of text and associated time series signals.

Preparing and utilizing datasets for T2S tasks requires purpose-built software for retrieving and sorting data along the time dimension. In many cases, data will be retrieved from one or more APIs, or web-scraped, further complicating dataset generation pipelines. `news-signals` exposes an intuitive interface for generating datasets that we believe will be straightforward for any data scientist or developer familiar with the Python data science software stack (see Section 2).

`news-signals` includes tooling for:

- calling 3rd party APIs to populate signals with text and time series data,
- visualizing signals and associated textual data,
- extending signals with new time series, feeds, and transformations,
- aggregations on textual clusters, such as abstractive and extractive summarization.

`news-signals` provides two primary interfaces: `Signal` and `SignalsDataset`. A `SignalsDataset` represents a collection of related signals. A `Signal` consists of one or more textual **feeds**, each connected to one or more time series. Time series have strictly one real value per-tick, while feeds are time-indexed buckets of textual data. For example, a news signal might contain a feed of all articles from a financial source that mention a particular company, linked to multiple time series representing relevant market signals for that company.

[3]`https://github.com/AYLIEN/news-signals-datasets`

`news-signals` datasets are designed to be easy to extend with new data sources, entities, and time series signals. In our initial release of the library, we work with three collections of entities: US politicians, NASDAQ-100 companies, and S&P 500 companies (see section 5).

The rest of the paper is organized as follows: section 2 gives an overview of library design and Section 3 describes the `Signal` and `SignalsDataset` APIs, the two main interfaces to time-indexed NLP datasets. Section 4 discusses how datasets can be created. Section 5 describes our example datasets, models, and end-to-end experiments, which are open-source, and can be used as templates for new research projects. Section 6 discusses applications, Section 7 reviews related work, and Section 8 gives conclusions and directions for the future.

2 Time-Indexed NLP Datasets

Traditional NLP and ML datasets consist of iid (X, Y) pairs. These pairs can be assigned indices, and be operated on by standard pre-processing procedures, such as randomly shuffling and splitting into `train`, `dev`, `test` subsets. However, for time series forecasting and related tasks, inputs are ordered along a time axis, and the distribution of later time steps is typically heavily dependent upon the distribution of earlier time steps; therefore, training, dev and test subsets are usually partitioned and split chronologically to reduce the potential for leakage, introducing additional complexity into data preparation.

Within the Python data science ecosystem, libraries such as Numpy (Harris et al., 2020), Pandas (Wes McKinney, 2010), and Pytorch (Paszke et al., 2019) have standardized a syntax for indexing and slicing multi-dimensional matrices and dataframes along axes. When a Pandas dataframe is indexed along a dimension with time-interval semantics, slicing between dates or timestamps is a very useful feature. For example, a user may want to work with the news articles and corresponding time series signals that occurred between particular `START` and `END` dates. Pandas in particular includes rich tooling for indexing and slicing datasets along time-indexed axes, and `news-signals` delegates slice commands and indexing to Pandas, exposing an interface for interacting with datasets using datetime indices[4].

2.1 `news-signals` Technical Requirements

The key technical desiderata we took into consideration when building `news-signals` are listed below:

- the complexity of data retrieval should be minimized: calling APIs, retrying failed requests, and parsing API output should be invisible to users.
- large datasets containing hundreds or thousands of signals, each lasting for thousands of "ticks", should be straightforward to configure and build.
- standard data science libraries such as Pandas should be used as much as possible to reduce maintenance burden over time.
- transformations on time series such as anomaly detection or trend/seasonality removal should be straightforward to implement.
- the complexity of compressing, saving, and loading datasets locally and remotely should be invisible to users.
- new types of signals should be easy to implement.
- Signals should be easy to use with standard machine learning libraries.

3 The `Signal` and `SignalsDataset` APIs

Signals consist of at least one time series coupled with zero or more textual data feeds. Figure 2 shows an example of creating and populating a `Signal`. Because most functions on the signal class return the signal itself, users can employ a convenient chaining syntax when performing multiple operations on a signal.

The library retrieves and stores the time series and news stories for the signal, and exposes a Pandas-like API to the underlying dataframes. We can add arbitrary textual data feeds to signals; in figure 2, `signal.sample_stories()` samples stories for every day of the time series (see library documentation on GitHub for more detailed information on how this works).

[4]https://pandas.pydata.org/docs/reference/api/pandas.DatetimeIndex.html

```
import datetime
from news_signals import signals

# wikidata QID for Twitter
qid = 'Q918'

signal = signals.AylienSignal(
    name='Twitter-Signal',
    params={"entity_ids": [qid]}
)

start = '2023-01-01'
end = '2023-06-01'
# retrieve a timeseries for the count of
# news articles per-day for this signal
signal = \
    signal(start, end).anomaly_signal()
# sample stories for every day in the signal
signal = signal.sample_stories()

# let's have a look at the biggest anomaly
top_day = signal.anomalies.idxmax()

# what was going on that day?
stories = signal.feeds_df.loc[top_day]['stories']
for s in stories:
    print(s['title'])

# Twitter experiencing outages nationwide
# Twitter experiencing international outages ...
# It's Not Just You, Twitter Is Acting Weird
# : Twitter briefly goes down
# Twitter outage: what happened, ...
#....
```

Figure 2: Creating and using a news signal

Once feeds and time series have been initialized, users can perform exploratory data analysis (EDA) in many ways, for example by examining and summarizing the news stories for an anomalous window of the signal's time series, or by plotting the signal.

Signals can also be easily mapped into a single dataframe representation by using the `.df` property. Signals' dataframe representations contain the textual and time series data associated with a signal, indexed along a `DatetimeIndex`, but they do not contain metadata such as how the signal is populated from one or more APIs, and transformation semantics such as how anomalies are computed.

Signals automatically differentiate between textual data and time series data types – for example, when `signal.plot()` is called, a signal's associated time series are automatically plotted in a multi-line plot.

3.1 API integrations

Most signals require retrieving data from one or more third-party APIs or on-disk datasets. In the current version of `news-signals`, we provide a deep integration with the Aylien NewsAPI, and additionally implement an interface to the Wikidata pageviews API for building pageview time series for Wikidata items [5].

3.2 The `SignalsDataset` API

Individual signals can be grouped into *datasets*. The `SignalsDataset` is a useful abstraction for working with groups of related signals — concretely, these might be signals for all politicians from a particular country, or for all companies connected to a specific market subset, such as the NASDAQ-100 or the S&P-500. Another dataset type could contain signals encapsulating content and time series related to different social media forums, such as Subreddits (Wang and Luo, 2021). The number of signals in a dataset can easily number in the hundreds or thousands, so we design a simple configuration DSL using `yaml` to allow easy construction of large datasets, which is documented in our GitHub repository.

Aylien NewsAPI and Wikimedia APIs Because our production use cases for `news-signals` are focused upon analyzing news data from the Aylien NewsAPI[6], the flagship Signal type in `news-signals` is currently[7] the `AylienSignal`. This signal type abstracts away API call semantics, allowing users to populate a signal by simply calling `signal(start_date, end_date)`. Of the data sources currently implemented in `news-signals`, Wikidata is completely free, but the Aylien NewsAPI requires a license key. However, we note that the Aylien NewsAPI currently has a two-week free trial allowing significant free API calls[8], and we hope to implement Signal types for fully public data sources beyond Wikidata in the near future.

3.2.1 Saving and loading Datasets

Local and remote serialization and persistence are essential features for dataset-focused libraries, and both Signal and SignalsDataset support saving and loading. We have also implemented persistent on Google Drive and Google Cloud Storage, that only require a remote path to be provided. Datasets are decompressed and cached locally so that the same dataset will not be re-downloaded if it is already available locally.

Library Documentation Section 3 has given only a small sample of the `news-signals` library capabilities, and we refer interested readers to the library documentation on GitHub, which also includes end-to-end example notebooks and video walkthroughs.

4 Building Signals Datasets

As discussed in section 3.2, `news-signals` provides an API for the creation of large-scale datasets representing collections of related signals.

Bootstrapping Datasets using Wikidata The Aylien NewsAPI links named entities in text to their Wikidata IDs (Vrandečić and Krötzsch, 2014). `news-signals` users can make use of the Wikidata Query Service[9] to easily build new datasets starting from SPARQL queries that return sets of matching entities (Prud'hommeaux et al., 2013). We build the datasets for NASDAQ-100, S&P 500, and US Politicians in this manner, and the SPARQL queries used to bootstrap these entity sets are available in our repository. For the purpose of this paper, and to exemplify use of the library, we build three example datasets: NASDAQ100, S&P 500, and US Politicians. Each of these datasets is bootstrapped from a list of Wikidata entities belonging to the respective set. To retrieve the entity sets, we build a SPARQL query returning the set of Wikidata entities that match the query, and then use this entity set to generate a dataset. This is a powerful way to generate arbitrary datasets for collections of related entities: for example, datasets for all politicians from a particular country or all American football players could be generated in this fashion. Note that in some cases Wikidata does not contain all entities in a particular set, for example, the NASDAQ100 dataset contains fewer than 100 entities. Dataset statistics are summarized in Table 1. Each of the entity sets is retrieved via one or more SPARQL queries[10]. We then use the Aylien

[5] `https://wikitech.wikimedia.org/wiki/Analytics/AQS/Pageviews`

[6] Aylien was acquired by Quantexa in February 2023

[7] as of August 2023

[8] https://aylien.com/news-api-signup

[9] https://query.wikidata.org/

[10] about SPARQL

NewsAPI[11] to sample up to 20 stories about each entity for each day of the time period Jan 2020-Jan 2023.

Multi-document Summarization (MDS) We provide a multi-document summarization model in `news-signals` for turning clusters of news articles associated with a particular timestamp into an easily readable summary. In particular, we use a hybrid extractive-abstractive approach that first uses a centroid-based sentence extraction method (Gholipour Ghalandari, 2017) to select 5 key sentences from the whole collection of provided news articles. We generate an abstractive summary from these sentences using a fine-tuned BART-large model (Lewis et al., 2020). The model was fine-tuned on such extractive summaries on the WCEP dataset (Gholipour Ghalandari et al., 2020), which contains compact event summaries with a neutral style.

Sampling News Data for Entities Importantly, we do not provide all news articles about each entity, rather, we provide only a sample of the news content about the entity for each day. This means that successful models should predict the time-series signal based upon the content of the article, rather than global numerical features [12].

Connecting Entities with Timeseries Signals In our example datasets, we focus upon entities that exist in the Wikidata knowledge graph. Different time series signal sources can be automatically linked to these entities. The Wikimedia API itself exposes several interesting time series signals, such as the number of pageviews and the number of edits for each page. We hypothesize that these signals are affected by events occurring in the real world – when an impactful event connected with an entity occurs, there is likely to be an observable change in signal behavior.

4.1 Dataset Release

To avoid potential licensing issues with releasing the news data content of the example datasets, at this stage we plan to only release the datasets containing article titles instead of full article texts and metadata. We also release a version of the datasets with daily abstractive summaries of the content, which do not reveal any source-specific content or data. Both versions will be available by email request to the authors[13].

Extending NewsSignals Because our datasets are grounded on the Wikidata knowledge graph, they are easy to extend with new inputs, entities, and signals. Obvious extensions to our work might include textual data from platforms such as Twitter and Reddit, and market signals such as stock price or other technical indicators for entities that are connected with publicly traded companies. Datasets should also be easy to extend with additional entities, and we provide a set of tools for extending NewsSignals in the accompanying code repository[14].

4.1.1 Docker Container and Example K8s Configuration

Because `news-signals` is designed to be used in both research and production settings, we have also provided a Dockerfile and an example Kubernetes (K8s) job configuration that can be deployed to Google Cloud Platform with minimal setup required. Together, these assets can be used to build signals datasets at a regular cadence, for example once a day or once a week.

5 Example Models and Experiments

This section presents a suite of example models and experiments for users to quickly adapt to their own task settings, and to verify the utility of `news-signals` by establishing baselines for a straightforward anomaly prediction task.

5.1 Binary Anomaly Prediction Task

In this work, we focus on a simple binary anomaly prediction task, which we treat as text classification. The goal is to predict whether a time series signal about a particular entity is anomalous during some window in the past, present, or future, based on textual information in news feeds about the entity. The input for an individual prediction is a set of news articles, an *aspect* (e.g. an entity) and the target a binary anomaly indicator. For simplicity, we predict the target value of a particular day from the textual input of the same day.

We transform time series signals into binary anomaly predictions with the following procedure:

[11] https://aylien.com/

[12] We may also consider models such as vector auto-regression that use signals derived from textual content as well as real-valued signals

[13] note also that all code used to produce the full datasets is open source

[14] `https://github.com/AYLIEN/news-signals-datasets`

Dataset Name	Start-End Date	Number of Signals	Total Articles	Time Series Targets
US Politicians	2020-01-01 to 2022-12-31	100	1285238	news volume, Wikimedia pageviews
NASDAQ-100	2020-01-01 to 2022-12-31	99	1569139	news volume, Wikimedia pageviews
S&P-500	2020-01-01 to 2022-12-31	100	1728179	news volume, Wikimedia pageviews

Table 1: Datasets Overview

5.2 Target Signals

We experiment with two different time series target signals: anomalies time series of NewsAPI volume counts and Wikimedia page views. One target time series consists of day-level binary values for the time range of our datasets. We use a simple anomaly detector to convert the raw time series signals into binary values, based on the Z-score: We treat each value x_t in a time series as an anomaly if the following is true:

$$\frac{x_t - \mu}{\sigma} > t \tag{1}$$

where μ is the mean and σ standard deviation of a time series. We set the anomaly threshold t (measured in standard deviations) to 3 which results in a proportion of 1-3% positive examples in our datasets.

5.3 Dataset Splits

Each of the three dataset is split chronologically into training (80%), validation (10%) and test (10%) sections. A trained model is informed about all entities in the training data and is tested to apply this knowledge to future data about these entities. The split can also be done across entities to test whether models can generalize to new entities. In this work, we focus on the simpler setting where the entities are known. Note that this does not apply to the zero-shot baselines using LLMs discussed below.

5.4 Balanced Sampling for Training

We preserve the validation and test dataset split as they are, i.e. with a small amount of 1-3% of positive labels, and as continuous time periods. Since training with this label imbalance results in poor results, we create modified training datasets from the time period of the training split: we randomly sample 10,000 positive and 10,000 negative examples for each dataset.

5.5 Compressing Textual Input

Since we are dealing with a large amount of text for each individual prediction task, i.e. a set of 20 news articles, we need to compress these articles into a shorter text to fit the input size of typical current deep learning models. In our experiments, we use the concatenation of all headlines of a day as the textual input. We leave a comparison to alternatives, e.g. multi-document summaries or representative articles, to future work.

5.6 Models for Anomaly Classification

We include several text classification baselines that predict the target based on one day of compressed textual content:

Fine-tuned Transformer Classifier: We fine-tune the pre-trained RoBERTa-base model (Liu et al., 2019) with an un-trained randomly initialized binary classification head. We fine-tune the model on 1 epoch of the label-balanced training examples with a batch size of 8, a learning rate of 2e-5 and a weight decay of 0.01, using the Adam optimizer.

Random Forest with Sparse Lexical Features: We train random forest models on binary lexical features, to explore how well the target signals are represented in surface-level text. We use `sklearn`[15] to extract sparse binary token-indicator features, with a vocabulary of 10,000 tokens, excluding stop words. We train the models with 100 trees and a maximum depth of 20. We determined these values on the validation datasets.

Zero-Shot Classification with Llama-2 (13B): We use Meta's `Llama-2-13b-chat` [16] model for zero-shot classification. We provide the 20 headlines of a day along with a prompt that describes the target signals as an input. The prompt used in the presented experiments is shown in Appendix B.

[15] `https://scikit-learn.org/`

[16] `https://huggingface.co/meta-llama/Llama-2-13b-chat`

5.7 Evaluation and Results

We evaluate the binary anomaly classification task using Precision, Recall and F1-score. We put the results into perspective by comparing them to two random baselines: random-uniform, i.e. randomly classifying each input as an anomaly with a 50% chance, and random-target, where we classify each input as an anomaly with a probability set to the proportion of positive examples in the test set. Table 2 shows the results for anomaly classification for news volume and Wikimedia pageviews as target signals. The trained models achieve above-random f1-scores on most of the dataset-target combinations, and obtain better results than the zero-shot baseline. We discuss the results in more detail in Appendix A. Figure 3 shows an example of predicted anomalies, compared to the ground-truth anomalies defined by the anomaly detection method. The predicted anomalies in this example consistently correspond to a spike of Wikipedia page views on the day or shortly after the day on which the input news stories were published.

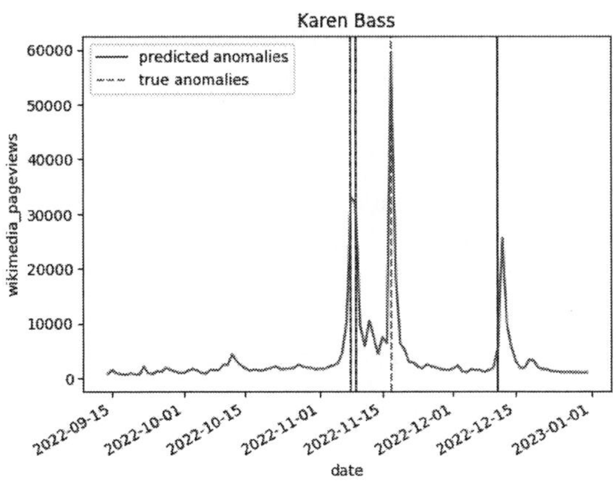

Figure 3: Predicted and ground-truth anomalies of a Wikipedia pageviews time series of US politician Karen Bass. The predictions are from a random forest model with sparse lexical features.

5.8 Extending to forecasting tasks

This experimental setup can easily be converted into forecasting tasks by pairing the text content of a particular day with the target signal shifted by some offset into the future. By sliding our forecasting window earlier than the input, we can also study how well today's news predicts signals that already happened. This may be more relevant for signals that imply significant information asymmetry, such as stock price, as opposed to signals that are public by definition, such as Wikimedia pageviews. Rather than binary anomaly targets, we can train models to directly predict the real-valued signal or quantized representations of the signal.

6 Intended Applications of NewsSignals

Time Series Forecasting using Texual Data As discussed, time series signal forecasting is an important task which is relatively unexplored in the context of models for natural language processing (NLP).

Financial Data Analysis We believe that this dataset and task setting should be straightforward to adapt to financial time series analysis. Financial time series such as stock price and trading volume are impacted by real-world events. The behavior of market signals reflects sentiment about particular entities, and is influenced by events happening in the world. However, market signals may contain opaque and confounding factors that make accurate prediction more challenging. Although this work deliberately does not consider market signals, it is very straightforward to add market time series such as stock price(s) or trading volume to signals.

NLP for Healthcare The `text2signal` task setting is well-suited to the emerging field of BioNLP or NLP for Healthcare – for example, predicting the number of hospital visits in subsequent months based upon a collection of doctor's notes from preceding months, or forecasting total medical expenditure in subsequent months based upon the content of a doctor's notes.

Sentiment To date, sentiment analysis datasets have been created by human annotation. However, the annotation task is difficult to fully specify, and impossible to scale to real-world volumes of data. An insight is that there are many real world signals that can be considered proxies to sentiment, most obviously market signals, especially when the definition of sentiment is constrained to specific (entity, aspect) pairs. Instead of using model-derived sentiment to forecast time series, market signals can be used as ground-truth proxies to sentiment annotations.

Social Sciences Social scientists may be interested in the tooling we have built around the Wikidata SPARQL endpoint, because `news-signals` allows users to easily build a set of signals connected to any set of Wikidata entities.

Target Signal	News Volume											
Model/Dataset	Nasdaq-100				Smp-500				US-politicians			
	prec	rec	f1	%pos	prec	rec	f1	%pos	prec	rec	f1	%pos
Random - uniform	0.01	0.43	0.02	0.5	0.01	0.49	0.02	0.49	0.03	0.5	0.05	0.51
Random - target	0.01	0.01	0.01	0.01	0.01	0.01	0.01	0.01	0.03	0.04	0.04	0.03
Sparse + RF	**0.19**	0.58	**0.28**	0.04	**0.12**	0.30	**0.18**	0.03	0.20	0.28	0.23	0.04
RoBERTa-base	0.12	**0.69**	0.2	0.08	0.1	**0.52**	0.17	0.05	**0.21**	**0.69**	**0.33**	0.08
Llama-2-13b-chat	0.03	0.71	0.06	0.16	0.03	0.47	0.05	0.1	0.05	0.46	0.1	0.22
Target Signal	**Wikimedia Pageviews**											
Model/Dataset	**Nasdaq-100**				**Smp-500**				**US-politicians**			
	prec	rec	f1	%pos	prec	rec	f1	%pos	prec	rec	f1	%pos
Random - uniform	0.02	0.46	0.03	0.5	0.02	0.52	0.04	0.49	0.02	0.51	0.03	0.5
Random - target	0.01	0.01	0.01	0.02	0.02	0.02	0.02	0.02	0.01	0.01	0.01	0.02
Sparse + RF	0.01	0.09	0.02	0.12	0.02	0.11	0.04	0.11	**0.22**	0.16	0.19	0.01
RoBERTa-base	0.01	0.09	0.03	0.11	0.03	0.19	0.05	0.13	0.18	**0.57**	**0.28**	0.05
Llama-2-13b-chat	**0.02**	**0.21**	**0.04**	0.3	**0.05**	**0.24**	**0.08**	0.24	0.04	0.52	0.07	0.22

Table 2: Evaluation results for anomaly classification experiments. %pos indicates the proportion of positive predicted labels.

In one of our example datasets, we produced a signal for every living US politician present in Wikidata, and we believe that many social scientists will be researching similar specific sets of entities and related time series signals.

This section discusses potential applications for `news-signals` and directions for future work.

Causality News-signals may be useful for NLP researchers working on tasks related to causality, because time series signals are well-suited to causality research. In general, we wish to find out what types of information are likely to impact time series signals. Concretely, we may believe that there is a true causal relationship between news and the edit rate on Wikimedia pages.

7 Related Work

NLP and Time Series Dataset Libraries `news-signals` can be seen as sitting between NLP-focused dataset libraries such as Huggingface Datasets (Lhoest et al., 2021) and time series focused libraries such as GluonTS and KATS (Alexandrov et al., 2019; Jiang et al., 2022). We specifically build tooling for working with datasets with textual inputs and time series outputs, and `news-signals` is complementary to and compatible with other popular NLP and time series libraries.

Granger Causality It is natural to consider whether the content of textual inputs "caused" an observed time series signal behavior. Granger causality (Granger, 1969) is a method of measuring the degree to which one signal may cause another. Marcinkevičs and Vogt (2021) propose a framework for discovering Granger Causality with interpretable neural networks.

Summary graphs (Peters et al., 2017) are a useful way of compressing relationships about Granger causality. Wen et al. (2017) introduce a flexible RNN architecture for time series forecasting. Nourbakhsh and Bang (2019) is a position paper discussing the use of PLMs for anomaly detection on financial data.

Time Series prediction with Textual Inputs As discussed in Section 1, one significant line of work focuses on predicting financial time series using signals derived from text, in particular aggregations of sentiment scores from social media posts (Chen et al., 2021, 2022; Arno et al., 2022; Li et al., 2014; Bing et al., 2014; Kim et al., 2016; Wang and Luo, 2021), inter alia.

PLMs and Transfer Learning Recently, significant work has been done to adapt transformer-based models in particular to time series forecasting tasks with flexible semantics (Wen et al., 2023).

Timeline Summarization from News Corpora A related line of work within the NLP community is constructing timelines of important events from large collections of news focused on long-term topics, e.g. disasters or entities (Martschat and Markert, 2018). The methods for identifying important events often make use of time-series-like signals defined over dates: the number of articles published per day or the number of times the date is mentioned in text (Tran et al., 2013; Ghalandari and Ifrim, 2020).

8 Conclusion

We have presented `news-signals`, an open source library for building and working with NLP datasets that predict time series signals based on textual inputs. We hope that this library can be useful to a broad group of researchers and data scientists in both academic and industry settings. Naturally, we would be very happy for additional contributions from the open source community to further improve the library.

References

Alexander Alexandrov, Konstantinos Benidis, Michael Bohlke-Schneider, Valentin Flunkert, Jan Gasthaus, Tim Januschowski, Danielle C. Maddix, Syama Sundar Rangapuram, David Salinas, Jasper Schulz, Lorenzo Stella, Ali Caner Türkmen, and Yuyang Wang. 2019. Gluonts: Probabilistic time series models in python. *CoRR*, abs/1906.05264.

Henri Arno, Klaas Mulier, Joke Baeck, and Thomas Demeester. 2022. Next-year bankruptcy prediction from textual data: Benchmark and baselines. In *Proceedings of the Fourth Workshop on Financial Technology and Natural Language Processing (FinNLP)*, pages 187–195, Abu Dhabi, United Arab Emirates (Hybrid). Association for Computational Linguistics.

Li Bing, Keith C. C. Chan, and Carol Ou. 2014. Public sentiment analysis in twitter data for prediction of a company's stock price movements. In *Proceedings of the 2014 IEEE 11th International Conference on E-Business Engineering*, ICEBE '14, page 232–239, USA. IEEE Computer Society.

Chung-Chi Chen, Hen-Hsen Huang, Hiroya Takamura, and Hsin-Hsi Chen, editors. 2021. *Proceedings of the Third Workshop on Financial Technology and Natural Language Processing*. -, Online.

Chung-Chi Chen, Hen-Hsen Huang, Hiroya Takamura, and Hsin-Hsi Chen, editors. 2022. *Proceedings of the Fourth Workshop on Financial Technology and Natural Language Processing (FinNLP)*. Association for Computational Linguistics, Abu Dhabi, United Arab Emirates (Hybrid).

Demian Gholipour Ghalandari and Georgiana Ifrim. 2020. Examining the state-of-the-art in news timeline summarization. In *Proceedings of the 58th Annual Meeting of the Association for Computational Linguistics*, pages 1322–1334.

Demian Gholipour Ghalandari. 2017. Revisiting the centroid-based method: A strong baseline for multi-document summarization. *EMNLP 2017*, page 85.

Demian Gholipour Ghalandari, Chris Hokamp, Nghia The Pham, John Glover, and Georgiana Ifrim. 2020. A large-scale multi-document summarization dataset from the Wikipedia current events portal. In *Proceedings of the 58th Annual Meeting of the Association for Computational Linguistics*, pages 1302–1308, Online. Association for Computational Linguistics.

C W J Granger. 1969. Investigating Causal Relations by Econometric Models and Cross-Spectral Methods. *Econometrica*, 37(3):424–438.

Charles R. Harris, K. Jarrod Millman, Stéfan J. van der Walt, Ralf Gommers, Pauli Virtanen, David Cournapeau, Eric Wieser, Julian Taylor, Sebastian Berg, Nathaniel J. Smith, Robert Kern, Matti Picus, Stephan Hoyer, Marten H. van Kerkwijk, Matthew Brett, Allan Haldane, Jaime Fernández del Río, Mark Wiebe, Pearu Peterson, Pierre Gérard-Marchant, Kevin Sheppard, Tyler Reddy, Warren Weckesser, Hameer Abbasi, Christoph Gohlke, and Travis E. Oliphant. 2020. Array programming with NumPy. *Nature*, 585(7825):357–362.

Xiaodong Jiang, Sudeep Srivastava, Sourav Chatterjee, Yang Yu, Jeffrey Handler, Peiyi Zhang, Rohan Bopardikar, Dawei Li, Yanjun Lin, Uttam Thakore, Michael Brundage, Ginger Holt, Caner Komurlu, Rakshita Nagalla, Zhichao Wang, Hechao Sun, Peng Gao, Wei Cheung, Jun Gao, Qi Wang, Marius Guerard, Morteza Kazemi, Yulin Chen, Chong Zhou, Sean Lee, Nikolay Laptev, Tihamér Levendovszky, Jake Taylor, Huijun Qian, Jian Zhang, Aida Shoydokova, Trisha Singh, Chengjun Zhu, Zeynep Baz, Christoph Bergmeir, Di Yu, Ahmet Koylan, Kun Jiang, Ploy Temiyasathit, and Emre Yurtbay. 2022. Kats.

Young Bin Kim, Jun Gi Kim, Wook Kim, Jae Ho Im, Tae Hyeong Kim, Shin Jin Kang, and Chang Hun Kim. 2016. Predicting fluctuations in cryptocurrency transactions based on user comments and replies. *PLOS ONE*, 11(8):1–17.

Mike Lewis, Yinhan Liu, Naman Goyal, Marjan Ghazvininejad, Abdelrahman Mohamed, Omer Levy, Veselin Stoyanov, and Luke Zettlemoyer. 2020. Bart: Denoising sequence-to-sequence pre-training for natural language generation, translation, and comprehension. In *Proceedings of the 58th Annual Meeting of the Association for Computational Linguistics*, pages 7871–7880.

Quentin Lhoest, Albert Villanova del Moral, Yacine Jernite, Abhishek Thakur, Patrick von Platen, Suraj Patil, Julien Chaumond, Mariama Drame, Julien Plu, Lewis Tunstall, Joe Davison, Mario Šaško, Gunjan Chhablani, Bhavitvya Malik, Simon Brandeis, Teven Le Scao, Victor Sanh, Canwen Xu, Nicolas Patry, Angelina McMillan-Major, Philipp Schmid, Sylvain Gugger, Clément Delangue, Théo Matussière, Lysandre Debut, Stas Bekman, Pierric Cistac, Thibault Goehringer, Victor Mustar, François Lagunas, Alexander Rush, and Thomas Wolf. 2021. Datasets: A community library for natural language processing. In *Proceedings of the 2021 Conference on Empirical Methods in Natural Language Processing: System Demonstrations*, pages 175–184, Online and Punta Cana, Dominican Republic. Association for Computational Linguistics.

Xiaodong Li, Haoran Xie, Li Chen, Jianping Wang, and Xiaotie Deng. 2014. News impact on stock price return via sentiment analysis. *Know.-Based Syst.*, 69(1):14–23.

Yinhan Liu, Myle Ott, Naman Goyal, Jingfei Du, Mandar Joshi, Danqi Chen, Omer Levy, Mike Lewis, Luke Zettlemoyer, and Veselin Stoyanov. 2019. Roberta: A robustly optimized bert pretraining approach. *arXiv preprint arXiv:1907.11692*.

Ričards Marcinkevičs and Julia E Vogt. 2021. Interpretable models for granger causality using self-explaining neural networks. In *International Conference on Learning Representations*.

Sebastian Martschat and Katja Markert. 2018. A temporally sensitive submodularity framework for timeline summarization. In *Proceedings of the 22nd Conference on Computational Natural Language Learning*, pages 230–240.

Armineh Nourbakhsh and Grace Bang. 2019. A framework for anomaly detection using language modeling, and its applications to finance.

Adam Paszke, Sam Gross, Francisco Massa, Adam Lerer, James Bradbury, Gregory Chanan, Trevor Killeen, Zeming Lin, Natalia Gimelshein, Luca Antiga, Alban Desmaison, Andreas Kopf, Edward Yang, Zachary DeVito, Martin Raison, Alykhan Tejani, Sasank Chilamkurthy, Benoit Steiner, Lu Fang, Junjie Bai, and Soumith Chintala. 2019. Pytorch: An imperative style, high-performance deep learning library. In *Advances in Neural Information Processing Systems 32*, pages 8024–8035. Curran Associates, Inc.

Jonas Peters, Dominik Janzing, and Bernhard Schölkopf. 2017. *Elements of Causal Inference: Foundations and Learning Algorithms*. Adaptive Computation and Machine Learning. MIT Press, Cambridge, MA.

Eric Prud'hommeaux, Steve Harris, and Andy Seaborne. 2013. SPARQL 1.1 Query Language. Technical report, W3C.

Giang Bihn Tran, Mohammad Alrifai, and Dat Quoc Nguyen. 2013. Predicting relevant news events for timeline summaries. In *Proceedings of the 22nd International Conference on World Wide Web*, pages 91–92. ACM.

Denny Vrandečić and Markus Krötzsch. 2014. Wikidata: A free collaborative knowledgebase. *Commun. ACM*, 57(10):78–85.

Charlie Wang and Ben Luo. 2021. Predicting $GME stock price movement using sentiment from Reddit r/wallstreetbets. In *Proceedings of the Third Workshop on Financial Technology and Natural Language Processing*, pages 22–30, Online. -.

Qingsong Wen, Tian Zhou, Chaoli Zhang, Weiqi Chen, Ziqing Ma, Junchi Yan, and Liang Sun. 2023. Transformers in time series: A survey. In *International Joint Conference on Artificial Intelligence(IJCAI)*.

Ruofeng Wen, Kari Torkkola, Balakrishnan (Murali) Narayanaswamy, and Dhruv Madeka. 2017. A multi-horizon quantile recurrent forecaster. In *NeurIPS 2017*.

Wes McKinney. 2010. Data Structures for Statistical Computing in Python. In *Proceedings of the 9th Python in Science Conference*, pages 56 – 61.

A Discussion of Anomaly Classification Results

The trained models, i.e. RoBERTa-base and the random forest with sparse features achieve considerable improvements over random results on most of the dataset-target combinations, with mixed rankings. In these cases, the models detect 50-70 % of the anomalies while only predicting 3-8% anomalies in total, which is a promising pattern. All baselines show close-to-random results on Nasdaq-100 and Smp-500 with Wikimedia Pageviews. Zero-shot anomaly prediction with `Llama-2-13b-chat` generally performs worse than the trained models, but still better than the random baselines. Our zero-shot approach suffers from over-prediction of the positive class - a behavior that is difficult to tune when designing prompts. We leave more systematic prompt tuning for this task to future work.

B Prompting for Zero-Shot Approach

We use the following prompt template for `LLama-2-13b-chat` to do anomaly classification from news:

Headlines: {{HEADLINES}} The stories above all involve {{ENTITY}} and were published on the same day. Do these news stories indicate one of the most significant events for {{ENTITY}}? Respond with 'no' or 'yes'.

We instantiate the placeholders with headlines and an entity name (person or company) for a specific data item.

We use the following system prompt: *You are an anomaly detector for news.*

We formatted the prompt according to the `LLama-2`-specific pattern.

A key issue in this zero-shot approach is to control the overall proportion of times an anomaly is detected in a dataset, i.e. to express the significance or importance of news stories to entities.

Signal-specific prompts, e.g. directly describing Wikipedia pageviews or news volume, turn out less effective than this generic description.

PyTAIL: An Open Source Tool for Interactive and Incremental Learning of NLP Models with Human in the Loop for Online Data

Shubhanshu Mishra*
shubhanshu.com
mishra@shubhanshu.com

Jana Diesner
University of Illinois at Urbana-Champaign
jdiesner@illinois.edu

Abstract

Online data streams make training machine learning models hard because of distribution shift and new patterns emerging over time. For natural language processing (NLP) tasks that utilize a collection of features based on lexicons and rules, it is important to adapt these features to the changing data. To address this challenge we introduce PyTAIL, a python library, which allows a human in the loop approach to actively train NLP models. PyTAIL enhances generic active learning, which only suggests new instances to label by also suggesting new features like rules and lexicons to label. Furthermore, PyTAIL is flexible enough for users to accept, reject, or update rules and lexicons as the model is being trained. Finally, we simulate the performance of PyTAIL on existing social media benchmark datasets for text classification. We compare various active learning strategies on these benchmarks. The model closes the gap with as few as 10% of the training data. Finally, we also highlight the importance of tracking evaluation metric on remaining data (which is not yet merged with active learning) alongside the test dataset. This highlights the effectiveness of the model in accurately annotating the remaining dataset, which is especially suitable for batch processing of large unlabelled corpora. PyTAIL will be open sourced and available at https://github.com/socialmediaie/pytail.

1 Introduction

Analysis of large scale natural language corpora often requires annotation of dataset in a given domain with pre-trained models. Generally, these models are pre-trained on a fixed training dataset which is often different from the domain of the dataset under consideration. This often leads to poor performance of the model on this new domain. One way to address this gap is to utilize domain adaptation (Sarawagi, 2008; Daumé III, 2007) to improve the model accuracy. However, efficient domain adaptation requires labeled training data from the new domain, which is costly to acquire. The problem gets compounded for social media data (Mishra et al., 2015, 2014; Mishra and Diesner, 2016, 2018), for which the vocabulary and language usage continuously evolve over time (Mishra et al., 2019, 2020b; Mishra and Mishra, 2019). Take the example of sentiment classification, where the ways of expressing the same opinion also change with time. For example, the opinion label of the phrase "you are just like *subject*", will depend on the general opinion about *"subject"* when the phrase was expressed. Similarly, many new words are coined on social media (Eisenstein, 2013; Gupta et al., 2010). This poses a challenge for maintaining these models retain their accuracy over time. In this work, we propose an approach to alleviate this issue by creating a system based on active human-in-the-loop learning which incrementally updates an existing classifier by requiring an user to provide few new examples from the new data. Traditionally, this setup, called active learning (Settles, 2009) only deals with suggesting new training examples to annotate. However, since many NLP models use feature based on existing rules or lexicons, with changing data characteristics it may be more desirable to also suggest rule and lexicon updates in the model. Our system PyTAIL (Python Text Analysis and Incremental Learning) addresses the issues highlighted here by allowing human-in-the-loop active learning systems to integrate new data points, rules, and lexicons. Our main contributions are as follows: (i) Introduce PyTAIL, an open source tool with an active learning workflow which uses new data, rules, and lexicons to continuously train NLP models. (ii) Introduce a social media text classification benchmark for active learning research. (iii) Introduce an evaluation setup on unconsumed

*Work done while at University of Illinois at Urbana-Champaign.

Proceedings of the 3rd Workshop for Natural Language Processing Open Source Software (NLP-OSS 2023), pages 190–198
December 6, 2023 ©2023 Association for Computational Linguistics

data in active learning to quantify how quickly a corpus can be fully annotated with a reasonable accuracy.

2 Incremental learning of models with human in the loop

In this section we describe `PyTAIL` (Python Text Analysis and Incremental Learning). `PyTAIL`'s goal is to enable efficient construction of training data using active learning, while supporting incremental learning of models using the most recent data. A description of `PyTAIL` workflow is shown in figure 1. `PyTAIL` is built with the following features in mind: (i) Low cost of continuous training data acquisition (ii) Incorporation of domain knowledge using lexicon and rules (iii) Efficient update of model using only the newly acquired training data.

Lexicons and Rules Traditional active learning systems usually rely on only using the data as an input. However, `PyTAIL`'s focus is on involving humans at multiple stages of the learning process. Hence, `PyTAIL` relies on data, a set of lexicons, and a set of rules. The lexicons are used for counting lexicon matches, e.g. positive or negative words from sentiment lexicons. Rules are arbitrary rules for generating features from the data, e.g. presence of a regular expression pattern. The lexicons are often used via a rule to count lexicon matches in the text. These lexicons and rules are used to help human annotators make better decisions on annotating the data and also help in the training of the model. Our rules are inspired from the Labeling function approach of Snorkel (Ratner et al., 2019), however, they differ as they are used as feature generator.

Overview As shown in figure 1, the user starts with a collection of artifacts in the Bootstrap Stage. This can include an pre-trained model, a small seed training dataset, existing rules, and lexicons. Next, the user introduces their unlabeled data stream from their domain of interest, e.g. social media corpora. The bootstrap artifacts are used to predict this data stream. These predictions are then fed to the query strategy (described below) to identify artifacts for the suggestion stage. The user can then accept, reject, update these suggestions or even introduce new suggestions. Next, the model is updated using updated artifacts such that the rules and lexicons are used for updating the model features and the annotated data is used for updating the model. Finally, `PyTAIL` shows continuous evaluation metrics which include metric on a test set, user accepted training set, and unobserved data stream. This process is repeated till a stopping criteria is met, e.g. the exhaustion of data stream or achieving reasonable evaluation score. `PyTAIL` supports two modes for training, one is human in the loop (HITL) mode, and another is simulation mode. The simulation model uses pre-defined heuristics to simulate human actions based on model prediction scores. The default model when applied to benchmark datasets is the simulation mode.

Human in the loop (HITL) mode In the HITL mode, `PyTAIL` uses the pre-trained model to suggest top K instances to the user. The user can sort the instances using the scoring criterion. In order to reduce the cognitive work of labeling an instance from scratch, the user is shown the model predictions (as well as the label probability). The user is only required to edit the labels if they disagree. Model predictions for all the unlabeled instances from the top suggestions are now used as gold labels and fed to the model during the update process (this is similar to self-supervision with the possibility of human intervention). The user is also shown the prominent features for that instance, the user can select these features and mark them as useful or useless. Lexicon matches with the annotations are also shown, along with prominent key phrases in the unlabeled data stream. The user can choose to update the lexicon with these new suggestions. Once the model update has happened, the user is provided feedback on the change in model evaluation on a held out data.

3 Benchmark for social media active learning

We introduce an active learning benchmark of 10 social media text classification datasets consisting of 200K posts. These datasets cover sentiment classification, abusive content identification, and uncertainty indication and is derived from the SocialMediaIE benchmark (Mishra, 2021, 2020a,b). The dataset is available at `https://zenodo.org/doi/10.5281/zenodo.7236429`.

3.1 Sentiment classification

For sentiment classification we use the same data as in (Mishra and Diesner, 2018). A description of these data is shown in table 1a. Clarin (Mozetič

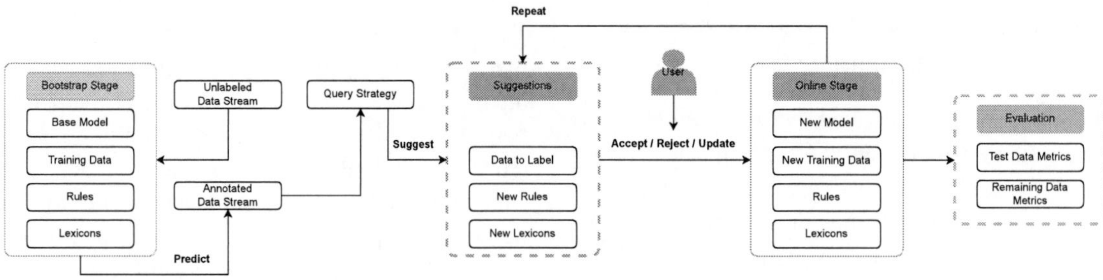

Figure 1: **`PyTAIL` Workflow**: Given a user and an unlabeled data stream, along with some bootstrapping artifacts, `PyTAIL` suggests data instances, rules, and lexicons which can be merged with bootstrapping artifacts to continuously create new model.

(a) Description of sentiment classification datasets. Datasets clustered together are enclosed between horizontal lines. Labels are *negative*, *neutral*, *positive*.

data	split	tokens	tweets	vocab
	dev	20079	981	3273
Airline	**test**	50777	2452	5630
	train	182040	8825	11697
	dev	80672	4934	15387
Clarin	**test**	205126	12334	31373
	train	732743	44399	84279
	dev	16339	803	3610
GOP	**test**	41226	2006	6541
	train	148358	7221	14342
	dev	15797	724	3304
Healthcare	**test**	16022	717	3471
	train	14923	690	3511
	dev	3472	209	1118
Obama	**test**	8816	522	2043
	train	31074	1877	4349
	dev	105108	4583	14468
SemEval	**test**	528234	23103	43812
	train	281468	12245	29673

(b) Description of abusive content classification datasets. Datasets which are clustered together are enclosed between horizontal lines. Labels for Founta are *abusive*, *hateful*, *normal*, and *spam*. Labels for WaseemSRW are *none*, *racism*, and *sexism*.

data	split	tokens	tweets	vocab
	dev	102534	4663	22529
Founta	**test**	256569	11657	44540
	train	922028	41961	118349
	dev	25588	1464	5907
WaseemSRW	**test**	64893	3659	10646
	train	234550	13172	23042

(c) Description of uncertainty indicators dataset. Datasets which are clustered together are enclosed between horizontal lines. Labels for Riloff are *sarcasm* and *not sarcasm*. Labels are for Swamy are *definitely no*, *definitely yes*, *probably no*, *probably yes*, and *uncertain*.

data	split	tokens	tweets	vocab
	dev	2126	145	1002
Riloff	**test**	5576	362	1986
	train	19652	1301	5090
	dev	1597	73	738
Swamy	**test**	3909	183	1259
	train	14026	655	2921

Table 1: Benchmark Datasets for Social Media Active Learning

et al., 2016) and SemEval are the two largest corpora. However, SemEval has a larger test set. All the sentiment datasets use the traditional labels of positive, neutral, and negative for labeling the tweets.

3.2 Abusive content classification

The second task we consider is abusive content classification. This task has recently gained prominence, owing to the the growth of abusive content on social media platforms. We utilize two datasets of abusive content. The first data is Founta from (Founta et al., 2018), which tags tweets as *abusive, hateful, normal, spam*. The second dataset is WaseemSRW from (Waseem and Hovy, 2016). It tags the data as *none, racism, sexism*. The rationale for including both these data under the same task it the core idea of identifing abusive content either direct or using racist or sexist variation. A description of these data is shown in table 1b.

3.3 Uncertainty indicators

Finally, we consider a collection of datasets for the task of identifying uncertainty indicators. Uncertainty indicators are defined as indicators in text which capture a level of uncertainty about the text, e.g., veridictality or sarcasm (uncertainty in intended meaning). We consider two datasets for this task as well. The first dataset is Riloff from (Riloff et al., 2013). This dataset consists of tweets annotated for sarcasm and non-sarcasm. The second dataset is Swamy from (Swamy et al., 2017). This dataset tries to identify the level of veridictality or degree of belief expressed in the tweet. The label set for this data is *definitely no, probably no, uncertain, probably yes, definitely yes*. A description of these data is shown in 1c.

4 PyTAIL for Social Media Text Classification

Model We use a logistic regression model with L_2 regularization. The regularization parameter is selected for each model using cross validation. We track the model scores on the held out test as well as validation data. Each text is represented using a set of features. Each tweet is tokenized and preprocessed by normalizing all mentions of hashtags, URLs, and mentions. We also use a large sentiment lexicon[1]. Furthermore, we suggest including a domain specific negative filter, i.e., words which should not be used to identify classification signals. For sentiment classification this can be entities in the corpora which should not bias the model.

[1] https://github.com/juliasilge/tidytext/blob/master/data-raw/sentiments.csv

Query selection strategies Active learning algorithms (Settles, 2009) identify most informative instances from unlabeled data that can be used to construct a high quality training dataset. The process of identifying informative instances is called **query selection**. Top instances $X_{selected}$ from the unlabeled data $X_{unlabeled}$ are identified based on a score. We consider two types of score: (i) $entropy = \sum_i p_i * log(p_i)$ - higher is better (ii) $min{-}margin = \max_{i \neq \star}\{p_i - p_\star \mid p_\star = \max_j p_j\}$ - lower is better. The entropy based scoring favors model predictions with highest randomness. The min-margin based scoring is useful in ensuring that the difference between the top prediction score and the second top prediction score is less. The selection is done using three strategies: (i) $Rand$: Instances are selected randomly without considering their scores, this acts as a baseline. (ii) X_{top}: Top K instances are selected based on their scores (X). (iii) X_{prop}: K instances are sampled proportional to their scores (X). This adds a degree of randomness to the top k strategy. These new instances are then added to the existing training instances $X_{train} = X_{train} \cup X_{selected}$, and the model is retrained.

Evaluation on remaining dataset Active learning systems often just track the test dataset performance. However, we observe another dataset which is not used for training, it is the left over dataset X_{left} after selecting the examples in each round. X_{left} is continously decreasing and tracking the performance of the model on X_{left} can reveal how fast can an in-distribution dataset be accurately annotated using the specific querying strategy. This is suitable for simulation mode where the whole dataset ($X_{left} = X_{unlabeled}$) is already annotated.

Simulation Experiments Human annotation for PyTAIL can be simulated.First, X_train is set to $N = 100$ random samples from $X_{unlabeled}$. In each round, X_{select} is K (K=100) instances from $X_{unlabeled}$ based on the scoring criterion described above. We conduct 100 rounds of active learning (200 for Clarin as it is a very large dataset) and evaluate the models using the micro-f1 score. We also compare against a model trained on the full

Table 2: Performance of query strategies across datasets using around 10% training dataset.

task	dataset	round	N	N_{left}	$\%_{used}$	Full	Rand	E_{top}	E_{prop}	M_{top}	M_{prop}
					Test Dataset						
ABUSIVE	Founta	42	41,861	37,661	0.10	0.79	0.77	0.78	0.78	0.79	0.77
	WaseemSRW	14	13,072	11,672	0.11	0.82	0.79	0.78	0.77	0.78	0.76
SENTIMENT	Airline	9	8,725	7,825	0.10	0.82	0.76	0.78	0.79	0.77	0.77
	Clarin	45	44,299	39,799	0.10	0.66	0.63	0.61	0.62	0.63	0.63
	GOP	8	7,121	6,321	0.11	0.67	0.63	0.64	0.63	0.62	0.64
	Healthcare	1	590	490	0.17	0.59	0.64	0.60	0.61	0.60	0.60
	Obama	2	1,777	1,577	0.11	0.63	0.56	0.60	0.58	0.59	0.57
	SemEval	13	12,145	10,845	0.11	0.65	0.59	0.60	0.61	0.58	0.61
UNCERTAINITY	Riloff	2	1,201	1,001	0.17	0.78	0.77	0.76	0.77	0.76	0.79
	Swamy	1	555	455	0.18	0.39	0.39	0.40	0.39	0.34	0.31
					Remaining Dataset						
ABUSIVE	Founta	42	41,861	37,661	0.10	NaN	0.77	0.80	0.78	0.81	0.78
	WaseemSRW	14	13,072	11,672	0.11	NaN	0.78	0.79	0.77	0.80	0.76
SENTIMENT	Airline	9	8,725	7,825	0.10	NaN	0.75	0.79	0.79	0.80	0.78
	Clarin	45	44,299	39,799	0.10	NaN	0.62	0.62	0.62	0.64	0.63
	GOP	8	7,121	6,321	0.11	NaN	0.62	0.64	0.62	0.63	0.63
	Healthcare	1	590	490	0.17	NaN	0.53	0.56	0.53	0.47	0.50
	Obama	2	1,777	1,577	0.11	NaN	0.54	0.56	0.57	0.56	0.56
	SemEval	13	12,145	10,845	0.11	NaN	0.61	0.62	0.62	0.63	0.62
UNCERTAINITY	Riloff	2	1,201	1,001	0.17	NaN	0.80	0.82	0.84	0.82	0.81
	Swamy	1	555	455	0.18	NaN	0.37	0.40	0.40	0.33	0.36

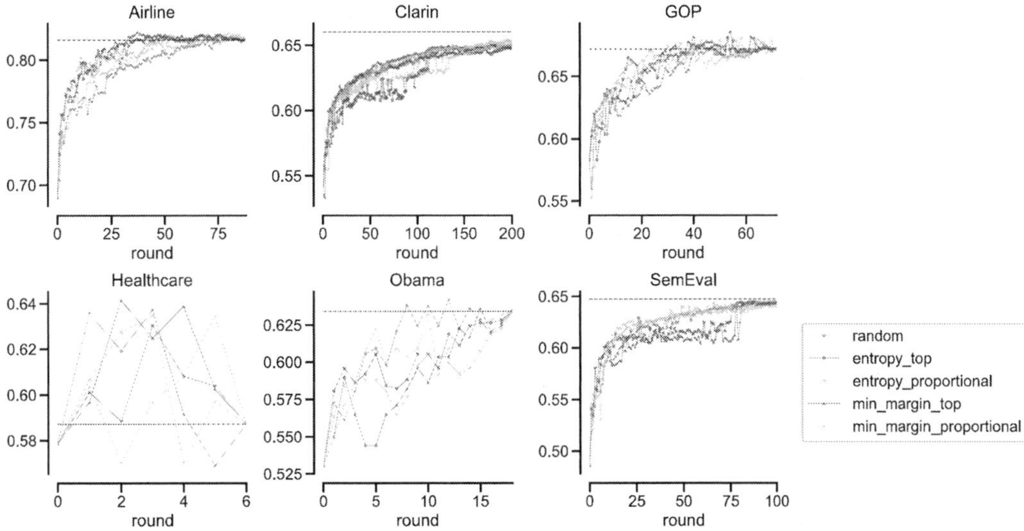

(a) Sentiment classification

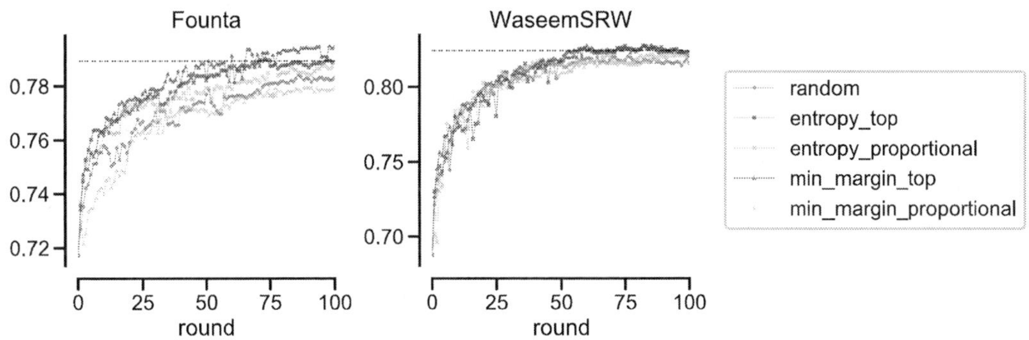

(b) Abusive content detection

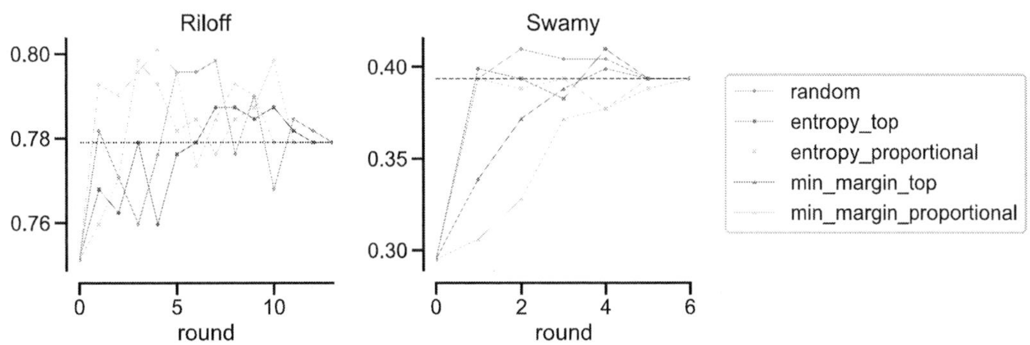

(c) Uncertainty indicators

Figure 2: Progression of active learning classifier performance (micro f1-score) on the respective test set across 100 rounds of active learning (200 for Clarin). The annotation budget for each round is 100 instances, and the model is warm started with 100 random samples of the training data. Black dotted line is the classifier performance when trained on all of the training data. Data ordered alphabetically and X and Y axes are not shared.

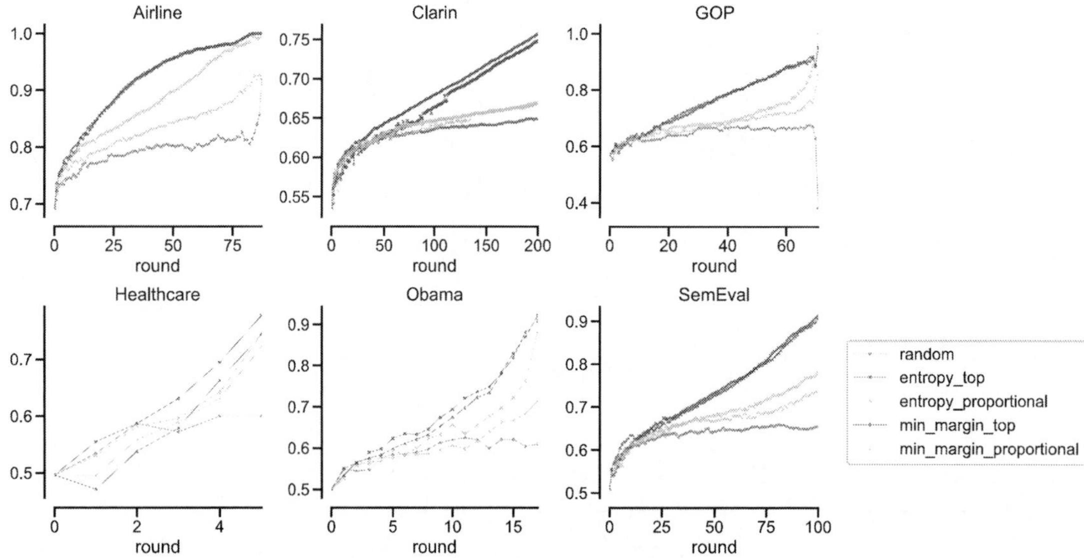

(a) Sentiment classification

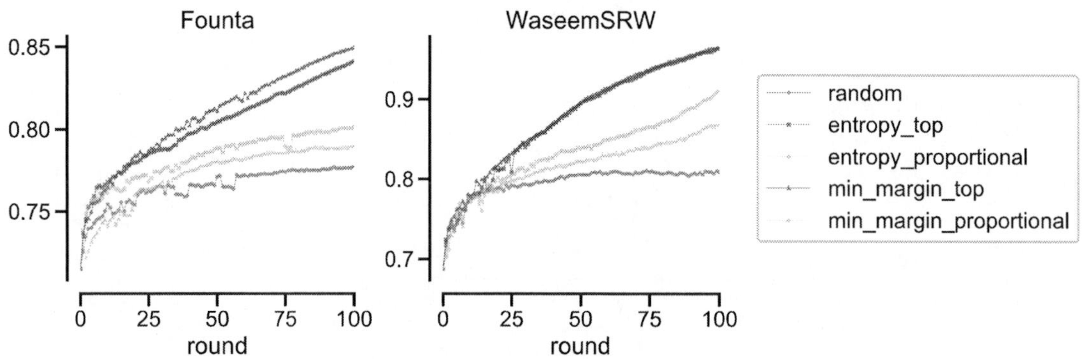

(b) Abusive content detection

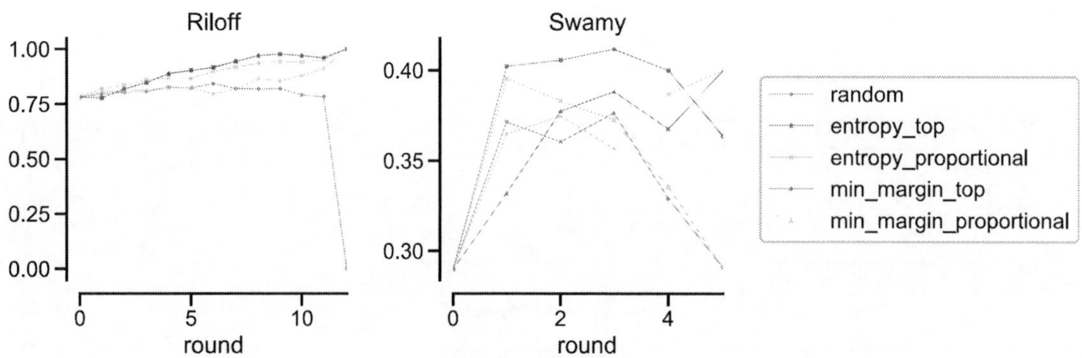

(c) Uncertainty indicators

Figure 3: Progression of active learning classifier performance (micro f1-score) on the respective unselected data set across 100 rounds of active learning (200 for Clarin). The annotation budget for each round is 100 instances, and the model is warm started with 100 random samples of the training data. Data ordered alphabetically and X and Y axes are not shared.

data (Full). The experimental results on the test split of each data are shown in figure 2 and table 2. We observe that the top K strategy is usually the best followed by the proportional strategy across all data. For larger datasets we see that the model closes the gap very soon. We also show experimental results on the X_{left} part of the training data in figure 3. We observe that the top K strategy is consistently the best, followed by the proportional strategy across all data. The increase in performance on the X_{left} is indicative of the fact that active learning ensures that the remaining data is actually easy to annotate without human correction. This evaluation presents a more practical usage pattern of ML models. This usage pattern requires annotating pre-selected and large $X_{unlabeled}$. In reality, once the dataset is selected, one is interested in reducing the size of X_{train} to efficiently annotate the data. We think, it is in this setting that the active learning is most beneficial. If the user can achieve high labeling accuracy by annotating few samples, then the user's job is done.

5 Conclusion

We described experiments for evaluating active learning approaches for text classification tasks on tweet data. We introduced, `PyTAIL`, an open source user interface for active learning of NLP models by only requiring the user to update the labels for the model prediction if required. We also release a benchmark dataset for social media active learning. One limitation of our work is that our experiments are only conducted using simple linear model as they are easier to experiment with for sparse text features which we used for feature importance. However, the API does not place any restriction on the type of model.

In the future we plan to extend this strategy to non classification tasks for Social Media datasets e.g. structured prediction tasks like Named Entity Recognition, POS tagging, and Chunking (Mishra and Diesner, 2016; Mishra et al., 2020a; Eskander et al., 2022; Mishra and Haghighi, 2021; Mishra, 2019; Mishra et al., 2022; Mishra, 2020c).

`PyTAIL` is available as an open source tool at `https://github.com/socialmediaie/pytail/` and our dataset is available at `https://zenodo.org/doi/10.5281/zenodo.7236429`.

References

Hal Daumé III. 2007. Frustratingly Easy Domain Adaptation. *Association for Computational Linguistic (ACL)s*, (June):256–263.

Jacob Eisenstein. 2013. What to do about bad language on the internet.

Ramy Eskander, Shubhanshu Mishra, Sneha Mehta, Sofia Samaniego, and Aria Haghighi. 2022. Towards improved distantly supervised multilingual named-entity recognition for tweets. In *Proceedings of the The 2nd Workshop on Multi-lingual Representation Learning (MRL)*, pages 115–124, Abu Dhabi, United Arab Emirates (Hybrid). Association for Computational Linguistics.

Antigoni-Maria Founta, Constantinos Djouvas, Despoina Chatzakou, Ilias Leontiadis, Jeremy Blackburn, Gianluca Stringhini, Athena Vakali, Michael Sirivianos, and Nicolas Kourtellis. 2018. Large Scale Crowdsourcing and Characterization of Twitter Abusive Behavior. In *International AAAI Conference on Web and Social Media*.

Manish Gupta, Rui Li, Zhijun Yin, and Jiawei Han. 2010. Survey on social tagging techniques. *ACM SIGKDD Explorations Newsletter*, 12(1):58.

Shubhanshu Mishra. 2019. Multi-dataset-multi-task Neural Sequence Tagging for Information Extraction from Tweets. In *Proceedings of the 30th ACM Conference on Hypertext and Social Media - HT '19*, pages 283–284, New York, New York, USA. ACM Press.

Shubhanshu Mishra. 2020a. Information Extraction from Digital Social Trace Data with Applications to Social Media and Scholarly Communication Data. *ACM SIGIR Forum*, 54(1).

Shubhanshu Mishra. 2020b. *Information extraction from digital social trace data with applications to social media and scholarly communication data*. Ph.d. dissertation, University of Illinois at Urbana-Champaign.

Shubhanshu Mishra. 2020c. Non-neural Structured Prediction for Event Detection from News in Indian Languages. In *Working Notes of FIRE 2020 - Forum for Information Retrieval Evaluation*, Hyderabad, India. CEUR Workshop Proceedings, CEUR-WS.org.

Shubhanshu Mishra. 2021. Information extraction from digital social trace data with applications to social media and scholarly communication data. *SIGWEB Newsl.*, 2021(Spring).

Shubhanshu Mishra, Sneha Agarwal, Jinlong Guo, Kirstin Phelps, Johna Picco, and Jana Diesner. 2014. Enthusiasm and support. In *Proceedings of the 2014 ACM conference on Web science - WebSci '14*, pages 261–262, New York, New York, USA. ACM Press.

Shubhanshu Mishra, Sneha Agarwal, Jinlong Guo, Kirstin Phelps, Johna Picco, and Jana Diesner. 2019. Tweet IDs annotated for enthusiasm and support towards social causes: CTE, cyberbullying, and LGBT.

Shubhanshu Mishra and Jana Diesner. 2016. Semi-supervised Named Entity Recognition in noisy-text. In *Proceedings of the 2nd Workshop on Noisy User-generated Text (WNUT)*, pages 203–212, Osaka, Japan. The COLING 2016 Organizing Committee.

Shubhanshu Mishra and Jana Diesner. 2018. Detecting the Correlation between Sentiment and User-level as well as Text-Level Meta-data from Benchmark Corpora. In *Proceedings of the 29th on Hypertext and Social Media - HT '18*, pages 2–10, New York, New York, USA. ACM Press.

Shubhanshu Mishra, Jana Diesner, Jason Byrne, and Elizabeth Surbeck. 2015. Sentiment Analysis with Incremental Human-in-the-Loop Learning and Lexical Resource Customization. In *Proceedings of the 26th ACM Conference on Hypertext & Social Media - HT '15*, pages 323–325, New York, New York, USA. ACM Press.

Shubhanshu Mishra and Aria Haghighi. 2021. Improved Multilingual Language Model Pretraining for Social Media Text via Translation Pair Prediction. In *Proceedings of the Seventh Workshop on Noisy User-generated Text (W-NUT 2021)*, pages 381–388, Online. Association for Computational Linguistics.

Shubhanshu Mishra, Sijun He, and Luca Belli. 2020a. Assessing Demographic Bias in Named Entity Recognition. In *Bias in Automatic Knowledge Graph Construction - A Workshop at AKBC 2020*.

Shubhanshu Mishra and Sudhanshu Mishra. 2019. 3Idiots at HASOC 2019: Fine-tuning Transformer Neural Networks for Hate Speech Identification in Indo-European Languages. In *Proceedings of the 11th annual meeting of the Forum for Information Retrieval Evaluation*.

Shubhanshu Mishra, Aman Saini, Raheleh Makki, Sneha Mehta, Aria Haghighi, and Ali Mollahosseini. 2022. Tweetnerd - end to end entity linking benchmark for tweets. In *Advances in Neural Information Processing Systems*, volume 35, pages 1419–1433. Curran Associates, Inc.

Sudhanshu Mishra, Shivangi Prasad, and Shubhanshu Mishra. 2020b. Multilingual Joint Fine-tuning of Transformer models for identifying Trolling,Aggression and Cyberbullying at TRAC 2020. In *Proceedings of the Second Workshop on Trolling, Aggression and Cyberbullying (TRAC-2020)*.

Igor Mozetič, Miha Grčar, Jasmina Smailović, H Alani, Igor Mozetič, and A Scala. 2016. Multilingual Twitter Sentiment Classification: The Role of Human Annotators. *PLOS ONE*, 11(5):e0155036.

Alexander Ratner, Stephen H. Bach, Henry Ehrenberg, Jason Fries, Sen Wu, and Christopher Ré. 2019. Snorkel: rapid training data creation with weak supervision. *The VLDB Journal*, 29(2-3):709–730.

Ellen Riloff, Ashequl Qadir, Prafulla Surve, Lalindra De Silva, Nathan Gilbert, and Ruihong Huang. 2013. Sarcasm as Contrast between a Positive Sentiment and Negative Situation. In *Proceedings of the 2013 Conference on Empirical Methods in Natural Language Processing*, pages 704–714, Seattle, Washington, USA. Association for Computational Linguistics.

Sunita Sarawagi. 2008. Information extraction. *Foundation and Trends in Databases*, 1(3):261–377.

Burr Settles. 2009. Active Learning Literature Survey. Technical report, University of Wisconsin–Madison.

Sandesh Swamy, Alan Ritter, and Marie-Catherine de Marneffe. 2017. "i have a feeling trump will win..................": Forecasting Winners and Losers from User Predictions on Twitter. In *Proceedings of the 2017 Conference on Empirical Methods in Natural Language Processing*, pages 1583–1592, Stroudsburg, PA, USA. Association for Computational Linguistics.

Zeerak Waseem and Dirk Hovy. 2016. Hateful Symbols or Hateful People? Predictive Features for Hate Speech Detection on Twitter. In *Proceedings of the NAACL Student Research Workshop*, pages 88–93, Stroudsburg, PA, USA. Association for Computational Linguistics.

Antarlekhaka: A Comprehensive Tool for Multi-task Natural Language Annotation

Hrishikesh Terdalkar and **Arnab Bhattacharya**
{hrishirt, arnabb} @cse.iitk.ac.in
Department of Computer Science and Engineering
Indian Institute of Technology Kanpur
Kanpur, India

Abstract

One of the primary obstacles in the advancement of Natural Language Processing (NLP) technologies for low-resource languages is the lack of annotated datasets for training and testing machine learning models. In this paper, we present *Antarlekhaka*, a tool for manual annotation of a comprehensive set of tasks relevant to NLP. The tool is Unicode-compatible, language-agnostic, Web-deployable and supports distributed annotation by multiple simultaneous annotators. The system sports user-friendly interfaces for 8 categories of annotation tasks. These, in turn, enable the annotation of a considerably larger set of NLP tasks. The task categories include two linguistic tasks not handled by any other tool, namely, sentence boundary detection and deciding canonical word order, which are important tasks for text that is in the form of poetry. We propose the idea of *sequential annotation* based on small text units, where an annotator performs several tasks related to a single text unit before proceeding to the next unit. The research applications of the proposed mode of multi-task annotation are also discussed. Antarlekhaka outperforms other annotation tools in objective evaluation. It has been also used for two real-life annotation tasks on two different languages, namely, Sanskrit and Bengali. The tool is available at https://github.com/Antarlekhaka/code.

1 Introduction and Motivation

Manual annotation plays an important role in natural language processing (NLP). It is particularly important in the context of low-resource languages for the creation of datasets.

There are a number of syntactic and semantic tasks in NLP which can utilize annotation by domain experts. Lemmatization, morphological analysis, parts-of-speech tagging, named entity recognition, dependency parsing, constituency parsing, co-reference resolution, sentiment detection, discourse analysis and so on are some examples of such common NLP tasks.

There's a need of considering historical context and respecting the perspectives of Indigenous language speaking communities when conducing NLP research involving these languages (Schwartz, 2022). Sanskrit, a classical language, has a large amount of text available digitally; however, it still suffers from poor performance in standard NLP tasks. Hence, manual annotation of text in Sanskrit is of prime necessity. Further, most of the classical Sanskrit literature is in poetry form following mostly free word order (Kulkarni et al., 2015), without any punctuation marks. Therefore, certain specialized tasks, such as sentence boundary detection and canonical word ordering, are needed for Sanskrit text processing

Consider an example[1] from a Sanskrit text, *Valmiki Ramayana*, (Dutt et al., 1891) shown in Fig. 1. The sentence boundaries are denoted using square brackets ([and]). The half-verse boundaries are marked by single forward slashes (/) and the verse boundaries by two forward slashes (//). It can be observed that the sentence boundaries do not coincide with the verse boundaries. In particular, there may be multiple sentences present in a single verse, or a sentence may extend across multiple verses. Further, the right side of the arrow shows that the canonical word order is different from the order in which words appear in the original text.

For such languages that either do not use punctuations or use them in a limited amount, sentence boundary detection is an important task. Additionally, in languages with relatively free word order, decision of a canonical word order is also relevant. These two tasks also play a vital role when dealing with the corpora in the form of poetry, making them potentially relevant for all languages.

Performing multiple annotation tasks on the

[1]Using IAST transliteration scheme: https://en.wikipedia.org/wiki/International_Alphabet_of_Sanskrit_Transliteration

Proceedings of the 3rd Workshop for Natural Language Processing Open Source Software (NLP-OSS 2023), pages 199–211
December 6, 2023

[na rocate mama-api-etad-ārye $]_1$ [yad-rāghavo vanam /
tyaktvā rājyaśriyaṃ gacchet $]_2$ [striyā vākyavaśaṃ gataḥ // 2
viparītaś ca vṛddhaś ca viṣayaiś ca pradharṣitaḥ /
nṛpaḥ kim iva na brūyāc codyamānaḥ samanmathaḥ // 3 $]_3$
[...]

→

[ārye etad mama api na rocate $]_1$
[yad rāghavo rājyaśriyaṃ tyaktvā vanam gacchet $]_2$
[viparītaḥ vṛddhaḥ ca viṣayaiḥ pradharṣitaḥ ca codyamānaḥ samanmathaḥ ca striyā vākyavaśaṃ gataḥ nṛpaḥ kim iva na brūyāt $]_3$
[...]

Figure 1: Sanskrit verses from Valmiki Ramayana. Original text appears on the left with sentence boundary markers added. The canonical word order is shown on the right.

same corpus is common, and the order of these tasks can be important due to their interdependence. Specifically, in cases[2] where sentence boundary detection is relevant, it must be performed before any other annotation task. For instance, determining the word order of a sentence requires finalizing the constituent words first. The same holds true for tasks such as dependency parsing, sentence classification, and discourse analysis.

In this paper, we describe *Antarlekhaka*[3], a tool for distributed annotation that provides user-friendly interfaces to facilitate the annotation process of various common NLP tasks in a straightforward and efficient way. We propose a sequential annotation model, where an annotator carries out multiple annotation tasks relevant for a small text unit, such as a verse, before proceeding to the next. The tool has full Unicode support and is designed to be language-agnostic, meaning it can be used with corpora from any language, making it highly versatile. The tool sports eight task-specific user-friendly annotation interfaces corresponding to eight general categories of NLP tasks: sentence boundary detection, canonical word ordering, free-form text annotation of tokens, token classification, token graph construction, token connection, sentence classification and sentence graph construction. The goal of the tool is to streamline the annotation process, making it easier and more efficient for annotators to complete multiple NLP tasks on the same corpus. Annotators can participate in the annotation without any programming knowledge. Additionally, the tool's easy setup and intuitive administrator interface make it accessible to administrators with minimal technical expertise.

2 Background

An annotation tool is crucial for the successful completion of any annotation task, and its success relies heavily on its usability for the annotators. Apart from this, the tool should be easily installable and should support web deployment for distributed annotation, allowing multiple annotators to work on the same task from different locations. The administration interface of the tool should also be intuitive and should provide convenient access to common administrative tasks such as corpus upload, ontology creation, and user access management. Additionally, often there is a need for multiple annotation tasks to be completed on the same corpus. A well-designed annotation tool should encompass these features to ensure a smooth, efficient, and accurate annotation process.

Numerous text annotation tools are available that target specific annotation tasks, such as WebAnno (Yimam et al., 2013), INCePTION (Klie et al., 2018), GATE Teamware (Bontcheva et al., 2013), FLAT (van Gompel, 2014), BRAT (Stenetorp et al., 2012), doccano (Nakayama et al., 2018) and more. However, each of these tools falls short in fulfilling all the requirements of an ideal annotation tool. For instance, WebAnno is rich in features but becomes complex to use and experiences performance issues as the number of lines displayed on the screen increases. Both WebAnno and BRAT lack full support for Firefox (Fort, 2016), an issue that was rectified in INCEpTION. GATE Teamware suffers from shortcomings such as inadequate support for relation and co-reference annotation (Herik et al., 2018), installation issues (Neves and Ševa, 2021) and complexity for average users (Yimam et al., 2013). FLAT uses a non-standard FoLiA XML data format and the system is not intuitive (Neves and Ševa, 2021). BRAT has not been actively[4] developed and exhibits issues such as slowness, limited scope for configuration and limitations regarding file formats (Yimam et al., 2013). The tool doccano, although simple to set up and intuitive, only supports labeling tasks. Sangrahaka (Terdalkar and Bhattacharya, 2021), while being easy to set up and use, focuses only on the annotation towards creation of knowledge graphs and lacks support towards general-purpose NLP annotation tasks.

Some annotation tools including INCEpTION

[2]For corpora without clear sentence boundaries, like languages with limited punctuation or poetic corpora

[3]*Antarlekhaka* is a Sanskrit word meaning 'annotator'.

[4]The latest version was published in 2012

Table 1: Comparison of NLP annotation tools based on primary features and supported tasks

	INCEpTION	GATE	BRAT	FLAT	doccano	Sangrahaka	**Antarlekhaka**
Distributed Annotation	✓	✓	✓	✓	✓	✓	✓
Easy Installation			✓	✓	✓	✓	✓
Sequential Annotation							✓
Querying Interface						✓	
Token Text Annotation	✓	✓	✓	✓			✓
Token Classification	✓	✓	✓	✓	✓		✓
Token Graph	✓	✓	✓	✓		✓	✓
Token Connection	✓	✓	✓	✓		✓	✓
Sentence Boundary	✓						✓
Word Order							✓
Sentence Classification	✓						✓
Sentence Graph							✓

use spans for marking most annotations, which a user by selecting and dragging mouse cursor over the corpus text. This method, while versatile, has a trade-off that the annotation process is slower and more tedious. Importantly, none of these tools address crucial tasks like canonical word ordering. Hence, there is a need for an annotation tool that is user-friendly, easy to install and deploy, and encompasses all the necessary tasks for NLP annotation.

Thus, for the general purpose multi-task annotation of NLP tasks, we present *Antarlekhaka.* The annotation is performed in a sequential manner on small units of text (e.g., verses in poetry). The application is language and corpus agnostic. The tool is able to process data in two different formats: the standard CoNLL-U[5] format and plain text format. Regular-expressions based tokenizer is applied when using the data in plain text format.

Tab. 1 shows a comparison of the prominent annotation tools. We also conduct an objective evaluation of *Antarlekhaka* using the scoring methodology proposed by (Neves and Ševa, 2021). We modify the criteria suitable to the domain of NLP annotation. Details of the evaluation are described in Sec. 4. It is important to note that while some of the existing tools, in theory, have the capability to support certain NLP tasks, they may not be designed with user-friendly interfaces.

3 Architecture

Antarlekhaka is a language-agnostic, multi-task, distributed annotation tool presented as a Web-deployable software. The tool makes use of several technologies, including *Python 3.8* , *Flask 2.2.2* , and *SQLite 3.38.3* for the backend, and *HTML5*, *JavaScript*, and *Bootstrap 4.6* for the frontend.

Flask web framework powers the backend of *Antarlekhaka* providing a robust and scalable infrastructure. A web framework is responsible for a range of backend tasks, including routing, templating, managing user sessions, connecting to databases and others. The recommended way to run the tool in a production environment is using a *Web Server Gateway Interface* (WSGI) HTTP server, such as *Gunicorn* , which can operate behind a reverse proxy server such as *NGINX* or *Apache HTTP Server* . However, any WSGI server, including the built-in server of Flask, can be utilized to run the application.

SQLite is used as the database management system to store and manage the data and metadata associated with the annotation tasks. An Object Relational Mapper (ORM) *SQLAlchemy*[6] is used to interact with the relational database. This allows the user to choose any supported dialect of traditional SQL, such as *SQLite*, *MySQL* , *PostgreSQL* , *Oracle* , *MS-SQL* , *Firebird* , *Sybase* and others[7].

The frontend of the tool, built using *HTML5*, *JavaScript*, and *Bootstrap*, provides user-friendly interfaces for annotators and administrators. The tool provides a feature-rich administrative interface to manage user access, corpus, tasks and ontology. The tool also includes eight types of intuitive annotation interfaces, explained in detail in Sec. 3.3.

The tool simplifies setup with a single configuration file that controls various customizable aspects. Overall, by combining the state-of-the-art technologies, *Antarlekhaka* offers a powerful and flexible solution for large-scale annotation projects.

3.1 Workflow

The workflow of the system is demonstrated in Fig. 2. The application is presented as a full-stack web-based software. It follows a single-file configuration system. An administrator may configure the tool and deploy it to web, making it immediately

[5]https://universaldependencies.org/format.html

[6]https://www.sqlalchemy.org/

[7]https://docs.sqlalchemy.org/en/20/dialects/

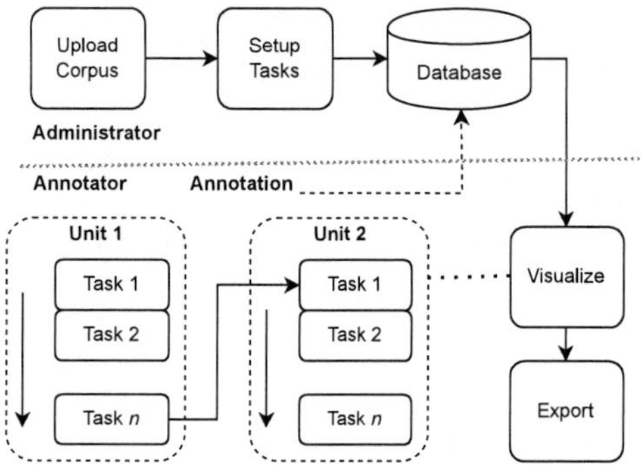

Figure 2: Workflow of *Antarlekhaka*

available for use. User registration is supported. User access is controlled by a 4-tier permission system, namely User, Annotator, Curator and Admin.

The tool has eight annotation interface templates corresponding to eight generic categories of NLP annotation tasks: sentence boundary detection, canonical word order, free-form token annotation, token classification, token graph construction, token connection, sentence classification, and sentence graph construction. Various NLP tasks can be modelled using each of these categories. More than one tasks of same category may be required for a specific annotation project. For example, named entity recognition (NER) and parts-of-speech (POS) tagging are both examples of token classification. To facilitate this, the administrative interface allows an administrator to create multiple tasks of each category. Additionally, an administrator can also control the set of active tasks, order of the tasks, ontology for the relevant tasks, corpus management and user access management.

We propose a streamlined sequential mode of annotation where an annotator completes multiple tasks for a single unit of text before moving on to the next unit. The set and order of tasks is customizable through an administrative interface. We consider a small logical block of text as a unit for the annotation, e.g., a verse from the poetry corpus.

3.2 Data

The data for corpus can be in either of two formats: *CoNLL-U* format or *plain text* format and can contain Unicode text. *CoNLL-U* is a widely used format for linguistic annotation, and it is based on the column format for treebank data. The format is designed to store a variety of linguistic annotations, including part-of-speech tags, lemmas, morphological features, and dependencies between words in a sentence. Data in *CoNLL-U* format can be obtained from treebanks such as Universal Dependencies (De Marneffe et al., 2021), which is a project that aims to develop cross-linguistically consistent treebank annotation. In addition, NLP tools such as Stanza (Qi et al., 2020) are capable of processing a general corpus of text and producing data in *CoNLL-U* format.

Plain text data is processed using a regular-expression based tokenizer, which is a process that splits the text into individual units of meaning, such as verses, lines and tokens using patterns defined in the form of regular expressions to identify the respective separators. The plain text processor module is a pluggable component. An administrator may reimplement it using any language specific features or tools as long as the data output by the module meets the current format specifications.

After the data has been imported, it is organized in a five-level hierarchy structure consisting of: Corpus, Chapter, Verse, Line, and Token. The hierarchical structure of the data provides a clear and organized framework for annotating and analyzing the data, making it easier to capture the relationships between different elements of the data.

3.3 Task Categories and Interfaces

The annotation supports annotation towards eight categories of annotation tasks and offers intuitive interfaces for each category. Annotators view the corpus in the form of text units (e.g., verses) on the left, and an annotation area on the right. After submitting annotations for a task, the interface automatically advances to the next task. Annotators are expected to complete all the tasks associated with a text unit before moving on to the next unit. This, however, is not strictly enforced, allowing annotator to still go back to modify annotations. Fig. 3 showcases the overall annotation interface.

The administrator can configure task-related information, including task titles, instructions, active tasks, and their order, through the administrative interface. This interface is illustrated in Fig. 5 (Appx. A). Tasks such as user access management, corpus creation, and ontology management also have intuitive administrative interfaces. Next, we provide a detailed description of each task category and its corresponding interface.

3.3.1 Sentence Boundary Detection

The importance of the sentence boundary task is not limited to languages without distinct sentence markers; it also pertains to poetry text, making it

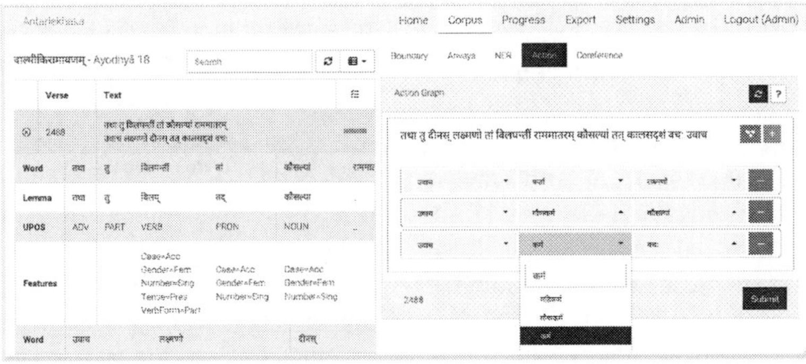

Figure 3: Annotation Interface: a Sanskrit corpus split into small units, and annotation area with task tabs

relevant to all languages.

The annotator's task is to identify and mark sentence boundaries by placing the delimiter '##' (two 'hash' symbols) at the end of each sentence in the provided editable text area prefilled with the original text. If the sentence does not end in the displayed unit, the user does not add any delimiters. After marking sentence boundaries, the user can proceed to the next annotation task. An illustration of this annotation task is shown in Fig. 6 (Appx. A).

It is worth mentioning that although the sentence boundary task is given primary citizen treatment, it can still be turned off for languages where it is not applicable. In such instances, the boundaries of annotation text units (e.g., verses) are treated as sentence boundaries.

3.3.2 Canonical Word Order

All sentences that end in the current unit of text are displayed to the annotator as a list of sortable tokens. The annotator can rearrange these tokens into the correct canonical word order by dragging them into place. Additionally, if any tokens are missing, the annotator can add them as well. A visual representation of this task is shown in Fig. 7 (Appx. A). The sorting capability is made possible through the use of the *jQuery UI (Sortable plugin)*[8].

3.3.3 Token Annotation

The token annotation interface allows an annotator to add free-form text associated with every token. This free-form text can have different purposes, such as to identify the root word of a word (lemmatization), to separate multi-word expressions into individual words (compound splitting), to analyze the morphological structure of a word (morphological analysis), etc. The token annotation interface is shown in Fig. 8 (Appx. A).

[8]https://api.jqueryui.com/sortable/

3.3.4 Token Classification

Token classification is a process of assigning predefined categories to individual tokens in text data. It is a special case of free-form token annotation, wherein the annotations are guided by an ontology. For such a task, an administrator must create an ontology. During the annotation process, an annotator is provided with a list of tokens, each accompanied by a dropdown menu, from which they can select the appropriate category for relevant tokens. Some common examples of token classification tasks include NER, dependency tagging, POS tagging, and compound classification. Fig. 9 (Appx. A) illustrates the token classification interface.

3.3.5 Token Graph

A token graph is a graph representation of the sentence, where the nodes are tokens belonging to a single sentence and the relations are based on an ontology. Tasks such as dependency parse tree, constituency graph, action graph are examples of tasks belonging to this category.

Semantic triple[9] is a standard format to represent and store graph-structured information in a relational database in a systematic manner. The interface allows an annotator to add multiple relations per sentence in the form of subject-predicate-object triples, where subject and object are tokens from the sentence and the predicate is a relation from the task specific ontology. The valid values of subject, object and predicate appear in individual dropdown menu elements for the annotator to choose from. Erroneous triples may also be removed. During the annotation process, an annotator can view the current status of the token graph at any time using the 'Show Graph' button. Fig. 10 (Appx. A) shows the token graph interface with graph visualization.

[9]https://en.wikipedia.org/wiki/Semantic_triple

3.3.6 Token Connection

Token connection is similar to token graph, however, there is a single type of relation to be captured. For example, when marking co-references, only connecting the two tokens to each other is sufficient, while the relationship 'is-coreference-of' is implicit. The tool provides a special simplified interface for this scenario. In addition to implicit relations, token connections can also be established across sentences. The annotator is presented with a list of clickable tokens from the current sentence as well as tokens from a context window of previous n (a configuration parameter with default as 5) sentences. The annotator can add a connection by clicking on the source token and the target token one after the other and confirming the connection. If a connection is added in error, it can be removed as well. In some cases, a connection might extend beyond the default context window. To address this, we have incorporated a button that an annotator can click to load additional context when needed. The token connection interface is shown in Fig. 11 (Appx. A).

3.3.7 Sentence Classification

Sentence classification is a task where sentences are classified into different categories, e.g., sentiment classification and sarcasm detection. This task is similar to ontology-driven token classification, with the difference being that classes are associated with sentences rather than tokens. The ontology is predefined by the administrator while setting up the task. The annotator can select the category for a sentence from a dropdown menu. Fig. 12 (Appx. A) illustrates the sentence classification interface.

3.3.8 Sentence Graph

Sentence graph is a graph representation of relationships between sentences, captured as subject-predicate-object triples. The connections can be between tokens or complete sentences. Tokens from the previous n (a configuration parameter with default as 5) sentences are presented as buttons arranged in the annotated word order. An annotator creates connections by clicking on the source and target tokens and selecting the relationship from a dropdown menu based on an ontology. A special token is provided to denote the entire sentence as an object. Tasks such as timeline annotation and discourse graphs are examples of tasks belonging to this category. Fig. 13 (Appx. A) shows the interface for creating sentence graph connections. Similar to the token graph task, an annotator can also visualize the sentence graph.

3.4 Clone Annotations

The administrative interface offers the capability to replicate annotations from one user to another. This feature proves valuable in cases where certain annotators possess expertise in specific tasks or if an annotator leaves a task incomplete, requiring another annotator to resume the task from their account. The cloned annotations are displayed just like regular annotations. However, they maintain the source information, including the annotator's ID and a reference to the original annotation.

3.5 Pluggable Heuristics

The tool supports the use of heuristics as 'pre-annotations' to assist annotators. Heuristics are custom functions that generate suggestions for the annotators to use or ignore. These heuristics are often specific to the language and corpus, and thus, must be implemented by the administrator when setting up the tool. The codebase of the tool outlines the format and type specifications of the heuristics, making them a pluggable component.

3.6 Progress Report

Detailed progress tracking serves multiple essential functions. Firstly, it provides project managers with the capability to allocate resources effectively and oversee the distribution of tasks among chapters. This facilitates the early detection of potential bottlenecks or areas needing extra focus. Moreover, the breakdown of progress contributes to streamlining the annotation process, guaranteeing the steady advancement of all chapters and tasks at an optimal rate. To facilitate this, we've developed an interface that offers a comprehensive overview of annotators' progress. This interface provides a detailed breakdown of advancements on a per-chapter and per-task basis, enabling thorough tracking and evaluation of their contributions.

3.7 Export

The export interface enables the access, retrieval and visualization of the annotated data for each task in a clear and straightforward manner. Annotator can easily view and export the data in two formats (1) a human-readable format for easy inspection and (2) a machine-readable format compatible with the standard NLP tools. The specifics of the standard format depend on the task. For example, a standard format for NER datasets is the BIO format (Tjong Kim Sang and De Meulder, 2003), which stands for *begin*, *inside*, and *outside*. The B-tag marks the beginning of a named entity, while the I-tag indicates the continuation of a named entity. The O-tag signifies that a word is not part of a named entity. Fig. 14 (Appx. A) illustrates the export interface showcasing the capability to export NER data in the standard BIO format. The interface facilitates the visualization and export of graph representations for tasks related to graphs. The export interface is accessible not only to annotators but also to curators, allowing them to review annotations made by other users. This feature serves as a mechanism for quality control.

3.8 Language Independence

Unicode is a widely used standard for encoding, representing, and handling text in a uniform and consistent way across various languages, computing platforms and applications. The standard assigns unique numerical codes to each character in a large number of scripts. Thus, full Unicode support allows users to work with text data in their preferred languages.

4 Evaluation

The tool is being used for annotation of a large corpus in Sanskrit, namely, *Valmiki Ramayana*. The details of this project are described in Sec. 4.3. Additionally, the tool is also being used for the annotation of plain text corpus in Bengali language.

Following (Terdalkar and Bhattacharya, 2021), we have evaluated our tool using a two-fold evaluation method of subjective and objective evaluation. We have not used the time taken for annotation as an evaluation metric since annotators often spend more time processing the text to identify the relevant information than physically annotating. Hence, it may not be a reliable measure.

4.1 Subjective Evaluation

For the subjective evaluation, an online survey was conducted, with participation from 16 annotators. They were asked to rate the tool on a scale of 1 to 5 across various categories including ease of use, annotation interface, and overall performance. The feedback from annotators was predominantly positive. The tool received a score of 4.3 for ease of use, 4.4 for annotation interface, and an overall score of 4.1. Furthermore, we gathered comments from users, and a word cloud over these comments can be found in Fig. 4.

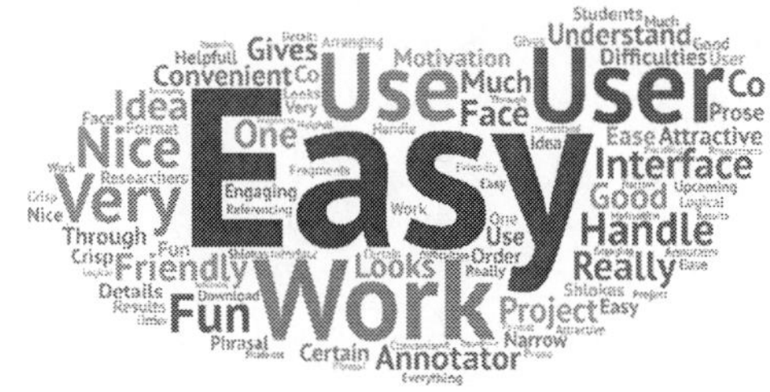

Figure 4: Word cloud of comments received in a survey

4.2 Objective Evaluation

The objective evaluation utilized a scoring mechanism similar to that employed in previous studies (Neves and Ševa, 2021; Terdalkar and Bhattacharya, 2021). We retained the additional categories introduced by (Terdalkar and Bhattacharya, 2021) while incorporating supplementary categories pertinent to the comprehensive assessment of a general-purpose NLP tool. These supplementary categories were designed to gauge the tool's support for a diverse range of NLP tasks. Consequently, a total of 29 categories were employed for the evaluation process. Each tool was assigned a rating: 1 for full support of a feature, 0.5 for partial support, and 0 for the absence of a feature.

In this evaluation, *Antarlekhaka* achieved a score of 0.79, outperforming other tools like *Sangrahaka* (0.74), *INCEpTION* (0.74) and *FLAT* (0.71). The detailed list of the 29 categories used for objectively scoring the annotation tools can be found in Tab. 2.

4.3 Case Study: Large Sanskrit Text

The *Valmiki Ramayana*, an ancient Sanskrit text, presents a rich and intricate narrative with a diverse array of characters, events, emotions, and settings, making it an ideal choice for annotation purposes. We employ Antarlekhaka, for this large-scale annotation task, as a case study. The text, sourced from the Digital Corpus of Sanskrit (DCS) (Hellwig, 2010–2021), comprises a total of 18754 verses distributed across 606 chapters.

The annotation is being performed with the help of 119 annotators to annotate 5 tasks per verse. These annotations have resulted in the following *task-specific datasets*:

- *Sentence Boundary*: 1972 sentence markers across 1499 verses;
- *Canonical Word Ordering*: 1886 sentences;

Table 2: Objective evaluation criteria for annotation tools. Each feature is evaluated on a ternary scale of 0, 0.5 and 1, where 0 indicates absence of the feature, 0.5 indicates partial support and 1 indicates full support for the feature.

Criteria			Tools					
ID	**Description**	**Weight**	**INCEpTION**	**doccano**	**FLAT**	**BRAT**	**Sangrahaka**	**Antarlekhaka**
P1	Year of the last publication	0	1	0	0	1	1	1
P2	Citations on Google Scholar	0	1	0	0	1	0	0
P3	Citations for Corpus Development	0	1	0	0	1	0	0
T1	Date of the last version	1	1	1	1	0.5	1	1
T2	Availability of the source code	1	1	1	1	1	1	1
T3	Online availability for use	1	0	0	1	0	0	0
T4	Easiness of Installation	1	0	1	1	0.5	1	1
T5	Quality of the documentation	1	1	1	1	1	0.5	0.5
T6	Type of license	1	1	1	1	1	1	1
T7	Free of charge	1	1	1	1	1	1	1
D1	Format of the schema	1	1	1	1	0.5	1	1
D2	Input format for documents	1	1	0.5	1	1	1	1
D3	Output format for annotations	1	1	1	1	0.5	0	0
F1	Allowance of multi-label annotations	1	1	0	1	1	1	1
F2	Allowance of document level annotations	0	0	0	0	0	0	0
F3	Support for annotation of relationships	1	1	0	0	1	1	1
F4	Support for ontologies and terminologies	1	1	0	1	1	1	1
F5	Support for pre-annotations	1	0.5	0	0.5	0.5	0	0
F6	Integration with PubMed	0	0	0	0	0	0	0
F7	Suitability for full texts	1	0.5	0.5	1	1	1	1
F8	Allowance for saving documents partially	1	1	1	1	1	1	1
F9	Ability to highlight parts of the text	1	1	1	1	1	1	1
F10	Support for users and teams	1	0.5	0.5	1	0.5	0.5	0.5
F11	Support for inter-annotator agreement	1	1	0.5	0	0.5	0.5	0.5
F12	Data privacy	1	1	1	1	1	1	1
F13	Support for various languages	1	1	1	1	1	1	1
A1	Support for querying	1	0	0	0	0	1	0
A2	Crash tolerance	1	0	0	0	0	1	0.5
A3	Web-based / Distributed annotation	1	1	1	1	1	1	1
A4	Sequential Annotation	1	0	0	0	0	1	1
A5	Support for Sentence Boundary Annotation	1	1	0	0	0	0	1
A6	Support for Word Order Annotation	1	0	0	0	0	0	1
A7	Support for Token Classification Tasks	1	1	1	1	1	1	1
A8	Support for Sentence Classification Tasks	1	1	0	0	0	0	1
	Total	29	21.5	16.0	20.5	18.5	21.5	**23.0**
	Score		0.74	0.55	0.71	0.64	0.74	**0.79**

- *Named Entity Recognition*: 1717 entities in 947 verses based on custom ontology with 89 labels;
- *Co-reference Resolution*: 2271 co-reference connections across 950 verses;
- *Action Graph*: 90 action graphs with 720 relations from 71 verses, where an *action graph* captures action-related words, encompassing verbs, participles, and other action-denoting words and their relationships with other words.

We continue to enhance these datasets through the ongoing annotation endeavour.

5 Potential for NLP Research

A natural language annotation tool simplifies the process of creating datasets for machine learning models, which is useful for NLP tasks such as lemmatization, NER, POS tagging, co-reference resolution, text classification, sentence classification, and relation extraction. Annotator-friendly and intuitive interfaces can simplify the otherwise tedious process of manual annotation process to a great extent. The effectiveness of higher-level tasks such as question-answering, grammatical error correction and machine translation often relies on the success of several low-level tasks, which can be handled by a multiple task annotation tool. The tool's ability to handle large amounts of data and multiple users simultaneously can contribute to faster completion of these tasks.

6 Conclusions

We have developed a web-based multi-task annotation tool called *Antarlekhaka* for sequential annotation of various NLP tasks. It is available at https://github.com/Antarlekhaka/code. The tool is language-agnostic and has full Unicode support. The tool sports eight categories of annotation tasks and an annotator-friendly interface for each category. Multiple annotation tasks from each category are supported. The tool enables creation of datasets for computational linguistics tasks without expecting any programming knowledge from the annotators or administrators. It is actively being used for a large-scale annotation project, involving a large Sanskrit corpus and a significant number of annotators, as well as another annotation task in Bengali language. *Antarlekhaka* has a potential to propel research opportunities in NLP by simplifying the conduction of large-scale annotation projects.

7 Limitations

While *Antarlekhaka* is a powerful tool for annotation, it does have some limitations. These include:

- *Subjectivity in annotations*: Manual annotation can introduce subjective biases and inconsistencies among annotators. Currently, there is no in-built automated mechanism to ensure inter-annotator agreement and quality check is performed manually with a small set of curators. Nevertheless, we plan to implement inter-annotator agreement metrics in future.
- *Language-specific challenges*: Antarlekhaka may encounter challenges specific to certain languages or linguistic phenomena, including variations in syntax, morphology, or semantic nuances that may require additional customization or fine-tuning. Additionally, languages with complex orthographic systems or unique writing conventions may pose difficulties.
- *Dependency on sequential annotation*: Sequential annotation is one of the strong features of the tool. However, if the sentence boundary detection task is enabled, it imposes a dependency in the sense that other tasks can be performed only after marking the sentence boundaries.
- *Constraints on AI-guided annotation support*: While Antarlekhaka supports incorporation of heuristics as pluggable components, the in-built support for AI-guided annotation is still limited in nature. The inherent language-specific characteristics and limitations of various NLP tools present challenges in delivering a fully language-agnostic guided annotation system. However, our future plans involve the integration of established NLP tools to offer more comprehensive guidance for annotators during the annotation process.

8 Ethics Statement

The research conducted in the development and use of *Antarlekhaka* adheres to ethical considerations and guidelines. The annotation tasks performed using the tool involve the analysis and processing of language data. We ensure the following ethical principles:

- *Informed Consent*: Prior to engaging in annotation tasks, all annotators participating in the research are informed about the nature of the tasks, their purpose, and the potential use of the annotated data. Annotators provide their voluntary consent to participate.
- *Anonymity and Privacy*: All personal information of annotators is kept confidential and handled securely. The data collected during the annotation process is anonymized to protect the privacy of individuals involved.
- *Data Usage*: The annotated data is solely used for research purposes and in compliance with relevant data protection regulations. It is not shared with any third parties without explicit consent or legal requirements.
- *Bias Mitigation*: We strive to minimize any biases that may arise during the annotation process. Annotators are provided with guidelines and training to ensure consistency and fairness in their annotations. Regular quality checks are being performed to address any potential bias issues for the Sanskrit text corpus.
- *Annotator Pool*: Annotators for the Sanskrit text corpus are under-graduate and post-graduate level Sanskrit students from various institutes and colleges. This ensured that annotations were of accepted quality. Participation in the annotation task was voluntary, and everybody who wanted to annotate was allowed to do so.

By adhering to these ethical principles, we aim to contribute to the responsible advancement of Natural Language Processing technologies and promote ethical practices in language annotation research.

References

Kalina Bontcheva, Hamish Cunningham, Ian Roberts, Angus Roberts, Valentin Tablan, Niraj Aswani, and Genevieve Gorrell. 2013. Gate teamware: a web-based, collaborative text annotation framework. *Language Resources and Evaluation*, 47(4):1007–1029.

Marie-Catherine De Marneffe, Christopher D Manning, Joakim Nivre, and Daniel Zeman. 2021. Universal dependencies. *Computational linguistics*, 47(2):255–308.

Manmatha Nath Dutt et al. 1891. *The Ramayana*, volume 1. Girish Chandra Chackravarti.

Karën Fort. 2016. *Collaborative annotation for reliable natural language processing: Technical and sociological aspects*. John Wiley & Sons.

Oliver Hellwig. 2010–2021. *The Digital Corpus of Sanskrit (DCS)*.

Hendrik Jacob Herik, Ana Paula Rocha, and Joaquim Filipe. 2018. *Agents and Artificial Intelligence: 9th International Conference, ICAART 2017, Porto, Portugal, February 24 {u2013} 26, 2017, Revised Selected Papers*. Springer International Publishing.

Jan-Christoph Klie, Michael Bugert, Beto Boullosa, Richard Eckart de Castilho, and Iryna Gurevych. 2018. The inception platform: Machine-assisted and knowledge-oriented interactive annotation. In *proceedings of the 27th international conference on computational linguistics: system demonstrations*, pages 5–9.

Amba Kulkarni, Preethi Shukla, Pavankumar Satuluri, and Devanand Shukl. 2015. How free is free word order in sanskrit. *The Sanskrit Library, USA*, pages 269–304.

Hiroki Nakayama, Takahiro Kubo, Junya Kamura, Yasufumi Taniguchi, and Xu Liang. 2018. doccano: Text annotation tool for human. Software available from https://github.com/doccano/doccano.

Mariana Neves and Jurica Ševa. 2021. An extensive review of tools for manual annotation of documents. *Briefings in bioinformatics*, 22(1):146–163.

Peng Qi, Yuhao Zhang, Yuhui Zhang, Jason Bolton, and Christopher D Manning. 2020. Stanza: A python natural language processing toolkit for many human languages. *arXiv preprint arXiv:2003.07082*.

Lane Schwartz. 2022. Primum non nocere: Before working with indigenous data, the acl must confront ongoing colonialism. In *Proceedings of the 60th Annual Meeting of the Association for Computational Linguistics*, volume 2.

Pontus Stenetorp, Sampo Pyysalo, Goran Topić, Tomoko Ohta, Sophia Ananiadou, and Jun'ichi Tsujii. 2012. Brat: a web-based tool for nlp-assisted text annotation. In *Proceedings of the Demonstrations at the 13th Conference of the European Chapter of the Association for Computational Linguistics*, pages 102–107.

Hrishikesh Terdalkar and Arnab Bhattacharya. 2021. Sangrahaka: A tool for annotating and querying knowledge graphs. In *Proceedings of the 29th ACM Joint Meeting on European Software Engineering Conference and Symposium on the Foundations of Software Engineering*, ESEC/FSE 2021, page 1520–1524, New York, NY, USA. Association for Computing Machinery.

Erik F Tjong Kim Sang and Fien De Meulder. 2003. Introduction to the conll-2003 shared task: language-independent named entity recognition. In *Proceedings of the seventh conference on Natural language learning at HLT-NAACL 2003-Volume 4*, pages 142–147.

Maarten van Gompel. 2014. Folia linguistic annotation tool. https://github.com/proycon/flat.

Seid Muhie Yimam, Iryna Gurevych, Richard Eckart de Castilho, and Chris Biemann. 2013. Webanno: A flexible, web-based and visually supported system for distributed annotations. In *Proceedings of the 51st Annual Meeting of the Association for Computational Linguistics: System Demonstrations*, pages 1–6.

A Screenshots of Various Interfaces

We showcase various interfaces of *Antarlekhaka* in this section. An administrative interface for managing tasks is shown in Fig. 5. Figs. 6 to 13 illustrate annotation interfaces for each task category. Fig. 14 highlights the export interface with the capability to export the data in the standard format.

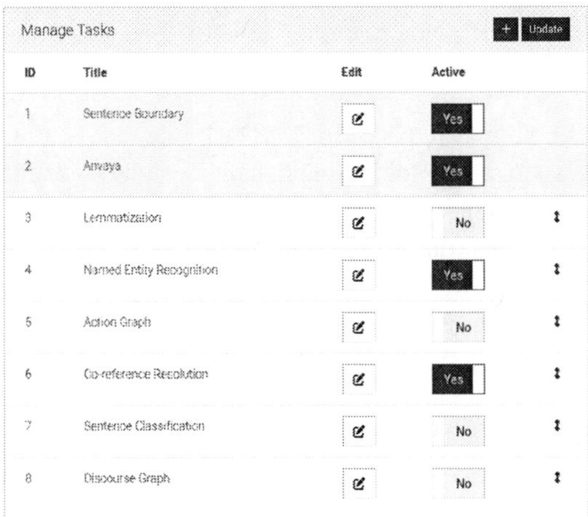

Figure 5: Task Management Interface: Add, Edit, Activate, Deactivate, Reorder Tasks

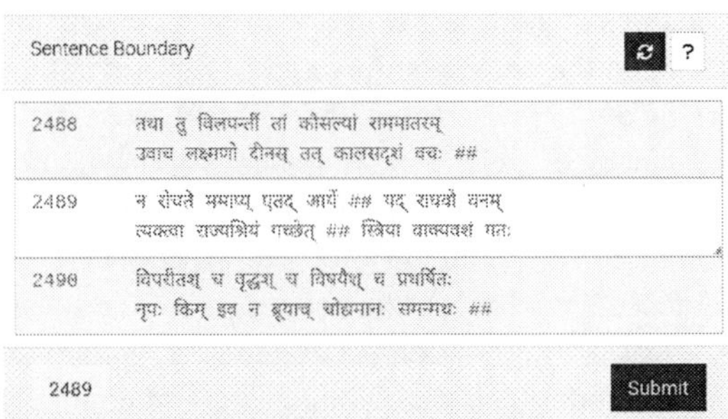

Figure 6: Sentence Boundary Annotation Interface

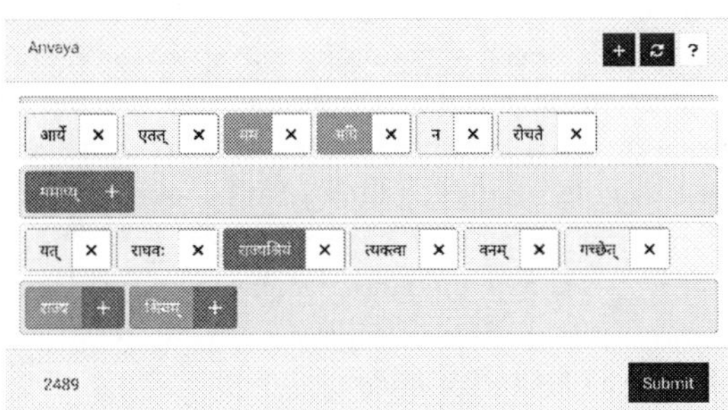

Figure 7: Word Order Annotation Interface

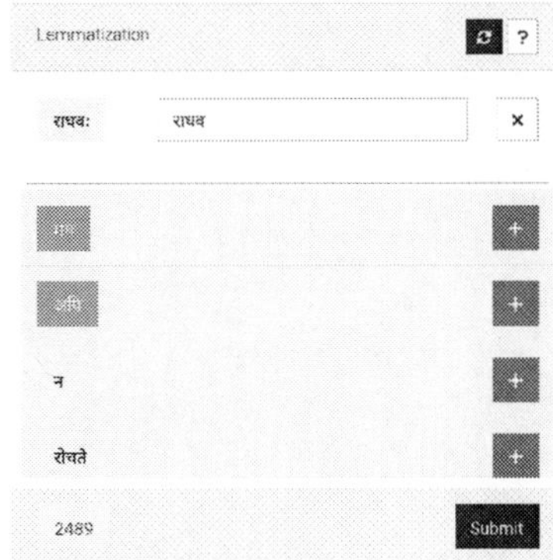

Figure 8: Token Annotation Interface: Lemmatization

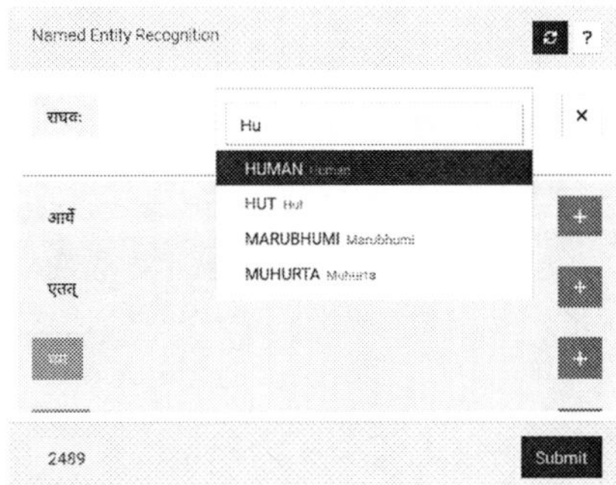

Figure 9: Token Classification Interface: Named Entity Recognition

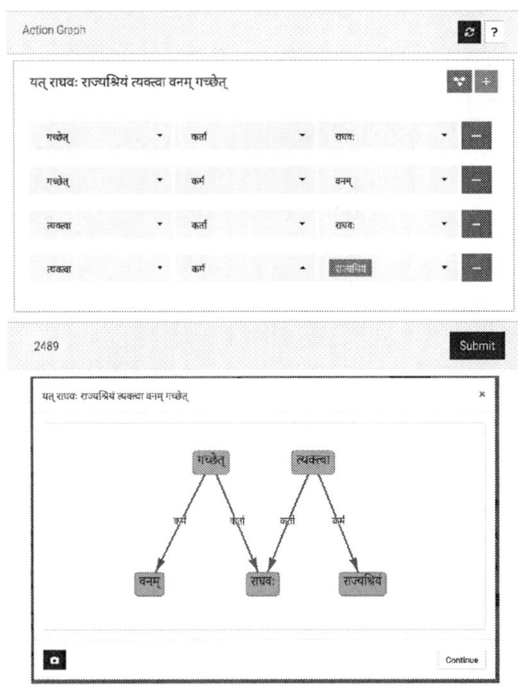

Figure 10: Token Graph Interface with Graph Visualization: Action Graph

Figure 11: Token Connection Interface: Co-reference Resolution

Figure 12: Sentence Classification Interface

Figure 13: Sentence Graph Interface

B Schema

Antarlekhaka utilizes a relational database to store information such as, corpus data, user data, task data and annotations. A relational database allows for efficient storage and retrieval of functional data, as well as the ability to establish relationships between different pieces of data. For example, annotations of specific verses by specific users can be linked allowing the system to quickly locate and display relevant annotations when needed.

B.1 Tasks

The information regarding tasks is stored in a single table within the relational database. This table serves as a centralized repository for information related to each task, including its title, category, and instructions for annotators. Each task is assigned a unique identifier known as a 'task id', which serves as a means of easily referring or linking to a specific task.

B.2 Ontology

Ontology is required for four task categories: token classification, token graph, sentence classification, and sentence graph. The ontology information is stored as a flat list of labels in four separate tables, each specific to a particular task category. There may be multiple tasks corresponding to each of these categories. Therefore, every ontology table also has a 'task id' column which associates the ontology entries with the corresponding tasks. This setup allows for clear organization and linking of the ontology information with the relevant tasks.

B.3 Annotations

There are eight annotation tables, each corresponding to a different category of annotation tasks. Annotations of all tasks belonging to each category are stored in the corresponding table. The annotations are linked to the semantic units of text, specifically, the sentences marked in the sentence boundary task. The other seven annotation tables include a reference to the 'boundary id'. In cases where the sentence boundary task is not necessary, the boundaries of the annotation text units (e.g., verse) are considered as sentence boundaries and annotated automatically in the background using a special annotation user. Additionally, to facilitate multiple instances of tasks from each task category, every annotation table contains a reference to the 'task id'. Finally, each annotation table sports a tailored schema to support the recording of task specific annotations. An 'annotator id' associated with every task annotation table, allows for proper organization and tracking of the annotations.

Fig. 15 shows the Entity Relationship (ER) diagram on a subset of tables from the relational database of *Antarlekhaka*.

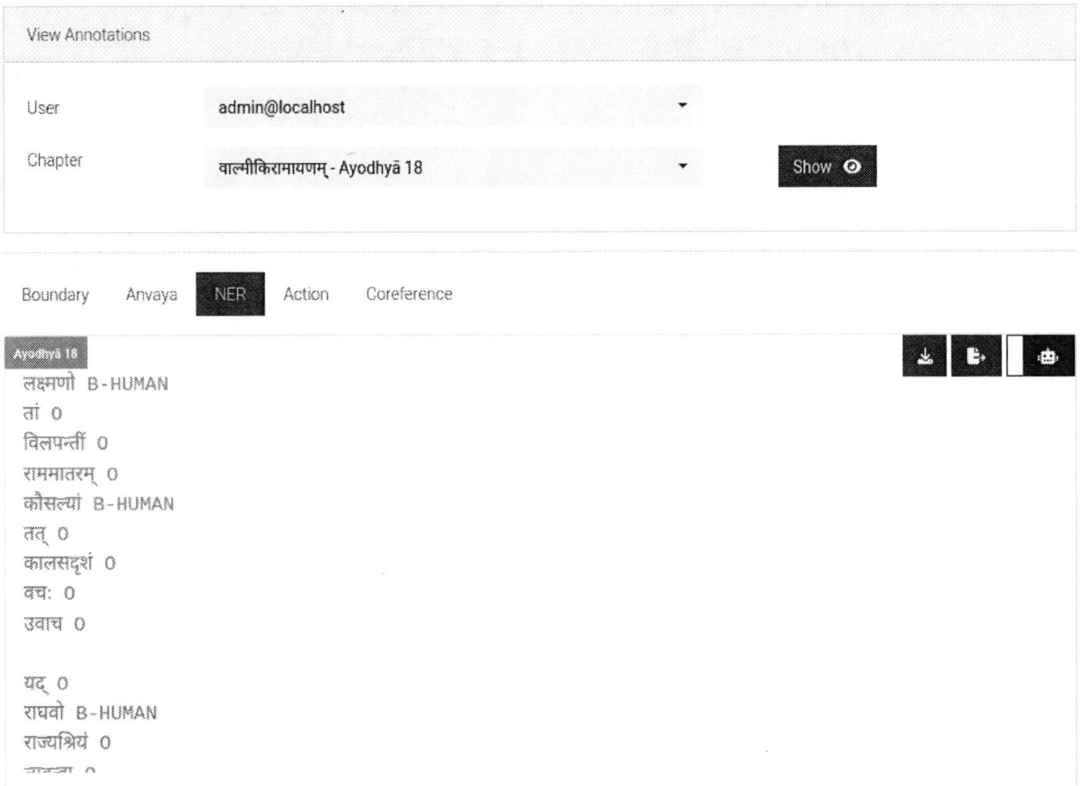

Figure 14: Export Interface: NER data in the standard BIO format

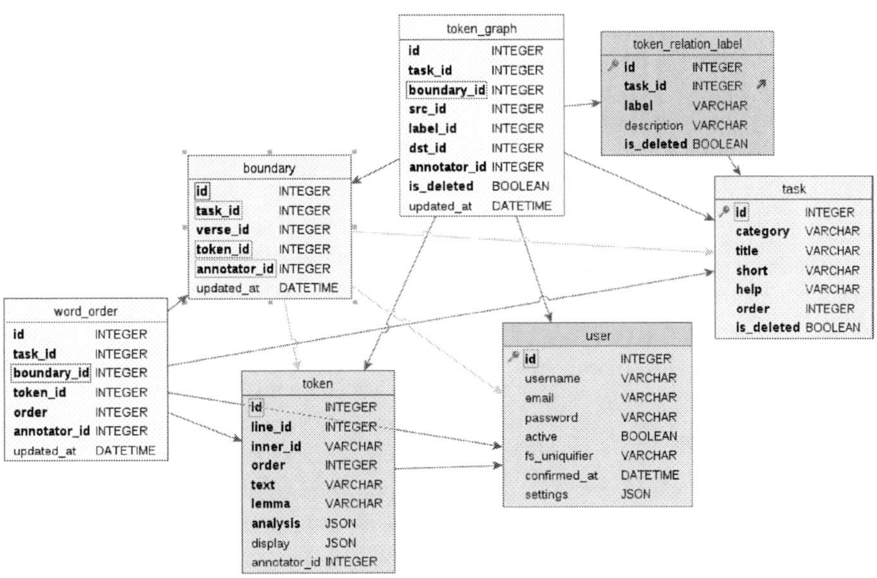

Figure 15: Entity Relationship Diagram illustrating some relevant links. Tables are color coded. Yellow: Annotation Tables, Orange: Ontology Tables, Blue: Corpus Tables, Pink: User Tables, Green: Task Information Table. The annotation table for 'Sentence Boundary' task is highlighted, showing the references incoming (red) and outgoing (green) references to other tables.

GPTCache: An Open-Source Semantic Cache for LLM Applications Enabling Faster Answers and Cost Savings

Bang Fu, Di Feng
Zilliz Inc.

Abstract

The rise of ChatGPT [1] has led to the development of artificial intelligence (AI) applications, particularly those that rely on large language models (LLMs). However, recalling LLM APIs can be expensive, and the response speed may slow down during LLMs' peak times, causing frustration among developers. Potential solutions to this problem include using better LLM models or investing in more computing resources. However, these options may increase product development costs and decrease development speed. GPTCache [2] is an open-source semantic cache that stores LLM responses to address this issue. When integrating an AI application with GPTCache, user queries are first sent to GPTCache for a response before being sent to LLMs like ChatGPT. If GPTCache has the answer to a question, it quickly returns the answer to the user without having to query the LLM. This approach saves costs on API recalls and makes response times much faster. For instance, integrating GPTCache with the GPT service offered by OpenAI can increase response speed 2-10 times when the cache is hit. Moreover, network fluctuations will not affect GPTCache's response time, making it highly stable. This paper presents GPTCache and its architecture, how it functions and performs, and the use cases for which it is most advantageous.

1 Introduction

Since OpenAI released ChatGPT, large language models have impressed many people and have been frequently integrated into our daily work and lives. At the same time, more open-source enthusiasts and tech companies have invested time and effort into developing open-source LLMs, such as Meta's LLama (Touvron et al., 2023a,b), Google's PaLM (Chowdhery et al., 2022), Stanford's Alpaca (Wang et al., 2023; Taori et al., 2023), and Databrick's Dolly (Conover et al., 2023).

There are two ways to use large language models: online services provided by companies like OpenAI, Claude, and Cohere or downloading open-source models and deploying them on your servers. Both methods require payment. Online services charge you based on tokens, while deploying models on your own server requires purchasing specific computing resources. The choice depends on individual needs.

While online services are more expensive, they are more convenient and effective and provide a better user experience than deploying models yourself. Costs and user experience are two critical considerations for building LLM applications. As your LLM application gains popularity and experiences a surge in traffic, the cost of LLM API calls will increase significantly. High response latency will also be frustrating, particularly during peak times for LLMs, directly affecting the user experience.

GPTCache is an open-source semantic cache designed to improve the efficiency and speed of GPT-based applications by storing and retrieving the responses generated by language models. Unlike traditional cache systems such as Redis, GPTCache employs semantic caching, which stores and retrieves data through embeddings. It utilizes embedding algorithms to transform the queries and LLMs' responses into embeddings and conducts similarity searches on these embeddings using a vector store such as Milvus. GPTCache allows users to customize the cache to their specific requirements, offering a range of choices for embedding, similarity assessment, storage location, and eviction policies. Furthermore, GPTCache supports both the OpenAI ChatGPT interface and the Langchain interface, with plans to support more interfaces in the coming months.

Through experiments using the `paraphrase-albert-small-v2` model (Reimers

[1] `https://openai.com/chatgpt`

[2] `https://github.com/zilliztech/GPTCache`

Proceedings of the 3rd Workshop for Natural Language Processing Open Source Software (NLP-OSS 2023), pages 212–218
December 6, 2023

and Gurevych, 2019) to embed input in the onnx runtime environment and running it on a local Mac with i7, 4CPU, and 32G memory, the time consumed when hitting the cache is approximately 0.3 seconds. Compared to accessing OpenAI ChatGPT with an average response latency of 3 seconds, the time consumed is only 1/10. Furthermore, no tokens are consumed when hitting the cache. Different embedding models and similarity evaluation algorithms must be selected in real development scenarios based on the tolerance for cache errors. Even so, the entire consumption time is about 3-4 times faster.

2 Related Works

2.1 Accelerating LLM Inference

Accelerating LLM Inference. Large language models (LLMs) typically take seconds to infer answers, prompting researchers to explore ways to reduce inference time and resource consumption. One approach is quantization (Dettmers and Zettlemoyer, 2023), which decreases the number of bits needed to represent each parameter and, therefore reduces the model size. However, this can result in a trade-off between accuracy and memory footprint. Another method is pruning, which can sparsify large-scale generative pre-trained transformer (GPT) models without retraining, as demonstrated by SparseGPT (Frantar and Alistarh, 2023). Additional methods include Compressing (Xu et al., 2020) and Inference with Reference (Yang et al., 2023).

2.2 Widespread application of Caching

Widespread application of Caching. Caching is a commonly used technique to reduce frequent and computationally expensive data accesses, which can improve system query performance. Many different caching schemes have been proposed for various scenarios. For example, semantic knowledge extracted from data can convert cache misses to cache hits, avoiding unnecessary access to web sources (Lee and Chu, 1999). Another example is in querying multiple databases with sensitive information, where a differentially private cache of past responses can answer the current workload at a lower privacy budget while meeting strict accuracy guarantees (Mazmudar et al., 2022). In addition, a cached memory architecture for new changes to embedding tables has been proposed during embedding. In this architecture, most rows in embeddings are trained at low precision, while the most frequent or recently accessed rows are cached and trained at full precision (Yang et al., 2020). As demonstrated, caching is applied in a variety of real-world development processes.

2.3 Embedding Models

Embedding models (Almeida and Xexéo, 2023) are a type of machine learning model that map discrete symbols or objects (such as text, images, audio, etc.) to continuous vector spaces. These vectors are called embedding vectors and are indispensable in many natural language processing (NLP) and computer vision (CV) tasks.

In NLP tasks, embedding models aim to map text into a low-dimensional continuous vector space. This makes it easier for machine learning models to process the text. The vectors can capture semantic information about the text, such as its meaning in context. In CV tasks, embedding models can map images, videos, or objects into a vector space. This approach allows them to be processed by computer vision algorithms, such as image search and identification. Common text embedding models include BERT (Devlin et al., 2019), GloVe (Pennington et al., 2014), and Word2Vec (Goldberg and Levy, 2014; Mikolov et al., 2013). These models generate embedding vectors by processing large amounts of text data. They can also perform well in many NLP tasks, such as semantic similarity calculation, part-of-speech tagging, named entity recognition, and sentiment analysis.

2.4 Vector Store

A vector database is designed for storing and managing vector data. Vector data consists of sequences of numbers commonly used to represent objects or features in high-dimensional spaces. For example, data types such as images, audio, and natural language text can be represented as vector data.

Vector databases improve the efficiency and accuracy of vector data retrieval by using vector similarity measures to index and query the data. This indexing technique allows the database to quickly find vectors most similar to a query vector, making it useful for various applications such as sentiment analysis, image search, speech recognition, and recommendation systems.

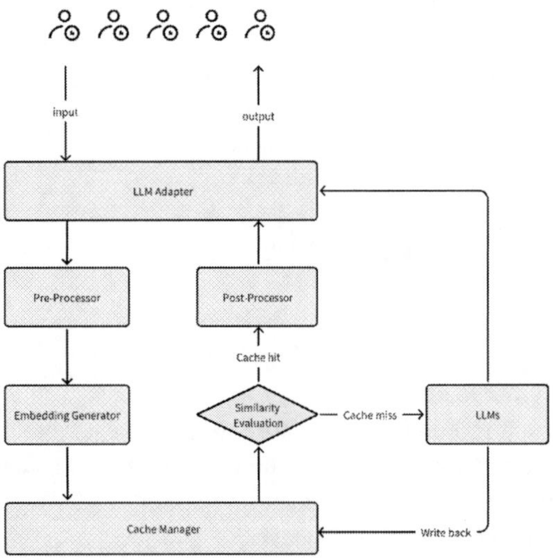

Figure 1: GPTCache: The architecture comprises six core components: adapter, pre-processor, embedding generator, cache manager, similarity evaluator, and post-processor.

3 GPTCache: Semantic Cache for LLMs

The overall workflow of GPTCache follows the general cache pattern - attempting to obtain results from the cache before fetching data or processing requests. If successful, the process terminates immediately. Otherwise, the processing path is the same as if the cache did not exist. However, before returning, the corresponding results are stored in the cache so that repeated actions will retrieve results directly from the cache next time. Using the cache significantly reduces workflow time, which explains why cache designs are ubiquitous in our lives, such as multi-level caches in computers, DNS caches in networks, and Redis/Memcache in management systems.

3.1 Adapter

The adapter serves as the interface for GPTCache to interact with the outside world. It is responsible for converting LLM requests into cache protocols, controlling the entire cache workflow, and transforming cache results into LLM responses. For easy integration of GPTCache into our systems or other ChatGPT-based systems without extra development effort, the adapter should be easy to integrate with all LLMs and flexible enough to integrate more multimodal models in the future.

3.2 Pre-Processor

The pre-processor handles the input of LLM requests primarily by formatting the information as the primary key for the cache data. This includes removing prompt information from inputs, compressing input information, and only retaining the last certain words for long texts or the last round in a multi-round conversation. These operations make the request data more distinguishable from each other and remove redundant and irrelevant information from the requests.

Pre-processing is a critical factor affecting the performance of the cache. For example, suppose both inputs contain a large portion of prompt information, where the key part of the information is only a small portion of the entire input. In that case, the cache cannot obtain the key information without eliminating the prompt. This can result in a high probability that all requests hit the cache. The preprocessed results are passed to the Embedding component for vector conversion.

3.3 Embedding Generator

The embedding generator can convert user queries into embedding vectors for later vector similarity retrieval. There are two methods to achieve this functionality. The first method generates embedding vectors through cloud services (such as OpenAI, Hugging Face, Cohere, etc.). The second method involves generating embedding vectors using local models that can be downloaded from sources such as HuggingFace or GitHub.

3.4 Cache Manager

The cache manager is the core component of GPTCache and has three functions:

- Cache storage: stores user requests and corresponding LLM responses.
- Vector storage: stores embedding vectors and retrieves similar results.
- Eviction management: controls cache capacity and clears expired data according to LRU or FIFO policy when the cache is full.

Before a piece of data is stored, an id will be generated. The id and scalar data will be stored in cache storage, and the id and vector data will be stored in vertor storage. In this way, cache storage and vertor storage are associated. Eviction management also records these IDs. When cache data needs to be cleared, the data corresponding to cache storage and vertor storage will be deleted based on the id.

The eviction manager releases the cache space by deleting data that has been unused for a long time or is furthest away from using in the GPT-Cache. If necessary, it removes data from both the cache and vector store. However, frequent deletion operations in the vector store can lead to performance degradation. Therefore, GPTCache only triggers asynchronous operations (e.g., index building, compression, etc.) upon reaching deletion thresholds.

3.5 Similarity Evaluator

GPTCache retrieves the Top-K most similar answers from its cache and uses a similarity evaluation function to determine if the cached answer matches the input query. The similarity evaluation module is also crucial for GPTCache. After research, we eventually adopted the fine-tuned ALBERT model. Of course, there is still room for improvement here, and other language models or LLMs (such as LLaMa-7b) can also be used.

3.6 Post-Processor

The post-processor is responsible for preparing the final response to be returned to the user. It can either return the most similar response or adjust the response's randomness based on the request's temperature parameter. If a similar response is not found in the cache, the LLM will handle the request to generate a response. The generated response will be stored in the cache before being returned to the user.

3.7 Key GPTCache Use Cases

Not all LLM applications are suitable for GPT-Cache, as the cache hit rate is a crucial factor for the cache's effectiveness. If the cache hit rate is too low, the return on investment cannot balance the input, and there is no need to spend effort on this feature. This is similar to traditional caching scenarios, where caching is usually done only on frequently accessed public nodes to maximize resource utilization and system performance and improve user experience.

This paper introduces three critical practical situations where GPTCache is most beneficial:

1. LLM applications designed for specific domains of expertise, such as law, biology, medicine, finance, and other specialized fields.

2. LLM applications applied to specific use cases, such as internal company ChatBots or personal assistants like chat-pdf and chat-paper. These applications can be enhanced with a cutting-edge AI technology stack called CVP[3] (ChatGPT+Vector DB]+prompt engineering). This combination overcomes the limitations of knowledge bases and enables further expansion and innovation.

3. LLM applications with large user groups can benefit from using the same cache for user groups with the same profile if user profiling and classification can be done. This approach yields good returns.

4 Experiments

To evaluate GPTCache, we randomly scrape some information from the webpage, and then let chatgpt produce a corresponding data (similar or exactly opposite). And then we created a dataset consisting of three types of sentence pairs:

- Similar sample pairs: two sentences with identical semantics
- Opposite sample pairs: two sentences with related but not identical semantics
- Unrelated sample pairs: two sentences with completely different semantics

Then we evaluate the effectiveness of cache through five indicators, which are:

1. Cache Hit, which successfully finds similar values based on the input, which consists of Positive Hits and Negative Hits.

2. Cache Miss, no similar value was found based on the input

3. Positive Hits, the obtained cache value is confirmed to be similar to the input value

4. Negative Hits, the obtained cache value is found to be not similar through inspection.

[3]https://zilliz.com/blog/ChatGPT-VectorDB-Prompt-as-code

Cache Hit	Cache Miss	Positive Hits	Negative Hits	Hit Latency
876	124	837	39	0.20 s

Table 1: Results for Caching Hit and Miss Samples, Caching Mixed Positive and Negative Queries, and Hit Latency

Cache Hit	Cache Miss	Positive Hits	Negative Hits	Hit Latency
570	590	549	21	0.17 s

Table 2: Results for Caching Hit and Miss Samples, Caching Mixed Positive and Negative Queries, and Hit Latency

5. Hit Latency, it includes pre-processing time, cache data search time, similarity calculation time and post-processing time. The pre-processing and post-processing do not use the model during the test process, and are just simple character or number comparisons.

In addition, we tried different similarity algorithms and found that they had no impact on the results, so we used the common cosine similarity.

First, we cached the keys of all 30,000 positive sample pairs. Next, we randomly selected 1,000 samples and used their peer values as queries. Table 1 presents the results.

We found setting the similarity threshold of GPTCache to 0.7 achieves a good balance between hit and positive ratios. So we used this for subsequent tests.

To determine if a cached result is positive or negative to the query, we used the similarity score from ChatGPT with a positive threshold of 0.7. We generated this by prompting:

> Please rate the similarity of the following two questions on a scale from 0 to 1, where 0 means not related and 1 means exactly the same meaning. And questions, "Which app lets you watch live football for free?" and "How can I watch a football live match on my phone?" The similarity score is.

We issued 1,160 queries with 50% positive and 50% unrelated negative samples. Table 2 presents the results. The hit ratio was about 50%, and the negative hit ratio was similar to Experiment 1, indicating GPTCache successfully distinguished related and unrelated queries.

Next, we tried to also cache all negative samples and queried with their peers. Surprisingly, despite high ChatGPT similarity scores (over 0.9) for some pairs, none hit the cache. The cause of the cache error could be the similarity evaluator's fine-tuning on this dataset correctly undervalued the similarity of negative pairs.

The initial experiments demonstrate that GPTCache can effectively utilize semantic similarity to cache LLM query-response pairs and achieve significant speedups. We plan to conduct more rigorous evaluations on larger and more diverse datasets. When tuning the similarity threshold, further investigation is required to balance cache hits versus false positives.

5 Future Challenges

One core factor affecting GPTCache's caching effectiveness is the choice of embedding model. Compared to other component selections, the choice of embedding model is crucial because subsequent vector database retrieval relies on the embedding vectors. If the vectors cannot adequately capture the features of the input text, the retrieval results will be very noisy or even counterproductive, returning completely irrelevant cached data. Our testing has shown that even the best cache hit rates do not exceed 90% with current embedding models. This means that negative cache hits are noticeable during use. While this may not greatly impact individual users, it would be unacceptable in real production scenarios. Although other methods, like more strict similarity evaluation, could improve positive cache hit rates, this would also decrease the overall hit rate. Most current embedding models are likely optimized for search scenarios but may not work as well for cache matching. For example, results with semantics opposite to the input text are acceptable in search since they have structural similarity, but this is unacceptable in caching scenarios. Naturally, how to obtain embeddings suitable for caching is an open area for exploration.

Even with a suitable embedding model, positive hit rates are unlikely to reach production requirements, such as 99%, without decreasing cache hits. The similarity evaluation module plays a core role in improving positive cache hit rates by filtering incorrect hits. Our current implementations include vector distance, retrieving distance, cohere rerank

API, and sbert cross-encoder. However, testing shows these methods do not sufficiently distinguish between positive and negative cache hits. To address this, we are using large models to judge sentence similarity and distill them into a small model to obtain a specialized model for textual similarity.

As large language models are widely adopted, their supported token counts have increased from 2k initially to 100k. However, if a single input exceeds the LLM's token count limit, it cannot process the request. Similarly, conversations with total tokens exceeding the limit must drop some information. Large token counts from long texts or conversations pose a challenge for caching, making it difficult to identify key information and generate representative vectors. Currently, we utilize summary models to pre-process and shorten long inputs, but this approach increases cache instability, and its effectiveness is not optimistic. Therefore, special cache lookup methods may be needed for long texts.

As mentioned earlier, is there any alternative to retrieving cache data using vector databases? For example, can we use traditional databases like MySQL, PostgreSQL, SQL Server, or Oracle to store cache data, with textual pre-rocessing to standardize user inputs? For instance, when the inputs are "tell me a joke" and "I want to get a joke", can we convert them to a certain string, like "tell a joke" , or a same number? Cache hits could then utilize string matching or numeric ranges instead of vectors.

6 Conclusion

GPTCache is a caching solution tailored for LLM applications. It brings the following benefits to the LLM app developers:

- Less costs: Most LLM services charge fees based on a combination of the number of requests and token count. GPTCache can effectively minimize expenses by caching query results, thereby reducing the number of requests and tokens sent to the LLM service.

- Faster response times: LLMs utilize generative AI to produce responses in real-time, which can be time-consuming. However, when a similar query is cached, the response time greatly improves, as the result is retrieved directly from the cache without interaction with the LLM service. In most cases, GPTCache can also offer better query throughput than standard LLM services.

- More scalable and available: LLM services often impose rate limits on the number of access requests within a given timeframe. If these limits are exceeded, additional requests are blocked until a cooldown period has elapsed, leading to service outages. GPTCache allows you to easily scale and handle increasing query volumes, ensuring consistent performance as your application's user base expands.

By utilizing semantic similarity search and vector embeddings, GPTCache provides an effective caching solution that enhances performance, reduces costs, and improves scalability for applications that use large language models. Our initial experiments have shown great potential, and we plan to conduct more comprehensive evaluations on diverse real-world datasets and application scenarios.

References

Felipe Almeida and Geraldo Xexéo. 2023. Word embeddings: A survey.

Aakanksha Chowdhery, Sharan Narang, Jacob Devlin, Maarten Bosma, Gaurav Mishra, Adam Roberts, Paul Barham, Hyung Won Chung, Charles Sutton, Sebastian Gehrmann, Parker Schuh, Kensen Shi, Sasha Tsvyashchenko, Joshua Maynez, Abhishek Rao, Parker Barnes, Yi Tay, Noam Shazeer, Vinodkumar Prabhakaran, Emily Reif, Nan Du, Ben Hutchinson, Reiner Pope, James Bradbury, Jacob Austin, Michael Isard, Guy Gur-Ari, Pengcheng Yin, Toju Duke, Anselm Levskaya, Sanjay Ghemawat, Sunipa Dev, Henryk Michalewski, Xavier Garcia, Vedant Misra, Kevin Robinson, Liam Fedus, Denny Zhou, Daphne Ippolito, David Luan, Hyeontaek Lim, Barret Zoph, Alexander Spiridonov, Ryan Sepassi, David Dohan, Shivani Agrawal, Mark Omernick, Andrew M. Dai, Thanumalayan Sankaranarayana Pillai, Marie Pellat, Aitor Lewkowycz, Erica Moreira, Rewon Child, Oleksandr Polozov, Katherine Lee, Zongwei Zhou, Xuezhi Wang, Brennan Saeta, Mark Diaz, Orhan Firat, Michele Catasta, Jason Wei, Kathy Meier-Hellstern, Douglas Eck, Jeff Dean, Slav Petrov, and Noah Fiedel. 2022. Palm: Scaling language modeling with pathways.

Mike Conover, Matt Hayes, Ankit Mathur, Jianwei Xie, Jun Wan, Sam Shah, Ali Ghodsi, Patrick Wendell, Matei Zaharia, and Reynold Xin. 2023. Free dolly: Introducing the world's first truly open instruction-tuned llm.

Tim Dettmers and Luke Zettlemoyer. 2023. The case for 4-bit precision: k-bit inference scaling laws. In *Proceedings of the 40th International Conference on Machine Learning*, volume 202 of *Proceedings of Machine Learning Research*, pages 7750–7774. PMLR.

Jacob Devlin, Ming-Wei Chang, Kenton Lee, and Kristina Toutanova. 2019. BERT: Pre-training of deep bidirectional transformers for language understanding. In *Proceedings of the 2019 Conference of the North American Chapter of the Association for Computational Linguistics: Human Language Technologies, Volume 1 (Long and Short Papers)*, pages 4171–4186, Minneapolis, Minnesota. Association for Computational Linguistics.

Elias Frantar and Dan Alistarh. 2023. SparseGPT: Massive language models can be accurately pruned in one-shot. *arXiv preprint arXiv:2301.00774*.

Yoav Goldberg and Omer Levy. 2014. word2vec explained: deriving mikolov et al.'s negative-sampling word-embedding method. *CoRR*, abs/1402.3722.

Dongwon Lee and Wesley W. Chu. 1999. Semantic caching via query matching for web sources. In *Proceedings of the Eighth International Conference on Information and Knowledge Management*, CIKM '99, page 77–85, New York, NY, USA. Association for Computing Machinery.

Miti Mazmudar, Thomas Humphries, Jiaxiang Liu, Matthew Rafuse, and Xi He. 2022. Cache me if you can: Accuracy-aware inference engine for differentially private data exploration.

Tomás Mikolov, Kai Chen, Greg Corrado, and Jeffrey Dean. 2013. Efficient estimation of word representations in vector space. In *1st International Conference on Learning Representations, ICLR 2013, Scottsdale, Arizona, USA, May 2-4, 2013, Workshop Track Proceedings*.

Jeffrey Pennington, Richard Socher, and Christopher Manning. 2014. GloVe: Global vectors for word representation. In *Proceedings of the 2014 Conference on Empirical Methods in Natural Language Processing (EMNLP)*, pages 1532–1543, Doha, Qatar. Association for Computational Linguistics.

Nils Reimers and Iryna Gurevych. 2019. Sentence-BERT: Sentence embeddings using Siamese BERT-networks. In *Proceedings of the 2019 Conference on Empirical Methods in Natural Language Processing and the 9th International Joint Conference on Natural Language Processing (EMNLP-IJCNLP)*, pages 3982–3992, Hong Kong, China. Association for Computational Linguistics.

Rohan Taori, Ishaan Gulrajani, Tianyi Zhang, Yann Dubois, Xuechen Li, Carlos Guestrin, Percy Liang, and Tatsunori B. Hashimoto. 2023. Stanford alpaca: An instruction-following llama model. `https://github.com/tatsu-lab/stanford_alpaca`.

Hugo Touvron, Thibaut Lavril, Gautier Izacard, Xavier Martinet, Marie-Anne Lachaux, Timothée Lacroix, Baptiste Rozière, Naman Goyal, Eric Hambro, Faisal Azhar, Aurelien Rodriguez, Armand Joulin, Edouard Grave, and Guillaume Lample. 2023a. Llama: Open and efficient foundation language models.

Hugo Touvron, Louis Martin, Kevin Stone, Peter Albert, Amjad Almahairi, Yasmine Babaei, Nikolay Bashlykov, Soumya Batra, Prajjwal Bhargava, Shruti Bhosale, Dan Bikel, Lukas Blecher, Cristian Canton Ferrer, Moya Chen, Guillem Cucurull, David Esiobu, Jude Fernandes, Jeremy Fu, Wenyin Fu, Brian Fuller, Cynthia Gao, Vedanuj Goswami, Naman Goyal, Anthony Hartshorn, Saghar Hosseini, Rui Hou, Hakan Inan, Marcin Kardas, Viktor Kerkez, Madian Khabsa, Isabel Kloumann, Artem Korenev, Punit Singh Koura, Marie-Anne Lachaux, Thibaut Lavril, Jenya Lee, Diana Liskovich, Yinghai Lu, Yuning Mao, Xavier Martinet, Todor Mihaylov, Pushkar Mishra, Igor Molybog, Yixin Nie, Andrew Poulton, Jeremy Reizenstein, Rashi Rungta, Kalyan Saladi, Alan Schelten, Ruan Silva, Eric Michael Smith, Ranjan Subramanian, Xiaoqing Ellen Tan, Binh Tang, Ross Taylor, Adina Williams, Jian Xiang Kuan, Puxin Xu, Zheng Yan, Iliyan Zarov, Yuchen Zhang, Angela Fan, Melanie Kambadur, Sharan Narang, Aurelien Rodriguez, Robert Stojnic, Sergey Edunov, and Thomas Scialom. 2023b. Llama 2: Open foundation and fine-tuned chat models.

Yizhong Wang, Yeganeh Kordi, Swaroop Mishra, Alisa Liu, Noah A. Smith, Daniel Khashabi, and Hannaneh Hajishirzi. 2023. Self-instruct: Aligning language models with self-generated instructions. In *Proceedings of the 61st Annual Meeting of the Association for Computational Linguistics (Volume 1: Long Papers)*, pages 13484–13508, Toronto, Canada. Association for Computational Linguistics.

Canwen Xu, Wangchunshu Zhou, Tao Ge, Furu Wei, and Ming Zhou. 2020. BERT-of-theseus: Compressing BERT by progressive module replacing. In *Proceedings of the 2020 Conference on Empirical Methods in Natural Language Processing (EMNLP)*, pages 7859–7869, Online. Association for Computational Linguistics.

Jie Amy Yang, Jianyu Huang, Jongsoo Park, Ping Tak Peter Tang, and Andrew Tulloch. 2020. Mixed-precision embedding using a cache.

Nan Yang, Tao Ge, Liang Wang, Binxing Jiao, Daxin Jiang, Linjun Yang, Rangan Majumder, and Furu Wei. 2023. Inference with reference: Lossless acceleration of large language models.

The Vault: A Comprehensive Multilingual Dataset for Advancing Code Understanding and Generation

Dung Nguyen Manh[1,*], **Nam Le Hai**[1,3,*], **Anh T. V. Dau**[1,3], **Anh Minh Nguyen**[1], **Khanh Nghiem**[1], **Jin Guo**[4,5], **Nghi D. Q. Bui**[2]

[1]FPT Software AI Center
{dungnm31, namlh35, anhdtv7, minhna4, khanhnv22}@fpt.com

[2]Fulbright University, Viet Nam
nghi.bui@fulbright.edu.vn

[3]Hanoi University of Science and Technology, Viet Nam
[4]School of Computer Science, McGill University, Canada
[5]Mila - Quebec AI Institute

Abstract

We present The Vault, an open-source dataset of high quality code-text pairs in multiple programming languages for training large language models to understand and generate code. We propose methods for thoroughly extracting samples that use both rules and deep learning to ensure that they contain high-quality pairs of code and text, resulting in a dataset of 42 million high-quality code-text pairs. We thoroughly evaluated this dataset and discovered that when used to train common code language models (such as CodeT5, CodeBERT, and CodeGen), it outperforms the same models train on other datasets such as CodeSearchNet. These evaluations included common coding tasks such as code generation, code summarization, and code search. The Vault can be used by researchers and practitioners to train a wide range of big language models that understand code. Alternatively, researchers can use our data cleaning methods and scripts to improve their own datasets. We anticipate that using The Vault to train large language models will improve their ability to understand and generate code, propelling AI research and software development forward. We are releasing our source code and a framework to make it easier for others to replicate our results.

1 Introduction

The advent of deep learning and advancements in large language models (LLMs) have spurred a revolution in the field of code representation learning. These developments, supported by the growing accessibility of vast open-source code repositories, have heralded the emergence of code large language models (CodeLLMs) for code generation and understanding tasks. The sheer volume of these repositories and the rich, unprocessed raw data they contain, serve as unparalleled resources for training LLMs. Consequently, current state-of-the-art models for coding tasks effectively utilize these expansive datasets for training. However, it is important to note that these datasets, including The Stack [Kocetkov et al., 2022] and The Pile [Gao et al., 2020a], often comprise unprocessed data.

Alternatively, there are established datasets, such as CONCODE [Iyer et al., 2018b], FunCom [LeClair et al., 2019], Deepcom [Hu et al., 2020] for code summarization tasks; APPS [Hendrycks et al., 2021] for text-to-code generation; and CodeSearchNet [Husain et al., 2019] for code search. These datasets contain carefully curated code-text pairs. Although considerably smaller in comparison to raw code datasets (e.g., 2.3M functions in CodeSearchNet [Husain et al., 2019] versus 197M files in The Stack [Kocetkov et al., 2022]), they provide high-quality code-text pairings that significantly enhance the effectiveness of model training.

Consequently, we identify two main types of datasets used to train CodeLLMs: large yet unprocessed, and smaller yet well-structured (e.g., arranged into code-text pairs). The scaling law [Kaplan et al., 2020, Gordon et al., 2021, Sorscher et al., 2022] indicates that the volume of training data is crucial for model performance. However, other studies underscore the importance of dataset quality over quantity in training superior LLMs [Zhou et al., 2023, Sorscher et al., 2022, Dau et al., 2022, Brown et al., 2020, Khan et al., 2020].

* Equal contribution

Proceedings of the 3rd Workshop for Natural Language Processing Open Source Software (NLP-OSS 2023), pages 219–244
December 6, 2023 ©2023 Association for Computational Linguistics

Given these observations, we propose that an ideal dataset for training CodeLLMs should combine both elements: it should be expansive in volume and meticulously processed to ensure quality.

In this paper, we present The Vault dataset, detailing its creation process, the toolkit developed for constructing and quality-controlling code-text pairs from raw source code, as well as an analysis of The Vault's metrics. We also share empirical results obtained from utilizing The Vault to fine-tune well-known foundational models. Our specific contributions include the following:

- A dataset with approximately 42M pairs of high-quality code-text pairs (approximately 10 times larger than CoDesc), 243M unimodal samples, and 69M pairs of line comments with context from 10 popular programming languages (Java, JavaScript, Python, Ruby, Rust, Golang, C#, C++, C, PHP), more diverse than CodeSearchNet, which has six programming languages.
- A novel approach to use a pre-trained language model for detecting and removing noisy samples to complement traditional rule-based methods.
- A thorough report of the process for transforming raw source code into code-text pairs and filtering noisy samples. We have released the toolkit used in this process to the open community via a public GitHub repository, including tools for parsing code and docstrings in different programming languages.
- We perform extensive evaluation where we fine-tuned different CodeLLMs with The Vault compared to other datasets, such as CodeSearchNet on various code understanding tasks, including code generation, code summarization and code search. The results show that models fine-tuned on The Vault outperform those fine-tuned on CodeSearchNet (code summarization, code search) and outperform the original model by a significant margin (code generation on pass@k over Human Eval dataset).

2 Related works

Code Large Language Models for Understanding and Generation Code large language models facilitate various code understanding and code generation tasks, including but not limited to code generation [Feng et al., 2020a, Wang et al., 2023, Elnaggar et al., 2021], code completion [Feng et al., 2020a, Wang et al., 2023, Peng et al., 2021], program repair [Xia et al., 2022], and code translation [Roziere et al., 2020]. A significant portion of recent research employs language models, originally developed for natural language processing, for handling code [Feng et al., 2020a, Wang et al., 2023, Guo et al., Ahmad et al., 2021b, Bui et al., 2021, Elnaggar et al., 2021, Peng et al., 2021, Kanade et al., 2020, Chakraborty et al., 2022, Ahmed and Devanbu, 2022, Niu et al., 2022]. Such approaches largely regard code as analogous to text and adapt pretraining strategies that mirror those used for natural languages. CodeBERT [Feng et al., 2020a], for instance, modifies a Roberta model [Liu et al., 2019] to pretrain a code model on multiple programming languages. CodeT5 [Wang et al., 2021] and CodeT5+ [Wang et al., 2023] employs unique identifier information from source code to pretrain the T5 model [Raffel et al., 2019] for code in a multi-modal fashion.

Datasets for Code Representation Learning: Code is commonly represented in training datasets for foundational LLMs, including the ROOTS corpus [Laurençon et al., 2023] for training BLOOM [Scao et al., 2022] and The Pile [Gao et al., 2020a] for training LLaMA [Touvron et al., 2023]. The code data represented in these datasets are unlabeled raw source code from GitHub. There is also a family of code-only datasets for training or fine-tuning coding-specific LLMs, including The Stack [Kocetkov et al., 2022], a 3TB corpus of permissively licensed source code, preceded by CodeParrot with 50GB of deduplicated source code [Tunstall et al., 2022]. These massive datasets are usually used to train CodeLLMs. However, labeled data are required for training and evaluating LLMs for coding tasks involving source code and natural language descriptions. CodeXGLUE is a benchmark dataset Lu et al. [2021] for 10 coding tasks that include 14 subsets, four of which are code-text pairs. Most of the code-text pairs in CodeXGLUE come from CodeSearchNet.

CodeSearchNet (CSN) has also been employed for pretraining LLMs, enabling supervised learning techniques to achieve state-of-the-art performance for models such as CodeT5+ [Wang et al., 2023] and UniXcoder [Guo et al., 2022]. A few code-text pair datasets set out to surpass CSN in size. CoDesc combines existing parallel datasets (CSN, DeepCom [Hu et al., 2020], CONCODE [Iyer et al., 2018a], and FunCom [LeClair et al., 2019]), and then refines the results from the superset, which yielded 4.2M Java data samples. PyMT5 [Clement et al., 2020] is a dataset with 7.7M Python code-text. However, both of these datasets each contains code for a single programming language. Notable datasets created from Stack Overflow [1] include the necessary code-text data for generating post titles [Gao et al., 2020b, Liu et al., 2022].

3 The Vault dataset

3.1 Overview

The Stack [Kocetkov et al., 2022] stands as the largest publicly accessible, multilingual, permissive-licensed source code dataset, with a size of 3TB. The Stack serves as the foundational dataset for constructing The Vault, wherein we transform raw source code into a compendium of high-quality code-text pairs. Our transformation pipeline is designed to efficiently extract data from source code, create text-code pairings, and remove noise, yielding three distinct output datasets, as detailed in Figure 2. We draw from a subset of The Stack, which comprises code in 10 prevalent programming languages, such as C, C#, C++, Java, JavaScript, GoLang, PHP, Python, Ruby, and Rust (out of the total 300 languages featured in The Stack). Each language-specific raw source code feeds into a custom-built tree-sitter[2] parser.

This parser is designed to extract functions, classes, methods, block code snippets, and their corresponding block or inline comments. The figure 1 illustrated a basic structure of a code file that contains multiple levels of code snippets. By applying a breadth-first search on the Abstract Syntax Tree (AST) of the root node, the parser is able to traverse down different node and leaf levels (class, function, and inline), result three separate datasets:

1. The first output dataset, referred to as D_{paired}, contains pairs of classes (node 1) and functions (node 3) with corresponding block comments that serve as docstrings (node 2). After the initial construction, this dataset proceeds through a pipeline that employs both rule-based filters and Deep Learning-based classification to remove noisy samples that fail to meet the criteria detailed in Section 3.2.

2. The second output dataset, denoted as D_{unimodal}, consists of standalone functions and classes, not paired with any docstring or comments, thereby forming a unimodal dataset.

3. The third and final dataset, D_{block}, includes pairs of arbitrary code blocks (node 4) and inline comments (node 5). To construct this set, we capture all inline comments. Each comment is paired with the preceding code block, tagged as the "previous context" (node $4a$), and the following code block, "next context" (node $4b$).

A large number of block comments adhere to widely accepted docstring formats (Appendix A.5), encompassing neatly organized details about the name (identifier) of the associated function or class, their parameters, arguments, and return types. We channel these block comments through docstring parsers, which we have developed and made publicly available, to extract this information as metadata for each sample in our dataset. We contend that this metadata could prove beneficial for downstream tasks, prompt settings, and other applications (Figure 8). Collectively, these three datasets (D_{block}, D_{unimodal}, and D_{paired}) constitute The Vault. Note that through the evaluation process, only D_{paired} is used since its contains data that is suitable for training and comparison with other datasets.

3.2 Data Cleaning Pipeline

From preliminary survey of the output dataset containing pairs of classes and functions with their corresponding block comments D_{paired}, we observe salient patterns that would impair the training quality for code related tasks. We implemented a set of rule-based filters (section 3.2.1) to remove irrelevant information or reformat textual data to be more descriptive of the corresponding code block. To address cases where the code-text pairs have inadequate or erroneous semantic correlation, we trained a deep-learning model based on CodeBERT (section 3.2.2) to score the semantic consistency of a code-text pair and remove low-scoring samples.

3.2.1 Remove Noisy Sample by Rules

Our data pipeline employs 13 rule-based filters to eliminate noisy patterns in the source dataset. These filters, detailed in Table 1, are categorized into three main groups: enhancing readability, promoting consistency, and preserving the intended usage of the code.

In terms of readability, we strip delimiters, math formulas, HTML tags, and metadata tags from the

[1] `https://stackoverflow.com/`

[2] `https://tree-sitter.github.io/tree-sitter/`

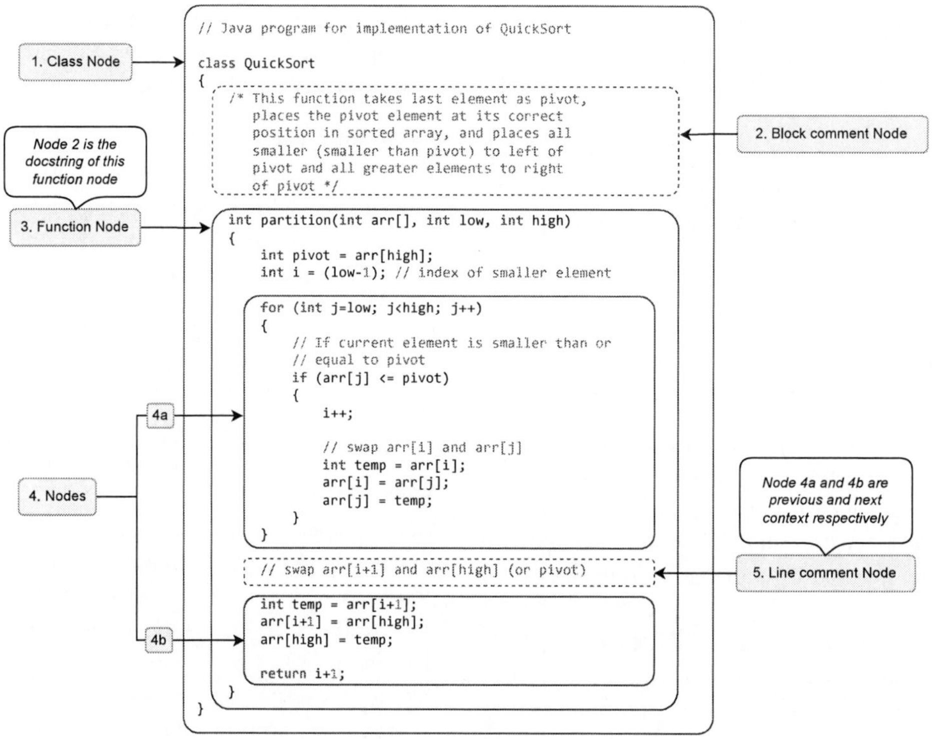

Figure 1: The tree-sitter node structure. Classes (1) and functions (3) are extracted along with their corresponding docstring, which may be in the form of a block comment (2) or a line comment (5). The line comments (5) are extracted along with their preceding ($4a$) and succeeding ($4b$) code nodes for the inline dataset.

text. This ensures a cleaner and more coherent code-text pairing. For consistency, we remove elements that may cause irregularities in the dataset. This includes stripping hyperlinks and embedded code, and removing empty comments, overly short or long comments, non-English comments, auto-generated blocks, and work-in-progress comments. Lastly, to preserve the original purpose of the code, we remove comments that are questions or serve as examples or notes. This rigorous filtering process guarantees a high-quality dataset, improving the effectiveness of code-focused language models.

3.2.2 Remove Low-Quality Samples with Classifier

Beyond the use of rule-based filtering methods, a crucial question arises: how do we ensure alignment between code and text? Random comments unrelated to the functionality of the code snippet can contaminate the dataset, necessitating the removal of such misaligned samples to guarantee quality. To address this issue, we constructed a classifier utilizing CodeBERT [Feng et al., 2020b], designed to score the semantic relationship between a function or class and its corresponding docstring.

Categories	Percentage (%)
Readability	
Strip Delimiters	13.430
Strip Math Formulas	0.021
Strip HTML Tags	3.180
Strip Metadata Tags	5.260
Consistency	
Strip Hyperlink	0.510
Strip Embedded Code	12.680
Remove Empty Comments	71.470
Remove Comments Too Short / Long	4.100
Remove Non-English Comments	3.230
Remove Auto-gen Blocks	0.050
Remove Work-in-Progress Comments	0.002
Intended usage	
Remove Comments as Questions	0.020
Remove Comments as Examples or Notes	0.460

Table 1: The percentage of constructed code-text pairs from The Stack caught by each rule-based filter.

In our scoring model, we input code snippets and docstrings separated by a token $< /s >$. Approximately 12% of the already rule-filtered code-text pairs dataset was randomly selected for training. As labeled data was unavailable, we generated negative samples by randomly pairing functions and

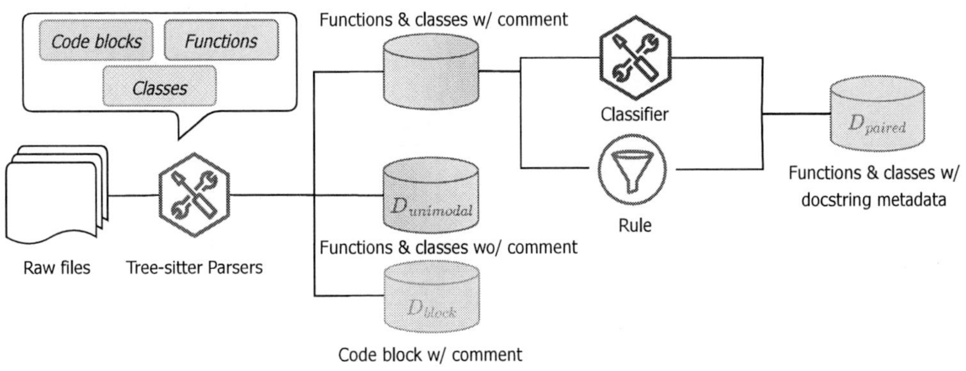

Figure 2: Pipeline to create datasets of code blocks with comments D_{block}, unimodal code $D_{unimodal}$, and code-text pairs D_{paired} from raw source code.

Language	Number of functions		#Repositories	#Tokens		
	w/docstring	All		#Unique code token	#Unique docstring token	#Unique identifier
Python	7,825,291	39,221,539	628,069	22,050,020	1,633,062	3,423,694
PHP	4,696,756	30,323,578	439,514	11,203,393	715,546	1,133,437
JavaScript	1,683,568	33,015,657	355,761	4,895,923	501,750	753,399
Java	6,667,422	69,744,181	321,129	16,536,979	1,749,151	2,525,492
C#	3,350,316	35,736,746	150,657	5,485,063	409,220	1,233,383
C++	1,709,448	28,684,400	116,897	5,630,067	678,063	1,155,241
C	1,685,966	13,762,988	88,556	5,764,837	750,146	1,197,164
Go	5,153,436	23,832,763	241,238	6,818,885	2,472,000	1,918,773
Rust	864,987	8,230,575	68,615	2,130,327	221,877	315,331
Ruby	461,585	4,342,191	61,804	1,436,713	146,237	213,005
Total	34,098,775	286,894,618	2,364,144	73,077,761	7,351,960	12,869,338

Table 2: The size of extracted function data in each programming language.

docstrings within the same programming language. We then passed the representation of the $< s >$ token to a linear layer, which produced a semantic correlation score between 0.0 and 1.0. Code-text pairs were then filtered using a binary classification gate with a threshold of 0.5.

To validate our model, we employed GPT 3.5-turbo for analogous predictions. A million predictions were generated from unseen instances, from which we selected 300 per language: 200 high-confidence instances (100 consistent and 100 inconsistent code-text predictions) and 100 low-confidence instances. GPT 3.5-turbo was instructed to assign a consistency score (1-10) for each instance's code-docstring pair, serving as a benchmark for our model's predictions. For high-confidence instances, our model agreed with the GPT 3.5-turbo scores over 80% of the time. Although our model faced challenges with ambiguous samples, the Area Under the Curve (AUC) metric proved suitable due to our primary goal of excluding misalignments while preserving matched examples. An average AUC of 0.89 indicates that our approach effectively reduced dataset noise without discarding numerous informative samples. Detailed configurations and evaluation results are available in Appendix A.2.

In addition, we use our model to find noisy examples in the rule-based noise-remove version of CodeSearchNet in CodeXGlue. Table 3 presents some inconsistent examples found by our model for Python, Java and JavaScript of CSN. It can be observed that detected pairs show strong inconsissency between docstring and code.

4 Empirical Evaluation

In this section, we aim to assess the quality of The Vault in comparison with other datasets, such as CSN. To substantiate this quality, we fine-tune prominent CodeLLMs on tasks that necessitate the involvement of both code and text, including code summarization, code search, and code generation.

Languages	Inconsistent pairs

Python	`// Handy for templates.`
	`def has_urls(self):`
	`    if self.isbn_uk or self.isbn_us or self.official_url or self.notes_url:`
	`        return True`
	`    else:`
	`        return False`

Java	`// only for change appenders`
	`public MapContentType getMapContentType(ContainerType containerType){`
	`        JaversType keyType = getJaversType(Integer.class);`
	`        JaversType valueType = getJaversType(containerType.getItemType());`
	`        return new MapContentType(keyType, valueType);`
	`    }`

JavaScript	`// we do not need Buffer pollyfill for now`
	`function(str){`
	`  var ret = new Array(str.length), len = str.length;`
	`  while(len--) ret[len] = str.charCodeAt(len);`
	`  return Uint8Array.from(ret);`
	`}`

Table 3: Examples of Inconsistent pairs in CodeSearchNet found by our model in Python, Java, and Javascript. "//" represents for docstring section. More examples are demonstrated in Table 15 in Appendix section.

Dataset	#PL	#Function	
		w/ docstring	w/o docstring
PyMT5 [Clement et al., 2020]	1	≈ 7,700,000	-
CoDesc [Hasan et al., 2021]	1	4,211,516	-
CodeSearchNet [Husain et al., 2019]	6	2,326,976	4,125,470
CodeXGLUE CSN [Lu et al., 2021]	6	1,005,474	-
Deepcom [Hu et al., 2020]	1	424,028	-
CONCODE [Iyer et al., 2018b]	1	2,184,310	-
Funcom [LeClair et al., 2019]	1	2,149,121	-
CodeT5 [Wang et al., 2021]	8	3,158,313	5,189,321
THEVAULT	**10**	**34,098,775**	**205,151,985**

Table 4: Comparison of THEVAULT function set to other code-text datasets.

We then compare these models, which have been fine-tuned on The Vault, with those fine-tuned on CSN. The comparison is made using the same test datasets and commonly employed metrics, such as BLEU, MRR, and pass@k.

4.1 Dataset Statistics

Table 2 provides the statistics of the samples for each programming language after undergoing our data-cleaning pipeline. In total, we have approximately 34M samples. The table also includes other information, like the number of tokens for code and docstrings, and the quantity of repositories.

Table 4 offers a comparison between The Vault and other parallel datasets frequently used for pretraining and fine-tuning downstream tasks. These datasets include Funcom [LeClair and McMillan, 2019], Deepcom [Hu et al., 2020], CONCODE [Iyer et al., 2018b], CSN [Husain et al., 2019], CoDesc [Hasan et al., 2021], and non-public data used for pretraining [Clement et al., 2020, Ciurumelea et al., 2020, Wang et al., 2021].

We split the training set into two smaller subsets: the small set and the medium set that contain 5% and 20% of the full training set, respectively. To reduce data leakage during training, we employed the MinHash LSH technique to filter training instance clusters that are close to samples in the validation and test sets of CSN, HumanEval, and MBPP. Additionally, during dataset partitioning, we prevented content from the same repository from appearing in multiple sets, thereby avoiding any potential internal data leakage. A more detailed analysis of The Vault's data samples at the class and code block levels can be found in Appendix A.4.

4.2 Experiment Setup

Data splitting: During the experiment phase, The Vault (D_{paired}) was split into three distinct datasets: training, validating, and testing sets. To avoid data leakage, we reinforced a policy where code samples from the same repository must all be in the same set. In the splitting algorithm, we also included as a goal the preservation of the token length distribution from The Vault's dataset in each subset.

For richer comparisons, the training set was further branched off to two smaller sets, the small and medium training sets, sampling 5% and 20% of the full training set, respectively. Details about experiment data can be found in Table 12. Note that TheVault/small has a comparable size with CSN, making it fair to assess and compare the quality of these two datasets.

Model	Dataset	Python	Java	JavaScript	Go	PHP	Ruby	Total/Avg
		CODESEARCHNET TESTSET (BLEU-4)						
CodeT5	raw-TheStack	16.18	9.06	6.23	19.05	7.07	5.78	11.84/10.56
	CodeSearchNet	19.55	20.38	16.15	19.83	26.26	15.38	**21.24/19.59**
	TheVault/small	18.94	17.72	13.96	19.92	20.43	15.22	18.83/17.70
PLBART	raw-TheStack	0.86	3.06	0.59	10.91	2.29	0.47	3.23/3.03
	CodeSearchNet	17.99	17.38	14.84	17.98	22.54	14.08	**18.78/17.47**
	TheVault/small	14.93	15.66	11.95	17.03	18.00	11.49	15.95/14.84
		THEVAULT TESTSET (BLEU-4)						
CodeT5	raw-TheStack	16.18	9.06	6.23	19.05	7.07	5.78	11.84/10.56
	CodeSearchNet	10.86	8.00	8.42	17.87	17.85	10.26	16.11/12.21
	TheVault/small	12.26	11.13	9.68	31.64	38.86	11.23	**25.12/19.13**
PLBART	raw-TheStack	1.69	4.02	0.43	24.60	4.83	0.49	7.19/6.01
	CodeSearchNet	10.24	7.26	7.64	16.90	13.83	9.60	14.39/10.91
	TheVault/small	10.23	9.28	8.95	22.78	34.32	9.74	**20.29/15.88**

Table 5: Smoothed BLEU-4 results for code summarization. The "Total" column demonstrates combined data in all languages to calculate BLEU, while "Avg" is the average BLEU score on the language level.

Model	Fine-tune data	Python	Java	JavaScript	Go	PHP	Ruby	Avg
		CODESEARCHNET TESTSET (MRR)						
CodeBERT	raw-TheStack	0.3713	0.3492	0.3148	0.5519	0.2731	0.2748	0.3559
	CodeSearchNet	0.3793	0.4636	0.4437	0.6201	0.4741	0.5219	0.4838
	TheVault/small	0.4074	0.4857	0.4466	0.6578	0.6578	0.5251	0.5301
RoBERTa	CodeSearchNet	0.3479	0.448	0.4254	0.5684	0.4623	0.5147	0.6952
	TheVault/small	**0.4849**	**0.5581**	**0.4962**	**0.7446**	**0.5166**	**0.59**	**0.5651**
UniXCoder	CodeSearchNet	0.3935	0.4549	0.4459	0.5861	0.489	0.5446	0.4857
	TheVault/small	**0.4427**	**0.4909**	**0.4506**	**0.6416**	**0.4515**	**0.5702**	**0.5079**
		THEVAULT TESTSET (MRR)						
CodeBERT	raw-TheStack	0.318	0.3245	0.1837	0.4194	0.1718	0.0878	0.2509
	CodeSearchNet	0.2881	0.3213	0.2409	0.4123	0.1854	0.2579	0.2843
	TheVault/small	**0.3501**	**0.4214**	**0.3216**	**0.4864**	**0.2351**	**0.2904**	**0.3165**
RoBERTa	CodeSearchNet	0.2644	0.3329	0.2371	0.2375	0.1577	0.2574	0.2478
	TheVault/small	**0.4533**	**0.5519**	**0.4386**	**0.5021**	**0.2876**	**0.3717**	**0.4342**
UniXCoder	CodeSearchNet	0.2959	0.344	0.2508	0.185	0.1646	0.2669	0.2512
	TheVault/small	**0.3852**	**0.4279**	**0.3491**	**0.4628**	**0.238**	**0.3201**	**0.3639**

Table 6: Comparison between the models fine-tuned on the CODESEARCHNET and on different THEVAULT training subsets on code search task.

Infrastructure: All experiments are conducted on 4 NVIDIA A100 GPUs.

Code search: We select CodeBERT [Feng et al., 2020a], RoBERTa [Liu et al., 2019] and UniXCoder [Guo et al., 2022] as the encoder for embedding source code and natural query, for all experiments. We train 10 epochs for each model with a sequence max length of 512, and a learning rate 2^{-5}.

Code summarization: CodeT5-base [Wang et al., 2021] is employed for the summarization task. We set the max input tokens to 512 and the max output tokens to 400. We train for 5 epochs with batch size of 512, the learning rate of 2^{-4}.

Code generation: We use CodeGen 350M and 2B Multi [Nijkamp et al., 2023] to evaluate code generation. We use the same configuration as in the code summarization task.

Additionally, we present supplementary results to demonstrate the efficiency of our process pipeline and offer a thorough evaluation of the dataset's versatility and adaptability with various architectures and frameworks in the Appendix A.8.

4.3 Evaluation Results

4.3.1 Code Summarization

For this task, we utilize the Vault and CSN to fine-tune CodeT5 [Wang et al., 2023] for the task of code summarization. The Vault and CSN exhibit significant differences in docstring format. The Vault retains the complete docstring format, offering comprehensive descriptions of core logic, parameters, arguments, and return types. This feature enables versatile applications in code documentation and various downstream tasks. Additionally, we save the first sentence of each complete docstring as metadata, termed as $short\_docstring$. To facilitate fair comparison between The Vault and CSN, we apply post-processing to our full docstrings and $short\_docstrings$ training sets, thereby reducing format distribution disparity.

Table 5 shows the results when comparing CodeT5 trained on CSN and The Vault for the code summarization task. Usage of full docstrings and $short\_docstrings$ are signified by "-L" and "-S" respectively. We use smoothed BLEU-4 score as the evaluation metric. We present further experimental outcomes using the Rouge-L and BERTScore metrics in Appendix, Table 14. The results show that CodeT5 fine-tuned on The Vault yields significantly better performance than on CSN. Although the performance gain when evaluated using the CSN test set is marginal (20.49 versus 19.59), it is worth noting that, despite the intermediary processing, CSN is a considerably smaller dataset with more consistent docstring patterns. In contrast, our dataset is substantially larger and exhibits greater diversity, thereby encouraging broader generalization. When evaluated against The Vault's test set, the model fine-tuned on CSN lags behind by over 10%.

4.3.2 Code Search

We utilize CodeBERT, RoBERTa and UniXCoder to fine-tune both The Vault and CodeSearchNet for the purpose of the code search task. The results of this task, when fine-tuning the model on The Vault and CodeSearchNet, are illustrated in Table 6. Remarkably, we attain superior results in most languages when fine-tund using the smallest dataset, TheVault/small, in contrast to solely fine-tuning on the CodeSearchNet corpus. We also furnish a baseline Mean Reciprocal Rank (MRR) score. MRR is a widely used metric for evaluating code search tasks, and in our case, it is trained on 10 different programming languages and assessed using the test set from CodeSearchNet and The Vault.

Model	Fine-tune dataset	pass@1	pass@10	pass@100
		HumanEval		
CodeGen 350M	-	6.67	10.61	16.84
	Py/CodeSearchNet	2.76	8.76	14.72
	(250k) Py/TheVault	3.74	10.57	16.26
	raw/PyTheVault	6.64	15.42	24.80
	Py/TheVault	**8.14**	**18.12**	**30.07**
CodeGen 2B	-	**14.51**	24.67	38.56
	Py/TheVault	14.00	**25.74**	**41.72**
		MBPP		
CodeGen 350M	-	7.46	24.18	46.37
	Py/TheVault	**10.13**	**33.96**	**53.20**
CodeGen 2B	-	18.06	45.80	**65.34**
	Py/TheVault	**27.82**	**50.06**	65.06

Table 7: Result on code generation benchmarks using CodeGen Multi 350M and 2B model.

4.4 Code Generation

We experiment with the CodeGen Multi-350M model [Nijkamp et al., 2023] on the HumanEval and MBPP datasets to generate code. The scope of our experiment was limited because the benchmarks only support Python. We use this checkpoint and continue fine-tuning this model on The Vault because CodeGen Multi-350M is trained on the dataset with multiple languages.

To create Multi-PyCSN and Multi-PyTheVault models, we fine-tuned the CodeGen pretrained model on Python subsets of CSN and TheVault. We sampled the training Python set of TheVault to match the size of the Python subset in CSN with 250K samples in the first round of fine-tuning. Additionally, raw-PyTheStack is a subset of Python data from The Stack mirroring the size of Python data present in The Vault dataset, which helps us to demonstrate the advancements achieved in our pipeline.

The results of this experiment are shown in table 7. We can see that fine-tuning the CodeGen Multi 350M on The Vault causes the model to improve significantly in terms of pass@1, pass@10, and pass@100 on the HumanEval and MBPP benchmarks. Additionally, CodeGen 2B is used to assess The Vault on larger scale models. Similar to experiments on small models, table 7 shows that The Vault can improve the performance of pre-trained large-scale models. These results validate The Vault's ability to improve the performance of pre-existing pretrained models. In the future, we will expand our evaluation to even larger scale models and assess The Vault's impact on them.

5 Conclusion

In this paper, we have presented The Vault, a large dataset of high-quality code-text pairs from 10 programming languages, totaling more than 41 million samples. The Vault was carefully curated to ensure that each pair meets quality standards, with detailed and informative descriptions and consistent coding styles. Our analysis has observed various intriguing patterns and trends that shed light on the characteristics of programming languages and coding practices. We are confident that The Vault will be a valuable resource for researchers and practitioners in this rapidly evolving field, providing a solid foundation for developing innovative approaches and advancing the state-of-the-art code large language models.

Limitations

In our approach, we employed 13 heuristic and context-specific rule-based filters, curated from manual data observations. While these filters effectively mitigated noisy patterns, their deterministic nature precluded comprehensive generalizability. To address this, we supplemented these rules with a deep learning approach as described in Section 3.2.2. However, the absence of labeled training data necessitated pseudo-random sample generation, which could compromise model soundness and potentially eliminate quality code-text pairs. Although cross-validation with GPT 3.5-turbo occasionally revealed scoring inconsistencies, we believe that human labeling and model fine-tuning could further refine the dataset.

Compared to The Stack and The Pile, our dataset is smaller, mainly due to our rigorous quality control procedures. Moreover, creating AST parsers for each programming language is a non-trivial task, limiting our dataset to 10 popular programming languages compared to The Stack's 300. Nonetheless, our framework's codebase is publicly available, encouraging future contributions to extend our parsers and rules to additional languages.

The current study primarily utilized small models with less than 2 billion parameters to illustrate the value of The Vault. These models effectively demonstrated the dataset's potential, but further research with larger models would shed light on its robustness and scalability across more complex tasks. In future work, we plan to conduct experiments using large-scale language models to further assess the impact of our dataset.

References

W. U. Ahmad, S. Chakraborty, B. Ray, and K. Chang. Unified pre-training for program understanding and generation. In K. Toutanova, A. Rumshisky, L. Zettlemoyer, D. Hakkani-Tür, I. Beltagy, S. Bethard, R. Cotterell, T. Chakraborty, and Y. Zhou, editors, *Proceedings of the 2021 Conference of the North American Chapter of the Association for Computational Linguistics: Human Language Technologies, NAACL-HLT 2021, Online, June 6-11, 2021*, pages 2655–2668. Association for Computational Linguistics, 2021a.

W. U. Ahmad, S. Chakraborty, B. Ray, and K. Chang. Unified Pre-training for Program Understanding and Generation. In K. Toutanova, A. Rumshisky, L. Zettlemoyer, D. Hakkani-Tür, I. Beltagy, S. Bethard, R. Cotterell, T. Chakraborty, and Y. Zhou, editors, *Proceedings of the 2021 Conference of the North American Chapter of the Association for Computational Linguistics: Human Language Technologies, NAACL-HLT 2021, Online, June 6-11, 2021*, pages 2655–2668. Association for Computational Linguistics, 2021b.

T. Ahmed and P. Devanbu. Multilingual training for software engineering. In *Proceedings of the 44th International Conference on Software Engineering*, pages 1443–1455, 2022.

T. B. Brown, B. Mann, N. Ryder, M. Subbiah, J. Kaplan, P. Dhariwal, A. Neelakantan, P. Shyam, G. Sastry, A. Askell, S. Agarwal, A. Herbert-Voss, G. Krueger, T. Henighan, R. Child, A. Ramesh, D. M. Ziegler, J. Wu, C. Winter, C. Hesse, M. Chen, E. Sigler, M. Litwin, S. Gray, B. Chess, J. Clark, C. Berner, S. McCandlish, A. Radford, I. Sutskever, and D. Amodei. Language models are few-shot learners. In H. Larochelle, M. Ranzato, R. Hadsell, M. Balcan, and H. Lin, editors, *Advances in Neural Information Processing Systems 33: Annual Conference on Neural Information Processing Systems 2020, NeurIPS 2020, December 6-12, 2020, virtual*, 2020.

N. D. Bui, Y. Yu, and L. Jiang. Self-supervised contrastive learning for code retrieval and summarization via semantic-preserving transformations. In *Proceedings of the 44th International ACM SIGIR Conference on Research and Development in Information Retrieval*, pages 511–521, 2021.

S. Chakraborty, T. Ahmed, Y. Ding, P. T. Devanbu, and B. Ray. Natgen: generative pre-training by "naturalizing" source code. In *Proceedings of the 30th ACM Joint European Software Engineering Conference and Symposium on the Foundations of Software Engineering*, pages 18–30, 2022.

A. Ciurumelea, S. Proksch, and H. C. Gall. Suggesting comment completions for python using neural language models. In *2020 IEEE 27th International Conference on Software Analysis, Evolution and Reengineering (SANER)*, pages 456–467, 2020.

C. B. Clement, D. Drain, J. Timcheck, A. Svyatkovskiy, and N. Sundaresan. Pymt5: multi-mode translation of natural language and python code with transformers. In B. Webber, T. Cohn, Y. He, and Y. Liu, editors, *Proceedings of the 2020 Conference on Empirical Methods in Natural Language Processing, EMNLP 2020, Online, November 16-20, 2020*, pages 9052–9065. Association for Computational Linguistics, 2020.

A. T. V. Dau, N. D. Q. Bui, T. Nguyen-Duc, and H. Thanh-Tung. Towards using data-influence methods to detect noisy samples in source code corpora. In *37th IEEE/ACM International Conference on Automated Software Engineering, ASE 2022, Rochester, MI, USA, October 10-14, 2022*, pages 148:1–148:3. ACM, 2022.

A. Elnaggar, W. Ding, L. Jones, T. Gibbs, T. Feher, C. Angerer, S. Severini, F. Matthes, and B. Rost. Codetrans: Towards cracking the language of silicon's code through self-supervised deep learning and high performance computing. *arXiv preprint arXiv:2104.02443*, 2021.

Z. Feng, D. Guo, D. Tang, N. Duan, X. Feng, M. Gong, L. Shou, B. Qin, T. Liu, D. Jiang, and M. Zhou. Codebert: A pre-trained model for programming and natural languages. In T. Cohn, Y. He, and Y. Liu, editors, *Findings of the Association for Computational Linguistics: EMNLP 2020, Online Event, 16-20 November 2020*, volume EMNLP 2020 of *Findings of ACL*, pages 1536–1547. Association for Computational Linguistics, 2020a.

Z. Feng, D. Guo, D. Tang, N. Duan, X. Feng, M. Gong, L. Shou, B. Qin, T. Liu, D. Jiang, and M. Zhou. CodeBERT: A pre-trained model for programming and natural languages. In *Findings of the Association for Computational Linguistics: EMNLP 2020*, pages 1536–1547, Online, Nov. 2020b. Association for Computational Linguistics.

L. Gao, S. Biderman, S. Black, L. Golding, T. Hoppe, C. Foster, J. Phang, H. He, A. Thite, N. Nabeshima, et al. The pile: An 800gb dataset of diverse text for language modeling. *arXiv preprint arXiv:2101.00027*, 2020a.

Z. Gao, X. Xia, J. Grundy, D. Lo, and Y. Li. Generating question titles for stack overflow from mined code snippets. *ACM Trans. Softw. Eng. Methodol.*, 29(4): 26:1–26:37, 2020b.

M. A. Gordon, K. Duh, and J. Kaplan. Data and parameter scaling laws for neural machine translation. In M. Moens, X. Huang, L. Specia, and S. W. Yih, editors, *Proceedings of the 2021 Conference on Empirical Methods in Natural Language Processing, EMNLP 2021, Virtual Event / Punta Cana, Dominican Republic, 7-11 November, 2021*, pages 5915–5922. Association for Computational Linguistics, 2021.

D. Guo, S. Ren, S. Lu, Z. Feng, D. Tang, S. Liu, L. Zhou, N. Duan, A. Svyatkovskiy, S. Fu, M. Tufano, S. K.

Deng, C. B. Clement, D. Drain, N. Sundaresan, J. Yin, D. Jiang, and M. Zhou. Graphcodebert: Pre-training code representations with data flow. In *9th International Conference on Learning Representations, ICLR 2021, Virtual Event, Austria, May 3-7, 2021*.

D. Guo, S. Lu, N. Duan, Y. Wang, M. Zhou, and J. Yin. Unixcoder: Unified cross-modal pre-training for code representation. In S. Muresan, P. Nakov, and A. Villavicencio, editors, *Proceedings of the 60th Annual Meeting of the Association for Computational Linguistics (Volume 1: Long Papers), ACL 2022, Dublin, Ireland, May 22-27, 2022*, pages 7212–7225. Association for Computational Linguistics, 2022.

M. Hasan, T. Muttaqueen, A. A. Ishtiaq, K. S. Mehrab, M. M. A. Haque, T. Hasan, W. U. Ahmad, A. Iqbal, and R. Shahriyar. Codesc: A large code-description parallel dataset. In C. Zong, F. Xia, W. Li, and R. Navigli, editors, *Findings of the Association for Computational Linguistics: ACL/IJCNLP 2021, Online Event, August 1-6, 2021*, volume ACL/IJCNLP 2021 of *Findings of ACL*, pages 210–218. Association for Computational Linguistics, 2021.

D. Hendrycks, S. Basart, S. Kadavath, M. Mazeika, A. Arora, E. Guo, C. Burns, S. Puranik, H. He, D. Song, and J. Steinhardt. Measuring coding challenge competence with APPS. In J. Vanschoren and S. Yeung, editors, *Proceedings of the Neural Information Processing Systems Track on Datasets and Benchmarks 1, NeurIPS Datasets and Benchmarks 2021, December 2021, virtual*, 2021.

X. Hu, G. Li, X. Xia, D. Lo, and Z. Jin. Deep code comment generation with hybrid lexical and syntactical information. *Empir. Softw. Eng.*, 25(3):2179–2217, 2020.

H. Husain, H.-H. Wu, T. Gazit, M. Allamanis, and M. Brockschmidt. Codesearchnet challenge: Evaluating the state of semantic code search. *arXiv preprint arXiv:1909.09436*, 2019.

S. Iyer, I. Konstas, A. Cheung, and L. Zettlemoyer. Mapping language to code in programmatic context. In E. Riloff, D. Chiang, J. Hockenmaier, and J. Tsujii, editors, *Proceedings of the 2018 Conference on Empirical Methods in Natural Language Processing, Brussels, Belgium, October 31 - November 4, 2018*, pages 1643–1652. Association for Computational Linguistics, 2018a.

S. Iyer, I. Konstas, A. Cheung, and L. Zettlemoyer. Mapping language to code in programmatic context. In *Proceedings of the 2018 Conference on Empirical Methods in Natural Language Processing*, pages 1643–1652, Brussels, Belgium, Oct.-Nov. 2018b. Association for Computational Linguistics.

A. Kanade, P. Maniatis, G. Balakrishnan, and K. Shi. Learning and evaluating contextual embedding of source code. In *International Conference on Machine Learning*, pages 5110–5121. PMLR, 2020.

J. Kaplan, S. McCandlish, T. Henighan, T. B. Brown, B. Chess, R. Child, S. Gray, A. Radford, J. Wu, and D. Amodei. Scaling laws for neural language models. *arXiv preprint arXiv:2001.08361*, 2020.

S. S. Khan, N. T. Niloy, M. A. Azmain, and A. Kabir. Impact of label noise and efficacy of noise filters in software defect prediction. In R. García-Castro, editor, *The 32nd International Conference on Software Engineering and Knowledge Engineering, SEKE 2020, KSIR Virtual Conference Center, USA, July 9-19, 2020*, pages 347–352. KSI Research Inc., 2020.

D. Kocetkov, R. Li, L. B. Allal, J. Li, C. Mou, C. M. Ferrandis, Y. Jernite, M. Mitchell, S. Hughes, T. Wolf, et al. The stack: 3 tb of permissively licensed source code. *arXiv preprint arXiv:2211.15533*, 2022.

H. Laurençon, L. Saulnier, T. Wang, C. Akiki, A. V. del Moral, T. L. Scao, L. V. Werra, C. Mou, E. G. Ponferrada, H. Nguyen, J. Frohberg, M. Šaško, Q. Lhoest, A. McMillan-Major, G. Dupont, S. Biderman, A. Rogers, L. B. allal, F. D. Toni, G. Pistilli, O. Nguyen, S. Nikpoor, M. Masoud, P. Colombo, J. de la Rosa, P. Villegas, T. Thrush, S. Longpre, S. Nagel, L. Weber, M. Muñoz, J. Zhu, D. V. Strien, Z. Alyafeai, K. Almubarak, M. C. Vu, I. Gonzalez-Dios, A. Soroa, K. Lo, M. Dey, P. O. Suarez, A. Gokaslan, S. Bose, D. Adelani, L. Phan, H. Tran, I. Yu, S. Pai, J. Chim, V. Lepercq, S. Ilic, M. Mitchell, S. A. Luccioni, and Y. Jernite. The bigscience roots corpus: A 1.6tb composite multilingual dataset, 2023.

A. LeClair and C. McMillan. Recommendations for datasets for source code summarization. pages 3931–3937. Association for Computational Linguistics, 2019.

A. LeClair, S. Jiang, and C. McMillan. A neural model for generating natural language summaries of program subroutines. In J. M. Atlee, T. Bultan, and J. Whittle, editors, *Proceedings of the 41st International Conference on Software Engineering, ICSE 2019, Montreal, QC, Canada, May 25-31, 2019*, pages 795–806. IEEE / ACM, 2019.

K. Liu, G. Yang, X. Chen, and C. Yu. Sotitle: A transformer-based post title generation approach for stack overflow. In *IEEE International Conference on Software Analysis, Evolution and Reengineering, SANER 2022, Honolulu, HI, USA, March 15-18, 2022*, pages 577–588. IEEE, 2022.

Y. Liu, M. Ott, N. Goyal, J. Du, M. Joshi, D. Chen, O. Levy, M. Lewis, L. Zettlemoyer, and V. Stoyanov. Roberta: a robustly optimized bert pretraining approach (2019). *arXiv preprint arXiv:1907.11692*, 364, 1907.

Y. Liu, M. Ott, N. Goyal, J. Du, M. Joshi, D. Chen, O. Levy, M. Lewis, L. Zettlemoyer, and V. Stoyanov. Roberta: A robustly optimized bert pretraining approach. *arXiv preprint arXiv:1907.11692*, 2019.

S. Lu, D. Guo, S. Ren, J. Huang, A. Svyatkovskiy, A. Blanco, C. B. Clement, D. Drain, D. Jiang, D. Tang, G. Li, L. Zhou, L. Shou, L. Zhou, M. Tufano, M. Gong, M. Zhou, N. Duan, N. Sundaresan, S. K. Deng, S. Fu, and S. Liu. Codexglue: A machine learning benchmark dataset for code understanding and generation. In J. Vanschoren and S. Yeung, editors, *Proceedings of the Neural Information Processing Systems Track on Datasets and Benchmarks 1, NeurIPS Datasets and Benchmarks 2021, December 2021, virtual*, 2021.

J. Mahmud, F. Faisal, R. I. Arnob, A. Anastasopoulos, and K. Moran. Code to comment translation: A comparative study on model effectiveness & errors, 2021.

E. Nijkamp, B. Pang, H. Hayashi, L. Tu, H. Wang, Y. Zhou, S. Savarese, and C. Xiong. Codegen: An open large language model for code with multi-turn program synthesis. In *The Eleventh International Conference on Learning Representations*, 2023. URL https://openreview.net/forum?id=iaYcJKpY2B_.

C. Niu, C. Li, V. Ng, J. Ge, L. Huang, and B. Luo. Spt-code: sequence-to-sequence pre-training for learning source code representations. In *Proceedings of the 44th International Conference on Software Engineering*, pages 2006–2018, 2022.

D. Peng, S. Zheng, Y. Li, G. Ke, D. He, and T.-Y. Liu. How could neural networks understand programs? In *International Conference on Machine Learning*, pages 8476–8486. PMLR, 2021.

C. Raffel, N. Shazeer, A. Roberts, K. Lee, S. Narang, M. Matena, Y. Zhou, W. Li, and P. J. Liu. Exploring the limits of transfer learning with a unified text-to-text transformer. *arXiv preprint arXiv:1910.10683*, 2019.

B. Roziere, M.-A. Lachaux, L. Chanussot, and G. Lample. Unsupervised translation of programming languages. *Advances in Neural Information Processing Systems*, 33:20601–20611, 2020.

T. L. Scao, A. Fan, C. Akiki, E. Pavlick, S. Ilić, D. Hesslow, R. Castagné, A. S. Luccioni, F. Yvon, M. Gallé, et al. Bloom: A 176b-parameter open-access multilingual language model. *arXiv preprint arXiv:2211.05100*, 2022.

B. Sorscher, R. Geirhos, S. Shekhar, S. Ganguli, and A. Morcos. Beyond neural scaling laws: beating power law scaling via data pruning. *Advances in Neural Information Processing Systems*, 35:19523–19536, 2022.

H. Touvron, T. Lavril, G. Izacard, X. Martinet, M.-A. Lachaux, T. Lacroix, B. Rozière, N. Goyal, E. Hambro, F. Azhar, A. Rodriguez, A. Joulin, E. Grave, and G. Lample. Llama: Open and efficient foundation language models, 2023.

L. Tunstall, L. Von Werra, and T. Wolf. *Natural language processing with transformers.* " O'Reilly Media, Inc.", 2022.

Y. Wang, W. Wang, S. R. Joty, and S. C. H. Hoi. Codet5: Identifier-aware unified pre-trained encoder-decoder models for code understanding and generation. In M. Moens, X. Huang, L. Specia, and S. W. Yih, editors, *Proceedings of the 2021 Conference on Empirical Methods in Natural Language Processing, EMNLP 2021, Virtual Event / Punta Cana, Dominican Republic, 7-11 November, 2021*, pages 8696–8708. Association for Computational Linguistics, 2021.

Y. Wang, H. Le, A. D. Gotmare, N. D. Q. Bui, J. Li, and S. C. H. Hoi. Codet5+: Open code large language models for code understanding and generation, 2023.

C. S. Xia, Y. Wei, and L. Zhang. Practical program repair in the era of large pre-trained language models. *arXiv preprint arXiv:2210.14179*, 2022.

C. Zhou, P. Liu, P. Xu, S. Iyer, J. Sun, Y. Mao, X. Ma, A. Efrat, P. Yu, L. Yu, et al. Lima: Less is more for alignment. *arXiv preprint arXiv:2305.11206*, 2023.

A Appendix

A.1 Rule-based filters

While some datasets eliminate all special characters (!@#$%&*()_-+=/.,'— ') and keep only the first sentence or the paragraph preceding the first double endline symbol [Hasan et al., 2021, Mahmud et al., 2021], our heuristic rules take a different approach. Instead of discarding such characters outright, we selectively remove the noisy elements while aiming to capture as many informative sections as possible.

We analyze each docstring block individually and retain the sections that meet our quality criteria. Table 8 provides comprehensive descriptions of our 13 rule-based filters, accompanied by illustrative examples. Additionally, table 9 presents the corresponding percentages of code-text pairs generated through the application of these rule-based filters.

A.2 Deep learning-based refinement method

To detect semantic inconsistency between code-text pairs, we considered fine-tuning on large foundational models such as CodeGen [Nijkamp et al., 2023], BLOOM [Scao et al., 2022] or leverage GPT 3.5-turbo APIs. However, these approaches would incur very high costs in terms of financial resources, time, and computational power. We decided to train a dedicated model to deal with this specific task and use GPT 3.5-turbo to cross-check the predictions.

Training: We trained our model based on CodeBERT, [Feng et al., 2020a]. The model assigns a score for semantic correspondence between code and text, before passing through binary classification into Consistent and Inconsistent categories. We randomly chose 5M samples (500K for each language in The Vault) and divided them into training, validation, and testing sets at a ratio of 3:1:1. The input to the model is the concatenation of the docstring and the code together with the $< /s >$ token used to separate them (Figure 3). We use the representation of the $< s >$ token and feed it into a linear layer to obtain the output logit.

Since labeled data was unavailable, we utilized self-supervised learning. We created negative samples by randomly pairing a function with a docstring from the same programming language (Figure 3).

Cross-check: We used GPT 3.5-turbo to perform similar classifications for semantic consistency of code-text pairs. We used a prompting template to ask GPT 3.5-turbo to score each pair of code-text on a scale of 1 to 10 for semantic correspondence with a detailed explanation and ran this prompting template on systematically selected 300 data points from each language with 100 data points in each of the following groups:

- Consistency group: Examples that the model gives high confidence prediction to class Consistent. We select the top 100 based on the output probability for class 1.
- Inconsistency group: Examples that the model gives high confidence prediction to class Inconsistent. We select the top 100 based on the output probability for class 0.
- Uncertainty group: Examples that the model gives uncertain predictions. We select the lowest top 50 examples for each class.

The systematic sampling scheme helped us select 2994 samples in function level to be scored out of millions, reducing the cost of requesting GPT 3.5-turbo API while enabling meaningful analysis. The prompt input to GPT 3.5-turbo is as follow:

```
I want you to act as an unbiased
    docstring evaluator for code. I will
     give you a docstring along with a
    source code, and you will give me a
    score for the consistency between
    them. The score will be on a scale
    of 1 to 10, 10 means the docstring
    can effectively summarize the code
    while 1 means they are inconsistent.
     The response answers must contain
    the score and the explanation that
    follows the format in the response
    format.

- Response format:
Score: X
Explanation: Y

- Docstring:
"{docstring}"

- Code:
"{code}"
```

Empirical Evaluation Results: Table 10 presents the performance of our model with GPT 3.5 turbo's scores as a reference, along with the scoring result for each group. In groups with high confidence, we witness a strong correlation between our model and GPT 3.5-turbo, with a high score for Consistency (7.81) and a low score for Inconsistency (3.15). A similar pattern is observed in the Uncertainty group, where the average score is close to the middle of the scale at 5.74.

Categories	Syntax Feature	Action	Docstring
Comment Delimiter	Unnecessary comment delimiter	Update	/** * Lexical essentially tokenizer. * */ → Lexical essentially tokenizer.
Hyperlink	URL Link	Update	Deletes a Mux asset @see https://docs.mux.com/v1/reference#deletean-asset → Deletes a Mux asset
Embedded Code	Inline or embedded code snippets, command lines, or script excerpts	Update	Set the trust level for a key in GPG keychain. code-block:: bash salt '*' gpg.trust-key key-id='3FAD9F1E' trust-level='marginally' → Set the trust level for a key in GPG keychain. code-block:: bash
Question	Question: Why? How?, ...	Update	isup <url> - Is it down for everyone, or just you? → isup <url>
Math formula	\sqrt(), \exp(), \mathbf, ...	Update	Recursive filter design using a least-squares method. {[}B,A{]} = YULEWALK(N,F,M) finds the N-th order recursive filter coefficients B and A. → Recursive filter design using a least-squares method.
Metadata Tag	Metadata tags or annotations	Update	Creates a slice of 'array' with 'n' elements dropped from the end. @static @memberOf_ @since 3.0.0 → Creates a slice of 'array' with 'n' elements dropped from the end.
HTML Tags	HTML tags: <p>... </p>, ... Special tags.	Update	Constructs a <code>GeneralStoresProductModel</code> from a plain JavaScript object. → Constructs a GeneralStoresProductModel from a plain JavaScript object.
Example and note	Code example, note from developers	Update	Pull packages data dir. note: Uses su to access package's data dir. → Pull packages data dir.
Unsuitable Length	Length < 5, length > 500	Remove	Write objects
Non-English	Not written in English	Remove	Retorna uma estrutura com os argumentos passados para o programa.
Auto-gen	Auto-generated	Remove	*<!-begin-user-doc-> <!-end-user-doc-> @generated
Under-dev	Under-development	Remove	Deprecate this build, so that it will be rebuilt if any other test run wants to use it.
No comment	No docstring/comment in function	Remove	null

Table 8: Rule-based filters and examples.

Categories	Python	PHP	JavaScript	Java	C#	C++	C	Rust	Ruby	Go	Total
Comment Delimiter	12.02	33.38	9.94	11.98	16.7	6.92	13.28	8.43	9.13	4.95	13.43
Hyperlink	0.95	0.44	0.66	0.25	0.71	0.15	0.11	0.59	1.11	0.65	0.51
Embedded Code	31.65	1.09	1.38	1.41	1.39	6.51	6.16	0.67	3.18	2.41	12.68
Question	0.03	0	0.02	0.02	0.01	0.03	0.02	0.06	0.13	0.02	0.02
Math formula	0.1	0	0.01	0.01	0.01	0.02	0.02	0.01	0	0	0.021
Metadata Tag	0.62	6.81	1.86	2.69	2.15	4.35	6.14	0.83	1.69	0.46	5.26
HTML Tags	0.79	0.68	0.8	2.7	17.15	0.31	0.45	1.13	1.56	0.13	3.18
Example and note	1.4	0.26	0.36	0.34	0.22	0.18	0.4	0.45	0.79	0.3	0.46
Unsuitable Length	5.11	8.79	3.90	2.20	2.75	4.58	3.86	2.26	5.19	4.37	4.10
Non-English	1.69	5.72	3.26	4.16	2.62	4.1	1.94	0.42	1.53	1.77	3.23
Auto-gen	0.01	0	0	0.2	0	0	0	0	0	0	0.05
Under-dev	0.02	0	0	0	0	0	0	0	0	0	0.002
No comment	60.54	49.0	78.5	77.15	76.16	80.95	72.28	80.43	71.55	69.75	71.47

Table 9: The percentage of constructed code-text pairs from The Stack caught by each rule-based filter, by programming language.

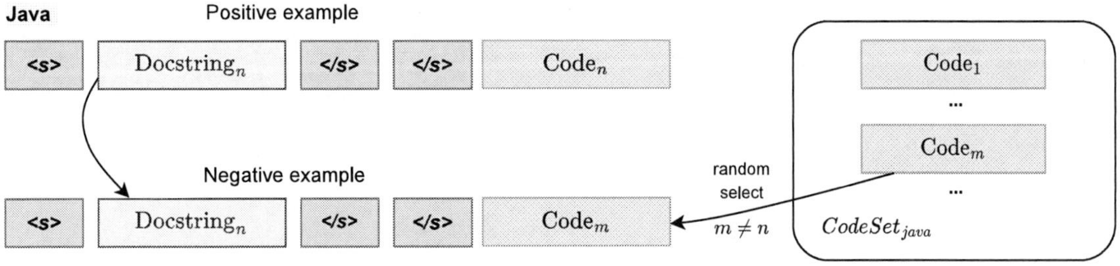

Figure 3: Input representation and Negative sample generation for code-docstring inconsistency detection.

In addition, we use GPT 3.5-turbo's scores to generate pseudo-labels and calculate accuracy and AUC for our model. We set a relative threshold of 5 to determine the labels. It can be witnessed that our model performs well in high-confidence groups but struggles in the uncertainty group. However, the accuracy is influenced by the choice of relative threshold, we consider Area Under the Curve (AUC) to measure the false positive and true positive rates. The metric shows a convincing result averaging 0.89, enabling us to effectively reduce a high amount of noise in our dataset while avoiding excluding too many informative examples. Finally, after removing noisy data using the proposed deep learning method, we notice a decrease of 1.3% in the dataset.

We use our model to find noisy examples in the rule-based noise-remove version of CodeSearchNet in CodeXGlue. Table 15 illustrates some examples found in 6 programming languages. It can be observed that detected pairs show strong inconsistency between docstring and code. For instance, the docstring of the first example in Python does not give much insight into what the code does or its purpose. The code defines a method named *'has_url'* which checks if the attributes have a non-empty value; however, the docstring mentions templates which does not provide enough context to fully understand how this code relates to templates or its broader purpose. A similar pattern also presents in the remaining examples. An example that provides more clarity is the second example in Ruby. The docstring describes a function with a *'YAML filePath'* parameter, but the function itself does not actually have this parameter. Besides, our model is able to identify non-English samples (the second example in PHP) that are not captured by the rule-based method.

A.3 Analysis of Function-Level Data in The Vault

Detailed description of function level data in The Vault can be found in Figure 4.

A.3.1 Code and Docstring Analysis

Token Length Distribution: When training seq-to-seq LLMs, maximum input and output lengths are typically required. By understanding the distribution of sequence lengths in the corpus, we can

Language	GPT 3.5-turbo score (accuracy)			Accuracy (%)	AUC
	Consistency	Inconsistency	Uncertainty		
Python	8.19 ± 1.15 (99%)	3.76 ± 1.96 (69%)	6.20 ± 2.12 (44%)	70.67	0.8559
PHP	7.73 ± 1.32 (96%)	3.01 ± 1.45 (90%)	4.90 ± 2.23 (49%)	78.33	0.8863
JavaScript	7.73 ± 1.25 (99%)	2.95 ± 1.40 (89%)	5.58 ± 2.29 (49%)	79.00	0.8984
Java	7.65 ± 1.71 (94%)	2.73 ± 1.32 (93%)	5.83 ± 2.12 (53%)	80.00	0.9014
C#	7.70 ± 1.35 (97%)	3.31 ± 1.56 (82%)	5.35 ± 2.09 (46%)	75.00	0.8606
C++	7.51 ± 1.64 (92%)	2.82 ± 1.46 (89%)	5.80 ± 2.33 (57%)	79.33	0.8787
C	7.79 ± 1.10 (98%)	2.99 ± 1.48 (88%)	5.81 ± 2.08 (47%)	77.67	0.9108
Go	8.08 ± 1.21 (99%)	3.68 ± 1.67 (74%)	6.09 ± 2.06 (50%)	74.83	0.8819
Rust	8.03 ± 1.20 (99%)	3.72 ± 1.77 (75%)	6.83 ± 1.62 (50%)	74.67	0.9051
Ruby	7.72 ± 1.03 (98%)	2.51 ± 1.04 (96%)	5.01 ± 2.23 (49%)	81.00	0.9203
All	7.81 ± 1.33 (97%)	3.15 ± 1.59 (84%)	5.74 ± 2.19 (49%)	77.05	0.8874

Table 10: Evaluate CodeBERT using the consistency score provided by GPT 3.5-turbo. We report the mean ± the standard deviation for the score in each subset.

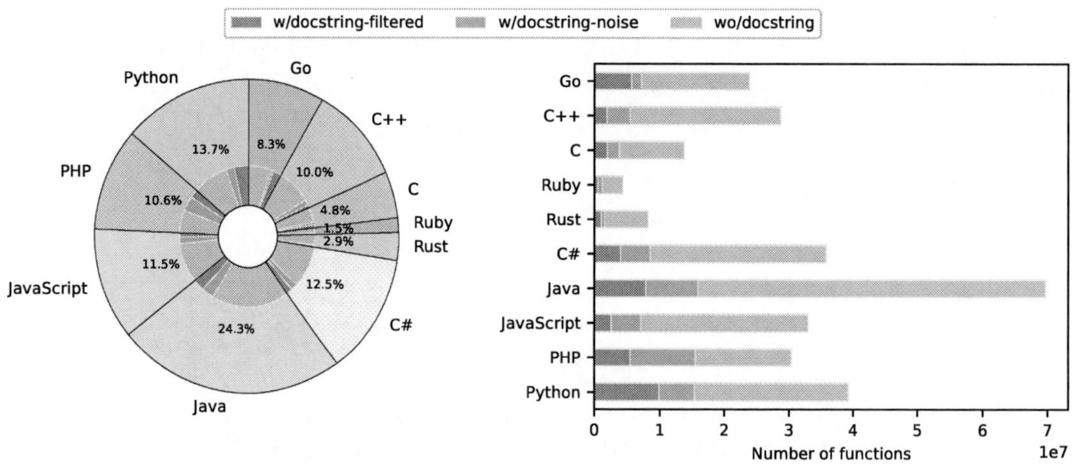

Figure 4: Distribution and the number of functions by the presence of docstrings. Functions with docstrings are further divided into two categories: functions removed by rule-based filters and functions in the final code-text dataset.

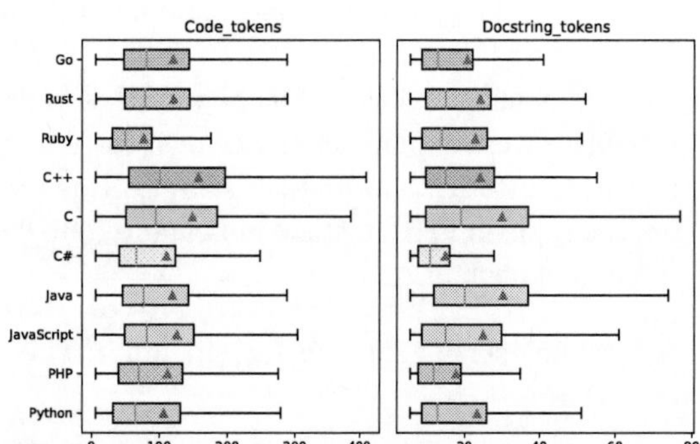

Figure 5: Code and Docstring tokens length distribution. The plot shows the lower to upper quartile values of the number of tokens in the data. The orange solid line | indicates the median and the green triangle ▲ presents the mean.

choose appropriate input and output lengths for training. This can help improve the performance of training a language model and prevent the resulting LLMs from producing outcomes too short or too long for the intended use cases [Kaplan et al., 2020, Brown et al., 2020].

Our tokenization process utilizes the tree-sitter framework to parse source code into nodes on an abstract syntax tree; each node is considered a token. For docstring tokenization, we tokenize by word and punctuation. The code and docstring tokens length distribution for each programming language is illustrated in Figure 5. The number of tokens present in a function (average of around 100 tokens) is considerably more than the number of tokens found in the docstrings (average of 15-30 tokens) that describe it. In particular, among the

10 programming languages, C and C++ have the highest number of tokens in a function. This can be attributed to the fact that these languages are low-level languages, which typically require more code to perform a task when compared to higher-level languages. In the case of docstrings, their number of tokens is determined not only by the naturalness of the description in practice but also by cleaning rules outlined in Section 3.2.1. From Figure 5-Right and Table 9, it can be observed that the docstrings in Java and C are lengthy but are slightly cleaned by update-action rules, indicating that the docstrings in these two languages are typically long and more detailed in practice. Meanwhile, the number of tokens of docstrings in C# is the lowest. The cleaning rules may have played a role, as a significant proportion of the samples in C# has been updated based on *Comment Delimite* (16,7%) and *HTML Tags* (17,15%) rules.

Table 2 depicts the overall number of distinct tokens for each programming language. As our dataset contains extensive unique tokens, we believe that model training on The Vault can effectively handle unseen tokens. Besides, we find that multiple function names are reused due to the relatively small number of unique identifiers compared to the total number of functions in the dataset. This finding implies that even for humans, naming functions might be a difficult task.

Docstring Styles: Alongside typical docstrings that provide brief descriptions of the source code, many adhere to formatting and style conventions like Google, Jsdoc, and reST styles, among others. Our toolkit, designed to parse docstrings and extract metadata into a dictionary, supports 11 prevalent docstring styles. The styles we support and the information we aim to extract are depicted in figures 10 and 8 in Appendix A.5. This rich dataset could inspire research on advanced problems, such as controlling docstring style during generation or crafting explanations for function parameters.

Figure 9 provides statistics on the number of docstrings following a standard style. The data suggests that styled docstrings constitute a small fraction of the overall code-text dataset. One possible explanation is that our style detection rules are stringent, excluding docstrings with even minor syntax deviations, which might result in underestimating the number of docstrings adhering to a specific format. For styled docstrings, Figure 9-bottom presents the distribution of the number of extracted attributes for each programming language, with most having between 1 to 5 elements. We make our docstring-style parser available to the community to facilitate easy customization and enhancement.

A.4 Analyzing for Class and Inline Comment Set

In Table 11, we provide a statistical analysis of the number of classes and inline comments in both the raw set and the filtered set. Since the class structure is not defined in C and Go, we do not have their information to give in this table.

Initially, we excluded a substantial number of class samples from the raw dataset that lacked docstrings. The remaining class-docstring pairs underwent additional processing. Since the nature of classes and functions is similar, their functionalities can be meaningfully defined by pairs of a code snippet and a docstring. However, one of the problems when constructing paired data for class-comment samples is the large code snippet length of the class structure. As a result, we set the maximum number of code tokens that a class can have to 5000. On average, the code-token length of the class set is approximately 500, which is around five times longer compared to the average token length in the function set, while the number of docstring-token lengths is similar between the two sets, as shown in Figure 6. Each pair of class-docstring is also examined via a rule-based filtering process, as described in Section 3.2.1, serving as a sample point in D_{pair} dataset.

In the D_{block} analysis, we initiate the initial formation of the sub-dataset by identifying and extracting inline comments within code functions. The extracted comments undergo a series of cleaning procedures similar to those applied to the docstrings (as discussed in Section 3.2.1). After eliminating noisy samples, we proceed to establish various intervals for the number of comment tokens, aiming to determine the optimal upper and lower bounds that yield high-quality collected comments. Our observations reveal that inline comments exceeding 15 tokens typically incorporate code snippets, while comments containing fewer than 3 tokens lack substantial meaningful information. Consequently, this interval serves as a filtering criterion to generate the final version of D_{block}. Figure 7 shows the distribution of code-token length and docstring-token length in D_{block} set.

Language	Number of raw classes		Number of classes	Number of raw	Number of inline comments
	w/ comment	wo/ comment	after filtering	inline comments	after filtering
Python	497,550	1,440,539	422,187	24,066,884	14,013,238
PHP	2,223,472	6,232,180	1,173,916	9,892,486	5,873,744
JavaScript	494,819	2,409,932	291,479	4,426,086	1,438,110
Java	8,438,772	11,997,783	4,872,485	24,982,298	17,062,277
C#	2,378,379	9,097,968	1,437,800	10,130,704	6,274,389
C++	285,184	791,355	174,370	20,770,494	10,343,650
Rust	188,517	3,591,465	93,311	2,998,368	2,063,784
Ruby	721,338	2,903,507	353,859	1,236,143	767,563
C	-	-	-	16,009,812	6,778,239
Go	-	-	-	7,574,542	4,390,342
Total	15,228,031	38,464,729	8,819,407	122,087,817	69,005,336

Table 11: The number of classes and inline comments associated with the class and inline set. The symbol '-' indicates that this information is unavailable due to the nonexistence of traditional classes in C and Go.

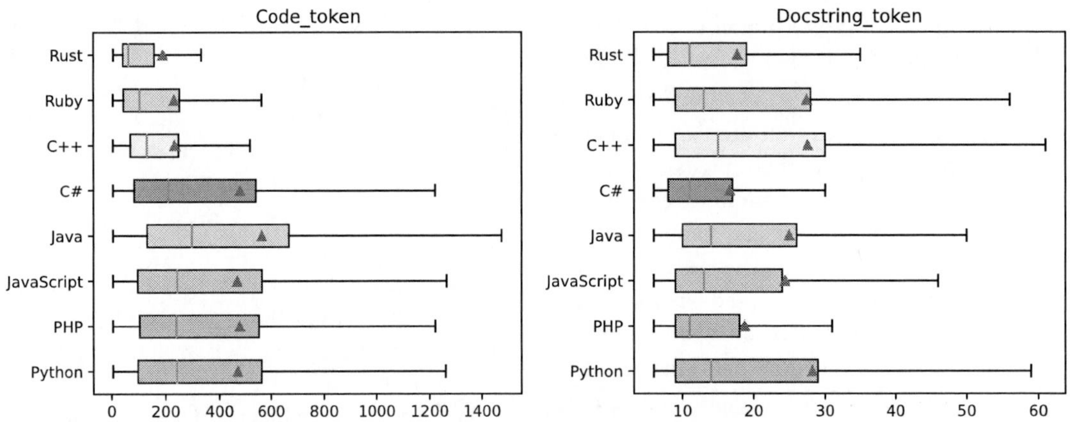

Figure 6: Code and Docstring tokens length distribution of the Class set after filtering.

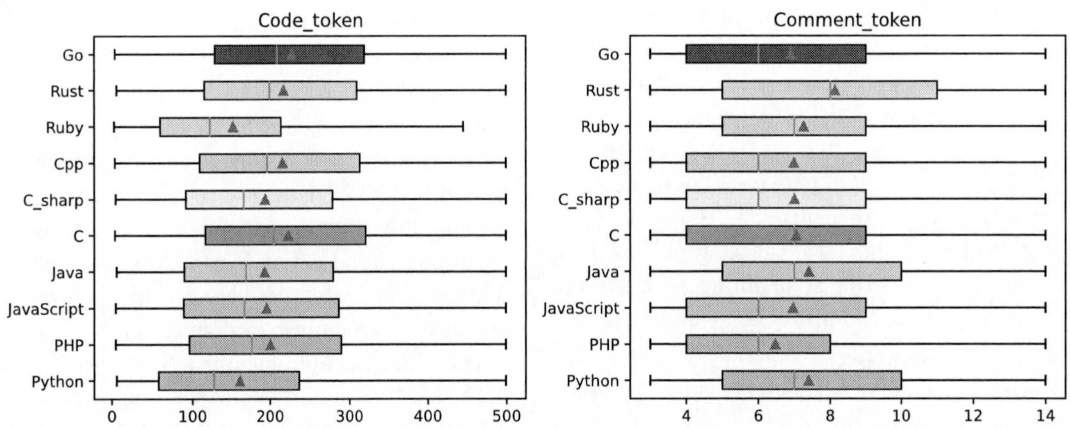

Figure 7: Code and Docstring tokens length distribution of D_{block} set after filtering.

A.5 Docstring Styling

A docstring is a string literal used as a form of documentation for a module, function, class, or method definition in programming languages. It is usually placed as the first statement in the code block (which can be inside or outside the code block itself) and enclosed by a comment delimiter (e.g., triple quotes (“‘) or a star slash (*)). Depending on developer comment habit or docstring style format, docstrings can form two types: one-line docstrings and multi-line (or block) docstrings. A docstring can provide a concise summary of the functionality while also providing a detailed description of the code block, including its parameters, return values, exceptions, and other relevant information (as illustrated in Figure 8)

The primary purpose of a docstring is to provide clear, concise, and easily accessible documentation for a code block. Docstring styles are conventions followed while writing docstrings to ensure consistency, readability, and ease of understanding throughout a codebase. This has become a standard for clean code in the industry and has developers saving tons of time when it comes to understanding or (auto-)generating documentation (using Sphinx, Doxygen, etc).

There are several popular docstring styles, such as Google Style, NumPy Style, reStructuredText (reST) Style for Python programmers, JavaDoc Style or Doxygen for Java users, each with its own formatting rules, structure and target programming language (docstring style examples and preferred language are listed in Figure 10). The statistic for docstring style corresponding to function level is presented in Figure 9. We believe that information inside a docstring is extremely useful and can provide numerous advantages for various applications in the fields of AI for source code, such as providing more precise and relevant search results for code search and retrieval tasks, or the performance of code analysis or refactoring can be significantly improved while the identifier of a parameter and its corresponding docstring information is available.

A.6 Experiment setup

Data splitting: During the experiment phase, The Vault (D_{paired}) was split into three distinct datasets: training, validating, and testing sets. To avoid data leakage, we reinforced a policy where code samples from the same repository must all be in the same set. In the splitting algorithm, we also included as a goal the preservation of the token length distribution from The Vault's dataset in each subset.

For richer comparisons, the training set was further branched off to two smaller sets, the small and medium training sets, sampling 5% and 20% of the full training set, respectively. Details about experiment data can be found in 12.

Language	Training set			Valid set	Test set
	Small	Medium	Full		
Python	370,657	1,952,110	7,772,647	30,992	21,652
Java	351,213	1,612,366	6,629,193	22,677	15,552
JavaScript	82,931	404,729	1,640,416	22,044	21,108
PHP	236,638	1,155,476	4,656,371	21,375	19,010
C	105,978	381,207	1,639,319	27,525	19,122
C#	141,090	783,166	3,305,891	24,787	19,638
C++	87,420	410,907	1,671,268	20,011	18,169
Go	267,535	1,319,547	5,109,020	19,102	25,314
Ruby	23,921	112,574	424,339	17,338	19,908
Rust	35,367	224,015	825,130	16,716	23,141
Total	1,702,750	8,356,097	33,673,594	222,567	202,614

Table 12: The proportion of training, validation, and test set of THEVAULT.

Infrastructure: All experiments are conducted on 4 NVIDIA A100 GPUs.

Code search: We select CodeBERT, as the encoder for embedding source code and natural query, for all experiments. We train 10 epochs for each model with a sequence max length of 512, and a learning rate 2^{-5}.

Code summarization: Codet5-base is employed for the summarization task. We set the max input tokens to 512 and the max output tokens to 400. The training batch size is set to 512, the learning rate is 2^{-4}, and training for 5 epochs.

Code generation: We use 350M parameters of CodeGen to evaluate code generation. We use the same configuration as in the code summarization task.

A.7 Experimental results on code summarization

We report Rouge-L, BERTScore, and BLEU-4 metrics on test sets of CSN and The Vault in Table 14. The results obtained from the experiments clearly indicate that models trained on our dataset consistently outperform CSN on all three evaluation metrics. This notable improvement across the metrics serves as strong evidence for the syntactic and semantic richness embedded within our dataset for code summarization. This highlights the effectiveness of our dataset in enabling models to grasp contextual information and generate high-quality summaries that accurately represent the underlying code functionality.

A.8 Ablation study

In this section, we assess TheVault's versatility and adaptability by providing additional experimental results on several architectures (RoBERTa [Liu et al., 1907], UniXcoder [Guo et al., 2022], PLBART [Ahmad et al., 2021a]) for code search

Model	Fine-tune data	Python	Java	JavaScript	Go	PHP	Ruby	Rust	C	C++	C#	Avg
		CodeSearchNet Testset (MRR)										
CodeBERT	CodeSearchNet	0.3793	0.4636	0.4437	0.6201	0.4741	0.5219	-	-	-	-	0.4838
	TheVault/small	0.4074	0.4857	0.4466	0.6578	0.6578	0.5251	-	-	-	-	0.5301
	TheVault/medium	0.6585	0.6945	0.6197	0.8571	0.638	0.7096		-	-	-	0.6962
	TheVault	**0.6952**	**0.7242**	**0.6562**	**0.8789**	**0.6646**	**0.7474**	-	-	-	-	**0.7278**
RoBERTa	CodeSearchNet	0.3479	0.448	0.4254	0.5684	0.4623	0.5147	-	-	-	-	**0.6952**
	TheVault/small	**0.4849**	**0.5581**	**0.4962**	**0.7446**	**0.5166**	**0.59**	-	-	-	-	**0.5651**
UniXCoder	CodeSearchNet	0.3935	0.4549	0.4459	0.5861	0.489	0.5446	-	-	-	-	0.4857
	TheVault/small	**0.4427**	**0.4909**	**0.4506**	**0.6416**	**0.4515**	**0.5702**	-	-	-	-	**0.5079**
		TheVault Testset (MRR)										
CodeBERT	CodeSearchNet	0.2881	0.3213	0.2409	0.4123	0.1854	0.2579	-	-	-	-	0.2843
	TheVault/small	0.3501	0.4214	0.3216	0.4864	0.2351	0.2904	0.326	0.2996	0.3015	0.3483	0.3165
	TheVault/medium	0.5929	0.6215	0.549	0.6862	0.3642	0.514	0.5705	0.5362	0.5264	0.5268	0.5488
	TheVault	**0.6448**	**0.6633**	**0.592**	**0.7111**	**0.3891**	**0.5607**	**0.6243**	**0.5947**	**0.5932**	**0.5616**	**0.5935**
RoBERTa	CodeSearchNet	0.2644	0.3329	0.2371	0.2375	0.1577	0.2574	-	-	-	-	0.2478
	TheVault/small	**0.4533**	**0.5519**	**0.4386**	**0.5021**	**0.2876**	**0.3717**	**0.4195**	**0.3805**	**0.37**	**0.4099**	**0.4342**
UniXCoder	CodeSearchNet	0.2959	0.344	0.2508	0.185	0.1646	0.2669	-	-	-	-	0.2512
	TheVault/small	**0.3852**	**0.4279**	**0.3491**	**0.4628**	**0.238**	**0.3201**	**0.363**	**0.2934**	**0.2861**	**0.3473**	**0.3639**

Table 13: Code search results of various architectures and training dataset.

and code summarization tasks. Besides, in order to validate the efficiency of our processing pipeline, we conduct a comparison between the performance of models trained on The Stack (raw data) and The Vault (processed data). Specifically, we established three function-level subsets, each approximately the size of TheVault/small ($\approx$1.7M code-text instances). These subsets were created by randomly sampling the raw function-level dataset extracted from The Stack, without applying any filtering (referred to as raw-TheStack). We use three different seeds to sample raw-TheStack and report the average result. Tables 13 and 14 illustrate the results for code search and code summarization, correspondingly. As a result, in the code search task, models trained on The Vault consistently outperform all baseline models, underscoring both the efficiency of our processing pipeline and the dataset's ability to generalize across different architectures. For code summarization, our pipeline has similarly witnessed strong effectiveness compared to raw-TheStack. Particularly, during training on the raw-TheStack dataset for the code summarization task, we found that the PLBART and CodeT5 generate outputs with substantial noise. These outputs are characterized by a prevalence of special tokens like // and *. This finding strongly underscores the efficacy of our filtering process in enhancing the quality of the dataset. However, the result using CSN shows superior performance on CSN's testset than using The Vault. The reason for this is our mention of the post-processing step (section 4.3.1) to reduce the difference between the CSN and The Vault filtering methods, where the syntactic distribution can still exhibit nonidentical characteristics, which can affect the BLEU score. However, this gap could be reduced by using the full version of The Vault as shown in Table 5.

Language	Finetune dataset	CodeSearchNet			The Vault		
		Rouge-L	BERTScore	BLEU-4	Rouge-L	BERTScore	BLEU-4
Python	CodeSearchNet	34.000	88.827	19.55 (20.36)	26.798	87.055	10.86
	TheVault/medium-S	34.676	88.905	19.74	30.335	87.633	13.06
	TheVault-S	**36.499**	**89.211**	**21.15**	31.786	87.929	14.14
	TheVault/medium-L	33.848	88.734	18.88	30.947	87.716	13.36
	TheVault-L	35.024	88.921	19.83	**32.251**	**87.954**	**14.33**
Java	CodeSearchNet	**35.625**	**89.132**	20.38 (20.46)	27.297	87.385	8.00
	TheVault/medium-S	33.385	88.490	18.62	31.320	87.897	11.17
	TheVault-S	35.495	88.907	**20.43**	**33.137**	**88.268**	12.00
	TheVault/medium-L	32.561	88.161	18.29	30.773	87.596	11.50
	TheVault-L	35.221	88.782	20.37	32.882	88.000	**12.47**
JavaScript	CodeSearchNet	28.330	**87.568**	16.15 (16.24)	24.895	86.519	8.42
	TheVault/medium-S	26.528	87.017	14.88	27.891	86.846	10.58
	TheVault-S	**28.345**	87.384	**16.30**	29.817	87.320	11.71
	TheVault/medium-L	27.062	87.057	14.95	28.290	86.936	10.83
	TheVault-L	27.869	87.276	15.63	**30.572**	**87.391**	**12.38**
PHP	CodeSearchNet	**41.346**	**89.981**	**26.26 (26.09)**	39.960	89.281	17.85
	TheVault/medium-S	34.802	88.125	21.78	63.984	93.287	37.72
	TheVault-S	37.297	88.676	23.53	65.401	93.580	38.30
	TheVault/medium-L	33.325	87.963	20.27	65.195	93.679	39.13
	TheVault-L	36.478	88.641	23.21	**67.089**	**94.012**	**40.13**
Go	CodeSearchNet	40.076	90.487	19.83 (19.76)	38.189	89.994	17.87
	TheVault/medium-S	42.011	90.816	21.38	54.030	92.372	34.47
	TheVault-S	**44.649**	**91.188**	**24.37**	54.889	92.541	35.44
	TheVault/medium-L	41.480	90.731	21.22	56.721	92.994	39.27
	TheVault-L	44.063	91.108	23.96	**57.681**	**93.130**	**40.38**
Ruby	CodeSearchNet	28.196	87.371	15.38 (15.69)	24.500	86.417	10.26
	TheVault/medium-S	29.680	87.559	16.09	26.904	86.964	12.26
	TheVault-S	**31.133**	**87.830**	**17.15**	28.535	**87.280**	13.79
	TheVault/medium-L	29.389	87.565	15.42	27.485	87.044	12.63
	TheVault-L	30.634	87.759	16.53	**29.141**	87.223	**14.24**
Total	CodeSearchNet	36.739	**89.341**	21.24	30.563	87.853	16.11
	TheVault/medium-S	34.935	88.755	19.91	39.589	89.278	26.02
	TheVault-S	**37.120**	89.163	**21.73**	41.079	89.591	27.41
	TheVault/medium-L	34.086	88.585	19.16	40.544	89.473	27.71
	TheVault-L	36.305	89.024	21.14	**42.187**	**89.753**	**29.32**
C	TheVault/medium-S	-	-	-	28.132	86.277	10.21
	TheVault-S	-	-	-	33.275	87.353	13.39
	TheVault/medium-L	-	-	-	29.151	86.566	11.32
	TheVault-L	-	-	-	**35.009**	**87.807**	**14.86**
C#	TheVault/medium-S	-	-	-	39.480	89.616	23.88
	TheVault-S	-	-	-	**46.854**	**90.819**	**31.11**
	TheVault/medium-L	-	-	-	39.720	89.652	24.30
	TheVault-L	-	-	-	46.594	90.788	31.05
C++	TheVault/medium-S	-	-	-	28.029	86.719	14.55
	TheVault-S	-	-	-	29.942	87.116	16.18
	TheVault/medium-L	-	-	-	28.815	86.827	14.85
	TheVault-L	-	-	-	**30.754**	**87.163**	**16.65**
Rust	TheVault/medium-S	-	-	-	30.416	87.758	13.30
	TheVault-S	-	-	-	32.535	88.126	14.72
	TheVault/medium-L	-	-	-	30.999	87.862	13.75
	TheVault-L	-	-	-	**32.857**	**88.142**	**15.18**

Table 14: Experimental results for code summarization. For models that are finetuned on The Vault, "-S" annotation refers to finetuning process using *short_docstring* field as summarization, while "-L" represents the *docstring* field.

Languages	Inconsistent pairs

Python	`// Handy for templates.`
	`def has_urls(self):`
	`    if self.isbn_uk or self.isbn_us or self.official_url or self.`
	`        notes_url:`
	`        return True`
	`    else:`
	`        return False`

	`// compresses the waveform horizontally; one of`
	`// ``"normal"``, ``"resync"``, ``"resync2"```
	`def phase_type(self, value):`
	`    self._params.phase_type = value`
	`    self._overwrite_lock.disable()`

Go	`// InWithTags, OutWithTags, Both, BothWithTags`
	`func Predicates(from Shape, in bool) Shape {`
	`    dir := quad.Subject`
	`    if in {`
	`        dir = quad.Object`
	`    }`
	`    return Unique{NodesFrom{`
	`        Quads: Quads{`
	`            {Dir: dir, Values: from},`
	`        },`
	`        Dir: quad.Predicate,`
	`    }}`
	`}`

	`// select Surf ro PhomtomJS`
	`func (self *DefaultRequest) GetDownloaderID() int {`
	`    self.once.Do(self.prepare)`
	`    return self.DownloaderID`
	`}`

Java	`// supplied callback function.`
	`public boolean rm(Pipe pipe, IMtrieHandler func, XPub pub)`
	`    {`
	`        assert (pipe != null);`
	`        assert (func != null);`
	`        return rmHelper(pipe, new byte[0], 0, 0, func, pub);`
	`    }`

	`// only for change appenders`
	`public MapContentType getMapContentType(ContainerType`
	`    containerType){`
	`        JaversType keyType = getJaversType(Integer.class);`
	`        JaversType valueType = getJaversType(containerType.`
	`            getItemType());`
	`        return new MapContentType(keyType, valueType);`
	`    }`

<table>
<tr><th>Languages</th><th>Inconsistent pairs</th></tr>
<tr><td rowspan="2">JavaScript</td><td>

```
// we do not need Buffer pollyfill for now
function(str){
  var ret = new Array(str.length), len = str.length;
  while(len--) ret[len] = str.charCodeAt(len);
  return Uint8Array.from(ret);
}
```

</td></tr>
<tr><td>

```
// WeakMap works in IE11, node 0.12
function (fn, name) {
  function proxiedFn() {
    'use strict';
    var fields = privates.get(this); // jshint ignore:line
    return fn.apply(fields, arguments);
  }

  Object.defineProperty(proxiedFn, 'name', {
    value: name,
    configurable: true
  });

  return proxiedFn;
}
```

</td></tr>
<tr><td rowspan="2">PHP</td><td>

```
// -> NEW
public function consumerId()
    {
        if (isset($this->session->data['customer_id']) === true) {
            return $this->session->data['customer_id'];
        }
        return null;
    }
```

</td></tr>
<tr><td>

```
// disini mo ba atur akan apa mo kamana
private function _parse_routes()
    {
        $uri=implode('/', $this->uri->segments());

        if (isset($this->router[$uri])) {
                return $this->_set_request(explode('/', $this->router
                    [$uri]));
        }

        foreach ($this->router as $key → $val) {
                $key = str_replace(':any', '.+', str_replace(':num',
                    '[0-9]+', $key));

                if (preg_match('#^'.$key.'$#', $uri)) {
                        if (strpos($val, '$') !== FALSE AND strpos($key,
                            '(') !== FALSE) {
                                $val = preg_replace('#^'.$key.'$#', $val,
                                    $uri);
                        }

                        return $this->_set_request(explode('/', $val));
                }
        }

        $this->_set_request($this->uri->segments());
    }
```

</td></tr>
</table>

<table>
<tr><th>Languages</th><th>Inconsistent pairs</th></tr>
<tr><td rowspan="2">Ruby</td><td>// Initialize a new page, which can be simply rendered or
// persisted to the filesystem.
def method_missing(name, *args, &block)
    return meta[name.to_s] if meta.key?(name.to_s)
    super
  end</td></tr>
<tr><td>// Accepts the path of the YAML file to be parsed into
// commands - will throw a CommandException should it have
// invalid parameters
// @param filePath [String] Path for YAML file
def action_options
    # Attempt resolution to outputs of monitor
    return @action_options unless @monitor_class.outputs.length >
        0
    action_options = @action_options.clone
    @monitor_class.outputs.each do |output, _type|
      action_options.each do |option_key, option_value|
        action_options[option_key] =
          option_value.gsub("{{#{output}}}", @monitor.send(output).
              to_s)
      end
    end
    action_options
  end</td></tr>
</table>

Table 15: Inconsistent pairs in CodeSearchNet found by our model. "//" represents for docstring section.

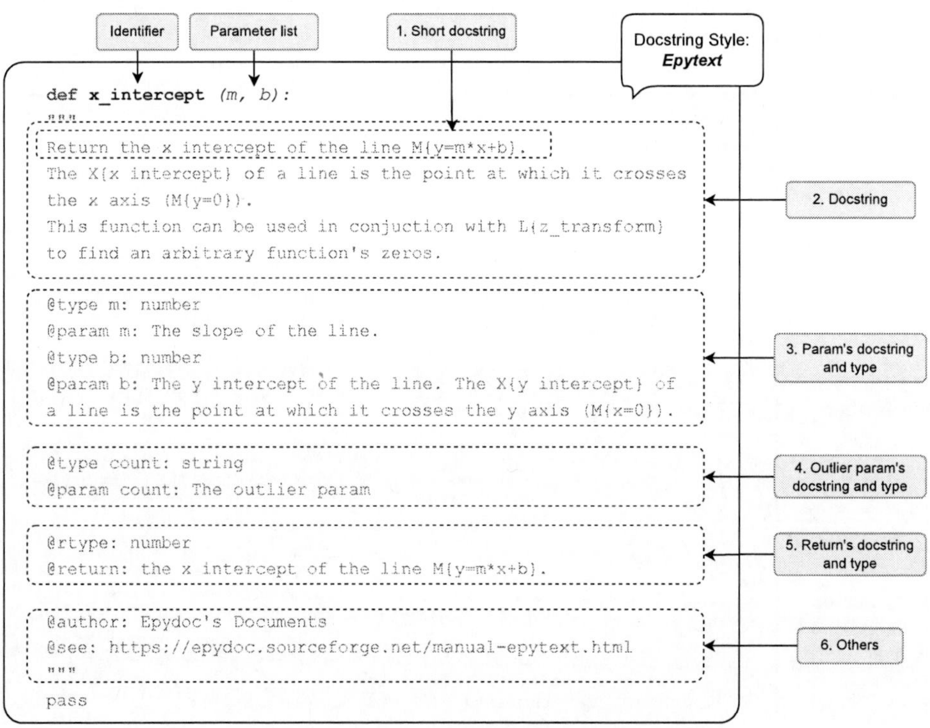

Figure 8: Structure of a docstring and its metadata.

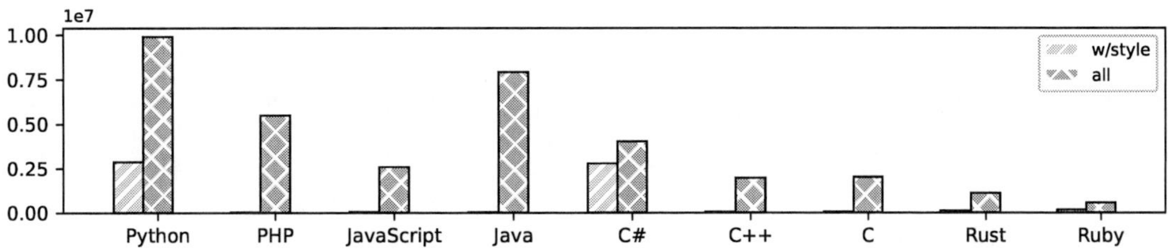

Languages	Python	PHP	JavaScript	Java	C#	C++	C	Rust	Ruby
w/style	2853520	8271	39295	14432	2754629	32517	25233	84427	156286
all	9893858	5455989	2562158	7886299	4011467	1934958	1978551	1076588	544867

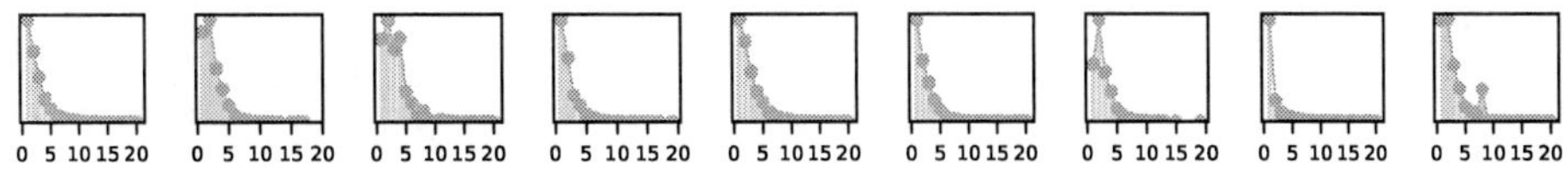

Figure 9: Number of docstrings follows a specific style over all extracted code-text pairs. **Upper** figure and **Middle** table illustrate statistics for docstrings with style. **Lower** figures present the histogram of extracted attributes in the range of 1-20 for docstrings in each language. Golang does not have a supported style.

Google Style — Python

```
"""
Test function.
Args:
    param1 (int): Description of param1.
    param2 (str): Description of param2.
Returns:
    bool: Description of the return value.
"""
```

JavaDoc — Java, C, C++, C#

```
/**
* Test function.
*
* @param param1 Description of param1.
* @param param2 Description of param2.
* @return Description of the return value.
*/
```

RustDoc — Rust

```
/**
* Test function.
** # Arguments
* `param1`: Description of param1.
* `param2`: Description of param2.
* # Returns
* Description of the return value.
*/
```

reST — Python

```
"""Test function.
:param param1: Description of param1.
:type param1: int
:param param2: Description of param2.
:type param2: str
:return: Description of the return value.
:rtype: bool
"""
```

Rdoc — Ruby

```
=begin
Test method.

@param param1 [Integer] Description of param1.
@param param2 [String] Description of param2.
@return [Boolean] Description of the return value.
=end
```

Jsdoc — JavaScript

```
/**
* Test function.
*
* @param {int} param1 - Description of param1.
* @param {string} param2 - Description of param2.
* @return {bool} Description of the return value.
*/
```

PHPdoc — PHP

```
/**
* Test function.
*
* @param int $param1 Description of param1.
* @param string $param2 Description of param2.
* @return bool Description of the return value.
*/
```

Doxygen — C, C++, C#

```
/**
* Test function.
* @brief Constructor.
* @param param1 Description of param1
* @param param2 Description of param2
* @see Test()
*/
```

XML — C#

```
/// <summary>
/// Test function.
/// </summary>
/// <param name="param1">Description of param1.
</param>
/// <param name="param2">Description of param1.
</param>
/// <returns>
/// Description of the return value.
/// </returns>
```

Epytext — Python

```
"""
Test function.
@type param1: int
@param param1: Description of param1
@type param2: string
@param param2: Description of param2
@rtype: bool
@return: Description of the return value.
"""
```

NumPy Style — Python

```
"""
Test function.
Parameters
----------
param1 : int
Description of param1.
param2 : str
Description of param2.
Returns
-------
bool
Description of the return value.
"""
```

Figure 10: Supported docstring styles.

trlX: A Framework for Large Scale Open Source RLHF

Louis Castricato
EleutherAI

Abstract

Reinforcement learning from human feedback (RLHF) utilizes human feedback to better align large language models with human preferences via online optimization against a learned reward model. Current RLHF paradigms rely on Proximal Policy Optimization (PPO), which quickly becomes a challenge to implement and scale up to large architectures. To address this difficulty we created the trlX library (Havrilla et al., 2023) as a feature-complete open-source framework for RLHF fine-tuning of models up to and exceeding 70 billion parameters. We implemented support for multiple types of distributed training including distributed data parallel, model sharded, as well as tensor, sequential, and pipeline parallelism.

Biography

Louis Castricato is a research scientist at EleutherAI, working on RLHF infrastructure and engineering. Previously, Louis was head of LLMs at Stability AI and team lead at CarperAI, the largest open source RLHF group, as well as a PhD student at Brown University.

References

Alexander Havrilla, Duy Van Phung, Maksym Zhuravinskyi, Aman Tiwari, Jonathan Tow, Shivanshu Purohit, Stella Biderman, Quentin Anthony, Ethan Kim, and Louis Castricato. 2023. trlx: A framework for large scale reinforcement learning from human feedback. In *Conference on Empirical Methods in Natural Language Processing*.

Proceedings of the 3rd Workshop for Natural Language Processing Open Source Software (NLP-OSS 2023), pages 245–245
December 6, 2023 ©2023 Association for Computational Linguistics

Southeast Asia LLMs: SEA-LION and Wangchan-LION

David Tat-Wee Ong,
AI Singapore

Peerat Limkonchotiwat
Vidyasirimedhi Institute of Science and Technology, Thailand

Abstract

SEA-LION (Southeast Asian Languages In One Network) (Singapore, 2023) is a family of multilingual LLMs that is specifically pre-trained and instruct-tuned for the Southeast Asian (SEA) region, incorporating a custom SEABPETokenizer which is specially tailored for SEA languages. The first part of this talk will cover our design philosophy and pre-training methodology for SEA-LION. The second part of this talk will cover PyThaiNLP's (Phatthiyaphaibun et al., 2023) work on Wangchan-LION, an instruct-tuned version of SEA-LION for the Thai community.

Biography

David Tat-Wee holds a M.Sc in Computer Science and a M.Sc in Financial Engineering from NUS. He started his career by spending a decade in tech as a software engineer, building early Internet applications and working in partnership with Apple, NEC, Siemens and the National Institute of Education. He spent the next decade in finance as a quantitative hedge fund manager with Octagon Capital Management, a Singapore quant fund, starting as a quant research analyst to managing global equities as a portfolio manager to becoming the Chief Investment Officer. He also developed Octagon's in-house financial applications and managed their IT systems.

He joined AI Singapore's (AISG) as an AI Engineer after graduating from its AIAP programme in 2021 and became the Head of the Computer Vsion Hub in 2022. David is presently the Head of Engineering in AISG's Products pillar, managing a team of software engineers to support AISG's Products research implementation.

Peerat Limkonchotiwat is pursuing a Ph.D. student in information science and technology (IST) at VISTEC, Thailand. His research experiences involve Natural Language Processing (NLP) and Information Retrieval (IR), including large language models, dense retrievals, semantic understanding, representation learning, question answering, and entity linking. He is currently working with Dr. Sarana Nutanong (VISTEC, Thailand) and Dr. Ekapol Chuangsuwanich (CU, Thailand).

Currently, he is a subject matter expert in a WangchanX project, a Thai NLP group developing applications based on research. His projects in WangchanX are Thai sentence embedding benchmarks, Thai text processing datasets (VISTEC-TP-TH-2021 and NNER-TH), and generative models, i.e. WangchanGLM (Polpanumas et al., 2023) and Wangchan-Sealion).

References

Wannaphong Phatthiyaphaibun, Korakot Chaovavanich, Charin Polpanumas, Arthit Suriyawongkul, Lalita Lowphansirikul, Pattarawat Chormai, Peerat Limkonchotiwat, Thanathip Suntorntip, and Can Udomcharoenchaikit. 2023. PyThaiNLP: Thai Natural Language Processing in Python. In *Proceedings of Second Workshop for NLP Open Source Software (NLP-OSS)*, Online. Association for Computational Linguistics.

Charin Polpanumas, Wannaphong Phatthiyaphaibun, Patomporn Payoungkhamdee, Peerat Limkonchotiwat, Lalita Lowphansirikul, Can Udomcharoenchaikit, Titipat Achakulwisut, Ekapol Chuangsuwanich, and Sarana Nutanong. 2023. WangChanGLM — The Multilingual Instruction-Following Model.

AI Singapore. 2023. Sea-lion (southeast asian languages in one network): A family of large language models for southeast asia. `https://github.com/aisingapore/sealion`.

Proceedings of the 3rd Workshop for Natural Language Processing Open Source Software (NLP-OSS 2023), pages 246–246
December 6, 2023 ©2023 Association for Computational Linguistics

Towards Explainable and Accessible AI

Brandon Duderstadt
Nomic AI

Yuvanesh Anand
Virginia Institute of Technology &
Nomic AI

Abstract

Large language models (LLMs) have recently achieved human-level performance on a range of professional and academic benchmarks. Unfortunately, the explainability and accessibility of these models has lagged behind their performance. State-of-the-art LLMs require costly infrastructure, are only accessible via rate-limited, geo-locked, and censored web interfaces, and lack publicly available code and technical reports. Moreover, the lack of tooling for understanding the massive datasets used to train and produced by LLMs presents a critical challenge for explainability research. This talk will be an overview of Nomic AI's efforts to address these challenges through its two core initiatives: GPT4All (Anand et al., 2023) and Atlas.

References

Yuvanesh Anand, Zach Nussbaum, Adam Treat, Aaron Miller, Richard Guo, Ben Schmidt, GPT4All Community, Brandon Duderstadt, and Andriy Mulyar. 2023. GPT4All: An Ecosystem of Open Source Compressed Language Models. In *Proceedings of Second Workshop for NLP Open Source Software (NLP-OSS)*, Online. Association for Computational Linguistics.

Biography

Brandon Duderstadt is the founder and CEO of Nomic AI, a series A startup whose mission is to improve the explainability and accessibility of AI. In 2018, Brandon dropped out of his biomedical engineering Ph.D. at Johns Hopkins to join Rad AI, a seed-stage medical generative AI startup. While at Rad AI, he built and deployed transformers that exceeded radiologist performance on a variety of medical summarization tasks. His experiences at Rad AI convinced him of both the profound impact that this new wave of AI technology would have as well as the need to improve the explainability and accessibility of AI models.

Yuvanesh Anand is a freshman computer science student at the Virginia Institute of Technology with broad interests in natural language processing and open-source software development. While still in high school, Yuvanesh joined Nomic AI as a software engineering intern, where he led the data collection and early development of the gpt4all project. He aspires to have an impact at the intersection of industrial AI R&D and open source.

Nomic AI was founded in 2022 by Brandon Duderstadt and Andriy Mulyar with the goal of improving the explainability and accessibility of AI. Nomic currently has two major projects: GPT4All and Atlas. GPT4All is an open-source ecosystem that enables anyone to run open-source language models on any machine. Atlas is a data visualization tool that enables anyone to interact with massive unstructured datasets, like those consumed and produced by AI models, using only their web browser.

Proceedings of the 3rd Workshop for Natural Language Processing Open Source Software (NLP-OSS 2023), pages 247–247
December 6, 2023

Author Index

Anand, Yuvanesh, 59, 247

Bang, Fu, 212
Beauchemin, David, 19
Bellew, Douglas, 102
Bhattacharya, Arnab, 199
Bollmann, Marcel, 83
Bui, Nghi D. Q., 219

Callison-Burch, Chris, 65
Caragea, Cornelia, 141
Castricato, Louis, 246
Chaovavanich, Korakot, 25
Chormai, Pattarawat, 25
Curtis, Brenda, 102

Dau, Anh T. V., 219
Di Eugenio, Barbara, 141
Diesner, Jana, 190
Duderstadt, Brandon, 59, 247
Dugan, Liam, 65

Garcia-Olano, Diego, 165
Geuter, Jonathan, 8
Ghaffari, Parsa, 179
Ghalandari, Demian Gholipour, 179
Giorgi, Salvatore, 102
Gowda, Thamme, 110
Grobol, Loïc, 54
Grundkiewicz, Roman, 110
Grypari, Ioanna, 37
Guntuku, Sharath Chandra, 102
Guo, Jin, 219
Guo, Richard, 59
Günther, Michael, 8

Hai, Nam Le, 219
Hokamp, Chris, 179
Hwang, Alyssa, 65

Jain, Rohit, 110
Jovanovic, Andrej, 130
Junczys-Dowmunt, Marcin, 110

Kashyap, Sanjna, 78
Khayrallah, Huda, 110
Kokhlikyan, Narine, 165
Kruse, Maya, 147
Kumar, Ritesh, 120
Köhn, Arne, 83

Landes, Paul, 141
Lignos, Constantine, 147
Limkonchotiwat, Peerat, 25, 245
Lowphansirikul, Lalita, 25
Lyris, Ioannis, 37

Madnani, Nitin, 78
Manh, Dung Nguyen, 219
Manola, Natalia, 37
Markosyan, Aram H., 165
Mastrapas, Georgios, 8
Mathur, Neerav, 120
Matsubara, Yoshitomo, 153
Miglani, Vivek, 165
Miller, Aaron, 59
Miranda, Lester James Validad, 1
Mishra, Shubhanshu, 190
Mulyar, Andriy, 59

Nawrot, Piotr, 95
Nghiem, Khanh, 219
Nguyen, Anh Minh, 219
Nussbaum, Zach, 59

Ong, David, 245

Papageorgiou, Haris, 37
Phatthiyaphaibun, Wannaphong, 25
Polpanumas, Charin, 25
Post, Matt, 83, 110

Ratan, Shyam, 120
Ross, Björn, 130
Rueda, Andrew, 147

Schmidt, Benjamin M, 59
Schneider, Nathan, 83
Sherman, Garrick, 102
Singh, Siddharth, 120
Stavropoulos, Petros, 37
Steimel, Kenneth, 78
Stollenwerk, Felix, 174
Suntorntip, Thanathip, 25
Suriyawongkul, Arthit, 25

Terdalkar, Hrishikesh, 199
Tjhi, William, 245
Treat, Adam, 59

Udomcharoenchaikit, Can, 25
Ungar, Lyle, 102

Wang, Bo, 8

Xiao, Han, 8
Xie, Zhaoyang, 78

Yang, Aobo, 165

Zhu, Andrew, 65

Association for Computational Linguistics
209 N. Eighth Street
Stroudsburg, Pennsylvania 18360

ISBN 978-1-7138-8605-1

9 781713 886051

CURRAN ASSOCIATES INC.
proceedings.com